Gateway to U.S. History

The Bridge to Success on Florida's EOC Test

Mark Jarrett, Ph.D. ■ Robert Yahng, J.D.

Florida Transformative Education

Copyright © 2020 by Florida Transformative Education

All rights reserved. Copying or projecting this book without permission of the publisher is a violation of federal copyright law. An exception is granted to teachers who wish to project pages of this book if an entire class set of these books is present and in use by students at the time of such projection. All other unauthorized copying or projecting of this material will be prosecuted by the publisher to the fullest extent permitted by law. For permission requests, write to the publisher, addressed "Attention: Permissions Coordinator," at the address below.

Florida Transformative Education
10 Folin Lane
Lafayette, CA 94549
Tel: (925) 906-9742 Fax: (925) 939-6557   www.floridasocialstudies.com

Florida Transformative Education and its logo are registered trademarks.

Printed in the United States of America

Our books are printed on long-lasting acid-free paper. When it is available, we choose paper that has been manufactured by environmentally responsible processes. These may include using trees grown in sustainable forests, incorporating recycled paper, minimizing chlorine in bleaching, or recycling the energy produced at the paper mill.

ISBN 978-0-9976835-3-0

Second Color Edition

25 24 23 22 21 20   10 9 8 7 6 5 4 3 2 1

About the Authors

Mark Jarrett studied at Columbia University (B.A.), the London School of Economics (M.A. in international history), Stanford University (Ph.D. in history), and the University of California at Berkeley, where he received a law degree with honors (Order of the Coif). He was an editor of the school's law review and received the American Jurisprudence Award for Comparative Legal History. Mark has taught at Hofstra University, at the Mander Portman School in London, and in the New York City Public Schools. He has served as a test writer for the New York State Board of Regents, and practiced law at Baker & McKenzie, the world's largest law firm. He is the co-author of more than 30 test preparation books and textbooks. James Sheehan, past President of the American Historical Association, describes Mark's recent book, *The Congress of Vienna and its Legacy* (London: I.B. Tauris, 2013), as "beautifully written" and providing "a fine sense of political structures without losing the human element," while Robert Jervis, past President of the American Political Science Association, calls his book a "model treatment." It was a *Choice* "Outstanding Title" for 2014.

Robert Yahng has taught Honors U.S. Government and Honors Micro- and Macroeconomics at Salesian High School in Richmond, California, for the past 16 years. He has been the school's Chairman of the Board of Directors for the past 10 years. Robert earned a B.A. in History at Berea College in Kentucky, the South's first interracial college, where his grandfather, father and mother were professors. He received his Juris Doctor degree from the University of Kentucky School of Law. Robert was a partner in the law firm of Baker & McKenzie for 21 years. He was the Managing Partner of its San Francisco and Palo Alto offices in the 1990s, and also founded its Taipei office. From 1999 to 2002, he served as a Public Governor on the Board of Governors of the Pacific Stock Exchange. He has been a member of the Board of Trustees of Berea College since 2003 and is its current Chairman. From 1997 to 2014 he was Chairman of American Bridge Company, which constructed the Bob Graham Sunshine Skyway Bridge shown on the cover. In 2019, Robert was inducted into the University of Kentucky College of Law's Hall of Fame.

The Cover

The cover shows the Bob Graham Sunshine Skyway Bridge, spanning Tampa Bay and constructed by the American Bridge Company.

Contents

Preface	Florida's End-of-Course Assessment in U.S. History	v
Introduction	Historians at Work	xiii

UNIT I — THE CIVIL WAR AND RECONSTRUCTION

Chapter 1	The Civil War	1
Chapter 2	Reconstruction	23
Chapter 3	"Go West!"	41
	Unit I Activities	

UNIT II — THE TRANSFORMATION OF AMERICAN SOCIETY

Chapter 4	The Triumph of Industry	59
Chapter 5	The Labor Movement	81
Chapter 6	Cities, Immigrants, and Farmers	95
Chapter 7	The Progressive Era	119
	Unit II Activities	

UNIT III — WORLD AFFAIRS THROUGH WORLD WAR I

Chapter 8	American Imperialism	141
Chapter 9	The United States in World War I	165
	Unit III Activities	

UNIT IV — THE INTERWAR PERIOD

Chapter 10	The Roaring Twenties	191
Chapter 11	The Great Depression and the New Deal	225
	Unit IV Activities	

UNIT V — WORLD WAR II AND THE COLD WAR

Chapter 12	World War II: America's Darkest and Brightest Hour	249
Chapter 13	The Cold War	285
	Unit V Activities	

UNIT VI — THE MODERN UNITED STATES: GLOBAL LEADERSHIP AND DOMESTIC ISSUES

Chapter 14	Postwar Prosperity and Civil Rights	309
Chapter 15	The Sixties: "The Times They are a-Changin'"	339
Chapter 16	U.S. Foreign Policy since 1972	367
Chapter 17	American Social Issues	387
	Unit VI Activities	

A Practice End-of-Course Assessment in U.S. History, 1850–present	EOC-1
Atlas	A-1
U.S. Constitution	C-1
Index	I-1

Dedications

*In loving memory of my father,
Paul Seymour Jarrett (1919–2013)*
—Mark Jarrett

To dear Tina
—Robert Yahng

Acknowledgments

The authors wish to thank the following individuals for their generous help and advice:

First and foremost, Dr. Alison McLafferty, formerly of the History Department at the University of California at Berkeley, for her diligence and scrupulousness in reviewing this manuscript; Dr. Mark Pearcy, formerly at Manatee School District and now teaching Social Studies methods at Rider University in Pennsylvania; Ms. Regina F. Stuck, AP and Honors U.S. History Teacher, former James Madison Fellow and Board Member on the Miami-Dade Council for the Social Studies; Ms. Mary Smith, recently retired Social Studies coordinator at Cypress-Fairbanks Independent School District, the third largest public school district in Texas; and Dovetail Publishing Services for their creativity in the design and layout of this book.

The authors also thank Dr. Louise Ball, Secondary Social Studies Curriculum Specialist, and Ms. Marie DiRito, of the Social Studies Department at Broward County, and Mr. Michael DiPierro, formerly at Broward County and now Social Studies Education Specialist at the Florida Department of Education, in particular for acquainting us with the CPALMS website; Ms. Jackie Viana and Dr. Sherrilyn Scott, District Supervisors at the Miami Dade County Public Schools; Ms. Christine Webber, formerly at Ben Gamla Charter Schools, who used draft chapters of this book with her students; Ms. Cherie Arnette, Social Studies Specialist for Escambia County School District; Ms. Polly Schlosser, Adjunct Professor of Social Studies Education at the University of Texas and former President of the Texas Council of the Social Studies; Ms. Montra Rogers, Secondary Social Studies Specialist for Houston Independent School District; the Seminole Tribe of Florida for information on the use of the term "American Indian" and "Native American," and finally, Dr. Jane Cho and Ms. Jacqueline Shine, both formerly at the University of California at Berkeley.

In addition, special mention should go to the late Dr. Randy Felton, Social Studies Coordinator at the Test Development Center of the Florida Department of Education, for his patience and willingness to direct us to public resources that supplied the answers to many of our questions. He is greatly missed.

This is not to be taken as an endorsement of this product by any of the individuals listed above. Any remaining errors are our own.

Preface

Florida's End-of-Course Assessment in U.S. History

This year you will be studying United States history. You will also be taking Florida's "U.S. History End-of-Course Assessment." This assessment will have 50 to 60 multiple-choice questions, testing your knowledge of 19 Social Studies Benchmarks:

Florida's 19 Tested Benchmarks

SS.912.A.1.1 Describe the importance of historiography, which includes how historical knowledge is obtained and transmitted, when interpreting events in history.

SS.912.A.2.1 Review causes and consequences of the Civil War.

SS.912.A.3.1 Analyze the economic challenges to American farmers and farmers' responses to these challenges in the mid to late 1800s.

SS.912.A.3.2 Examine the social, political, and economic causes, course, and consequences of the second Industrial Revolution that began in the late 19th century.

SS.912.A.4.1 Analyze the major factors that drove United States imperialism.

SS.912.A.4.5 Examine causes, course, and consequences of United States involvement in World War I.

SS.912.A.5.3 Examine the impact of United States foreign economic policy during the 1920s.

SS.912.A.5.5 Describe efforts by the United States and other world powers to avoid future wars.

SS.912.A.5.10 Analyze support for and resistance to civil rights for women, African Americans, Native Americans, and other minorities.

SS.912.A.5.11 Examine causes, course, and consequences of the Great Depression and the New Deal.

SS.912.A.6.1 Examine causes, course, and consequences of World War II on the United States and the world.

SS.912.A.6.10 Examine causes, course, and consequences of the early years of the Cold War (Truman Doctrine, Marshall Plan, NATO, Warsaw Pact).

SS.912.A.6.13 Analyze significant foreign policy events during the Truman, Eisenhower, Kennedy, Johnson, and Nixon administrations.

SS.912.A.7.1 Identify causes for post-World War II prosperity and its effects on American society.

SS.912.A.7.4 Evaluate the success of 1960s-era presidents' foreign and domestic policies.

SS.912.A.7.6 Assess key figures and organizations in shaping the Civil Rights Movement and Black Power Movement.

SS.912.A.7.8 Analyze significant Supreme Court decisions relating to integration, busing, affirmative action, the rights of the accused, and reproductive rights.

SS.912.A.7.11 Analyze the foreign policy of the United States as it relates to Africa, Asia, the Caribbean, Latin America, and the Middle East.

SS.912.A.7.12 Analyze political, economic, and social concerns that emerged at the end of the 20th century and into the 21st century.

Most of these Benchmarks will incorporate additional information from related Benchmarks found in Florida's Social Studies Standards. The questions on the End-of-Course Assessment will be distributed as follows:

Time Period	Chapters in this Book	Percentage
Late Nineteenth and Early Twentieth Century, 1860–1910	Chapters 1–7	32%
Global Military, Political and Economic Challenges, 1890–1940	Chapters 8–11	34%
The United States and the Defense of the International Peace, 1940–Present	Chapters 12–17	32%

In addition to these Benchmarks, this book incorporates all of the most important terms and individuals listed by the Florida Department of Education in the "Remarks/Examples" section of the CPALMS website (collaborate-plan-alignment-learn-motivate-share). Some of these terms may also appear on the End-of-Course Assessment.

This book also includes a large number of primary source documents to improve your skills in interpreting key ideas and details in a nonfiction text, as required by the Common Core Standards.

This book can therefore help you both to learn more about U.S. history *and* to perform your very best on the End-of-Course Assessment. It can be used either by itself or alongside another textbook. It contains everything you need to learn about American history to do well on the statewide test.

Special Features of *Gateway to U.S. History*

- We often learn best when we have some general idea of what we are about to learn in advance. Every content chapter in this book begins with information that tells you what the chapter is about. First, there is the **title** of the chapter, which describes its topic. This is followed by a **list of Florida Social Studies Standards** that are covered in the chapter. This includes not only the 19 Benchmarks listed on pages v and vi, but also all related Benchmarks.

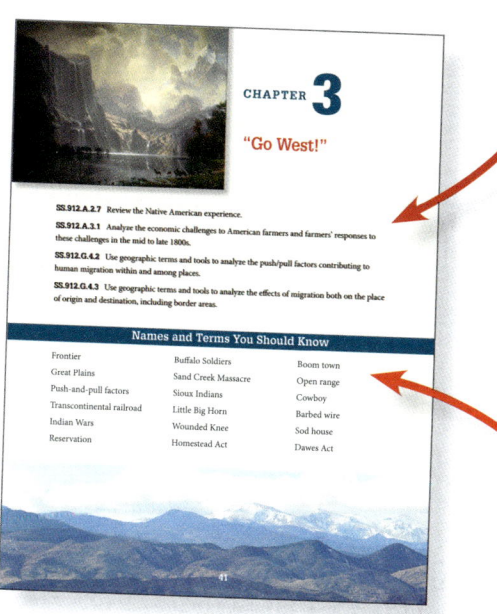

- At the bottom of the first page there is a list of **Names and Terms You Should Know**. You can use this list to guide your way through the chapter. Most of these terms are either listed in the Benchmarks or in the "Specifications" provided to those teachers who are writing your test.

- This is followed by **Florida "Keys" to Learning**. No, these aren't the real Florida Keys on the southern end of the state! They are the keys to what you should know for the test. This section provides a summary of important ideas and facts, forming the backbone to the chapter. You might look at these before you read the chapter to see how many of these "Keys" you already know. You will then see that the rest of the chapter simply expands on these key ideas and facts. When you have finished the chapter, you can read through these "Keys" again to review the chapter. If you don't understand or remember one of these "Keys," you might want to look back at the more detailed discussion in the chapter. Finally, you may want to review all of the 17 **Florida "Keys" to Learning** sections (one for each content chapter) just before you take the statewide U.S. History End-of-Course Assessment.

- The "Keys" are followed by the main text of the chapter. You will find that each chapter is divided into sections, and that the text is accompanied by illustrations, charts, graphs, and maps. Information in the chapter is organized around core concepts and developments to make it easier to understand and learn.

- Most chapters include a "**Focus on Florida**," where you learn about important events that took place in Florida at the same time as the other events in the chapter.

Preface | Florida's End-Of-Course Assessment in U.S. History

▶ At the end of each section of the text, you will find **The Historian's Apprentice**. This feature recommends activities for you and your classmates to complete under the supervision of your teacher. In these activities, you will be asked to conduct research, interpret a historical document, or use your historical imagination to think about what it might have been like to have lived in the past—just as real historians do.

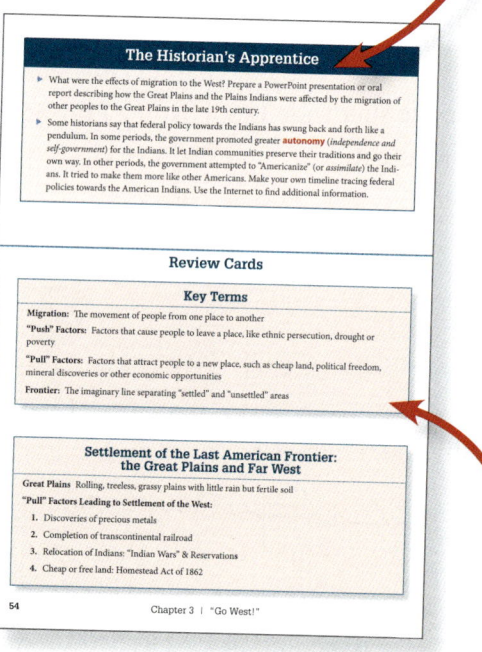

▶ At the end of each chapter, there are several special features to help you review concepts in the chapter, reinforce your understanding, and check your knowledge. First, there is a series of **Review Cards**. These cards summarize the most important information in the chapter, most likely to be found on Florida's End-of-Course Assessment. You can use these **Review Cards** in a variety of ways. You might cover part of the **Review Card** and check your ability to recall the information you have covered. You might copy the card by hand and make pictures to illustrate it or add further information. You can also use the **Review Card** to test your friends, or to make sample test questions. As you read through the book, you can copy these cards by hand to assemble a whole collection of them. Scramble them up to see if you can recall their contents when they are not in order.

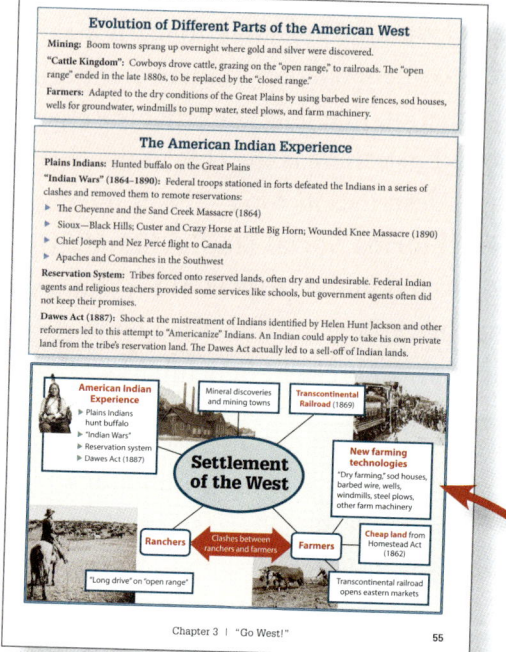

▶ The **Review Cards** are followed by a **Concept Map**. This map provides an overview showing how all the developments in the chapter are related.

▶ Each content chapter concludes with **What Do You Know?** This is a series of practice multiple-choice questions, similar in format to the assessment items on Florida's U.S. History End-of-Course Assessment.

Each group of related chapters forms a unit. Every unit of the book ends with a list of key terms and people for you to identify or define, followed by a crossword puzzle. The last chapter of the book provides a final practice test covering all the Benchmarks in the book, so that you can see what you have learned. The questions on this test follow the same test specifications and the same distribution (by time period) as the actual Florida U.S. History End-of-Course Assessment. By taking this practice test and by reviewing any errors you may commit, you can be sure to have prepared your very best for the test!

There are many ways to use this book. You may want to use this book as your main resource in the course of the school year. It covers everything you need to know for the test. You may also use it with another textbook. After you complete each unit in your textbook, you can review it by using one or more chapters in *Gateway to U.S. History*. Finally, you may want to use this book for a final review in the weeks just before the test. You can focus on the **Florida "Keys" to Learning, Review Cards,** and practice questions. With its lively text and special learning features, reading through this book may be a great way for you to recall everything you have studied this school year to prepare for the test.

How to Answer a Multiple-Choice Question

Besides possessing the knowledge and skills that are being tested, you have to be a good test-taker to do your best on this or any test. Here are the three basic steps we recommend for answering multiple-choice questions on Florida's U.S. History End-of-Course Assessment. In fact, these same steps should be used to answer multiple-choice questions on almost any test.

1 Understand the Question

Make sure you read the question carefully. Take special care in examining any document or data that may be contained in the question itself. Also, make sure you understand what the question asks for. Questions on the U.S. History End-of-Course Assessment will most likely ask you one of the following:

- to identify the **cause** of something: *what made it happen?*
- to identify or analyze the **effect** or **impact** of something: *how did it influence people or change things?*
- to **explain** or **describe** an event or development: *how did it happen? what was it like?*
- to **identify** or **define** something: *what is it?*
- to **compare** two or more things: *what are their similarities and differences?*
- to **sequence** events: *in what order did they occur? which was first or last?*
- to **interpret** a document, an illustration, a cartoon, a map, a table, or a graph: *what issue is addressed in this cartoon?*
- to provide an **example** of something: *which best illustrates this principle?*
- to make a **prediction**: *what is most likely to happen next?*
- to **categorize** people, events, places, or concepts: *which action furthered the goal of international peace?*
- to make a **generalization** or to draw a **conclusion:** *Based on the photograph, what conclusion can be made about child labor in the United States in the 1880s?*

2 Think About What You Know

Here comes the hardest part! Many students wish to rush ahead: they want to finish the test early. To do your best, however, you have to take your time. Once you have read and understood the question, take a moment to think about the topic that it asks about. For example, if the question asks about the causes of the Civil War, think about what you can remember about the causes of the Civil War. You might think about sectionalism, states' rights, slavery, the abolitionists, and the conflicts and compromises in Congress. You might also recall how the election of Abraham Lincoln in 1860 divided the nation. Then think how you might answer the question, based on what you can recall, *without looking at the answer choices*.

Preface | Florida's End-Of-Course Assessment in U.S. History

3 Answer the Question

Now you are ready to answer the question. Review the question. Look carefully at the answer choices. Eliminate any answer choices that are obviously wrong or irrelevant (*not related to the question or its topic*). Then choose the best of the remaining answer choices, based on your knowledge and understanding.

If you have extra time after you have finished the test, be sure to check your work again to eliminate any careless mistakes.

Special Types of Questions

Many questions on Florida's End-of-Course Assessment will ask about a "graphic" that is a part of the question. It is important for you to be able to interpret these different types of graphics, including maps, graphs, charts, tables, political cartoons, illustrations, photographs, and timelines. Each of these is simply another way of presenting or displaying information. Questions may ask what the graphic shows, or they may ask you to make an inference or draw a conclusion about the graphic. You might also be asked to identify the causes or effects of the situation or event described by the picture, timeline, photograph or other graphic. Often you will have to apply your knowledge of U.S. history to answer the question. The rest of this chapter looks at six of the most important types of graphics that may appear on the test.

Maps

A map is used to show geographical information. It may show the boundaries between countries, the location of cities, or the physical characteristics of a place. A *key* or *legend* will often explain any symbols on the map. Maps may also have a *scale* to show what their dimensions represent in real life, and a *compass* (or *direction indicator*).

▶ What does this map show?

▶ Based on the map, which states permitted slavery in 1850?

▶ What conditions led to the divisions shown on this map?

▶ What conclusions can you draw from this map?

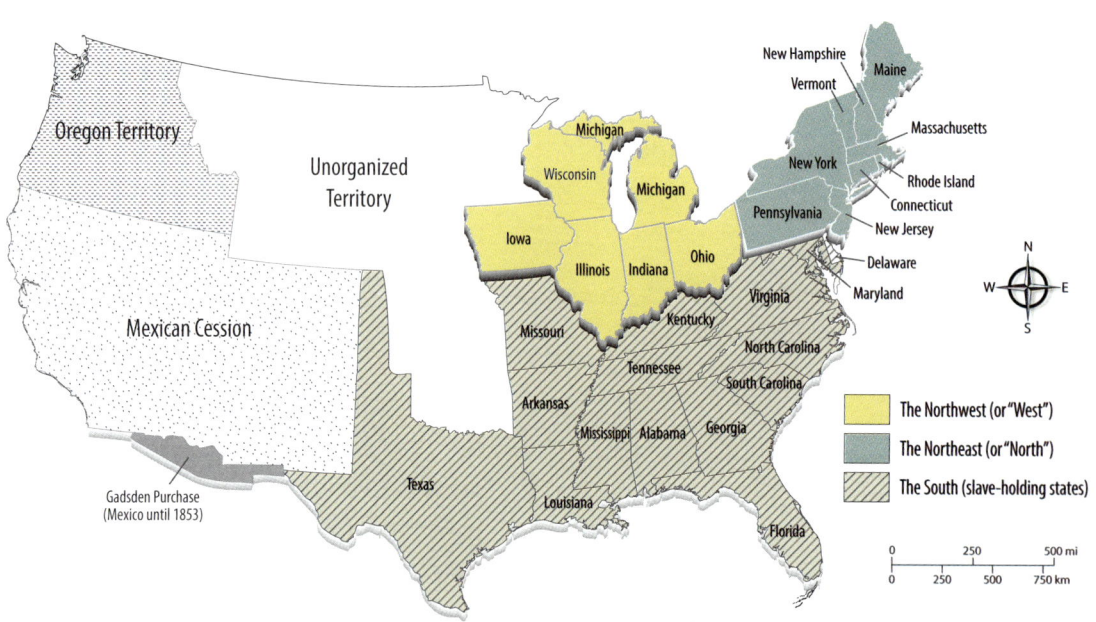

Graphs

Graphs are used to display quantitative information. A *bar graph* has bars representing different amounts. Often it is used to compare things, such as the number of Union and Confederate soldiers killed in the Civil War, or the number of battleships of each power in the 1920s. *Line graphs* show how the amount or size of something has changed over time. For example, a line graph might show the number of workers in the coal industry from 1850 to 1950. Or it could show the average income for Americans from 1900 to 2000. To interpret a line graph, be sure to understand both the "Y-axis" on the left side and the "X-axis" on the bottom. Usually the Y-axis is a "yard stick" providing the numbers for measuring, such as how many thousands of workers, while the X-axis indicates the passage of time.

Workers in U.S. Coal Mining

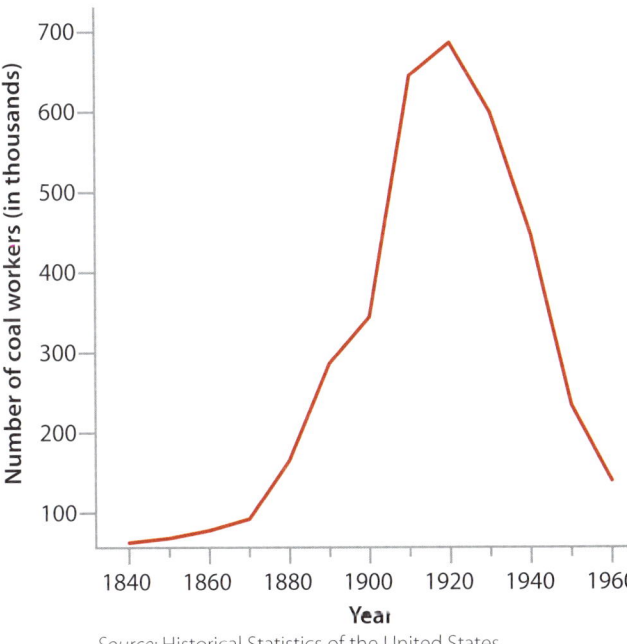

Source: Historical Statistics of the United States

▶ On a separate sheet of paper, turn this line graph into a bar graph showing the number of American coal miners in 1860, 1900 and 1960.

Charts and Tables

Charts and tables often present information in rows and columns. This format makes it easy to locate particular facts or numbers. The top row usually provides headings, telling the reader what each column stands for. The left column lists the individual items the chart or table describes.

▶ From the line graph above, create a your own table showing the number of American coal miners every decade from 1850 to 1920.

Political Cartoons

A political cartoon is a cartoon by an artist commenting on current affairs, social conditions or events. Political cartoonists often question authority, draw attention to corruption, or expose insincerity and hypocrisy. Cartoonists frequently use satire, exaggerate features, or make comparisons with their art to make their point. For example, a cartoonist might draw the American President with a crown and the robes of a king. What would the artist be trying to say? The artist probably thinks the President is assuming too much power, or acting without consulting Congress or the public. When looking at a cartoon, be sure to understand what it shows. What is the time period of the cartoon? Who is represented? What are the people in the cartoon doing? Are there any special symbols or references? What were some of the key issues of that time period? Finally, what is the cartoonist's point of view?

▶ Andrew Jackson was President of the United States from 1829 to 1837. What is this cartoonist's view of Andrew Jackson?

▶ Which features of the cartoon helped you to determine the cartoonist's point of view?

Photographs and Illustrations

A photograph, drawing or painting gives us a snapshot into the past. Historians use these sources to understand what the past was really like. To interpret a photograph or illustration, you have to be a good detective. What details does the picture show? Consider the faces and clothing of any people in the photograph or picture. Also, consider the setting or background. What can you learn from it? Think of the photograph or illustration as a piece of evidence. A photograph might be used, for example, to show conditions for workers in an early 20th century coal mine. From the picture, you could see what equipment was used, how crowded the mine was, how much personal space each worker had, and how safe conditions were. You might also judge how energetic or tired the workers seem, their ages, and their gender and racial background. Questions on a photograph or illustration may also ask you what the picture shows or to draw conclusions from it.

▶ How old are the workers in this coal mine?
▶ What equipment are they using?
▶ Why do you think this photograph was taken?
▶ What conclusions can you draw from this photograph?

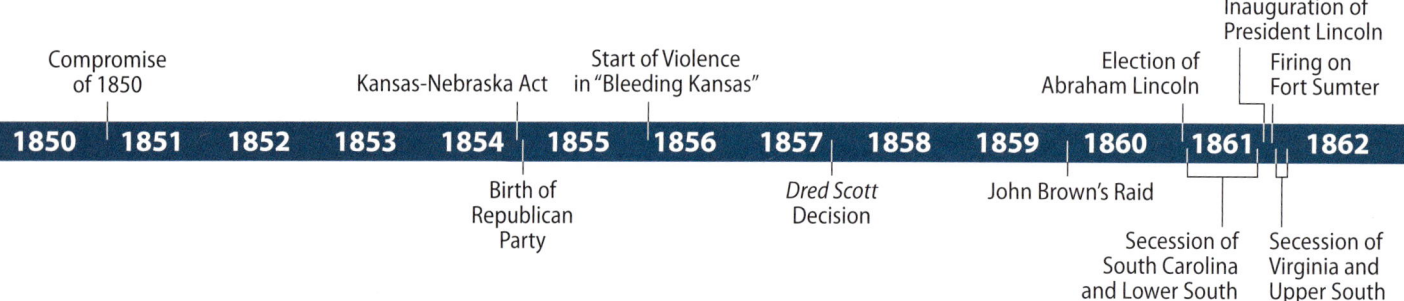

Timelines

A timeline shows a series of events arranged along a line in the order, or sequence, in which they occurred. Usually, the left side of the timeline marks the beginning of the time period it shows, and the right side marks the end. As dates move from left to right, they move closer to the present. A timeline usually shows a series of related events. It is useful because we can see exactly when they occurred and how they relate to each other. Questions on timelines may ask about how the events on the timeline are related, or they may ask you to make an inference or draw a conclusion about the events that are shown.

▶ What other events might be placed on this timeline?
▶ What were some of the consequences of the events shown on the timeline?
▶ Make your own timeline showing how you spent yesterday.

Introduction

Historians at Work

SS.912.A.1.1 Describe the importance of historiography, which includes how historical knowledge is obtained and transmitted, when interpreting events in history.

SS.912.A.2 Utilize a variety of primary and secondary sources to identify author, historical significance, audience, and authenticity to understand a historical period.

What Is History?

What, exactly, is *history*? Historians, of course, study the past. They try to understand exactly what took place in the past. They also often focus on the causes and effects of past events.

You probably know that many historians study politics and wars. But that is not all that historians study. There are many varieties of history. Many historians try to understand what it was like for ordinary people living in the past. Others try to understand how standards of living, beliefs and values, machines and technology, and ways of relating to one another have changed over time. Still others study the struggles of minority groups or women to achieve equal rights, or a country's foreign relations.

Here are some of the most common forms of history that you should know:

Political History: Political historians study government, political parties and political events. Much of what you study in high school is political history.

Economic History: Economic historians study how goods are made and distributed, how economies grow, and why they sometimes fail. This year you will study several topics in economic history: why did the U.S. economy grow in the late 19th century, why did farmers on the Great Plains face economic difficulties, what were the causes of the Great Depression, and what were the causes of the prosperity of the 1950s?

Social History: Social historians study what it was like to live in the past for ordinary people. They also study particular social groups. This year you will study how ordinary Americans were affected by industrialization. You will consider what life was like for many different social groups, including American Indians, Western farmers, factory workers, immigrants, and women.

Labor History: Labor historians study conditions for workers. They also study how workers organized themselves to improve their conditions and standards of living. This year you will learn how working conditions declined for many with industrialization. Then you will learn how different groups of industrial workers formed labor unions.

Women's History: Historians of women study the rights and living conditions of women in the past, and how they organized to achieve equal rights and opportunities with men. This year you will learn how women struggled to achieve the right to vote, and how they later fought for social and economic equality.

Black History: These historians study the African-American experience from slavery to the present. This year you will learn about the conditions of African Americans under slavery, how they were freed by the Civil War, their conditions in the South during Reconstruction and afterwards, the Great Migration and Harlem Renaissance, and how they ended segregation and secured equal rights during the Civil Rights Movement of the 1950s and 1960s.

Intellectual History: Intellectual historians look at past ideas, how they changed and developed, and the impact these ideas had on society. This year you will learn about such ideas as capitalism, Social Darwinism, Communism, socialism, and anarchism.

Military History: Military historians examine past wars and how they were fought. They review military strategies and consider why wars are won or lost. They study how nations prepare for war and the impact of the military on society as a whole. This year you will study the Mexican-American War, the Spanish-American War, World War I, World War II, the Vietnam War, the Korean War, the Persian Gulf War and the Iraq War.

Environmental History: Environmental historians study how people make use of their physical environment, and how they in turn affect it. This year you will study how Americans transformed the Great Plains; how industry, railroads and automobiles changed our country's environment; and how environmental changes led to the Dust Bowl in the 1930s.

You already know that history is the study of the past. But what is *historiography*?

Historiography is the study of history itself. In other words, it is the study of how historians reach their conclusions and often disagree. It is also the study of how our views on the history of an event often change over time. In short, historiography is the study of how historical knowledge is learned and transmitted. Historiographers look at how groups of historians often interpret and explain events. Often they will agree on certain fundamental points but just as often they will disagree on their interpretation of the past. They may disagree on particular facts or disagree on the interpretation and importance of those facts. When you compare the views of different historians on the same topic, you are studying historiography.

The Historian's Apprentice

- Select one of the types of history from the list above. Using the Internet, find one historian who works in that field of history and find the name of one book that this historian has written.
- If you became a historian, which type of history would you choose to study? Explain your answer in a short personal essay of two to three paragraphs.
- How does history differ from historiography?

Who Cares about History?

In today's busy and rapidly changing world, you may wonder if it is worthwhile at all to study history. In fact, there are many reasons why it is important for each of us to know something about the past:

- History helps us to understand how we got to where we are today.
- In many cases, past events still affect how we think today.
- Knowledge of history can give us insight into where we are going in the future.
- The record of the past often has lessons that we can apply in facing our nation's challenges, or even in dealing with our personal problems. By knowing about the past, we can often avoid making the same mistakes. Sometimes we can even "recycle" good ideas from the past to solve present problems.
- History teaches us that terrible things can happen when people neglect the study of history or have a partial and distorted view of the past. For example, the rulers of Nazi Germany and other totalitarian regimes deliberately controlled knowledge of history in order to "brainwash" the public into believing certain historical myths that furthered their own goals.
- If we don't study the past, the struggles and accomplishments of those who went before us will be forgotten. By implication, our own struggles and achievements will be ignored by those who come after us, robbing our own lives of meaning and significance.
- Studying history is fun, while it also helps develop our critical thinking skills. In learning about the past, you will discover new facts and ideas, analyze and evaluate information, compare theories and explanations, make connections, and draw conclusions. These are skills that will be important for participation as a citizen in our democracy as well as for your future work.

As you can see, there are many good reasons for learning about history—in addition to wanting to perform your very best and earning a top score on Florida's End-of-Course Assessment!

The Historian's Apprentice

- What is your own family's history? Ask your mother, father or guardian what they can tell you about your family's history. What did your parents and grandparents do for a living? When did members of your family first come to the United States—in recent decades or centuries ago?
- Were any members of your family ever direct participants in a national event—such as fighting in a war, surviving the Great Depression, or marching in the Civil Rights Movement?
- Can you think of one way in which your own life or beliefs might have been influenced by your family history? Write a short essay describing one detail of your family's history and how it may have affected you.

Introduction | Historians at Work

Where Do Historians Get Their Information From?

You are probably used to learning about history from your textbook, or maybe even by watching movies and television. But a historian does not usually go to a textbook to discover what happened in the past. In order to learn what happened in the past, historians look at a variety of sources.

Primary Sources

Everything we know about the past can ultimately be traced back to primary sources. **Primary sources** are original writings or artifacts created at the time of the events or conditions they describe. A report to Congress in 1901 describing fighting at the time in the Philippines would be a primary source. So would a series of photographs showing the conditions of migrant workers harvesting fruits and vegetables on California farms in the 1920s. A letter from President Kennedy to his brother Robert about the Cuban Missile Crisis, written in October 1962, would be another primary source. Even if a person writes about events he or she personally witnessed some years later, this is still considered a primary source, although it may be less reliable than if it had been written at the time of the event.

Secondary Sources

Historians also use secondary sources. A **secondary source** is any writing or other source of information about the past that is *not* a primary source. It is often the work of a historian or scholar who has reviewed the primary sources and other secondary sources. This very book, *Gateway to U.S. History*, is a secondary source.

Secondary sources can be very useful for obtaining an overview of an event. They often summarize what is found in a large number of primary sources. Secondary sources are often used to present information about history to students or to the general public.

To write a secondary source, such as a history book or textbook, a historian usually first reads other secondary sources about the same topic. Then the historian reads several primary sources. These may be published autobiographies, letters, or collections of documents. Or the historian may go to the archives, such as the National Archives in Washington, D.C., to find actual letters and other documents in the original. The historian then pieces all of this evidence together—what other historians say in their secondary sources, and what the historian has learned by examining some of the primary sources.

How Historical Knowledge is Developed and Transmitted

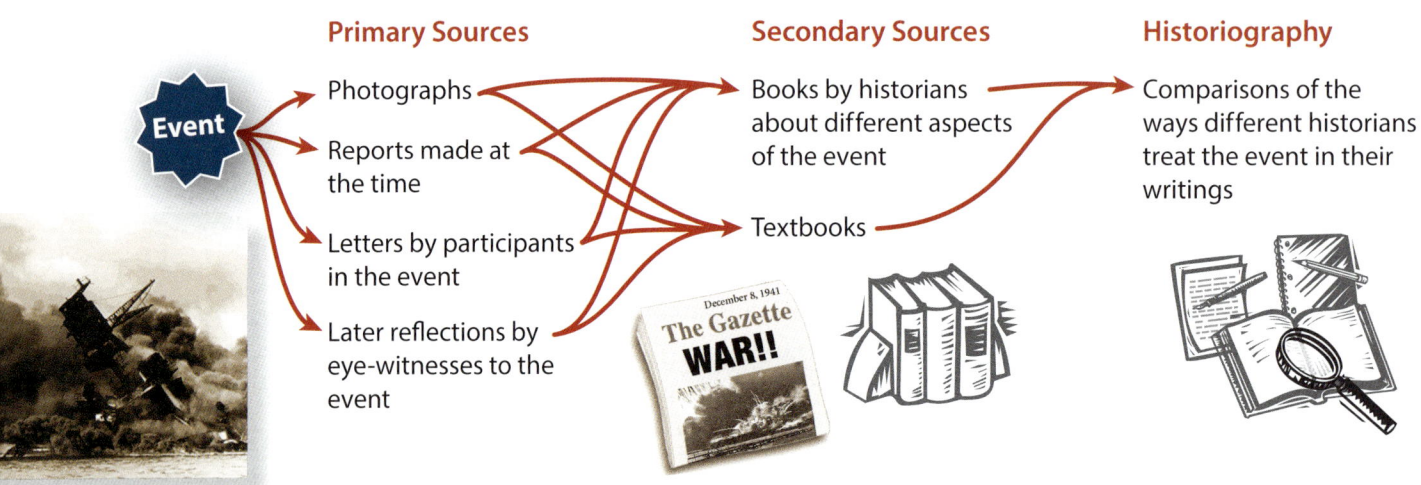

Introduction | Historians at Work

The Historian's Apprentice

You are assisting a public historian in your community. She is preparing an exhibition about the Civil War in Florida for your local museum. She has asked you to determine which of the following are primary or secondary sources. Provide your answers and explain what made you decide whether each of these is a primary or secondary source.

	Primary	Secondary	Comments
A letter in 1859 from a slave owner to his wife describing his slaves' living quarters.	☐	☐	_____
The film "Yellowneck," released in 1955, which depicts Confederate deserters during the Civil War, who are wading through the Everglades to escape to Cuba.	☐	☐	_____
An original rifle used by a Confederate soldier in the Battle of Olustee (1864).	☐	☐	_____
A copy of Tracy Revels' book, *Grander in Her Daughters: Florida's Women during the Civil War*, published in 2004.	☐	☐	_____
A printed copy of the "Ordinance of Secession," passed by Florida's General Assembly in 1861.	☐	☐	_____

Evaluating Primary and Secondary Sources

Have you ever noticed that you often use different reasoning with your parents than with your friends? For example, suppose you feel you didn't do your very best on a test in school. You might tell your friends that you didn't really care that much and that you just didn't study enough. But you probably wouldn't say that to your parents. You might tell them, instead, that everyone in your class did poorly on the test, or at least that your best friend did much worse than you did. Or you might even tell them that your teacher didn't do a good job at explaining the topic, and that you would try much harder to do better next time.

Introduction | Historians at Work

Now suppose you were a historian in the future reading these different explanations 100 years from now. Which explanation would you believe?

Historians are very aware that they cannot take every written document or artifact at "face value." They cannot assume it is true just because it is written down. They have to evaluate the document.

There is a reason why every document was created. That reason may affect how accurate that document is, and what it says. Historians therefore consider very carefully who wrote each document and why it was written.

> When judging a document, especially a primary source, a historian will generally ask these questions:
>
> ▶ Who wrote the document?
> ▶ When was it written?
> ▶ Why was it written?
> ▶ What is known about the author of the document?
> ▶ How did the social position and/or personal biases of the author influence what was written in the document?
> ▶ How does the information in this document relate to other available evidence?

Using a Variety of Sources to Understand the Past

To understand a particular historical period, you should use a variety of primary and secondary sources just like a real historian. This will provide you with several points of view.

- ▶ For each source, first consider the *author*. Think about what you already know about that person. What is his or her social background, education, and occupation? Does the author have any special interests or biases that might have slanted his or her viewpoint?

- ▶ Next, consider the *audience* towards which the writer or speaker is directing his or her message.

- ▶ Third, consider its *authenticity*. Based on what you know, does the document seem to be *authentic*? Does it seem real or fake? Does it fit in with what you already know? Is it a genuine expression of the author's views? Or does the information in the document seem like a wild exaggeration? Does this source agree with other sources? Does the language in this source sound like the way people spoke at the time?

- ▶ Finally, you should consider the *historical significance* of any source that you use to learn about the past. How does the information in this source compare to what you have read in other sources? What does this source tell you about this historical period?

When reading a historical document, be sure to use *context clues* to help you determine the meaning of any words or terms you do not know. Sometimes you can determine the basic meaning of a document even without knowing the definitions of some of its more difficult terms.

Historians not only use written texts, such as letters, court decisions, government orders, newspapers, and legislative debates. They also look at **artifacts** (*objects*), political cartoons, photographs, maps and artwork to learn about the past. A photograph can show what conditions were once like. A painted portrait may reveal something of the sitter's personality. Old maps show historians where things were once located. Political cartoons often reflect popular feelings. Artifacts tell us what everyday life was like in a different time period.

Florida's U.S. History End-of-Course Assessment will ask you to answer some questions in which you must interpret a historical document contained in the question. By reading original sources, you will get the practice you need to answer this kind of question.

In this book, you will have an opportunity to look at many different primary sources. **The Historian's Apprentice** activities will sometimes ask you to interpret a source or to find additional primary and secondary sources on your own.

The Historian's Apprentice

Here is a primary source about Florida, written in the 1930s. It is a description from a travel brochure "Souvenir Folder of Tropical Florida: The Sun Porch of America," published by J. N. Chamberlain.

"Florida, the very name entices and draws people from every section of the country . . . Florida was admitted as the twenty-seventh State in the Union in 1845, with a population of some 60,000, which number has grown until there are now 1,253,600 people who are permanent residents. During the winter months this is about doubled, and each year sees a greater number of winter visitors pouring into the State by rail and automobile.

Florida furnishes an all-year climate, ideal in winter and pleasant in summer. The balmy breezes and bright sunshine of Florida in the winter months have made this State the Nation's playground. The summer months in Florida are pleasant ones. Temperatures are even, the heat is tempered by constant breezes, and the nights invariably comfortable. No part of the state is far from the sea. Every section is swept by mild zephyrs from the Atlantic Ocean and the Gulf of Mexico.

Florida offers exceptional recreational advantages every day in the year. There are more than one hundred golf courses in the State, where links are green and inviting all the time. Motoring is a favorable pastime on the more than 10,000 miles of highways which wind through orange groves, pine forests, along rivers, lakes and ocean. Surf bathing may be enjoyed every day in the year, as well as horseback riding, tennis, polo, aviation and other sports which are outdoor features of this great land.

Florida is ideally situated as a winter playground. There is but one Florida and it calls to all nature-loving people. Not only is it a playground for the leisure class and a winter home for the wealthy, but it is a year-round place in which to live, to transact business on a large or a small scale as befits your ability; a place where you may grow your own vegetables every day in the year.

Life, love and laughter—that is Florida . . . Health, happiness and opportunity await you in Florida. Nowhere else in America is there greater reward for energy, enthusiasm or capital than in this wonder State at the nation's door. Nowhere else may one find the joy of relaxation, rest or recreation so fully satisfied as in Florida."

▶ What are the author's main ideas in this document?
▶ What was the author's purpose in writing this description? Who is the audience?
▶ How has the author's purpose influenced the details included in the description?
▶ Do you think all Floridians in the 1930s would have agreed with this description?
▶ How might a historian today make use of this historical document?

This year you will study the history of the United States. In many ways, it is an inspiring story, full of struggle, defeat and triumph.

Above all, the American story has been one of the expansion of human rights—slowly bringing to life the ideal expressed in the Declaration of Independence, that all Americans "are created equal." You will learn how Americans at one time were deeply divided by bigotry and racism. Gradually, we have overcome slavery, segregation, the denial of civil rights, and racially-inspired violence. You will also learn how American women of all races and backgrounds were once treated as second-class citizens and only won the right to vote less than a century ago, and the right to equal opportunities in education and employment five decades ago. Through popular protests, legislation, and the actions of our nation's courts, similar rights have been extended to other groups, from ethnic minorities to the elderly and those with disabilities.

The American story is also one of innovation and accelerating economic growth, which has led to increasing prosperity and modern conveniences. You will learn how what was once a rural society of isolated communities was transformed by industrialization and urbanization. You will see how modern society was forged by a series of American inventions: the telegraph, the telephone, the electric light bulb, and the assembly line. Great entrepreneurs turned America into a modern industrial society, based on steel, oil, electricity, and automobiles. Industrialization also brought new challenges—the increasing exploitation of workers and immigrants, overcrowded cities, corrupt officials, and the accumulation of monopoly power and political influence by the very rich.

A third theme in our history is the relationship of Americans to their government. You will learn how some reformers looked to government to curb the worst abuses of industrialization. Progressives in government broke up business monopolies, challenged unfair practices and introduced regulations to protect consumers. People later appealed to government leaders in the depths of the Great Depression in the 1930s, when millions of Americans lost their jobs and homes, and were reduced to begging in the streets. Related to this is the issue of the proper ratio between government spending and taxation. You will see how, throughout our history, people have held different views of how government should obtain its money—from tariff duties, income taxes, or selling bonds that increase our national debt.

A fourth theme of American history that you will study this year concerns our relations with the rest of the world. In the century before the Civil War, America was relatively isolated from the powers of Europe. After expanding their frontiers to the Pacific and engaging in a great Civil War, Americans were ready to expand outward. They acquired overseas colonies in 1898, and afterwards became drawn into two world wars and the "Cold War" in defense of democracy and American values. You will consider how these commitments have had enormous costs, and how new weapon technologies have made modern wars vastly more destructive than conflicts in the past.

What would you like to know about American history? Identify one thing you would like to learn more about this year on a separate sheet of paper and keep it in a safe place. This spring, when you have completed this course, return to the page you have written to see if you have met your objective!

Introduction | Historians at Work

CHAPTER 1

The Civil War

SS.912.A.2.1 Review causes and consequences of the Civil War.

SS.912.A.3.13 Examine key events and peoples in Florida history as they relate to United States history.

Names and Terms You Should Know

Sectionalism	Ostend Manifesto	Fort Sumter
Abolitionists	Republican Party	Anaconda Plan
Frederick Douglass	*Dred Scott* decision	Emancipation Proclamation
Missouri Compromise	John Brown's raid	Gettysburg
Freeport Doctrine	Abraham Lincoln	Gettysburg Address
Compromise of 1850	States' rights	Vicksburg
Fugitive Slave Act	Secession	Appomattox
Kansas–Nebraska Act	Jefferson Davis	

Florida "Keys" to Learning

1. The Civil War had multiple causes, including sectionalism, slavery, and differing views of states' rights.

2. Sectionalism refers to the loyalty many Americans felt towards their own geographic region—the North, South, or West—rather than to the country as a whole.

3. The Northeast saw the rise of manufacturing; the West was populated by independent farmers growing food and raising livestock; the South focused on growing cash crops for export, such as cotton and rice, and remained dependent on the use of slave labor.

4. Abolitionists wanted to end the practice of slavery. Pro-slavery apologists argued that Southern slaves were better treated than Northern workers.

5. The issue of the extension of slavery to new territories arose as the nation expanded westward. A series of compromises at first seemed able to resolve the issue. Under the Missouri Compromise (1820), Missouri became a slave state and Maine became a free state. Slavery was not otherwise to be permitted in the lands of the Louisiana Purchase above 36°30′N. Thus, the later admission of Florida as a slave state was balanced by the addition of Iowa as a free state. In the Compromise of 1850, California was admitted as a free state and a stricter fugitive slave law was enacted.

6. The system of compromise broke down with the passage of the Kansas–Nebraska Act (1854), "Bleeding Kansas" (1855–1856), the *Dred Scott* decision (1857), and John Brown's raid on Harpers Ferry (1859).

7. In the Presidential election of 1860, Democrats were divided. Republican candidate Abraham Lincoln won the election with only 39% of the popular vote and no electoral votes from Southern states. South Carolina and six other Southern states immediately seceded (*withdrew from the Union*). The seceding states formed the Confederate States of America.

8. In his inaugural address, Lincoln called on Southern states to remain in the Union and promised not to end slavery in the South. When he sent supplies to Fort Sumter in Charleston Harbor, South Carolina fired on the fort, beginning the Civil War. Rather than fight fellow Southerners, four more states seceded.

9. The North had many advantages: a larger population, greater revenues, more railroad lines and factories, and superior naval power. The South had its military traditions and the fact that white Southerners were fighting to preserve their way of life. The existence of a large population of Southern slaves created an additional element of uncertainty, while the South's specialized export economy and devotion to states' rights further weakened the Confederacy.

10. In the early campaigns, the South repelled Northern invasions, but could not successfully advance into the North itself. Meanwhile the North relied on its naval power to strangle the South—imposing a naval blockade of the Atlantic Coast and attempting to obtain control of the Mississippi.

11. In September 1862, Lincoln issued the Emancipation Proclamation. It announced the emancipation of slaves in those states still in rebellion on January 1, 1863.

12. The turning point of the war was reached in 1863, when the North defeated Southern forces at Gettysburg and General Ulysses S. Grant captured Vicksburg. Lincoln put Grant in supreme command of Union forces. Grant aimed at destroying Confederate forces and their sources of support. General Sherman's "March to the Sea" further divided the South and destroyed farms, towns, and railroad lines.

13. In April 1865, General Robert E. Lee surrendered to Grant at Appomattox. Less than a week later, President Lincoln was assassinated.

14. The Civil War ended slavery, preserved the Union, and strengthened the federal government.

The Civil War

The Civil War was the most divisive conflict in American history. More Americans were killed in this war than in any other. The wounds left by the Civil War took decades to heal.

Causes of the Civil War

A complex event like the Civil War has many causes. Historians often consider both the long-term and short-term causes of such events:

▶ **Long-term** causes are those economic, social, cultural, and political factors that make an event possible or even likely.

▶ **Short-term** causes usually consist of a specific problem or crisis and how it is handled, which then leads directly to the event.

Although a war or revolution may appear to have been inevitable when looking backwards at events, such conflicts can sometimes be avoided if leaders skillfully steer through a crisis and introduce reforms to address the underlying problems.

In looking at the Civil War, historians frequently consider sectionalism, slavery, and disagreements over the interpretation of the Constitution as the long-term causes of the conflict. Did they make the conflict inevitable?

1. Sectionalism

The first factories and steamboats made their appearance only a few years after the U.S. Constitution was ratified. Meanwhile, the United States doubled its size with the Louisiana Purchase in 1803.

Economic development and westward expansion affected each part of the country differently. Each region of the United States gradually evolved its own distinct social system.

Chapter 1 | The Civil War

- The **South** was distinguished by the continuation of slavery—its "peculiar institution"—long after it had been abolished in the North. The invention of the cotton gin and the increased demand for raw cotton from factories in the North and Britain overseas led to an expansion of slavery in the South. By 1860, almost four million people—about one-third of the population of the South—were African-American slaves. A majority of them worked on the large plantations of the Southern elite.

- The **Northwest** was dominated by small, independent farmers. The Northwest became the "bread basket" of the United States, growing grain that was shipped by river and canal to both the Northeast and the South.

- The **Northeast** became a center of manufacturing. In the early years of the nineteenth century, the Northeast witnessed the growth of a new class of factory workers.

These economic and social differences led to the rise of "**sectionalism**" as early as the 1820s. *Sectionalism* refers to the greater loyalty that many Americans felt towards their "section" (or region)—the North, South or West—than to the country as a whole.

Political leaders in each section generally wanted federal policies favorable to their sectional interests. This led to frequent clashes. Northerners wanted high tariffs to protect their manufactured goods from competition with cheaper British goods. Southerners opposed high tariffs because they sold raw cotton

The United States in Early 1850

Economic Specialization in the United States, circa 1850

Section	Population in 1850	Leading Economic Activities
Northeast (9 states)	9 million	Manufacturing (textiles, ironwares, and machinery), shipping, small farms and fishing.
South (15 states)	9 million (including about 3.5 million slaves)	Small farms and large plantations using slave labor to grow cash crops like cotton, tobacco, rice, and sugar for export.
Northwest (6 states)	5 million	Family farms on fertile lands produced wheat, corn, oats, and livestock for sale in the Northeast and South.

Source: *Historical Statistics of the United States*

Important National Issues, 1820–1850

Issue	Northeast	South	Northwest
Protective Tariff	Yes	No	Yes
National Bank	Yes	No	No
Federal Financing of Roads and Canals	Yes	No	Yes
Cheap Federal Land	No	Yes	Yes
Extension of Slavery to New Territories	No	Yes	No

to Britain and wanted to be able to buy cheap British imports. In general, Northerners favored a more active federal government that would take steps to promote the growth of American industry (such as the creation of a strong central bank). Southerners wanted as little interference from the federal government as possible. They feared high tariffs and federal meddling with their system of slavery.

2. Slavery

The most explosive issue facing Americans was that of slavery. **Abolitionists** were reformers (often Protestant preachers) who saw slavery as a great moral evil that ought to be abolished. The abolition of slavery in the British Empire in 1833 greatly inspired these American abolitionists. So did the efforts of many former slaves, such as **Frederick Douglass**, **Sojourner Truth** and **Harriet Tubman**, who gave speeches and wrote books about the horrors they had endured in the South. Publications like William Lloyd Garrison's journal, *The Liberator,* and a popular book by **Harriet Beecher Stowe**, *Uncle Tom's Cabin* (1852), helped to create a sense of moral outrage against slavery across much of the North.

Frederick Douglass

In fact, in Southern states about two-thirds of the white population owned no slaves at all. Nevertheless, much of the Southern economy was based on profits gained through the use of slave labor. Pro-slavery Southerners argued that African Americans were inferior and actually better off as slaves. They claimed that Southern slaves were better treated than factory workers in the North, because slaves were fed, clothed, and housed by their masters. Finally, they feared that emancipating millions of slaves might lead to social disorder and violence against whites.

Was the existence of slavery the main cause of the Civil War? Surely it would have been difficult to eliminate the Southern system of slavery—the South's "peculiar institution"—without a war. And the main reason the Southern states seceded from the Union was certainly because they thought their system of slavery was threatened. African Americans also saw the war as a struggle to obtain their freedom. On the other hand, the Civil War did not at first start over the question of slavery in the South, but over the issue of whether individual states had the right to secede from the Union. And several slave-holding border states, such as Missouri, refused to secede. Northern leaders did not want to drive these border states away by threatening an end to slavery.

3. Westward Expansion

Tensions between the North and South might have been controlled had it not been for the acquisition of new lands in the West. Expansionist policies in the 1840s led to American control of half of the Or-

Slaves waiting to be sold in Richmond, Virginia

egon Territory and a large section of Mexico. These annexations created the problem of determining which way of life was to be adopted in the new territories—one based on slavery or free labor?

Many Northerners were appalled at the possibility of the further spread of slavery. Others feared competition with slave labor. Lincoln's Republican Party, formed in 1854, did not oppose the existence of slavery in the South, but opposed its extension to the new territories.

Most Southerners felt that only by extending slavery to some of the new states could they keep control of half of the United States Senate. They saw this as vital since the Senate was their main weapon in defending the slave system against abolitionist attacks from the more populous North.

4. The Breakdown of Compromise

Despite sectional differences, the nation managed to preserve its fragile unity through a series of clever compromises.

The Missouri Compromise, 1820

When Missouri applied for admission as a slave state, there were exactly eleven free states and eleven slave states. Neither the North nor the South wanted to give the other side a majority in the Senate. A compromise was eventually worked out:

Free versus Slave States

Year	Free States	Slave States
1790	7	8
1800	8	9
1821	12	12
1837	13	13
1846	14	15
1848	15	15
1858	17	15
1861	19	15

▸ Missouri was admitted as a slave state.

▸ Maine was admitted as a free state.

▸ No other slavery was to be allowed in the Louisiana Purchase north of the southern boundary of Missouri (the 36°30'N line of latitude).

It was in the spirit of the Missouri Compromise that Florida was admitted as a slave state and Iowa was admitted as a free state in the 1840s.

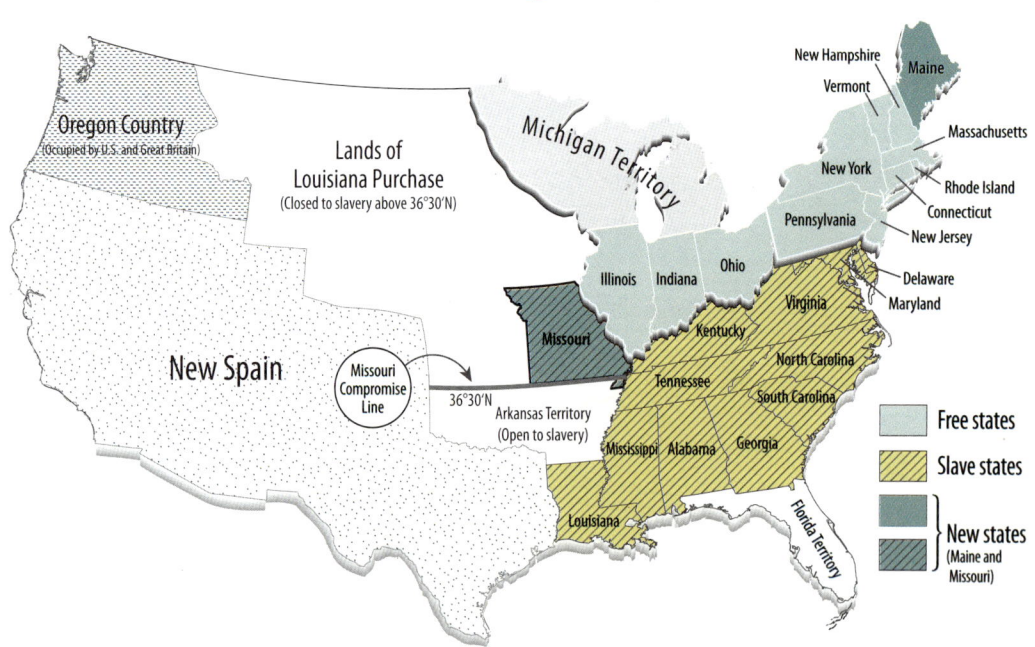

The Missouri Compromise, 1820

The U.S. Senate debates the Compromise of 1850

The Compromise of 1850

Another crisis occurred thirty years later when California threatened to upset the balance in the Senate by applying for admission as a free state. In fact, all of the lands taken from Mexico during the **Mexican-American War** (1846–1848) posed the same problem. Again, a compromise was arranged:

- California was admitted as a free state.
- The system of "popular sovereignty" was applied to the other territories taken from Mexico. This meant that the people living in those territories would decide for themselves whether or not to permit slavery.
- A new and harsher fugitive slave law was passed, requiring free states in the North to cooperate in returning runaway slaves to their owners in the South. The Fugitive Slave Act of 1850 was greatly resented in the North.
- The sale of slaves was banned in Washington, D.C.

The Embittered Climate of the 1850s

In the 1850s, a series of new events tore these earlier compromises apart. Was this breakdown inevitable or did it demonstrate a failure of American political leadership? An alarming rise of violence in events such as "Bleeding Kansas" and John Brown's raid was symptomatic of the new climate.

The Kansas–Nebraska Act, 1854

The change in climate began with the Kansas–Nebraska Act. Senator Stephen Douglas of Illinois, who had helped to arrange the Compromise of 1850, introduced the **Kansas–Nebraska Act** to win Southern support for a railroad line to be built from the Midwest to California. The act divided the Nebraska Territory into Nebraska and Kansas. It further repealed the Missouri Compromise by applying the principle of "popular sovereignty" to both the Kansas and Nebraska Territories. This reintroduced

The Compromise of 1850

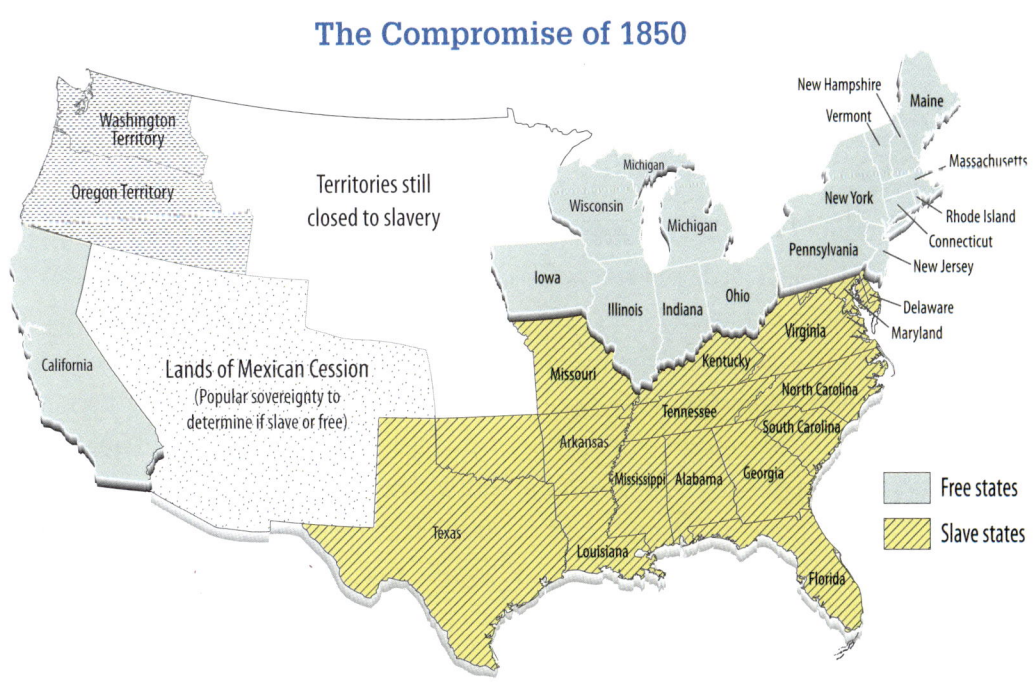

Chapter 1 | The Civil War

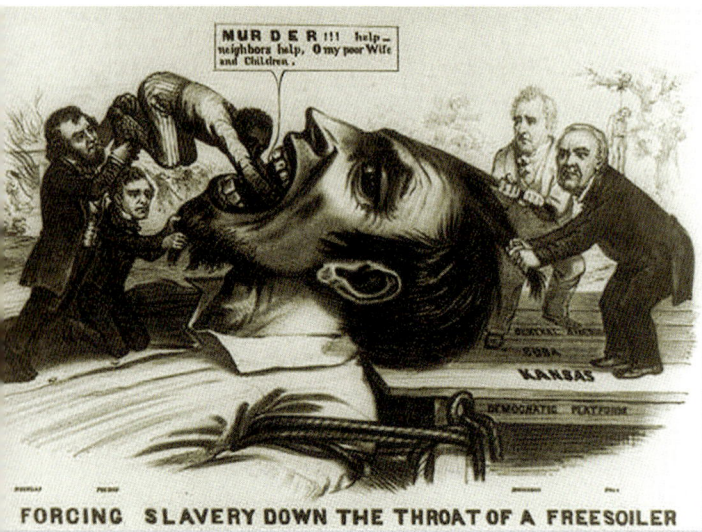

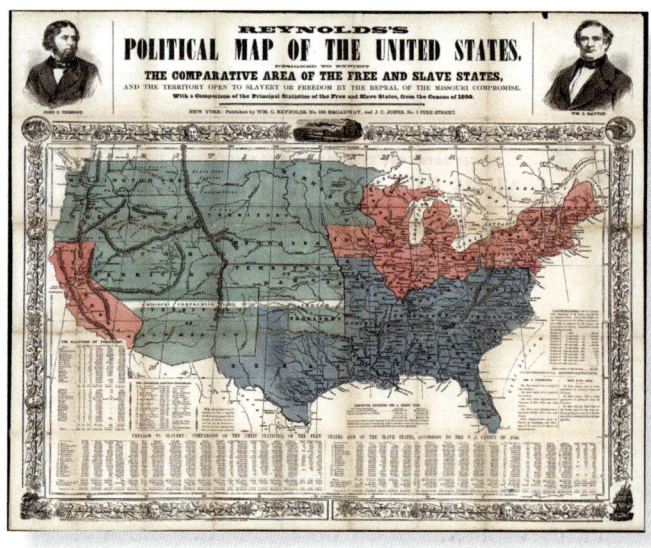

the possibility of slavery where it had previously been prohibited. Douglas argued that "popular sovereignty" offered the most democratic way of resolving the slavery question and would remove the issue from national politics. Many Northerners, however, were shocked. The **Republican Party** was formed in 1854 in direct response to the Kansas–Nebraska Act. Republicans opposed the extension of slavery to any new territories. Northerners were further outraged when U.S. diplomats in Europe from the South schemed to annex Cuba as a new slave state in a report known as the **Ostend Manifesto** (see page 143).

"Bleeding Kansas," 1855–56

Both pro-slavery and anti-slavery forces tried to influence the outcome in Kansas by bringing in their own groups of settlers. By 1855, two rival state governments were formed—one pro-slavery and one opposed to slavery. The federal government eventually had to send in troops to restore order. Violence even reached the U.S. Senate in May 1856. In one of his speeches, Senator Charles Sumner of Massachusetts denounced Senator Butler of South Carolina with insults for embracing slavery. A few days later, Butler's nephew beat Sumner unconscious with a gold-tipped walking cane on the floor of the Senate.

The *Dred Scott* Decision, 1857

Dred Scott, a Missouri slave, had lived with his owner, an army officer, for several years in Illinois (a free state) and in the Wisconsin territory where slavery was barred by the Missouri Compromise. During this time, Scott had married another slave, and they had two children. After the Scotts returned with their master to Missouri, Dred Scott sued for their freedom. The Scotts were

Dred Scott

in fact freed by a Missouri jury in 1850, but the Missouri Supreme Court reversed this decision in 1852. Dred Scott then appealed his case to the United States Supreme Court. Five years later, the Supreme Court reached its decision. Chief Justice Roger Taney announced that Dred Scott, as an African American, was not a U.S. citizen and therefore had no right to sue in federal court. Moreover, the Supreme Court held that the prohibition of slavery in northern territories by the Missouri Compromise was unconstitutional. According to the Court, a slave was simply the property of another person and Congress did not have the right to take that citizen's property away, or even to limit his property rights—including the right to take that property into federal territory.

> "[African Americans] had no rights which the white man was bound to respect; and that the negro might justly and lawfully be reduced to slavery for his benefit. He was bought and sold and treated as an ordinary article of merchandise, whenever profit could be made by it. [Referring to language in the Declaration of Independence] it is too clear for dispute, that the enslaved African race were not intended to be included, and formed no part of the people who framed and adopted this declaration. . . ."
>
> —Chief Justice Taney, *Dred Scott v. Sandford* (1857)

This ruling by the Justices of the U.S Supreme Court, a majority of whom came from the South, raised a storm of protest throughout the North. In the **Freeport Doctrine**, Stephen Douglas insisted that the residents of a territory could still ban slavery through local laws. Ironically, Dred Scott himself was freed by his owners only two months after the Supreme Court's decision was announced. The troubles caused by the case remained.

The Historian's Apprentice

Pretend your class is putting Chief Justice Roger Taney on trial for his opinion in *Dred Scott v. Sandford*. Did the Supreme Court act fairly and reasonably in reaching its decision? Did the Justices follow the U.S. Constitution, based on the views of that time? Should they have reached a different decision?

John Brown's Raid, 1859

John Brown, a white Northern abolitionist, had moved to "Bleeding Kansas" where he had fought and killed pro-slavery agitators. Brown next drew up plans for launching slave revolts across the South. In 1859, Brown captured a federal arsenal in Harpers Ferry, Virginia, but his tiny force was soon overwhelmed by U.S. troops. Not a single slave joined his uprising. Brown was hanged two months later, but his attempt to stir the slaves to revolt created a wave of fear among Southern whites.

5. Differences in Constitutional Interpretation: States' Rights

Southerners were strong supporters of states' rights. They argued that the states themselves had created the federal government by ratifying the Constitution. Since each state had joined the Union voluntarily, it also had the power to withdraw if it wished.

These ideas were tested during the Presidency of Andrew Jackson. **John C. Calhoun**, a famous Senator from South Carolina and Vice President under

Harpers Ferry Insurrection

Chapter 1 | The Civil War

Jackson, wrote that states had the right to "nullify" (or *cancel*) federal laws within their borders if they believed they were unconstitutional. In 1832, South Carolina nullified the federal tariff, which had raised import duties on goods from England. When Jackson threatened to use force against South Carolina, however, the state backed down. South Carolina continued to maintain that it had the right to nullify federal laws or even to secede from (or *leave*) the Union if it wished.

Many Northerners took a different view. They saw the Constitution as the work of the American people as a whole—"We the People"—and not as the product of the individual states. States therefore did not have the right to pull out of the Union whenever they pleased.

The Immediate Cause of the Civil War: Lincoln's Election and the Secession of the South

The frictions of the previous thirty years created a climate of tension in which an armed conflict between the states became possible. In the Presidential election of 1860, the new Republican Party nominated **Abraham Lincoln**, a former Congressman from Illinois who had made a name for himself in a series of debates with Stephen Douglas. Democrats were divided: Southern Democrats nominated the Vice President, John Breckinridge, and Northern Democrats nominated Stephen Douglas. Another new party, the Constitutional Union, was made up of Southerners who supported the Union; they nominated John Bell. These divisions allowed Lincoln to win the election with only 39% of the popular vote. Not a single Southern state gave its electoral votes to Lincoln.

As soon as Lincoln was elected, South Carolina announced its **secession** from the Union. Six other states from the lower South quickly followed. Florida was the third state to secede. Southern leaders nevertheless hoped to avoid war. Could they peacefully establish a separate nation of slaveholders and slaves, with an economy based on export agriculture, bordering the United States?

President Buchanan declared that these states had no right to secede, but he also felt the federal government had no power stop them. Meanwhile, the Southern states organized themselves into the "**Confederate States of America**." They drew up their own constitution and elected their own President, **Jefferson Davis**. In his inaugural address, Davis emphasized that in their secession from the Union, Southerners had "merely asserted a right which the Declaration of Independence defined to be inalienable." Since the South had no designs of aggression and was largely agricultural, while the North was industrial, Davis hoped the two nations could live side-by-side in peace and prosperity.

In his own inaugural address, Lincoln tried to calm the fears of white Southerners. He pledged not to interfere with slavery where it already existed. He hoped that a show of firmness would avoid bloodshed, but he was equally determined to go to war if necessary to bring the Southern states back to the Union: "[T]he Union of these states," he declared, "is perpetual," and "no state can lawfully get out of the Union."

President Lincoln did recognize the existence of a vague "right of revolution," based on the Declaration of Independence. This right justified rebellion against great moral wrongs, such as taxation without representation. However, Lincoln believed this right did not apply to the circumstances of 1861 because the Southern states were acting unjustly. He was therefore determined to take steps to preserve the Union.

Shots Fired at Fort Sumter

When Lincoln sent food and supplies to **Fort Sumter**, a federal fort in the harbor of Charleston, South Carolina, Confererate forces fired on the fort on April 12, 1861. Lincoln called on all other states to supply militia to put down the rebellion. Virginia and three other states from the upper South joined the seceding states rather than fight against them. West Virginia broke off from Virginia to form a new state loyal to the Union. The border states of Missouri, Kentucky, Maryland, and Delaware also sided with the North.

Once blood was shed, all the frustrations of the past thirty years quickly came to the surface. In both the North and the South, the public seemed to welcome the outbreak of war as a great release and as an opportunity to demonstrate their own superiority. Most people thought their side would win quickly and easily. Unfortunately, they were wrong.

The Historian's Apprentice

Your teacher will organize your class to hold a debate on the proposition that the Southern states had the right to secede from the Union. You can base your arguments in part on the principles found in the Declaration of Independence, the writings of John Locke, the Articles of Confederation, and the U.S. Constitution (popular sovereignty).

The Course of the Civil War

Advantages of the North

When the Civil War began, the North had many advantages over the South. With the border states, it had a population of 22 million, compared to only 5.5 million free persons in the South. It was more industrialized with more railroads, factories, mines, roads, and canals than the South. Its factories could produce arms and ammunition. The North had more coal, iron, gold, and other natural resources.

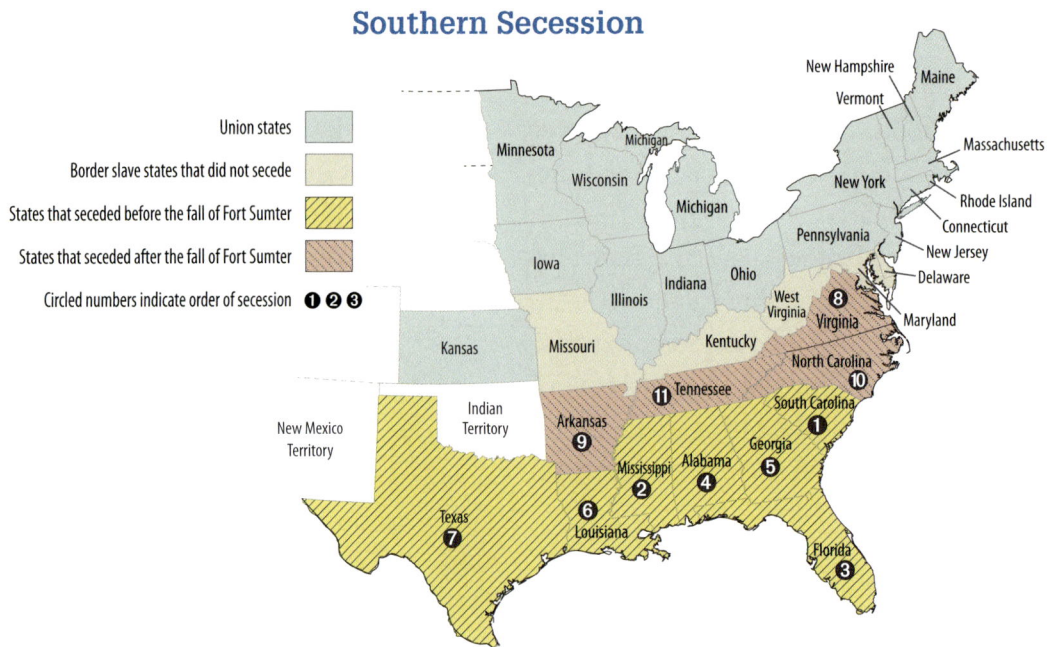

Southern Secession

The Southern economy was dangerously dependent on exports of a few cash crops and lacked diversification. The North had merchant ships and control of the U.S. Navy, while at the start of the war, the South had no navy at all. The South was home to a large slave population, which created an immense element of uncertainty. Would these slaves assist their masters or initiate a series of uprisings to win their freedom and assist the North? Given all the North's advantages, it is remarkable that the war lasted as long as it did. This may have been due to the fact that white Southerners were defending their way of life. They also possessed a strong military tradition and many gifted military commanders, such as **Robert E. Lee** and "Stonewall" Jackson.

General Robert E. Lee

Military Strategies

Northerners adopted a strategy first suggested by General Winfield Scott, which became known as the "**Anaconda Plan**." An anaconda is a giant snake. To limit the bloodshed, Scott proposed strangling the South with a naval blockade of Southern ports and the use of Northern naval power to seize control of the Mississippi and divide the Confederacy in two.

Southerners hoped to ward off Northern attacks. After showing Northerners that they could not win easily, Southern leaders thought the public in the North would lose interest in the war and recognize the Confederacy. They also hoped to win support from foreign countries that depended on Southern cotton.

Lincoln acted quickly. He ordered a naval blockade of the South, suspended *habeas corpus* (which prevents the government in peacetime from imprisoning a person without charge), and issued paper money to pay for wartime expenses. Later, Lincoln even introduced military **conscription** (*obligatory service*).

The opening campaign took place on the peninsula separating Washington, D.C., and Richmond, Virginia, the capital of the Confederacy. A Northern army marched south towards Richmond but was stopped by Confederate forces at the Battle of Bull Run. Farther to the west,

The U.S. Navy captures New Orleans

the U.S. Navy captured New Orleans, while federal troops farther north began pushing down the Mississippi River.

Lee counter-attacked, trying to bring the war to the North. He led his troops into Maryland, but his advance was stopped at the **Battle of Antietam**, on the single bloodiest day of the Civil War.

The Emancipation Proclamation

Lincoln had been reluctant to identify slavery as the cause of the Civil War because this would have risked losing the support of the border states—Maryland, Kentucky, Missouri and Delaware—which permitted slavery but stood by the Union. However, Lincoln was pressured by African Americans like Frederick Douglass and other abolitionists to use the war to end slavery. There was also the problem created by the slaves themselves, who had fled their plantations to join Union forces. Equally important, Lincoln feared that Britain and France might intervene to assist the Confederacy. By making the war more about the continuation of slavery, he would avoid this risk. Finally, there can be no doubt that Lincoln hated slavery.

For all these reasons, Lincoln issued the **Emancipation Proclamation** on September 22, 1862, just days after the Battle of Antietam. Lincoln acted on the basis of his emergency wartime powers. The Emancipation Proclamation announced that all slaves in states still in rebellion on January 1, 1863, would be freed. It did not emancipate any slaves in the border states loyal to the Union. This meant that Lincoln was not actually freeing any slaves at all in states that recognized the authority of the federal government.

But his proclamation did finally make the war into a contest over slavery. It encouraged slaves in the South to join the Union, and discouraged Britain and France from helping the Confederacy. The Union even began recruiting African-American troops for combat, such as the 54th Massachusetts Regiment.

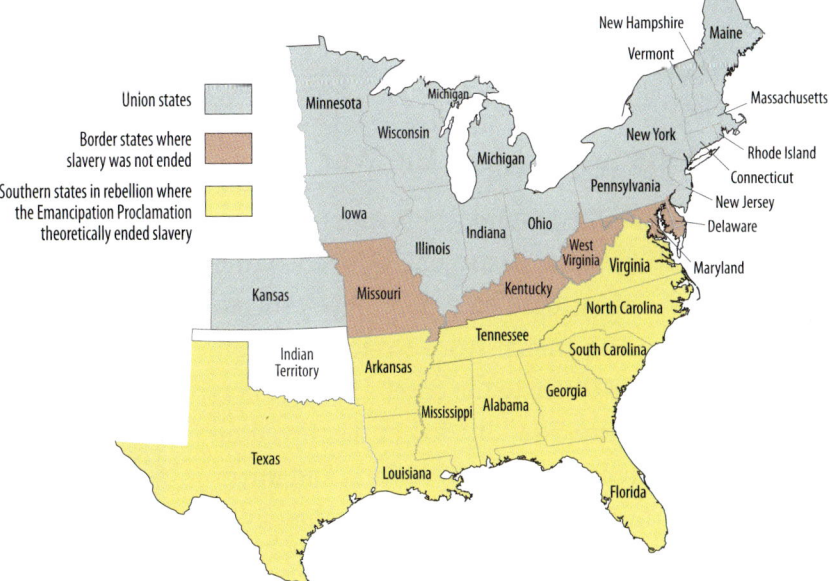

Chapter 1 | The Civil War

1863—The Turning Point of the War

The turning point of the war was reached less than a year later. General Lee again advanced into the North. This time Confederate forces were defeated at **Gettysburg**, Pennsylvania, in July 1863. More than 50,000 troops were injured or killed in the battle. Lincoln honored Union losses in his famous Gettysburg Address. Lee retreated and never advanced into the North again. The day after the Battle of Gettysburg ended, General **Ulysses S. Grant** took **Vicksburg**, a major fortified town farther to the west, giving the North control over the entire Mississippi River Valley.

The Gettysburg Address

Four score and seven years ago our fathers brought forth on this continent a new nation, conceived in liberty, and dedicated to the proposition that all men are created equal. Now we are engaged in a great civil war, testing whether that nation, or any nation, so conceived and so dedicated, can long endure.

We are met on a great battlefield of that war. We have come to dedicate a portion of that field, as a final resting place for those who here gave their lives that that nation might live. . . .

The brave men, living and dead, who struggled here, have consecrated it, far above our poor power to add or detract. . . . It is rather for us to be here dedicated to the great task remaining before us—that from these honored dead we take increased devotion to that cause for which they gave the last full measure of devotion—that we here highly resolve that these dead shall not have died in vain—that this nation, under God, shall have a new birth of freedom—and that government of the people, by the people, for the people, shall not perish from the earth.

—Abraham Lincoln, November 19, 1863

▶ What was the "new birth of freedom" to which Lincoln referred?

▶ Do you think the reputation of this famous speech is justified?

Grant and the Last Year of the War

Lincoln now appointed Grant as his supreme commander. Grant aimed at destroying both the Confederate army and its base of support. He ordered General Sherman to march from western Georgia to Atlanta and then down to the coast. During Sherman's "**March to the Sea**," his forces destroyed all Confederate sources of supply by looting and burning farms and tearing up railroad lines; they even burned the city of Atlanta to the ground.

Lincoln with General Grant and other Union leaders

Following these new battlefield victories, Lincoln was able to win the Presidential election of 1864. By 1865, Confederate forces were dwindling, allowing Grant to advance on the Confederate capital of Richmond. Confederate forces were surrounded at Petersburg and forced to retreat, leaving Richmond vulnerable to attack. On April 9, 1865, Lee surrendered to Grant at **Appomattox**, virtually ending the Civil War. President Lincoln was assassinated by Southern-sympathizer John Wilkes Booth less than one week later.

The Consequences of the War

The Civil War ended slavery, re-affirmed the existence of the Union, and strengthened the power of the federal government. It also led to the loss of 600,000 lives. In Chapter 2, you will learn about the Reconstruction Era—the post-war period of adjustment and recovery in the South. In Chapter 4, you will learn how the North experienced rapid industrialization in the decades following the Civil War.

The Historian's Apprentice

Make a chart summarizing the effects of the Civil War. Consider the war's political, economic, and social effects.

The Blue and the Gray: Soldiers in the Civil War

When the war began in 1861, most soldiers were volunteers with little knowledge of the military. They often enlisted with their friends and formed companies together. They had to learn to march together, to load and fire their rifles, to cook their food, and to set up tents. A few officers had experience in the Mexican-American War but most had no experience at all. Later in the war, soldiers were conscripted (*required to serve*).

Early volunteers wore their own clothes. After confusion at the Battle of Bull Run, Union soldiers were supplied with standard blue uniforms. Confederate soldiers wore uniforms of gray.

For most of the war, Union soldiers enjoyed a steady supply of food. Each carried a canteen, cup, knife, fork, frying pan, coffee can and lantern in his knapsack. Although Southern farms grew food, they often had no way of bringing it to their soldiers. Confederate soldiers therefore sometimes went hungry. In general, soldiers ate salted meat, coffee, and "hardtack" (*a hard biscuit*). The hardtack had to be dipped in coffee or broken up and mixed with water. They also received flour, beans, potatoes and dried vegetables. Soldiers might seize fresh vegetables and livestock from farms they passed on their march.

The armies of the Civil War were young. The average age of a soldier was only 24 years old. Many soldiers were only in their teens. Drummer boys could be even younger. Soldiers in the Union army were most often farmers, factory workers or immigrants. Soldiers in the Confederacy were often farmers or students.

At first the war seemed like a great adventure. But after the Battle of Bull Run, attitudes changed. Hardships increased such as long marches, hunger, disease, and the terror of battle.

Weapons were more deadly than in earlier wars. **Rifling** is a way of placing grooves along the inside barrel of a gun. It causes the bullet to spin as it leaves the rifle. This makes a rifle much more accurate than a musket. During the Civil War, soldiers stood in lines or ran into each other as in earlier wars, but their weapons were much more accurate. The result was that many more people were injured or killed.

Imagine you are a soldier in the Civil War. Your officers order you to attack. A drummer boy sounds the beat. You and your fellow men begin walking towards the enemy. As you get closer, you start to run. Then you stop from time to time to load your rifle, aim and fire. Meanwhile, the soldiers you are attacking have formed two lines. One line is made up of soldiers who are kneeling and loading their weapons. The other stands, aims and fires. In the background there are cannons firing, the smell of gunpowder and lots of smoke. The bodies of injured and dead soldiers begin to clutter the field.

Doctors and nurses played a critical role in the war. For the first time, the wounded were carried to tents that served as hospitals. Doctors took out bullets and **amputated** (*cut off*) limbs. They did not know to wash their hands or sterilize their instruments, so many died of infection. But a large number miraculously survived. And twice as many soldiers died from disease as from wounds in battle.

Chapter 1 | The Civil War

Two Civil War Generals

Robert E. Lee was born in Virginia in 1807. Lee came from a famous family. He was a cousin of Richard Henry Lee, who had proposed the independence of the United States to the Continental Congress in 1776. His father had fought in the American Revolution and was Governor of Virginia. Lee attended the U.S. Military Academy at West Point and graduated second in his class. Winfield Scott considered him one of the best officers in the Mexican-American War. In 1859, Lee put down John Brown's rebellion at Harpers Ferry. When the Civil War broke out, Lincoln offered Lee command of all Union forces. Lee did not feel, however, that he could fight against his native state of Virginia. So he turned Lincoln down. Lee opposed secession but joined the Confederacy once Virginia seceded. Lee advised Jefferson Davis, commanded the forces of Virginia and became commander-in-chief of the Confederate army. Lee was known for his masterful moves on the battlefield. He felt if he could make the war last long enough, public opinion in the North would turn against it.

Ulysses S. Grant was born in Ohio in 1822. His father was a tanner (*someone who makes leather goods*). Like Lee, Grant went to West Point and served in the Mexican-American War. Grant was forced to leave the army in 1854 because of drunkenness. He tried several jobs, including farming and running a small leather and saddle store. When the Civil War broke out, Grant raised a company of volunteers. He became a colonel and later a general. Grant lost a battle at Shiloh with heavy casualties, but Lincoln refused to dismiss him: "I can't spare this man—he fights." Grant was one of the first generals to use African-American soldiers. In 1863, Grant was put in charge of the Union effort to take Vicksburg, a fortress on a cliff overlooking the Mississippi River. Grant surrounded the city and starved it into surrender. Because of his successes in the West, Lincoln appointed Grant as the commander of all Union forces in 1864. Grant's plan was to use the North's greater resources by sending several Union armies against the Confederates at once. Grant introduced the idea of "total war." He ordered General Sherman to "get into the interior of the enemy's country as far as you can [and to make] all the damage you can against their war resources." In May 1864, Grant began his own march towards Richmond. He refused to give up his advance despite defeats and heavy casualties.

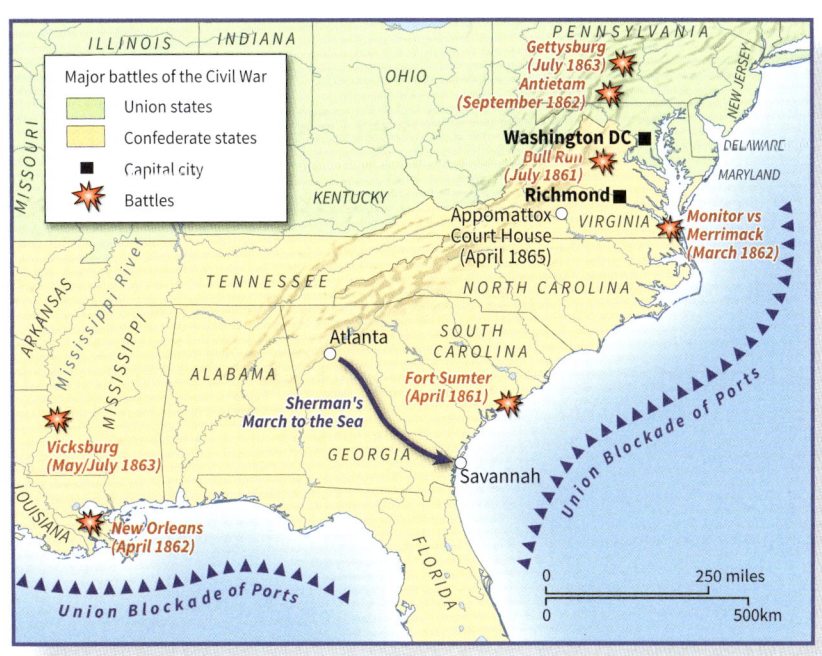

Chapter 1 | The Civil War

Florida in Focus

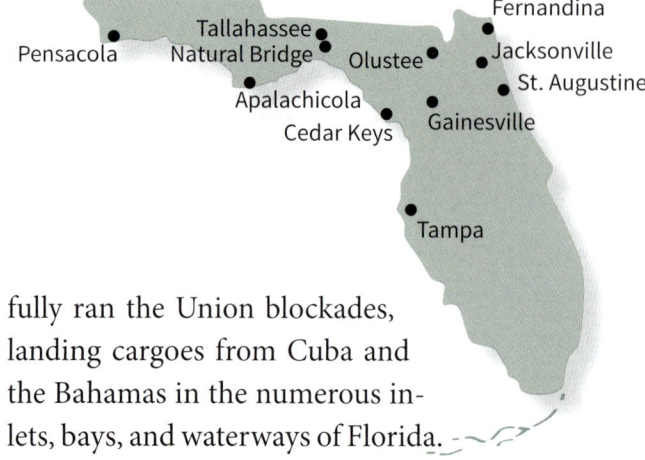

In 1860, the population of Florida was just over 140,000 inhabitants, of whom approximately 40% were slaves. The Seminole Indians had, over the previous half century, been confined to reservations through a series of bloody conflicts. The state's economy centered on the production of cotton and timber goods, both of which depended heavily on the use of slave labor. It was therefore not surprising that on January 10, 1861, a constitutional convention called for by Florida's General Assembly adopted an ordinance of secession by a vote of 62 to 7. The "nation of Florida" thus seceded from the United States. The following month, Florida joined the Confederate States of America.

For much of the war, the North sought to control Florida's coastline and to enforce a blockade preventing the supply of Confederate forces with food, arms, and materials from Florida. For these purposes, Union troops occupied Fort Pickens near Pensacola off the Gulf of Mexico, and made the fort their headquarters in Florida for the duration of the war. Key West remained in Union hands as well.

Federal forces also invaded and seized control of Apalachicola, Cedar Keys, Fernandina, Jacksonville, St. Augustine, and Tampa. Floridians often successfully ran the Union blockades, landing cargoes from Cuba and the Bahamas in the numerous inlets, bays, and waterways of Florida.

The Confederate commander, Robert E. Lee, hoped to preserve the interior of Florida as a source of agricultural produce and cattle for the South. A number of battles were therefore fought in this region. In 1864, 5,200 Confederate troops, led by General Joseph Finnegan, defeated 5,500 Union soldiers at the **Battle of Olustee.** Further Confederate victories followed at Gainesville, Cedar Keys, and Natural Bridge. This was despite the fact that these Confederate forces were often comprised of young boys and old men. Many of the slaves in Florida, in fact, remained loyal to their masters and stayed to help their owners' wives and daughters manage the land and nurse the wounded. The war in Florida ended on May 10, 1865, when Tallahassee was occupied by federal troops.

Review Cards

Long-term Causes of the Civil War

Sectionalism: People felt greater loyalty to their section—the North, South, or West—than to the nation as a whole.

Slavery: Abolitionists wanted to end slavery. Escaped slaves like Frederick Douglass spoke out against the horrors of slavery. Pro-slavery apologists in the South argued that slaves were better off than Northern factory workers.

Extension of Slavery: Many Northerners did not want to see slavery extended to new territories; Southerners feared being outnumbered by free states if slavery did not spread.

States' Rights: Many Southerners believed states had the right to leave the Union if they wished.

Causes of the Civil War

The Breakdown of Compromise

Early Compromises over the Slavery Question:

(a) Missouri Compromise (1820) Missouri admitted as a slave state and Maine as a free state; slavery prohibited in the Louisiana Purchase north of 36°30'N.

(b) Compromise of 1850 California admitted as a free state; the sale of slaves banned in Washington, D.C.; tough Fugitive Slave Act of 1850 enacted; popular sovereignty applied to the slavery question in the rest of Mexican Cession.

The Breakdown of Compromise:

Kansas-Nebraska Act (1854) Popular sovereignty to determine the slavery question in remaining territories of Louisiana Purchase, reopening the slavery issue there.

Birth of Republican Party (1854) Republicans opposed the extension of slavery.

The Ostend Manifesto (1854) Attempt by U.S. diplomats from the South to purchase Cuba as a new slave state.

"Bleeding Kansas" (1855–1856) Anti-slavery and pro-slavery settlers violently contested control of the Kansas Territory.

***Dred Scott* decision (1857)** Supreme Court ruled that Dred Scott, an African American, was not a citizen and had no right to sue in court; the Court also ruled that Congress had no right to forbid slavery in the territories.

Freeport Doctrine (1858) View of Stephen Douglas that local communities could still choose to ban slavery despite the *Dred Scott* decision.

John Brown's Raid (1859) John Brown, a white abolitionist, attacked a federal arsenal in Virginia, hoping to stir up slave revolts throughout the South.

Causes of the Civil War

The Secession Crisis

Presidential Election of 1860: Democrats were divided, helping Republican candidate Abraham Lincoln to win the election with 39% of the vote.

Secession: South Carolina immediately seceded. Six Southern states followed, forming the Confederacy. Four states of the upper South seceded after war broke out.

Fort Sumter: Lincoln sent supplies to this fort in Charleston Harbor. Confederate forces fired on the fort, starting the Civil War. Border states stayed loyal to the Union.

Course of the Civil War

- The North had a larger population, more industry and resources, and the navy. Lincoln imposed a naval blockade on the South. The Anaconda plan was the North's strategy for winning the war.
- Lincoln issued the Emancipation Proclamation in September 1862, freeing all slaves in states still in rebellion on January 1, 1863. He acted on the basis of his emergency wartime powers.
- Florida was valued for its cattle and food supplies; the Battle of Olustee was fought in northern Florida in 1864.
- The Battle of Gettysburg (1863) was the turning point of war; Lincoln gave the Gettysburg Address; Grant captured Vicksburg and became Union commander; Lee surrendered at Appomattox in April 1865.

Consequences of the Civil War

- Preservation of the Union
- Abolition of slavery
- Tremendous loss of life and destruction of property
- Power of the federal government strengthened

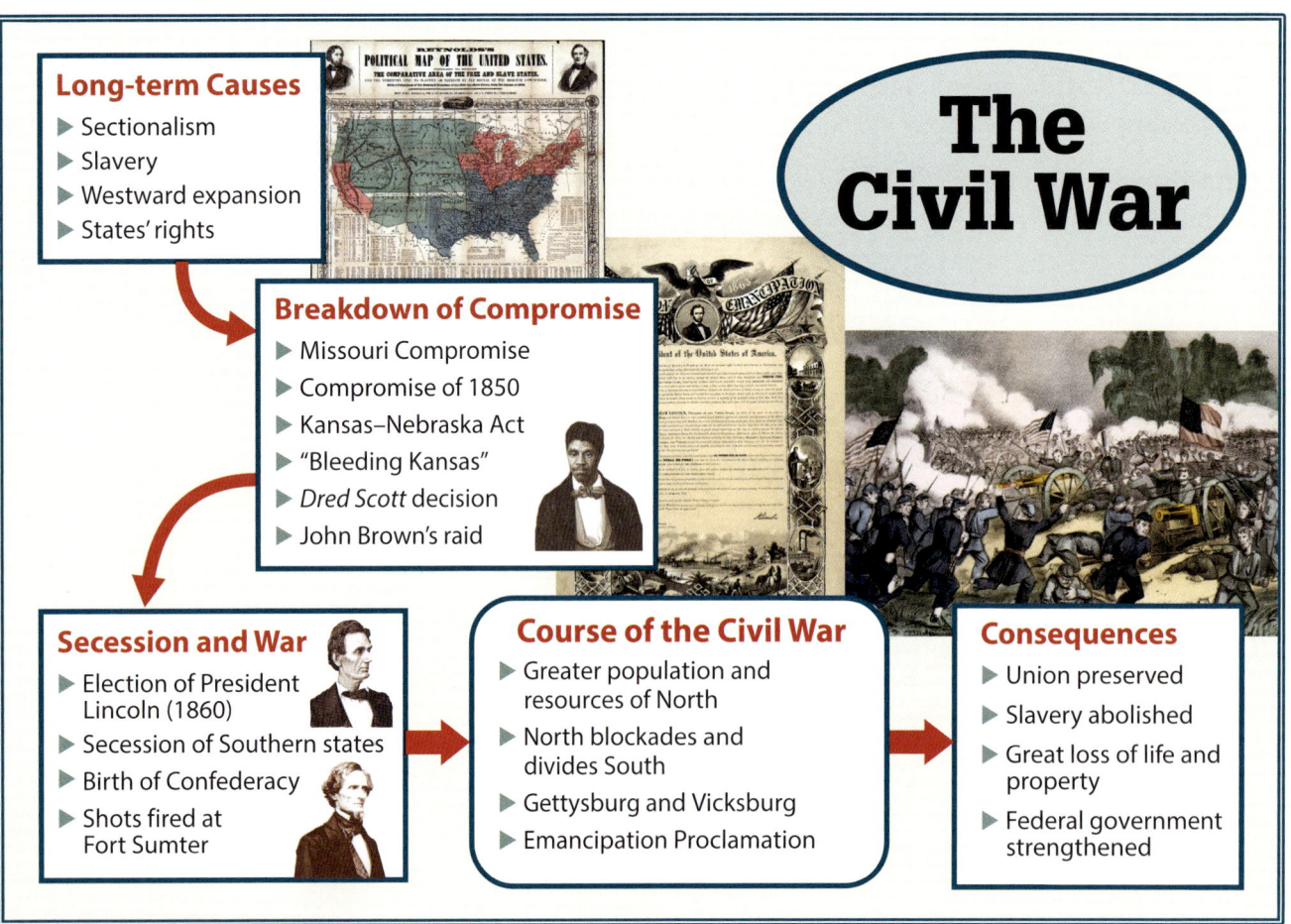

What Do You Know?

SS.912.A.2.1

1. Which sequence of events correctly identifies a rise in tensions, bringing the nation closer toward armed conflict?

    A. John Brown's raid → Missouri Compromise

    B. Compromise of 1850 → *Dred Scott* decision

    C. Kansas-Nebraska Act → Admission of California to statehood

    D. "Bleeding Kansas" → Admission of Maine and Missouri to statehood

SS.912.A.2.1

2. Which event was the catalyst for the secession of the first seven Southern states in 1861?

    A. passage of a higher protective tariff

    B. issuance of the Emancipation Proclamation

    C. the election of Abraham Lincoln as President

    D. the shipment of Union supplies to Fort Sumter

SS.912.A.3.13

3. The diagram below provides details about the Civil War.

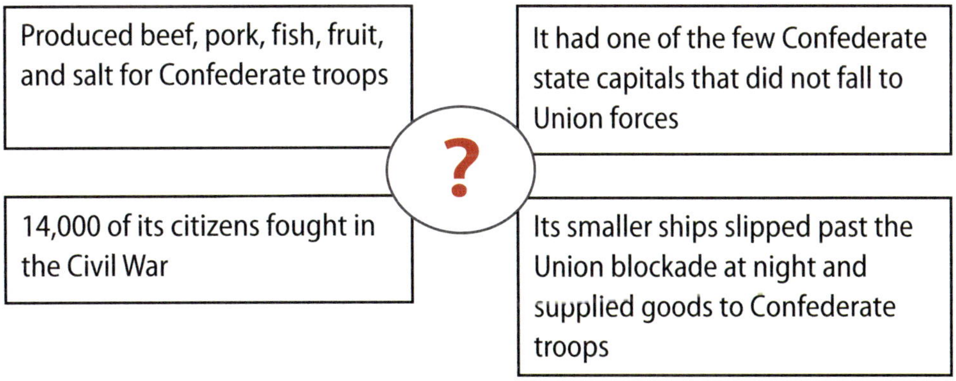

Produced beef, pork, fish, fruit, and salt for Confederate troops	It had one of the few Confederate state capitals that did not fall to Union forces
14,000 of its citizens fought in the Civil War	Its smaller ships slipped past the Union blockade at night and supplied goods to Confederate troops

?

Which title best completes the diagram?

   A. Union Troops Occupy Fort Pickens

   B. Slaves in Florida Fought for the Union

   C. The Florida Economy Booms during the Civil War

   D. Florida's Contribution to the South during the Civil War

SS.912.A.2.1

4. The excerpt below is from a letter by General Winfield Scott written in 1861.

> **The Anaconda Plan**
>
> "[S]o as to envelope the insurgent States and bring them to terms, with less bloodshed than by any other plan."

What was the main objective of the plan described in General Scott's letter?

A. to attack and bring under control a few key Southern cities

B. to disrupt Southern supply lines by controlling the railroad junctions in the South

C. to sign treaties with Britain and France to prevent them from assisting the South

D. to suffocate the South by controlling the Mississippi River and the Southern ports

SS.912.A.2.1

5. Why did the Union impose a naval blockade on the South during the Civil War?

A. to promote domestic industries in the South

B. to strangle the shipment of supplies to the Confederacy

C. to motivate enslaved African Americans to migrate to the North

D. to encourage Union sympathizers to persuade their states to rejoin the Union

SS.912.A.2.1

6. The graph below compares the resources of the North and South during the Civil War.

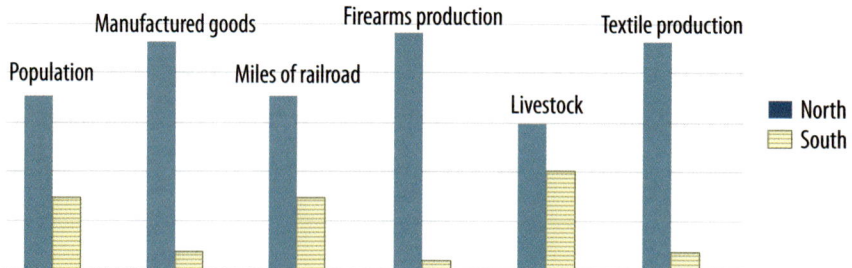

Which of these strategies was NOT used by the South to counter the North's advantages in resources shown in the graph?

A. The South would invade and capture major Union cities.

B. The South would fight a defensive war on its own terrain.

C. The South would use its pool of talented military experience.

D. The South would conscript troops and print its own paper money.

SS.912.A.2.1

7. What was a significant impact of the Emancipation Proclamation?

    A. Slaves in Northern states were freed.
    B. The war became a moral contest over slavery.
    C. Slaves in border states were immediately freed.
    D. African Americans were admitted into the Confederate army.

SS.912.A.2.1

8. What were the major consequences of the Civil War?

    A. the end of slavery and a strengthening of the power of the federal government
    B. recognition of the rights of states to leave the Union and to nullify federal laws
    C. an end to racial discrimination and establishment of social equality throughout the nation
    D. the abolition of slavery in all Northern states and in all federal territories north of 36° 30' N

SS.912.A.2.1

9. Which of the following contributed to the outbreak of the Civil War?

    A. Southerners feared that Northerners intended to abolish slavery.
    B. Southern states wanted a free hand in suppressing local slave revolts.
    C. The *Dred Scott* decision led Northern state officials to defy federal law.
    D. Northerners opposed the shipment of Southern cotton to Great Britain.

SS.912.A.2.1

10. The excerpt below is from a recently written history of the Civil War.

    > What were the rights and liberties for which Confederates contended? The right to own slaves; the liberty to take this property into the territories; freedom from the coercive powers of a centralized government.
    >
    > —James McPherson, *The Battle Cry of Freedom*

    What contradiction does this Civil War historian find in the secession of the Southern states?

    A. Confederates were outnumbered by Northerners.
    B. Confederates demanded the freedom to enslave others.
    C. Confederates believed that states had the right to leave the Union.
    D. Confederates felt that slaves were better treated than Northern factory workers.

SS.912.A.2.1

11. This cartoon was published in 1850.

Which social issue is addressed in the cartoon?

A. the safety of workers
B. the need for public education
C. the conditions of Southern slaves
D. the polluted air in the new industrial towns

SS.912.A.2.1

12. Which best expresses the viewpoint of the artist in the cartoon above?

A. Farm life is healthier than city living.
B. Slavery is a moral evil that should be abolished.
C. Factory owners should use slave labor in factories.
D. Southern slaves are better treated than factory workers.

SS.912.A.2.1

13. Which view was held by most Southerners of the secession crisis of 1860–1861?

A. Revolution against properly elected officials is never justified.
B. Since the Union was created by the states, they could leave it at any time.
C. The Union was formed by the American people, and not by individual states.
D. Because of their economic connections with the North, secession would be disastrous.

CHAPTER 2

Reconstruction: America's "Unfinished Revolution"?

SS.912.A.2.2 Assess the influence of significant people or groups on Reconstruction.

SS.912.A.2.3 Describe the issues that divided Republicans during the early Reconstruction era.

SS.912.A.2.4 Distinguish the freedoms guaranteed to African Americans and other groups with the 13th, 14th, and 15th Amendments to the Constitution.

SS.912.A.2.5 Assess how Jim Crow Laws influenced life for African Americans and other racial/ethnic minority groups.

SS.912.A.2.6 Compare the effects of the Black Codes and the Nadir on freed people, and analyze the sharecropping system and debt peonage as practiced in the United States.

SS.912.A.3.13 Examine key events and peoples in Florida history as they relate to U.S. history.

Names and Terms You Should Know

Reconstruction	Equal Protection	Literacy tests
Thirteenth Amendment	Fifteenth Amendment	"Grandfather clauses"
Freedman	Impeachment	Poll taxes
Freedmen's Bureau	Carpetbagger	Solid South
Andrew Johnson	Scalawag	Nadir
Radical Republicans	Sharecropping	"Jim Crow" laws
"Black Codes"	Debt peonage	Segregation
Civil Rights Act of 1866	Ku Klux Klan	*Plessy v. Ferguson*
Fourteenth Amendment	Suffrage	African-American migration

Florida "Keys" to Learning

1. During Reconstruction, Southern states had to be readmitted into the Union, incorporate the emancipated freedmen into public life, and rebuild their war-torn economies.

2. Lincoln had proposed to treat the South leniently. After he was assassinated in April 1865, the next President, Andrew Johnson, at first seemed to be sterner on former Confederates. However, Johnson soon began pardoning almost all former Confederates.

3. One of the greatest issues facing the South was the fate of the freedmen. How would four million people, suddenly emancipated from slavery, enter into public life and the free market economy? There was a struggle over the control of Southern land and the labor of the freedmen. Despite several experiments and promises during the war, the freedmen were not given their own land. The federal government set up the Freedmen's Bureau, with offices throughout the South, to help the freedmen adjust and to set up schools to educate them.

4. Southern state legislatures had to accept the end of slavery, but quickly passed "Black Codes," based on older slave codes. These limited the civil rights and freedom of movement of the freedmen.

5. Northern Republicans in Congress were outraged by the election of former Confederates to Congress and by the passage of the Black Codes throughout the South. Republicans passed the Civil Rights Act, granting freedmen their civil rights. This federal law later became the basis for the Fourteenth Amendment.

6. Congress also passed its own program for Reconstruction, dividing the South into five districts—each occupied by the Union army. Former Confederate leaders lost their political rights, while freedmen were given the right to vote.

7. The Republicans in Congress impeached President Johnson. He was impeached (*accused*) in the House of Representatives, but the Senate failed to remove him from office.

8. During Reconstruction, three amendments were added to the Constitution. The Thirteenth Amendment abolished slavery. The Fourteenth Amendment guaranteed all citizens the "equal protection of the laws" and "due process." The Fifteenth Amendment prohibited any denial of voting rights on the basis of race.

9. During Reconstruction, freedmen, carpetbaggers, and scalawags held power in Southern governments. For the first time, African Americans were elected to government office. Hiram Rhodes Revels became the first African American elected to Congress.

10. Reconstruction governments built roads and schools and took steps towards racial equality. However, after Northern troops were withdrawn, Southern states started passing segregation laws in the late 1870s.

11. Southerners also developed a new economy during Reconstruction. Former slave owners often did not have money to pay laborers. The emancipated slaves did not have land. Many former slaves became sharecroppers, giving a share of their crops to the landowner in exchange for use of the land. Other freedmen became tenants, and soon owed debts to their landlords (usually their former master under slavery).

12. After the end of Reconstruction, Southern state governments passed "Jim Crow" laws requiring racial segregation (separation of "white" and "colored") in public places. These laws were upheld by the U.S. Supreme Court in *Plessy v. Ferguson* (1896). The Ku Klux Klan and similar groups terrorized African Americans and prevented them from exercising their rights.

The Challenges of Reconstruction

By April 1865, when the Civil War ended, much of the South had been destroyed. Plantations, towns, and farms were in ruins. Railway lines had been torn up by advancing Union armies. A large number of Southerners had fought for years in the Confederate army for a cause that had lost. President Lincoln's Emancipation Proclamation had abolished slavery throughout the rebelling states. Escaping slaves had fled to the Union army. Some had been given plots of land from plantations abandoned by Confederate owners, in an experiment in the Sea Islands of South Carolina. Confederate paper money had lost all its value. There was no way for Southerners to return to the ways of the antebellum years.

To "**reconstruct**" means to rebuild. To rebuild the South, Americans had to overcome a series of major political, economic, and social hurdles:

1. How should Southern states be readmitted to the Union?

2. Was it the President or Congress that had the power to set conditions for their readmission?

3. Should former Confederate leaders be permitted to participate in public life, or should they be excluded or otherwise punished?

4. What was to be the position of the millions of former slaves (known as *freedmen*) in Southern society? Most historians today consider this as the greatest challenge of Reconstruction.

5. How could the economy of the South be rebuilt?

Historians such as Eric Foner believe that the **Reconstruction Era** was one of great promise, but that America's leaders failed to seize the initiative for fundamental change. Indeed, Foner considers Reconstruction to be America's great "Unfinished Revolution."

Early Plans for Reconstruction

Even before the end of the war, people started thinking about Reconstruction. A special **Freedmen's Bureau** was established by Congress in March 1865 to help the former slaves adjust to freedom. President Lincoln promised in his second Inaugural Address that he had lenient plans for Reconstruction "with malice toward none, with charity for all." As early as November 1863, he proposed that once ten-percent of a state's voters pledged allegiance to the Union and accepted the Emancipation Proclamation, the state should be admitted into the Union. Congress rejected Lincoln's "**Ten-Percent Plan**" and passed a more stringent bill for Reconstruction in July 1864, known as the Wade-Davis Bill, but Lincoln had refused to sign it. In April 1864, the U.S. Senate also proposed the **Thirteenth**

Chapter 2 | Reconstruction: America's "Unfinished Revolution"?

Amendment, prohibiting slavery throughout the United States. This amendment passed the House in January 1865 and was ratified by the states by the end of the year. This freed slaves in the border states and confirmed the emancipation of Southern slaves, since the President's authority in issuing the Emancipation Proclamation was unclear. In the meantime, President Lincoln was suddenly assassinated in April 1865, only a few days after the South had finally surrendered.

The Politics of Reconstruction

Presidential Reconstruction

Lincoln's successor was his Vice President, **Andrew Johnson**, a former slaveholder from Tennessee, one of the states that had joined the Confederacy. In the months before the new Congress assembled, President Johnson enjoyed a relatively free hand over Reconstruction policy. Coming from a modest background, Johnson had resented wealthy slaveholders.

At first, it was believed that he would impose harsh conditions on the Southern Confederates. Indeed, he refused to issue a general pardon to former Confederate leaders. Each leader had to personally request amnesty. However, Johnson soon began issuing thousands of individual pardons, allowing former Confederates to regain their former properties as well as their rights of citizenship.

President Johnson did not consider African Americans to be on equal terms with whites. Instead, he hoped for reconciliation between Northern and Southern whites as quickly as possible, with little actual change in the South. Johnson even recognized the newly formed Southern state governments, largely made up of former Confederate leaders. The President soon came under the suspicion of many Northerners, including many Congressmen, for being too sympathetic to the South.

The Black Codes

Under these conditions, Southern whites became more daring. In new elections, Southern voters chose former Confederate leaders, including several generals and colonels, to represent them in the new Congress. Southern states also took steps to withhold the right to vote from freedmen.

At the same time, they passed new "**Black Codes**." These were in fact based on the slave codes of the past. Each Southern state wrote its own code, but they all had several features in common: they first defined the freedmen as "persons of color," and then prevented such persons from voting, serving on juries, testifying in court against whites, holding office, or serving in the state militia. They also regulated freedmen's marriages and labor contracts between freedmen and whites. "Such persons are not entitled to social and political equality," proclaimed the South Carolina Black Code of 1865, "with white persons." Likewise in Florida, a law decreed that the "jurors of this state shall be white men."

Most of all, the Black Codes made it illegal for freedmen to travel freely or to leave their jobs. Each freedmen had to show that he had work for the current year. This forced the former slaves to stay on plantations as workers. Black workers could also be whipped for showing disrespect to their employers—often their former masters. Black children were "apprenticed" to white employers, and black convicts were turned over to white employers for hard labor. The whole aim of the Black Codes was to preserve the structure of Southern society with as little disruption as possible, despite the abolition of slavery.

Congressional Reconstruction

Public opinion in the North was outraged at the election of former rebel leaders by Southern states and by the enactment of the new Black Codes. The blood-stained victory of the Civil War itself seemed to be at stake. Congress refused to seat the newly-elected Southern members. Moderate Republicans joined hands with the "**Radical Republicans**," a smaller group of Republicans who believed that the South should be punished and that African Americans should be granted full political and civil equality.

Republicans passed a "Civil Rights" bill and a bill to enlarge the Freedmen's Bureau. President Johnson vetoed both bills, but the Republicans had enough votes to override his veto.

The new **Civil Rights Act of 1866** prohibited discrimination based on race, thus overturning the Black Codes. It made all persons born in the United States into citizens, including the freedmen, and guaranteed them the same rights as "white citizens."

The Fourteenth Amendment

To insure these rights against a challenge by the Supreme Court, Congress rewrote the terms of the Civil Rights Act into the **Fourteenth Amendment**. This amendment prevents states from denying African Americans or other minorities the rights and privileges of citizens, including a fair trial and equal protection of the laws.

Although written to protect the rights of freedmen from the actions of Southern state governments, the Fourteenth Amendment actually guaranteed the same rights to all citizens. Based on this amendment, state governments as well as the federal government must respect the rights listed in the Bill of Rights even today.

To be readmitted to the Union, each Southern state was forced to ratify the Fourteenth Amendment, while former Confederate leaders were deprived of the right to hold elected office. The effect of these changes was to shift the balance of power in Southern governments.

The Impeachment of President Andrew Johnson

President Johnson opposed the terms of **Congressional Reconstruction**. However, Northern voters in the 1866 mid-term Congressional elections supported the Radical Republicans.

After President Johnson failed to win support in these elections, the Radical Republicans became the dominant force in Congress. The continuing exclusion of representatives from the Southern states helped them to maintain their majority.

All persons born or naturalized in the United States, and subject to the jurisdiction thereof, are citizens of the United States and of the State wherein they reside. No State shall make or enforce any law which shall abridge the privileges or immunities of citizens of the United States; nor shall any State deprive any person of life, liberty, or property, without due process of law; nor deny to any person within its jurisdiction the equal protection of the laws.

—An excerpt from the Fourteenth Amendment

- ▶ What is meant by "due process of law"?
- ▶ What is meant by the "equal protection of the laws"?
- ▶ How do these concepts differ?
- ▶ How did this amendment overturn the earlier *Dred Scott* decision?

The Radical Republicans passed their own bill for Reconstruction. They divided the South into five districts. Each district was occupied by a division of the Union army and placed under martial law.

To enforce its program, Congress also passed a law, known as the Tenure of Office Act. This act limited the President's power to dismiss his own cabinet members. President Johnson refused to obey this law. When he dismissed the Secretary of War, Congressional leaders attempted to remove Johnson from the Presidency through the process of **impeachment**. Johnson was successfully impeached by the House of Representatives in February 1868, but in the Senate three months later the Radical Republicans failed to remove him by only one vote. Johnson was the first President to have been impeached. Later that same year, Ulysses S. Grant was elected as the next President of the United States.

The **Fifteenth Amendment** was ratified in 1870. It prohibited states from denying any citizen the right to vote, known as **suffrage**, on the basis of race or previous "servitude" (*slavery*).

President Andrew Johnson's impeachment hearing in the U.S. House of Representatives

The chart below summarizes the early plans for Reconstruction by President Johnson, the Southern States, and the Radical Republicans in Congress:

	President Johnson	Southern States	Radical Republicans
Who should control the readmission of Southern States?	The President		Congress
When should Southern States be readmitted?	Immediately, so long as they support the Union and the end of slavery.	Immediately, with each state in charge of its own affairs.	Only when most citizens in the state agree to support the Union and black citizens are given their full civil and political rights.
Should Southern leaders be punished?	Almost all Southern rebels are individually pardoned by the President.	No punishment for former Confederate leaders.	Confederate leaders should be punished and all who served in the Confederacy should lose their political rights.
Should the freed slaves be entitled to vote?	Johnson recommends that state governments give the franchise to educated freedmen and black veterans, but refuses to use the federal government to force them to do so.	No.	Yes.

28   Chapter 2 | Reconstruction: America's "Unfinished Revolution"?

The Historian's Apprentice

1. Imagine you are a U.S. Senator in 1864. Write a letter to a friend explaining how the Thirteenth Amendment differs from the Emancipation Proclamation.
2. Make an illustrated timeline showing the development of Presidential and Congressional policies for Reconstruction.
3. Pretend your class is the United States Senate in May 1868 deciding whether to remove President Andrew Johnson from office. One team should present the grounds for removal. A second team should defend his actions. Then put his impeachment and removal from office to a vote. Members of the "Senate" should write a paragraph explaining how they voted. Did President Johnson narrowly survive impeachment in your classroom, as he did in 1868?
4. Write a paragraph on whether you think President Johnson's impeachment was justified. Examine the grounds for impeachment in the U.S. Constitution. For what reasons do you believe a President should be impeached?
5. Reread the language of the 14th Amendment. Do you think this language entitled women to vote? Use the Internet to find out what happened when Susan B. Anthony voted on the basis of this amendment in 1872. Would you have agreed with the judge in this case? Give two reasons to support your answer.

The Reconstruction Governments in the South

Giving the vote to freedmen while excluding former Confederate leaders created new conditions in the South. New Southern governments were elected. They often fell under the control of new arrivals from the North, known as "**carpetbaggers**." This was a term of abuse applied by Southern newspapers. It meant that many of the new arrivals were poor whites, able to fit all of their belongings into a few bags made of carpet, who came to exploit the South. In fact, many of these Northerners came for an idealistic goal—to help the freedmen. Others came for new business opportunities. The new Reconstruction governments in the South also included "**scalawags**"— Southern whites who supported Reconstruction. Most of all, new African-American voters made up a large portion of the Southern electorate in the Reconstruction Era.

One of the most important aspects of Reconstruction was the active participation of African Americans in state and local governments across the South. Over 600 served as state legislators. African Americans filled numerous posts in state governments, including Governor of Louisiana. In South Carolina, African Americans became a majority of the state legislature and chose an African-American Speaker of the House. **Hiram Rhodes Revels**, a Protestant minister, became the first African American to sit in Congress when he was elected as Senator from Mississippi in 1870. Fifteen other African Americans sat in Congress during Reconstruction.

Among the greatest areas of accomplishment of the Reconstruction governments were the creation of a system of public schools, laws banning racial discrimination, and the encouragement of investment in railroads. Reconstruction leaders generally favored modernization of the South. Nonetheless, Reconstruction governments faced great financial difficulties, were often guilty of the corruption that was widespread in that era, and never won the support of the majority of white Southerners. White

Southerners especially resented Northern interference and did not recognize their former slaves as social equals. Without changing white Southern attitudes or giving African Americans greater resources, Reconstruction policies were ultimately doomed to fail once the North withdrew.

African-American Migration

During Reconstruction, thousands of African Americans chose to leave the South. Some applied to go to Liberia in Africa; others migrated to Northern cities such as New York, Philadelphia, Chicago or Pittsburgh. Still others went west. African Americans from Louisiana, Mississippi and Kentucky migrated to towns in Kansas, where they established their own farming communities.

The Historian's Apprentice

Imagine you are an African-American freedman, a Northern "carpetbagger," or a white "scalawag" in a Southern state. Write a paragraph for an editorial in a local newspaper explaining your views on Reconstruction in your state.

With the end of slavery and the widespread destruction of the Civil War, one of the major tasks of Reconstruction was to repair the economy of the South. Without slave labor, the old plantation system could not be restored. Some plantation owners were forced to sell off sections of their lands. For the most part, however, plantation owners entered into **sharecropping** arrangements with their former slaves, who had no resources of their own. The landowner provided a cabin, a mule, tools, and a plot of land to the sharecropper. The sharecropper, in turn, gave a large share of his crop to the landowner. Most freedmen became sharecroppers, but others became **tenant farmers**. They rented land from the landowner but provided their own tools and provisions. Very few freedmen ever became landowners themselves.

If a sharecropper or tenant farmer owed any money at all to the landlord for cash loans or the use of tools, he or she could not leave until the debt was paid—in effect tying the freedman down in a system of **debt peonage**.

Some Southerners saw the end of slavery as a good thing for the South. They thought the South could develop a more diversified economy by growing many types of crops and carrying out its own manufacturing. They called this the "**New South**." After the war, new farming methods increased the yield per acre. The cultivation of new crops like fruits and vegetables was added to old staples like cotton, tobacco, rice, and sugar. Most important of all, railroads, cotton mills, and steel furnaces were built and more people moved into Southern cities. Although manufacturing in the South did not rival the North, it was much greater than in pre-Civil War times.

Sharecroppers planting sweet potatoes

Reconstruction Comes to an End

Reconstruction governments lasted different lengths of time in different states, but none for more than ten years. In 1876, the outcome of the narrow Presidential election contest between Republican candidate Rutherford B. Hayes and Democrat Samuel Tilden was disputed. Tilden won the popular vote but did not have enough votes in the Electoral College.

The results were disputed in Oregon and three Southern states: Florida, Louisiana and South Carolina. If all 20 disputed votes were given to Hayes, he would win the election. There were accusations of fraud in all three states, including Florida. A special Congressional commission was formed to decide the disputed electoral votes. In the end a compromise was worked out. Under the "Compromise of 1877," all the disputed electoral votes were given to Hayes, who agreed to withdraw Northern troops from the South and end Reconstruction.

By 1877, Northern troops left the South, and local governments entirely returned to local white Southern rule. Former Confederate leaders could now vote and state legislatures quickly moved to bar African Americans from voting or participating in the political process.

There were several reasons why Reconstruction failed to achieve complete equality for African Americans:

1. *A Legacy of Racism*—White Americans, in the North as well as the South, were not ready to recognize African Americans as their social equals. In the South, Reconstruction was keenly resented because it placed blacks in the position of exercising authority over whites. The weight of centuries of prejudice prevented most white Americans, both in the North and the South, from changing their attitudes.

2. *The Economic Dependence of African Americans*—The failure to divide up the plantations and give the freedmen their own plots of land after the Civil War meant that Southern blacks remained dependent on their former masters for their livelihoods.

3. *The Freedmen Lacked Education and Political Experience*—Most of the freedmen were uneducated, which further weakened their ability to compete with hostile whites.

4. *White Terrorism*—Secret societies, like the **Ku Klux Klan**, Knights of the White Camelia, the White League, Red Shirts and Pale Faces, terrorized those Southern blacks who attempted to assert their full political and social rights. This frightened many into submission.

5. *Loss of Northern Interest in Southern Reconstruction*—The Reconstruction governments were established right after the Civil War, when Northern voters and politicians were anxious to assert supremacy after a hard-fought struggle. When Americans were hit by an economic depression in 1873, most Northerners lost interest in the South.

The Aftermath to Reconstruction: The Segregated South

The system that replaced Reconstruction in the South was one of racial segregation and white supremacy. African Americans were deprived of their basic political and civil rights until the Civil Rights movement nearly a century later. Some historians refer to this period as the "**Nadir**," or low point, in American race relations.

Freedmen voting during Reconstruction

African Americans in Southern States Lose the Right to Vote

The Fifteenth Amendment had guaranteed the right to vote to all adult males. However, in the ten years following Reconstruction, Southern state governments systematically stripped African Americans of this right. Southern blacks were economically dependent on white owners of land and businesses and were unlikely to challenge them politically. Moreover, African Americans were terrorized by the Ku Klux Klan, the White League, The Knights of the White Camelia, and similar groups. Armed bands openly threatened African Americans who tried to vote. They especially targeted teachers and community leaders. Lynchings of African Americans became common. (A **lynching** is a public hanging by a local mob of an accused person without a trial.) Southern sheriffs and police were all white, as were Southern judges and juries, and they enforced laws selectively against blacks.

Finally, Southern legislators passed a series of laws in the decades after Reconstruction specifically designed to prevent African Americans from voting without actually violating the 14th and 15th Amendments.

Literacy Tests—A **literacy test** determines if someone can read. Literacy is not normally a requirement for voting, but it was not unconstitutional for a state to make it one. Literacy tests were made more difficult for black citizens, while white citizens were often exempted from this requirement.

Poll Taxes—**Poll Taxes** were special registration fees for voting. They were not only burdensome to the poor, but usually had to be paid long in advance and could not be paid on the day of the election.

"Grandfather Clauses"—These laws allowed people who had been qualified to vote at the beginning of 1867, their descendants, and relatives to vote without passing a literacy test or paying a poll tax. In effect, this exempted "poor whites" from these requirements but not poor blacks, since few African Americans had been qualified to vote in the South in January 1867. "**Grandfather clauses**" were declared unconstitutional by the Supreme Court in 1915, but the other requirements, such as poll taxes, were upheld.

As a result of these measures, whites regained control of their state governments and representation in Congress. Thus, even though a majority of citizens in Louisiana, Mississippi, and South Carolina were African Americans, few could vote. Resentful of Republican reconstruction, for the next hundred years white Southerners consistently voted for the Democratic Party. For this reason, they became known as the "**Solid South**" in national elections.

The System of Racial Segregation: the Reign of "Jim Crow"

The new white state legislatures quickly passed a series of **segregation laws**, which separated blacks from whites. By state law, whites and blacks attended different schools, rode in separate railway cars, ate in different restaurants, used different public toilets and water fountains, and sat on different public benches. The facilities given to African Americans were generally inferior.

The laws establishing racial segregation in the South became known as the "**Jim Crow**" **laws**, named after a character in earlier song-and-dance shows. Segregation denied black citizens equal opportunities and rights, reinforced white racism and fear of blacks, and conveyed the message that whites were superior. Poor whites were especially afraid of competition from black workers and welcomed the "Jim Crow" laws for keeping blacks "in their place." The purpose of these laws was to *circumvent*—or get around—the 13th, 14th, and 15th Amendments.

In 1890, Louisiana passed a "Jim Crow" law requiring railroad companies to "provide equal but separate" facilities to members of different races. Opponents of segregation persuaded Homer Plessy, who was one-eighth African American, to challenge this law. Plessy sat in a railroad car for whites, told the conductor of his mixed ancestry, and was arrested. He fought his case all the way up to the U.S. Supreme Court. In 1896, the Supreme Court upheld racial segregation in **Plessy v. Ferguson.**

The Court saw nothing in the Louisiana law itself that stated that some races were inferior to others:

> *"We cannot say that a law which requires the separation of two races is unreasonable. We consider the [error] of [Plessy's] argument to consist in the assumption that the enforced separation of the two races stamps the colored race with a badge of inferiority."*

Segregation was also practiced in the North, but generally as a matter of custom rather than law. For example, riots took place in Chicago in 1919 when a black swimmer went ashore on a "white" beach and was murdered by white bathers.

The African-American Response

African Americans responded to these adverse conditions in a variety of ways. A small trickle migrated northwards. From 1910 onwards, this trickle became a flood and close to 2 million African Americans migrated to Northern cities over the next two decades. Another way Southern blacks responded was by developing strong community and church ties. These became especially important during the later Civil Rights Movement.

Focus on Florida

Florida was fortunate in suffering less damage than most Southern states during the Civil War. After 1865, growing cotton in Florida became secondary to a wide variety of other occupations, including growing citrus fruits and winter vegetables, raising cattle, cutting timber, and tourism. The state's population nearly doubled in the two decades after 1860, reaching 270,000 inhabitants by 1880. Almost half of these were African Americans.

African Americans took a very active role in the government of Florida during Reconstruction. They made up 19 of the 53 members elected to the state legislature in 1868. **Jonathan C. Gibbs**, a preacher and graduate of Dartmouth College, became Florida's Secretary of State. **Josiah T. Walls**, a former slave and Union veteran, was the first black Floridian elected to the U.S. House of Representatives, where he served three terms.

Josiah T. Walls

Southern Democrats regained control of Florida's state government in 1877. They followed the example of other Southern states in enacting their own "Jim Crow" laws. A state constitutional convention was held in 1885, which imposed poll taxes, literacy tests, and residency qualifications as requirements for voting. The con-

Jonathan C. Gibbs

vention also endorsed racial segregation in schools. In 1889, Florida's state legislature introduced multiple ballot boxes at elections in order to confuse and discourage African-American voters. These laws were accompanied by acts of violence against those African Americans who still dared to exercise their political rights. Despite these threats, some African Americans bravely continued to assert their rights. For example, Joseph H. Lee, an African American who moved to Florida in 1873, actually served in the state legislature from 1880 until 1913.

A unique form of **debt peonage** developed in the pine forests of Florida at the end of Reconstruction, which lasted until the 1940s. African Americans who sought work in a turpentine camp were offered a bus ride to the camp. For their ride, they became indebted to the owner and were unable to leave the camp until the debt was paid. They became further indebted to the owner for their housing and food. Thus they became virtual prisoners. One victim later remembered:

> "You is born into the teppentime, with no hope of getting out."

The system exploited thousands of African Americans, who worked in the camps that produced one-fifth of the world's turpentine.

Review Cards

The Battle over Reconstruction

Freedmen's Bureau was set up to help freedmen; **13th Amendment** abolished slavery.

Presidential Reconstruction

- Lincoln wanted to readmit Southern states when 10% voters pledged allegiance to the Union and recognized end of slavery.
- Johnson insists Confederate leaders seek personal pardons.

Black Codes: New Southern state governments with former Confederate leaders pass **"Black Codes,"** restricting the rights of freedmen.

Congressional Reconstruction

- Shocked at the Black Codes and the election of Confederate leaders, Radical Republicans refuse to seat Southerners in Congress.
- **Civil Rights Act,** passed over Johnson's veto, grants freedmen rights of citizenship, overturning Black Codes.
- Civil Rights Act is rewritten as **14th Amendment,** granting all citizens:
  - **"Due process of law":** right to fair procedures before a state government takes away a person's property or freedom
  - **"Equal protection of the laws":** state laws should treat people equally
- **Reconstruction Act (1867)** divides the South into military occupation zones.

Impeachment of President Andrew Johnson

▶ Radical Republicans pass the Tenure of Office Act: The President needs Senate consent to remove cabinet members.

▶ Johnson impeached for removing his Secretary of War. He is the first President to be impeached. When tried in the Senate, Johnson is saved from removal by one vote.

Reconstruction Governments

▶ **Carpetbaggers, scalawags,** and **freedmen** participate in Reconstruction governments.

▶ African Americans vote and serve in government during this experiment in biracial democracy. **Hiram Rhodes Revels** becomes the first African American in Congress.

▶ Reconstruction governments ban racial discrimination, establish public schools, and encourage railroad construction—but they are also guilty of corruption.

Reconstruction Economics

▶ **Sharecropper:** uses the land and tools of the landlord in exchange for part of crop

▶ **Tenant farmer:** rents land from landlord

▶ **Debt peonage:** loss of freedom to move away because of debts to landlord or business owner

▶ **"New South":** new economy of South with greater crop diversity, more railroads, and some manufacturing

The End of Reconstruction

▶ North loses interest after economic depression in 1873.

▶ Rutherford B. Hayes withdraws troops in a deal to win the disputed 1877 Presidential election.

▶ Southern Democrats return to power.

▶ **Ku Klux Klan** and other groups terrorize African Americans.

The "Jim Crow" Laws: the "Nadir" in Race Relations

▶ Southern state governments take steps to stop African-American voting: literacy tests, poll taxes, residency requirements. Whites exempted by "grandfather clauses."

▶ African Americans were intimidated by violence and economic dependence.

▶ Southern state governments pass **"Jim Crow" laws** requiring racial segregation, or separation of whites and blacks, in schools, railroads, restaurants and other public places.

▶ "Jim Crow" laws upheld by the Supreme Court in *Plessy v. Ferguson* (1896): Facilities can be "separate but equal." Many consider this the "**nadir**," or low point, in race relations.

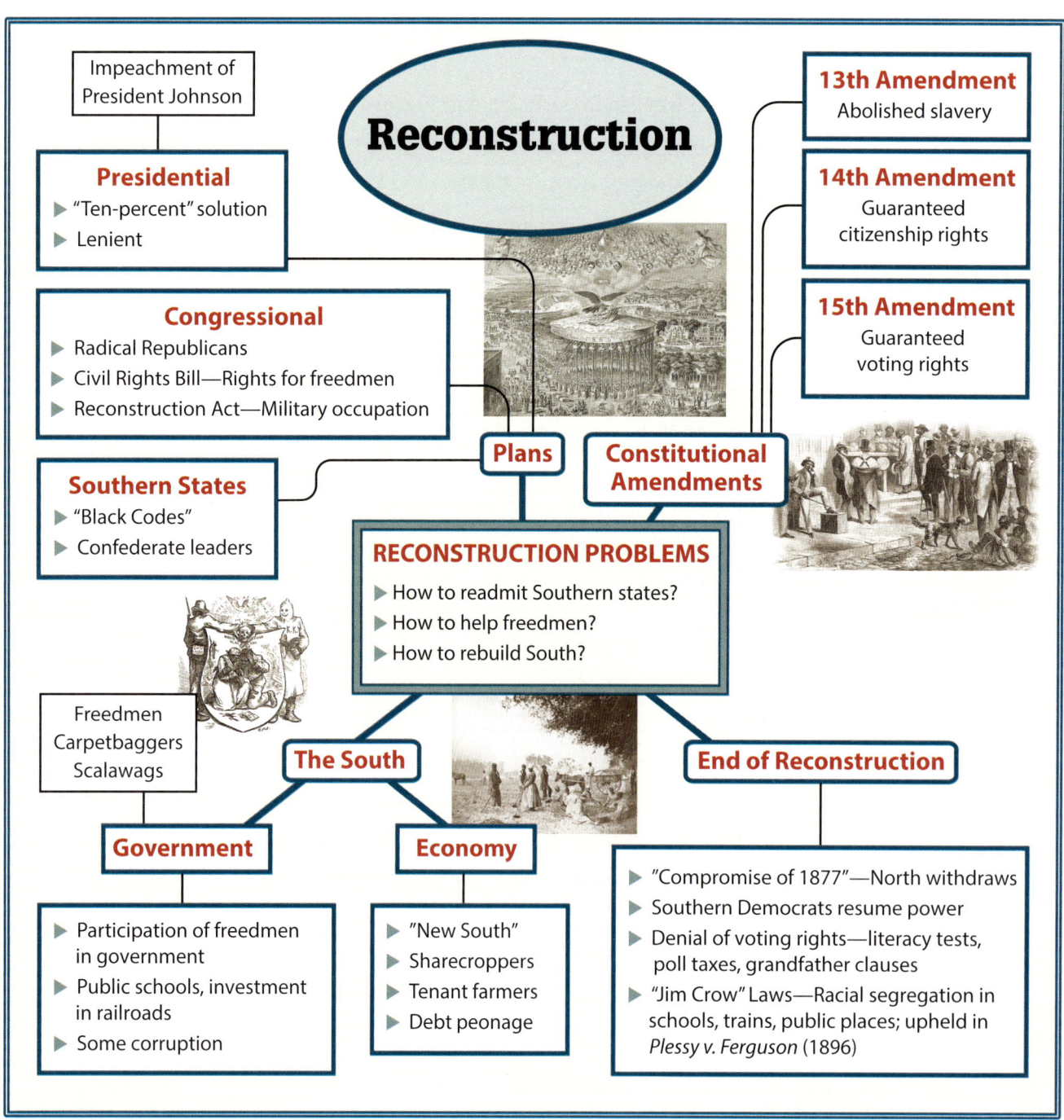

What Do You Know?

SS.912.A.2.3

| How should former Confederate leaders be punished? | How should Southern states be readmitted to the Union? |

| How should four million freedmen enter into public life and the free market economy? | How should the economy of the South be rebuilt? |

1. What was one impact of these issues on Republicans following the Civil War?

    A. They rejected the idea of creating a group of new African-American voters sympathetic to their party.

    B. They disagreed over whether the President or Congress should set conditions for Reconstruction.

    C. They agreed to let Southerners govern their own affairs without federal interference.

    D. They refused to treat the Southern states as conquered areas.

22.912.A.2.3

Congressional Reconstruction

▶ Created five districts and imposed martial law on the South.
▶ States had to ratify the 14th Amendment before readmission into the Union.
▶ Confederate leaders could not hold elected office.

2. What was an immediate effect of the changes described above, which were implemented by Congressional Reconstruction?

    A. The citizenship rights of African Americans were withheld.

    B. The balance of power in Southern state governments shifted.

    C. Northern and Southern whites were reconciled more quickly.

    D. Confederate leaders automatically regained their confiscated properties.

SS.912.A.2.4

3. Which amendment guaranteed the "equal protection" of the laws to all American citizens?

    A. 1st Amendment

    B. 13th Amendment

    C. 14th Amendment

    D. 15th Amendment

Chapter 2 | Reconstruction: America's "Unfinished Revolution"?

22.912.A.2.2

4. The statement below was by Thaddeus Stevens, a Radical Republican leader.

   > If [African-American] suffrage is excluded in the rebel states, then every one of them is sure to send a [Democratic] representation to Congress and pass a solid [Democratic] electoral vote [for President].

   What reason did Stevens give in this statement for granting voting rights to African Americans?

   A. African Americans deserved to vote after contributing their unpaid labor for centuries.

   B. Democrats and Republicans were in agreement on the fairness of letting all races vote.

   C. Republicans must offer voting rights to freedmen before Southern Democrats do.

   D. Black voters would help Republicans to maintain control of the Congress and Presidency.

SS.912.A.2.3

5. What impact did Radical Republicans in Congress have on Reconstruction?

   A. They opposed the passage of the Fourteenth Amendment.

   B. They encouraged the freedmen to exercise their new political rights.

   C. They persuaded President Johnson to pardon former Confederate leaders.

   D. They prevented President Johnson from sending federal troops to the South.

SS.912.A.2.2

6. Which is the best contemporary definition of a "scalawag"?

   A. a Northern abolitionist who supported the Freedmen's Bureau

   B. a Northerner who came to the South after the Civil War

   C. a white Southerner who supported Reconstruction

   D. a freedman entitled to vote

SS.912.A.2.2

7. What was a positive long-term impact of Radical Reconstruction on the South?

   A. Women were given the right to vote.

   B. Confederate leaders never again held elected office.

   C. Public education systems were established for students of all races.

   D. The South remained divided into five districts governed by martial law.

SS.912.A.2.6

8. What was an important effect of the sharecropping system and debt peonage?

   A. Freedmen achieved social and political equality in the South.

   B. Freedmen played an important role in local and state government.

   C. Freedmen achieved economic independence from their former masters.

   D. Freedmen often remained in a state of economic dependence on their former masters.

SS.912.A.2.2

9. The cartoon on the left by Thomas Nast was published in 1874. What was the main message of this cartoon?

   A. Opponents of Reconstruction were using violence to intimidate the freedmen.

   B. Different groups of Southerners were cooperating to rebuild the South after the war.

   C. The Ku Klux Klan and other private associations in the South were assisting the freedmen.

   D. The 14th Amendment protected the rights of freedmen despite the activities of the Ku Klux Klan.

SS.912.A.2.6

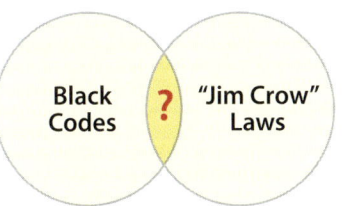

10. Which phrase completes the diagram on the left?

    A. Discriminated against African Americans

    B. Required racial segregation in all public places

    C. Provided Americans of all races with equal rights under the law

    D. Denied African Americans freedom of movement and basic civil rights

SS.912.A.2.5

11. The excerpt below is from the Supreme Court's decision in *Plessy v. Ferguson* (1896).

    > Laws permitting, or even requiring, the separation of the races do not place a badge of inferiority upon one group over another. Thus it is not a violation of the Fourteenth Amendment.

    What practice did this ruling uphold?

    A. job training for freedmen

    B. free public schooling for all races

    C. racial segregation in public places

    D. African-American participation in politics

Chapter 2 | Reconstruction: America's "Unfinished Revolution"?

SS.912.A.2.5

> Be it enacted by the Legislature of the State of Florida:
> **Section 1.** It shall be a penal offense for any individual, body of individuals, corporation or association to conduct within this State any school of any grade, public, private or parochial wherein white persons and negroes shall be instructed or boarded within the same building, or taught in the same class, or at the same time by the same teachers.
> —Florida State Legislature, 1895

12. How did this law influence conditions for African Americans in Florida?

    A. Schools for African-American children received fewer resources than schools for white children.

    B. African-American adults were permitted to attend night school to improve their literacy skills.

    C. African Americans were given the right to attend free public schools in Florida for the first time.

    D. African-American parents who opposed racial segregation sent their children to private schools.

SS.912.A.2.2

13. Which two groups most helped the freedmen during the Reconstruction Era?

    A. Radical Republicans and carpetbaggers

    B. Northern Democrats and Ku Klux Klan members

    C. Southern Democrats and supporters of the Black Codes

    D. Confederate veterans and supporters of President Andrew Johnson

SS.912.A.2.5

> The right of citizens of the United States to vote shall not be denied or abridged by the United States or by any state on account of race, color, or previous condition of servitude.
> —The 15th Amendment

14. Which practices were introduced in Southern states after Reconstruction to circumvent this amendment?

    A. African-American freedmen increased their participation in government in the nation's first experiment in biracial democracy.

    B. Poll taxes, literacy tests, and residency requirements were passed, which affected African Americans more than other citizens.

    C. White and black children in Southern states were required to attend separate, racially segregated public schools, and to use separate playgrounds.

    D. "Jim Crow" laws imposed racial segregation in public places, including trains, restaurants, and hotels.

CHAPTER 3

"Go West!"

SS.912.A.2.7 Review the Native American experience.

SS.912.A.3.1 Analyze the economic challenges to American farmers and farmers' responses to these challenges in the mid to late 1800s.

SS.912.G.4.2 Use geographic terms and tools to analyze the push/pull factors contributing to human migration within and among places.

SS.912.G.4.3 Use geographic terms and tools to analyze the effects of migration both on the place of origin and destination, including border areas.

Names and Terms You Should Know

Frontier	Reservation system	Boom town
Great Plains	Buffalo Soldiers	Open range
Western expansion	Sand Creek Massacre	Cowboy
Push-and-pull factors	Sioux Indians	Barbed wire
Transcontinental railroad	Little Big Horn	Sod house
Indian Wars	Wounded Knee	Dawes Act
	Homestead Act	

Florida "Keys" to Learning

1. The American frontier was the line separating areas of settlement from less densely populated areas. By the end of the Civil War, the frontier was at the Great Plains, Rocky Mountains, and deserts of the Southwest.

2. Geographers use push/pull factors to explain human migration. Push factors, like economic hardships, cause people to leave a place. Pull factors, like economic opportunity, attract people to new areas.

3. People went to the American West to find new economic opportunities. Miners came because of discoveries of gold and silver. Others came to establish their own farms and ranches. The completion of the transcontinental railroad in 1869, the defeat of the Indians in the "Indian Wars," and the availability of cheap land under the Homestead Act (1862) encouraged their migration.

4. In 1865, the Great Plains and Southwest were still occupied by Indian tribes. The destruction of the buffalo on the Great Plains took away the main source of food for the Plains Indians. After a series of wars with federal troops, Indian tribes were forced onto reservations. Often the reservations were on undesirable land. Many promises to Indians were broken.

5. Regions of the American West often went through different stages. Some places were first dominated by mining or cattle grazing. Later, farmers and ranchers took over. Farmers developed new technologies to farm on the dry but fertile Great Plains. They dug wells and built windmills to pump water found deep in the ground. They built sod houses and surrounded their fields with barbed wire to keep livestock in and other animals out. They used steel plows to break up the tough sod and made greater use of farm machinery.

6. In 1887, Congress passed the Dawes Act. This act attempted to help the Indians. It gave them the right to create private property from reservation land, and tried to "Americanize" them. However, the Dawes Act was a failure because it lacked respect for Indian traditions. It led to a massive sell-off of Indian lands.

America's Last Frontier

The American **frontier** was the line separating areas of denser settlement from "unsettled" territory. From a different perspective, the frontier divided areas where traditional native peoples lived, often as nomadic hunter-gatherers, from those areas where more technologically advanced peoples drastically altered the landscape by creating farms, ranches, towns, and cities to meet their needs. Since the arrival of the first colonists, the American frontier—or line of advanced settlement— had shifted steadily westwards. The United States was firmly committed to **western expansion**.

Over a century ago, Frederick Jackson Turner, a prominent American historian, argued that the existence of the frontier was one of the most important influences in shaping America. According to Turner, the essential American character was forged in the West, not the East. Rugged individualism, social equality, democracy, and a spirit of optimism had all been fostered by the conditions of American frontier life. The frontier had also acted as a "safety valve," allowing ambitious and discontented people in the East to escape to the West, where they could recreate themselves as "self-made" men and women.

The Last Frontier: The Great Plains and the Far West

By the end of the Civil War, the United States controlled all of the territory from the Atlantic to the Pacific. Much of this vast area was settled and divided into states, reaching from Texas to Minnesota. American settlers had also occupied lands along the Pacific Coast from California to Oregon. Between these regions remained a vast expanse of territory— almost equal in size to the rest of the United States— consisting of the Great Plains, the Rocky Mountains, the Great Basin, and the deserts of the Southwest. This was the final frontier, with largely unsettled territories that had yet to apply for statehood.

The **Great Plains** were rolling, treeless plains that stretched from Texas to North Dakota. They received little rainfall, especially on their western side closer to the Rockies. In 1870, the plains were covered with short, thin grasses, which provided a home

The United States in 1870

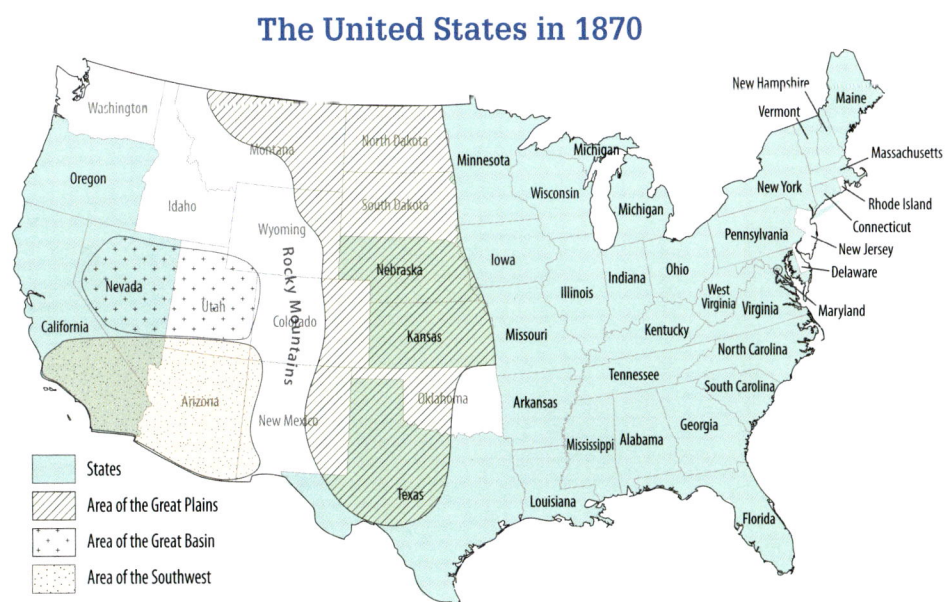

Chapter 3 | "Go West!"

both to millions of American buffalo and to the Great Plains Indians who lived off them. The Great Plains were only vaguely known to most Americans as the "Great American Desert." In reality, the soil of the northeastern plains was extremely fertile. In the short space of twenty years, between 1870 and 1890, most of the buffalo were killed, the Indians were forcibly moved to reservations, and the Great Plains were divided up into ranches and farms. In 1890, the U.S. Census Bureau officially announced the frontier was "closed"—no areas remained with fewer than two people per square mile.

Factors Leading to the Settlement of the Last Frontier

Geographers point to a combination of "**push**" and "**pull**" **factors** to explain the **migration**, or movement, of people from one place to another. "Push" factors are those that push people to leave a place. People may leave to escape from religious persecution, ethnic prejudice, war, drought, or grinding poverty. "Pull" factors are those that attract people to a place—such as hopes for religious freedom or the promise of economic opportunity. In the decades after the Civil War, a number of "pull" factors encouraged migration to the American West.

The Discovery of Precious Metals

The California Gold Rush of 1849 and later discoveries of gold and silver in Colorado, Nevada, South Dakota, Arizona, and other western states brought prospectors westward, led to the growth of mining towns, and often resulted in clashes with the Indians.

The Completion of the Transcontinental Railroad

In the days before the Civil War, only a few stage coach lines, the telegraph, ships sailing to the Pacific Coast, and, for a brief period, the Pony Express, kept the Far West in contact with the rest of the country. During the war, Congress passed the Pacific Railway Act and the federal government put aside land for the first **transcontinental railroad**. Construction began in 1863, while the Civil War was still raging. Laborers, mainly Irish immigrants, worked on building the Union Pacific line from Omaha westwards,

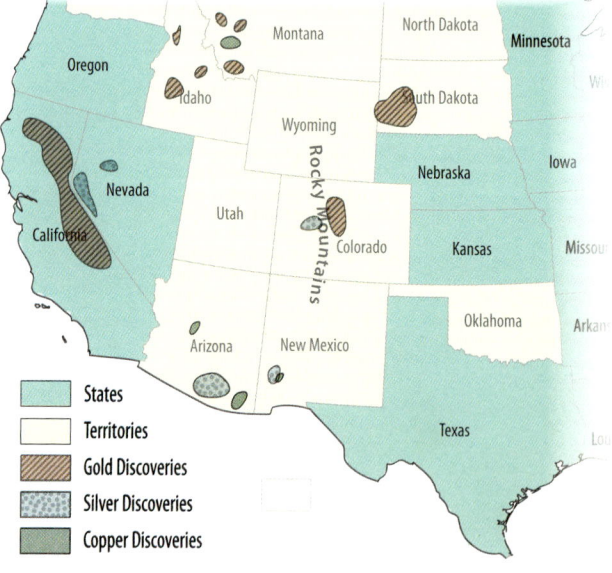

Precious Metals in the West

- States
- Territories
- Gold Discoveries
- Silver Discoveries
- Copper Discoveries

44 Chapter 3 "Go West!"

Transcontinental Railroad

The painting, "The Last Spike," depicts completion of the the transcontinental railroad in Promontory, Utah.

while crews of Chinese workers laid the track for the Central Pacific Railroad from Sacramento, California eastwards. After 1865, these workers were joined by army veterans and African-American freedmen. The first transcontinental railroad was completed when the two sides met in Utah in May 1869. A six-month sea voyage was suddenly replaced by a train ride that took just over a week. Four more transcontinental lines were built over the next 25 years.

The railroads provided the principal stimulus for the settlement of the Great Plains:

- They made it easier for settlers to move westward and to receive supplies from the East.
- They made it possible for farmers and ranchers to ship their grain and cattle to Northeastern urban markets for sale.
- The railroads sold land grants they had received from the government to settlers.
- Railroad advertising in Europe and the United States encouraged westward migration.

The Relocation of the American Indians

Before the new settlers could divide up the Great Plains, its existing inhabitants had to be relocated. In fact, back in 1830, Congress had already ordered the removal of all Indians in Southern states to west of the Mississippi. Nearly one-quarter of the Cherokee tribe had perished on their journey westward, which became known as the "Trail of Tears." Forty years later, some of the tribes found on the Great Plains were the very same ones that had been forcibly moved westward, like the Cherokee. Others, like the Sioux and Cheyenne, had lived on the Great Plains for centuries, where they had developed a distinct way of life, based on the large buffalo herds.

The "Indian Wars" of 1864–1890 The completion of the transcontinental railroads made these western lands highly desirable. Even where the Indians had been promised particular lands, they were asked to move again if settlers found their territory attractive. The Indians naturally resisted further resettlement. Clashes between land-hungry miners, ranchers and farmers with the Indians of the Great Plains became inevitable. A series of skirmishes, known as the "**Indian Wars**," lasted about twenty-five years. Federal troops, stationed in forts in the West, acted to protect the settlers. Some of these were African-American troops, often known as the "**Buffalo soldiers**." Some of the heaviest fighting occurred in the Southwest against the Apache Indians in Arizona and the Comanche in

Chapter 3 "Go West!"

Buffalo Soldiers

Texas and New Mexico. The federal government had guaranteed a vast expanse of territory to the Cheyenne and Sioux in the Treaty of Fort Laramie in 1851. In 1864, Union troops attacked a Cheyenne camp at *Sand Creek* in eastern Colorado. Despite a white flag, soldiers killed more than a hundred Indians, mainly women and children. Lands reserved for the Plains Indians were reduced by the Second Treaty of Fort Laramie in 1868.

On the northern Plains, the Great Sioux War lasted from 1876 to 1877 (see next page). In the Pacific Northwest, Chief Joseph of the Nez Perce tribe led a band of 200 warriors and their families on a 1,200-mile retreat towards Canada in 1877. They defeated federal troops several times before their final surrender just miles from the Canadian border.

Indian warriors were generally no match for federal troops, battle-hardened from the Civil War and assisted by such superior weapons as the revolver and the Winchester rifle. In the end, their technological superiority and greater numbers simply overwhelmed the Indian tribes. Because most Americans did not regard the Indians as equals, they were quite willing to break their treaties with them.

With the completion of the transcontinental railroad, sharpshooters began shooting at the massive herds of buffalo that roamed the plains, to collect and sell their hides. After only a few years, the American buffalo was on the edge of extinction. The destruction of millions of buffalo in the early 1870s took away the main source of food for the Plains Indians and sealed their fate. In the end, they had no choice but to submit to federal authority, and were confined to ever smaller and more remote "reservations."

The Reservation System   Once a tribe of Indians submitted to federal authority, they were settled on a **reservation**. The government "reserved" particular lands for the tribe and signed a treaty with them. The tribe promised not to go beyond the borders of its lands. Those who did were captured and brought back. In effect, the Indians became the "wards" of the federal government. The government promised to provide food, blankets, and seed, but all too often the officials charged with delivering these supplies ignored or deliberately cheated the Indians.

In the 1860s and 1870s, most U.S. government officials believed the Indians should enjoy a large degree of independence on their reservations. Reservation lands, however, were usually quite different from the lands the tribe had lived on before. Frequently they were located in infertile and undesirable areas. Moreover, tribal customs generally encouraged hunting and discouraged men from farming. Teachers sent to instruct children in the reservation schools attempted to convert them to Christianity while telling them that their most cherished tribal beliefs were wrong.

Thousands of buffalo skulls in a pile

Case Study

> Note: You are not required to know details about the Sioux Indians or the Indian Wars for the EOC Assessment

The Sioux Indians of the Great Plains

The treatment of the Sioux Indians provides one example of the American Indian experience.

▶ **1862** When a tribe of Sioux braves are denied their promised supplies, they massacre hundreds of settlers in Minnesota. In response, thirty-eight of the Sioux are executed.

Mass hanging of Sioux in Mankato, Minnesota

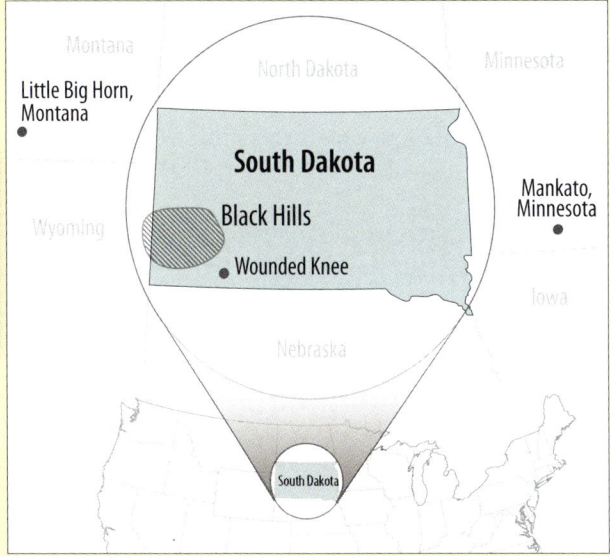

▶ **1868** Sioux leaders agree to withdraw to the Black Hills of South Dakota, sacred to them as the home of the "Great Spirit." The United States agrees to abandon several of its forts in the area in a second Treaty of Fort Laramie.

▶ **1871–1874** Hunters slaughter millions of buffalo, upon which the Sioux rely for their food.

▶ **1874** Gold is discovered in the Black Hills of South Dakota.

▶ **1876** The Sioux are asked to move out of the Black Hills. **Sitting Bull**, a Sioux holy man, inspires some of them to resist. **Crazy Horse** and other warriors surround **Colonel Custer** and his 700 men at **Little Big Horn.** Custer and 267 of his men are killed.

▶ **1877** Crazy Horse surrenders and is killed in captivity; the Sioux are forced onto reservations.

▶ **1881** Sitting Bull surrenders. He later joins Buffalo Bill's "Wild West" show, entertaining audiences in the Northeast and Midwest with shows dramatizing the defeat of the Indians.

▶ **1890** The Sioux on reservations begin the "Ghost Dance" in the belief that the "Great Spirit" is about to return control of the Great Plains to them and to restore the buffalo; fearing another Sioux rebellion, U.S. Army troops massacre as many as 200 Sioux men, women, and children with rapid-fire artillery guns in the final tragedy of the "Indian Wars," at **Wounded Knee**, South Dakota.

Custer and his men are defeated at Little Big Horn

Chapter 3 | "Go West!"

The Availability of Cheap Land

The slaughter of the buffalo and the removal of the Indians opened up vast tracts of new land for settlement. Immigrants from Europe and farmers from the East and Midwest of the United States were attracted by the prospect of cheap land. Railroads often misled settlers by advertising that farming conditions on the dry western plains were the same as those back east.

▶ The **Homestead Act** of 1862 promised settlers 160 acres of land for $1.65 an acre after improving it for six months, or for free if they farmed it for five years.

▶ Railroads sold land cheaply to attract settlers. The railroads expected to make later profits by charging the settlers for shipping their freight.

▶ In 1889, the federal government authorized the sale of two million acres of land in Oklahoma—formerly known as "Indian Territory." This land had been set aside for the Indians, but the government yielded to public pressure. On April 12, 1889, fifty thousand eager settlers waited along the border of the Oklahoma Territory for America's first and greatest "land run."

The Historian's Apprentice

▶ Have your class hold a debate on Frederick Jackson Turner's "frontier thesis." Do you think Turner was right in emphasizing the impact of the frontier on the American character?

▶ Place American government leaders on trial for their treatment of the Plains Indians. Should they be condemned for the way they took the Indians' land away?

▶ Which do you think was the most important factor behind the closing of the American frontier: the discovery of mineral resources, government land grants and promotions, or the completion of the railways? Use evidence to support your answer.

▶ Why did Congress make cheap land available under the Homestead Act?

Stages in the Evolution of the American West

America's "last frontier" generally evolved through a series of stages based on different economic activities. Particular regions differed in their development, depending upon their local resources.

The Mining Boom

In many parts of the West, miners were the first to arrive. Gold and silver discovered in California, the Rocky Mountains, and the Black Hills doubled the world's gold supply during the second half of the nineteenth century. Once a discovery was made, thousands of prospectors and adventurers were attracted to the spot in the hopes of striking a fortune. A rough-and-ready "**boom**" **town** sprang up overnight. There were few women: in 1860, Nevada and Colorado had nine men for every woman. Even as late as 1880, California was still 60% male. Boom towns often arose before a system of laws could be adopted. Violence was controlled by citizens' committees, known as "vigilantes."

Individual miners, with few resources, were generally limited to primitive techniques, like panning streams and rivers for gold. After the surface minerals wore out, many mining towns became abandoned "**ghost towns**" almost as suddenly as they had arisen. In others, mining companies with heavy machinery moved in to exploit valuable mineral ores that still lay beneath the surface. Remaining miners were reduced to laborers and frequently clashed with the mining companies that employed them. The mining companies also brought in immigrants—often Europeans skilled at mining. Some California miners moved to Nevada where silver was discovered in the Comstock Lode; others moved to Colorado where gold was discovered only a decade after the California Gold Rush.

The Cattle Kingdom and the "Open Range"

The "Cattle Kingdom" was a short-lived boom, which lasted about twenty years. At the end of the Civil War, there were several million wild longhorn cattle grazing on the Great Plains in Texas. Some Texans decided to drive these cattle northwards to the nearest railroad lines in Kansas. From Kansas, the cattle were shipped by rail to Chicago to be slaughtered. Then the cuts of beef were shipped in new refrigerated railroad cars to cities in the Northeast.

It took about three months to drive the cattle herds northward from Texas to Kansas, along the Chisholm Trail. On this "**long drive**," the cattle grazed on the short grasses of the "**open range**"—public lands not belonging to anyone and not fenced. The plains had abundant grass and water to support the moving herds. **Cowboys**, who had learned special techniques of riding, roping, branding, and dehorning cattle from the

CARAMBO!—CARAJA!—SACRAMENTO!—SANTA MARIA!—DIAVOLO!

Chapter 3 | "Go West!"

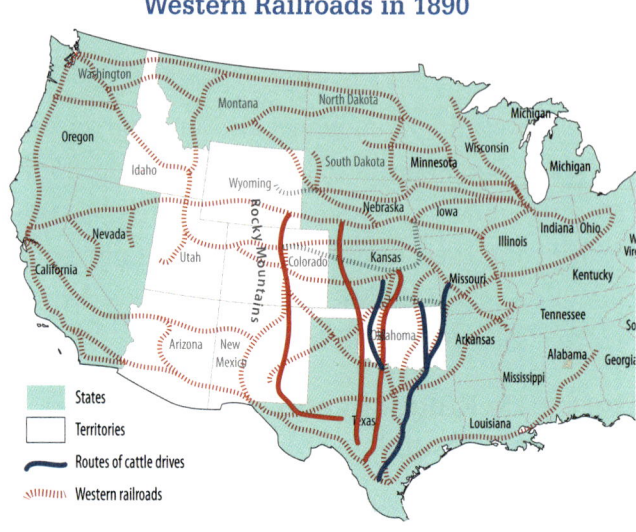

Western Railroads in 1890

Mexican *vaqueros*, kept the herds moving together northward. As many as one in five American cowboys was African-American. The image of the "cowboy" has since become a romantic symbol of the American spirit, but many cowboys led lonely, isolated lives.

In the late 1870s and 1880s, the cattle herds were driven farther north a year before they were ready for slaughter. The cattle then fattened themselves by grazing on the northern plains of Montana, Wyoming, and the Dakotas. However, by 1886 overgrazing had destroyed much of the grass. Moreover, sheepherders and farmers had bought up much of the "open range" and enclosed it with **barbed wire** fences. Economic hard times in the Northeast also meant prices fell and some cattle went unsold. Two severe winters and an unusually hot and dry summer killed millions of cattle in the years 1886 and 1887, finally putting an end to the "long drive."

Cattle ranchers nonetheless remained on the plains. They bought their own lands, bred cattle on the "closed range," and sent their young cattle eastwards by train to be fattened and slaughtered. Before long, railroad lines reached Texas.

The Farming Frontier

The railroads made it far easier for farmers to occupy the Great Plains. The Homestead Act and the sale of land by railroads greatly encouraged farmers' movement westwards. The railroads also enabled them to sell their produce back east. Many of the settlers on the Great Plains were immigrants arriving directly from Europe; others were the children of farmers in the East and Midwest.

At first, these farming families had faced the hostility of both the Plains Indians and the cattlemen. The Indians, however, were soon defeated by federal troops and moved onto reservations. The cattlemen formed their own associations to oppose the farmers. Some even hired gunmen to commit acts of violence against the homesteaders. Eventually, the farmers won the contest against the ranchers. They came in greater numbers and began enclosing their properties with barbed wire fences.

Even more serious than the opposition of Indians and ranchers were the many natural obstacles that the farmers faced. From the railroad advertisements, they had expected to find amply watered, wooded lands like those in the East. Instead, they were shocked to find little rainfall, tough soil, few trees, extreme temperatures, plagues of grasshoppers, and a painful sense of isolation caused by the wide distances between neighboring farms. Some of the earliest settlers even starved or died of exposure. Large numbers of homesteaders gave up and moved back east. In those families that stayed, women and small

A Texas longhorn

children were often forced to engage in strenuous physical labor for countless hours. During the cold, snowy winters, families might be locked in complete isolation for months at a time. Nevertheless, with technological ingenuity, the farmers were eventually able to overcome many of the obstacles they faced:

- **Obstacle:** Remoteness of markets
  Solution: The railroads allowed the farmers to ship their produce eastwards.

- **Obstacle:** Lack of wood, clay, or rock for homes
  Solution: The farmers built "**sod houses**," made from thick clumps of grass and soil cut into bricks.

- **Obstacle:** Lack of wood for fencing
  Solution: The farmers used barbed wire, first invented in 1874. Wire was twisted together at intervals to create sharp barbs that kept cattle and other animals from jumping over or crawling through the fence.

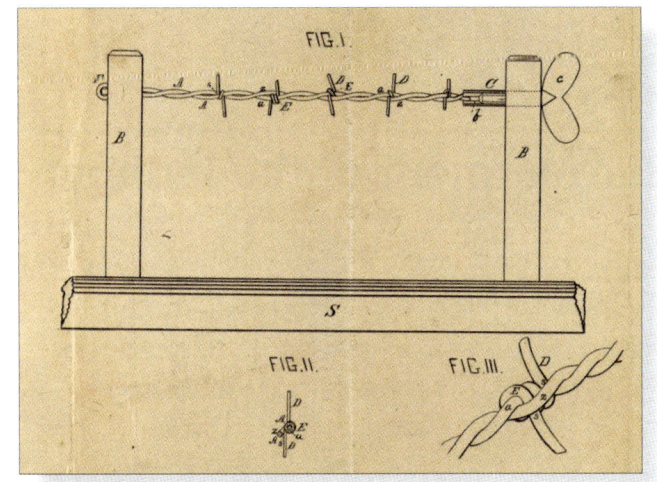

Patent drawing for barbed-wire fencing

- **Obstacle:** Lack of rainfall
  Solution: Farmers on the Great Plains used drilling equipment to dig wells hundreds of feet deep in order to tap into groundwater. Windmills powered pumps that brought this water to the surface.

- **Obstacle:** Tough, dry soil
  Solution: Farmers used steel or chilled-iron plows and plowed more deeply to preserve surface moisture in the soil. These new techniques came to be known as "dry farming."

- **Obstacle:** Lack of fuel
  Solution: The farmers burned "buffalo chips" (*dried buffalo manure*) for fuel.

- **Obstacle:** Lack of manpower
  Solution: They used machinery, such as horse-drawn harvesters and threshers, to farm more acres with fewer workers. In fact, some machinery was actually easier to use on the treeless plains than elsewhere.

With the use of these techniques, combined with the development of new varieties of wheat that needed less water and were more resistant to cold, farmers were able to turn the Great Plains into productive farmland and the main source of America's wheat.

A Diversity of Experiences

Earlier historians—and popular literature—once depicted the American West as an area of conflict between American Indians and white settlers, or between white ranchers and farmers. Today, historians see the settling of the West as much more of a multicultural affair. While it is true that there were Indians and white, English-speaking Americans, there were also many others. These included German, Scandinavian, Irish, Chinese, Italian, French, Russian, and Japanese immigrants; African-American freedmen and soldiers; and Spanish-speaking Mexicans who occupied the same lands they had lived on before the Mexican-American War. Chinese and Irish immigrants helped to build the railroads, and large numbers of Chinese, mainly men, remained in California. German and Scandinavian farming families came by steamship to America to settle the northern Great Plains. "The west," concludes historian Rodman W. Paul, "was a land of many races, many ethnic backgrounds, many national origins."

The Historian's Apprentice

- Pretend you are working for a railroad company in 1870. Design a poster to attract farming families to the Great Plains.
- Pretend you are a newspaper reporter in 1882. Write an imaginary article reporting violence between ranchers and farmers on the Great Plains in Wyoming. Use the Internet to gather information.
- Imagine you are a settler on the Great Plains. Write a letter to your relatives back home, describing the conditions around you.
- Earlier in this chapter, you learned about the **push-and-pull factors** that led to the migration of people from one place to another. Identify two such factors and explain how they led different groups—miners, ranchers or farmers—to migrate to the Great Plains or the Far West.
- During periods of migration, **border areas** where migrants first arrive are often especially affected. Write a short essay explaining how border areas of the West were affected by the mixture of peoples who came there.
- In one sense, the diversity of the American West can be explained by its location at a crossroads where peoples from many different regions interacted—from the expanding United States in the east, from Mexico to the south, and from Asia across the Pacific. There were African Americans coming from the South, Indians being moved onto reservations, and immigrants arriving directly from Europe and Asia. Make your own map or chart illustrating this diversity.

A Public Outcry against the Mistreatment of the Indians

While farmers were developing new techniques for transforming the Great Plains into productive farmland, conditions for the Indians on the reservations only worsened. Some bold reformers began to protest their mistreatment. Helen Hunt Jackson criticized the federal government for breaking its promises to the Indians in her popular books, *A Century of Dishonor* (1881) and *Ramona* (1884). Indeed, new associations formed to protect Indian interests.

"Americanization"

Some reformers urged the Indians to become "**Americanized**." By adopting so-called "American" ways and institutions, such as private property, it was thought that the Indians could become part of "mainstream" society. These well-intentioned reformers did not fully appreciate that "Americanization" might actually endanger the survival of traditional Indian culture.

The Dawes Act, 1887: A Misguided Attempt at Reform?

Congress passed the **Dawes Act** to "Americanize" the Indians. Each male Indian was permitted to claim 160 acres of reservation land as his own private property (the same amount of land given to homesteaders). The reformers hoped that private property would gradually replace communal tribal lands and that the Indians would be transformed into a class of prosperous farmers. Those who exercised the right to claim their own lands were to be rewarded with U.S. citizenship and the right to vote.

Shortcomings of the Dawes Act:

- Despite its good intentions, the Dawes Act threatened the survival of Indian culture. Individual farm ownership was contrary to Indian traditions of tribal sharing, and many tribes had never even engaged in farming. Assimilation into American "mainstream" society meant the destruction of tribal ways.

- Indians continued to face severe economic hardships. Often reservation lands were arid and infertile. The federal government never gave the assistance it had promised to Indian farmers. Reservation schools provided an inferior education. Indians suffered from malnutrition and health problems on the reservations without proper medical attention.

- The Dawes Act actually led to a sell-off of reservation lands. Tribal lands in excess of 160 acres per family were immediately sold off by the government. The act prohibited individual Indians from selling their 160 acres for a period of 25 years. However, even this restriction was lifted in 1906. Speculators and other buyers quickly persuaded many Indians to sell their private plots at low prices. Almost two-thirds of all reservation lands were sold before the government put a halt to this practice. What was left was often the most infertile and undesirable land. Meanwhile, those Indians who bravely left their reservations for the cities usually faced discrimination, unemployment, and poverty.

The Historian's Apprentice

▶ What were the effects of migration to the West? Prepare a PowerPoint presentation or oral report describing how the Great Plains and the Plains Indians were affected by the migration of other peoples to the Great Plains in the late 19th century.

▶ Some historians say that federal policy towards the Indians has swung back and forth like a pendulum. In some periods, the government promoted greater **autonomy** (*independence and self-government*) for the Indians. It let Indian communities preserve their traditions and go their own way. In other periods, the government attempted to "Americanize" (or *assimilate*) the Indians. It tried to make them more like other Americans. Make your own timeline tracing federal policies towards the American Indians. Use the Internet to find additional information.

Review Cards

Key Terms

Migration: The movement of people from one place to another

"Push" Factors: Factors that cause people to leave a place, like ethnic persecution, drought or poverty

"Pull" Factors: Factors that attract people to a new place, such as cheap land, political freedom, mineral discoveries or other economic opportunities

Frontier: The imaginary line separating "settled" and "unsettled" areas

Settlement of the Last American Frontier: the Great Plains and Far West

Great Plains Rolling, treeless, grassy plains with little rain but fertile soil

"Pull" Factors Leading to Settlement of the West:

1. Discoveries of precious metals
2. Completion of transcontinental railroad
3. Relocation of Indians: "Indian Wars" & Reservations
4. Cheap or free land: Homestead Act of 1862

Evolution of Different Parts of the American West

Mining: Boom towns sprang up overnight where gold and silver were discovered.

"Cattle Kingdom": Cowboys drove cattle, grazing on the "open range," to railroads. The "open range" ended in the late 1880s, to be replaced by the "closed range."

Farmers: Adapted to the dry conditions of the Great Plains by using barbed wire fences, sod houses, wells for groundwater, windmills to pump water, steel plows, and farm machinery.

The American Indian Experience

Plains Indians: Hunted buffalo on the Great Plains

"Indian Wars" (1864–1890): Federal troops stationed in forts defeated the Indians in a series of clashes and removed them to remote reservations:

- The Cheyenne and the Sand Creek Massacre (1864)
- Sioux—Black Hills; Custer and Crazy Horse at Little Big Horn; Wounded Knee Massacre (1890)
- Chief Joseph and Nez Percé flight to Canada
- Apaches and Comanches in the Southwest

Reservation System: Tribes forced onto reserved lands, often dry and undesirable. Federal Indian agents and religious teachers provided some services like schools, but government agents often did not keep their promises.

Dawes Act (1887): Shock at the mistreatment of Indians identified by Helen Hunt Jackson and other reformers led to this attempt to "Americanize" Indians. An Indian could apply to take his own private land from the tribe's reservation land. The Dawes Act actually led to a sell-off of Indian lands.

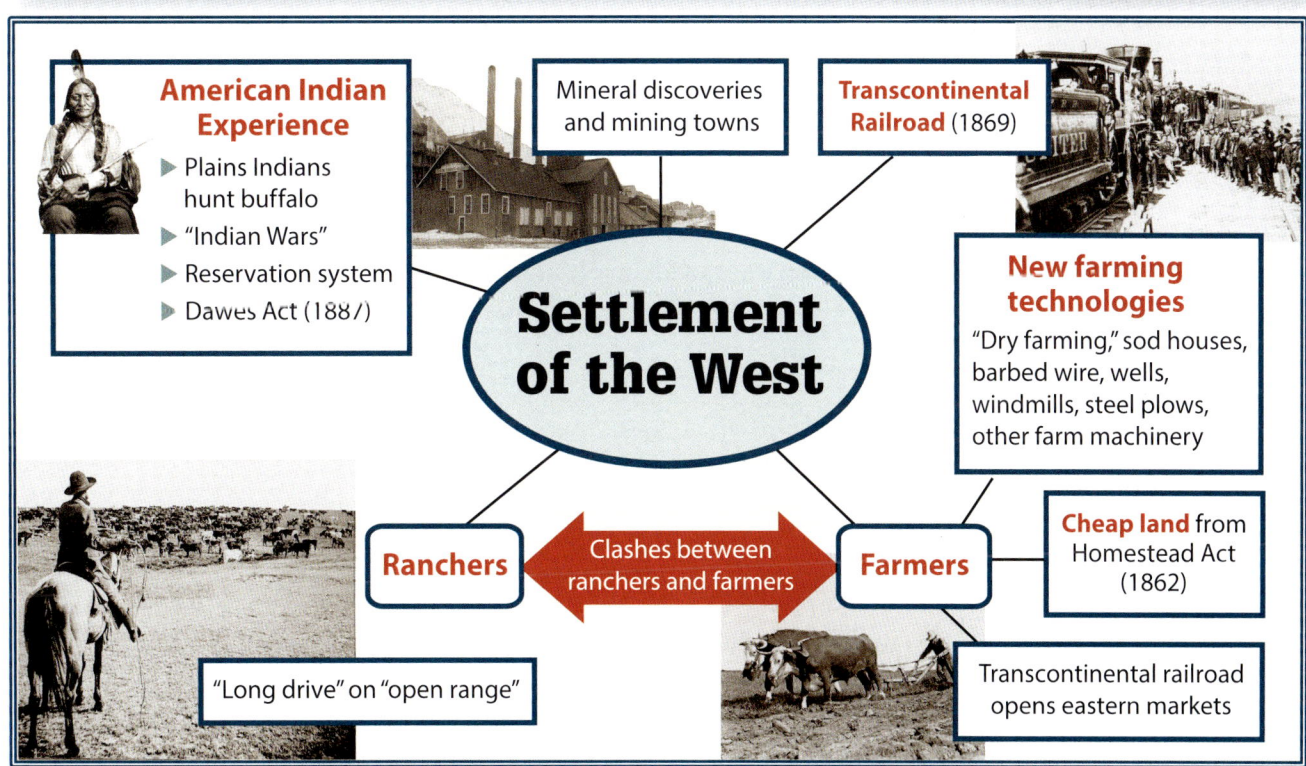

Chapter 3 | "Go West!"

What Do You Know?

SS.912.A.2.7

1. What was the main purpose of the reservation system?

    A. to make the new transcontinental railroad safer to operate

    B. to clear federal lands for settlement by railroads, ranchers, and farmers

    C. to provide employment for Union troops and veterans after the Civil War

    D. to make it easier for Indians to assimilate into mainstream American culture

SS.912.G.4.2

2. How did completion of the first transcontinental railroad in 1869 encourage settlement of the American West?

    A. The railroad led to new discoveries of precious minerals.

    B. The railroad required immense quantities of iron and coal to build.

    C. The railroad frightened Indian tribes, who retreated to reservations.

    D. The railroad made it easier for ranchers and farmers to ship goods back east.

SS.912.G.4.2

3. Which of the following would geographers consider a "pull" factor that contributed to the settling of the Far West?

    A. The amount of farmland available for sale in the Northeast and Midwest was limited.

    B. After the Depression of 1873, many craftsmen in Northeastern cities could not find work.

    C. The children of large farming families in Germany and Scandinavia often did not have enough land of their own.

    D. Only a decade after the California Gold Rush, new discoveries of gold and silver were made in Nevada, Colorado, and South Dakota.

SS.912.A.2.7

4. What was a negative aspect of the "Americanization" policy of the late 1880s for American Indians?

    A. Indians attended reservation schools and learned a trade.

    B. Indians could own and farm 160 acres of their own land.

    C. Indians learned English and could gain the right to vote.

    D. Indians saw the survival of their traditional cultures threatened.

SS.912.A.3.1

5. Which conflict is described in the newspaper shown on the left?

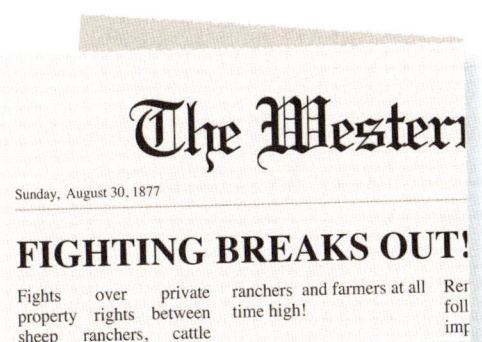

   A. Ranchers with herds on the open range opposed farmers and ranchers with fenced properties.

   B. American Indians opposed ranchers and homesteaders for control of the Great Plains.

   C. Different ranchers with cattle herds competed for grazing along the Chisholm Trail.

   D. Farmers on the Great Plains contested the shipping rates set by railroad companies.

SS.912.A.2.7

6. The cartoon below was published in the late 1800s.

   What is the main idea of the cartoon?

   A. Federal Indian agents assisted Indians in growing crops on the reservation.

   B. The federal government provided Indians with all the supplies needed.

   C. Indians went hungry while federal Indian agents grew wealthy.

   D. The livestock raised on the Indian reservations were diseased.

SS.912.A.3.1

- Built sod houses
- Used dry farming techniques
- Used barbed wire fences
- Burned cow and buffalo chips for fuel
- Windmills pumped water
- Steel plow used for tough soil

7. What would be the best title for the box above?

   A. Methods Used by Forty-Niners to Stake Claims

   B. Sources of Conflict between Ranchers and Farmers

   C. How Farmers Adapted to Conditions on the Great Plains

   D. How American Indians and Western Farmers Cooperated

Chapter 3 | "Go West!"

SS.912.A.2.7

8. How did the Dawes Act (1887) mark a departure from earlier federal Indian policy?
   A. It led to conflicts between new settlers and Indian tribes on the Great Plains.
   B. It moved Indian tribes still on the Great Plains to reservations farther west.
   C. It permitted Indians to withdraw private plots from the tribal reservation.
   D. It encouraged the shooting of buffalo herds from new railroad lines.

SS.912.G.4.3

9. People in the American West had different points of view about how land should be used. Which of the following does **NOT** show a conflict over land use?

   A. Farmers — barbed-wire fence — Ranchers
   B. Miners — polluted water — Farmers
   C. Indians — gold in holy site — Miners
   D. Railroad — sale of land grants to private owners — Farmers

SS.912.G.4.2

10. Which would be the best title for the chart below?

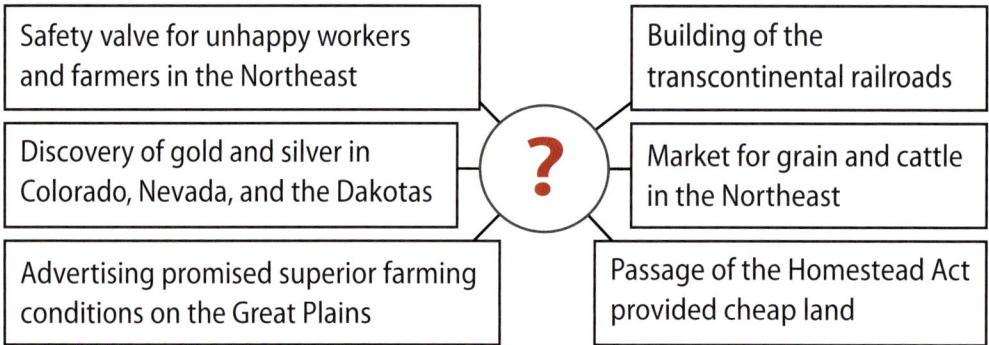

   A. Reasons for the Success of the Nebraska Land Rush
   B. Factors Contributing to the Settlement of the West
   C. Conditions Leading to the Spread of Cholera
   D. Sparks for the Second Industrial Revolution

SS.912.G.4.2

11. What did the passage of the Homestead Act of 1862 and the Pacific Railway Act demonstrate about the federal government?
    A. It was committed to settling the western territories.
    B. It was concerned about conserving natural resources.
    C. It was unwilling to move American Indian tribes to reservations.
    D. It was determined to break up business trusts harmful to free enterprise.

Unit I: The Civil War and Reconstruction (Chapters 1–3)

Identify or define each of the following terms.

Missouri Compromise _____
_____

Compromise of 1850 _____
_____

Kansas-Nebraska Act _____
_____

Dred Scott decision _____
_____

Gettysburg _____
_____

Reconstruction _____
_____

Freedmen's Bureau _____
_____

"Black Codes" _____
_____

Radical Republicans _____
_____

Fourteenth Amendment _____
_____

Sharecropping _____
_____

"Jim Crow" laws _____
_____

Homestead Act _____
_____

Transcontinental Railroad _____
_____

Reservation System _____
_____

Crossword Puzzle

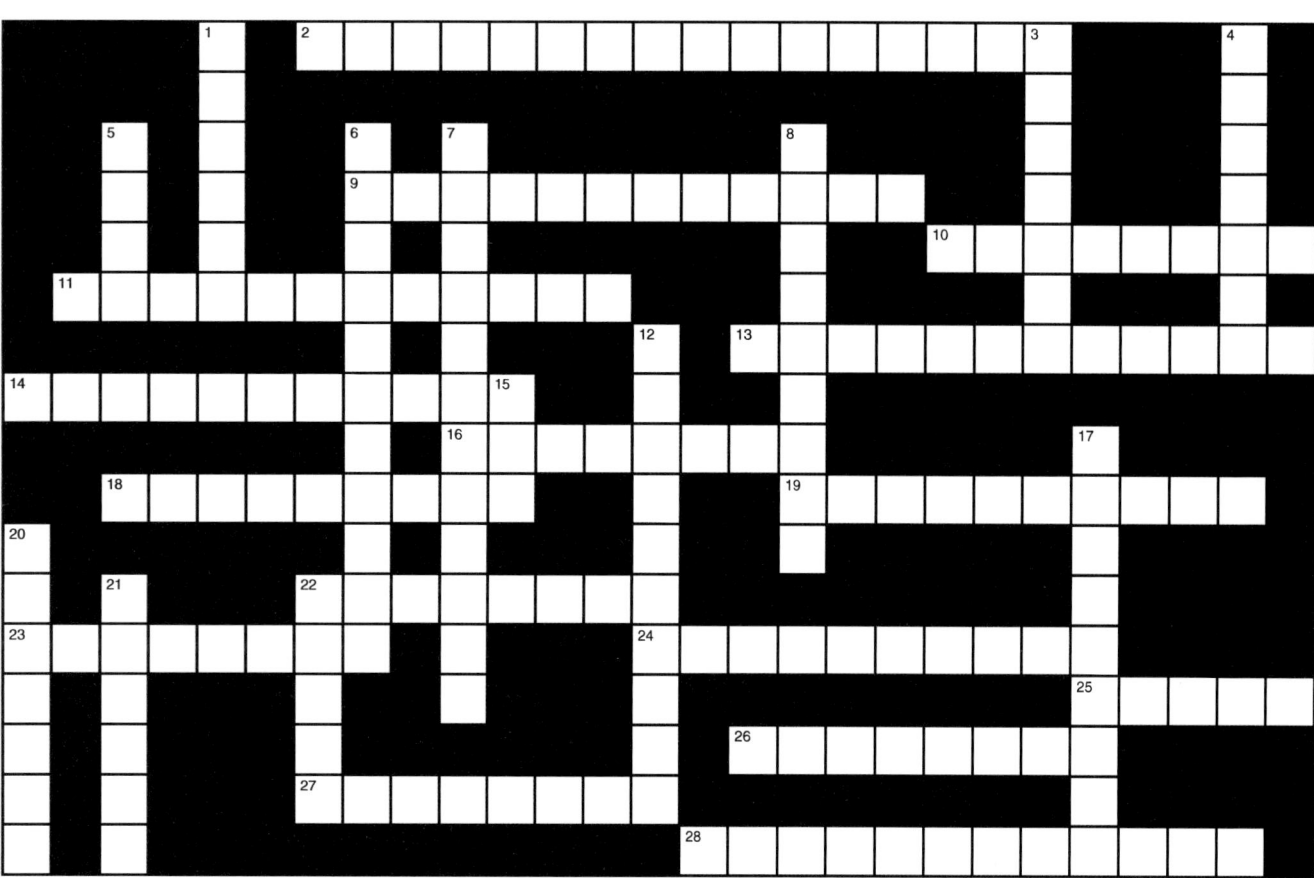

Across

2. Name of the railroad that was completed in 1869
9. Lincoln's _____ Proclamation declared that slaves in states in rebellion would be free in January 1863
10. Line separating areas of settlement from less densely populated areas
11. Term for a freedman who enters into a farming deal with former owner to work the land and divide the harvest
13. Loyalty felt by many Americans to their region of the country
14. Bill which prohibited discrimination based on race
16. Town that sprang up overnight, often in a mining area
18. The government act that granted free land to settlers after improving it for six months
19. Constitutional amendment that prohibits slavery throughout the United States
22. Frederick _____ wrote about his experiences as a former slave
23. An emancipated slave
24. Just after the Civil War, _____ _____ were written by Southern states to prevent freedmen from having the same rights as whites
25. Indian tribe native to the Black Hills of South Dakota
26. A compromise reached in 1820 to keep slave and nonslave states equal in the Senate
27. Southern white who supported Reconstruction
28. A person who agitated to end slavery

Down

1. Federal fort in the harbor of Charleston
3. Republican who won the 1860 Presidential election
4. The 14th Amendment established everyone's right to due _____
5. Type of factor that causes people to leave one place for another
6. The enforced separation of different racial groups
7. Derogatory term for people from the North who arrived to help the freedmen
8. Constitutional amendment that prohibits denial of voting rights on the basis of race
12. Lee's 1863 advance on the North resulted in the battle at _____, Pennsylvania
15. Thick clumps of grass and soil used to construct houses
17. The action of formally withdrawing from membership in the United States
20. African-American troops in the West were called _____ soldiers
21. First African American to sit in Congress
22. A misguided attempt by the United States to "Americanize" Indians was known as the _____ Act

Unit I | Activity 2

CHAPTER 4

The Triumph of Industry

SS.912.A.3.2 Examine the social, political, and economic causes, course, and consequences of the Second Industrial Revolution that began in the late 19th century.

SS.912.A.3.3 Compare the First and Second Industrial Revolutions in the United States.

SS.912.A.3.4 Determine how the development of steel, oil, transportation, communication, and business practices affected the United States economy.

SS.912.A.3.5 Identify significant inventors of the Industrial Revolution, including African Americans and women.

SS.912.A.3.13 Examine key events and peoples in Florida history as they relate to United States history.

Names and Terms You Should Know

First Industrial Revolution	Telegraph	Corporation
Market economy	Alexander Graham Bell	Stock
Capitalism	Transatlantic cable	Entrepreneur
Innovation	Thomas Edison	Andrew Carnegie
Second Industrial Revolution	Wilbur and Orville Wright	John D. Rockefeller
Transportation	African-American inventors	J. P. Morgan
Railroads	Madam C. J. Walker	Trusts
George Pullman	Elijah McCoy	Monopoly
George Westinghouse	Sarah Goode	Government regulation
Bessemer process	Garrett Morgan	Sherman Antitrust Act
Samuel Morse	Lewis Howard Latimer	Henry Flagler
	Jan Ernst Matzeliger	

Florida "Keys" to Learning

1. In the decades following the Civil War, Americans experienced a "Second Industrial Revolution." The first Industrial Revolution, 70 years earlier, had been based on the use of the steam engine and the new factory system. The Second Industrial Revolution witnessed the expansion of the railways, increased production of steel, the introduction of telecommunications and electricity, and the emergence of a truly national market.

2. Many factors prepared the way for America's Second Industrial Revolution. The United States possessed abundant natural resources, including water, timber, coal, iron ore, and oil. A growing population provided labor. The free enterprise system and the American work ethic encouraged individual initiative, entrepreneurship, and economic growth. The government provided a system of laws, established patents and copyrights, regulated the currency, sold public lands, and established tariffs favorable to growth.

3. New inventions helped to trigger the Second Industrial Revolution. These included the Bessemer process for making steel, the sewing machine, telegraph, telephone, electric light bulb, typewriter, elevator, refrigerated railway car, and cash register. African-American men and women contributed to a steady stream of new inventions: these inventors included Madam Walker, Elijah McCoy, Sarah Goode, John Burr, Lewis Howard Latimer, Jan Ernst Matzeliger, Sarah Boone, and Garrett Morgan.

4. The expansion of the railroads and new methods of communication created a truly national market. Americans developed new ways to sell and distribute goods, such as the department store and mail-order catalog.

5. New forms of doing business, such as the corporation, made it easier to raise the huge sums of money required by heavy industry. Large enterprises enjoyed certain economies of scale. They could purchase large quantities of goods at a discount, or even acquire their own sources of supply. They could design larger production facilities and take full advantage of mechanization and the latest technologies. They could also engage in cutthroat practices against competitors and equally harsh tactics against their own workers.

6. The entrepreneurs who built these enterprises—among them, Andrew Carnegie in steel, John D. Rockefeller in oil, and J. P. Morgan in electricity, banking and steel—amassed immense personal fortunes. Many of the richest gave part of their fortunes away through acts of philanthropy.

7. The federal government attempted to prevent some of the worst abuses of "Big Business" through legislation. The Interstate Commerce Act (1887) prevented unfair practices by railroads. The Sherman Antitrust Act (1890) allowed the government to break up monopolies that engaged in harmful business practices against the public interest.

America's Second Industrial Revolution

In 1860, most Americans were farmers living in the countryside. They made most things for themselves—from clothes to furniture—and bought only a few small luxuries or scarce items in the local general store or from a traveling peddler. People depended on torches or whale oil lamps once the sun went down. American manufacturing consisted mainly in making textiles and ironwares, and in processing foods. Railroads and canals linked together Northeastern cities but much of the American West was still unsettled. Many Americans had limited contact with the world outside their own community in the course of a lifetime.

By 1920, the United States had changed dramatically. Half of all Americans now lived in cities. Large corporations produced goods for the entire nation. Railroads and telephone lines spanned the country from coast to coast. Americans bought their goods in department stores, chain stores, specialty shops, or from mail-order catalogs. Electric lights illuminated the evening hours, and a large number of factories were driven by electricity. People went to motion picture shows for entertainment. The use of the automobile was spreading. America had become the world's leading industrial power. How did all these great changes come about?

Background: The Foundations for Economic Growth

Economists generally agree that the foundations for America's spectacular economic growth had already been laid by the end of the Civil War.

1. Abundant Natural Resources

The United States was generously endowed with valuable natural resources: fertile soil, swift-flowing streams, vast quantities of timber, and rich deposits of coal, iron ore, oil, phosphates, and copper.

2. The "Free Enterprise" System

The United States enjoyed the benefits of the "free enterprise," or **capitalist**, system of economic organization. Under this system, tools, factories, and other means of production (including the money needed to buy these things)—known as *capital*—are privately owned. People are free to buy and sell goods and labor on an open market. For this reason, this is also known as a **market economy**. The producers of better and cheaper goods are generally able to compete more effectively and stay in business. The market acts to eliminate less efficient producers. While each person pursues his own interest, the market guides all individual activity towards the most efficient means of production.

A competitive "work ethic" strengthened belief in the virtues of the free enterprise system. American culture emphasized individualism and material success. American individualism encouraged entrepreneurs, farmers, and laborers to work hard. The nineteenth-century philosophy of **Social Darwinism** likewise stressed the necessity of free competition. Based on the evolutionary theory of biologist Charles Darwin, Social Darwinists believed that the most successful individuals were those endowed with superior talents who had the ability to adapt, survive, and thrive. Wealthy people often viewed poverty as the fault of the poor themselves rather than as the product of circumstances or of injustices in the social system.

Chapter 4 | The Triumph of Industry

3. The Role of Government

Under the theory of *"laissez-faire"* **capitalism**, the government was supposed to interfere in the free market as little as possible. Although the government officially followed this "hands-off" policy, it actually encouraged industrialization in many ways. The **patent system**, established in the U.S. Constitution, encouraged inventiveness by guaranteeing an inventor exclusive rights to the use of his or her invention for a limited period, if a *patent* was filed and issued. The aim of this system was to encourage inventors to share their discoveries and innovations with the public, secure in the knowledge that they could reap the benefits of their invention for a reasonable length of time.

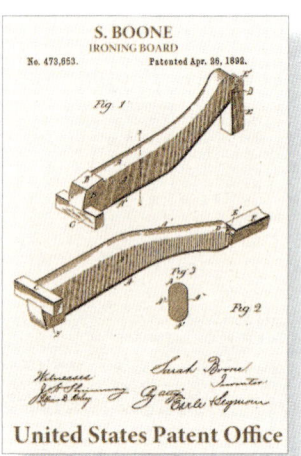

Tariffs protected American manufacturing from foreign competition by imposing customs duties on foreign-made goods. Other laws protected property and business agreements (*contracts*). Congress had the power to regulate the currency and banks. Finally, federal land policies encouraged westward expansion and development. Grants of franchises to railroad companies over vast tracts of federal land encouraged the construction of railroads.

4. The Legacy of the First Industrial Revolution

In the late 18th century, the **First Industrial Revolution** in Great Britain introduced the use of steam power and the mass production of goods in factories. The United States became the first nation to follow Britain's lead. By the 1850s, the use of steam power was firmly established in the United States. Northeastern states became the main centers of American manufacturing. Steamboats and railroads began linking together distant regions of the country. In the South, railroads and steamboats led to an expansion of the "Cotton Belt," producing raw cotton for export to British factories. The Midwest produced livestock and wheat for both the Northeast and the South.

5. The Economic Stimulus Provided by the Civil War

The value of Northern manufacturing doubled in the decade of the Civil War. Wartime needs for uniforms, guns, processed foods, and other goods stimulated production. Huge wartime profits were re-invested in manufacturing. The abolition of slavery at the end of the war united the North and South in a giant free-labor, free-market economy.

Finally, the secession of the South temporarily freed Northern Congressmen to enact federal laws favorable to the growth of Northern industry.

> **Civil War Legislation Encouraging Economic Growth**
>
> **Morrill Tariff** (1861) was enacted to protect American manufacturing from European competition.
>
> **National Banking Acts** (1863 and 1864) created a national banking system through nationally chartered banks and a national currency through the regulation of bank notes.
>
> **Homestead Act** (1862) offered free land to settlers occupying farms in the West.
>
> **Morrill Act** (1862) gave land grants to states to support technical and agricultural colleges.
>
> **Pacific Railway Act** (1862) gave federal loans and land grants to railroad companies to complete a transcontinental railroad.

The Historian's Apprentice

▶ Create your own illustrated concept map or web showing those factors that set the stage for America's spectacular economic growth in the late 19th century.

▶ Use the Internet or your school library to conduct further research on one of the factors supporting American economic growth. Then write a brief report describing that factor and explaining why it was important.

America's Second Industrial Revolution: Emergence of the Modern Industrial Economy

After the Civil War, America was united by new railroad lines, making possible a truly national market for the first time. Manufacturers were able to produce and sell goods more easily across the entire nation. New forms of business organization enabled producers to raise the vast sums of money needed to cover their larger production and distribution costs. These developments transformed how goods were made and used. Historians generally refer to this new burst of economic growth as America's **Second Industrial Revolution**.

The Spread of Railroads

Improvements in transportation were crucial to both the First and Second Industrial Revolutions. By the end of the Civil War, the United States had 35,000 miles of railroad track. Only 25 years later, it had more than five times that mileage—in fact, more than all of Europe. The greatest growth in this period occurred in the West. The first transcontinental railroad was completed in 1869; four additional trans-continental lines were built by 1893. Soon other lines were extended from these first trunk lines. Federal and state governments encouraged railroad construction by granting franchises over vast tracts of land to railroad companies. Steel rails replaced iron ones. A uniform track width (or "gauge") was adopted, making it possible to travel on the tracks of different railroad companies without disruption. The railroads were made safer and more comfortable by laying double tracks. **George Pullman** invented the sleeping car, and **George Westinghouse** invented the air brake, which stopped all the cars of a train at

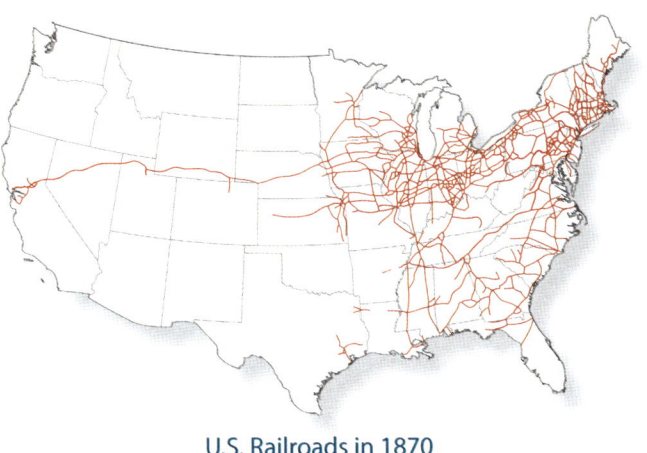

U.S. Railroads in 1870

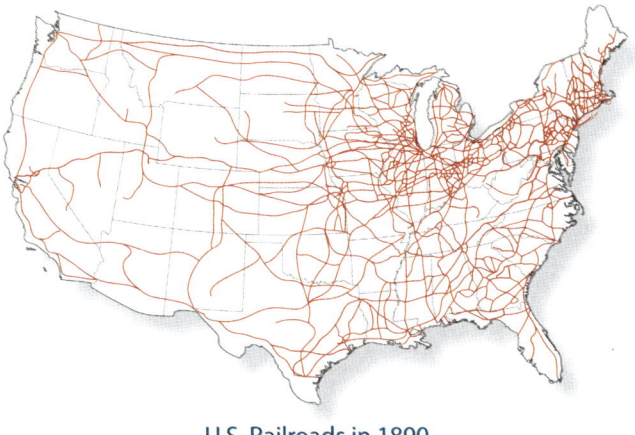

U.S. Railroads in 1890

Chapter 4 | The Triumph of Industry

the same time. Gustavus Swift developed the first refrigerated railroad cars. Meat was stored in the bottom of a heavily insulated railroad car, while chunks of ice were placed at the top.

Railroads affected just about every aspect of American life. Railroad schedules created the need for uniform time zones across the country. The construction of the railroads provided a tremendous stimulus to the steel, iron, and coal industries. The railroads brought settlers to the Great Plains and connected them with urban markets in the Northeast. Railroads encouraged the growth of cities by enabling workers to commute and allowing farmers to ship their crops and livestock over longer distances. It became possible to slaughter cattle, hogs, and sheep in the stockyards of Chicago, and then to pack and ship the cuts of meat to urban markets in the Northeast. Railroads connected raw materials to factories, and factories to consumers across the nation. Railroad hubs like Chicago and Atlanta mushroomed into major urban centers. Railroads transformed America into a nation on the move as never before.

Technological Innovation

Just as the "First Industrial Revolution" had depended upon new inventions and innovations, such as the invention of the steam engine and its adaptation for manufacturing in factories, the "Second Industrial Revolution" was also largely based on the twin processes of invention and innovation. The patent system continued to encourage Americans to create inventions and to share those inventions with others. Some of the most striking advances occurred in the fields of steel, communications, electricity, oil and transportation.

Steel

In Britain, Henry Bessemer invented the "**Bessemer process**" in 1855, making the production of steel much more economical. Bessemer blew air through molten pig iron (created by heating iron ore with carbon) to remove impurities before it turned into steel.

His new process took place in a lined "Bessemer converter." Hot pig iron was poured into the mouth of the converter and air was blown in through the sides. Impurities burned off the top as gas or dropped to the bottom of the converter as "slag."

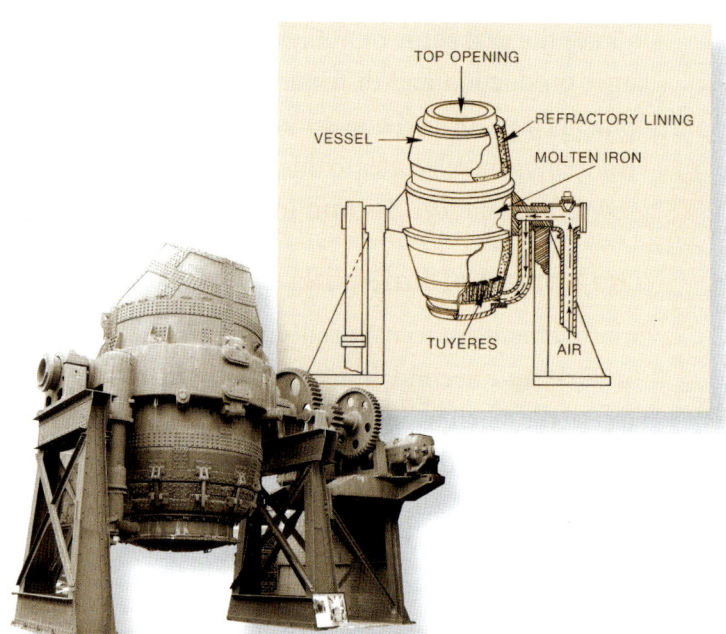

Invention or Innovation?

Invention is the process of developing something for the first time, especially new machines, methods and products. **Innovation** refers to the process of putting these new ideas and methods into practice. An inventor might design and build the first refrigerator; an innovator is the first to build a factory that manufactures them.

The Bessemer process reduced the cost of making steel by more than 80%. Cheaper steel made it possible for Americans to produce thousands of miles of railroad track and to build giant steamships, towering steel suspension bridges, massive turbines and engines, and skyscrapers made with steel beams.

Communications

A series of exciting new inventions, most coming from America, completely revolutionized the field of communications.

Samuel Morse (1791–1872) Morse's wife suddenly fell ill and died while she and Morse were apart. This heart-stricken painter then began a search for a faster means of long distance communication. Morse developed the **telegraph** using electromagnetism. He also invented a code of long and short spaces capable of transmitting the alphabet. By breaking and closing the circuit, the telegraph operator could move a distant telegraph device on the same circuit. Morse's telegraph made instant communications possible, even over long distances.

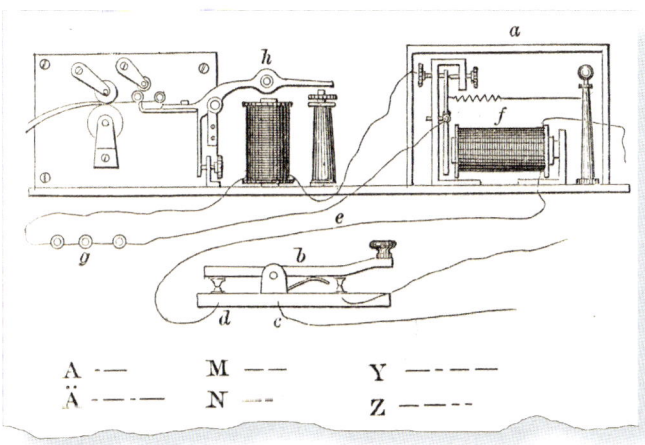

Cyrus Field (1819–1892) Field made a fortune in paper manufacturing. He then became interested in laying the first **transatlantic cable** to carry telegraphic messages between America and Europe. Field organized a company that successfully laid the first cable in 1858, but the cable failed after only three weeks. Field organized a new company and laid a heavier and more durable cable seven years later.

Alexander Graham Bell (1847–1922) The mother and wife of this Scottish immigrant were both deaf, while his father and grandfather had both been teachers of speech. Bell began investigating how to reproduce the sounds of speech electronically to help the deaf. He patented the **telephone** in 1875, which carries a variable current to a receiver capable of reproducing the human voice. Bell's invention made it possible to communicate over long distances using natural speech instead of Morse code.

Electricity

Both the telegraph and telephone made use of electrical current. A young telegraph operator, **Thomas Alva Edison**, invented a new "stock-ticker" machine for following the prices of stocks; he also invented an improved telegraph machine. With the money he earned from these first inventions, Edison hired a team of researchers to work in his laboratory in Menlo Park, New Jersey. In 1877, Edison patented the **phonograph** (record player). After testing various carbon filaments (wires) and gases, Thomas Edison invented a practical **electric light bulb** in 1879, which could burn brightly

Chapter 4 | The Triumph of Industry

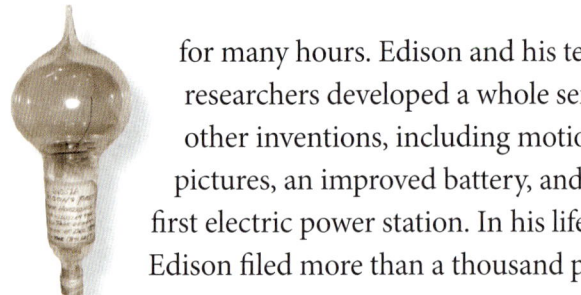

for many hours. Edison and his team of researchers developed a whole series of other inventions, including motion pictures, an improved battery, and the first electric power station. In his lifetime, Edison filed more than a thousand patents.

Electricity was also used to run the new **electric motor**, based on the application of electromagnetism to create motion. Electric motors proved to be more adaptable to different uses than steam engines. By the end of the 19th century, electricity was being used to power factories and to operate electric streetcars and subway trains.

Nicola Tesla was a Serbian immigrant who came to the United States in 1884 to work for Edison. Two years later, Tesla started his own company. Tesla challenged Edison's reliance on direct current and developed a motor for producing alternating current ("AC"), which could travel longer distances. George Westinghouse, the inventor of the air brake, became Tesla's financial backer. In 1893, they used their high-voltage alternating current to light up the Chicago World's Fair. Tesla also conducted early experiments with X-rays and radio waves.

Oil

In the early 19th century, people had used the blubber (or fat) of whales to make oil for lubrication and lighting. The first oil well was drilled by **Edwin Drake** in Pennsylvania in 1859.

Improvements in refining allowed products from **petroleum**—a liquid hydrocarbon formed over millions of years from the decayed remains of sea organisms—to be used for lighting and machine lubrication. Kerosene was used in lamps in millions of homes. By the end of the century, **gasoline**, another petroleum derivative, was being used to run the new internal combustion engine.

Other Industries

Invented at the end of the 19th century, the **internal combustion engine** used controlled explosions of gasoline to move pistons in a cylinder. It was small yet powerful enough to run automobiles, made by **Henry Ford** and other manufacturers. The internal combustion engine also powered the first airplane, invented by two Ohio bicycle makers, **Wilbur and Orville Wright** in 1903.

Other important American inventions in these decades included the typewriter, vacuum cleaner, cash register, fountain pen, linotype (a machine for printing newspapers), and an improved sewing machine.

Women and African-American Inventors

Women had fewer opportunities but could also be inventors. For example, **Josephine Cochran** (1839–1913) was a wealthy woman who invented the first automatic dishwasher.

Although often deprived of opportunities for educational and professional advancement, African Americans also made significant contributions to the innovations of this period.

John Albert Burr This African-American inventor patented an improved rotary-blade lawn-mower in 1899. Its blades were designed so that they would not get plugged up with lawn clippings.

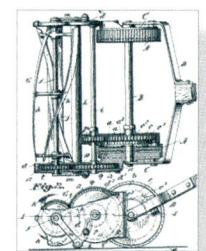

Granville T. Woods (1856–1910) patented a series of inventions for trains and streetcars, including a multiplex telegraph that could send signals between stations and moving trains.

Elijah McCoy (1844–1929) Born to fugitive slaves who had fled to Canada, this African-American inventor trained as a mechanical engineer in Scotland before returning to the United States, where he opened up his own machine shop. McCoy obtained several patents for lubricators for steam engines. These lubricators,

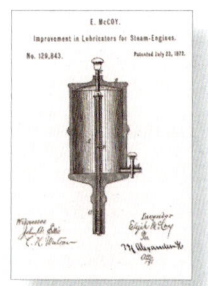

or oil-drip cups, automatically added oil to lubricate the engines of railroad locomotives and steamships, enabling them to run better.

Sarah Goode (b. 1850)   Born into slavery, she became the first African-American woman to receive a U.S patent. After the Civil War, she moved to Chicago where she opened a furniture store. In 1885, she received a patent for a fold-away bed that could be tucked into a desk. This was especially useful for the millions of Americans living in small apartments.

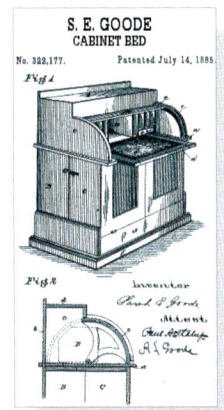

Madam C. J. Walker (1867–1919) American cosmetic companies generally ignored the needs of African-American women. Born to former slaves in Louisiana, Madam Walker made a fortune developing and selling hair care and cosmetic products for African-American women. Because of the general lack of indoor plumbing, many people washed their hair infrequently and suffered from scalp diseases. Madam Walker invented new remedial shampoos based on sulfur. She may have been the first African-American millionaire.

Lewis Howard Latimer (1848–1928)   The son of fugitive slaves, he served in the navy towards the end of the Civil War. Latimer became a patent draftsman and worked for both Alexander Graham Bell and Thomas Edison. In 1881, he patented an improved method for producing the carbon filaments used in the new electric light bulb.

Jan Ernst Matzeliger (1852–1889)   Born in South America, he moved to the United States at the age of 19 and worked in a shoe factory. In 1883, Matzeliger was awarded a patent for inventing a machine that attached the upper part of a leather shoe to its sole (the bottom of the shoe). By hand, an expert shoemaker could attach no more than 50 soles a day; with the new machine, a worker could attach 150 to 700 soles a day. Matzeliger's invention cut the price of shoes in half.

Garrett Morgan (1877–1963)   Born in Kentucky to former slaves, he moved to Ohio at the age of 14 in search of work. Morgan began repairing sewing machines and later opened his own shop. He discovered that he had a talent as an inventor. Morgan developed a safety hood and smoke protector for firefighters—a type of gas mask that used a wet sponge as a filter and a long tube that dropped to the ground for the intake of air. He used his safety hood to save workers in an explosion in 1916. Morgan also patented a type of traffic signal for automobiles in 1923.

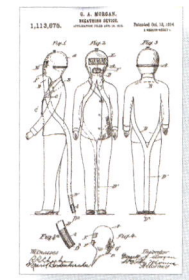

The Historian's Apprentice

▸ Was the "Second Industrial Revolution" of greater importance to Americans than the "First"? Write an essay defending your point of view.

▸ Make your own chart or timeline showing the most important inventions of this period with their inventors. Be sure to include an explanation of how each invention changed the ways that people lived.

▸ Write an imaginary newspaper headline and article announcing the patenting of a new invention, such as the telephone or electric light bulb.

▸ Which invention from this period do you think had the greatest impact on society? Write an essay justifying your selection.

▸ How was the U.S. patent system important to the development and sharing of these American inventions? Write a paragraph explaining its role.

A Growing Population

The use of machinery and the increased acreage under cultivation made it possible for American farmers to feed many more people than ever before. Between 1860 and 1920, the population of the United States more than tripled. This increase was fueled in part by a constant stream of European and Asian immigrants. Population growth created conditions favorable for business growth: there was a steadily rising demand for goods and a ready supply of cheap labor.

	1860	1920
Total U.S. population	31,443,321	106,021,557
U.S. labor force	7,442,705	42,918,000
Foreign-born population	4,138,697	13,920,692

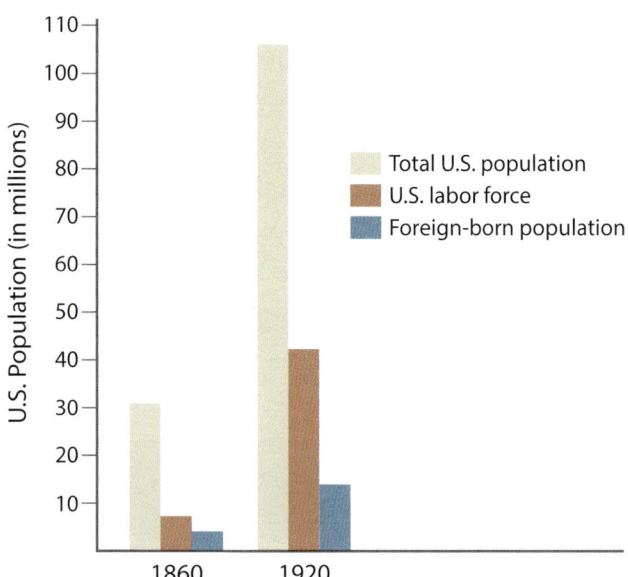

Source: U.S. Census; Weiss, *US Labor Force Estimate and Economic Growth*

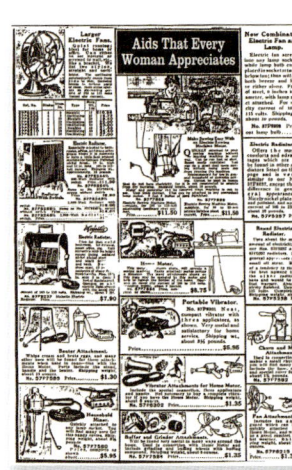

tions, the population itself expanded, and new methods of advertising and selling were developed. More of the population became concentrated in large cities, where goods were easier to sell. Large corporations developed specialized marketing and advertising departments. New types of retailers—department stores, chain stores (Woolworths), mail-order houses (Sears & Roebuck), and specialty shops—bought items in large quantities from producers at a discount, in order to sell to consumers at a profit.

While the growing population needed consumer goods, expanding industries needed steel, coal, oil, and machinery. National producers could make and ship these capital goods more cheaply than local producers. The high investment costs of modern mass production required a large market to remain profitable.

The Emergence of a National Market

The spread of railroads and innovations in communications and manufacturing led to the replacement of separate regional markets by a single national market. Railroads made it cheaper to transport goods to other parts of the country, the telegraph and telephone improved communica-

New Business Practices: The Rise of the Corporation

Before the Civil War, most American businesses had been owned either by an individual or by a group of partners. Owners were personally **liable** (*responsible*) for the debts of their company. When owners died, their business usually dissolved.

68   Chapter 4 | The Triumph of Industry

In the years following the Civil War, a new form of enterprise became more common. A **corporation** is a company chartered by a state and recognized in law as a separate "person." The corporation issues **stocks**, or shares of ownership in the corporation, to investors.

Each stockholder is a partial owner of the corporation and receives a share of its profits in the form of dividends. Stockholders elect a board of directors, who in turn appoint a general manager (or "CEO") to run the company.

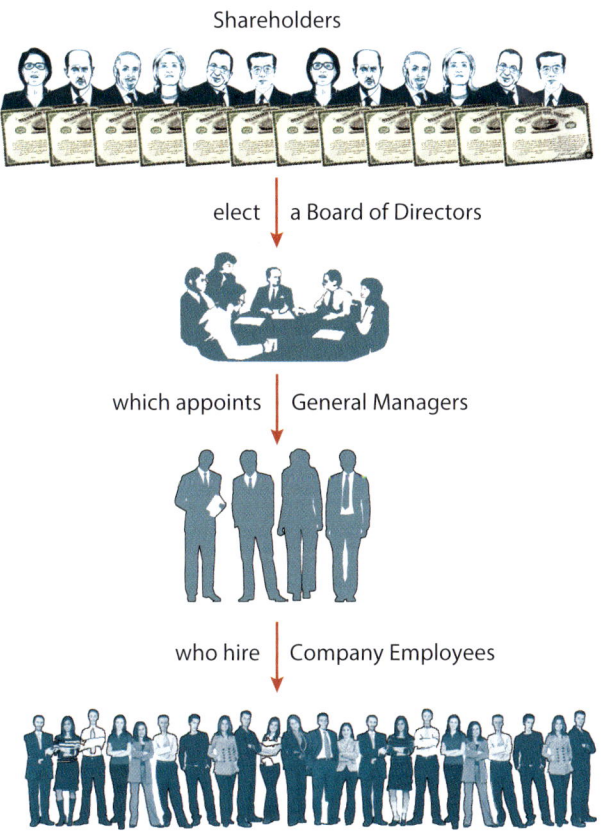

Corporate stocks are transferable and can be inherited or sold. The death of a stockholder does not affect the survival of the corporation, which can continue indefinitely. Nor are individual shareholders personally responsible for the debts of the company, although they do risk losing their investment.

Building railroads, producing steel, refining petroleum, laying telegraph and telephone wires, and building factories required enormous sums of capital investment. By issuing stocks, corporations were able to raise greater sums of money than ever before. Individuals were able to pool their money together by investing in a corporation. The corporate form of business organization thus allowed the creation of larger businesses. Large-scale enterprises enjoyed many advantages over smaller competitors.

Economies of Scale in Production Larger businesses could build larger production facilities and modernize more rapidly. Such facilities were often more efficient because they could introduce a greater division and specialization of labor, more mechanization, and an increased use of water, steam, or electrical power. They could also invest more money in developing a superior factory design, such as the use of assembly lines.

Cheaper Sources of Supply Giant corporations could obtain raw materials more cheaply from suppliers because the large size of their bulk purchases

Chapter 4 | The Triumph of Industry   69

gave them greater bargaining power and the ability to obtain discounts. Eventually some large corporations even acquired their own sources of supply. A few companies took control over all stages of production and distribution, known as **vertical integration**: they owned their own sources of raw materials, their own transportation networks, and their own manufacturing facilities.

More Efficient Management The larger size of corporations allowed them to develop better management. Large corporations generally had specialized departments headed by expert managers—accounting, purchasing, processing, marketing, and research and development. They adopted the practice of cost-accounting—determining the exact cost of each step in the production and distribution process—to guide their decisions. They pioneered new methods for marketing their products, such as the use of brand names. Corporations could afford to hire engineers, chemists, and scientists to conduct continuous research to improve their existing products and develop new products.

The Entrepreneurial Spirit

The creation of the modern industrial economy would not have taken place without the guiding hand of the great entrepreneurs. **Entrepreneurs** are those who take risks by engaging in business to make a profit. The leading entrepreneurs of America's "Second Industrial Revolution" considered themselves to be "captains of industry" who adopted new technologies and took advantage of new forms of corporate organization to make cheaper and better products. They had the vision to see the possibilities created by the latest advances in transportation, technology and corporate finance. They also had the drive to sacrifice the interests of others to their own ambitions. Critics called them "Robber Barons" who exploited workers, used dishonest tactics, and exercised their monopoly control over individual industries to overcharge the public. They amassed legendary personal fortunes and frequently turned to **philanthropy** in their old age.

A Portrait Gallery of the Great Entrepreneurs of the Gilded Age

Because of the displays of great wealth by leading industrialists, often obtained through unethical tactics and covering serious social problems, historians sometimes refer to America's Second Industrial Revolution as the "**Gilded Age**." A *gilded* surface has a thin layer of gold on top concealing a less expensive metal beneath. The name is taken from the title of a novel by Mark Twain and Charles Dudley Warner, published in 1873, which humorously criticized greed and corruption in American society.

Andrew Carnegie (1835–1919) was a penniless immigrant from Scotland as a child. He worked as a factory worker, messenger boy, and telegraph operator. He worked his way up to a managerial position in a railroad company and became friends with the owner, who helped him with his own investments. During the Civil War, Carnegie helped manage Union railroad lines.

Carnegie's birthplace

After the war, Carnegie left the railroad industry to start the Keystone Bridge Company. He hoped to build bridges of iron instead of wood. His company became the subcontractor that built much of the first bridge to carry trains across the Mississippi River. To span this distance, he had to build a structure of steel. Carnegie became one of the first to adopt the Bessemer process for producing steel. He used the corporate form of enterprise to raise additional capital and bought out competing local companies in the 1870s.

He joined with Henry Clay Frick to gain access to Frick's coke operations, since coke (*carbon made by heating coal in a furnace without air*) was needed to make pig iron, an essential ingredient for making steel. Carnegie began producing steel girders for building

Andrew Carnegie in 1878, age 33

70   Chapter 4 | The Triumph of Industry

construction, as well as steel rails for railroad tracks.

Carnegie hired chemists to improve his production and introduced cost-accounting. He eliminated middlemen and made use of immigrant labor at low wages. Carnegie's workers worked 12-hour shifts, and his mills operated day and night.

Carnegie pretended to be a friend to labor, and so he hid in Scotland while Frick broke the back of the steelworkers' unions during the Homestead Strike (see the next chapter). Carnegie opposed all attempts at worker organization during the 1892 Homestead Strike.

Meanwhile, he bought iron ore mines, a coke works, a limestone company, railroads, and a fleet of ore boats in the Great Lakes. This gave him complete control over all stages of the production and distribution process, known as **vertical integration**.

By the end of the century, Carnegie was producing

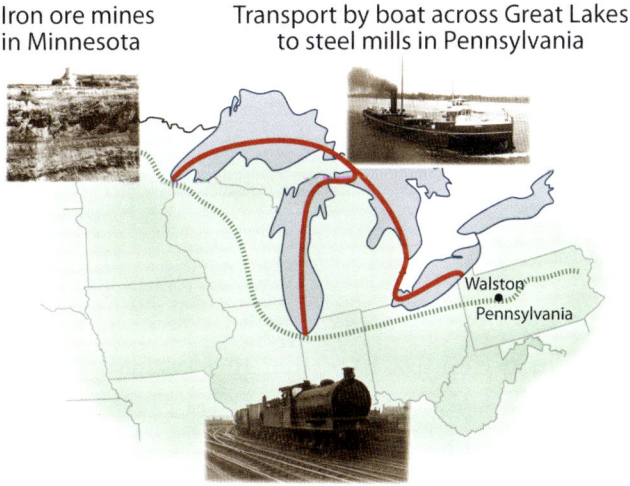

one-quarter of all the steel made in the United States. He sold his company to J. P. Morgan in 1901 for $225 million. He spent the rest of his life giving his money away in acts of philanthropy, including millions to establish public libraries and Carnegie Hall in New York City.

Carnegie expressed his views on philanthropy in his book *The Gospel of Wealth*. He believed that a rich man should not die

Carnegie, age 78

with his wealth but should give it away in his lifetime, especially to institutions that promoted self-improvement.

John D. Rockefeller (1839–1937) made profits during the Civil War by investing in oil refineries in Ohio. In 1870, he formed the Standard Oil Company, taking advantage of the corporate form of enterprise.

Rockefeller purchased local rivals in the 1870s and expanded to other Northeastern states. He entered into agreements with railroad companies to give him secret rebates for shipping his oil, while they charged higher prices to his competitors. Later, he started building pipelines to transport his oil, bypassing the railroads altogether. In 1882, Rockefeller formed the Standard Oil Trust, the first great industrial **trust** (see page 73 for an explanation of a trust). It brought 90% of all oil refining in the United States under his control, a form of **horizontal integration** (*when one owner controls all companies and facilities at one stage of production of a good or commodity*).

"King" Rockefeller

At the same time, Rockefeller lowered the price of kerosene and other oil products by more than 80%. This made it possible for ordinary people to afford to light their homes at night. The demand for kerosene

A Standard Oil Company refinery

Chapter 4 | The Triumph of Industry

soared. Just when the invention of the electric light bulb threatened to make Rockefeller's oil less valuable, the invention of the automobile required gasoline, another product made from oil. Like Carnegie, Rockefeller introduced cost-accounting, hired chemists, eliminated middlemen, used cheap labor, and bought out rivals. Also, like Carnegie, he turned to philanthropy in his old age, giving funds to both education and science.

John Pierpont ("J. P.") Morgan (1837–1913) was the son of a banker and gifted financier. Much of his early career was spent reorganizing and consolidating failing railroad companies. But Morgan wanted to start his own industry. In 1892, Morgan helped Thomas Edison to form the Edison Electric Company. Edison opposed the use of alternating current, which he thought was too dangerous. When Edison proved to be wrong, Morgan pushed him out of the company, which he renamed as General Electric, and adopted Tesla's system of alternating current. In 1895, Morgan formed the J. P. Morgan & Company, a commercial and investment banking institution. In 1901, Morgan bought Carnegie's steelworks and joined them with other steel companies to form U.S. Steel, the first billion-dollar company in the United States.

J. P. Morgan and the "Gilded Age" mansion he had built for his sister.

The Historian's Apprentice

▶ Were these leaders of American businesses "Captains of Industry" or "Robber Barons"? Select one of the great entrepreneurs above or others such as Cornelius Vanderbilt, Jay Gould, James Fisk, Andrew Mellon, James Duke, or Henry Flagler. Conduct your own research on the Internet or in your school library. Then present your findings to classmates by pretending to be that entrepreneur. In a short speech to your classmates, justify the actions you took to ensure the success of your business.

▶ Choose one of the following industries and write a one-page essay explaining how its development affected the U.S. economy: steel, oil, transportation, or communications.

The Consolidation of Big Business and the Government Response

The mania for laying new railroad lines led first to speculation and then to financial collapse in 1873. In the **depression** (*a prolonged business downturn with high unemployment*) that followed, successful entrepreneurs like Carnegie and Rockefeller drove many smaller competitors out of business and bought up their companies or facilities. In other cases, falling prices and "**cutthroat competition**" (*lowering prices temporarily to drive competitors out of business*) led rival companies to join together.

Business consolidations took a variety of forms. **Pooling agreements** were informal agreements to fix prices or divide markets on a regional basis, often used by railroad companies. **Trusts** became popular because various state laws placed restrictions on companies operating in more than one state. To get around these restrictions, stockholders of existing companies gave their stocks over to the board of directors of a "trust" in exchange for "trust certificates," entitling them to dividends based on the profits of the entire trust. The trustees exercised control over the different companies in the trust and managed them as a single enterprise. By combining all the companies producing a particular product (or stage of production) into a single trust, the trustees could obtain complete control over that commodity. Similar to a trust, a **holding company** was a company that owned a controlling number of shares in other companies.

The Dangers of Monopoly

The aim of all these forms of business consolidation was to eliminate competition and to establish a **monopoly**—complete control over the production of a good or service. Monopolies had important disadvantages for the general public:

- Monopolists had less incentive to improve their products since they faced no competition.

- Monopolists could raise their prices at any time to earn excessive profits. Consumers had no choice but to pay because of the lack of alternative products.

Early Government Regulation of Business

Munn v. Illinois (1877)	In this case, the U.S. Supreme Court ruled that states could regulate businesses affecting the public "interest," such as railroads.
Wabash v. Illinois (1886)	Here, the U.S. Supreme Court ruled that states could not regulate railroads running through several states since this was "interstate commerce." Only Congress could regulate interstate commerce.
Interstate Commerce Act (1887)	In response to *Wabash v. Illinois*, Congress passed this law against unfair practices by railroads. Railroads were prohibited from pooling agreements or giving rebates. All customers were required to pay the same rates, which were to be "reasonable and just." Finally, a special regulatory commission was established to enforce the act.
Sherman Antitrust Act (1890)	In this law, Congress forbade all trusts, combinations, and conspiracies that limited or restricted interstate trade. The act simply stated: "Every contract, combination in the form of trust or otherwise, or conspiracy, in restraint of trade or commerce among the several States, or with foreign nations, is declared to be illegal." The language of the act was extremely vague, weakening its effect. In the 1890s, it was even used against labor unions instead of against "Big Business."
U.S. v. E.C. Knight Company (1895)	In this case, the U.S. Supreme Court ruled that the Sherman Antitrust Act could not be used to break up a monopoly controlling over 90% of all U.S. sugar refining. The Court held that this was a manufacturing monopoly and therefore not within the congressional power to control "interstate trade." This decision greatly weakened the reach of the Sherman Antitrust Act over "Big Business."

The Government Response

During the Gilded Age, the federal government took few steps to curb the power of "Big Business." In general, government helped business by its absence of regulations or corporate taxes, and its failure to protect either workers or consumers. Under the *laissez faire* ideology of the Gilded Age, government was not supposed to interfere in relations between producers and buyers, or with employers and employees. The operation of the free market was expected to eliminate inefficient businesses, leading to the best and cheapest goods. A series of Supreme Court decisions affirmed that government had no right to interfere in the relationship between employers and their free employees. Meanwhile, business leaders often gave hefty campaign contributions and some even secretly bribed government officials. They used government support to break up unions and prevent strikes, at the very same time that they argued that government should not interfere in business.

Reformers therefore demanded that the government take measures to regulate "Big Business" and to prevent the formation of monopolies. The abuses of some businesses were so glaring that U.S. lawmakers finally acknowledged that monopolies posed a greater danger to free enterprise than the risks of **government regulation**. The first **antitrust laws** (*laws against monopolies*) were weakly enforced, but they established the fundamental principle that Congress could regulate (*make rules for*) business in some circumstances.

The Historian's Apprentice

▸ What is the cartoonist's view of Andrew Carnegie and trusts?

▸ Write a newspaper editorial agreeing or disagreeing with the Supreme Court's decision in *U.S. v. E.C. Knight Company*. Be sure to interpret the Sherman Antitrust Act in your editorial.

▸ Write an outline for an essay on the causes or the consequences of the Second Industrial Revolution.

▸ Write a three-paragraph essay on the rise of corporations and the effects of business consolidation and other business practices on the United States economy during the "Gilded Age."

"A trustworthy beast"

Florida in Focus

Any study of Florida in the late nineteenth century would be incomplete without mentioning **Henry Morrison Flagler** (1830–1913). Flagler was a partner of John D. Rockefeller in the creation of Standard Oil Company, which gained monopoly control of all oil refineries in the United States by 1892. Rockefeller gave Flagler full credit for its formation. "I wish I had the brains to think of it," he said, but "it was Henry M. Flagler."

From his first visit to Florida in 1876 until his death in 1913, Flagler was fascinated with Florida. He devoted much of his time and money to developing the Sunshine State. In 1887 and 1888, he built the Ponce de Leon Hotel (now Flagler College), a luxury resort in St. Augustine. He later built similar luxury hotels in Palm Beach and Miami, forming the basis for the tourism industry in Florida. Flagler's enterprises also included railroads, real estate, and shipping. Flagler's

contributions to the growth of Miami were so important that he was given an unofficial title as the "Father of Miami".

It was in railroad building that Flagler had his greatest impact. With his vast wealth and grants of land and rights-of-way obtained from both the State of Florida and private landowners, Flagler was able to buy and build railroads connecting the entire length of Florida from Jacksonville to Miami, and eventually all the way south to Key West. Flagler merged several smaller railroads together to form the **Florida East Coast Railroad**. His railroad brought tourists to fill his hotels, but also made it possible for Floridians to export their agricultural products, including citrus fruits, vegetables, tobacco and cigars, cotton, beef, and cattle. The same railroads transported supplies, laborers, tourists, and settlers in Florida. A deep-water port at Key West anticipated future shipping from the Panama Canal. Even before the Panama Canal was completed, Flagler constructed a railroad junction at Key West to help Floridians ship their exports to the Caribbean and beyond. Flagler hoped his railroads would transport both goods and passengers. His railroad to Key West was destroyed by hurricane in 1935, but provided the foundation for the Overseas Highway that goes to Key West today.

Review Cards

Factors behind American Economic Growth

▶ Abundant natural resources
▶ Growing population provided labor
▶ Free enterprise system—market economy: *laissez faire* capitalism encouraged individual initiative
▶ Legacy of First Industrial Revolution: use of new source of power (steam); mass production; factory system
▶ Role of government:
  • Patents encouraged new inventions.
  • Tariffs protected American manufactured goods.
  • Laws protected property and contracts.
  • Land grants encouraged railroad construction.
  • Government regulated currency and banks.
▶ Stimulus of the Civil War—tariffs, Banking Act, Pacific Railway Act, Homestead Act

America's Second Industrial Revolution

▶ Spread of railways
▶ Technological innovation
  • Bessemer Process
  • Telegraph
  • Telephone
  • Transatlantic cable
  • Elevator
  • Sewing machine
  • Electric light bulb
  • Internal combustion engine
▶ Emergence of national market
▶ Rise of corporations (limited liability; ability to raise more capital)
▶ Contributions of entrepreneurs

Spread of Railways

▶ Provided stimulus to iron, coal, and steel industries
▶ Provided cheaper transportation costs for carrying raw materials and finished goods
▶ Forged a national market
  • Henry Flagler—Florida East Coast Railroad

Chapter 4 | The Triumph of Industry

Key Industries

- Steel
  - **Bessemer process:** air blown into hot pig iron to remove impurities; reduces cost of making steel by 80%
  - Andrew Carnegie adopted Bessemer process; built large steelworks
- Communications
  - **Telegraph:** Samuel Morse/"Morse Code" (dots and dashes)
  - **Telephone:** Alexander Graham Bell
  - **Transatlantic Cable:** Cyrus Field
- Electricity
  - **Thomas Edison:** phonograph (1877); electric light bulb (1879); motion pictures (1896); improved battery; electric power station backed by J. P. Morgan
  - **Nicola Tesla:** alternating current
- Oil
  - **Edwin Drake:** first oil well drilled in Pennsylvania (1859)
  - **John D. Rockefeller:** Standard Oil Company; kerosene and gasoline; railroad rebates; pipeline transport
- Transportation
  - Internal combustion engine: at end of 19th century: used controlled explosions to move piston in cylinder
  - **Henry Ford:** less expensive automobile
  - **Wilbur** and **Orville Wright:** airplane (1903)

African-American and Women Inventors

- **Elijah McCoy:** oil-drip cups for trains
- **Sarah Goode:** fold-away bed
- **Lewis Howard Latimer:** new process for making carbon filaments in lightbulbs
- **Jan Ernst Matzeliger:** machine for attaching soles to shoes
- **Garrett Morgan:** breathing apparatus for use by firemen; a patent for a traffic signal
- **Madam C. J. Walker:** hair-care products, especially for African-American women
- **Granville Wood:** multiplex telegraph

Other Women Inventors
- **Josephine Cochran:** first "automatic" dishwasher

"Captains of Industry" or "Robber Barons"?

- **Andrew Carnegie** (steel)
  adopted Bessemer process; Homestead Strike; vertical integration; *Gospel of Wealth*
- **John D. Rockefeller** (oil refining)
  secret rebates from railroads; Standard Oil; horizontal integration
- **John Pierpont Morgan** (financier)
  financed Edison; formed General Electric; formed U.S. Steel in 1901

Invention vs. Innovation

- **Invention:** to design something new
- **Innovation:** to apply or adopt new machines, processes and/or products

New Business Practices

- Advantages of large companies:
  - Economies of scale
  - Cheaper sources of supply
  - More efficient management
- Dangers of monopoly:
  - Less incentive to improve products
  - Monopolists can overcharge consumers
- Forms of business consolidation: Pooling agreement; trust; holding company

Chapter 4 | The Triumph of Industry

U.S. Supreme Court Cases

▶ *Munn v. Illinois:* State governments can regulate grain elevators
▶ *Wabash v. Illinois:* State governments cannot regulate interstate railroads

Federal Laws Regulating Business

▶ *Interstate Commerce Act:* Congress regulates interstate railroads; sets up enforcement agency
▶ *Sherman Antitrust Act:* Combinations "in restraint of trade" are prohibited

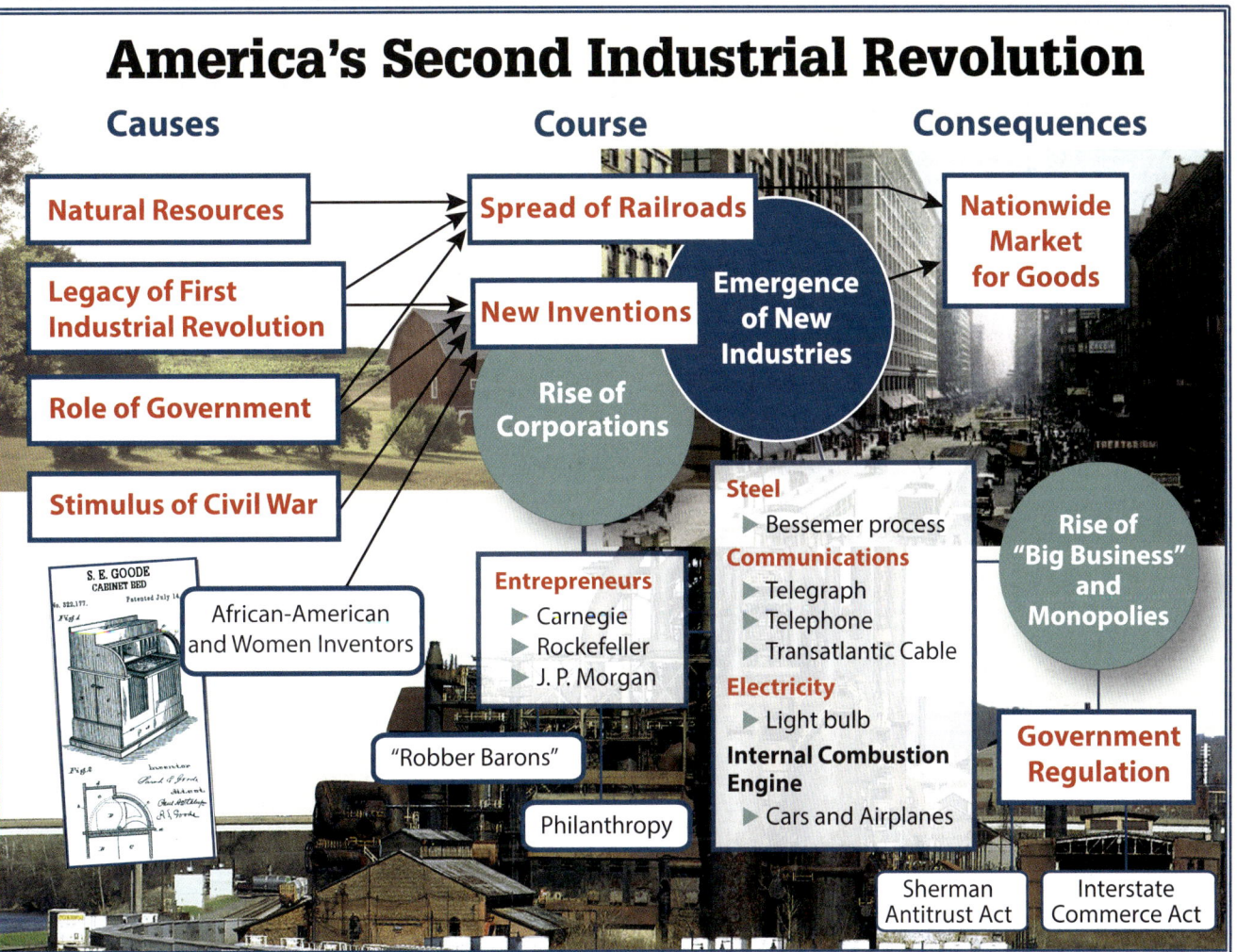

What Do You Know?

SS.912.A.3.2

1. What was one consequence of the acts listed on the right, passed by Congress during the Civil War years?

   A. economic decline in the South

   B. increased trade with Latin America

   C. delay in completion of the transcontinental railroad

   D. post-war economic growth of the Northeast and West

Federal Legislation Passed during the Civil War
- Morrill Tariff
- National Banking Act
- Homestead Act
- Morrill Land Grant Act
- Pacific Railway Act

Chapter 4 | The Triumph of Industry

SS.912.A.3.2

2. How did the patent system encourage inventiveness?
   A. It guaranteed an inventor sole rights to the use of his or her invention for a limited time.
   B. It guaranteed inventors a fee if they successfully applied and were granted a patent.
   C. It ensured that inventors could locate manufacturers to produce their inventions.
   D. It advertised an invention so that the inventor could sell more products faster.

SS.912.A.3.5

3. Which inventor predicted that, "The day is coming when telephone wires will be laid on to houses just like water and gas—and friends will converse with each other without leaving home," by using his invention?
   A. Thomas Edison
   B. Henry Bessemer
   C. Lewis Howard Latimer
   D. Alexander Graham Bell

SS.912.A.3.4

4. Which entrepreneur is NOT correctly paired with his field?
   A. John D. Rockefeller → telecommunications
   B. Andrew Carnegie → steel
   C. Gustavus Swift → meat-packing
   D. J. P. Morgan → finance

SS.912.A.3.4

5. These steps are all performed by a single company.

   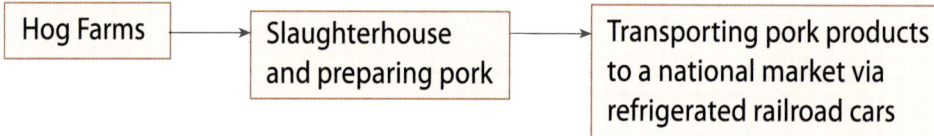

   Which of the following best describes the diagram?
   A. horizontal integration
   B. vertical integration
   C. trust company
   D. holding company

SS.912.A.3.2

6. What was the significance of the passage of the Interstate Commerce Act (1887) and the Sherman Antitrust Act (1890)?
   A. They encouraged Big Business to grow by passing protective tariffs.
   B. They prevented poor quality goods from being shipped across state lines.
   C. They were both used to break up labor unions that interfered with free enterprise.
   D. They established the principle that Congress could regulate business in certain circumstances.

SS.912.A.3.5

7. Which African-American inventor is credited with over 50 patents on lubricating systems for steam engines?
   A. Garrett Morgan
   B. Elijah McCoy
   C. Sarah Goode
   D. John Burr

SS.912.A.3.3

8. What would a comparison of the First and Second Industrial Revolutions show?

   A. The first depended on new inventions but the second did not.

   B. Both the first and second relied almost entirely on steam power.

   C. Both used natural resources and relied on telecommunications to send messages over long distances.

   D. Both saw improvements in transportation but a truly national market only emerged in the second.

SS.912.A.3.5

9. Which invention was patented in 1885 by Sarah Goode, the first African-American woman ever to receive a U.S. patent?

   A. a curved ironing board for shirt sleeves

   B. a lubricator oil-cup for steam engines

   C. a unique shampoo to fight hair loss

   D. a fold-away bed

SS.912.A.3.5

10. Which identifies an accomplishment of Thomas Edison and his team of researchers at Menlo Park, New Jersey?

    A. the first telephone

    B. the first steam engine

    C. the first practical light bulb

    D. the first internal combustion engine

SS.912.A.3.4

11. How were Americans influenced by the growth of railroads during the Second Industrial Revolution?

    A. Railroads led to shortages of raw materials for factories and of workers on farms.

    B. Railroads stimulated the construction of steamships to trade up and down rivers.

    C. Railroads created time zones, the growth of cities, and the first truly national market.

    D. Railroads caused cotton, rice, and wheat production to move from the Southeast to the West Coast.

SS.912.A.3.3

12. The diagram on the right compares two industrial revolutions.

    Which phrase completes the diagram?

    A. Mass production of goods

    B. Changes in a market economy

    C. New methods of telecommunication

    D. Successful entrepreneurs gain great wealth

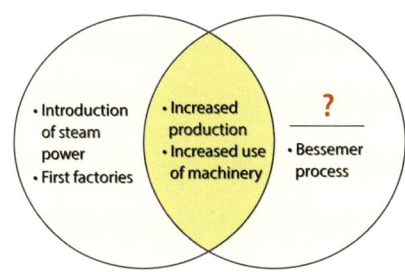

Chapter 4 | The Triumph of Industry

SS.912.A.3.4

The cartoon below was published in *Puck* magazine in 1883.

HOPELESSLY BOUND TO THE STAKE.

13. Which issue is addressed in the cartoon?

   A. the influence of labor unions

   B. the excessive power of Big Business

   C. the dangerous conditions of factory labor

   D. the corruption of political machines in American cities

SS.912.A.3.2

14. Based on the cartoon above (in question 13), what conclusion can be reached about the United States in the early 1880s?

   A. Most American manufacturing was controlled by business monopolies.

   B. Some American critics felt workers were being oppressed by business monopolies.

   C. Government leaders were finally taking steps to curb the power of business monopolies.

   D. Business monopolies overcharged their customers but were essential to American economic growth.

SS.912.A3.13

15. What goal motivated Henry Flagler to build the Florida East Coast Railway?

   A. to encourage the U.S. government to build a canal in Panama

   B. to bring tourists to the luxury hotels he had built along the Florida coastline

   C. to create a refuge for people immigrating to the United States from Latin America

   D. to build a "dream town" with money he had made from his partnership with John D. Rockefeller

CHAPTER 5

The Labor Movement

SS.912.A.3.9 Examine causes, course, and consequences of the labor movement in the late 19th and early 20th centuries.

SS.912.A.3.10 Review different economic and philosophic ideologies.

Names and Terms You Should Know

Child labor	American Federation of Labor	Ideology
Labor Union	Samuel Gompers	Capitalism
Strike	Haymarket Riot	Social Darwinism
Lockout	Homestead Strike	Communism
Knights of Labor	Pullman Strike	Socialism
		Anarchism

Florida "Keys" to Learning

1. America's Second Industrial Revolution led to worsening conditions for many industrial workers. They labored in unpleasant or dangerous conditions for long hours at monotonous and repetitive jobs, and received low wages. Even many children were forced to work.

2. Individual workers had no bargaining power with large corporations. Some workers began to organize into labor unions to improve their conditions. Through their union, they could negotiate wages and working conditions collectively with their employer. They could also go on strike.

3. Two early national unions were the Knights of Labor and the American Federation of Labor. The Knights of Labor invited skilled and unskilled workers to become members, including women and African Americans. However, after a series of unsuccessful strikes, it collapsed. The American Federation of Labor was a federation of unions of skilled workers with more limited objectives.

4. Management had many advantages over labor unions in the late nineteenth century. Government leaders and the public generally sympathized with management and were suspicious of labor unions. Management could fire or lockout workers, blacklist union leaders, and obtain government support to put down strikes.

5. Early major strikes were largely unsuccessful. People blamed union organizers when a bomb went off in Chicago during the Haymarket Riot. A large group of steel workers striking against Carnegie's Homestead steel mill were defeated when the state militia intervened. President Cleveland used federal troops to break up the Pullman strike.

6. An ideology is a set of related beliefs about people, society and government. Several new economic and philosophical ideologies emerged in response to the Industrial Revolution. Capitalists continued to support *laissez-faire* policies. Social Darwinists thought the wealthy at the top of society were simply superior to others. Communists predicted a violent proletarian revolution would overthrow the wealthy ruling class and create a more just and egalitarian society in which property was held in common. Socialists also desired social change but sought to achieve this through peaceful means. Anarchists opposed organized government.

Workers Face New Problems

One of the main factors behind America's rapid economic growth was the increasing exploitation of the industrial worker. Gains in industrial productivity were often achieved at terrible human costs. Critics of industrial capitalism complained that industrial workers were being treated as no better than "wage-slaves."

Impersonal Conditions As factories and workplaces grew larger, individual workers lost personal contact with their actual employers and all influence over their own personal working conditions.

Long Hours Workday hours were long by today's standards. Workers faced a six or even seven-day workweek of ten to fourteen hours labor each day. Steel workers in Carnegie's mills, for example, worked 12-hour shifts seven days per week.

Boring, Repetitive Tasks Skilled workers, like carpenters or mechanics, have extensive training and perform a wide range of specialized tasks. But as industrialists broke up manufacturing into a series of simple tasks to achieve greater speed and efficiency, each worker became nothing more than a human cog in a vast machine. Industrial work became less skilled, more repetitive, monotonous and boring. There was little pleasure or job satisfaction in repeating the same task for hours on end. And factory rules often prohibited talking among employees during working hours.

Low Wages Wages were so low that many workers could not afford minimal requirements for food, shelter and clothing. Every member of the family had to work to make ends meet, even though women and children were especially low paid. Immigrants from overseas and migrants from the countryside flooded the labor market with workers willing to work for very low wages.

Dangerous Conditions Conditions at work in the late 19th and early 20th centuries were often extremely hazardous. There were insufficient safeguards around machinery and overworked employees were often extremely tired. Hundreds of thousands of workers were injured or killed in accidents each year, especially on the railroads or in the coal mines. Others suffered debilitating illnesses from unhealthful working conditions.

Child Labor Textile mills and coal mines made use of child laborers to perform special tasks and because they were paid less than adults. As many as one out of every five children under 15 years old was working outside the home in 1910. These children were deprived of opportunities for sunshine, fresh air, play, or to improve their lives by attending school.

Periodic Unemployment Today, we have workers' compensation to pay workers for injuries they receive on the job. But in the late nineteenth century, workers' compensation did not exist. Employers also did not provide health insurance or contribute to a pension for an employee's old age. There was no unemployment insurance when a worker lost his or her job. Most companies gave no paid "sick days."

Lack of Opportunity for Advancement It was difficult to move from an unskilled to a skilled position or to find a new job with higher wages. There were generally no promotions or automatic increases in pay for being at a job a long time. In times of recession or intense competition with rival companies, pay might even be cut or workers could be laid off.

Unpleasant Living Conditions Most workers lived in crowded, inner-city slums or in company towns. With their low wages, they could not afford better housing. In company towns like Pullman, the company controlled not only the workers' wages, but what workers paid in rent and for food and other supplies in the company store. The company controlled town officials and the police, making it almost impossible for workers to complain or to organize against the company.

Workers Organize

With the rise of large corporations, individual workers lost all their bargaining power with employers. Since most work was unskilled, workers could be easily replaced. The only way to achieve better conditions seemed to be through better worker organization. Therefore, industrial workers began to organize. Such organizations, known as **labor unions**, generally had three main purposes.

Goals of Unions

- **To Obtain Higher Wages and Better Working Conditions** By joining together, workers felt they could demand better pay, shorter hours and better working conditions. If an employer refused their demands, all the workers at a factory, steel mill, mine, or other workplace might **strike** (*walk off their jobs at the same time*). The business owner's operations would halt, forcing the owner to come to terms with the striking workers to get things going again.
- **"Mutual Aid" Societies** Members of unions regularly contributed to special funds to provide pensions and insurance benefits in times of need, such as injury, illness, strike, or death.
- **To Place Pressure on Government** Unions also acted as "pressure groups" on government. Union leaders tried to coordinate workers' votes to influence politicians in favor of their demands. Unions also contributed directly to campaign funds and lobbied in legislatures. Some labor leaders wished to go further and use unions to create a new political party that would represent workers.

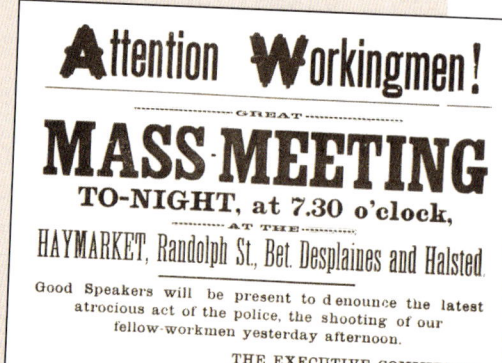

The Historian's Apprentice

- Imagine you are an industrial worker in the late 1870s. Write a letter to a friend describing your conditions at work and how organizing a union might help to improve those conditions.
- Pretend you are a union organizer entering a factory in 1875. Give a speech explaining to the workers there why they should form a union.

Workers Seek a National Voice

In the decades after the Civil War, worker organizations were generally weak. To oppose national corporations, labor leaders reasoned they needed to form their own national unions.

The Knights of Labor

Founded by **Terrence Powderly** in 1869, the **Knights of Labor** formed a single nationwide union. Both skilled and unskilled workers were encouraged to join.

Terrence Powderly

African Americans, women, and rural farm workers were all welcomed. The Knights demanded an 8-hour workday, higher wages, and safety codes in factories. They opposed child labor and convict labor and favored equal pay for women. The Knights of Labor also strongly supported restrictions on immigration, since they saw immigrants as competitors willing to work for lower wages. Membership in the Knights soared in the prosperous 1880s. By 1886, they reached their peak strength of 700,000 members.

The Knights preferred the arbitration of disputes to strikes, but they were willing to support strikes whenever they believed they were necessary. In the end, however, the Knights proved to be too loosely organized. Skilled workers resented being grouped together with unskilled laborers. The general public associated the Knights with unpopular radical political ideas. After a series of unsuccessful strikes, members started leaving for other organizations and the Knights of Labor finally fell apart.

The American Federation of Labor

A new nationwide labor organization was founded in 1881 by **Samuel Gompers**, a Jewish immigrant who worked making cigars. In 1886, it adopted a new name as the **American Federation of Labor**, or AFL. Unlike the Knights of Labor, the AFL was a federation of several national craft unions, including those of carpenters, cigar-makers, and shoemakers. Its membership was restricted to skilled workers. The AFL also did not admit women. At first, Gompers insisted that the affiliated craft unions admit African-American workers, but when several refused to do so, Gompers backed down. As a result, only the United Mine Workers and a few other AFL unions admitted African Americans in these years. African-American leaders complained that the unions were holding African Americans back, especially by refusing to admit young blacks as apprentices. Gompers also failed to counteract ethnic prejudice against different nationalities within particular craft unions.

Gompers limited the goals of the AFL to obtaining immediate benefits for its members—higher pay, an 8-hour workday, better conditions in the workplace, and a "closed shop" policy (in which the employer promised to hire only union members). Gompers believed that the worker's interests were best served, not by resisting industrial capitalism, but by bargaining for a greater share of its profits. To counter the concentration of industry in the hands of a few owners, Gompers believed workers had to band together to speak in a single voice. While Gompers favored peaceful bargaining with employers, he was willing to use strikes and boycotts when necessary. He also supported political candidates who backed union demands.

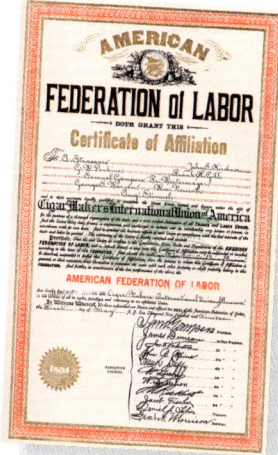

The American Federation of Labor soon became the leading voice of organized labor. By 1900, it had half a million members. It was weakened, however, by the fact that in its early years it excluded unskilled workers. These constituted the bulk of the American labor force. By 1910, fewer than 5% of American workers were unionized.

The Historian's Apprentice

- ▶ Create a Venn diagram comparing the Knights of Labor and the American Federation of Labor.
- ▶ Write one or two paragraphs explaining why the AFL was more successful than the Knights of Labor.

The Tactics of Labor and Management

Organized labor had a number of tactics at its disposal. While on strike, union workers carried signs outside their place of employment—known as the "**picket line**"—to win public support and prevent the use of **strike-breakers** (*temporary workers hired by management to operate the factory, mine or mill while the regular workers were out on strike*). To support themselves during a strike, union members made contributions while they were working to a **strike fund**.

In the early days of unions, employers had many more weapons at their disposal than today:

- The company's **managers**—those people running the company—could simply fire striking workers and hire new ones.
- If management did not agree to worker demands, they could close the factory to keep the workers from their jobs. This was known as a **lockout**.
- When workers went on strike, management often brought in temporary workers known as "**strike-breakers**" (or "**scabs**"). These worked in factories or mines until the dispute with the striking workers was settled. Often the strike-breakers were African-American workers or immigrant workers with different ethnic backgrounds than the strikers.
- Employers might force their employees to sign agreements, known as "**Yellow Dog" Contracts**, that they would not join a union. (Such agreements were later made illegal.)
- Union leaders and members were often fired. Their names might be circulated to other employers so that they could not get another job. This practice was known as "**blacklisting**."
- Employers hired private detectives, known as *Pinkertons*, to spy on union leaders and to break up strikes, often with violence and sometimes even murder.
- Finally, employers might seek a court order prohibiting a strike. Once such an **injunction** (court order) was issued, employers could count on the government to break up the strike. Police or even state troops might be used to break up the strike.

The Historian's Apprentice

Pretend that the Old Virginny Spinning Mule Textile Co. (or "Mule Co.") is a textile company in Roanoke, Virginia, in 1885. Factory employees work at the company for ten hours a day for six days a week. They receive very low wages. Factory workers have organized into a union. The managers of the factory and union leaders are about to meet. Your teacher will appoint 3 students as managers representing the company and 5 as the Board of Directors of Mule Co. Your teacher will appoint 2 students to act as mediators who work openly and behind the scenes to resolve deadlocked issues. Finally, your teacher will appoint 3 students as union leaders. The rest of the class will act as union members.

Positions of Management:
1. Wages must remain low in order for the company to be profitable.
2. Working hours must remain the same.
3. The company has to invest in equipment and issue some dividends to shareholders.
4. The company may have to use strike-breakers, hire a new workforce, or temporarily close its factory to remain competitive.

Positions of Workers:
1. 10% raise in pay.
2. Eight-hour workday.
3. More protection needed against factory accidents.
4. If their demands are not met, they may go out on strike.

▸ Have both sides meet separately to prepare their respective positions for the negotiations. The members of the management team should present their proposals to the union leaders. The union members should gather behind their union leaders, shouting encouragement, defiance, and support for their union leaders.

▸ Several sessions may be required with the use of mediators, as necessary.

▸ If an agreement is reached, it will have to be accepted by Mule Co.'s Board of Directors, and separately by the union members.

▸ What did you learn about collective bargaining from this activity?

The Role of Government

The attitude of government was critical to the fortunes of the early labor movement. In the late 19th century, government leaders were often partial towards business and took a hostile view of unions. There were many reasons why the federal and state governments favored management over unions:

▸ Only a small number of workers were actually unionized.

▸ Government leaders saw their proper role as providing protection to private property. Strikers seemed to threaten the security of property.

▸ Public opinion was hostile to unions. The public believed that union demands would raise prices.

▸ Union activity was associated in the public mind with violence, anarchism, socialism and ideas brought over by recent European immigrants.

▸ Businesses contributed to politicians' campaign funds, while business and government leaders often shared the same general outlook. Government officials believed America owed much of its economic success to its business leaders.

▸ *Laissez-faire* attitudes gave businessmen the power to hire or fire employees as they pleased.

▸ Government leaders feared the disruptive effect of strikes. In 1895, the Supreme Court applied the Sherman Antitrust Act to union activities, ruling that strikes were an illegal interference with interstate commerce. In several strikes, state governors or even the President of the United States sent in troops to suppress the strike and restore order.

Milestones of the Early Labor Movement

One effect of the organization of labor was the occurrence of strikes. There were more than 20,000 strikes involving six million workers in the twenty years from 1880 to 1900. Early strikes were often violent and workers were sometimes killed. Here are three of the milestones of the early labor movement.

The Haymarket Riot (1886)

A nationwide strike in favor of the eight-hour workday was held on May 1, 1886. Two days later, striking workers gathered in front of the McCormick Harvesting Machine factory in Chicago. Strikers began fighting with strike-breakers until police fired into the crowd, killing several demonstrators. Anarchist leaders, most of them immigrants, called for a rally to be held the next evening at Haymarket Square in response. **Anarchists** believed in overthrowing capitalist society and establishing self-governing communities. Their advertisements, in English and German, accused the police of killing strikers on behalf of business interests. On the evening of May 4th, the rally at Haymarket Square began peacefully. However, after several speakers addressed the rally, a large police force approached the speaker's stand and ordered the crowd to disperse. A dynamite bomb was thrown at the police, killing one policeman instantly. What happened next is unclear, but according to most reports the police opened fire as the crowd ran in all directions. Six other policemen and four demonstrators later died from their wounds. In the public mind, unions became associated with anarchism and violence. Police arrested several labor leaders and searched their meeting halls and offices. Eight (five of them German immigrants) were put on trial and found guilty, even though only one was linked by any evidence at all to the explosion. Seven of the eight were sentenced to death. Two of the sentences were changed to life imprisonment by the governor, while one of the defendants committed suicide; four others were hanged. Much of the public wrongly associated these events with the Knights of Labor, which dissolved soon afterwards.

Mathias J. Degan, policeman killed in the Haymarket Riot

Homestead Strike (1892)

In 1882 and 1889, the steel workers' union held two successful strikes at Andrew Carnegie's steelworks at Homestead, Pennsylvania. Carnegie and his partner **Henry C. Frick** believed that union rules were slowing down steel production and preventing the use of more advanced machinery, so they decided to break the union when it came time to negotiate a new contract. Carnegie, who had spoken in favor of unions, put Frick in charge and left for Scotland. Frick made unrealistic offers in the next contract negotiations and locked out the workers from the steel mill at Homestead. The workers went on strike and surrounded the plant with their picket lines. Frick hired **Pinkerton detectives** to reopen the steel mill. The Pinkertons attempted to break through the picket lines at night, leading to a violent battle with the strikers. After the strikers defeated the Pinkertons, the state militia was called in to restore order—allowing Frick to bring in **strike-breakers** ("scabs") to run the mill. A misguided attempt to assassinate Frick further increased public sympathy for the company and against the unions. Members of the steel workers union were fired and "blacklisted" from employment in the steel industry, while their union collapsed.

Henry C. Frick

Pullman Strike (1894)

George Pullman invented railroad cars in which passengers could sleep, and made a vast fortune. His workers lived in Pullman, Illinois—a **company town**. Pullman owned their houses and company stores in the town. His workers went on strike when Pullman lowered their wages but refused to lower his own rents and food prices. After their rent was deducted, many Pullman workers were only being paid a few cents a day. Labor leader **Eugene V. Debs** had helped form the American Railway Union (the "A.R.U."). He called on its members not to handle any trains with Pullman cars during the Pullman Strike. The strike thus brought railroads in the western United States to a virtual standstill. President Cleveland sent in federal troops to end the strike, on the grounds

Violence erupts as troops intervene in the Pullman Railroad strike

that he needed to guarantee delivery of the mails. In fact, the strikers had not interfered with the mail. The government also used a court injunction to stop the strike, on the grounds that it interfered with interstate commerce. The U.S. Supreme Court upheld the injunction in 1895. The collapse of the strike destroyed the American Railway Union. Eugene Debs was sent to prison for six months, where he became a socialist.

These three strikes demonstrated the continuing sympathies of the government and the public in favor of employers and against labor unions. However, attitudes would change in the early 20th century.

Pullman railroad cars allowed passengers to travel in luxury and even provided sleeping berths.

The Historian's Apprentice

▶ Make an illustrated timeline of the most important events in the early labor movement, including the formation of the Knights of Labor and AFL and the three strikes described above.
▶ Use the Internet or your school library to find out more information about one of these strikes. Then present your findings in the form of a research report or oral presentation to the class. Be sure to include contemporary illustrations or photographs that depict these events.

The Rise of Ideology

Responses to industrialization also led to the rise of different **ideologies**. An *ideology* is a system of related beliefs and ideas about people, society, economics, and government.

Capitalists believed that free market capitalism was the best system. Influenced by the earlier writings of Adam Smith, they argued that capitalism gave enterprising individuals the freedom to develop new businesses. By pursuing their own profit, these entrepreneurs also benefitted all of society by producing better goods at lower costs.

Social Darwinists were influenced by the works of Charles Darwin, the biologist who first formulated the theory of evolution. Social Darwinists argued that societies were subject to the same laws as other organisms. Both individuals and whole societies were in fact in competition with one another, and only the strongest would survive. Although some people might suffer, it was natural that the best and strongest people would rise to the top and enjoy positions of power, wealth and authority. Likewise it was only fitting that more advanced societies, like the United States, should rule over less advanced ones.

Communists followed the ideas of Karl Marx. They challenged the class structure of industrial society. In *The Communist Manifesto* (1848), Marx and his co-author Friedrich Engels declared that all of history was the history of class struggle, in which the rich took advantage of the poor. In the new industrial society, the *bourgeoisie* (factory owners, employers, and professionals) exploited the *proletariat* (workers). Although the proletariat added value to raw materials with their labor, most of this added value went to the factory owner as profit. Eventually, Marx and Engels predicted, the proletariat would rise up and overthrow the bourgeoisie in a violent revolution. Then they would establish an ideal classless, Communist society. Private property would be abolished.

Socialists believed that workers were generally oppressed but that their conditions could be gradually improved without a violent revolution. By electing government officials favorable to labor, they could introduce needed reforms like social security and free public schools. Socialists believed that the government might even take over some businesses, such as railroads and the telephone, to operate them for the public good. Eugene Debs was one of the founders of the American Socialist Party and several times became its candidate for President of the United States.

Anarchists were alarmed at the influence of the rich on government. They favored abolition of central governments, by violence if necessary.

Eugene Debs poster in 1912

The Historian's Apprentice

Make your own three-column chart comparing these ideologies. Make the first column "Ideology," the second column "Famous People," and the third column "Important Ideas." Then fill in the chart using information from this chapter and from your own research in your school library or on the Internet.

Review Cards

Problems Faced by Industrial Workers

- Impersonal conditions / boring, repetitive tasks
- Long workdays
- Low wages / periodic unemployment
- Dangerous conditions / No workers' compensation
- Lack of opportunity for advancement
- Child labor

The First National Labor Unions

Knights of Labor: Terrence Powderly / skilled and unskilled workers / Women & minorities welcomed as members / collapsed shortly after Haymarket Riot

American Federation of Labor (AFL): a federation of different unions of skilled workers (such as carpenters, shoemakers, etc.) / Samuel Gompers / focused on improving conditions and raising wages / hostile to immigration / most member unions refused women or African Americans

Milestones of Early Labor Movement

In the early days of the labor movement, public attitudes and government officials were often hostile to labor:

Haymarket Riot (1886) After an explosion during a demonstration in Haymarket Square, labor leaders were arrested and put on trial. Four were hanged. In the public mind, the labor movement became associated with violence and anarchism.

Homestead Strike (1892) Carnegie and Frick decided to "break" the union and locked out workers from Homestead Steelworks when they failed to negotiate a new contract. Workers went on strike, surrounded the mill with picket lines, and defeated Pinkertons in the pitched battle. The state militia was called out to protect the plants, and Frick sent in strike-breakers. Workers gave in, ending unionization in steel mills.

Pullman Strike (1894) Pullman workers went on strike when Pullman lowered wages but not prices in his company town. Eugene Debs' American Railway Union joined in sympathy and would not work on Pullman cars, bringing trains in the west to a standstill. President Cleveland sent in federal troops to end the strike.

Advantages of Labor Unions

Collective Bargaining	Workers act together in negotiating new contracts for higher wages and better working conditions
Mutual Aid Society	Save money for emergencies
Strikes	Workers walk off their jobs and picket the factory or workplace
"Closed Shop"	Only union members can work there

Tactics of Management

Lockout	Closing down a factory or mill so that workers cannot work there
Strike-breakers ("scabs")	Temporary workers who fill jobs during a strike, often from a different ethnic group than most of the strikers
Blacklisting	Circulating names of fired employees to other employers
"Yellow-Dog" contract	Forcing workers to sign an agreement not to unionize
Pinkertons	Private detectives used to break up strikes
Injunction	A court order to end a strike

Ideologies of the Industrial Age

Ideology	A system of beliefs about society
Capitalism	Market-based economic system in which individuals or corporations privately own the means of production
Socialism	Ideology in favor of government ownership of the means of production to improve conditions for workers
Communism	Ideology developed by Karl Marx, calling for violent revolution by workers (*proletariat*) to overthrow the "bourgeoisie" and establish a classless society
Anarchism	A radical political theory opposing all forms of government in favor of self-governing communities
Social Darwinism	Belief that humans, like other forms of life, compete for survival and that those who are naturally superior will meet with the greatest success

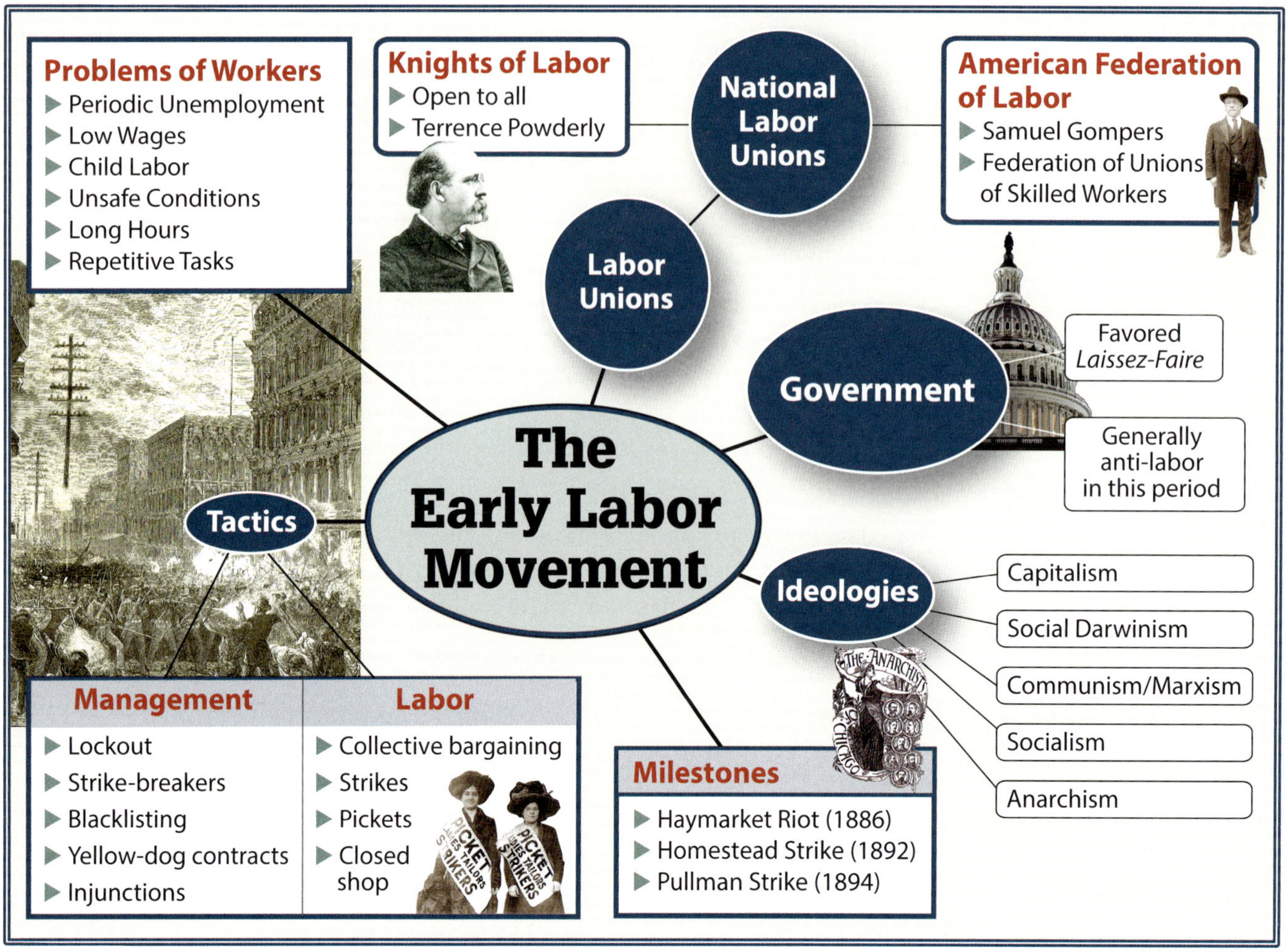

The Early Labor Movement

Problems of Workers
- Periodic Unemployment
- Low Wages
- Child Labor
- Unsafe Conditions
- Long Hours
- Repetitive Tasks

Knights of Labor
- Open to all
- Terrence Powderly

National Labor Unions

American Federation of Labor
- Samuel Gompers
- Federation of Unions of Skilled Workers

Labor Unions

Government
- Favored *Laissez-Faire*
- Generally anti-labor in this period

Tactics

Ideologies
- Capitalism
- Social Darwinism
- Communism/Marxism
- Socialism
- Anarchism

Management
- Lockout
- Strike-breakers
- Blacklisting
- Yellow-dog contracts
- Injunctions

Labor
- Collective bargaining
- Strikes
- Pickets
- Closed shop

Milestones
- Haymarket Riot (1886)
- Homestead Strike (1892)
- Pullman Strike (1894)

What Do You Know?

SS.912.A.3.9

1. Which was NOT a problem faced by most American factory workers in the late 19th century?
   - A. boring, repetitive tasks
   - B. periodic unemployment
   - C. long hours and low wages
   - D. demanding hiring requirements

SS.912.A.3.9

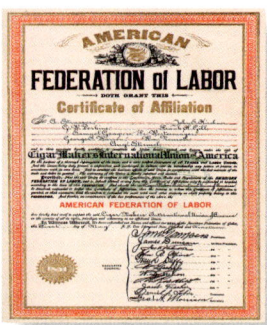

2. The certificate on the left was issued in 1919.

   What was the primary goal of the organization that issued this certificate?
   - A. to obtain better conditions for workers in its affiliate unions
   - B. to assist in the transition from a capitalist to a socialist society
   - C. to help cigar workers obtain better housing and U.S. citizenship
   - D. to replace individual labor unions with a single union for all workers

SS.912.A.3.13

3. The drawing on the left was published in England in 1894. Which ideology was most similar to the ideology identified in this drawing?

   A. capitalism
   B. imperialism
   C. Communism
   D. Social Darwinism

SS.912.A.3.9

4. The flier on the left appeared on May 4, 1886. Based on the flier, which conclusion can be made about the Haymarket Riot?

   A. The protesters intended to overthrow the U.S. government.
   B. The protesters were members of the American Federation of Labor.
   C. The rally was held in support of the Homestead and Pullman strikes.
   D. A large number of the participants were German-speaking immigrants.

SS.912.A.3.9

5. The picture below depicts the Haymarket Riot in May 1886.

   Based on the picture, which sentence best describes the viewpoint of the artist?

   A. The police were largely responsible for the violence.
   B. The lives of women and children were endangered.
   C. The protestors' demands were largely justified.
   D. The protestors were prepared to use violence.

SS.912.A.3.9

6. Which tactic was sometimes used by management to resist the demands of labor?

   A. strike
   B. boycott
   C. lockout
   D. picket line

SS.912.A.3.9

7. What was an important consequence of the Haymarket Riot?

   A. decline of the Knights of Labor
   B. rally of public opinion in favor of workers
   C. victory of workers in the Homestead Strike
   D. break up of the American Federation of Labor

Chapter 5 | The Labor Movement

SS.912.A.3.9

8. The timeline below shows events from the early American labor movement.

   1869: Formation of Knights of Labor
   1881: Formation of future American Federation of Labor
   1892: ?
   1886: Haymarket Riot
   1894: Pullman Strike

   Which completes the timeline by replacing the question mark?

   A. Arrest of Eugene V. Debs
   B. Collapse of American Railway Union
   C. Homestead Strike at Carnegie's steelworks
   D. Supreme Court applies antitrust laws to unions

SS.912.A.3.13

9. Why did government leaders generally sympathize with business owners against labor in the late 19th century?

   A. Government leaders received money from business and also believed in *laissez-faire*.
   B. Government leaders were followers of new ideologies from Europe such as socialism.
   C. Government leaders did not believe that conditions for industrial workers were all that bad.
   D. Government leaders feared violence from business owners if they took the side of workers.

SS.912.A.3.9

10. The newspaper on the left depicts the Homestead Strike. What was the main cause of the event depicted in the newspaper?

    A. Andrew Carnegie had wanted to employ Civil War veterans in his steelworks.
    B. Anarchists intended to blow up Andrew Carnegie's steelworks near Pittsburgh.
    C. Andrew Carnegie and Henry Frick wanted to break up the power of the steelworkers' union.
    D. Steelworkers left their jobs to enlist as soldiers when a future war with Spain became likely.

SS.912.A.3.9

11. How were the Homestead and Pullman Strikes similar?

    A. Both were ended by federal court injunctions.
    B. Both were led by union organizer Eugene V. Debs.
    C. Both ended in important defeats for organized labor.
    D. Both involved armed confrontations between workers and Pinkertons.

CHAPTER 6

Cities, Immigrants, and Farmers

SS.912.A.3.1 Analyze the economic challenges to American farmers and farmers' responses to these challenges in the mid to late 1800s.

SS.912.A.3.6 Analyze changes that occurred as the United States shifted from an agrarian to an industrial society.

SS.912.A.3.7 Compare the experience of European immigrants in the east to that of Asian immigrants in the west (the Chinese Exclusion Act, Gentlemen's Agreement with Japan).

SS.912.A.3.11 Analyze the impact of political machines in United States cities in the late 19th and early 20th centuries.

SS.912.G.4.2 Use geographic terms and tools to analyze the push/pull factors contributing to human migration within and among places.

SS.912.G.4.3 Use geographic terms and tools to analyze the effects of migration both on the place of origin and destination, including border areas.

Names and Terms You Should Know

Urban centers	Ellis Island	Interstate Commerce Act
Urbanization	Angel Island	Farmers Alliance
Tenement	Chinese Exclusion Act	Populist Party
Political machine	Gentlemen's Agreement	Populism
Tammany Hall	Nativism	Omaha Platform
Boss Tweed	Agricultural surplus	William Jennings Bryan
Immigrant	Sherman Silver Purchase Act	"Cross of Gold" Speech
Old Immigrants	Grange Movement	
New Immigrants	Granger Laws	

Florida "Keys" to Learning

1. The rise of industry led to urbanization: the movement of people from the countryside to cities. The growth of cities posed new problems: (1) traffic congestion; (2) overcrowding and slums; (3) inadequate garbage collection and sewage treatment; and (4) vast differences in wealth, sharpening social antagonisms.

2. The problems of cities led to the rise of political machines like Tammany Hall in New York. The machine, usually led by a "Boss" like Boss Tweed, provided services to immigrants and the poor. The machine then encouraged immigrants and the poor to vote for its candidates. Officials elected by the machine made huge fortunes by charging excessive amounts on public contracts or receiving "kickbacks."

3. The "Old Immigrants" had come from Great Britain, Ireland and Germany before 1880. The "New Immigrants" came from Southern and Eastern Europe (Poland, Russia, Italy, Greece) after 1880. Most were Catholic, Jewish, or Greek Orthodox. Many spoke no English and were desperately poor.

4. Steamship companies made coming to America more affordable. Poorer immigrants travelled "steerage" class. Europeans in steerage class were processed at Ellis Island, where they could be sent back if they did not pass a medical examination. After 1910, Asians were processed on Angel Island in San Francisco Bay, where they often faced long delays—sometimes for several months. Most immigrants went to live in ethnic neighborhoods in cities, known as "ghettos," where they lived with others speaking the same language and practicing the same traditions. Usually the children of the immigrants were the first to be "Americanized."

5. Asian immigrants faced special challenges. Chinese men began arriving after the California Gold Rush and helped to build the railroads in California. The Chinese Exclusion Act (1882) banned almost all immigrants from China. Japanese Americans began arriving at the end of the century; their immigration was restricted by the Gentlemen's Agreement (1907) between Japan and the United States.

6. Nativists believed that white, Protestant, native-born Americans were superior to others, and that immigrants with other cultural traits were undesirable.

7. In the late 19th century, most Americans were still farmers. They began experiencing difficulties when food prices fell even though their costs remained high. Farmers organized into social and political groups to meet these challenges. The Grange Movement was a national association of farmers' social clubs, which served social and educational purposes.

8. Grangers entered state legislatures and passed laws to regulate grain elevators and railroads. The Supreme Court upheld state regulation of a grain elevator in *Munn v. Illinois* (1877). It overruled a state law regulating railroad rates in *Wabash v. Illinois* (1886) on the grounds that only Congress could regulate interstate commerce. Congress passed the Interstate Commerce Act in 1887, the first federal law to regulate business practices.

9. The Populist Party was formed in the early 1890s to represent the interests of farmers and workers. The "Omaha Platform" of 1892 included many far-reaching proposals that were later adopted: direct election of U.S. Senators, a secret ballot, a progressive income tax, initiative and referendum procedures, the eight-hour workday, and restrictions on immigration. In 1896, William Jennings Bryan was chosen as the Democratic and Populist candidate for President after giving his "Cross of Gold" speech. In his campaign, Bryan focused on "bimetallism"—the proposal to base money on silver as well as gold in order to raise prices. Bryan lost the election to William McKinley in a close contest.

In this chapter, you will learn about some of the changes that occurred as America shifted from an agrarian to an industrial society.

Cities

One of the most important effects of America's Second Industrial Revolution was the explosive growth of cities. In 1865, most Americans lived in the countryside. By 1920, half of all Americans lived in cities. New York, Chicago and Philadelphia had over a million residents. This movement of people from the countryside into **urban centers** (*larger towns and cities*) is known as **urbanization**.

The Reasons for Urbanization

Why did so many people move into cities in these years? Both "push" and "pull" factors contributed to urbanization:

- Railroads and improved roads made it easier for people to move to cities. Cities grew with special rapidity at railroad "hubs" like Chicago and Atlanta, where goods had to be loaded and unloaded to change their routes or forms of transportation.

- Many people were attracted by the cultural opportunities and variety of city life. They sought the convenience and pleasures of music halls, museums, libraries and universities.

- The rise of factories and the needs of growing urban populations created more jobs. At the same time, farm machinery meant not as many laborers were needed to grow food on farms. This caused people to move to cities in search of work.

The Historian's Apprentice

- Use the Internet to research a large city close to where you live. When did it first become a city? What factors caused its population to grow?

City	1870	1880	1890	1900	1910
New York*	1,338,391	1,772,962	2,321,644	3,437,202	4,766,883
Philadelphia	674,022	847,170	1,046,964	1,293,697	1,549,008
St. Louis	310,864	350,518	451,770	575,238	687,029
Chicago	298,977	503,185	1,099,850	1,698,575	2,185,283
Baltimore	267,354	332,313	434,439	508,957	558,485
Boston	250,526	362,839	448,477	560,892	670,585
Cincinnati	216,239	255,139	296,908	325,902	363,591
San Francisco	149,473	233,959	298,997	342,782	416,912

* Includes Brooklyn

Cities Face New Problems

American cities grew so rapidly that municipal authorities often could not deal adequately with all their needs. Many cities lacked sufficient hospitals, police forces, public schools, fire departments, and street-cleaning and garbage-collection services for the large influx of people.

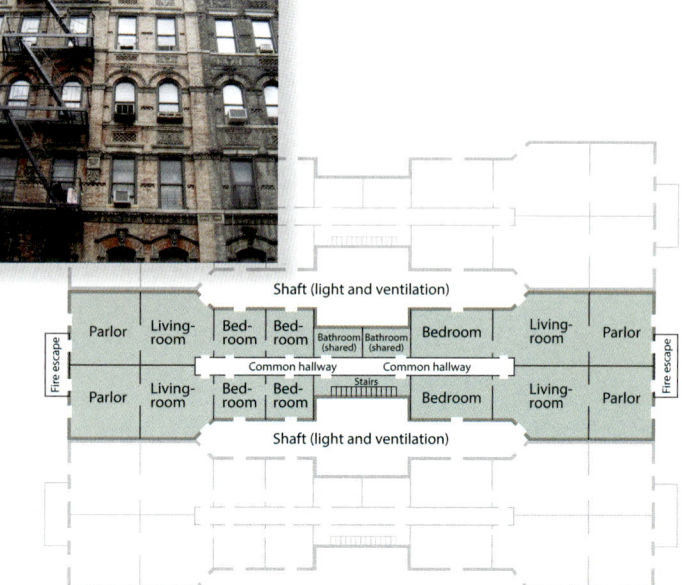

A photo and floorplan of a tenement row.

Overcrowding and slums

As workers poured into the inner city in search of jobs, the middle classes moved out of the industrial districts for better housing. Middle-class homes in city centers were converted into **tenements**—low-cost rental housing barely meeting minimal living requirements. Whole families were crowded into single-room apartments, often without heat or lighting. Many families shared a single toilet.

Lack of Sanitation and Pollution

In the 1870s, most cities lacked sewer systems. Raw sewage sometimes flowed into sources of drinking water. People died from epidemics of cholera or typhoid, spread from contaminated water. The lack of ventilation in tenement housing also contributed to the spread of disease. Garbage-collection and street-cleaning services were generally inadequate. Factories and railroads polluted the air, water, and ground with smoke, ashes, and chemicals. These problems were only gradually eliminated as cities built sewer systems and took other steps to improve public health.

Traffic Congestion

Until the turn of the century, horse-drawn cars crowded the streets of larger cities, making movement difficult when people traveled to and from work. Most cities had developed haphazardly and their streets were often not wide enough for the increased traffic. This problem was gradually reduced by the introduction of the cable car, the electric trolley, and the electric subway for urban transport.

Vast Differences in Wealth

In American cities, the very rich often lived just around the corner from the very poor. Rich city-dwellers spent lavish amounts of money on parties, clothes, and other luxury items just to display their wealth. They also built walls and hired guards to protect themselves. The very proximity of the rich and poor increased the tensions of city-life and made it all the more difficult for the poor to endure their squalid conditions.

Political Corruption

Many American cities were run by "political machines." A **political machine** is an organization, usually controlled by a strong leader or "**boss**," that gets citizens to vote for its candidates on election day. People worked for the "machine" in exchange for political favors and other rewards.

In the 19th century, political bosses provided jobs and services to immigrants and other poor residents in return for their votes. The political machine then used its control of city government to make profits by overcharging on city contracts. It might overcharge on construction or for other services. The most famous political machine was **Tammany Hall** in New York City. Founded in 1789, Tammany Hall named and elected mayors and other government officials of New York City from the 1850s to the 1930s. Tammany Hall assigned its own "ward boss" to each local district of the city (known as a *ward*), to help gather votes. Tammany Hall especially welcomed Irish immigrants, who generally supported its candidates. **Boss Tweed**, the most corrupt politician of his day, amassed a personal fortune from city contracts and "kickbacks."

William Marcy "Boss" Tweed

Another Tammany Hall member, George Washington Plunkitt, was a New York State legislator. He made a fortune by buying up property he knew the government was about to purchase, and then selling it at exorbitant prices. Plunkitt distinguished between "dishonest graft," which was only for personal gain, and "honest graft" for the benefit of one's party and state as well as oneself.

Tammany Hall became the object of reformers' attacks. Washington Gladden, a Protestant pastor and editor of a religious newspaper, condemned Boss Tweed. **Thomas Nast**, the satirical artist, attacked Boss Tweed and Tammany Hall in his political cartoons, published in *Harper's Weekly* and *The New York Times*. Tweed complained that his voters could not read but they were moved by Nast's drawings. The inability of Tweed's political machine to prevent a city riot in 1871 turned New York's elite against him, and Tweed was arrested later in the year. After a series of trials and an escape to Spain, Tweed was returned to the United States and finally died in jail in 1878.

For all their shortcomings, the bosses and their machines did provide important social services to those in need at a time when government's role in resolving social problems was strictly limited. Political machines lent money, provided jobs, and gave emergency assistance for food, coal, or rent. Boss Tweed, for example, provided jobs to Irish laborers and helped them to complete their applications for becoming American citizens. Tweed and his followers also encouraged the uptown expansion of New York City and the construction of the Brooklyn Bridge, and arranged a generous grant of land to the Metropolitan Museum of Art.

The "BRAINS"
That achieved victory at the Rochester Democratic Convention

The Historian's Apprentice

Use the Internet to research the impact of political machines. Select one American city in the late 19th century and investigate its "political machine." Present your findings in the form of a short oral report or PowerPoint presentation to your class.

Immigrants

The industrialization of America and the rapid growth of cities were greatly spurred by a flood of immigrants to American shores.

Shifting Patterns of Immigration

The United States is unique in that most of its citizens are descended from immigrants. Historically, the migration of people to the United States has resulted from a combination of "**push**" and "**pull**" factors: conditions in immigrants' home countries propelled them to leave, while conditions in the United States attracted them to come here.

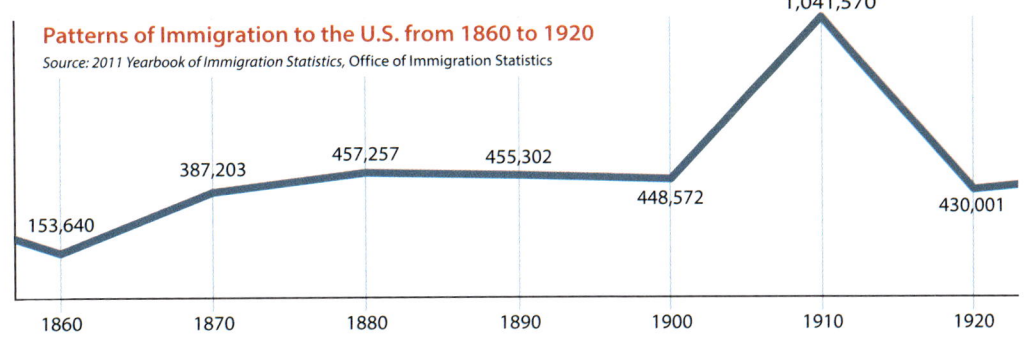

Patterns of Immigration to the U.S. from 1860 to 1920
Source: 2011 Yearbook of Immigration Statistics, Office of Immigration Statistics

1860: 153,640
1870: 387,203
1880: 457,257
1890: 455,302
1900: 448,572
1910: 1,041,570
1920: 430,001

Chapter 6 | Cities, Immigrants, and Farmers

The "Old Immigrants" (before 1880)

The "Old Immigrants" generally came to escape religious and political persecution or to find new economic opportunities. Most spoke English. Often they came to escape great hardships. For example, the Irish potato famine led to a mass exodus from Ireland to America in the 1840s.

Depiction of mother and children during the Irish potato famine

The "New Immigrants," 1880–1924

Existing patterns of immigration changed in the 1880s. Conditions in Western Europe improved, while lower transportation costs brought migration to America within the grasp of other Europeans. The "New Immigrants" came chiefly from Southern and Eastern Europe, especially Austria-Hungary, Italy, Russia, and Greece. Italians, Poles, Jews, and Greeks came in large numbers. The "New Immigrants" were generally Catholic, Jewish or Orthodox Christian rather than Protestant. They spoke little or no English and had different appearances and habits from Northern Europeans. Many were extremely poor and uneducated. Like the "Old Immigrants," many of the "New Immigrants" came to escape religious or political persecution. Jews from Russia, for example, came to escape *"pogroms"* (violent mob attacks on Jewish communities, generally supported by government authorities, in which property was destroyed and community members were often killed).

Most "New Immigrants," however, simply came to escape grinding poverty. In their own countries, land and wealth were controlled by small elites and most people were desperately poor. Because of cheaper steamship travel, many could now afford the voyage to the United States. There were no legal restrictions on European immigration to America at that time. Letters from relatives and accounts in newspapers spread optimistic reports of the benefits of American life. Advertisements from steamship companies selling tickets, railroads selling land grants, and industrialists recruiting labor also attracted newcomers.

Immigrants were drawn by the promise of greater freedom, higher standards of living, and economic opportunity. By 1900, more than 13% of those living in the United States were foreign-born.

The Historian's Apprentice

Make a Venn diagram comparing the characteristics of the "Old" and "New" Immigrants.

Establishing a New Life

The Voyage Across

Usually the "New Immigrants" traveled by train to a port in Europe and then crossed the Atlantic in the cheapest class (known as "steerage"), sleeping in spaces without windows below the water level. Many carried their belongings in a single bag. Most landed in New York Harbor, where they passed the Statue of Liberty, a gift from France that came to symbolize America's willingness to accept the "tired" and "poor . . . huddled masses" of other lands, "yearning to be free."

After 1892, most immigrants arriving in New York City landed at **Ellis Island** for medical examinations and to be processed

Thousands of immigrants arrived at Ellis Island every week

for admission to the United States. They could be sent back to Europe for poor health, especially signs of tuberculosis (TB), or for other reasons, such as a criminal history, but most were admitted to the United States. Many immigrants were given new names by officials who could not pronounce their old ones. Once admitted, a large number of the immigrants remained in New York City; others took trains to join relatives and friends in towns and cities across America.

Challenges in the New Land

The vast majority of the "New Immigrants" settled in the cities of the Northeast and Midwest, where they took unskilled jobs. A few, especially those coming from Scandinavia and Germany, went to farms on the Great Plains. They all faced many challenges:

- They were unfamiliar with American customs and ways—from foods and kitchen implements to voting in elections.

- They could only find employment at unskilled jobs for long hours with low pay.

To cope with these problems, immigrants usually settled down in urban neighborhoods with other immigrants of the same nationality, known to historians as "**ghettos**." Different parts of the Lower East Side of New York City, for example, were Jewish or German (*Kleindeuschland*), while Chinatown and Little Italy sprang up on opposite sides of Canal Street. In these ethnic neighborhoods, immigrants could converse with one another in their native language. Here they found churches and synagogues they could attend, and they helped one another to find housing and work. Often they had friends and relatives from the "Old Country" in the same neighborhood. They had groceries with ethnic foods, clothing stores with their traditional garments, and their own banks and insurance companies. There might even be one or more community newspapers printed in their native language. The immigrants felt comfortable surrounded by those who spoke the same language, followed the same customs, and shared the same experiences. But the fact that they lived in these ethnic ghettos also meant that they were cut off from the American mainstream.

The Process of "Americanization"

Only gradually did the immigrants become "**Americanized**"—*assimilated into mainstream American society by learning its values and behaviors*. Often it was the children of the immigrants, and not the immigrants themselves, who were the first to become "Americanized."

While some adult immigrants attended night school to learn English, most were too busy working or caring for their families to spend time learning a new language. It was left to the children of the immigrants to attend public schools, learn English, and become familiar with American customs. Immigrant children were eventually "**assimilated**"—or made similar to other Americans. The process of assimilation was frequently accompanied by conflict between generations. The immigrants and their

Mulberry Street in New York City was home to Italian immigrants

Chapter 6 | Cities, Immigrants, and Farmers

children had to choose which new customs to accept and which older traditions to preserve. Often different generations did not agree on the proper mix. Immigrant children, for example, might be embarrassed by the clothes or speech of their elders. Their parents might insist on arranged marriages, while the children insisted on finding their own marriage partners, according to the American custom.

Immigrants from Asia

Chinese Americans

Apart from three Chinese sailors who arrived by ship in 1785, and three Chinese residents listed in the Census of 1830, there is little evidence of Chinese immigration to the United States before the discovery of gold in California in 1848. "Pushed" by warfare and economic hard times in China, and "pulled" by the lure of gold, Chinese immigrants began arriving in "Gold Mountain"—California—shortly thereafter. At first, most worked panning for gold. Just as the gold was running out, Chinese workers were recruited as laborers for the construction of the transcontinental railroad. Men in China left their villages, borrowed money from a broker for the journey, and repaid the broker's loan with earnings in America. Most left their wives and families behind. Railroad workers earned wages in America ten times higher than they could in China. They worked tirelessly, lived in meager dwellings, and sent most of their pay back to their families in China. Charles Crocker, one of the railroad owners, noted that "wherever we put them, we found them good, and they worked themselves into our favor to such an extent that if we found we were in a hurry for a job, it was better to put Chinese on at once."

In 1868, the United States signed the Treaty of Burlingame, permitting the "free migration" of Chinese immigrants to America. After the railroad was completed, many Chinese immigrants moved to San Francisco, where they lived in "Chinatown" and

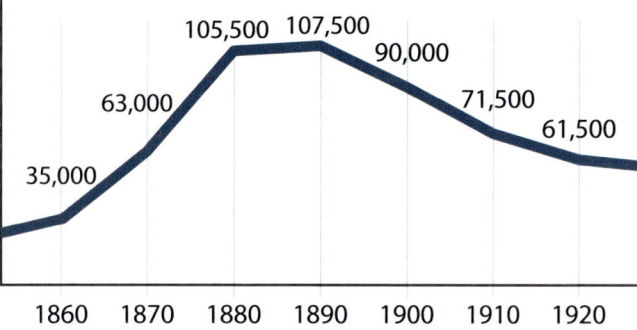

The Population of Chinese Immigrants and their Descendants in the United States

Chinese gold miners in California

worked as tailors, cigar-makers and at other jobs; others worked as field hands, dug wine cellars in vineyards, or labored at other tasks. Because of discrimination, many left their jobs and started their own small businesses—especially Chinese laundries.

Like the "New Immigrants" from Europe, the Chinese looked and dressed differently and spoke an alien language. They often lived in "Chinatowns" in a society of men where prostitution, gambling and other vices flourished. It was feared that a "Chinese invasion" would threaten the "racial purity" of traditional America. Prejudice against Chinese immigrants found expression in politics, the laws, and the courts. In the 1850s, George Hall, a

Chinese workers on the Central Pacific, part of the transcontinental railroad

102   Chapter 6 | Cities, Immigrants, and Farmers

white man, was convicted in California of murdering a Chinese resident based on the testimony of three Chinese witnesses. The California Supreme Court ruled that Chinese individuals could not testify in court and that the evidence of the three witnesses was inadmissible. The conviction was reversed and Hall, the murderer, was set free. Decisions like *People v. Hall* gave license to others to abuse the Chinese.

The U.S. Naturalization Act of 1870 permitted "whites and persons of African descent" to become U.S. citizens, but denied Asians this same right: only by being born in the United States could a person with Asian parents qualify as an American citizen. The Page Act of 1875 further prohibited the immigration of "undesirables" from Asia (such as convicted criminals or prostitutes).

In the Presidential election of 1876, both candidates promised to introduce laws ending Chinese immigration to the United States. In 1882, Congress then passed the **Chinese Exclusion Act**. This law placed a ban on the immigration of Chinese skilled and unskilled laborers to the United States for a period of ten years. Afterwards, the act was periodically renewed. All Chinese already living in the United States had to obtain a special certificate before leaving for a visit to China, or they would not be permitted to re-enter the United States. Six years later, the law was amended so that any Chinese who left could never return. As a result of the Chinese Exclusion Act, many Chinese residents in America were permanently separated from their families in China.

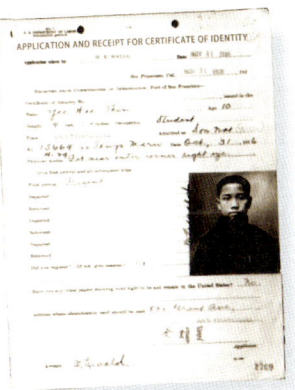
Re-entry application

After 1910, the limited Chinese immigration that remained (such as merchants) was processed at **Angel Island**, a facility in San Francisco similar to Ellis Island. However, Chinese immigrants generally received worse treatment than those arriving from Europe. They might be kept on Angel Island in prison-like conditions for days, weeks or even months before being permitted to enter the United States.

Japanese Americans

Japanese immigration to the United States began shortly after the Meiji Restoration (1868) caused major unrest and social change in Japan. "Pushed" by changes in Japan and "pulled" by the lure of greater economic opportunities in America, the first wave of Japanese settlers was sponsored by the Wakamatsu Tea and Silk Farm Company. They arrived in California in 1869. The 1870 Census showed 55 Japanese living in the United States; there were still only 148 in 1880, and just 2,038 by 1890. Similar to the Chinese, the first Japanese immigrants provided a source of cheap labor, working on farms and in mines, and building railroads in the northwest. Almost all of the earliest Japanese immigrants were men. Like the Chinese, they were unable to become naturalized citizens.

Japanese immigrants—1860s

Because of racist prejudices, American leaders finally negotiated a "**Gentlemen's Agreement**" with the Japanese government in 1907. The Japanese government agreed to prevent the further immigration of workers from Japan to the United States. An exception was made for the wives and children of those Japanese already in America. Japanese men living in the United States could therefore return to Japan, get married, and come back to America with their wives. Those who could not afford the trip across the Pacific sometimes arranged marriages by exchanging photographs. Their weddings took place according to Japanese custom, even though the bride and groom were in different places and had never even seen one another. In this way, some Japanese women, known as "picture brides," became the wives of men in the United States and were able to immigrate to join their husbands.

Chapter 6 | Cities, Immigrants, and Farmers

The Historian's Apprentice

- Compare the experiences of the "New Immigrants" from Southern and Eastern Europe with those of Chinese and Japanese immigrants coming from Asia. Consider why they came, how they came here, what they did, and how they were treated. Present your results in the form of a table or chart. Use the Internet or your school library to obtain additional information.

- Look on the Internet or in your school or public library for pictures showing how immigrants from Europe and Asia lived in their home countries and in the United States between 1870 and 1920. Make a slide show to share with your classmates. What conclusions can you draw from these pictures about the immigrant experience?

The Rise of Nativism

Before World War I, there were no limits on European immigration to the United States. The Statue of Liberty in New York Harbor symbolized the spirit of welcome. Americans felt that their country was so large that it could easily absorb newcomers. Because America was populated mainly by immigrants and their descendants, many Americans felt a strong sense of empathy towards new arrivals at its shores. Employers welcomed immigration as a source of cheap labor.

The huge flood of immigration at the end of the 19th century, however, led to a rise in **nativism**—*the belief that native-born Americans were superior to others, and that immigrants and their diverse cultural influences were undesirable.* Nativists believed that the only "true" Americans were native-born, white, English-speaking and Protestant—characteristics that a majority of American citizens shared at that time. Nativists looked at other races, religions, and nationalities as inferior. They viewed the "New Immigrants" as dirty and unhealthy, and feared that they would lower American standards of living, spread disease, and bring down the wages of other workers. Nativists further blamed the immigrants for selling their votes to political "bosses," undermining American democracy and spreading corruption. The "New Immigrants," they concluded, could never be assimilated into mainstream American life.

Anti-immigration societies began to spring up across America, such as the "Immigration Restriction League." In California, prejudice against Asians led to riots even before the Chinese Exclusion Act. The Ku Klux Klan also re-emerged as a racist and nativist organization that favored "white supremacy." Klan members disliked African Americans, Catholics, Jews and immigrants. Nativism would eventually lead to the passage of federal laws severely restricting immigration. You will learn more about these laws later in this book.

1880s cartoon showing a skilled American worker being displaced by newly arriving immigrants

Farmers

As late as 1900, four out of ten Americans still lived on farms. These farmers, like other Americans, were greatly affected by the Second Industrial Revolution. Most of them were no longer self-sufficient: they were market-oriented and grew crops or raised livestock for sale in America's burgeoning towns and cities. They sold their wheat, cotton, corn, beef or milk to others for cash and then used the money that they earned to buy other foods and goods. This made American farmers extremely vulnerable to changes in market prices for crops and livestock.

In the late 19th century, farmers experienced increasing difficulties as food prices dropped lower and lower. By 1890, the average price of wheat was less than one-third what it had been in 1870. Farmers blamed the railroads and bankers for their troubles. Because so many Americans were still farmers, their discontent had important social and political effects.

The Problems of Farmers, 1870–1920

Most farmers found their incomes were steadily falling, even as their expenses remained high. Why were crop and livestock prices dropping?

Agricultural Overproduction

The main reason for the drop in crop prices was overproduction. The opening of the Great Plains had greatly increased the number of acres under cultivation. At the same time, improvements in machinery and farming techniques had increased the amount grown on each acre. The result of all this was that American farmers were producing more crops than ever before. With so many crops, food prices naturally fell. City-dwellers benefitted from greater farm production and cheaper food. But many farmers were driven out of business.

International Competition

Railroad and steamship transportation created a new international market for food crops. Wheat-growers faced new competition from Canada, Argentina, Russia and Australia. Less of the American crop could be sold abroad. At home, even when American farmers had bad years because of poor weather, imported foreign grain kept prices low.

The Scarcity of Money

Another reason for the drop in food prices was the scarcity of money. Because of fluctuations in gold and silver prices, the government stopped minting silver dollars. Yet, as the population of the United States and the value of its goods and services grew, there was no longer enough money in circulation. This caused some prices to drop.

Meanwhile, even as their own prices dropped, American farmers continued to face high production costs and other difficulties, making it ever harder for them to make ends meet.

The Profits of "Middlemen"

Farmers usually did not sell their crops directly to urban consumers but to "middlemen" who connected them with urban markets. These middlemen were brokers or grain elevator owners, who bought crops at harvest time when prices were low. The farmer, who needed cash, had no choice but to sell to the broker or grain elevator operator at a low price. The middlemen made profits by selling later to urban markets when prices were higher. In some cases, farmers paid grain elevator owners to store their grain. Often the elevator owner charged exorbitant rates. Farmers resented middlemen for taking a share of what they thought should be their own profit.

A farmer and grain dealer negotiating price of wheat

High Shipping Costs

Farmers who shipped crops to grain elevators or urban markets had to pay for shipping by the railroads. Rates were often extremely high. Railroad companies generally charged less to carry freight over a longer than a shorter distance. This was because there were usually competing railroad lines for "long hauls" between major cities. Railroad companies tried to make up for what they lost in the cutthroat competition for long hauls by raising their rates for "short hauls"—shipments from small communities served by only one railroad. Railroad companies knew that whatever rate they charged, local farmers would have to pay it to reach their markets. In effect, a single railroad usually enjoyed a monopoly on local shipping.

The High Cost of Manufactured Products

While farmers were paid low prices for their crops, they paid high prices for manufactured or processed goods like kerosene, fertilizer, farm machinery, clothing and furniture. A high protective tariff kept out many cheaper foreign goods. In some cases, monopoly practices in American industry also kept the prices of manufactured products artificially high. Trusts kept up the prices of fertilizer, barbed wire, and harvesters.

Farm Debt and the Cost of Money

Farmers often borrowed money to buy land, make improvements, or purchase farm machinery. If the harvest was poor, farmers also took out loans simply to survive. They used their own farms as security for these loans. Banks and other lenders saw farmers as poor credit risks and charged them high rates of interest. If a family could not meet its payments, the bank might foreclose and seize the family farm.

Because most farmers were in debt, they favored a policy of "**cheap money**,"—that is, *inflated* currency. If prices rose, the real value of a farmer's payments to a bank to pay off his debt would be less.

> **Inflation** occurs when prices rise—for example, when the price of a quart of milk increases from $2.00 to $3.00. The quart of milk is the same, but the money has changed its value. Because of inflation, the same amount of money ($2.00) has actually become worth less. To remember inflation, think of blowing up a balloon. Pumping air into the balloon causes it to increase in size—or *inflate*. Inflation occurs when prices increase, just like the size of a balloon when pumped with air.

Unfortunately, just the opposite of what the farmers wanted was happening: because of the scarcity of money (and other factors), food prices were continuing to drop. This **deflation** made farmers' loan payments increasingly hard to pay.

Many farmers believed that if the government would just print more paper money or flood the economy with silver coins and paper money backed by silver as well as gold, prices would rise again. This would then make it possible for them to raise their own prices and to repay their debts.

With recent mining discoveries of silver, it was hoped

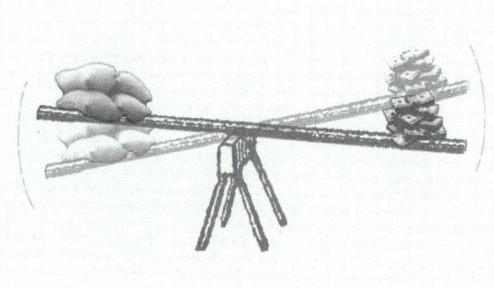

For example, a farmer might buy tools and seed for $10.00. He borrows the money from the bank. Suppose the farmer needs to sell 100 bushels of wheat to earn $10.00 to repay the loan. If prices go down, he will need to sell more wheat to earn the same $10.00 to pay off the loan. If prices go up, it will become easier for him to pay the loan because he can sell less wheat to make $10.00.

that the government could in fact make more silver coins and silver-backed paper money. In 1890, Congress passed the **Sherman Silver Purchase Act**. This law required the federal government to purchase a large amount of silver each month. Supporters predicted this would lead to an increase in the amount of money in circulation. However, the law was repealed in 1893 when the country entered into a depression.

Natural Disasters

In addition to these other problems, farmers were constantly subject to the forces of nature. A single bad year could wipe out the savings of many good years, increase the amount that a farmer borrowed, or even force a farmer to sell his land. In the 1880s, Southern cotton-growers suffered from the spread of boll weevils (*a type of beetle that eats cotton buds*), while wheat farmers on the Great Plains lost crops to grasshoppers and **droughts** (*lack of rainfall*).

Rural Isolation

The problems of farm life were made worse by the psychological effects of isolation. A farming family worked long hours on the land, miles from neighbors and without the conveniences we have today, such as cars, telephones, radios, or televisions. Social life centered on market days and church services in the nearest small town. The problems of rural isolation and loneliness were especially acute on the vast Great Plains.

Farmers Organize to Overcome Their Problems

In the last quarter of the 19th century, farmers united to overcome the challenges confronting them in an industrial society.

The Grange Movement

In 1867, **Oliver Hudson Kelley** organized the "Grange Movement." (The name *grange* comes from the old French word for "barn.") The **Grange** was a national association of farmers' social clubs. Kelley hoped to break 

A Grange hall and a painting depicting a Grange meeting

the rural isolation of farmers and to spread information about new farming techniques. He wished to modernize farming by providing farmers with the same opportunities for education and social interaction that existed in cities. The Grangers organized picnics, lectures, and other social activities. Within ten years, the Grange had more than 1.5 million members.

Grangers tried to replace middlemen by forming their own "farmers' cooperatives." These cooperatives bought machinery, fertilizers, and manufactured goods in bulk at a discount. They also sold their crops directly to markets in towns and cities. But because of their lack of experience and expertise, most of these cooperatives eventually failed.

Granger Laws

Once farmers had organized into Granger clubs, they quickly turned to politics. They especially blamed the railroad companies for their problems. In several states in the Midwest, Grangers elected candidates to their state legislature. These states passed new laws regulating railroad and grain storage rates.

The railroad companies protested bitterly against the "Granger laws," arguing that these new regulations took away the value of their property illegally, without "due process."

In *Munn v. Illinois* (1877), the U.S. Supreme Court upheld one of the "Granger laws" as constitutional. Illinois had passed a law regulating grain elevators. A grain elevator owner challenged the law as a violation of his private property. The Supreme Court ruled that a state government could regulate a private utility if that utility was serving the public interest.

Chapter 6 | Cities, Immigrants, and Farmers

Nine years later, the Supreme Court limited this ruling. In *Wabash, St. Louis and Pacific Railroad v. Illinois* (1886), the Supreme Court held that state governments could not regulate railroads running through more than one state, since the Constitution had given the power to regulate interstate commerce exclusively to Congress. Since most railroads ran through several states, the *Wabash* decision invalidated many of the "Granger laws."

The Historian's Apprentice

"[A] statute of a state, intended to regulate or to tax or to impose any other restriction upon the transmission of persons or property or telegraphic messages from one state to another, is not within that class of legislation which the states may enact in the absence of legislation by Congress, and that such statutes are void even as to that part of such transmission which may be within the state."

—U.S. Supreme Court, *Wabash, St. Louis, and Pacific Railroad v. Illinois* (1886)

▶ Write a paragraph explaining, in your own words, why the U.S. Supreme Court ruled differently in the *Munn* and *Wabash* decisions.

The Interstate Commerce Act (1887)

In reaction to the *Wabash* decision, Congress passed the **Interstate Commerce Act** only one year later. The act marked the first step towards federal regulation of unfair business practices. It prohibited giving different rates to different customers for hauling freight the same distance. It also banned price-fixing agreements ("**pooling**") or charging more for "short hauls" than for "long hauls" along the same route. Railroad companies were required to publish their rates, which were to be "fair and reasonable." An **Interstate Commerce Commission** was created to investigate complaints against railroads and to enforce the act. It was the first federal regulatory agency created to watch over an industry

The Populist Party, 1892–1896

Even after passage of the Interstate Commerce Act, farmers continued to have difficulties. Farmers—mainly Grange members—formed regional political associations, known as "**Farmers Alliances**," in the Northwest and the South. The Farmers Alliances generally focused on local politics. In the early 1890s, the leaders of the Farmers Alliances formed a new national political party—the "People's Party"—better known as the **Populist Party**. "Populism" refers to a belief in the "people"—ordinary citizens, rather than the elite. The Populists were convinced that rich industrialists and bankers had a stranglehold on government, and that the Democratic and Republican Parties had both "sold out" to the bank-

ing interest. They further believed that bankers were using their control of government to restrict the money supply so that their own gold would become even more valuable. To fight this conspiracy, the Populists wanted to unite all laboring men—both farmers and industrial workers.

The Populist Platform of 1892

The Populists held a national convention at Omaha, Nebraska, in 1892. They nominated a candidate to the Presidency and drew up a party platform with many innovative proposals. The "**Omaha Platform**" contained many ideas that were later enacted into law.

In the election of 1892, the Populists elected five Senators and received more than a million votes for their Presidential candidate. Their main strongholds were areas where prices had dramatically dropped: cotton prices in the South, wheat prices in the Northwest, and silver in the Mountain states.

The Election of 1896

The Depression of 1893 began only a few months after the election. Populists blamed the depression on the scarcity of money, which at that time was backed by gold. Without enough money, prices kept spiraling downwards. Free coinage of silver, the Populists reasoned, would increase the money available through **bimetallism**. This would raise farm prices and make farm loans easier to repay. Populist leaders focused their attention on this issue to attract "free silver" Republicans and Democrats to their party.

Key Provisions of the "Omaha Platform"

▶ Free and unlimited coinage of silver at a ratio of 16:1 (1 ounce of gold should be equal in value to 16 ounces of silver).

▶ The direct election of Senators, instead of their selection by state legislatures.

▶ Government ownership of railroads, telegraphs and telephones.

▶ The use of the secret ballot in elections so voters could not be unfairly pressured.

▶ Introduction of a graduated (or progressive) income tax—taxing the wealthy at higher rates than others—to reduce the government's dependence on tariffs for revenue.

▶ Postal saving banks, so that people would not need to rely on private banks to protect their savings.

▶ Use of the "initiative" and "referendum," to make politicians more responsive to the people (see page 126).

▶ Restrictions on immigration.

▶ An eight-hour workday for industrial workers.

▶ Limit the Presidency to one term in office.

▶ Use government warehouses to store farm goods until food prices were higher.

The Historian's Apprentice

Which of these Populist proposals later passed into law and are still with us today?

> "There are two ideas of government. There are those who believe that, if you will only legislate to make the well-to-do prosperous, their prosperity will leak through on those below. The Democratic idea, however, has been that if you legislate to make the masses prosperous, their prosperity will find its way up through every class which rests upon them. You come to us and tell us that the great cities are in favor of the gold standard; we reply that the great cities rest upon our broad and fertile prairies. Burn down your cities and leave our farms, and your cities will spring up again as if by magic; but destroy our farms and the grass will grow in the streets of every city in the country... Having behind us the producing masses of this nation and the world, supported by the commercial interests, the laboring interests, and the toilers everywhere, we will answer their demand for a gold standard by saying to them: "You shall not press down upon the brow of labor this crown of thorns; you shall not crucify mankind upon a cross of gold."
>
> —William Jennings Bryan, Speech at the Democratic National Convention

The Democratic Convention. The incumbent President, Grover Cleveland, was a Democrat. Many farmers and workers saw his policies, however, as increasingly conservative. As President, Cleveland had halted the government purchase of silver, had used federal troops to put down the Pullman Strike, and had failed to lower tariffs significantly. As a result, Democrats became divided.

At the Democratic Convention of 1896, "free silver" Democrats—those who thought the government should allow unlimited coinage of silver—defeated Cleveland's supporters after a bitter struggle. **William Jennings Bryan**, a 36-year-old Congressman, won his party's nomination after delivering his brilliant **"Cross of Gold" speech**, exalting the farmer and denouncing banking interests for attempting to "crucify mankind upon a cross of gold."

William Jennings Bryan

The Democratic nomination of Bryan on a "free silver" platform placed Populist leaders in an awkward position. They decided to nominate Bryan too, rather than to divide the "free silver" vote. This brought Populists under the control of the Democratic Party and ended their independence as a separate party.

The Election: McKinley versus Bryan. Republicans nominated William McKinley, who favored the gold standard, a high protective tariff, and the non-interference of government in business. Behind McKinley stood the organizing ability of wealthy Ohio businessman Marcus Hanna. Hanna solicited money from large business owners and raised ten times as much campaign money as Bryan's supporters. John D. Rockefeller was frightened by Bryan, and his company contributed to McKinley's campaign. In the Northeast, many people blamed President Cleveland for the depression and looked upon the Democratic candidate, Bryan, as a lunatic. Hanna's propaganda convinced workers that Bryan's election would bring about a general economic collapse and cost them their jobs. Most newspapers also supported McKinley. In the West, people viewed the silver issue with religious devotion. Bryan campaigned throughout the country, giving more than 600 speeches. The election itself turned out to be very close. Bryan swept the South, the Great Plains, and the Rocky Mountain states, winning 6.5 million votes. But McKinley won the Northeast, the Midwest, and the Pacific states of California and Oregon—giving him 7 million votes and a majority of the electoral votes. Bryan ran for the Presidency again in 1900 and 1908, but lost each time. Although the Populists disbanded, many of their ideas were later adopted. You will learn about these changes in the next chapter.

Cities

Urbanization—the movement of population from the countryside to cities

Problems of Cities

- Overcrowding and slums—cheap tenement housing often lacked air ventilation or proper sanitation
- Traffic congestion—horse-drawn cars, trains, narrow streets
- Lack of garbage collection services and proper sewage—led to water contamination and diseases like cholera
- Vast differences in wealth—sharpened social antagonisms

Political Machines—corruption—Example: Boss Tweed and Tammany Hall

- The "Boss" and members of the machine provided various social services to the immigrants and the poor.
- The "political machine" encouraged immigrants and the poor to vote for its candidates.
- Officials elected by the "political machine" then charged excessive amounts on public contracts or received "kickbacks," making huge fortunes.

Immigration

Before 1880: "Old Immigrants" came from Great Britain, Ireland and Germany. Most people spoke English.

1880–1924: "New Immigrants"

- The "**New Immigrants**" came from Southern and Eastern Europe: Poland, Russia, Italy, Greece.
- Most were Catholic, Jewish, or Greek Orthodox. Many spoke no English. Most were desperately poor.
- They had different traditions than most "mainstream" Americans and faced prejudice and discrimination.

Asian Immigrants

- Chinese men began arriving during the California Gold Rush and helped to build the transcontinental railroad in California. Afterwards, they faced prejudice and discrimination.
- The **Naturalization Law of 1870** prevented Asian immigrants from becoming naturalized citizens.
- The **Chinese Exclusion Act** (1882) banned almost all immigrants from China, and was the first restriction ever placed on immigration to the United States (other than against criminals or unhealthy persons).
- Japanese Americans began arriving at the end of the century; their immigration was cut off by the **Gentlemen's Agreement** (1907) between Japan and the United States.

The Immigrant Experience

The Voyage: Steamship companies made it more affordable to come to America.

Admission: After 1892, poorer Europeans in "steerage" class were processed at **Ellis Island**. They could be sent back if they did not pass a medical examination. After 1910, Asians generally were processed on **Angel Island** in San Francisco, where they faced even longer delays—sometimes for several months.

Ethnic "Ghettos": Most immigrants went to live in ethnic neighborhoods in cities, known to historians as "**ghettos**." There they lived with others who spoke the same language and practiced the same traditions.

"Americanization": Usually the children of the immigrants were the first to be "**Americanized**"—or assimilated into "mainstream" society by learning the values and behaviors of American culture. By attending public schools, immigrant children learned English and American ways. This often led to conflict between generations.

Nativism: **Nativists** generally believed that white, Protestant native-born Americans were superior to others, and that immigrants and their diverse cultural influences were undesirable. Nativist feelings led to the Chinese Exclusion Act of 1882, and later restrictions on immigration in the 1920s.

Farmers' Problems

In the late 19th century, a large number of Americans were still farmers, growing crops or raising livestock for sale. They began experiencing problems when food prices fell, even though their costs remained high.

Why Food Prices Fell
- Agricultural overproduction
- International competition
- Scarcity of money kept food prices low: the **Sherman Silver Purchase Act** was passed in 1890 but repealed three years later.

Other Problems Faced by Farmers
- High costs of manufactured products—protective tariffs and trusts
- Profits of middlemen
- High shipping costs—unfair railroad rates
- Farmer indebtedness
- Natural disasters
- Rural isolation

Farmers Organize

Farmers organized into social and political groups to meet these challenges.

Grange Movement: National association of farmers' social clubs—served social and educational purposes

Farmers' Cooperatives: Attempts by Grangers to set up their own businesses for buying and selling bulk

Populist Party: Grangers formed "Farmers' Alliances," which formed the **Populist Party** in the early 1890s—a new national political party to represent the common interests of farmers and workers.

Granger Laws

- Grangers entered state legislatures and passed laws to regulate grain elevators and railroads.
- The Supreme Court upheld state regulation of a grain elevator in *Munn v. Illinois* (1877).
- The Supreme Court overruled a state law regulating railroad rates in *Wabash v. Illinois* (1886) on the grounds that only Congress could regulate interstate commerce.

Interstate Commerce Act (1887)
- Passed by Congress after the *Wabash* decision.
- The first federal law to regulate business practices.
- Railroads could not give different rates for hauling the same freight the same distance.
- Railroads could not charge more for short hauls than long hauls.
- Congress set up a new agency, the *Interstate Commerce Commission*, to oversee enforcement of the act.

The Populist Party

- **Populist Platform of 1892 ("Omaha Platform")**
  - Included many far-reaching proposals that were later adopted: direct election of U.S. Senators, secret ballot, progressive income tax, initiative and referendum procedures, eight-hour workday, restrictions on immigration.
  - Other ideas were never adopted: government ownership of railroads and utilities, postal savings banks, unlimited silver coinage.
- **William Jennings Bryan's "*Cross of Gold*" Speech**—Bryan chosen as Democratic Party nominee in 1896. Populist party follows suit rather than divide the "free silver" vote.
- 1896 Presidential election campaign: Populists and Democrats focused on **"bimetallism"**—basing money on silver as well as gold to raise prices and make it easier for farmers to repay their debts.
- Bryan lost to McKinley in a close election: Populists won support in the South, Great Plains and the Rocky Mountain states.

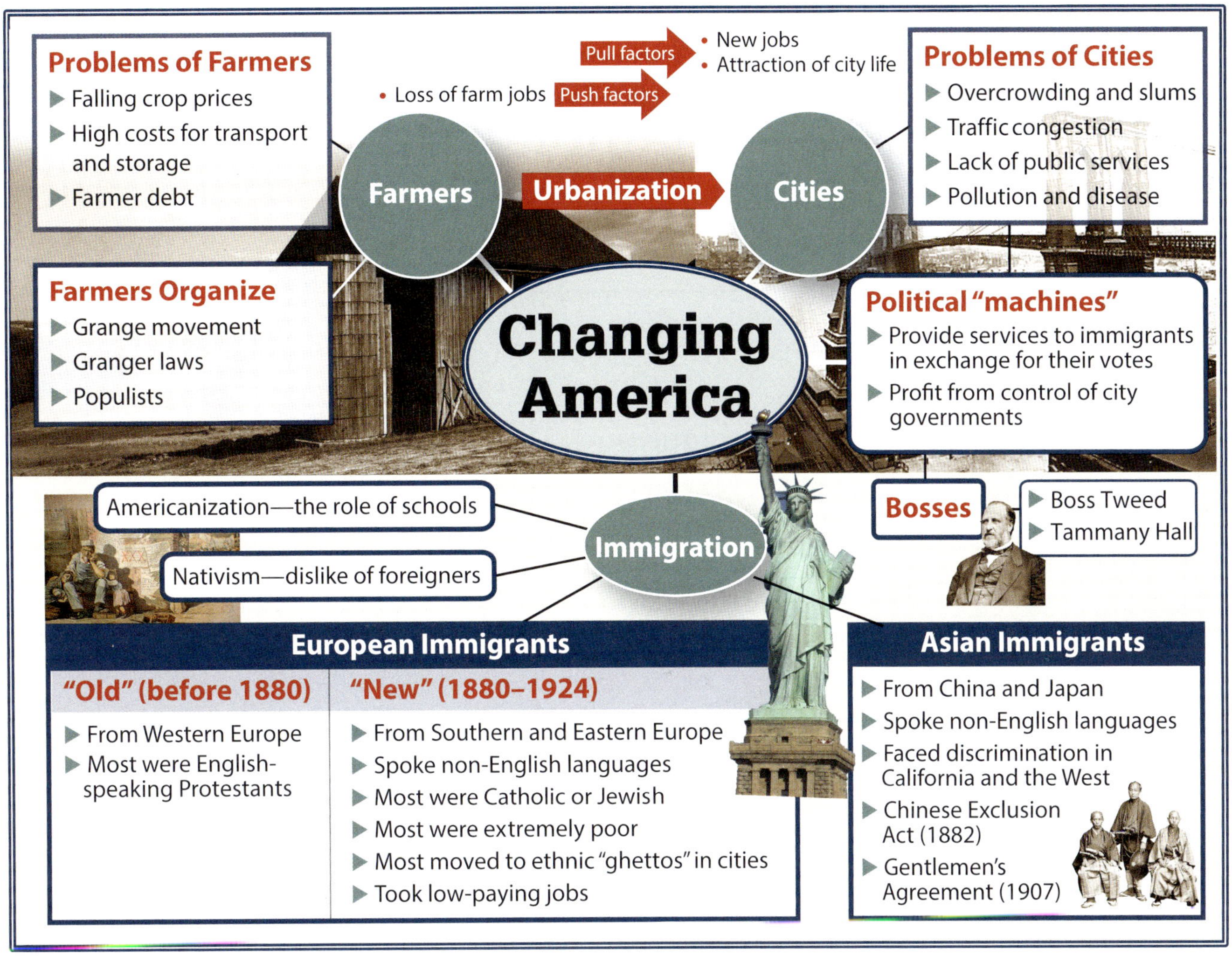

Changing America

Problems of Farmers
- Falling crop prices
- High costs for transport and storage
- Farmer debt

Farmers Organize
- Grange movement
- Granger laws
- Populists

Push factors: Loss of farm jobs
Pull factors: New jobs, Attraction of city life

Farmers → Urbanization → Cities

Problems of Cities
- Overcrowding and slums
- Traffic congestion
- Lack of public services
- Pollution and disease

Political "machines"
- Provide services to immigrants in exchange for their votes
- Profit from control of city governments

Bosses
- Boss Tweed
- Tammany Hall

Immigration
- Americanization—the role of schools
- Nativism—dislike of foreigners

European Immigrants

"Old" (before 1880)
- From Western Europe
- Most were English-speaking Protestants

"New" (1880–1924)
- From Southern and Eastern Europe
- Spoke non-English languages
- Most were Catholic or Jewish
- Most were extremely poor
- Most moved to ethnic "ghettos" in cities
- Took low-paying jobs

Asian Immigrants
- From China and Japan
- Spoke non-English languages
- Faced discrimination in California and the West
- Chinese Exclusion Act (1882)
- Gentlemen's Agreement (1907)

What Do You Know?

SS.912.A.3.6 & SS.912.G.4.2

1. The graph below shows the proportion of rural and urban population of the United States from 1870 to 1900.

   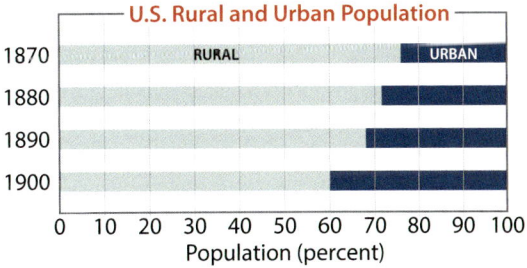
   U.S. Rural and Urban Population

   Which factor contributed to the shift in population shown on the graph?

   A. Not enough families took advantage of the Homestead Act.

   B. Great Plains Indians left their reservations to buy new farmland.

   C. Houses in cities were less expensive than those in the countryside.

   D. Better jobs in industry attracted farmers and farm laborers to cities.

Chapter 6 | Cities, Immigrants, and Farmers

SS.912.A.3.6

2. What was a consequence of the rapid growth of cities in the late 1800s?

   A. the decline of political machines in the Midwest

   B. the migration of poor workers to the suburbs

   C. a decrease in the gap between rich and poor

   D. the rapid growth of tenements and ghettos

SS.912.A.3.11

3. The cartoon at the left by Thomas Nast was published in 1871.

"Who stole the People's money?"   'Twas him

   Which problem is addressed in the cartoon?

   A. New citizens were often unable to exercise their voting rights.

   B. City governments were providing inadequate services to residents.

   C. Political machines were profiting from kickbacks on public contracts.

   D. The deadlock between political parties was costing taxpayers money.

SS.912.A.3.11

4. Which useful function was served by the political machines of the late 1800s?

   A. They prevented corruption in local government.

   B. They helped provide a supply of cheap and skilled labor for industry.

   C. They served as role models for future city governments by acting as city managers.

   D. They assisted in the social and political assimilation of immigrants into the community.

SS.912.A.3.7 & SS.912.G.4.2

5. The statement below was made by a 19th-century immigrant to the United States.

   > My family was lucky. We survived the pogrom in our village in Russia. The Tsarist government acted in support of these anti-Jewish attacks. We had a cousin in Chicago who sent us enough money to pay for our passage by steamship to America.

   Based on this statement, why did her family immigrate to the United States?

   A. Religious persecution pushed them out of Russia.

   B. A drought in western Russia pushed them out of Russia.

   C. The discovery of gold in the Black Hills pulled them towards the United States.

   D. The promise of jobs in the oil industry in Chicago pulled them towards the United States.

SS.912.A.3.7

6. How did the "New Immigrants" differ from the "Old Immigrants"?

    A. Most of them were Protestants.

    B. Most of them spoke very little English.

    C. They came seeking new economic opportunities.

    D. They were generally accepted by native-born Americans.

SS.912.A.3.7 & SS.912.G.4.3

7. Why were immigrants from Southern and Eastern Europe in the late 19th century welcomed by industrialists?

    A. The immigrants found it difficult to learn English and assimilate.

    B. The immigrants voted for candidates from the local political machine.

    C. The immigrants lived in ghettos with other people from the same background.

    D. The immigrants were willing to work for lower wages than most other workers.

SS.912.A.3.7 & SS.912.G.4.3

8. This diagram provides details about late 19th-century America. Which title completes the diagram?

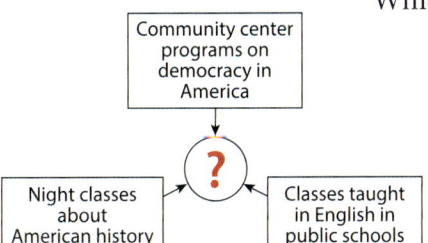

    A. Programs for Americanization

    B. Factors Promoting Immigration

    C. Activities of the Freedmen's Bureau

    D. Goals of the Temperance Movement

SS.912.A.3.7

9. Which group most favored the passage of the Chinese Exclusion Act in 1882?

    A. imperialists in Congress

    B. nativists on the West Coast

    C. Progressives from the Midwest

    D. anarchists who immigrated from Europe

SS.912.A.3.7

10. How did the experiences of Chinese immigrants differ from those of the "New Immigrants" from Southern and Eastern Europe?

    A. They often took the least desirable and lowest paying jobs.

    B. They frequently faced prejudice and discrimination from nativists.

    C. They were unable to use all of the same skills that they possessed at home.

    D. They could not own property, testify in some state courts, or become citizens.

Chapter 6 | Cities, Immigrants, and Farmers

SS.912.A.3.6 & SS.912.G.4.3

11. The table below provides information about the population of several cities in 1870 and 1900.

Place	1870			1900			
	Total Population	Foreign born		Total Population		Foreign Born	
	Number	Number	% of Total	Number	% Change	Number	% Change
New York, NY*	942,292	419,094	44.5	3,437,202	265	1,270,080	37
Chicago, IL	298,977	144,557	48.4	1,698,575	468	587,112	34.6
Philadelphia, PA	674,022	183,624	27.2	1,293,697	92	295,340	22.8
St. Louis, MO	310,864	112,249	36.1	575,238	85	111,356	19.4
Boston, MA	250,526	87,986	35.1	560,892	124	197,129	35.1
San Francisco, CA	149,473	73,719	49.3	342,782	129	116,885	34.1
Los Angeles, CA	5,728	2,004	35	102,479	1,698	19,964	19.5
Seattle, WA	1,107	279	25.2	80,671	7,187	22,003	27.3

* Does not include Brooklyn

Source: U.S. Census

Which describes a trend indicated by the information in the table?

A. Immigrants formed a larger proportion of more cities in 1900 than in 1870.

B. There were fewer immigrants in the United States in 1900 than in 1870.

C. The number of immigrants increased but the size of major cities increased even faster.

D. The percentage of foreign-born residents increased in cities in the West but not in cities in the East.

SS.912.A.3.6 & SS.912.G.4.3

12. Which was NOT a major issue faced by the cities on the table above?

A. the growth of nativist attitudes against immigrants

B. rising food prices caused by labor shortages on farms

C. increased corruption in city government from political machines

D. increased traffic congestion from pedestrians, carriages and trains

SS.912.A.3.7 & SS.912.G.4.3

13. How did many nativists feel about the rapid influx of immigrants between 1870 and 1900?

A. They worried that the costs of urban housing would go down.

B. They feared that the immigrants might take their jobs for lower wages.

C. They hoped that the growth of the city would bring more concerts and parks.

D. They welcomed the arrival of diverse peoples with different foods and traditions.

SS.912.A.3.7 & SS.912.G.4.3

Source: Library of Congress

14. The photograph on the left shows immigrants on Ellis Island in 1904. What was the primary purpose of this facility?
    A. processing permanent residents applying for U.S. citizenship
    B. processing highly skilled workers arriving from China and Japan
    C. processing first-class passengers arriving on European steamship lines
    D. processing immigrants who mainly came from Southern and Eastern Europe

SS.912.A.3.7

15. The timeline below displays the sequence of some events affecting Asian immigrants.

    1854: *People v. Hall*   1882: Chinese Exclusion Act
    1854   1870   1882   1907
    1870: U.S. Naturalization Act   1907: "Gentlemen's Agreement"

    What was the goal of these measures?
    A. to keep Asian immigrants out of American society
    B. to assimilate Asian immigrants into American society
    C. to encourage Americans to become more multicultural
    D. to give Asian and European immigrants the same treatment

SS.912.A.3.1

16. Which was NOT a problem faced by farmers in the late 19th century?
    A. Overproduction on the Great Plains led to a drop in crop prices.
    B. Rising city populations were willing to pay higher prices for food.
    C. Railroads and grain elevator owners were making huge profits on farmers.
    D. Famers owed money on loans for farm machinery, improvements and bad times.

SS.912.A.3.1

17. What demand was made in the Populist Party platform of 1892?
    A. higher tariffs
    B. a graduated income tax
    C. unrestricted immigration
    D. selection of U.S. Senators by state legislatures

Chapter 6 | Cities, Immigrants, and Farmers

SS.912.A.3.1

18. The excerpt below is from a law enacted by Congress in 1887.

> **Section 4.** That it shall be unlawful for any common carrier subject to the provisions of this act to charge or receive any greater compensation in the aggregate for the transportation of passengers or of like kind of property, under substantially similar circumstances and conditions, for a shorter than for a longer distance over the same line, in the same direction, the shorter being included within the longer distance . . .

Why did Congress pass this law?

A. Only Congress had the right to regulate economic activities even within a single state.

B. Congress wanted to save natural resources by discouraging shipments over long distances.

C. The Supreme Court had overruled state laws prohibiting unjust practices by interstate railroads.

D. Political machines influenced Congress to pass legislation favoring some companies over others.

SS.912.A.3.1

19. The excerpt below is from William Jenning Bryan's speech at the Democratic Convention in 1896.

> Having behind us the producing masses of this nation and the world, supported by the commercial interests, the laboring interests, and the toilers everywhere, we will answer their demand for a gold standard by saying to them: "You shall not press down upon the brow of labor this crown of thorns; you shall not crucify mankind upon a cross of gold."

Based on this speech, what did Bryan demand in his subsequent campaign for the Presidency?

A. the acquisition of colonies to increase employment opportunities

B. the creation of a national park system to protect the nation's wildlife

C. a policy of bimetallism that would help farmers by raising crop prices

D. higher tariffs to protect American manufacturers from foreign competition

SS.912.A.3.1

20. What was the purpose of the Grange movement?

A. to fight the corruption of political machines in cities

B. to break the rural isolation of farmers and represent their interests

C. to halt the influx of immigrants from Southern and Eastern Europe

D. to agitate for government ownership of railroads, telegraphs and telephones

CHAPTER 7

The Progressive Era

SS.912.A.3.2 Examine the social, political, and economic causes, course, and consequences of the Second Industrial Revolution that began in the late 19th century.

SS.912.A.3.6 Analyze changes that occurred as the United States shifted from an agrarian to an industrial society.

SS.912.A.3.8 Examine the importance of social change and reform in the late 19th and early 20th centuries (class system, migration from farms to cities, Social Gospel movement, role of settlement houses and churches in providing services to the poor).

SS.912.A.3.10 Review different economic and philosophic ideologies.

SS.912.A.3.11 Analyze the impact of political machines in United States cities in the late 19th and early 20th centuries.

SS.912.A.3.12 Compare how different nongovernmental organizations and progressives worked to shape public policy, restore economic opportunities, and correct injustices in American life.

SS.912.A.3.13 Examine key events and peoples in Florida history as they relate to United States history.

Names and Terms You Should Know

Nongovernmental organization	Settlement house	17th Amendment	William Howard Taft
Progressives	Jane Addams	Women's Suffrage	16th Amendment
Social Gospel Movement	National Woman Suffrage Association	Child labor	Woodrow Wilson
Temperance Movement	Municipal reform	Susan B. Anthony	Graduated income tax
Consumers	Political machines	Alice Paul	Federal Reserve Act
Muckrakers	City manager	Theodore Roosevelt	Clayton Antitrust Act
Ida Tarbell	Secret ballot	Government regulation	Federal Trade Commission
Upton Sinclair	Initiative	"Square Deal"	Everglades
Jacob Riis	Referendum	Coal Strike of 1902	Governor Broward
Social change	Recall	Meat Inspection Act	
	Direct primary	Pure Food and Drug Act	

Florida "Keys" to Learning

1. The Progressive Movement flourished from 1890 until the outbreak of World War I. Its aim was to remedy the political and economic injustices that had resulted from America's rapid industrialization. Progressives believed in using government power to correct these abuses.

2. Progressivism had multiple roots: (1) the appearance of the new problems of an industrial society, such as brutal working conditions, urban crowding, the need for more public services, and political corruption; (2) the American reform tradition; (3) the Populist Party; (4) the "Social Gospel" movement—Protestant ministers who helped the poor out of a sense of moral responsibility based on Christian teachings; (5) new forms of journalism—"muckrakers" exposed the abuses and corruption of industrial society; (6) rising consumer consciousness; and (7) the support of women reformers and organized labor.

3. In contrast to the Populists, the Progressives were middle class and urban. Progressive leaders were generally members of the professional classes: professors, lawyers, doctors, religious ministers, and writers. Their followers were members of the lower middle classes: technicians, clerical workers, small business owners, and service personnel.

4. Through their writings in magazines and newspapers, "muckrakers" like Ida Tarbell and Upton Sinclair exposed many evils and stimulated a public outcry for reform. Social Reformers like Jane Addams established "settlement houses" for immigrants and the poor. They also formed associations such as the National Woman Suffrage Association, the NAACP, and the Anti-Defamation League.

5. Municipal reformers attacked the political machines and created new forms of municipal government such as by city manager. At the state level, Progressives elected governors and state legislators such as Robert La Follette of Wisconsin and Napoleon Broward of Florida. They also introduced several reforms to reduce corruption in state government, including the secret ballot, initiative, referendum, recall, direct primary, direct election of U.S. Senators, and women's suffrage in many states. Many of these political reforms were first suggested by the Populists. Progressives also introduced social and economic reforms at the state level, including child labor laws, laws regulating conditions in urban housing, laws regulating safety and health in factories, laws limiting the number of hours that women could work in factories, and workers' compensation for work-related injuries.

6. A series of Progressive Presidents brought Progressivism to the federal government. Theodore Roosevelt saw himself as the steward of the people's interest. His efforts were meant to give Americans a "square deal." He tried to break up "bad" trusts; introduced federal regulation of meat, food and drugs; intervened to end the 1902 coal strike; and took steps to conserve the nation's natural resources and wildlife. William Howard Taft largely followed Roosevelt's policies. When Roosevelt became critical of Taft and ran as an independent in the 1912 election, the Republicans lost to the Democrats. Democratic candidate Woodrow Wilson was in fact another Progressive. He attacked the "triple wall of privilege"—banks, tariffs, and trusts. Wilson lowered tariffs, introduced the graduated income tax, created the Federal Reserve System, and strengthened antitrust legislation with the Clayton Antitrust Act.

The **Progressive Era** took place in the decades between 1890 and the outbreak of the First World War. The primary aim of the Progressives was to remedy the political and economic injustices that had resulted from America's rapid industrialization. Progressives believed in human "progress." They did not oppose industrialization, but they wanted to use the power of government to correct its abuses so that Americans could enjoy better lives. In order to achieve this, they felt they had to reform government itself, which had been corrupted by Big Business and political bosses. Progressive reforms moved Americans from a *laissez-faire* economy to one in which government regulations prevented the worst abuses of economic power.

Roots of the Progressive Movement

Why did the Progressive Movement suddenly emerge at this time? Historians look at several factors to explain the rise of Progressivism.

The Reform Tradition

Reform has been a continuing process in American history. Reform movements, such as abolitionism and Progressivism, have been based on the belief that society can be improved or made better. Americans have experienced periodic demands for reform, especially when they are beset with economic difficulties or social injustices.

The Legacy of Populism

Progressives borrowed many ideas from the earlier Populists and often received strong rural support.

The Problems of Industrial Society

The rise of industry was accompanied by grave new social problems: brutal working conditions, child labor, political corruption, urban overcrowding, exploitation of the environment, extreme inequalities of wealth, and the sale of misleading, defective or even dangerous products. *Laissez-faire* policies were not very successful in curbing these evils. The Progressives called for limited government intervention to stop abuses and overcome these problems. Through moderate reform, the Progressives hoped to avoid the worst abuses of the new industrial age while still preserving the benefits of free enterprise.

The Influence of the Middle Class

Populism was largely rural and appealed mostly to the South and West. In contrast, Progressivism, writes historian Richard Hofstadter, "was urban, middle-class and nationwide." Members of the professional classes—college professors, lawyers, doctors, religious ministers, and writers—provided its core leadership; members of the lower middle-classes—technicians, clerical workers, small business owners, and service personnel—provided a following. Hofstadter notes that while Populists protested against worsening economic conditions, Progressives generally acted in times of prosperity. They felt psychologically challenged by the rise of industrial society: the rise of industrialists of vast wealth made ordinary professional men and women feel almost insignificant.

Children playing in a dirty urban environment, near open sewers and a dead horse. Such scenes prompted reformers to campaign for better sanitation in U.S. cities.

Another historian, Robert Wiebe, provides a more optimistic viewpoint. Wiebe argues that Progressivism was a middle-class "revolution in values." It represented the rise of new professional classes with modern views, who admired "continuity and regularity, functionality and rationality, administration and management." As America changed from a nation of small, independent, rural communities to an urban society subject to vast impersonal forces, the Progressives called for greater social organization and regulation. They felt professionals of all kinds could help both business and government run more smoothly and efficiently according to scientific principles.

In general, the Progressives felt that the rise of Big Business, organized labor, and political machines had closed the door to individual opportunity. Such large concentrations of economic and political power failed to engage in fair business practices or to allow equal competition. In short, both business and government had become corrupt. The Progressives therefore aimed at removing this corruption and regulating business and government practices so that the average American would have more of a chance to compete on a fair basis.

The "Social Gospel" Movement

Middle-class Progressives often acted out of a sense of moral responsibility derived from religion. Towards the end of the 19th century, many Protestant ministers grew concerned at the plight of the poor in the new industrial society. They were disgusted by living conditions in the slums, by child labor, by poor schools, by the horrendous working conditions of industrial laborers, and by the selfishness of the wealthy business owners. Some believed that God would not return to Earth for the "Second Coming" until people made greater efforts to eliminate these social evils. Many Protestant ministers called for **social change**, including safer working conditions, better public schools, and the abolition of child labor; some even called for a form of "Christian Socialism" in place of indifference to the sufferings of others. Groups like the **Salvation Army** emphasized the Christian duty to help the less fortunate. Methodists in Colorado established a free hospital, night schools for adults, and a free summer camp for children. Others began "settlement houses" to help immigrants (see below). All of these efforts became known as the "**Social Gospel**" movement. The Social Gospel movement called on governments, churches and private charities to work together to help people in need. They especially wanted to educate the poor and downtrodden to help themselves. Members of the movement also promoted **temperance**, calling for a ban on alcoholic drinks, which they saw as one of the chief causes of many of these social problems.

New Forms of Journalism

With the expansion of cities, newspapers and magazines reached larger audiences than ever before. Advertisers were the major source of revenue for these newspapers and magazines, but publishers needed to attract more readers to attract advertisers. Readers liked human-interest stories, often focusing on the rich, the poor, and the corrupt. Investigative reporting gave widespread exposure to the abuses of industrial society and stimulated the desire for reform.

Rising Consumer Consciousness

With the growth of modern industries, most products were no longer produced locally. Americans began buying mass-produced goods manufactured by large, impersonal companies. The Progressives realized it was in the interests of American consumers that these goods should be safe to use, and that manufacturers not misrepresent their products. Progressives believed that government intervention was needed to police the market and to protect the public interest.

Socialism, Anarchism, Communism

The abuses of industrial capitalism led some critics in Europe and America to demand an end to capitalism itself. American **Socialists**, led by union-organizer Eugene Debs, believed that government should take over basic industries. **Anarchists** desired that the country should break up into self-governing communities. **Communists** believed that workers should seize control of the means of production through violent revolution and abolish private property. Progressives rejected all of these schemes. However, they felt that some moderate reforms were necessary if a more radical social revolution were to be avoided.

The Support of Women and Workers

Many Progressives favored women's suffrage. Since they believed women were more "virtuous" than men, they thought women voters would create a more civilized and kinder society. Women and industrial workers tended to support the Progressives because they favored social reform and more regulation of Big Business.

The Historian's Apprentice

▸ Create a chart showing the different influences that came together in the Progressive Movement.

▸ Use the Internet or your school library to learn more about the Social Gospel movement and make an oral report or PowerPoint presentation to your class.

▸ Write a paragraph comparing the views of Richard Hofstadter and Robert Wiebe on the role of the middle classes in the Progressive Movement. In your conclusion, be sure to state your own views.

▸ Create your own chart or Venn diagram comparing the Populists and Progressives.

The Early Progressives

Progressivism was a diverse movement, operating at many levels of society and government. **Nongovernmental organizations**—such as churches, settlement houses, and newspaper organizations—often played as important a role in the Progressive Movement as governments.

The Muckrakers

The first influential Progressives were journalists, writers and social scientists who exposed the abuses and corruption of industrial society. These writers became known as "**muckrakers**" because they "raked" through the **muck** (*moist dirt or filth*) of American life, exposing some of the most ugly problems of the new industrial society.

The muckrakers wrote for magazines like *McClure's* and *American Magazine*. These magazines put money and research assistance at the disposal of muck-raking journalists, enabling them to uncover the "inside story." The muckrakers examined the rise of industry and the abuses and corruption that had led to the accumulation of large fortunes. They also examined business

practices affecting consumers, and the lives of the very poor and wretched, eliciting sympathy in their readers. They wrote in a graphic style that appealed to a wide readership. The muckrakers exposed many evils and stimulated a public outcry for reform. In so doing, they set a model for investigative journalism that is still at work today. Newspaper, magazine, television, and online journalists now act as watchdogs over government. They expose problems, inform the public, and stimulate debate.

"Muckrakers" of the Progressive Era

Writer	Book	What it Did
Jacob Riis	How the Other Half Lives	Examined the conditions of the urban poor.
Ida Tarbell	History of the Standard Oil Company	Tarbell's investigative journalism revealed how Rockefeller's success was largely based on ruthless business practices.
Lincoln Steffens	The Shame of the Cities	Looked at corruption in city governments.
Ray Stannard Baker	Following the Color Line	Reported on the conditions of African Americans in both the South and North.
Frank Norris	The Octopus	A popular novel that depicted the stranglehold of railroads over California farmers.
Upton Sinclair	The Jungle	A novel about poverty-stricken immigrants in Chicago. It included a description of the harmful practices in the meatpacking industry, such as putting dead rats and rat poison in sausage meat.

Ida Tarbell studied public documents from court cases and interviewed many of Rockefeller's associates to piece together an accurate history of John D. Rockefeller and his company. She then published a series of 19 articles in *McClure's Magazine*, which were eagerly read by a large audience. These articles later became the basis for her book, *History of the Standard Oil Company*.

> "The strides the firm of Rockefeller and Andrews made . . . were attributed for three or four years mainly to his extraordinary capacity for bargaining and borrowing. Then its chief competitors began to suspect something. John Rockefeller might get his oil cheaper now and then, they said, but he could not do it often. He might make close contracts for which they had neither the patience nor the stomach. He might have an unusual mechanical and practical genius in his partner. But these things could not explain all. They believed they bought, on the whole, almost as cheaply as he, and they knew they made as good oil and with as great, or nearly as great, economy. He could sell at no better price than they. Where was his advantage? There was but one place where it could be, and that was in transportation. He must be getting better rates from the railroads than they were.
>
> —Ida Tarbell (1904)

The Historian's Apprentice

- What made the publication of Tarbell's *History of Standard Oil* so important?
- According to Tarbell, what was one of the most important advantages that Rockefeller had?
- Tarbell's father was a small oil producer whose business was ruined by Rockefeller. How might this have shaped her views?
- Use the Internet or your school library to examine the writings of at least one other muckraker listed in the table above. Write a paragraph describing your reactions.

The Social Reformers

Some Progressives were so outraged at the injustices of industrial society that they made their own individual efforts at social reform. **Jane Addams** ran a "settlement house" in Chicago known as Hull House. **Settlement houses** were usually situated in "slum" neighborhoods and provided services to immigrants and the urban poor, such as classes, English lessons, childcare, nursing of the sick, and help in obtaining naturalization. Some settlement houses had dining halls, gymnasiums, auditoriums, nurseries and classrooms. The middle-class, educated women who ran these settlement houses often lived in them alongside the immigrant poor who used them. They also went out into the community and campaigned for better trash collection and sewers, hospitals, and other public services. At one time there were more than 400 settlement houses operating in the United States.

Other Progressives formed associations to promote social change and professional responsibility. Progressives organized charities, clubs, and other associations. The American Bar Association, the National Woman Suffrage Association, the **NAACP** (National Association for the Advancement of Colored People), and the **Anti-Defamation League** (which opposed anti-Semitism and religious prejudice generally) were all founded or active during the Progressive period.

Municipal Reform
Progressives "clean up" city government

In the last chapter you learned how cities had mushroomed so fast in the late 19th century that they were incapable of dealing with many of their problems. "**Municipal**" refers to the town or city level of government. Municipal government in many large cities had come to be dominated by a political machine, like Tammany Hall in New York City. The machine, in turn, used its control over city government to make a fortune out of lucrative public contracts. To work for the city, each contractor had to promise to pay a share of his receipts secretly to the machine. This graft made city government overly expensive and inefficient. Progressives mobilized the votes of citizens who were tired of corruption. They exposed corruption through the efforts of muckrakers in newspapers, magazines, and books like Lincoln Steffens' *The Shame of the Cities*. Progressive reformers replaced the rule of "bosses" and political machines with public-minded Progressive mayors. Progressive reformers expanded city services to take care of urban overcrowding, fire hazards, inadequate sanitation, and the lack of public services. In some cases, cities acquired direct control of utilities like water, electricity, and gas.

In many cities, Progressives actually introduced new forms of city government to discourage corruption, such as the use of a **city commission** or a **city manager**. In government by commission, the city was governed by a panel of experts, each of whom directed a department delivering an essential city service. In government by city manager, an elected board of citizens appointed a specially-trained "manager" to run the city government more efficiently. The city manager had to answer to the board and therefore was far weaker than a traditional mayor. In this way, the Progressives hoped to make city government more democratic and transparent, and less open to corruption.

The Reforms by State Governments

Progressives also elected state legislators and officials to promote reform at the state level. Progressives were found in both parties—Democratic and Republican. The leading Progressive Governor was **Robert La Follette**, Governor of Wisconsin from 1900 to 1906. He broke the power of local political bosses and the influence of the railroads over the state legislature. La Follette began taxing railroads at the same rate as other property, and he set up a special commission to regulate railroad rates. He started other regulatory commissions to regulate public utilities and acted to conserve Wisconsin's forests and waters against industrial exploitation and pollution. To carry out his policies, he relied heavily on advice from professors at the University of Wisconsin, reflecting the Progressives' faith in solving problems more scientifically.

Other important Progressive Governors were Theodore Roosevelt and Charles Evans Hughes in New York, Hiram Johnson in California, and Woodrow Wilson in New Jersey. These states acted as laboratories for political and social reforms. Many of the measures they took were later adopted at the federal level.

Political Reforms

Progressives took special steps to free state government from corruption and the influence of "Big Business." Innovative reforms, some borrowed from the Populists, were designed to make government more responsive to the people:

- **Secret Ballot**—Voters marked their ballots in private instead of voting openly, making them less subject to pressure and intimidation.

- **Initiative**—Voters could directly introduce bills into the state legislature.

- **Referendum**—Voters could repeal a law already passed by the legislature through a special election known as a "referendum."

- **Recall**—Elected officials could be "recalled" (*dismissed from office*) by voters in a special election.

- **Direct Primary**—Party members voted in a special election to indicate their preferences for their party's nominees. Up until this time, party leaders generally chose their party's candidates.

- **Direct Election of Senators**—The Constitution originally gave state legislatures the power to select U.S. Senators. The **17th Amendment** (1913) changed the Constitution itself, giving voters the power to directly elect their Senators.

- **Women's Suffrage**—"Suffrage" refers to the right to vote in elections. The **National Woman Suffrage Association** was founded in 1869. It

Marchers supporting women's suffrage parade down Fifth Avenue in New York City.

represented millions of women and was active during the Progressive Era in the struggle to achieve voting rights for women. Under the U.S. Constitution, individual states actually control the requirements for voting, even in federal elections. During the Progressive Era, many states, especially in the West, gave the vote to women.

Social and Economic Reforms

States also enacted new laws to deal with some of the worst social and economic effects of industrialism. These included laws regulating conditions in urban housing; laws against the employment of young children; laws regulating safety and health conditions in factories; laws limiting the number of hours that women could work; laws forcing employers to give compensation to workers injured on the job ("workmen's compensation"); laws regulating railroads and public utilities; laws conserving natural resources and wildlife preserves; and laws prohibiting the sale of alcohol (the Temperance Movement).

For example, in 1911, a fire at the **Triangle Shirtwaist Factory** in New York City led to the deaths of 146 female workers because its doors were bolted and there were no adequate fire escapes. Striking workers had previously protested against these conditions but the owners had refused to make any changes. The fire led to widespread public sympathy for the garment workers and the passage of new state laws providing fire safety codes for factories.

The actions of state reformers, however, were severely limited by the U.S. Supreme Court. In *Lochner v. New York* (1905), the Court held that a New York State law limiting the working hours of bakers to 60 hours a week was unconstitutional. The Court believed that New York's regulation of hours took away the freedom of employers and employees to negotiate their own contracts and working conditions. On the other hand, in *Muller v. Oregon* (1908), the Supreme Court upheld an Oregon law limiting the working hours of women, on the grounds that special circumstances justified state intervention. The Court feared that long hours of hard labor were endangering women's health.

The Historian's Apprentice

- Which of the political reforms introduced by Progressives at the state level (such as initiative, referendum, recall, direct primaries) would you consider as most important? Explain your answer.
- Imagine you are a muckraker in 1900. Write a short article exposing one injustice in society that you would like to remedy.
- Use the Internet or your school library to conduct research on Progressive Era reforms in one state. Then prepare a written or oral report to share your findings.
- Imagine you were an attorney arguing before the Supreme Court in *Lochner v. New York*. Write an opening statement explaining why a state government should, or should not, be able to limit the hours of private workers.

Four Women Reformers

In the late 19th century and early 20th centuries, women faced many obstacles to participation in public life. Most could not vote, few attended college, and they could not enter most professions. Women were still considered intellectually inferior to men. Despite these obstacles, some women managed to become active reformers. Four of the most important were Susan B. Anthony, Florence Kelley, Carrie Chapman Catt, and Alice Paul.

Susan B. Anthony (1820–1906) grew up in a Quaker family in Massachusetts. She began her reform activities in support of the Temperance Movement and as an abolitionist. After the Civil War, Anthony believed the time had come for women to have the right to vote. She started publishing *The Revolution*, a weekly journal for women's rights, and co-founded the National Woman Suffrage Association (NWSA). Anthony voted in the Presidential election of 1872 on the basis of the 14th Amendment, but the court ruled that these rights of citizenship did not extend to women. For the next 28 years, she was a tireless fighter for women's rights. Although she did not live to see passage of a constitutional amendment for women's suffrage, she predicted it would soon come.

Florence Kelley (1859–1932) was a prominent social reformer. She studied at Cornell University and in Switzerland. From 1891 to 1899, she lived in Hull House in Chicago. Kelley fought to establish a minimum wage and the 8-hour day, and against child labor and conditions in sweatshops. In 1893, the Governor of Illinois, a Progressive, made Kelley the state's chief factory inspector. Kelley worked on the brief that persuaded the Supreme Court to limit women's workday hours in *Muller v. Oregon*. In 1909, she became one of the founders of the NAACP.

Carrie Chapman Catt (1859–1947) became active in Iowa's suffrage movement and developed a close friendship with Susan B. Anthony. Catt succeeded Anthony as President of the National American Woman Suffrage Association (NAWSA) in 1900. In 1920, Catt founded the League of Women Voters. Catt also fought for women's rights overseas and for international peace. In 1933, she was one of the first to protest against the persecution of Jews in Nazi Germany (see Chapter 12, pages 253, 265–266).

Alice Paul (1885–1977) was the daughter of wealthy Quakers. She attended Swarthmore College and later obtained both a Ph.D. and a law degree. She visited England, where she became active in the suffrage movement. Paul brought back knowledge of their more militant tactics when she returned to America. Paul organized a march in Washington, D.C. on behalf of women's suffrage in 1913, the day before President Woodrow Wilson's inauguration. In 1916, Paul left the NAWSA to form her own more militant group. They picketed the White House and were arrested in 1917. Alice Paul went on a hunger strike in prison and had to be force-fed. Her tactics helped persuade President Wilson that the time had come for an amendment giving women the right to vote. In 1923, Alice Paul then proposed the "Equal Rights Amendment" (see Chapter 15, page 355).

The Historian's Apprentice

▸ Your teacher should select four students to represent these four reformers. Then hold a press conference with the four reformers at the front of the room. The rest of the class should act as reporters asking questions.
▸ What role did family and educational background play in the work of these reformers?
▸ Make a chart comparing the backgrounds, views and accomplishments of these four reformers.

The Progressive Presidents

The Progressive Movement spread from municipal and state governments to the federal government itself. From 1901 to 1919, a remarkable trio of Progressive Presidents sat in the White House: Theodore Roosevelt, William Howard Taft, and Woodrow Wilson.

Theodore Roosevelt and the "Square Deal," 1901–1909

The Character of the President

Theodore Roosevelt came from a wealthy New York family. Sickly as a child, he built up his strength through rigorous exercise and sports such as boxing and big game hunting. For a brief time, Roosevelt tried his hand at ranching in the Dakotas. Afterwards, he was Civil Service Commissioner, Police Commissioner of New York City, and Assistant Secretary of the Navy. During the Spanish-American War, Roosevelt resigned his post in Washington to form a voluntary cavalry regiment known as the "Rough Riders," which he led on a famous charge up San Juan Hill in Cuba. Roosevelt became so popular from his war exploits that Republican Party bosses chose him to become Governor of New York in 1899. When they were unable to block his efforts to uncover corruption in state government, party bosses tried to remove him from New York by making him Republican candidate for Vice President (in those days, a less active office than today). Then in 1901, President McKinley was assassinated. Roosevelt, only 42 years old, suddenly became the youngest person ever to be raised to the Presidency.

Roosevelt's Conception of the Presidency

In the late 19th century, American Presidents had left the conduct of public affairs mainly to Congress. Roosevelt reversed this trend. He saw the President as the one individual who represented all Americans, and therefore he believed that the President should act vigorously in the public interest. His personal popularity encouraged him to expand the powers of the Presidency. According to Roosevelt's "stewardship" theory, the President acted as the "steward" (or *manager*) of the people's interests. Above all, Roosevelt believed in taking action. He promised Americans a "**Square Deal**," by which he meant fair play and equality of opportunity—especially conservation of natural resources, control of corporations and the protection of consumers.

Roosevelt and the Coal Strike of 1902

Roosevelt's views on the Presidency were quickly put to the test when coal miners went on strike in 1902 and the nation was threatened with a winter without coal. Roosevelt acted quickly to protect the public interest. He brought the representatives from the unions and the mine owners to the White House. When the mine owners refused to negotiate, Roosevelt threatened to seize their mines and operate them with the army. This finally convinced the mine owners to submit to arbitration. Roosevelt formed a special commission to resolve the dispute. The final outcome was a compromise: the coal miners wanted a 20% pay raise and got 10%; they also wanted an eight-hour workday and were given a nine-hour one. The main victory went to Roosevelt, who showed that he meant to protect the public interest.

Roosevelt as "Trust-Buster"

Roosevelt revived the use of the Sherman Antitrust Act against large business consolidations. He did not attack all monopolies or trusts (see the top of page 93 for an explanation of trusts, a form of business organization). What Roosevelt stood for was "fair play." He therefore distinguished between "good trusts" and "bad trusts." Bad trusts were those business combinations that acted against the public interest.

In 1902, Roosevelt filed an antitrust lawsuit against Northern Securities Company, a holding company controlled by the financier J. P. Morgan. It was the first time the government had challenged a major industrialist. Thus, Roosevelt reassured the public that even Big Business was subject to the law. In a later antitrust suit, Roosevelt challenged Rockefeller's Standard Oil Company, which controlled 90% of all oil refining in the country. After Roosevelt left office, the Supreme Court affirmed the decision to break up Standard Oil. The Supreme Court even borrowed Roosevelt's distinction between good and bad trusts by applying the Sherman Antitrust Act to "unreasonable" trusts—those trusts that harmed the public interest by such unfair business practices as price-fixing or "cutthroat" competition.

Roosevelt did not actually break up many trusts, and in fact more new trusts were formed during his Presidency. But he established the principle that the federal government could break up harmful trusts, thereby earning his reputation as "trust buster." Under Roosevelt, the federal government had shifted away from unquestioned support of Big Business and towards consumers.

Government Regulation of Meat, Food and Drugs

As part of his "Square Deal," Roosevelt launched new laws to protect consumers. Roosevelt had been shocked by Upton Sinclair's account of the meat-packing industry in *The Jungle*. Roosevelt pushed the **Meat Inspection Act** through Congress in 1906, establishing government inspection of meat shipped between states. The **Pure Food and Drug Act**, also passed in 1906, prohibited the adulteration of foods or the use of poisons as preservatives. Medicine containers were required to bear labels indicating their contents.

Meat inspectors

President Roosevelt with John Muir above Yosemite Valley

Regulation of Railways

Under Roosevelt, Congress passed new laws strengthening the Interstate Commerce Act. In 1906, a new law permitted the Interstate Commerce Commission to set its own "just and reasonable" rates for railroads. Shortly after Roosevelt left office, the **government regulation** of communications (telephone and telegraph) was also placed under the Interstate Commerce Commission.

Conservation of Natural Resources

Roosevelt was a great outdoorsman. As President, he drew the nation's attention to the need to conserve forests, wildlife, and natural resources. The Newlands Reclamation Act of 1902 provided funds for irrigation projects and dams to reclaim wastelands. Roosevelt also appointed noted conservationists, such as **Gifford Pinchot**, who became head of the national forestry service. In 1903, Roosevelt spent three days camping in Yosemite with naturalist John Muir. Before his Presidency, the federal government had been selling off public lands for development. Roosevelt withdrew 1.5 million acres from public sale. He created five new national parks—doubling their number. Roosevelt was unable to obtain the approval of Congress to create national parks for the Devils Tower in Wyoming and the Petrified Forest and Grand Canyon in Arizona. So he protected these natural landmarks by using his power as President instead to designate them as "national monuments," under a new law passed in 1906. Roosevelt also called together the White House Conservation Commission in 1908, which led to the formation of the **National Conservation Commission**. It prepared a detailed report of American natural resources.

The Presidency of William Howard Taft, 1909–1913

Although still young, Roosevelt left office in 1909 because of a public pledge not to run for a third term. In his place, he promoted a conservative Progressive, his close friend William Taft. Taft was elected on the basis of Roosevelt's popularity. Once in office, Taft continued many of Roosevelt's policies, such as trust-busting and civil service reform. Taft opposed restrictions on immigration, and he met with Booker T. Washington and other African-American leaders. He pre-

vented railroad companies from raising their rates unreasonably and pushed a workman's compensation bill for railroad employees through Congress. He proposed the first corporate income taxes as well as the **16th Amendment**, which permits the federal government to collect income taxes on individuals.

However, Taft was a clumsy politician who alienated many Progressive Republicans. He often went forward with his own ideas without bothering with delicate political negotiations or considering the views of other members of his party. For example, he promised a lower tariff but did not get the promised reductions through Congress. He returned to public sale some of the wildlife areas that Roosevelt had withdrawn, and he dismissed Gifford Pinchot.

The Election of 1912 and the "Bull Moose" Party

Roosevelt became unhappy with Taft's policies and decided to challenge him for the Republican nomination in 1912. Although Roosevelt enjoyed greater popular support, Taft controlled the Republican Convention and won the nomination. Roosevelt then decided to accept the nomination of a new third party, the "Progressive Party," formed by Progressive Republicans in 1911. After Roosevelt accepted its nomination, the party became popularly known as the "Bull Moose" Party, since Roosevelt had announced he felt as strong as a bull moose. Roosevelt actively campaigned for further Progressive reforms, including the direct election of U.S. Senators; adoption of the initiative, referendum, and recall in all states; women's suffrage; and an eight-hour work day.

The division of the Republican Party between Taft and Roosevelt helped the Democrats to capture the White House. The Democrats had also nominated a Progressive candidate: Woodrow Wilson. The 1912 election thus marked the high water mark of Progressivism. All four candidates—Wilson, Roosevelt, Taft and the Socialist candidate, Eugene Debs—shared Progressive beliefs of varying degrees.

Woodrow Wilson and the "New Freedom," 1913–1920

Born in Virginia, Woodrow Wilson was the son of a Presbyterian Minister and the first Southerner in the White House since Andrew Johnson. Wilson had been a college professor, President of Princeton University, and Governor of New Jersey before his election as President.

Where Roosevelt had been emotional and enthusiastic, Wilson was cool and logical. Wilson was an excellent public speaker and revived the practice of personally delivering the annual "State of the Union" address to Congress. He frequently made appeals directly to the public to build support for his programs. Wilson received African-American support in the election of 1912, but as a Southerner he practiced racial discrimination. He encouraged racial segregation in many government departments and made it harder for African Americans to enter government service.

In the campaign of 1912, Wilson had promised Americans a "**New Freedom**." Like other Progressives, Wilson wanted to tame Big Business by opening the way for greater competition. He planned to do this by attacking what he called the "triple wall of privilege"—the tariff, the banking system, and the trusts. Roosevelt had drawn public attention to the power of the Presidency by introducing government regulation to protect consumers from the worst abuses of industrial society; Wilson went even further by passing a whole series of major legislative reforms, reshaping American society in ways that still affect us today.

The Underwood Tariff of 1913

Since the Civil War, high tariffs had protected American manufacturers. Even though many American manufacturers were already extremely wealthy, tariffs let them keep their prices artificially high by keeping out cheaper foreign goods. Wilson believed that high tariffs only benefitted rich monopolists at the expense of the average American, so he lowered tariff duties by 25%.

> A **graduated income tax** is a direct tax on incomes in which wealthier people are taxed at higher rates than others—that is, rich people pay a higher percentage of their income in tax than poorer people do. Progressives believed it was fair to tax people on the basis of their ability to pay.

The Graduated Income Tax

At the same time that Wilson reduced tariff duties, he introduced the graduated income tax.

Wilson was able to introduce federal income tax because Taft had pushed through the 16th Amendment. Ratified in 1913, it gave Congress the power to tax personal incomes directly. Today, the income tax is the chief source of revenue for the federal government.

The Federal Reserve Act

This important act, passed in 1913, solved many of the nation's longstanding banking problems. The act created a more elastic currency that could expand or contract according to the nation's needs. The new system was a compromise between private and government control of the nation's banking system.

The act created the **Federal Reserve System** (or the "Fed"). The Federal Reserve System regulates banks and serves as a "bank to the banks." It also sets U.S. monetary policy.

The Federal Reserve is able to expand or contract (*reduce*) the money supply in three ways:

1. The Federal Reserve sets a "**reserve requirement**" for all banks. Banks are required to hold a certain percentage of their deposits on reserve with their regional Federal Reserve Bank. They can then lend the rest of their deposits to borrowers. If a bank has $1,000 on deposit and the reserve requirement is 10%, the bank can lend out $900, but it must keep $100 on reserve. A higher reserve requirement means that banks can lend out less money. This reduces the amount of money in circulation. A lower reserve requirement means they can lend out more and expands the money supply.

2. The Federal Reserve sets the **interest rate** (or "discount rate") that it charges to other banks to lend them money. A higher interest rate means these banks charge higher interest to their own customers. People are able to borrow less, reducing the amount of money in circulation. A lower interest rate makes it easier to borrow and increases money supply.

3. The Federal Reserve buys and sells U.S. government securities (bonds and bills) in its "open market operations." When it sells government bonds to banks and businesses, it removes money from circulation. This reduces the money supply. When it buys government securities, it returns money into the economy and increases money supply.

> **Monetary policy** determines the amount of money (known as "money supply") circulating in an economy. Monetary policy generally aims at promoting economic growth while controlling inflation.

Chapter 7 | The Progressive Era

The Clayton Antitrust Act

In 1914, Wilson strengthened the Sherman Antitrust Act by proposing the **Clayton Antitrust Act** and the **Federal Trade Commission Act**. The Clayton Antitrust Act prohibited certain unfair business practices. It also stated that the antitrust laws could not be used against labor unions or farmers cooperatives. Courts could only issue orders (injunctions) against strikes where permanent damage to property was threatened. The Federal Trade Commission Act established the **Federal Trade Commission**—a regulatory agency with powers to investigate corporate activities and to issue orders forcing a corporation to discontinue a business practice until its fairness was decided in court. The Federal Trade Commission was created to put "teeth" into antitrust legislation.

Later Reforms

In 1916, Wilson sponsored a final series of reforms, including federal aid to vocational education, limiting the workday of railroad workers to 8 hours, and a national law against the sale of goods produced by **child labor**. By then his attention was mainly focused on foreign affairs, since war had broken out in Europe in 1914. The Supreme Court later held that Wilson's prohibition of child labor was unconstitutional.

The Historian's Apprentice

▶ Make a Venn diagram comparing the policies of Theodore Roosevelt and Woodrow Wilson as Presidents.

▶ Imagine you are a citizen living in Florida in November 1912. Decide which candidate you would vote for in the Presidential election: Taft, Roosevelt, Wilson or Debs? Then write a letter to a friend explaining your choice.

▶ Hold a class debate on this proposition:

Resolved: Woodrow Wilson achieved more for the Progressive Movement than Theodore Roosevelt did.

▶ In what way did the Progressives offer an alternative to socialism, anarchism or Communism?

▶ Look at a recent newspaper for articles about the Federal Reserve. Then read and summarize one article. Which of the powers of the Federal Reserve does the article discuss?

The Progressive Era Reaches an End

In 1917, Americans entered a world war with a reforming impulse. Many saw the war as a crusade "to make the world safe for democracy." After the war, many Americans became disillusioned. By then, the Progressive Movement had lost much of its appeal. Nevertheless, both women's suffrage and Prohibition were passed at the very end of the war—as the final reforms of the Progressive Era. A few historians even claim that Progressivism actually continued throughout the 1920s, although most would disagree. You will learn more about these events later in this book.

Focus on Florida

The Progressive Movement that swept through the entire country affected Florida as well. **William Sherman Jennings**, Governor of Florida from 1901 to 1905, struck one of the first blows against Big Business by reclaiming land from the railroad barons to whom Florida had generously given vast expanses of land in the late 19th century. Jennings greatly increased the power of the Florida Railroad Commission in regulating the practices of the state's railroads. His wife, **May Mann Jennings**, (1872–1963) was a pivotal figure in promoting reforms. She championed women's suffrage, child labor laws, public education, and better treatment of the Seminole Indians. Her early efforts in nature conservation later led to the creation of the **Everglades National Park** in 1947.

Another prominent reformer in Florida during the Progressive Era was **Napoleon Bonaparte Broward**, Governor from 1905 to 1909. Broward stood up for farmers and small businesses. Although he had parts of the Everglades drained to create land for agriculture, he generally advocated conservation of forests, fish, and game. He spoke against the exploitation of child labor. Broward built roads to improve trade for farmers and supported social welfare programs, prison reform, and public education. In fact, many historians refer to the Progressive Era in Florida as the "Broward Era." Little was done during the Progressive Era, however, to improve conditions for the state's minority populations. Indeed, African Americans continued to suffer from racism and segregation.

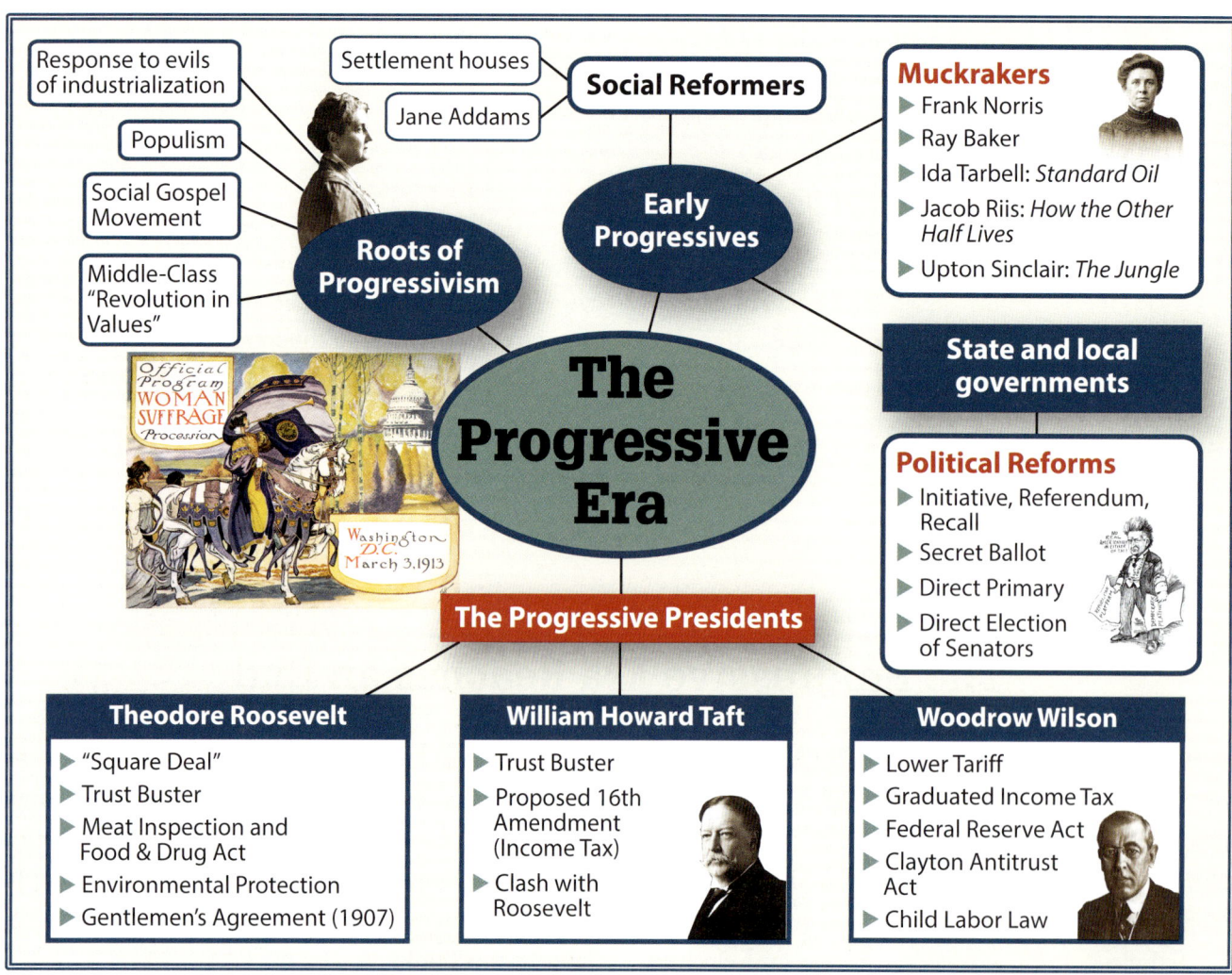

Chapter 7 | The Progressive Era

Review Cards

The Progressive Movement

- **Progressivism** flourished from 1890 until the outbreak of World War I.
- The aim of Progressivism was to remedy the political and economic injustices that had resulted from America's rapid industrialization.
- Progressives believed in using government power to reform and to correct these abuses.

Roots of Progressivism

1. Many new problems created by industrial society needed to be addressed:
   - Brutal working conditions
   - Urban overcrowding
   - Child labor
   - Political corruption
   - Environmental exploitation
   - Extreme inequalities of wealth
   - Defective, substandard consumer products.
2. The Reform Tradition: Reform has been a continuing process in American history, based on the belief that society can be made better.
3. The legacy of the Populists: Progressives adopted many of their ideas.
4. The influence of the middle class:
   - Progressivism was middle class, urban, and nationwide in contrast to Populism, which was rural and had its main support in the South and West.
   - Progressive leaders were generally members of the professional classes: professors, lawyers, doctors, religious ministers, and writers. They were supported by the lower middle-classes: technicians, clerical workers, small business owners, and service personnel.
   - The middle classes saw Progressive reform as preferable to socialism, Communism or anarchy.
5. The **"Social Gospel"** movement: Progressives often acted out of a sense of moral responsibility based on religion. Protestant ministers of the Social Gospel movement inspired the Progressives.
6. New forms of journalism: The **"Muckrakers"** gave widespread exposure to the abuses of industrial society and stimulated the desire for reform.
7. Rising consumer consciousness: Progressives believed that government intervention was needed to control the market and ensure that mass-produced goods were safe.
8. Progressives favored women's suffrage, social reform, and better regulation of Big Business. Women reformers and organized labor supported the Progressives.

The Early Progressives

- **Muckrakers** published articles in magazines and newspapers exposing abuses and corruption and stimulating a public outcry for reform. For example, **Ida Tarbell** exposed the unfair business practices of Rockefeller in her *History of the Standard Oil Company*. Upton Sinclair exposed the unhealthy practices of the meat-packing industry in *The Jungle*.
- **Social reformers** like **Jane Addams** established **"settlement houses"** for the poor; others formed associations and clubs to promote social change, such as the National Woman Suffrage Association, the NAACP and the Anti-Defamation League.
- **Municipal reformers** cleaned up city government by eliminating political machines and introducing new forms of municipal government such as by a commission or a professional **city manager.**

Progressive Reforms in State Government

Progressives elected state governors and legislators to promote reforms. One example was Governor **Napoleon Broward** of Florida.

Progressive Political Reforms

- **Initiative**: voters could directly introduce bills into the state legislature.
- **Referendum**: voters could repeal a law passed by the legislature.
- **Recall**: voters could dismiss elected officials in a special election.
- **Secret ballot**
- **Direct primary**: party members voted on candidates to represent their party in running for office.
- Direct election of U.S. Senators: **17th Amendment**
- **Women's suffrage**: many individual states gave women the right to vote.

Progressive Social and Economic Reforms

Many state governments also passed the following:

- Laws regulating conditions in urban housing
- Child labor laws
- Laws regulating safety and health in factories
- Workers' compensation for work-related injuries
- Laws limiting the number of hours that women could work in factories
- Laws conserving natural resources and wild life
- Laws prohibiting the sale of alcohol (Temperance Movement)

The Progressive Presidents

Theodore Roosevelt (1901–1909)

- Believed that the President was the steward of the people's interests.
- Greatly expanded the powers of the Presidency.
- His efforts were meant to give Americans a **"Square Deal,"** especially in natural resource conservation, control of corporations and protection of the consumers:
  - **Meat Inspection Act** and **Pure Food and Drug Act**
  - **Trust buster:** "good" vs. "bad" trusts
  - **1902 Coal Strike:** intervened to settle the dispute and get coal to consumers.
  - **Conservation:** appointed **Gifford Pinchot;** created new national parks and monuments; formed the National Conservation Commission.

William Howard Taft (1909–1913)

- Continued many of Roosevelt's policies, but was a clumsy politician and later came into conflict with Roosevelt.
- Introduced **16th Amendment,** making a federal tax on individual incomes possible.
- **Election of 1912:** Republicans divided between Taft and Roosevelt's new Progressive Party—gave Democrats the election.

Woodrow Wilson (1913–1921)

- His "New Freedom" attacked the "triple wall of privilege": banks, tariffs and trusts.
- Lowered tariffs, introduced the **graduated income tax,** created the **Federal Reserve System** (1913), and strengthened antitrust legislation with the **Clayton Antitrust Act.**
- Passed a federal law prohibiting **child labor** in 1916, which the Supreme Court declared unconstitutional.
- Progressive Era came to an end with World War I.

What Do You Know?

SS.912.A.3.12

1. The information below identifies examples of the work of the muckrakers.

   - Upton Sinclair exposed the unhealthy practices of Chicago's meat-packing plants.
   - Ida Tarbell revealed the dishonest business tactics of Rockefeller's Standard Oil Company.
   - Jacob Riis wrote *How the Other Half Lives*, showing the conditions of the residents of New York City tenements.

   What was the impact of these muckraking activities during the early 1900s?

   A. Society changed in response to their promotion of Social Darwinism.

   B. Voters agreed to let the owners of Big Business create more profitable monopolies.

   C. Reports of these works in publications abroad led to a sudden decrease in immigration.

   D. Public reaction to their books led to new laws addressing the abuses of industrialization.

SS.912.A.3.8

2. This photograph was taken by Lewis Hines in 1907 for *The Survey*, a magazine promoting social reform.

   > My name is Luther Watson. I am 14 years old. My right arm was cut off by a veneering saw. I was using a board to [press on] the belt operating the saw. I lost my job in the factory because of the accident.

   Which laws addressed concerns raised by the case of Luther Watson?

   A. Sherman Antitrust Act and Clayton Antitrust Act

   B. Meat Inspection Act and Pure Food and Drug Act

   C. workers' compensation act and child labor laws

   D. graduated income tax and Federal Reserve Act

SS.912.A.3.12

3. In 1913, President Wilson proposed a reduction in tariffs. How did Wilson plan to make up for the loss of these revenues by the federal government?

   A. reducing federal expenditures

   B. introducing a new federal income tax

   C. requiring contributions by state governments

   D. having government ownership of some industries, such as electricity

Chapter 7 | The Progressive Era

SS.912.A.3.12

4. Which reformer is correctly paired with her accomplishments?

A.	Florence Kelley	→ fought for better conditions for workers and helped found the NAACP
B.	Carrie Chapman Catt	→ wrote a book criticizing the Standard Oil Company in 1904, which led to its breakup
C.	Ida Tarbell	→ organized a march for women's suffrage in 1913 and wrote the Equal Rights Amendment
D.	Alice Paul	→ became a close friend of Susan B. Anthony and succeeded her as President of the National American Woman Suffrage Association

SS.912.A.3.12

5. The information on the left identifies some of the key reforms of the Progressive Era. Which characteristic was shared by all five reforms?

- Initiative
- Referendum
- Recall
- Direct Primary
- 17th Amendment

A. They were reforms of state government.

B. They gave citizens a greater voice in government.

C. They were directly aimed at reducing corruption in state government.

D. They successfully brought economic relief to the urban working classes.

SS.912.A.3.12

6. The information below describes the position of a city manager.

> In the city-manager form of municipal government, an elected city council hires a city manager. The city manager is an expert in public administration who runs city services.

What was a DISADVANTAGE of this new form of city government?

A. City government became more efficient than before.

B. The city manager was not directly responsible to the electorate.

C. Experts with special training in public administration ran the city.

D. The influence of political machines on city government was reduced.

SS.912.A.3.12

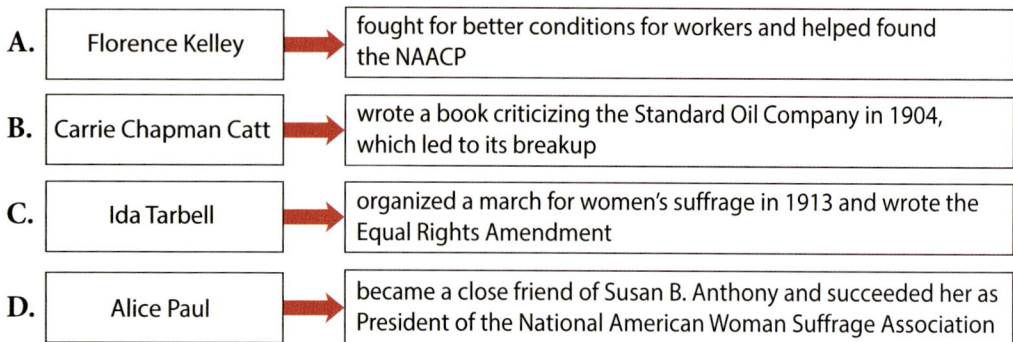

7. The newspaper headline on the left describes a significant event in domestic affairs. Which set of Progressive reforms is illustrated by this article?

A. state and federal regulation of the food and drug industry

B. the breakup of "bad" trusts engaged in unfair business practices

C. government support for large businesses in order to encourage industry

D. the introduction of measures of direct democracy at the local and state level

Chapter 7 | The Progressive Era

SS.912.A.3.12

8. The cartoon below, "The Bosses of the Senate," was published in 1889.

Source: U.S. Senate

What is the viewpoint of the artist?

A. Trusts mainly compete against one another for profits.

B. Trusts have been subjected to unfair regulation by Congress.

C. Trusts have too much influence over the United States Senate.

D. Trusts play an essential role in promoting American economic growth.

SS.912.A.3.12

9. The timeline below displays the sequence of some events during the Progressive Era:

1890: Sherman Antitrust Act		1906: Antitrust lawsuit filed against Standard Oil Company		1911: Supreme Court affirms break up of Standard Oil Company
1890	**1900**	**1905**	**1910**	**1915**
	1902: Antitrust lawsuit filed against Northern Securities Company	1904: Supreme Court affirms break up of Northern Securities Company		1913: Clayton Antitrust Act

What was the primary goal of the government in these actions?

A. to break up all trusts since every trust tries to prevent competition

B. to break up trusts that adopt unfair or dishonest business practices

C. to increase the role of government in guaranteeing full employment

D. to make examples discouraging business owners from establishing new trusts

SS.912.A.3.12

10. This cartoon was published in the *New York-American Journal* in 1902. Which legislation was directed at remedying the evils depicted in the cartoon?

A. Prohibition

B. child labor laws

C. Meat Inspection Act

D. workers' compensation laws

Chapter 7 | The Progressive Era   139

SS.912.A.3.12

11. The excerpt below was published in 1904 by Ida B. Tarbell in her book *The History of the Standard Oil Company*.

> So long as Standard Oil Company can control transportation as it does today, it will remain master of the oil industry, and the people of the United States will pay for their indifference and folly in regard to transportation a good sound tax on oil, and they will yearly see an increasing concentration of natural resources and transportation systems in the Standard Oil crowd.

Which action took place in response to these criticisms?

   A. The federal government purchased its own oil wells and refineries.

   B. President Roosevelt filed a lawsuit to break up the Standard Oil Company.

   C. The powers of the Interstate Commerce Act were extended to set railroad rates.

   D. John D. Rockefeller sold all his shares in the Standard Oil Company to the public.

SS.912.A.3.8

12. In 1902, Lincoln Steffens and Claude Wetmore published the article below about St. Louis in *McClure's* magazine.

> About 1890, public franchises and privileges were sought, not only for legitimate profit and common convenience but for loot. Taking but slight and always selfish interest in the public councils, the big men misused politics. The riff-raff, catching the smell of corruption, rushed into the Municipal Assembly, drove out the respectable men, and sold the city—its streets, its wharves, its markets, and all that it had—to the now greedy businessmen and bribers.

Which type of activity does this article illustrate?

   A. reporting by muckrakers

   B. Social Gospel movement

   C. government by city-manager

   D. operation of settlement houses

SS.912.A.3.12

13. What was the purpose of the Federal Reserve System?

   A. to regulate banks and create a more elastic currency

   B. to keep better track of government income and expenditure

   C. to meet the demands of Populists and Progressives for bimetallism

   D. to reassure bondholders that America would remain on the gold standard

Unit II: The Transformation of American Society (Chapters 4–7)

Identify or define each of the following terms.

Second Industrial Revolution _____

_____

Corporation_____

_____

Andrew Carnegie _____

_____

Labor union_____

_____

Haymarket Riot_____

_____

Political machine_____

_____

Communism _____

_____

Nativism _____

_____

Chinese Exclusion Act_____

_____

Populist Party _____

_____

Progressives_____

_____

Muckrackers _____

_____

Referendum_____

_____

Theodore Roosevelt_____

_____

Woodrow Wilson _____

_____

Crossword Puzzle

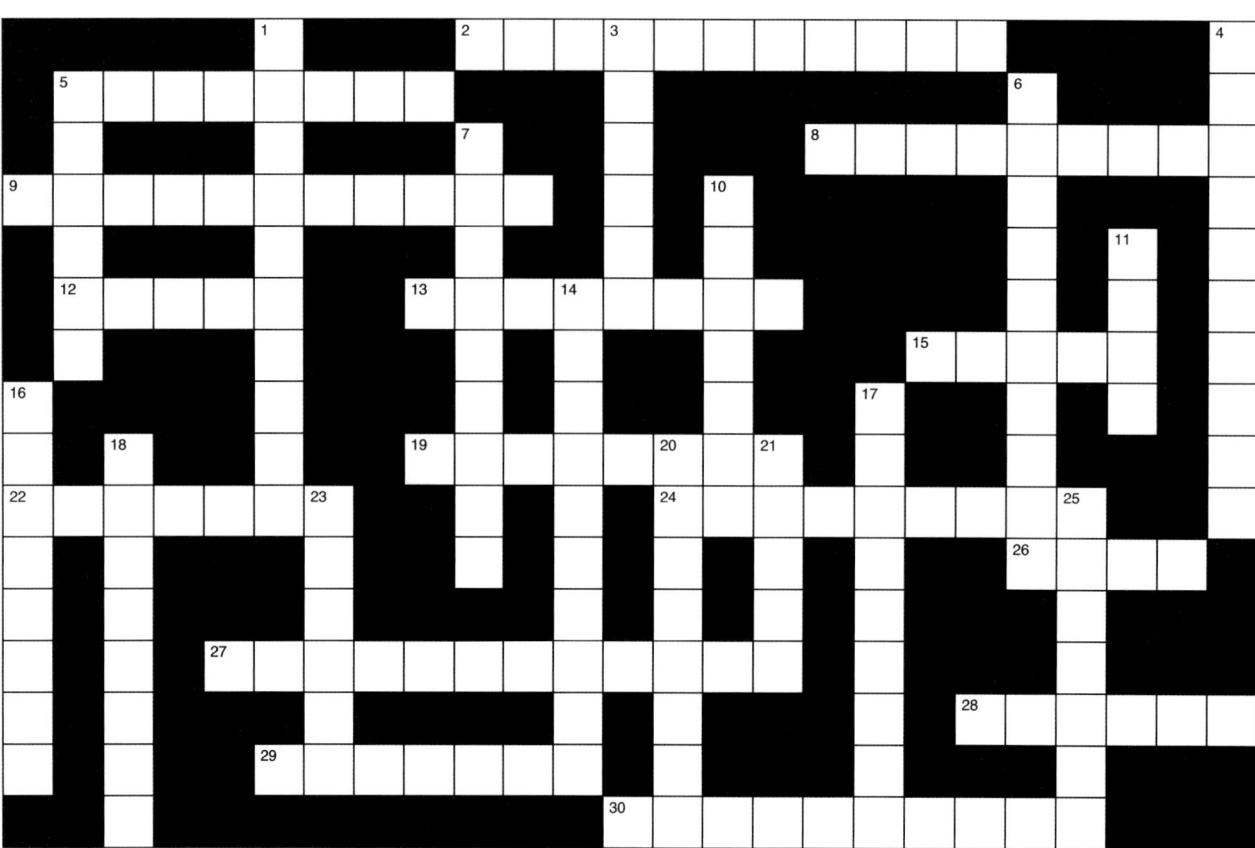

Across

2. _____ reforms moved the economy to one in which government regulations prevented abuses of economic power
5. In 1887, Congress passed the Interstate _____ Act, which provided for federal regulation of practices by railroads
8. Ideology in favor of government ownership of the means of production to improve conditions for workers
9. A _____ is a company chartered by a state and recognized in law as a separate "person"
12. The island that processed immigrants arriving in New York City during the late 1800s
13. In 1855, the _____ process was invented for making low-cost steel
15. In 1892, political candidates from the People's Party ran on the _____ Platform
19. When a business owns its own raw materials, transport, and manufacturing facilities, this is known as _____ integration
22. _____ agreements are informal arrangements to fix prices or divide markets on a regional basis
24. A radical political theory opposing all forms of government in favor of self-governing communities
26. Communism was an ideology developed by Karl _____
27. A person who takes risks by engaging in business to make a profit
28. In the late 1800s, workers began to organize into labor _____ to improve their working conditions
29. If management did not agree to worker demands, they could close the factory to keep the workers from their jobs in what is called a _____
30. The _____ Movement wanted to ban alcohol

Down

1. A business downturn resulting in high unemployment
3. A national association of farmers' social clubs
4. The internal _____ engine was invented at the end of the 19th century
5. A "_____ shop" is a workplace in which only union workers can be hired
6. An economic system in which a country's trade and industry are controlled by private owners for profit
7. In 1892, the _____ Strike took place at Carnegie's steelworks
10. The _____ Silver Purchase Act required the federal government to purchase a large amount of silver each month
11. Congress passed the _____ Inspection Act in 1906, establishing government inspection of this product shipped between states
14. _____ houses in poor neighborhoods provided services such as classes, childcare, and nursing to immigrants
16. Party formed by farmers in the early 1890s
17. Journalist or writer who exposes the abuses and corruption of industrial society
18. Complete control over the production of a good or service
20. By the end of the 19th century, _____ was producing one-quarter of all the steel made in the U.S.
21. The American Federation of _____ was a federation of unions comprising skilled workers
23. Neighborhood consisting of immigrants of the same nationality and speaking the same language
25. A political _____ is an organization that gets citizens to vote for its candidates and uses its officeholders to make profits

Unit II | Activity 2

CHAPTER 8

American Imperialism

SS.912.A.4.1 Analyze the major factors that drove United States imperialism.

SS.912.A.4.2 Explain the motives of the United States' acquisition of territories.

SS.912.A.4.3 Examine the causes, course, and consequences of the Spanish-American War.

SS.912.A.4.4 Analyze the economic, military, and security motivations of the United States to complete the Panama Canal as well as major obstacles involved in its construction.

SS.912.A.4.11 Examine key events and peoples in Florida history as they relate to United States history.

Names and Terms You Should Know

Spanish-American War	Philippines	Hawaii
Cuba	Expansionism	Queen Liliuokalani
José Marti	Imperialism	"Open Door" policy
Ostend Manifesto	Alfred Thayer Mahan	Boxer Rebellion
Yellow press	"White Man's Burden"	Treaty of Portsmouth
William Randolph Hearst	Anti-Imperialist League	Panama Canal
De Lôme letter	Mark Twain	Yellow fever
USS *Maine*	Puerto Rico	Monroe Doctrine
Rough Riders	Teller Amendment	Roosevelt Corollary
Commodore Dewey	Platt Amendment	"Big Stick" policy

Florida "Keys" to Learning

1. José Marti landed in Cuba in 1895 and launched a war for independence. Spain attempted to suppress the rebellion with great brutality. Sensationalist reports in the Hearst and Pulitzer newspapers—referred to as "yellow journalism" or the "yellow press"—fanned the desire to intervene. Americans were motivated by both humanitarianism and self-interest. De Lôme, the Spanish ambassador, wrote a letter criticizing President McKinley as weak, which was leaked to the press. Shortly afterwards, the USS *Maine* exploded in Havana Harbor. These events led to a public outcry.

2. The Spanish-American War lasted only a few months. Theodore Roosevelt organized the "Rough Riders," who fought in Cuba. Commodore Dewey defeated Spanish naval forces in the Philippines. Congress promised not to annex Cuba in the Teller Amendment. Cuba became independent but fell under indirect control.

3. A debate arose over American imperial expansion. Anti-imperialists argued that: (1) Americans had once fought against British imperialism and should not become imperialists themselves; (2) imperialism was anti-democratic; and (3) ownership of colonies might pull America into international conflicts. Imperialists argued that: (1) colonies were needed to provide natural resources and markets; (2) America had a moral obligation to help colonial peoples; (3) Americans should grab remaining territories before Europeans did; and (4) colonies would provide strategic naval bases, encourage trade, and bring wealth and power.

4. The outcome of the debate was that America annexed the Philippines. A local rebellion was put down with brutality. American plantation owners in Hawaii overthrew Queen Liliuokalani in 1893 with the support of U.S. troops. President Cleveland refused to annex Hawaii, but President McKinley and Congress agreed to do so in 1898. Midway, Guam, and Samoa also became U.S. possessions in the Pacific. In the Caribbean, Americans annexed Puerto Rico in 1898 and purchased part of the Virgin Islands in 1917.

5. In 1899, Secretary of State John Hay announced the "Open Door" policy, declaring that trading rights in China should remain open to all foreign powers. In 1900, an international military expedition, which included U.S. forces, put down the Boxer Rebellion. Hay announced the United States would oppose any attempt to divide China into colonies.

6. President Roosevelt helped Japan and Russia negotiate the Treaty of Portsmouth in 1905.

7. Roosevelt wanted to build a canal through the Isthmus of Panama to provide easier access between the Atlantic and Pacific Oceans. When talks with Colombia for building a canal stalled, Roosevelt supported Panamanian rebels. In exchange for U.S. recognition and protection, Panama gave control of the canal zone to the United States. The canal took a decade to build and was the most complicated engineering project of its day.

8. The "Roosevelt Corollary to the Monroe Doctrine" asserted that America would act as a policeman in Latin America, leading to repeated U.S. interventions in Central America and the Caribbean.

In previous chapters, you studied events occurring within the United States. In this chapter and the next, you will study U.S. foreign relations: how Americans have interacted with the rest of the world.

The Spanish-American War

Spain once had the greatest of all colonial empires. But from the 18th century onwards, Spanish power had been in continual decline. By 1898, all that remained of the once great Spanish empire was Cuba, the Philippines, Puerto Rico, and several smaller possessions. That year, the United States went to war with Spain to liberate Cuba from Spanish rule. Most Americans thought they were fighting to help the oppressed people of Cuba, but as a result of the war, the United States acquired its own overseas empire. The Spanish-American War thus marked a major turning point in the history of American foreign relations.

Origins of the Spanish-American War

Most Cubans were laborers working on the sugar and tobacco plantations of wealthy landlords. Cuban revolutionary **José Marti** organized a rebellion while living in exile in the United States. In 1891, he announced his plans to the community of Cuban cigar makers in **Ybor City** in Tampa. In April 1895, Marti declared Cuban independence and returned to Cuba. He was killed one month later. Cuban rebels continued to wage guerilla warfare, destroying plantations and sugar mills. General Weyler was sent from Spain to suppress the rebellion. Weyler used brutal methods, forcing Cuban peasants into "concentration camps" surrounded with barbed wire in order to separate them from the rebels. In fact, terrible atrocities were committed by both sides.

Humanitarian Concerns

Many Americans felt they had a moral obligation to intervene in Cuba. The same Progressive impulse that had promoted reform at home now encouraged intervention abroad.

The Impact of "Yellow Journalism"

American humanitarian concerns were deliberately stirred up by "yellow journalism," or the "yellow press." The **yellow press** was a new technique for selling more newspapers by sensationalizing and even distorting news events to arouse interest and evoke sympathy. In the 1890s, Joseph Pulitzer's *New York World* and William Randolph Hearst's *New York Journal* deliberately sensationalized news from Cuba to sell more papers. They depicted Spaniards as murderous brutes and Cuban rebels as helpless victims. These newspaper publishers distorted events and even printed false stories of fictitious atrocities. Through such methods, Hearst was able to increase his newspaper circulation substantially, but Americans received an inaccurate picture of the Cuban civil war.

Economic Interests

U. S. government and business leaders were concerned to protect American investments in Cuba, which exceeded $50 million. They believed that the Cuban civil war was hurting American trade. And some American businessmen even thought that American intervention in Cuba might lead to new business opportunities after the war.

Imperial Interests

Even before the Civil War, some Americans had expressed their desire to annex Cuba. In 1854, the U.S. minister to Spain discussed the possible purchase of Cuba with Spanish officials. Some Southerners believed that adding Cuba to the Union as a large territory with slaves might counter-balance the admission of new free states. The minister's

Chapter 8 | American Imperialism

report back to Washington, D.C. caused a sensation among Northerners when it appeared in American newspapers as the "**Ostend Manifesto**." The report urged Americans to seize Cuba if Spain would not sell it. Forty years later, a small but influential group of Americans saw the crisis in Cuba as a new opportunity for the United States to chase Spain out of the Americas and to obtain this important possession.

The Triggering Events: The De Lôme Letter and the Explosion of the Maine

In February 1898, a letter by Enrique Dupuy de Lôme, the Spanish ambassador to the United States, was published in the Hearst press. The letter caused a public outcry for calling President McKinley "weak." It indicated that the Spaniards were not being totally honest in their negotiations with the United States over events in Cuba. This leak was followed almost immediately by the explosion of the American battleship USS *Maine* in Havana Harbor in Cuba. The *Maine* had been sent to Havana to protect American lives and property. Historians still do not know why the ship exploded, but the Hearst press immediately blamed Spain for an act of sabotage. The De Lôme letter and sinking of the *Maine* so inflamed public opinion that President McKinley found it hard to resist the outcry for war. The Spanish government agreed to McKinley's demands for a cease-fire with the rebels and even for opening up the camps where they were forcing Cubans from the countryside to go in order to isolate the rebels. However, Spain refused to grant formal independence to Cuba. Given the climate of American public opinion, President McKinley felt he had no other choice but to ask Congress for a declaration of war.

The Course and Consequences of the War

The Spanish-American War lasted only four months. The technological superiority of the U.S. Navy assured an early victory. American land forces overwhelmed Spanish troops on Cuba. Theodore Roosevelt, Assistant Secretary of the Navy, resigned his post and gathered a group of volunteers, known as the "**Rough Riders**." Roosevelt arranged for these volunteers to serve along with regular army units. Most of the

"Rough Riders" take San Juan Hill

Rough Riders were recruited in Texas and the Southwest. From there, they took a train to Tampa, Florida, where they waited for orders to embark for Cuba. About one-third of the Rough Riders remained in Tampa for the course of the war; the rest sailed from Tampa to Cuba, where they fought in several battles. Under Roosevelt's command, they led a famous cavalry charge against Spanish artillery up San Juan Hill. Their victory helped the U.S. Army capture Santiago, the capital of Cuba. On the other side of the globe, the U.S. Navy under **Commodore George Dewey** defeated the Spanish fleet in Manila Bay and occupied the Philippines. The American triumph in the Spanish-American War advertised to the world the fact that the United States was now a "great power."

As a result of the war, Spain lost Cuba, the Philippines, Puerto Rico and Guam. The United States annexed all of these territories except Cuba. It paid Spain $20 million for the Philippines. Cuba became independent in name but fell under the indirect control of the United States.

Cartoon depicting U.S. victory over Spain in the Philippines

Chapter 8 | American Imperialism

The Debate over Imperial Expansion

Imperialism is the rule of one country by another. Most Americans had traditionally opposed imperialism. As citizens of a former colony that had won its independence, they felt they should not impose colonial rule on others. The rule of one country by another was simply seen as a violation of the democratic principles upon which America was based. Democracy, by definition, implied self-government. Many Americans also feared that the acquisition of colonies would drag them into conflicts with other imperial powers. For these reasons, President Cleveland and the U.S. Congress had refused to annex Hawaii in 1894 (you will learn more about this later in this chapter). Anti-imperialist sentiment was still strong in the United States in 1898. For example, in authorizing the Spanish-American War, Congress had passed the **Teller Amendment**. This was an amendment (*or addition*) by Congress to its original declaration of war, promising that the United States would not annex Cuba, even if it won the war. It received overwhelming support in the House of Representatives.

> "[The United States] disclaims any disposition of intention to exercise sovereignty, jurisdiction, or control over said island except for pacification thereof, and asserts its determination, when that is accomplished, to leave the government and control of the island to its people."
>
> —Teller Amendment, April 1898

The Logic of Imperialism

In the aftermath of the Spanish-American War, however, the United States became an imperial power. Some Americans opposed ratification of the **Treaty of Paris**, the peace treaty with Spain ending the war, since its terms made the United States an imperial power. But others argued that new factors had made the acquisition of colonies extremely desirable. They pointed to the following:

The Need for Raw Materials and Markets for American Industry

The rise of industry had created new needs. Imperialists argued that colonies could provide raw materials for American factories and guarantee markets for American manufactured goods. The expansion of American industry thus propelled the United States overseas. Farmers hoped to sell their surplus crops to colonial populations. Imperial expansion seemed all the more necessary because high protective tariffs limited trade among the industrialized countries. A colonial empire would provide Americans with a protected market for trade.

New Technological Capabilities

The steamboat, railroad, improved rifle, machine gun, telegraph, and telephone, as well as better medicines, made it possible to colonize many new areas, especially in the Tropics.

The Importance of Naval Power

The most influential imperialist thinker, Captain **Alfred Thayer Mahan**, published his book *The Influence of Sea Power Upon History* in 1890. President of the Naval College at Annapolis, Mahan believed that it was sea power that made a nation truly great. He urged the United States to increase its wealth and power by developing a strong navy. To provide sailors for the navy and to encourage trade, Mahan argued, the United States also needed a large fleet of merchant ships and overseas colonies. The navy would safeguard ocean-shipping lanes to protect the country's colonies and merchant fleet. "England's naval bases have been in all parts of the world," he observed, "and her fleets have at once protected them, kept open the communications between them, and relied upon them for shelter." He concluded that "colonies attached to the mother-country afford, therefore, the surest means of supporting abroad the sea power of a country." The key to world power thus lay in overseas colonies, strategic naval bases, a large merchant marine, and a powerful navy.

Mahan recommended that the United States build a canal through Panama, annex colonies in the Pacific and Caribbean to serve as naval bases, and develop greater trade with East Asia. Mahan's most famous disciple, Theodore Roosevelt, put much of Mahan's program into effect during his Presidency.

Competition with the European Powers

In the 1880s and 1890s, European powers were carving up Africa, Asia, and the Pacific into colonies and "spheres of influence." American imperialists urged the United States to follow suit and to grab some territories of its own before nothing was left.

Clipper ships and steamships brought tea and other goods from China and the rest of East Asia to the United States. Colonies in the Pacific like the Philippines and Hawaii could help to protect America's growing trade with Asia.

A Golden Opportunity

Imperialists argued that the final collapse of the Spanish empire had created a "golden opportunity" for the United States by placing these last Spanish possessions in America's lap. President McKinley reasoned in the following way in deciding the fate of the Philippines: he could not return them to Spain or give them to any other European power; at the same time, the Filipinos did not appear to be ready for self-government. McKinley concluded that the United States had no choice but to assume control over the Philippines itself.

The New "Manifest Destiny"

The United States had already expanded from the Atlantic to the Pacific Coast. So the earlier ideal of Manifest Destiny seemed to have been fulfilled. But in the 1890s, "Manifest Destiny" suddenly took on a whole new meaning: it became America's divine mission, not simply to reach the shores of the Pacific, but to extend beyond. This notion was also closely tied to feelings of Anglo-Saxon superiority.

The "White Man's Burden"

Many Americans believed in the superiority of "Anglo-Saxons" (those of British ancestry). They thought that white Protestants—especially Anglo-Saxons—were a superior race that deserved to rule over others. Their conviction in Anglo-Saxon superiority also satisfied deep psychological needs in many Americans.

Social Darwinists borrowed their ideas from Charles Darwin's theory of evolution. They believed in the "survival of the fittest" and in the superior nature of the most powerful—not only among plants and animals—but also among human racial groups and social classes. Such beliefs reinforced popular racist attitudes. Josiah Strong, a popular Protestant preacher and writer, even predicted that Anglo-Saxons would multiply and eventually take over the Earth.

There was also a strong humanitarian impulse behind these beliefs. Many Americans genuinely wanted to help other peoples around the world. Such humanitarians thought that by spreading American institutions and Protestant Christianity, they were doing native peoples in other parts of the world a great favor.

The Anti-Imperialist Argument

Other Americans opposed imperialism. These **anti-imperialists** felt that imperialism—the rule of one people by another—was immoral and went against the most basic values of American democracy. Some dreaded negative economic repercussions. Labor leader Samuel Gompers feared colonies would become a source of cheap labor, leading to lower wages in the United States. The industrialist Andrew Carnegie was a pacifist and thought that the possession of colonies would lead to rivalry and armed conflict with other imperial powers. In 1898, the same year as the Spanish-American War and the annexation of Hawaii, critics of imperialism formed a new organization called the **Anti-Imperialist**

British author Rudyard Kipling wrote a poem about the "White Man's Burden" (1899) to help others. Kipling was specifically addressing the American acquistion of the Philippines, and he published his poem in the Progressive magazine, *McClure's*.

The White Man's Burden, by Rudyard Kipling

Take up the White Man's burden—
Send forth the best ye breed—
Go, bind your sons to exile
To serve your captives' need;
To wait, in heavy harness,
On fluttered folk and wild—
Your new-caught sullen peoples,
Half devil and half child. . . .

Take up the White Man's burden—
The savage wars of peace—
Fill full the mouth of Famine,
And bid the sickness cease;
And when your goal is nearest
(The end for others sought)
Watch sloth and heathen folly
Bring all your hope to nought.

▶ According to Kipling, how did imperialism actually help colonial peoples? Use evidence from the poem to support your answer.

▶ What were Kipling's ideas about colonial peoples? Use evidence from the poem to support your answer.

League. In April 1899, ten thousand members gathered in Chicago to merge several local leagues into the **American Anti-Imperialist League**. Former President Grover Cleveland, Andrew Carnegie, Samuel Gompers, Jane Addams, and William Jennings Bryan all became members of the League.

The most famous member of the Anti-Imperialist League was the celebrated writer Mark Twain, a bitter critic of imperialism. Originally, he had favored American intervention in the Philippines: "I said to myself, here are a people who have suffered for three centuries. We can make them as free as ourselves, give them a government and country of their own, put a miniature of the American constitution afloat in the Pacific, start a brand new republic to take its place among the free nations of the world. It seemed to me a great task to which we had addressed ourselves." But he was shocked when he learned that such liberation was not the true aim of American leaders: "I have seen that we do not intend to free, but to subjugate the people of the Philippines. We have gone there to conquer, not to redeem. We have pledged the power of this country to maintain and protect the abominable system established in the Philippines by the [Spanish monks]. It should, it seems to me, be our pleasure and duty to make those people free, and let them deal with their own domestic questions in their own way. And so I am an anti-imperialist. I am opposed to having the eagle put its talons on any other land."

The Historian's Apprentice

Imagine it is 1898 after the Spanish-American War. Write your own newspaper editorial explaining either the advantages or the disadvantages of becoming an imperialist power for the United States.

The American Colonial Empire

In the aftermath of the Spanish-American War and a vigorous debate, the United States acquired a colonial empire in the Pacific Ocean and the Caribbean Sea. The United States also asserted informal control over much of the Caribbean area, which became an "American lake."

Possessions in the Pacific

The Philippines

When the Spanish-American War broke out, Filipino rebels were already at war with Spain. They were bitterly disappointed when McKinley decided to annex the Philippines instead of granting them their independence. Filipino rebels, led by Emilio Aguinaldo, rejected annexation by the United States and launched a rebellion against American rule that lasted for another three years. The rebels used guerilla warfare against the occupiers, while American military commanders ironically used methods similar to those previously used by Spain in Cuba, such as burning villages. The war against the Filipino rebels actually cost more in money and lives than the shorter Spanish-American War. As many as 200,000 Filipinos may have died from warfare and disease. Filipino forces were only finally defeated in 1902. Afterwards, the United States built roads, hospitals, and schools in the Philippines. The Jones Act gave Filipinos the right to elect both houses of their own legislature in 1916, and promised eventual independence.

Hawaii

Hawaii is an archipelago (*a chain of islands*) in the Pacific Ocean. It provided a useful coaling station on trips from the United States to East Asia. In the mid-nineteenth century, Hawaiians had welcomed American settlers, who built sugar and pineapple plantations and then imported Chinese and Japanese laborers. By the 1880s, however, native Hawaiians and American plantation owners were coming into increasing conflict. Wealthy American landowners forced the King of Hawaii to accept a constitution that gave only property owners like themselves the right to vote. In 1893, a new ruler, **Queen Liliuokalani**, tried to take back political power. She announced that she would issue a new constitution. In response, the American minister to Hawaii and leading American landowners, with the help of the U.S. Marines, seized power. The Americans formed a provisional government and asked for Hawaii to be annexed by the United States. President Cleveland, however, refused

Filipino soldiers

Queen Liliuokalani

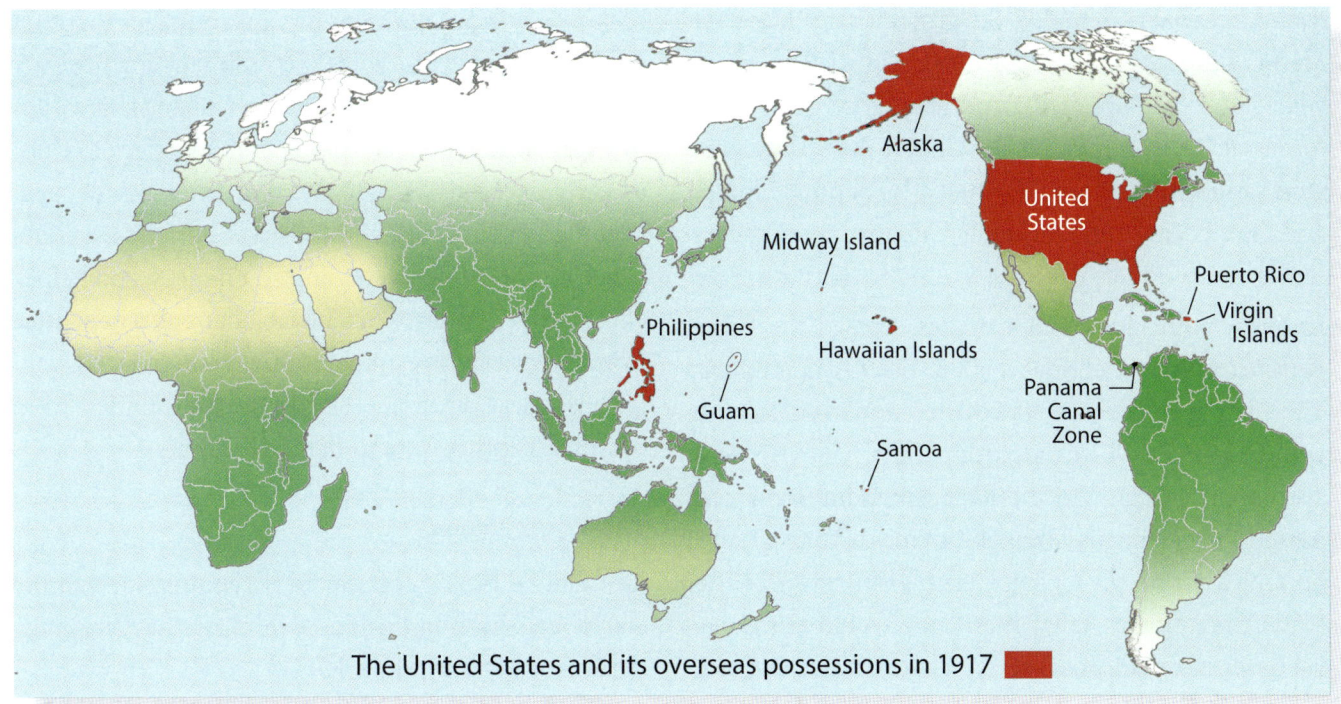

The United States and its overseas possessions in 1917

because the landowners had overthrown the queen by force. Congress also voted not to interfere in Hawaiian affairs in 1894. After the outbreak of the Spanish-American War and the rise of new imperialistic sentiment in the United States, American businessmen in Hawaii petitioned for annexation again in July 1898. This time, Congress voted overwhelmingly for annexation.

Other Pacific Islands: Guam, Samoa, and Midway

In these years, Americans also acquired a number of smaller islands in the Pacific. **Midway** had been an American possession since 1867. **Guam** was taken from Spain after the Spanish-American War. **Samoa** was placed under the joint control of Britain, Germany and the United States in 1889. In 1899, it was divided between Germany and the United States. These islands provided valuable coaling stations for American ships sailing to Asia, where they could obtain coal, fresh water, food and other supplies.

New Interests in the Caribbean

Puerto Rico

Puerto Rico also became an American possession after the Spanish-American War. It was not until 1952 that Puerto Rico became a self-governing "Commonwealth." Today, the United States provides for the island's defense and sets its foreign policy. Puerto Ricans themselves have rejected both total independence and statehood. They enjoy rights of unrestricted immigration to the United States.

Cuba: An Informal Protectorate

When President McKinley asked Congress for a declaration of war against Spain in 1898, he promised to establish "a stable government" in Cuba. Congress responded with a joint resolution authorizing him to use force against Spain but promising "recognition of the independence of the people of Cuba" when the war was over. Senator Henry Teller proposed a further amendment to this resolution, promising that the United States had no "intention to exercise sovereignty, jurisdiction, or control over [Cuba] except for pacification thereof," and that when the war was over, the United States would "leave the government and control of the island to its people." Both Houses of Congress passed the **Teller Amendment**, ensuring that the United States would not annex Cuba after the war. Consequently, Cuba was not annexed and Cubans were given their independence once Spain was defeated. However, American influence was so strong in Cuba that the

Chapter 8 | American Imperialism

island became a virtual U. S. "protectorate" (*an area under American protection and control*). For three years after the Spanish-American War, American forces actually remained on Cuban soil. They created sanitation systems, trained a local police force, and gave voting rights to male Cubans meeting certain property qualifications.

In 1901, both Houses of Congress passed the **Platt Amendment**, which replaced the Teller Amendment. The Platt Amendment stated the conditions for the withdrawal of U.S. troops from Cuba. Cubans were also forced to agree to the Platt Amendment, which passed the Cuban Assembly by a vote of 16 to 11 and became a part of the Cuban Constitution in 1902. The Platt Amendment stated that Cuba would place naval bases at the disposal of the United States and not borrow any amounts from foreign countries that they could not repay. The Platt Amendment further gave Americans the right to intervene in Cuban affairs at any time. Indeed, American troops were sent back to Cuba as early as 1906. Meanwhile, the American occupation did benefit Cuba in some ways. Americans established a school system, organized finances, and helped eliminate yellow fever in Cuba. Cubans also benefitted from American investment in sugar and tobacco plantations, sugar refineries, electricity and utilities. Most of Cuba's exports went to the United States.

The Virgin Islands

The United States completed its acquisitions in the Caribbean by purchasing several of the Virgin Islands from Denmark in 1917.

The Platt Amendment, 1901

I. That the government of Cuba shall never enter into any treaty or other compact with any foreign power or powers which will impair or tend to impair the independence of Cuba, nor in any manner authorize or permit any foreign power or powers to obtain by colonization or for military or naval purposes or otherwise, lodgement in or control over any portion of said island.

II. That said government shall not assume or contract any public debt [they would not have sufficient income to repay.]

III. That the government of Cuba consents that the United States may exercise the right to intervene for the preservation of Cuban independence, the maintenance of a government adequate for the protection of life, property, and individual liberty, and for discharging the obligations with respect to Cuba imposed by the Treaty of Paris on the United States, now to be assumed and undertaken by the government of Cuba. . . .

VII. That to enable the United States to maintain the independence of Cuba, and to protect the people thereof, as well as for its own defense, the government of Cuba will sell or lease to the United States lands necessary for coaling or naval stations at certain specified points to be agreed upon with the President of the United States.

▶ Review these four articles from the Platt Amendment. Which article do you think was the most important? Why?

▶ Were Cubans really independent after they accepted the Platt Amendment? Why or why not? Use evidence from the Platt Amendment to support your point of view.

The Historian's Apprentice

Create your own map showing American territorial acquisitions between 1867 and 1917, as well as areas where the United States exercised strong military or commercial influence.

American Foreign Policy, 1898–1914

In the years after the Spanish-American War, the focus of American foreign policy was mainly on developing advantageous commercial relations with East Asia and Latin America, strengthening America's hold over its new colonies, and building a canal in Central America.

American and Trade with East Asia

The United States was in an advantageous location for trade with East Asia. Only the Pacific Ocean separated this region from the West Coast of the United States. In the late 19th century, Americans developed an active trade with China and Japan. Other Asian territories, like the Dutch East Indies (present-day Indonesia), were important sources of spices, rubber and other goods. Control of the Philippines transformed the United States into an important power in the Pacific. Midway, Hawaii, Guam, and Samoa provided naval bases and coaling stations for ships going back and forth to East Asia.

The "Open Door" Policy in China, 1899

American leaders were especially concerned that European powers claiming exclusive "**spheres of influence**" in China would cut off American trade. U.S. Secretary of State John Hay sent notes to the major European powers in 1899, proposing equal trading rights for all foreign nations throughout China. Although the other powers gave evasive replies, Hay declared that his "**Open Door**" **policy** was now in effect.

Only months after Hay declared the "Open Door" policy, the **Boxer Rebellion** erupted in China. The "Boxers" were groups of Chinese opposed to foreign influence in China. During their rebellion, the Boxers murdered Chinese Christians and threatened the lives of foreigners in China. An international military expedition, in which the United States participated, put down the rebellion and saved the foreign inhabitants of Beijing. Americans feared that European and Japanese intervention in China would lead to dismemberment of the country. Hay announced that the United States would oppose any attempts to divide up China. Partly because of Hay's efforts, Chinese territorial integrity was preserved.

Troops from the "Eight Nations Alliance" helped to end the Boxer Rebellion: Britain, United States, Italy, Germany, Russia, Austria-Hungary, and Japan.

The "Opening" of Japan

In 1822, a young naval officer named Matthew Perry was the first to sail to Key West and to plant the American flag there after the U.S. acquisition of Florida from Spain. Just over thirty years later, Commodore Perry entered Tokyo Bay with U.S. gunships and opened up

Chapter 8 | American Imperialism

Commodore Perry's fleet entering Tokyo Bay in 1853

isolationist Japan to Western trade. Fearing the fate of China, Japanese leaders made Japan the first non-Western country to adopt Western ways and industrialize. By the 1890s, Japanese leaders were seeking to make their country an imperialist power in its own right. They were anxious to sell their industrial goods, to obtain raw materials, and to find a home for their surplus population on the Asian mainland. Japan challenged and defeated China in the Sino-Japanese War (1894–95), allowing it to take both Taiwan and Korea away from Chinese rule.

Japan next surprised the Western world by defeating the Russians in the **Russo-Japanese War** (1904–1905). President Theodore Roosevelt accepted a Japanese invitation to mediate the conflict. Roosevelt persuaded both sides to agree to the terms of the **Treaty of Portsmouth** (1905), and won the Nobel Peace Prize for his work. Nonetheless, many Japanese and Russian leaders felt Roosevelt had treated them unfairly. Bad feelings between the United States and Japan increased in 1907 when Roosevelt negotiated the "**Gentlemen's Agreement**" to reduce immigration from Japan. Japanese leaders were unhappy at the treatment of Japanese immigrants and agreed to let only the most qualified Japanese—rather than workers—emigrate to the United States.

The United States and Latin America
The Panama Canal

The Spanish-American War had demonstrated the importance of building a canal in Central America connecting the Atlantic and Pacific Oceans. Without it, the Atlantic fleet would have been forced to sail all around South America if it had needed to come to the aid of the Pacific fleet in the Philippines. By 1903, President Theodore Roosevelt therefore decided it was essential to build a canal across the Isthmus of Panama, then a part of Colombia. The United States offered $10 million and an annual fee to Colombia for a strip of land on which to build the canal. Colombians wanted more money, however, and delayed. Roosevelt then struck a deal with rebels in Colombia who were attempting to establish a new country in Panama. A U.S. warship prevented the Colombian government from suppressing the rebellion in Panama, while Roosevelt immediately gave Panama diplomatic recognition. In return, the new nation of Panama agreed to give the United States complete control over a 10-mile strip running through the center of Panama, known as the "Panama Canal Zone," for building the canal. Colombia and other Latin American countries were greatly angered by Roosevelt's high-handed and self-serving policies.

Roosevelt ordered the construction of the canal almost at once. It was a monumental undertaking, requiring engineers and workers to cut through hills and jungle. There were a large number of difficulties. The tropical jungles of Panama were home to mosquitoes carrying malaria and yellow fever. American engineers had to drain swamps and spray insecticides. Next, American engineers rebuilt the

Early stages of Panama Canal construction

152   Chapter 8 | American Imperialism

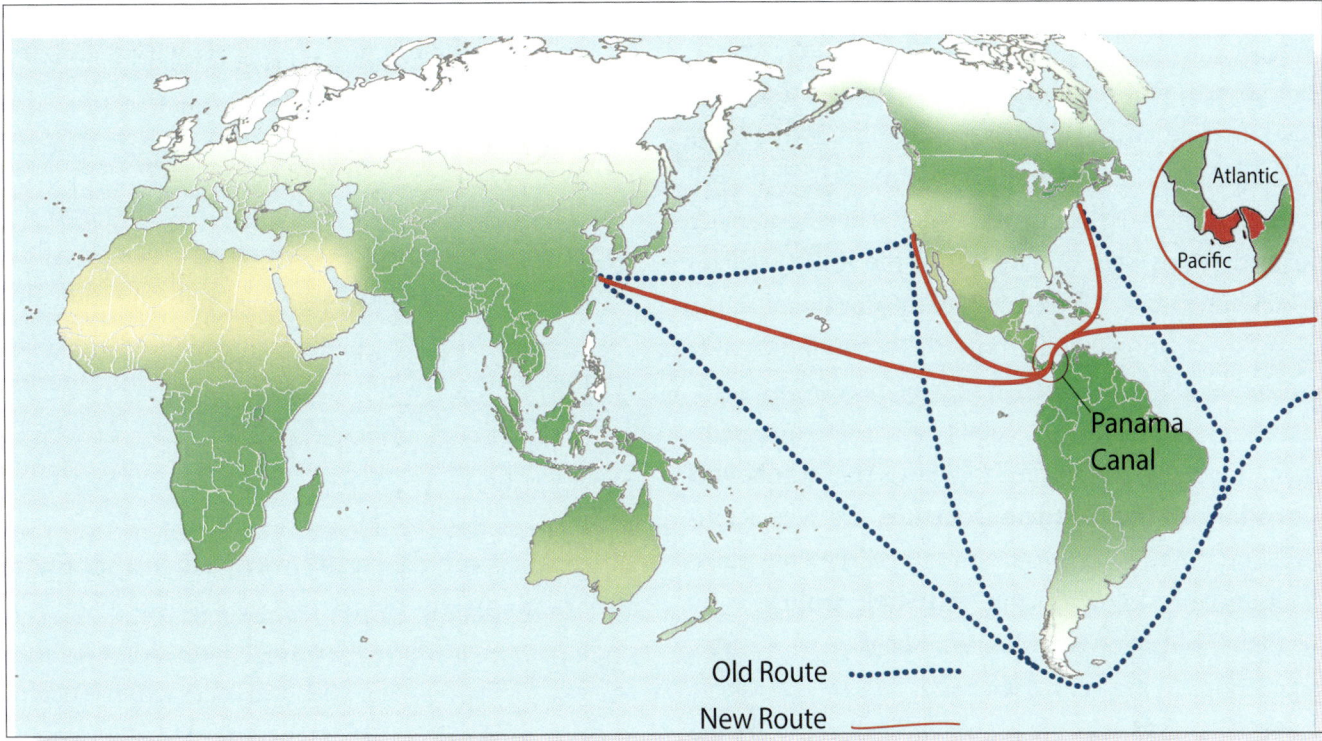

Shipping routes were dramatically shortened by the Panama Canal

Panama Railway to carry equipment for constructing the canal. Modern steam shovels and other expensive equipment were used to build a reservoir and locks at each end of the canal to raise ships over the highlands and lower them back down to sea level. Ships crossing the canal today sail into a lock, which is then filled with water to raise the ship. At the other end of the canal, locks are drained to lower the ship. The Panama Canal took more than ten years to complete, costing thousands of lives and $400 million.

The "Roosevelt Corollary to the Monroe Doctrine"

Almost a century earlier, President Monroe had announced the **Monroe Doctrine** in 1823. He had stated that the United States would oppose any attempt

The Panama Canal connected the Pacific to the Atlantic.

The Historian's Apprentice

Use the Internet or the school library to research the construction of the Panama Canal. Describe the problems encountered in building the canal. Then explain the advantages to the United States of building the canal.

Chapter 8 | American Imperialism

by European Powers to establish new colonies in the Western Hemisphere. In the late 19th century, American governments extended the meaning of the Monroe Doctrine. In 1904, when the Dominican Republic owed debts to European countries, President Roosevelt refused to let those countries use force to collect them. Instead, Roosevelt declared that the United States would intervene and collect the debts for them, acting as an "international police power." Roosevelt took over collection of the Dominican Republic's customs, turning more than half the receipts over to foreign creditors. This approach became known as the "**Roosevelt Corollary to the Monroe Doctrine**." Because Roosevelt's motto was to "speak softly and carry a big stick," it also became known as the "**Big Stick**" **policy**. Under this policy, the United States sent troops to the West Indies and Central America so often that the Caribbean became known as an "American lake." Haiti, Nicaragua, Honduras, and the Dominican Republic joined Cuba as virtual American protectorates. The "Roosevelt Corollary" was deeply resented by most Latin Americans.

> Note: You are not required to know about Dollar Diplomacy and Watchful Waiting for the EOC Assessment

Taft and "Dollar Diplomacy"

Roosevelt's successor, President Taft, encouraged American bankers to invest in the countries of the Caribbean. Whenever Latin American countries became unable to repay these loans, the United States sent in troops to ensure that the money was collected. American bankers lent money to Nicaragua, for example, to help that country pay its foreign debts. In return, the Nicaraguan government promised to give American bankers control over Nicaraguan railroads, customs duties, and the national bank. When Nicaraguans refused to carry out this arrangement, Taft sent in the U.S. Marines to enforce it. Taft's use of American investment to promote American foreign policy objectives became known as "**Dollar Diplomacy**."

Wilson and Mexico: "Watchful Waiting"

As a Democrat, Woodrow Wilson had opposed the imperialist policies of the three previous Republican Presidents—McKinley, Roosevelt, and Taft. But once he became President, Wilson similarly ended up intervening in Haiti, Nicaragua, and the Dominican Republic. Wilson even added to the American colonial empire by purchasing the Virgin Islands from Denmark in 1917.

Wilson became especially involved in the affairs of Mexico. Many of his closest advisors, such as Colonel Edward House, were Texans with business experience in Mexico. The Mexican dictator Porfirio Diaz had been overthrown by moderate revolutionaries in 1910. The new democratic government of Mexico faced immense difficulties, including local revolts. In February 1913, General Huerta and the Mexican army turned against the elected government and murdered its leaders. Huerta established a new government, but Wilson refused to extend diplomatic recognition to it. Wilson announced he would only recognize democratically elected governments, not governments established by murder. Wilson's policy of waiting to see what would happen became known as "**watchful waiting**." In 1914, Wilson sent troops to the Mexican port of Vera Cruz to prevent Germans from landing arms there for General Huerta. Later in 1914, Huerta finally resigned and fled to Spain. Wilson immediately recognized the new government. This annoyed **Pancho Villa**, a Mexican rebel leader who feared the new government would not help the Mexican peasants. In 1916, Villa's rebel troops murdered a small band of American workers in Mexico. Then they crossed over the border and attacked a town in the United States. Wilson reacted to these events by sending U.S. troops into Mexico under the command of General Pershing. They remained almost a year but never caught Pancho Villa. Wilson finally withdrew American forces from Mexico in 1917, when the threat of involvement in World War I overshadowed the difficulties in Mexico.

The Historian's Apprentice

▶ What was the difference between the original Monroe Doctrine (1823) and the "Roosevelt Corollary"?
▶ Use the Internet to find political cartoons that illustrate President Theodore Roosevelt's "Big Stick" policy toward Latin America, Taft's "Dollar Diplomacy," or Wilson's "Watchful Waiting." Then write a short analysis of one cartoon. In your analysis, consider these key questions: (1) who are the characters in the cartoon? (2) what objects or symbols does the cartoonist use and what does each represent? (3) what is the cartoonist's overall message? (4) how would this cartoon have affected views at the time when it was created?

Florida in Focus

By the late 19th century, Florida already had substantial Cuban communities in Key West and other towns. Because there was a tariff on cigars but not on tobacco, Vicente Martinez Ybor moved his cigar-making operations to Ybor City in Tampa in the 1880s. The Cuban immigrants in Florida contributed their money and support to José Marti and other Cuban revolutionaries. You have already learned how Marti gave an important speech on behalf of Cuban independence in Ybor City.

In the months before the outbreak of the Spanish-American War, Floridians began to fear the bombardment of their coastal cities by Spanish forces. The industrialist Henry Plant had already established a railroad line, a steamship line, wharves, and luxury hotels at Tampa. Plant sent a letter to the U.S. Secretary of War, asking the government to build defensive fortifications there. As war grew more certain, a new question arose: where should U.S. forces intended for an invasion of Cuba be based? Tampa's local press and politicians used all their influence in Washington. Plant sent a prominent company official to plead for Tampa, which was eventually chosen as the port of embarkation. Troops began arriving in Tampa by train as early as April 20, even before war was declared. Several camps were set up around Tampa, while army headquarters were established in Henry Plant's beautiful Tampa Bay Hotel. Theodore Roosevelt stayed at the Tampa Bay Hotel as well. Additional camps were set up in Jacksonville ("Camp Cuba Libre"), Lakeland, Miami, and Fernandina. As a result of over-crowding in the camps, typhoid quickly broke out among the soldiers. More men would eventually die from disease than from the fighting.

The triumph of American imperialism likewise affected Florida. Inspired by the construction of the Panama Canal, Henry Flagler decided to extend his Florida East Coast Railway to Key West, then Florida's largest city. Tampa, the center of Plant's transportation network, became a major port for shipping goods to Latin America. On the other hand, Cuba and America's new overseas colonies became competitors to Florida in the production of duty-free sugar.

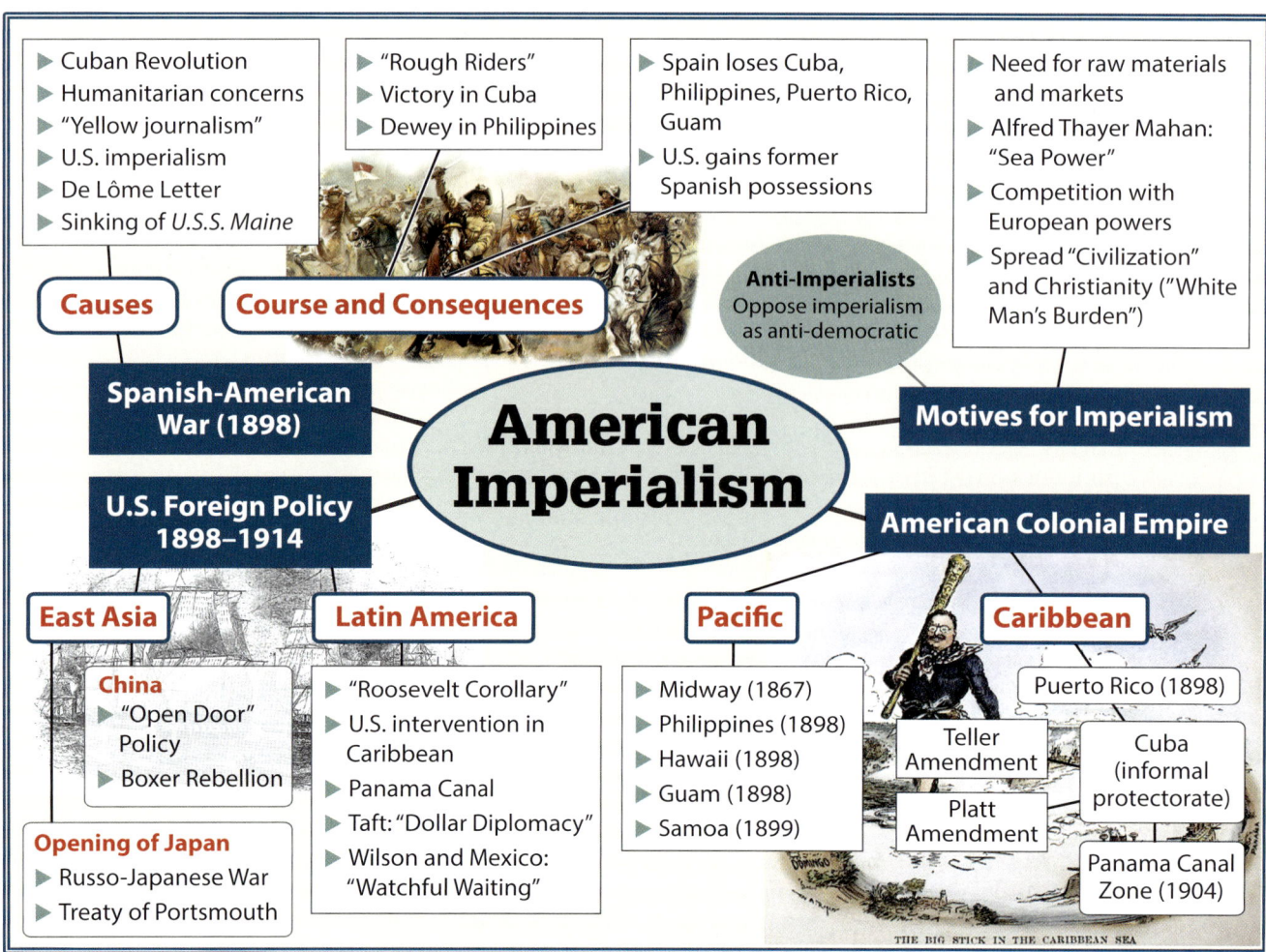

Review Cards

The Debate over Imperial Expansion

Imperialism is when a country rules over foreign areas. Since America had once been a colony, many Americans opposed imperialism on principle. Yet newly acquired territories from Spain turned the United States into an imperial power.

Arguments of the Imperialists:
(1) Colonies were needed to provide raw materials and as markets for American industry.
(2) America had a moral obligation to help colonial peoples and spread Christianity and American institutions. It was an extended part of our "Manifest Destiny" as a superior nation.
(3) Americans should grab remaining territories as colonies before European powers did.
(4) **Alfred Thayer Mahan** argued that colonies would provide strategic naval bases and encourage trade; America would develop a larger merchant marine and strengthen its navy; increased naval power would bring wealth and power.

Arguments of the Anti-imperialists:
(1) Americans had fought British imperialism and should not become imperialists themselves.
(2) Imperialism was anti-democratic.
(3) Colonies created a danger of being pulled into future global conflicts.
(4) Organized labor feared cheap colonial labor would lead to lower wages in the United States.
(5) The **American Anti-Imperialist League** included prominent members such as Mark Twain and Andrew Carnegie.

The Spanish-American War (1898)

Background:
- **Cuba** was a Spanish colony. Cubans wanted their independence and rebelled in 1895. Spain suppressed Cuban guerilla warfare with brutal force.

Motives for Intervention: Americans were motivated by both humanitarian concerns and self-interest to help Cuba.
- Sensational works of **yellow journalism** (Hearst and Pulitzer) distorted events, which fanned the American desire to intervene.
- Some Americans argued that their business investments and opportunities in Cuba needed protection.
- Others believed Cuba would provide greater security and wealth to the United States.

Immediate Causes:
- Spanish ambassador **De Lôme's** letter was leaked to the press. De Lôme criticized President McKinley as incompetent.
- **USS *Maine*** exploded in Havana Harbor. Yellow journalists blamed Spain.
- The De Lôme letter and the explosion of the American battleship fueled popular support for a more aggressive U.S. foreign policy. **President McKinley** gave in to popular pressure and asked Congress for a declaration of war on Spain.

Course of War:
- U.S. quickly defeated Spain with the aid of Theodore Roosevelt's "Rough Riders" in Cuba; Commodore Dewey quickly defeated the Spanish navy in the Philippines.

Consequences:
- U.S. annexed the former Spanish colonies: Philippines, Puerto Rico and Guam.
- Based on **Teller Amendment**, Cuba remained independent but came under indirect U.S. control.

The American Colonial Empire

New U.S. territories in the Pacific and Caribbean provided raw materials, coaling stations, and naval stations for the U.S.

- **Philippines**: Instead of granting independence, the United States annexed this former Spanish colony. Filipinos fought a guerilla war for self-rule for several years. The United States finally ended the rebellion in 1902 and assisted in rebuilding the defeated colony. The Jones Act in 1916 announced that the United States would eventually grant the Philippines its independence.
- **Hawaii**: These islands provided a useful coaling station in the Pacific Ocean. American merchants established profitable sugar cane and pineapple plantations. When **Queen Liliuokalani** of Hawaii began her reign in 1893, she sought to rewrite her country's constitution. With the help of U.S. Marines, American landowners in Hawaii forcibly removed the queen and set up a republic. The U.S. Congress voted not to annex Hawaii but the anti-imperialist tide then turned. After the United States defeated Spain, Congress approved the annexation of Hawaii. The United States also annexed **Guam** and **Samoa** in the Pacific Ocean.
- **Puerto Rico:** became an American possession in the Caribbean.
- **Cuba:** Although Cuban independence was guaranteed by the **Teller Amendment,** Cuba became an American protectorate. In 1901, the **Platt Amendment** gave the United States military bases in Cuba and the right to intervene in Cuban affairs at any time.

Chapter 8 | American Imperialism

U.S. Foreign Policy in East Asia

- European powers had established their own "**spheres of influence**" in China. Americans feared European powers might cut off their trade in China. In 1899, Secretary of State **John Hay** declared the "**Open Door**" policy, stating that trading rights in China were open to all foreign powers.
- In 1900, groups of Chinese known as **Boxers** threatened foreigners in China. An international military expedition, which included the United States, put down the **Boxer Rebellion.** However, the United States announced it would oppose any attempts to turn China into colonies.
- **Commodore Perry** had opened Japan to the west, which then adapted Western ways, including creation of a modern army and navy. Japan defeated China in the Sino-Japanese War, giving it control of Taiwan and Korea. Japan next defeated the Russians in the **Russo-Japanese War**. President Theodore Roosevelt mediated, and war ended with the two sides agreeing on the **Treaty of Portsmouth** (1905). The United States concluded the **Gentlemen's Agreement** (1907), halting Japanese immigration to America.

U.S. Foreign Policy in Latin America

- **Panama Canal**: Influenced by the ideas of Alfred Thayer Mahan and the experience of the Spanish-American War, Theodore Roosevelt and other U.S. leaders wanted to build an American-controlled canal through Central America for easier access between the Atlantic and Pacific Oceans. At first, Roosevelt negotiated with Colombia to build the canal across the Isthmus of Panama. When talks stalled, Roosevelt supported a Panamanian revolution. In exchange for recognition and protection, the newly formed country of Panama granted perpetual control of the **Panama Canal Zone** to the United States. This project firmly established American power while antagonizing Latin American nations. The Canal took a decade to build and was the most complicated engineering project of its day.
- **Caribbean Region**: The Monroe Doctrine (1823) had stated that the United States would oppose any new European intervention in the Western Hemisphere. At the turn of the 20th century, debt-ridden Latin American nations were unable to pay their European investors. European powers in turn sent military ships to collect their debts. The U.S. government appointed itself the arbiter and collected customs duties to repay the debts and avoid European interference in the Western Hemisphere. This approach, known as the **Roosevelt Corollary to the Monroe Doctrine** or the "**Big Stick**" **policy**, asserted that the United States would intervene in any Latin American disputes with foreign powers by acting as "policeman."

What Do You Know?

SS.912.A.4.3

1. Which of the following provides the best evidence in support of the view that Americans went to war with Spain in 1898 for humanitarian purposes?
   A. Anti-imperialists feared colonies would eventually become a source of cheap labor.
   B. Mark Twain said, "We do not intend to free but to subjugate the people of the Philippines."
   C. President Cleveland had previously refused to annex Hawaii when U.S. landowners had overthrown Queen Liliuokalani by force.
   D. Congress passed the Teller Amendment promising that the United States would not annex Cuba, even if it won the war.

SS.912.A.4.3

2. How did the Platt Amendment differ from the Teller Amendment?
   A. The Platt Amendment promised that the United States would never intervene again in Cuba.
   B. The Platt Amendment overturned the Teller Amendment by authorizing the United States to annex Cuba.
   C. The Platt Amendment preserved Cuban independence but claimed the right to intervene in Cuban affairs.
   D. The Platt Amendment promised that the United States would leave Cuba as soon as its independence from Spain was secured.

SS.912.A.4.1

3. Before 1898, most Americans had opposed imperialism. Why did imperialism suddenly become more popular in the United States by the end of the century?
   A. Americans felt it was against the principles of democracy to rule over others.
   B. Americans wanted to sell goods to new markets and buy raw materials for new industries.
   C. Americans wanted to rule others because America had once been a British colony.
   D. Americans feared imperialism would bring the United States into conflict with other powers.

SS.912.A.4.3

4. Why is the Spanish American War of 1898 often considered a major turning point in U.S. history?
   A. It revealed that the United States had become a world power.
   B. It marked the first American victory over a European power.
   C. It demonstrated the need for better communications in wartime.
   D. It showed American support for European economic interests in East Asia.

Chapter 8 | American Imperialism

SS.912.A.4.4

5. The excerpt below is from Alfred Thayer Mahan's *The Influence of Sea Power upon History,* published in 1890.

> England's naval bases have been in all parts of the world and her fleets have at once protected them, kept open the communications between them, and relied upon them for shelter. . . . Colonies attached to the mother-country afford, therefore, the surest means of supporting abroad the sea power of a country. . . . Britain's power was everywhere that her ships could reach.

In this book, Mahan urged Americans to build a large navy and acquire colonies as Britain had. What other strategy did Mahan advocate for the United States to succeed as a naval power?

A. developing an air force

B. having a large standing army

C. placing military bases in Europe

D. building a canal through Central America

SS.912.A.4.2

6. The political cartoon on the right appeared on the cover of *Puck* magazine on December 1, 1897. Its caption says "Another Shotgun Wedding, with Neither Party Willing." The cartoon depicts President William McKinley as a minister conducting a wedding. He is reading from a book entitled "Annexation Policy." The man in the Confederate uniform holding the shotgun is U.S. Senator John Tyler Morgan, a former Confederate general and a prominent imperialist. Kneeling before the minister are Uncle Sam and a Hawaiian woman.

Source: Bishop Museum Archives, Honolulu, Hawaii

What is the main idea of this political cartoon?

A. President McKinley would have preferred to let Hawaii remain independent.

B. The annexation of Hawaii was popular with most Americans but not among Hawaiians.

C. Most Hawaiians would have preferred to be annexed by Japan rather than by the United States.

D. President McKinley and the Senate pushed through the annexation of Hawaii despite opposition at home and in Hawaii.

SS.912.A.4.2

7. The timeline below provides details about American imperialism.

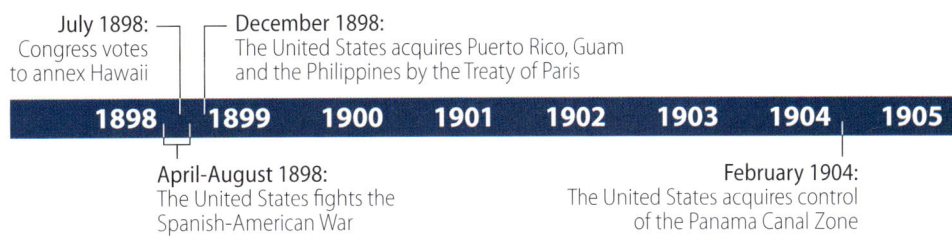

What was one of the arguments used in favor of these changes?

   A. American industries need raw materials and markets found overseas.

   B. The system of imperialism is contrary to American democratic principles.

   C. Colonial peoples are inviting American leadership to develop their economies.

   D. Imperialist expansion threatens to bring the United States into conflict with European powers.

SS.912.A.4.1

8. H. T. Johnson wrote "The Black Man's Burden" in response to Rudyard Kipling's poem, "The White Man's Burden."

The White Man's Burden

Take up the White Man's burden—
Send forth the best ye breed—
Go, bind your sons to exile
To serve your captives' need;
To wait, in heavy harness,
On fluttered folk and wild—
Your new-caught sullen peoples,
Half devil and half child . . .
Take up the White Man's burden—
The savage wars of peace—
Fill full the mouth of Famine,
And bid the sickness cease;
And when your goal is nearest
(The end for others sought)
Watch sloth and heathen folly
Bring all your hope to nought.

—Rudyard Kipling, 1899

The Black Man's Burden

Pile on the Black Man's Burden.
'Tis nearest at your door;
Why heed long bleeding Cuba,
or dark Hawaii's shore?
Hail ye your fearless armies,
Which menace feeble folks
Who fight with clubs and arrows
and brook your rifle's smoke.
Pile on the Black Man's Burden
His wail with laughter drown
You've sealed the Red Man's problem,
And will take up the Brown,
In vain ye seek to end it,
With bullets, blood or death
Better by far defend it
With honor's holy breath.

—H. T. Johnson, 1899

What point of view does Johnson express?

   A. Imperialism is beneficial because it brings Christianity to heathens.

   B. Imperialism feeds colonial peoples and saves them from famine and disease.

   C. Imperialism seeks to conquer and exploit weaker peoples rather than to help them.

   D. Imperialism is worthwhile because more advanced societies have better technology.

SS.912.A.4.4

> **Geography of Panama**
> ▸ Tropical climate with prolonged rainy season
> ▸ Coastal plains and rugged mountainous interior
> ▸ Large interior lake elevated above sea level

9. How did engineers overcome the obstacles that the geography of Panama posed to the building of the Panama Canal?

   A. They built new paved roads so that a greater number of dump trucks could remove the excavated earth.

   B. They sprayed insecticides to kill mosquitoes and built concrete locks to raise ships to a higher elevation.

   C. They used steam shovels to dredge the interior lake and bring its elevation down to sea level to build a sea-level canal.

   D. They used pneumatic drills and dynamite to remove several of Panama's mountains, making construction of the canal easier.

SS.912.A.4.4

10. The political cartoon on the right was published in December 1903. The hill in the background says "Bogota," the capital of Colombia. Eight years later, Theodore Roosevelt stated: "I took the Canal Zone and let Congress debate; and while the debate goes on, the Canal does also."

    To what event do the cartoon and President Roosevelt's statement refer?

    A. a debate in Congress over whether to appropriate funds to build the Panama Canal

    B. the many obstacles that the geography of Panama posed to the construction of a canal

    C. the debate over whether construction of the canal would be useful to U.S. national security

    D. Roosevelt's decision to help Panamanian rebels against Colombia in exchange for the Canal Zone

SS.912.A.4.4

11. Which of these was a negative result of the construction of the Panama Canal?

    A. The shortest water route between the Atlantic and Pacific Oceans was reduced by 8,000 nautical miles.

    B. Colombia and other Latin American countries resented U.S. interference in the Panamanian revolt against Colombia.

    C. Vast quantities of war materials and troops could now move quickly between the East and West Coasts of the United States in the event of war.

    D. Large numbers of ocean-going merchant vessels could pass through the canal annually, most of which were headed to or from U.S. ports.

SS.912.A.4.1

12. After observing how the European great powers had carved out "spheres of influence" in China, what action did U.S. Secretary of State Hays propose?
    A. The United States would help the Boxers to overthrow foreign influence in China.
    B. The United States and other foreign nations should enjoy equal trading rights in China.
    C. The United States would help China to recover all of the lands taken by European powers.
    D. The United States would blockade all Chinese ports if it was not given control of Hong Kong.

SS.912.A.4.1

13. The excerpt below is from a speech by Senator Albert J. Beveridge to the U.S. Senate on January 9, 1900.

    > Mr. President, the times call for [honesty]. The Philippines are ours forever, "territory belonging to the United States," as the Constitution calls them. And just beyond the Philippines are China's [unlimited] markets. We will not retreat from either. We will not repudiate our duty in the archipelago. We will not abandon our opportunity in the Orient.

    Based on this speech, what conclusion can be made about the views of American imperialists in 1900?
    A. They intended to spread the democratic form of government to China.
    B. They feared the growing economic and naval power of the Japanese Empire.
    C. They believed that the Constitution required U.S. acquisition of the Philippines.
    D. They saw the Philippines as a useful base for increasing American trade with East Asia.

SS.912.A.4.2

14. The diagram below provides details about United States involvement in the Philippines during the early 1900s.

    Which phrase completes the diagram?
    A. U.S. Senate refuses to annex the Philippines
    B. Filipino leaders invite the United States to annex the Philippines
    C. American businessmen overthrow the local ruler of the Philippines
    D. U.S. forces fight a three-year war against Filipino rebels seeking independence

Chapter 8 | American Imperialism

SS.912.A.4.1

15. The map below shows the world in 1917.

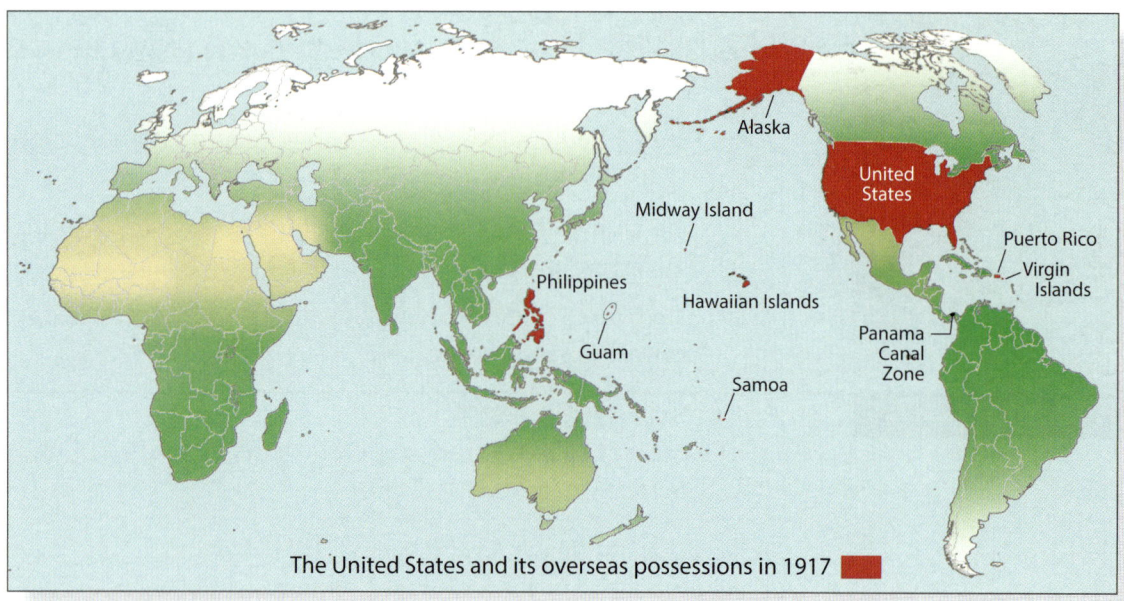

Which conclusion can best be drawn from this map?

A. American imperialists were mainly concerned with maintaining U.S. trade with Europe.

B. American imperialists saw their nation's main opportunities in the Pacific and the Caribbean.

C. American imperialists believed it was their "Manifest Destiny" to take over both Canada and Mexico.

D. American imperialists intended to challenge European control of Africa, the Middle East and South Asia.

SS.912.A.4.11

16. Which exiled Cuban leader raised money in Ybor City and other cities in Florida to organize a new revolt against Spanish rule in Cuba?

A. Enrique Dupuy de Lôme
B. Vicente Martinez Ybor
C. Emilio Aguinaldo
D. José Marti

SS.912.A.4.11

17. Which American city served as the main port of embarkation for the "Rough Riders" and other American forces sent to Cuba during the Spanish-American War?

A. New Orleans, Louisiana
B. Jacksonville, Florida
C. Galveston, Texas
D. Tampa, Florida

CHAPTER 9

The United States in World War I

SS.912.A.4.5 Examine causes, course, and consequences of United States involvement in World War I.

SS.912.A.4.6 Examine how the United States government prepared the nation for war with war measures (Selective Service Act, War Industries Board, war bonds, Espionage Act, Sedition Act, Committee of Public Information).

SS.912.A.4.7 Examine the impact of airplanes, battleships, new weaponry, and chemical warfare in creating new war strategies (trench warfare, convoys).

SS.912.A.4.8 Compare the experiences Americans (African Americans, Hispanics, Asians, women, conscientious objectors) had while serving in Europe.

SS.912.A.4.9 Compare how the war impacted German Americans, Asian Americans, African Americans, Hispanic Americans, Jewish Americans, Native Americans, women, and dissenters in the United States.

SS.912.A.4.10 Examine the provisions of the Treaty of Versailles and the failure of the United States to support the League of Nations.

SS.912.A.4.11 Examine key events and peoples in Florida history as they relate to United States history.

Names and Terms You Should Know

Entangling Alliances	Airplanes	Home Front	*Schenck v. United States*
Militarism	Chemical warfare	Selective Service Act	Great Migration
Nationalism	Naval blockade	War Industries Board	German Americans
Archduke Francis Ferdinand	Convoys	War bonds	Conscientious objectors
Serbia	Lusitania	Espionage Act	Fourteen Points
Austria-Hungary	Sussex Pledge	Sedition Act	Armistice
Allied Powers	Zimmerman Telegram	Committee of Public Information	Big Four
Central Powers	Unrestricted Submarine Warfare	Propaganda	Treaty of Versailles
Trench warfare	American Expeditionary Force (AEF)	Eugene Debs	Reparations
			League of Nations

Florida "Keys" to Learning

1. World War I in Europe had several long-term causes: (1) nationalism; (2) economic rivalries and imperialism; (3) entangling alliances; and (4) militarism. Archduke Ferdinand of Austria-Hungary was assassinated by Serb nationalists in June 1914. Austria invaded Serbia in response. Russia and Germany entered the conflict to honor their alliance commitments. Germany invaded France by marching through Belgium, drawing Britain into the war.

2. New weapons prevented either side from winning quickly. To avoid machine gun fire, soldiers dug trenches running for hundreds of miles. These trenches were separated by barbed wire and land mines. A British naval blockade of the North Sea prevented foreign arms and food from reaching Germany. Germans used submarines ("U-boats") to prevent ships with supplies from reaching Britain.

3. Americans tried to stay out of the war. In 1915, a German submarine sank the *Lusitania,* a British passenger ship, stirring anti-German sentiment. In 1916, Germany pledged not to use submarine warfare against passenger ships, but in 1917, it resumed "unrestricted submarine warfare." Publication of the Zimmerman Telegram, promising the return of U.S. territories to Mexico if it allied with Germany, outraged American public opinion. The sinking of U.S. merchant ships led to American entry into the war.

4. The Selective Service Act required adult males to register for possible conscription. The Committee of Public Information influenced public opinion; the War Industries Board coordinated wartime manufacturing; the Railroad Administration temporarily nationalized the railroads; and the War Labor Board resolved labor disputes. To pay for the war, the government increased taxes and sold war bonds (known as "Liberty Bonds").

5. During the war, individual rights were restricted in the interests of national security. The Espionage Act of 1917 permitted censorship of the mails and imprisonment of those who interfered with the draft. The Sedition Act of 1918 prohibited the use of "disloyal" language. Socialist leader Eugene Debs was imprisoned for criticizing the war. In *Schenck v. U.S.* (1919), the Supreme Court held that free speech could be restricted whenever a "clear and present danger" was evident.

6. As men went off to war, women and minorities filled their places in factories, farms, and railroads. African Americans left the South for Northern jobs in the "Great Migration." Mexicans crossed the border to work on U.S. farms. Women supported the war effort by selling war bonds, knitting socks, cooking meatless dinners, joining the Red Cross, or serving as nurses. During the war, German Americans faced prejudice and more than 4,000 were imprisoned. Over 100,000 African Americans joined the armed services, but were forced to serve in segregated units. Asian Americans also enlisted, although they too were segregated.

7. The arrival of the American Expeditionary Force (AEF) gave the Allies overwhelming superiority. Germany surrendered in November 1918. Wilson had already announced America's war aims in the "Fourteen Points": self-determination for the peoples of Europe; freedom of the seas; equal trade terms; a reduction in armaments; an end to secret diplomacy; and the creation of the League of Nations.

8. Wilson traveled to Paris to negotiate the treaties ending the war. Under the Treaty of Versailles and related treaties, Germany lost territory to both France and Poland. Germany further lost its colonies and its navy, while its army was reduced to a police force. German leaders agreed to the "War Guilt" clause, accepting blame for starting the war, and consented to pay reparations to the Allies. Austria-Hungary was divided into several smaller national states. A League of Nations was established to prevent aggression and to protect the peace. The U.S. Senate failed to ratify the treaty and the United States never joined the League of Nations.

World War I was a global war fought with new destructive technologies that resulted in the deaths of millions of people. Americans managed to stay out of this maelstrom for almost three years—from its outbreak in Europe in August 1914 until April 1917. American intervention on the side of the Allies brought an end to the war in just over a year. The war changed the face of Europe, toppling empires and creating new states. In the United States, the war led to temporary government controls over the economy, a massive mobilization of manpower in the armed services, a rise in taxation and the national debt, an increased use of women and minorities as workers in American industry, and new limits on civil rights. The results of the war disappointed those American idealists who had hoped to make the world "safe for democracy." It led to two decades of relative American isolation from world affairs. The war also turned the United States into the world's preeminent economic power.

Origins of the War in Europe

What circumstances led the statesmen of Europe to plunge their countries into the devastation of total war? As with the Civil War, it is possible to identify several long-term causes as well as to trace the specific events that triggered the conflict. Historians still debate the long-term causes of the conflict, but most would agree on the following:

▶ **Nationalism**. Nationalism—pride in one's nation and often, belief in its superiority—led to rivalries between the European "Great Powers," such as France and Germany. Nationalist feelings also led some ethnic groups to demand their own nation-states. Before the war, Austria-Hungary was composed of many different ethnic groups and several of these now demanded independence. Such demands threatened Austria-Hungary with dismemberment, and became a major factor leading to war.

▶ **Economic Rivalries and Imperialism**. Behind the nationalistic rivalries of the great powers were competing economic interests. German industrialization threatened British economic supremacy. Russian desires to expand their influence in the Balkans threatened both Austria-Hungary and Ottoman Turkey. Competing colonial claims also created an atmosphere of tension.

▶ **The Alliance System**. Starting in the 1890s, Europe had divided into two separate alliance systems. On one side stood Germany and Austria-Hungary; on the other, Russia, France and Great Britain. Although these alliances originally sought to preserve the existing balance of power, every dispute involving any two of these countries threatened to involve all the others.

▶ **Militarism**. Glorification of the military, military planning, and arms races also played key roles in pushing Europeans towards war. Germany and Britain competed to build the largest, most powerful navy. Because the British depended on their sea power, they were especially suspicious of Germany's naval expansion program. Germans, in turn, worried about facing a two-front war against both Russia and France. They felt they needed an army large enough to defeat both powers at once. Large armies and armaments made military leaders tense. Once a crisis started, each side's generals were afraid to back down. They even thought that whoever attacked first would most likely end up winning the war.

The Flashpoint of the War

On June 28, 1914, **Archduke Francis Ferdinand**, the heir to the throne of Austria-Hungary, was assassinated in Sarajevo by Slavic nationalists. The Austrian government decided to teach Serbia a lesson. They sent an ultimatum, making demands that Serbia could not meet. Austria then invaded Serbia (see map on page 179). Because of their alliances, Russia backed Serbia and Germany supported Austria. France was pulled into the war by its alliance with Russia. When Germany marched through neutral Belgium to advance on Paris, Britain also became involved. What should have been a minor regional crisis escalated into a major European war—between the **Central Powers** (Germany and Austria-Hungary, joined by Ottoman Turkey) and the **Allied Powers** (Britain, France, Russia, and, after it changed sides, Italy).

Fighting in Europe

Military leaders thought the contest would be over quickly. They were wrong. In fact, the war became a struggle lasting several years. A host of new and improved weapons were used to fight the war—machine guns, poison gas, submarines, airplanes, and tanks. These new weapons prevented either side from quickly defeating the other.

Soldiers required gas masks to avoid the effects of poison gases

▶ **Trench Warfare**. The Germans at first advanced through Belgium and northern France. However, their advance was stopped by the use of machine gun fire, which made it difficult to advance any further. Both sides dug **trenches** that soon extended for hundreds of miles. Soldiers in the trenches suffered from loud shelling, rats and lice, dampness, trench foot, and disease. The trenches were separated by an area of barbed wire and land mines known as "no man's land." Anyone advancing into "no man's land" would be fired at by machine guns. **Tanks** were still new and unable to break through. Each side bombarded the other with heavy artillery and even tried using **poison gas**—a form of **chemical warfare**—but neither side could defeat the other.

▶ **Naval Blockade**. With the stalemate in Western Europe, Great Britain set out to use its naval power to starve Germany into submission. The British established a naval blockade of the North Sea, preventing foreign arms or foodstuffs from reaching Germany. The Germans did not have enough battleships to defeat the British navy. They responded by using their submarines to prevent ships from bringing supplies to Great Britain. The submarines used their torpedoes to sink enemy ships.

▶ **Airplanes**. Overhead, a new invention, the airplane, dominated the sky. Airplanes were often used for reconnaissance—to see what was happening on the battlefield below. Airmen and allied pilots sometimes engaged in "dogfights"—duels in the sky in which each pilot tried to shoot down the other. However, airplanes were still new and did not play as important a role as they would in later wars.

America Goes to War

While the armies of Europe were locked in ferocious combat, Americans attempted to follow their traditional policy—first announced in Washington's "Farewell Address" more than a century earlier—of avoiding entanglement in European conflicts. The United States was not a member of either European alliance. Americans felt relatively safe, protected by the oceans. President Wilson declared that America would remain neutral. Two years later, Wilson was re-elected President in 1916 with the campaign slogan, "He kept us out of war!" Pacifists, isolationists, and German Americans were especially opposed to being dragged into a war on behalf of the Allies. Despite these efforts at maintaining neutrality, the Americans did eventually enter the war in April 1917. Why did this happen?

Cultural Ties

Most Americans already favored the Allies in the war. Many Americans traced their ancestry to Britain. A common language and a common history also tied Americans to Britain. The United States, Great Britain, and France further shared the same political system—democracy. Although Germany had a Parliament, its government was controlled by an autocratic **Kaiser** (*Emperor*). Most Americans detested German militarism. On the other hand, a large number of Americans could trace their ancestry to Germany.

German Atrocities and Allied Propaganda

Americans were especially shocked at the German invasion of Belgium. German war plans had called for the German army to march through neutral Belgium as the quickest way to invade France and encircle Paris. Germany went ahead with these plans even though Belgium had not declared war and the invasion was a violation of international law. When the German army encountered unexpected resistance, they shot civilians without trial and destroyed buildings. Such atrocities were widely reported in the American press. American newspapers even carried exaggerated stories of German soldiers cutting off children's hands and slicing babies with bayonets. Even though these stories were false, American public opinion was horrified.

Isolation of the Central Powers

The British blockade cut off the Central Powers from the United States. Americans grew more favorable to the Allies because they heard only their side of the story. While American trade to Germany dropped to almost nothing, American trade to Britain and France increased four-fold between 1914 and 1916. American bankers lent $2 billion to the Allied Powers—and only one-tenth of that amount to the Central Powers. The United States became the main source of arms, supplies, and food for Britain and France.

German Submarine Warfare and the United States

To break the British blockade, to save their own people from starvation, and to win the war, the German government resorted to submarine warfare. This was the main factor leading to American entry into World War I.

The British Blockade

The British blockade of Germany was in violation of international law. The British put explosive mines in the North Sea. They forced all ships to land in Britain before entering the North Sea. They prevented food as well as arms from going to Germany. They also blockaded neutral countries like Norway, Sweden and Denmark. President Wilson protested against these violations, but he did not cut off American trade with the Allies. U.S. merchant ships travelled in groups, or **convoys**, escorted by battleships. Meanwhile, hundreds of thousands of Germans were starving to death from the lack of food and fertilizers.

The German Counter-Blockade

The German fleet was not powerful enough to challenge the British navy. However, the Germans did have a strong fleet of submarines ("U-Boats"). A few months after the British declared their naval blockade of Germany, Germans retaliated by announcing a submarine blockade of Britain. Germany threatened to sink all Allied merchant ships sailing in the blockaded area. Because their submarines were underwater and so small, the Germans were unable to provide traditional warnings before attack or even to rescue survivors. All this violated international law. The

Germans did not intend to attack American ships, but those Americans travelling on Allied ships would be affected. Most Americans felt this violated "freedom of the seas."

Sinking of the Lusitania, May 1915

On May 7, 1915, a German submarine shot a single torpedo at close range at the *Lusitania*, a British passenger ship that had sailed from New York and was just off the Irish coast. The ship sank in just 18 minutes, far faster than the *Titanic* had three years earlier. Although there were sufficient lifeboats, people simply did not have time to get in them. More than a thousand passengers were killed, including 128 Americans and 94 children. American newspapers widely reported this disaster. The sinking of the *Lusitania* had a powerful impact on the American public, stirring up anti-German feelings and creating a desire for revenge. Germans claimed the *Lusitania* had secretly concealed armaments. President Wilson sent a strong protest to Germany, but he refused to declare war over this incident.

German U-boats at anchor at Kiel in Northern Germany. The U-20 on the far right sank the *Lusitania*.

The "Sussex Pledge," 1916

After a German submarine attack on an unarmed French passenger ship, the *Sussex*, Wilson threatened to break off diplomatic relations with Germany. The German government then pledged not to sink any more ocean liners or merchant ships without prior warning or making provisions for passengers. However, Germany agreed to these terms only on the condition that the United States persuade the Allies to lift the naval blockade of Germany. Meanwhile the British continued to use convoys—groups of merchant ships traveling together and protected by one or more battleships—to reduce their losses to submarines.

Germany Declares "Unrestricted Submarine Warfare," January 1917

German leaders realized that a resumption of submarine warfare would probably result in war with the United States. But they were suffering desperately from the lack of supplies and food due to the British blockade. Moreover, along the Eastern Front, Russia was almost defeated, while on the Western Front, several French units had mutinied. German military leaders felt that with unrestricted submarine warfare, they could probably defeat Britain and France before the United States could effectively intervene. They therefore took a calculated risk by announcing that they would sink all ships—neutral as well as Allied—traveling in the area of their blockade around Britain. This new policy was a clear violation of the American principle of "freedom of the seas"—the right claimed by the United States, as a neutral country, to ship non-military goods, even to nations at war.

The Zimmerman Telegram, March 1917

Popular feelings against Germany were further inflamed when a secret telegram was discovered and decoded by the British from the German Foreign Minister, Arthur Zimmerman, promising the return of New Mexico, Arizona and Texas to Mexico if it allied with Germany against the United States. The telegram was printed in American newspapers on March 1, 1917.

German Submarines Sink American Merchant Ships, March 1917

Even after the German announcement of unrestricted submarine warfare and the publication of the Zimmerman telegram, Wilson still hoped to avoid war. He decided he would not ask Congress for a declaration unless Germany actually committed "overt acts" against American shipping. In March 1917, German submarines then sank several unarmed American merchant vessels. Wilson addressed Congress and obtained a declaration of war in early April 1917.

American Idealism—Making the World "Safe for Democracy"

An idealistic Progressive, Wilson expanded the American war effort from a defense of "freedom of the seas" to a crusade for democracy. By the time that Americans entered the war in April 1917, Russia had been shaken by the first of two revolutions. In April 1917, Russia was a democracy, and the Allies had become a league of democratic nations. Wilson therefore told Congress that the United States was not going to war against the German people, but against their leaders. America's aim in entering the war was to establish the ultimate peace of the world and to free its peoples: "The world must be made safe for democracy." Most Americans found it inspiring to endure the rigors of the war for such high-minded ideals. With a strong sense of moral superiority, they set out to save and remake the world.

The Historian's Apprentice

Have your class hold a debate on the following:

"Resolved: That American intervention in World War I was justified."

Those in favor of the resolution should show why the United States was right to enter the war. Those opposed should show why Americans should not have become involved.

America at War, 1917–1918

Mobilization

Allied leaders in Europe hoped that the United States would send fresh troops to fill their own ranks. Instead, Wilson announced he would keep American troops together as the million-man **American Expeditionary Force** (AEF). The AEF was placed under the command of General Pershing—the same general whom Wilson had unsuccessfully sent into Mexico chasing Pancho Villa. Despite more than three years of conflict across the Atlantic, Americans were not prepared for war in April 1917. The first task ahead was **mobilizing** (*bringing into use*) America's vast resources.

The Selective Service Act

Wilson hesitated between raising a voluntary army or relying on conscription. He finally decided on **conscription** (or compulsory military service, also known as the "draft"). Because the notion of "service" was in the air, Congress called its conscription law the "**Selective Service Act**." Ten million men immediately registered for the "draft." Dates of birthdays were chosen out of a glass jar to determine the order in which men would be called to serve. Eventually, almost three million men were drafted into the armed services, while another two million volunteered.

Some men refused to serve because it violated their religious beliefs to kill others. These men became

Chapter 9 | The United States in World War I

known as **conscientious objectors**. Even if they weren't prepared to fight, they were still expected to report to military camp if they were drafted. Many conscientious objectors were sent to France to serve in noncombatant roles, such as driving an ambulance or caring for the wounded. Others were permitted to work on farms in the United States, where there was a shortage of labor, or to serve as fire fighters. Still others were assigned to the American Friends Service Committee, a Quaker organization, provided different forms of alternative service for conscientious objectors. Several hundred conscientious objectors were imprisoned during the war. Some of these were subjected to unfair treatment, and two even died at the hands of their jailers.

The Historian's Apprentice

To be a conscientious objector, a person generally had to belong to a recognized religious group opposed to warfare of any kind, such as the Amish, Mennonites or Quakers. Simple political opposition to World War I was not considered to be enough to excuse a man from military service. Write a short essay (2–3 paragraphs) explaining why, in your opinion, this policy was either fair or unfair.

The Committee of Public Information

George Creel was appointed to run the **Committee of Public Information** (CPI). This agency created posters, printed pamphlets, made billboards, offered news releases to newspapers, made short newsreels to be shown in movie theaters, and provided other forms of propaganda in favor of the war effort. **Propaganda** is one-sided information designed to persuade listeners. Creel's "four-minute men" were trained speakers who gave short speeches on behalf of the war during intermissions in movie theaters and at public assemblies. Hollywood helped in the effort by making patriotic, anti-German films.

The War-Time Economy

The United States now had to train and equip a large body of troops as well as continue helping its European allies. American leaders continued to lend money to Britain and France, thinking that this might help reduce the future cost of the war in American lives. Americans also had to manufacture arms and equipment.

In peacetime, Wilson had acted to curb Big Business in favor of free competition. After the outbreak of the war, however, he collaborated with the leaders of Big Business and organized labor to coordinate the economy and direct it towards the war effort.

The war saw a vast expansion of the federal government. Wilson was given sweeping powers by Congress to regulate wartime production. For this purpose, he established a number of special agencies:

▶ The **War Industries Board**, headed by Bernard Baruch, coordinated America's wartime manufacturing. Wilson and Baruch hoped to persuade businesses to take voluntary action. Baruch offered high prices for products, using profits rather than state controls to stimulate wartime industries. The War Industries Board also set standard specifications for all kinds of goods.

▶ The **Food Administration** oversaw the production and distribution of food. The head of the Food Administration, **Herbert Hoover**, expanded agricultural production by raising food prices. He guaranteed farmers a minimum price for wheat. Hoover wanted to avoid the rationing of food. He preferred voluntary methods, persuading the public to eat less wheat

and meat so that these could be sent overseas. Hoover also instructed farmers in more efficient farming methods. Farm incomes rose, food production increased and home consumption fell, creating a surplus of food for American troops and their overseas allies.

- The **Fuel Administration** regulated coal and gasoline, and called for voluntary conservation.

- Railroads were nationalized and placed under the control of the **Railroad Administration**, headed by Treasury Secretary William McAdoo. Fares were standardized, and the facilities of different railroad companies were shared. McAdoo provided money for railroad repairs and provided higher wages to railroad workers.

- The **Emergency Ship Corporation**, another government agency, built a fleet of merchant ships to transport men and supplies to Europe.

- Wilson recognized organized labor, supported the 8-hour workday and even addressed the American Federation of Labor (AFL) in November 1917. He created the **War Labor Board**, a new body for mediating disputes between owners and workers. AFL leader Samuel Gompers promised Wilson that workers would not go on strike before the end of the war. During the war, workers' wages went up, and membership in the AFL almost doubled.

Paying for the War

At first, Wilson and his cabinet thought they would pay for most of the war with the new graduated income tax and special taxes on "war profits" (*extra profits made by companies supplying the government with wartime goods*). This would have placed most of the burden of paying for the war on the wealthy, and was strongly supported by Progressives such as Robert La Follette. The costs of the war turned out to be far greater than anyone had ever expected. William McAdoo, Secretary of the Treasury, gave up all hopes of paying for even half of the war through taxation. In the end, the war cost over $30 billion, an unimaginable sum at that time and more than 30 times the total revenue of the federal government in 1916. Taxes, mainly on the wealthy, paid for about one-third of the war, while war bonds, sold to the public, paid for the rest. The national debt rose from $1 billion in 1916 to $20 billion by the war's end.

The war bonds became widely known as "**Liberty bonds**." They paid low interest rates. The government whipped up enthusiasm for the war effort to encourage people to buy them. Purchasing Liberty bonds became a patriotic act. There were posters, newspaper advertisements, and public drives to sell war bonds. Some Americans, especially German Americans, were pressured into buying war bonds to demonstrate their patriotism.

Large numbers of people actually borrowed money from the bank to buy these bonds. The new Federal Reserve System also created new money, inflating the economy to meet wartime needs.

As much as one-third of the money spent during the war was lent to the Allies. As a result, the United States turned from a *debtor* to a *creditor* nation— instead of owing money to foreign countries for

> A **bond** is a note sold by the government. The government promises to pay interest to the holder of the bond at a fixed rate for a period of time, and then promises to buy the bond back at the end of this period. A war bond is sold by the government in time of war to meet wartime expenses.

their earlier investments, these countries now owed money to the United States.

Civil Rights on the Home Front

In wartime, there are often demands to reduce the scope of individual rights in the interests of national security. In the case of World War I, Wilson and his government became suspicious of critics; other Americans grew distrustful of the nation's large German-American population. As a result, Congress passed emergency measures restricting free speech.

In 1917, Wilson pushed the **Espionage Act** through Congress. This law created procedures for detecting and imprisoning spies. It allowed the federal government to censor the mails and to arrest anyone interfering with the enforcement of the draft.

This was followed the next year by the **Sedition Act of 1918**. This law made it a crime to use "disloyal" or "abusive language" about the government, the flag, or the Constitution.

The government prosecuted more than 2,000 people under these acts. Postmaster General Albert Burleson had his employees read through the mail. Burleson refused to allow socialists and other groups critical of Wilson's policies to mail their newsletters and magazines at the lower rates generally given to periodical publications. He also required advance translation of all foreign periodicals into English for government review. The expense and delay involved in translating and obtaining government approval meant that many foreign language newspapers had to close down.

Socialists viewed the war as a capitalist quarrel using workingmen as cannon fodder. The Socialist Party became the rallying point for those who opposed the war. In June 1918, **Eugene Debs**—the former Socialist candidate for the Presidency—gave an anti-war speech in Ohio and was arrested. Debs claimed that he had a right to exercise his free speech, which was protected by the First Amendment, but he was imprisoned all the same. Other leading socialists against the war, such as Bill Haywood and Emma Goldman, were also sent to prison.

Charles Schenck was arrested for violating the Espionage Act of 1917 when he mailed leaflets advising young men to resist the draft. Schenck claimed his arrest violated his free speech rights. In ***Schenck v. U.S.*** (1919), the Supreme Court upheld limits on free speech whenever "a clear and present danger" is evident.

In the cases of *Debs v. U.S.* (1919) and *Abrams v. U.S.*, the Supreme Court again upheld these restrictions on free speech. Not only the federal government, but also the state governments took steps against those people they suspected of disloyalty.

The Historian's Apprentice

One of the most famous Supreme Court Justices, Justice Oliver Wendell Holmes, wrote the unanimous opinion of the Court in *Schenck v. U.S.*:

> "The most stringent [strict] protection of free speech would not protect a man in falsely shouting fire in a theatre and causing a panic. . . . The question in every case is whether the words used are used in such circumstances and are of such a nature as to create a clear and present danger that they will bring about the substantive evils that Congress has a right to prevent."

▶ Do you think Schenck's actions created a "clear and present danger"?
▶ In times of war, which actions should be permitted as forms of free speech and which ones should be prohibited?

The Experiences of Women and Minorities—at Home and Overseas

Women

In January 1917, Jeanette Rankin became the first woman in Congress. When Congress declared war a few months later, many women's rights organizations were actively campaigning for a constitutional amendment granting women the right to vote. Others thought it would be better to achieve women's suffrage state-by-state. Suffragists were angry at Wilson's failure to support women's rights more actively. Most women's organizations were strongly opposed to U.S. entry into the war. However, once the United States entered the conflict, they wanted to display their patriotism. The National American Woman Suffrage Association (NAWSA) gave strong support to the war effort. A special Woman's Committee was created to coordinate women's efforts. Ida Tarbell, the muckraker, acted as vice-chairman of this group. Alice Paul's National Woman's Party, on the other hand, continued to oppose American involvement in the war.

Women performed every sort of task on the home front. They sold war bonds, knitted socks, cooked meatless dinners, and wore shorter skirts to save cloth for uniforms. Others joined the Red Cross or volunteered to serve as nurses overseas. Because of the labor shortage at home, many women took men's jobs in factories and other places.

German Americans

Prejudice against **German Americans** became especially widespread. In 1914, as many as one quarter of the U.S. population were descended from German immigrants. There were German-American clubs, music halls, restaurants, schools and foods. German was the leading foreign language taught in the United States. When President Wilson addressed the Congress asking for a declaration of war on Germany, he pointedly reminded them that most German Americans were loyal Americans; but he also announced that the German government had sent spies to the United States. After the declaration of war, posters by Creel's Committee of Public Information frequently depicted Germans as bloodthirsty "Huns." Rumors of German atrocities, most of them untrue, spread. German books were taken out of libraries and burned. Foods were renamed: sauerkraut (pickled cabbage) became "liberty cabbage," and hamburgers became "liberty steaks." Many German Americans changed their last names to sound more "American." German immigrants in the United States had to be fingerprinted, answer a detailed questionnaire, and take an oath of allegiance. More than 4,000 German Americans were imprisoned during the war as suspected spies. The federal government also seized $200 million in assets of German Americans. Robert Prager, a German immigrant and a socialist, was attacked by a mob, covered with a flag, dragged through his town, and hanged. His only crime was being a German American.

A Century of German Immigration to the United States, 1821–1920

Decade	Total Number	Percentage of Total Immigration to USA
1821–1830	7,729	5.1
1831–1840	152,454	25.4
1841–1850	434,626	25.3
1851–1860	951,667	36.6
1861–1870	787,468	34.0
1871–1880	718,182	25.5
1881–1890	1,452,970	27.7
1891–1900	505,152	13.7
1901–1910	341,498	3.9
1911–1920	143,945	2.5

Source: Roger Daniels, *Coming to America* (New York, 1990), p. 146.

Other minority groups saw the war as an opportunity to show their patriotism.

American Indians

Even before the United States entered the war, some members of American Indian tribes enlisted in Canada in order to fight in Europe. Young American Indians, trained in military values in non-reservation boarding schools, were especially enthusiastic volunteers. Even many American Indians who were not U.S. citizens enlisted. When the draft was introduced, the Commissioner of Indian Affairs was sent to register all American Indian males, ages 21 to 30, who either were citizens or intended to become so. About 6,000 American Indians volunteered and another 6,000 were drafted—or 20% of all eligible males—a higher proportion than in the general population. More than 2,000 of them saw action in France. Unlike African-American soldiers, American Indian troops were integrated into white units. Six hundred Oklahoma Indians, mostly Choctaw and Cherokee, were assigned to a unit widely recognized for its courage in battle and several of them received military decorations in France. So many American Indians were recognized for bravery that the Army actually conducted special tests to see what accounted for their superiority in warfare. The Army also used Choctaw soldiers to send messages by radio in their native language to prevent German listeners from deciphering them and discovering Allied plans. On the home front, costumed Indians were used by the government for recruiting purposes and to sell war bonds. Indians themselves purchased $15 million in war bonds. American Indian children volunteered for the Red Cross. The Indian Citizenship Act of 1919 gave those Indians who had served in the armed forces during the war the right to become U.S. citizens.

Jewish Americans

Like other minority groups in the early 20th century, Jewish Americans faced prejudice. Only a year before the war had broken out in Europe, Leo Frank, a Jewish man, was lynched by an angry mob in Georgia. In reaction, American Jews had formed the **Anti-Defamation League** to oppose anti-Semitism and religious prejudice generally. American Jews signed up to fight in World War I in disproportionate numbers. Although only three percent of the American population was Jewish, they made up five percent of the U.S. Army. The American Jewish community also raised funds to help people in Europe. The American Jewish Joint Distribution Committee raised $63 million in relief funds.

African Americans

African Americans had supported Wilson in 1912 but had been very disappointed by his record on race relations. Wilson, who was from Virginia, actually brought racial segregation back to the Post Office and U.S. Treasury Department. He also refused to integrate the armed services. In late July 1917, 15,000 African Americans silently marched down Fifth Avenue, New York, to protest "Jim Crow" laws and lynchings in the South.

Thousands of African Americans nonetheless volunteered for service when the war broke out. More than 100,000 of them eventually went to France. African-American leaders encouraged their followers to enlist so that, by fighting for freedom and democracy abroad, they could help to achieve it more rapidly at home. A special segregated facility was set up in Iowa to train African-American officers. Some African-American combat units were assigned directly to French forces. They fought in France and marched into Germany with the French army. The first two Americans to receive the French *Croix de Guerre* for heroism in combat were African Americans: Henry Johnson and Needham Roberts.

African-American soldiers sometimes resisted discrimination. In Houston, Texas, townspeople shouted insults at an African-American regiment, and the soldiers fired back. Seventeen were killed. Thirteen of the soldiers were later executed. After living in France, a less racist society than the South, many African-American soldiers were eager for a real change.

Hispanic Americans

Mexican Americans, especially from Texas, enlisted to show their patriotism. Some received special English language training at Camp Cody, New Mexico. Many, like Marcelino Serna, fought with great bravery. In March 1917, Congress extended U.S. citizenship to Puerto Ricans, making them subject to the draft. About 18,000 of them served in the war. Because of a shortage of farm laborers, U.S. officials made it easier for Mexican workers to enter the country. Meanwhile Cuba entered the war as an ally of the United States and sent officers here for training.

Asian Americans

By 1917, about 180,000 Asian Americans lived in the United States. The three major groups were Japanese Americans, Chinese Americans and Filipinos. A handful of Filipinos had recently graduated from the two military academies—West Point and Annapolis. Filipino men who had gone to Hawaii as workers suddenly found themselves subject to the new draft. In the military, Asian Americans were assigned to separate units as "non-whites" and few saw combat. There were notable exceptions: Marine Private Tomas Mateo Claudio and Army Sergeant Sing Kee fought at the Battle of Château-Thierry: Claudio was killed, but Kee survived to receive the Distinguished Service Medal. Sergeant Major Tokukiro Nishimura Slocum fought with distinction as a member of the 328th Infantry Regiment, 82nd Infantry Division. Asian Americans who served in the armed forces were permitted to become naturalized citizens. At the same time, Congress passed the Immigration Act of 1917, barring any further Japanese or Chinese immigration. In 1918, the Philippines actually equipped a force of 25,000 men from the Philippine National Guard to join Pershing's forces in France, but an armistice ending the war was signed before they could be sent.

The Labor Shortage and the Great Migration

When men left for training and the battlefields of Europe, this created a labor shortage at home. Women, African Americans, and members of other minorities filled much of this gap by taking jobs in factories, farms, and railroads. Labor agents appeared in the South to recruit workers for Northern factories. This started the flow of African Americans known as the **Great Migration**. Thousands of African Americans left the South, with its "Jim Crow" laws and rural poverty, for cities in the Northeast and Midwest. Southerners sometimes resorted to violence to prevent the loss of more African Americans, whom they needed for their labor.

The Historian's Apprentice

Choose one of the groups above and write a brief report describing their experiences during World War I.

"Over There"—Allied Victory in Europe

The United States entered the war in April 1917. That same spring, German submarines aggressively attacked Allied ships until the use of the convoy system reduced shipping losses in the Atlantic. American troops did not begin arriving in France for several months and at first only in a trickle. In the meantime, Russia dropped out of the war, allowing Germany to concentrate all its efforts on the Western Front. The Germans launched a great offensive in March 1918. But German leaders miscalculated when they thought they could achieve a breakthrough. The German offensive was unable to reach Paris and soon collapsed. By June 1918, American troops began arriving in large numbers—about 10,000 a day. Almost two million American troops eventually reached Europe. The new American Expeditionary Force gave the Allies overwhelming superiority. The German army finally surrendered in November 1918. An **armistice**, or ceasefire, was signed and all fighting stopped. Although Americans had only been in the war just over a year, they suffered heavy casualties with 117,000 killed.

American soldiers celebrate the announcement of peace.

The Peace Settlement: Wilson and the Treaty of Versailles

The Fourteen Points

Even before the war had ended, President Wilson announced America's aims in a famous speech to Congress in January 1918. Wilson enumerated "**Fourteen Points**." These reflected his view that the war should become a crusade for democracy. The Fourteen Points demanded national self-determination for the peoples of Europe. The map of Europe would be redrawn so that each nationality had its own nation-state and government. Austria-Hungary would be broken up into smaller states. Poland, divided up by neighboring European monarchs more than a century before, would be reunited.

Woodrow Wilson

Wilson called for a "New Diplomacy" to replace the older policies of militarism and balance-of-power politics that had led to the war. He also demanded freedom of the seas, equal trade terms, reduced armaments, an end to secret diplomacy, and the creation of a new international peace-keeping organization, the "League of Nations." Wilson thus hoped to create a world of peaceful democratic states in which future world wars would no longer be possible. Inspired by Wilson's promises and hoping to get better peace terms, Germans overthrew the Kaiser (*the German Emperor*) in November 1918.

The Historian's Apprentice

The Fourteen Points

1. Open covenants of peace, openly arrived at . . . [D]iplomacy shall proceed always frankly and in the public view.
2. Absolute freedom of navigation upon the seas . . .
3. The removal, so far as possible, of all economic barriers and the establishment of equality of trade conditions among all the nations . . .
4. Adequate guarantees given . . . that national armaments will be reduced . . .
5. A free, open-minded, and absolutely impartial adjustment of all colonial claims . . .
6. The evacuation of all Russian territory and such a settlement of all questions affecting Russia as will secure the best and freest cooperation of the other nations of the world . . .
7. Belgium, the whole world will agree, must be evacuated and restored . . .
8. All French territory should be freed and the invaded portions restored, and the wrong done to France by Prussia in 1871 in the matter of Alsace-Lorraine, which has unsettled the peace of the world for nearly fifty years, should be righted . . .
9. A readjustment of the frontiers of Italy should be effected along clearly recognizable lines of nationality.
10. The peoples of Austria-Hungary, whose place among the nations we wish to see safeguarded and assured, should be accorded the freest opportunity to autonomous development.
11. Romania, Serbia, and Montenegro should be evacuated; occupied territories restored . . .
12. The Turkish portion of the present Ottoman Empire should be assured a secure sovereignty, but the other nationalities which are now under Turkish rule should be assured an . . . opportunity of autonomous development.

13. An independent Polish state should be erected which should include the territories inhabited by indisputably Polish populations . . .
14. A general association of nations must be formed under specific covenants for the purpose of affording mutual guarantees of political independence and territorial integrity to great and small states alike . . .

▶ Explain two of Wilson's Fourteen Points in your own words.
▶ In what ways did the Fourteen Points represent American values? Use specific evidence from the Fourteen Points to support your answer.

The Paris Peace Conference and the Treaty of Versailles

Even though the armistice was concluded, the Allies and defeated powers still had to negotiate a final peace. Wilson personally traveled to Paris to negotiate the peace treaties. Most historians agree that Wilson made a crucial mistake in not inviting influential Senators to accompany him, since the U.S. Senate would eventually have to ratify each treaty. In Paris, the peace settlement was decided by the "**Big Four**": Britain, France, Italy and the U.S. Wilson came into conflict with other Allied leaders who wanted to impose a harsher treaty on Germany. Wilson eventually made many concessions to their views in order to win their support for the League of Nations, which was included in the peace treaty at Wilson's insistence. The final terms of the **Treaty of Versailles** and its related treaties were extremely harsh on Germany and the other defeated Central Powers:

1. Germany lost territory to France and Poland, and lost all of its colonies.
2. Germany lost its navy, while its once powerful army was reduced to the size of a police force.
3. Germans were forced to sign the "**War Guilt**" clause, accepting blame for starting the war. For this reason, they were required to pay huge **reparations** (*payment for damages*) to the Allies.
4. Austria-Hungary was divided into several smaller national states.
5. Like the Tsar and the Kaiser, the Sultan was overthrown and Turkey became a republic. The Ottoman Empire lost most of its territories in the Middle East. Although the Allies had made various promises to local peoples, most of these territories were given to Britain or France to govern as "mandates."

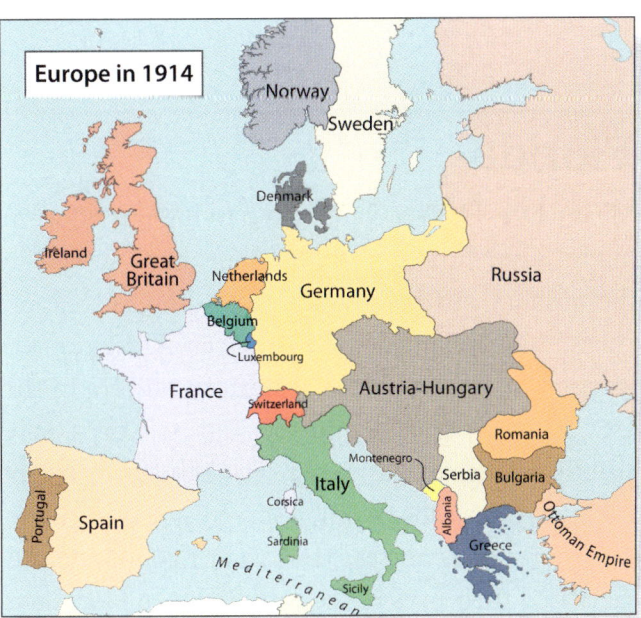

The League of Nations

Just as Wilson had demanded, the Versailles Treaty created the **League of Nations**—an organization of nations that would defend each other against aggressors. It was believed that this new institution could discourage aggression and prevent future wars. Since the League had no army of its own, however, it depended entirely on the good will of its members to stop acts of aggression. **Article X** of the **Covenant of the League of Nations** (*the agreement inserted into the Treaty of Versailles creating the League*) stated that League members would help other League members facing aggression.

The United States Rejects the Versailles Treaty and Retreats into Isolationism

When Wilson returned back home, he needed the support of two-thirds of the U.S. Senate to ratify the treaty. But many Americans were disillusioned with what had been achieved after the heavy costs of the war. Their disillusionment was reflected in the 1918 Congressional elections, in which Republicans gained control of the Senate. Republicans especially objected to Article X.

When the Versailles Treaty was debated in the Senate in 1919, Wilson refused to accept any compromises offered by Senator Henry Cabot Lodge and other leading Republicans. He instructed Democrats to oppose ratification of the Treaty with Lodge's modifications. Wilson decided to appeal directly to voters by giving speeches throughout the country. Three weeks after he began this exhausting campaign to win public support, Wilson suffered a major stroke, which left him partially paralyzed.

The Senate then rejected Wilson's treaty. Republicans won further support in the 1920 Presidential election. In fact, the United States never joined the League of Nations. Instead, it signed a separate peace with Germany in 1921. Americans once again decided to avoid entanglements with Europe. They became more concerned with their own well-being at home and less committed to foreign affairs.

The Historian's Apprentice

Pretend your classroom is the U.S. Senate in 1919. Hold your own debate on the Treaty of Versailles, including the League of Nations. One class member should act as Woodrow Wilson addressing the Senate. Another should act as Henry Cabot Lodge, opposing the treaty and proposing amendments. Other class members should speak as Senators. Then hold a vote on whether to ratify the treaty.

Focus on Florida

During World War I, Florida had one of its most colorful governors. In 1916, Sidney J. Catts was elected as Governor of Florida after campaigning against alcoholic drinks and Catholics. He toured the state in his Model-T automobile, shouting speeches through a bullhorn. Florida passed "Prohibition" of alcoholic beverages in 1917. Catts remained Governor until January 1921. During the war, he encouraged anti-German sentiment and even accused African Americans of conspiring with Germany.

Meanwhile, Florida contributed to the war effort in many ways. Just over 42,000 Floridians served in the military during the war. According to state records, these included 13,024 African-American enlistees and seven African-American officers in the U.S. Army. The Navy and the Marine Corps were strictly segregated at the time and refused to accept African Americans. Women served as secretaries in the Navy and as nurses. More than 1,000 Floridians sacrificed their lives in the war. Eighteen Floridians received the Distinguished Service Cross for extreme gallantry and courage.

Florida further contributed to the war by providing food and other products. Its farms produced cotton for making uniforms, vegetables, and fruits—especially citrus fruits. Its forests provided timber. Shipyards in Tampa and Jacksonville built Allied ships. A submarine base in Key West, five flight schools in Pensacola and other Florida cities, and other military camps helped to train troops. Thomas Edison spent time in Key West developing depth charges for use against submarines in naval warfare. Wartime experiences in turn affected Florida. Many who trained in Florida later returned as tourists or residents.

Racial relations actually worsened as a result of the war. African Americans who had served in the war had witnessed how Northern states and Europe treated them with greater respect and grew hopeful for changes in Florida after the war. A historic African-American voter registration drive was launched in Jacksonville in January 1919. Black churches, unions, clubs, and meeting places held workshops on voter registration. African-American veterans from the war and newly enfranchised women attempted to assert their rights. But the 1920 election proved to be one of the bloodiest in Florida history. Many of those African Americans who attempted to vote were beaten and a few were even killed. The state remained rigid in its segregationist policies.

Review Cards

Long-Term Causes of World War I

- **Nationalism.** Nationalist feelings increased the rivalries between the "Great Powers" of Europe and encouraged ethnic groups in multi-national empires to form their own nation-states.
- **Economic Rivalries and Imperialism** of the "Great Powers" increased spirit of competition and conflict.
- **The Alliance Systems** (Germany and Austria vs. Russia, France, and Great Britain). Any conflict between nations in the opposing alliances threatened to draw in all the others.
- **Militarism.** Glorification of the military, military planning, and arms races played key roles in pushing Europeans to war. Generals felt they had to be the first to mobilize and attack.

"Flashpoint" of World War I

- **Flashpoint:** the assassination of **Archduke Ferdinand** of Austria-Hungary on June 28, 1914, by Serb nationalists.
- Austria invaded Serbia to teach the Serbs a lesson.
- This brought Russia and the other Great Powers into the conflict because of their alliances. Germany invaded France by marching through Belgium, ensuring British entry into the war.

Fighting in Europe

New weapons employed in the war prevented either side from quickly defeating the other.
- **Trench warfare.** The use of **machine guns** led soldiers to dig **trenches.** The trenches were separated by barbed wire and land mines known as "no man's land." Heavy artillery and **chemical warfare** (*poison gas*) were sometimes used.
- **Naval Blockade.** British blockade of the North Sea prevented foreign arms and food from reaching Germany. In retaliation, Germany used submarines (**U-boats**) to prevent supply ships from reaching Britain.
- **Airplanes.** Used for reconnaissance and "dogfights." They did not play a major role but this was a precursor for later wars.

Why Americans Went to War

- **Cultural Ties:** a common language and history with Britain.
- **Allied Propaganda** and **German Atrocities:** The German invasion of neutral Belgium led to exaggerated stories of German atrocities—largely false—which shocked Americans.
- **Isolation of the Central Powers:** Because of the British naval blockade, the Central Powers were isolated from the United States. Because Americans only heard the British side of the story, they grew more favorable to the Allies. U.S. trade with Germany dropped to almost nothing while the United States became the main provider of arms, food and supplies to the Allies.
- **Zimmerman Telegram** (March 1917): Germany promised the return of New Mexico, Arizona, and Texas to Mexico, if Mexico allied itself with Germany. The publication of this telegram in U.S. newspapers outraged the public.
- **Submarine Warfare:** *see next page*

German Submarine Warfare

- **British Blockade:** The British blockade of Germany led to German submarine warfare against ships bringing supplies to Britain. German submarines were too small to announce themselves in advance of attack or to carry survivors.
- **Lusitania:** In May 1915, a German submarine sank the *Lusitania*, a British passenger ship. The attack led to over a thousand deaths, including 128 Americans and 94 children, and greatly stirred anti-German feelings among Americans.
- **Sussex Pledge:** Another German submarine sank the *Sussex*, a French passenger ship in 1916. Germany pledged not to sink any more ocean liners or merchant ships without warning or rescuing survivors.
- **Unrestricted Submarine Warfare:** In January 1917, Germany declared "unrestricted submarine warfare." German leaders felt they could defeat the Allies before the United States entered the war. The sinking of more U.S. merchant ships in 1917 led to a U.S. declaration of war on Germany. Wilson called for intervention not only to protect freedom of the seas but as a crusade to make the "world safe for democracy."

America at War

- **Mobilization:** President Wilson appointed General Pershing to command the million-man **American Expeditionary Force** (AEF).
- **Selective Service Act** required **conscription** (*compulsory military service known as the "draft"*).
- **Conscientious Objectors (COs):** Those who refused to fight on moral grounds. They still had to serve in noncombatant roles, such as ambulance drivers, caring for the wounded, working on farms, or as firefighters. Some were imprisoned and treated unfairly.
- **The Committee of Public Information:** This federal agency was responsible for propaganda in favor of the war effort, creating posters, pamphlets, billboards, press releases, newsreels, and anti-German films.

The War-Time Economy

The U.S. government collaborated with Big Business and organized labor to further the war effort:

- **War Industries Board:** Coordinated wartime manufacturing.
- **Food Administration:** Oversaw the production and distribution of food.
- **Fuel Administration:** Regulated coal and gasoline, and called for voluntary conservation.
- **Railroad Administration:** Nationalized the railways during the war.
- **The Emergency Ship Corporation:** Built a fleet of ships to transport men and supplies to Europe.
- **War Labor Board:** Mediated disputes between owners and workers.

Paying for the War

- Total war costs were $30 billion—30 times the total revenues of the federal government in 1916.
- Higher taxes on the wealthy raised 1/3 of the war costs.
- **Liberty Bonds.** The rest of the war was financed through borrowing. Liberty bonds were government bonds sold to the public and paid a low interest rate. The national debt rose from $1 billion in 1916 to $20 billion by the war's end.
- One-third of this money was lent to the Allies. The United States turned from being a "debtor" to a "creditor" nation.

Civil Rights on the Home Front

During the war, individual rights were restricted in the interests of national security:
- **Espionage Act of 1917** allowed government censorship of the mails and imprisonment of those who interfered with the draft.
- **Sedition Act of 1918** made it a crime to use "disloyal" language.
- These wartime restrictions were upheld by the U.S. Supreme Court:
  - *Schenck v. U.S.* (1919)—speech can be restricted whenever a "clear and present danger" is evident.
  - *Debs v. U.S.* and *Abrams v. U.S.* (1919)—also upheld restrictions on speech.

U.S. Minorities during World War I

When men went off to war, women, African Americans, and other minorities filled the gap by taking jobs in factories, farms, and railroads.
- **Women:** At the time war was declared, many women were campaigning for a constitutional amendment granting them the right to vote. The National American Woman Suffrage Association and its members supported the war effort by selling war bonds, knitting socks, cooking meatless dinners, joining the Red Cross, and serving as nurses. The National Woman's Party opposed the war.
- **German Americans:** Great prejudice was shown against German Americans. More than 4,000 were imprisoned. One German American was attacked by a mob and killed.
- **American Indians:** American Indians enlisted in World War I and fought bravely in Europe.
- **Jewish Americans:** Despite prejudice against them, a great number enlisted. The American Jewish community raised funds to help people in Europe.
- **African Americans:** African-American leaders urged their followers to fight for freedom and democracy abroad so they could achieve them more rapidly at home. Over 100,000 joined the war in Europe, although they were forced to serve in segregated units. African Americans were also recruited in large numbers for jobs in cities in the Northeast and Midwest. They left the South in the **Great Migration.**
- **Hispanic Americans:** Large numbers crossed the Mexican border to work on U.S. farms. Puerto Ricans were given U.S. citizenship and drafted. Many Latinos, like Marcelino Serna, fought with great bravery.
- **Asian Americans:** Japanese Americans, Chinese Americans, and Filipino Americans enlisted in the armed services even though they faced discrimination.

Allied Victory in 1918

- The **American Expeditionary Force** (AEF) gave the Allies overwhelming superiority. The German army surrendered in November 1918. An **armistice** for a ceasefire was signed and the fighting stopped.

The Fourteen Points

In January 1918, Wilson announced America's war aims in the **"Fourteen Points."** These reflected his view that the war was a crusade for democracy. The Fourteen Points included:
- self-determination for the peoples of Europe
- freedom of the seas
- equal trade terms
- reduced armaments
- an end to secret diplomacy
- creation of the League of Nations

Treaty of Versailles and Related Treaties
▶ Treaty terms were determined by the **Big Four**: Britain, France, Italy and the United States
▶ Germany lost territory to France and Poland, and lost all of its colonies.
▶ Germany lost its navy, while its once powerful army was reduced to the size of a police force.
▶ Germans were forced to sign the **"War Guilt"** clause, accepting the blame for starting the war. On these grounds, they were also required to pay huge **reparations** (*payment for damages*) to the Allied victors.
▶ Austria-Hungary was divided into several smaller national states.
▶ The Sultan was overthrown and Turkey became a republic. The Ottoman Empire lost most of its territories in the Middle East. These territories became mandates of Britain and France.
▶ A **League of Nations** was established to prevent aggression and protect the peace.

The U.S. Senate Rejects the Treaty of Versailles
▶ Americans were generally disappointed with the war's outcome.
▶ Many Americans retreated into isolation.
▶ The Congressional elections of 1918 reflected this disappointment and gave control of the Senate to Republicans. Wilson ordered his supporters to reject the Treaty of Versailles rather than accept it with Republican changes.
▶ The United States never joined the League of Nations; instead, it signed a separate peace treaty with Germany in 1921.

What Do You Know?

SS.912.A.4.5

1. The diagram below provides details about the origins of World War I.

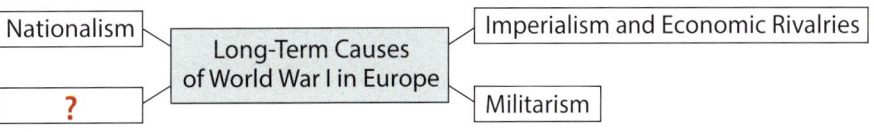

Which phrase completes the diagram?

   A. Alliance System

   B. Social Revolution

   C. Drought and Famine

   D. Worldwide Economic Depression

SS.912.A.4.6

2. Which group of adult males, ages 21 to 30, was NOT required to serve in the U.S. military during World War I?

   A. African Americans

   B. Conscientious objectors

   C. People who opposed the war

   D. American Indians with U.S. citizenship

SS.912.A.4.5

3. The table below gives details about United States trade.

United States Foreign Trade during World War I			
	1914	1915	1916
With the Allied Powers	$824,860,237.00	$1,991,747,493.00	$3,214,480,547.00
With the Central Powers	$169,289,775.00	$11,878,153.00	$1,159,653.00

Which event was responsible for the changes in trade shown on the table?

A. The United States boycotted Germany after it invaded neutral Belgium.

B. Submarine warfare made it difficult to ship goods safely to the Central Powers.

C. The convoy system helped protect American ships carrying supplies to Germany.

D. The British naval blockade of the North Sea cut off American trade to the Central Powers.

SS.912.A.4.5

4. The cartoon on the left was published on February 1, 1917. The letter from Germany to Uncle Sam reads:

> "Ruthless warfare at sea. Ships enter blockade zone at their risk. Pledges as to warnings cancelled."

What was the effect of the message shown in this cartoon?

A. The United States declared war after the *U.S.S. Maine* was blown up in Havana Harbor.

B. The United States declared war after Germany sank American ships in the blockaded zone.

C. The Zimmerman telegram offered Texas and California to Mexico in exchange for an alliance.

D. Germany announced it would not attack passenger ships or merchant ships without warning.

SS.912.A.4.6

5. The card on the left was used by a 33 year-old man to register with the Selective Service in 1917.

Why did Congress feel this registration was necessary?

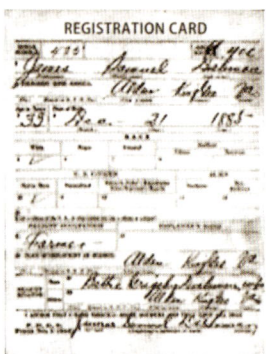

A. The United States needed to raise troops to fight overseas.

B. The United States needed to increase its agricultural production.

C. The United States needed laborers to replace men in the armed services.

D. The United States needed to produce war goods, such as ships and uniforms.

SS.912.A.4.5

6. The message below was sent in secret code by the Foreign Minister of Germany to the German Ambassador to Mexico in January 1917. It was discovered and deciphered by the British government.

> We intend to begin on the first of February unrestricted submarine warfare. We shall try in spite of this to keep the United States of America neutral. If this does not succeed, we will make a proposal of alliance to Mexico on the following terms: we make war together, we make peace together, we give generous financial support and an understanding that Mexico is to regain the lost territory in Texas, New Mexico, and Arizona. . . . Please call the attention of the President [of Mexico] to the fact that the ruthless employment of our submarines now offers the prospect of compelling England to make peace in a few months.

What was the impact of the publication of this letter?

A. Mexico allied with Germany in World War I.

B. American public opinion was outraged against Germany.

C. The United States Senate immediately declared war on Germany.

D. The United States paid Mexico compensation for its lost territories.

SS.912.A.4.9

7. The graphic organizer on the left gives details about American society, April 1917–November 1918.

What would be an appropriate title for the graphic organizer?

A. The Impact of World War I on Women

B. The Impact of World War I on Food Production

C. The Impact of World War I on German Americans

D. The Impact of World War I on the Federal Government

SS.912.A.4.9

8. What caused African-American demographic patterns in the United States to shift during World War I?

A. the closing of factories in the South

B. effects of the Civil Rights movement

C. more job opportunities in Northern cities

D. the availability of cheap farmland in the North

SS.912.A.4.8

9. Which sentence describes the experiences of African-American soldiers during World War I?

A. They were unable to engage in combat because of racial prejudice.

B. They successfully persuaded the government to desegregate the army.

C. They were segregated but many engaged in combat under French command.

D. They were treated as equals with ample opportunity for advancement through the ranks.

Chapter 9 | The United States in World War I

SS.912.A.4.6

10. Which step was taken by Herbert Hoover as head of the U.S. Food Administration during World War I?

   A. persuading Americans to eat less wheat and meat

   B. rationing food on the home front with ration coupons

   C. prohibiting the migration of farm workers to jobs in cities

   D. directing farmers to grow fewer crops to maintain food prices

SS.912.A.4.6

11. The cartoon on the left was published on May 16, 1917.

   What was the purpose of the bonds being sold in the cartoon?

   A. To avoid an economic depression

   B. To keep the United States out of war

   C. To help finance the American war effort

   D. To make emergency loans to Britain and France

SS.912.A.4.7

12. The photograph on the left shows American infantry in France in 1918.

   What would be the best caption for this photograph?

   A. The introduction of tanks ends trench warfare

   B. Battlefield devastation from aircraft bombardment

   C. Crossing "No Man's Land" to reach an enemy trench

   D. Troops get exercise by running along an Allied trench

SS.912.A.4.10

13. Why did the United States Senate fail to ratify the Treaty of Versailles in 1919?

   A. Many Senators opposed the severe sanctions that the treaty placed on Germany.

   B. Many Senators feared the League of Nations would involve the United States in foreign wars.

   C. Many Senators felt the League of Nations would interfere with American plans in the Philippines.

   D. Many Senators predicted that membership in the new League of Nations would be too expensive.

SS.912.A.4.6

14. The cartoon below was published in May 1917.

Which was NOT one of the "new bureaus" referred to in this cartoon?

   A. War Industries Board
   B. Railroad Administration
   C. American Federation of Labor
   D. Committee of Public Information

SS.912.A.4.9

15. The excerpt below is from Supreme Court Justice Oliver Wendell Holmes' opinion in *Schenck v. United States* (1919).

> The question in every case is whether the words used are used in such circumstances and are of such a nature as to create a clear and present danger that they will bring about the substantive evils that Congress has a right to prevent.

Based on the excerpt, with which statement would Oliver Wendell Holmes have agreed?

   A. Freedom of speech is not absolute.
   B. Prayer in public schools is unconstitutional.
   C. Immigration from other countries cannot be permitted during wartime.
   D. Criticism of the policies of allied countries must be temporarily prohibited in wartime.

SS.912.A.4.10

16. The excerpt below is from the Covenant of the League of Nations, a part of the Treaty of Versailles.

> **ARTICLE 10**
> The Members of the League undertake to respect and preserve the territorial integrity and existing political independence of all Members of the League against external aggression. In case of any such aggression or threat of such aggression, the [Executive] Council shall advise on the means by which this obligation shall be fulfilled.

Why did many U.S. Senators object to this article?

   A. They had plans to seize new overseas territories for the United States.
   B. They were afraid that the League would be controlled by hostile powers.
   C. They feared Americans would be required to act against aggression in Europe.
   D. They thought it demanded that Americans grant Philippine independence.

SS.912.A.4.11

17. Which sentence best describes the impact of World War I on Florida?

   A. Governor Sidney J. Catts lifted the state's prohibition of alcoholic drinks during wartime.
   B. Large numbers of Cubans moved to Florida to find work in America's wartime industries.
   C. Military training centers were located in Florida, the state's farmers sold more crops, and a thousand Floridians gave their lives.
   D. After fighting for democracy abroad, most Floridians became more willing to grant equal rights to African Americans at home.

SS.912.A.4.9

18. Which best describes how American women reacted to American participation in World War I?

   A. Some protested but most supported the war effort and many filled men's jobs.
   B. Because of a shortage of enlisted men, many women served in combat for the first time.
   C. Women's continuing protests for women's suffrage dangerously impeded the war effort.
   D. Large numbers of women were forced to move from their homes to meet wartime needs.

SS.912.A.4.10

19. Which was NOT one of President Woodrow Wilson's Fourteen Points?
   A. creation of an independent Poland
   B. lenient treatment of the Central Powers
   C. creation of a peace-keeping association of nations
   D. autonomous development for the peoples of Austria-Hungary and the Ottoman Empire

Unit III: World Affairs through World War I (Chapters 8–9)

Identify or define each of the following terms.

Spanish-American War _____

Platt Amendment _____

Imperialism _____

Philippine-American War _____

Annexation of Hawaii _____

"Open Door" policy _____

Panama Canal _____

Alliance System _____

Zimmerman Telegram _____

Unrestricted submarine warfare _____

Committee of Public Information _____

Schenck v. United States _____

Great Migration _____

Fourteen Points _____

Treaty of Versailles _____

Unit III | Activity 1

Crossword Puzzle

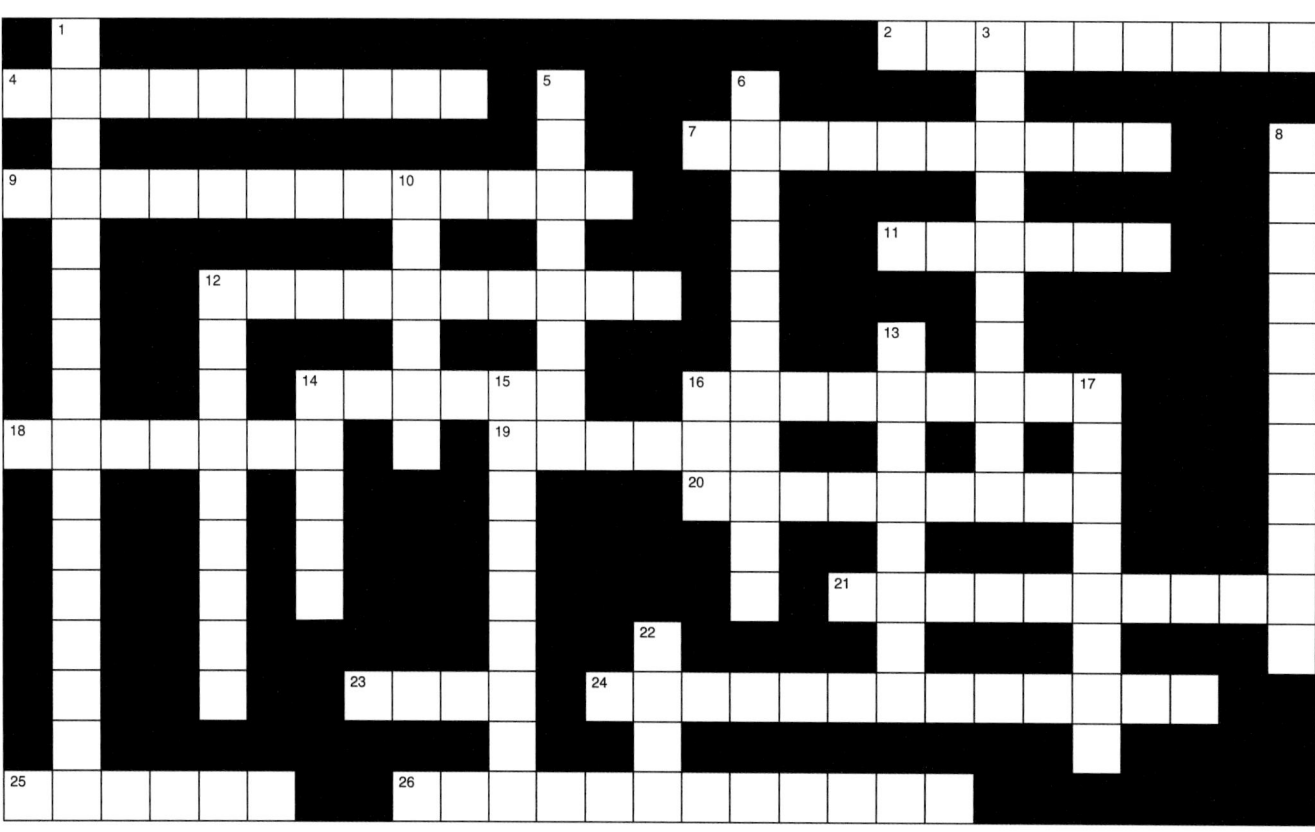

Across

2. In 1917, Congress passed the _____ Act, which created procedures for detecting and imprisoning spies
4. The final peace treaty negotiated by Wilson at the end of World War I was the Treaty of _____
7. Roosevelt won the Nobel Peace Prize for negotiating the terms of the Treaty of _____ between Russia and Japan
9. During World War I, the head of the Food Administration, _____ _____, requested voluntary food reduction by the public to reduce the risk of food shortages
11. Owner of the *New York Journal* who sensationalized news in order to sell more papers
12. Glorification of the military and the consideration of military over civilian interests
14. Canal built in Central America that connected the Atlantic and Pacific Oceans
16. The invention of _____ was a great help in reconnaissance from the sky during World War I
18. The _____ Powers consisted of Germany, Austria–Hungary, and Ottoman Turkey
19. The _____ Powers consisted of Britain, France, and Russia
20. Archduke Francis _____, the heir to the throne of Austria-Hungary, was assassinated by Slavic nationalists in 1914 sparking what would lead to World War I
21. The War _____ Board coordinated American's wartime manufacturing
23. The Teller Amendment promised that the U.S. would not annex _____, even if it won the Spanish-American war
24. Men who refused to serve in World War I because it violated their religious beliefs were called _____ objectors
25. Colorful term for a style of journalism that sensationalizes and distorts the news
26. Compulsory military service, or the "draft," is also known as _____

Down

1. Conscription was established by the _____ _____ Act
3. One-sided information designed to persuade listeners
5. The use of poison gas to kill in war is called _____ warfare
6. The volunteers who served along with regular army units during the Spanish-American War were known as the "_____ _____"
8. Term for the rule of one country by another
10. The _____ Manifesto urged Americans to seize Cuba if Spain would not sell it to the U.S.
12. After World War I, thousands of African Americans left the South for work in the North and Midwest in what became known as the Great _____
13. A group of friendly nations formed to support a common cause is known as an _____
14. The _____ Amendment replaced the Teller Amendment and stated, among other things, that Cuba would place naval bases at the disposal of the U.S.
15. Famous writer who was a strong voice for anti-imperialism
16. Acronym for Woodrow Wilson's million-man force
17. In 1918, the _____ Act made it a crime to use "disloyal" or "abusive language" about the government, flag, or Constitution
22. The Spanish-American War lasted _____ months

Unit III | Activity 2

CHAPTER 10

The Roaring Twenties

SS.912.A.5.1 Discuss the economic outcomes of demobilization.

SS.912.A.5.2 Explain the causes of the public reaction (Sacco and Vanzetti, labor, racial unrest) associated with the Red Scare.

SS.912.A.5.3 Examine the impact of United States foreign economic policy during the 1920s.

SS.912.A.5.4 Evaluate how the economic boom during the Roaring Twenties changed consumers, businesses, manufacturing, and marketing practices.

SS.912.A.5.5 Describe efforts by the United States and other world powers to avoid future wars.

SS.912.A.5.6 Analyze the influence that Hollywood, the Harlem Renaissance, the Fundamentalist Movement, and prohibition had in changing American society in the 1920s.

SS.912.A.5.7 Examine the freedom movements that advocated civil rights for African Americans, Latinos, Asians, and women.

SS.912.A.5.8 Compare the views of Booker T. Washington, W.E.B. Du Bois, and Marcus Garvey relating to the African American experience.

SS.912.A.5.9 Explain why support for the Ku Klux Klan varied in the 1920s with respect to issues such as anti-immigration, anti-African American, anti-Catholic, anti-Jewish, anti-women, and anti-union ideas.

SS.912.A.5.10 Analyze support for and resistance to civil rights for women, African Americans, Native Americans, and other minorities.

SS.912.A.5.12 Examine key events and people in Florida history as they relate to United States history.

SS.912.H.1.5 Examine artistic response to social issues and new ideas in various cultures.

Names and Terms You Should Know

Roaring Twenties
Demobilization
Disarmament
Red Scare
Palmer Raids
J. Edgar Hoover
Sacco and Vanzetti
Warren Harding
Normalcy
Tariffs
Fordney-McCumber Act
Teapot Dome scandal
Nativism
Quota system
National Origins Act
Foreign economic policies

Dawes Plan
League of Nations
Washington Naval Conference
Four-Power Treaty
Kellogg-Briand Pact
Women's International League for Peace and Freedom
Henry Ford
Assembly line
Consumerism
Installment buying
Fundamentalist Movement
Eighteenth Amendment
Volstead Act
Prohibition
Nineteenth Amendment
Flappers

Hollywood
Great Migration
Booker T. Washington
W.E.B. Du Bois
Marcus Garvey
Harlem Renaissance
Jazz Age
Universal Negro Improvement Association
NAACP (National Association for the Advancement of Colored People)
Ku Klux Klan
100 Percent Americanism
Rosewood
Seminole Indians

Florida "Keys" to Learning

1. When the war ended in November 1918, Americans had to demobilize—discharge soldiers and return to peacetime production.

2. The triumph of Bolshevism in Russia and strikes and bombings in the United States led many Americans to fear anarchists and Communists during the "Red Scare" of 1919. Foreign-born radicals were arrested and deported in the "Palmer Raids." Two Italian anarchists, Sacco and Vanzetti, were convicted for murder in 1920 on flimsy evidence.

3. Republican Presidents Warren Harding, Calvin Coolidge, and Herbert Hoover pursued policies favorable to business: low taxation, high tariffs (Ford–McCumber Act), and lax enforcement of regulations. The Teapot Dome scandal exposed corruption in Harding's administration.

4. The Emergency Quota Act of 1921 and the National Origins Act of 1924 placed new restrictions on immigration in order to preserve America's existing ethnic composition.

5. While refusing to join the League of Nations, Harding attempted to promote world peace. At the Washington Naval Conference, the world's naval powers agreed to limit the numbers of their battleships. In the Kellogg–Briand Pact, countries agreed to give up war except for self-defense.

6. Americans had lent money to the Allies during the war and insisted on being repaid. France and Britain used reparations money from Germany to repay their debts to the United States. The Dawes Plan lent money to Germany and reduced its reparations payments.

7. The spread of the automobile and new electric appliances contributed to economic prosperity. Assembly-line production lowered prices, while installment payment plans made buying goods easier. Speculation on the stock market, including buying on margin, added to the prosperity.

8. Traditional values confronted new ones. The inhabitants of small towns and even in many cities supported Prohibition and Fundamentalist Christianity. John Scopes was put on trial for teaching evolution. The Ku Klux Klan experienced a resurgence in these years.

9. Others supported greater freedom for women and young people. The Nineteenth Amendment gave women the right to vote, while flappers wore loose clothing and went out without chaperones. Novelists, Hollywood, aviation, and sports supplied new popular heroes.

10. African Americans continued to face Jim Crow laws, lynchings, and economic inequality in the South. Booker T. Washington urged them to seek vocational training, but W.E.B. Du Bois favored a struggle for full civil rights. Many moved north in the Great Migration. Even in Northern cities, they faced racism, discrimination, and violence. One of the worst race riots occurred in Florida at Rosewood in 1923.

11. The Harlem Renaissance saw a flourishing of African-American culture, with jazz music, essays, novels, short stories, and poetry. Marcus Garvey encouraged African Americans to rely more on themselves and to separate from whites.

12. Most minorities did not share in the prosperity of the 1920s. The number of Hispanic Americans increased since immigration from Mexico was unrestricted. American Indians were made citizens in 1924 but continued to suffer from widespread poverty. The Seminoles of Florida increased their interaction with tourists. Asian Americans continued to face discrimination.

After the reforms of the Progressives and the sacrifices of World War I, many Americans embraced the call of Warren Harding, elected President in 1920, for a "return to normalcy." America needed a rest. Instead of trying to save the world, Americans would focus on earning money and spending it. But this was a far cry from a simple return to the pre-war days: the Twenties were a period of profound economic, social, and cultural change.

Demobilization and Adjustment to Peace, 1920

The postwar period opened with the challenge of adjusting to peace. **Mobilization** is the task of directing all resources towards achieving a goal, such as winning a war. **Demobilization** is just the opposite—the transition process during which a nation at war returns to a state of peace. Soldiers retire from active service while economic production reverts back to civilian purposes. When World War I ended, the federal government no longer needed to buy vast quantities of guns, bullets, uniforms, and battleships. Factories temporarily shut their doors to convert from wartime to peacetime production. Farmers could no longer sell the same amounts of food to the army and navy.

Some Progressives had hoped that President Wilson would continue federal control of the railroads and other businesses into peacetime, but these restraints on industry were quickly lifted. Railroads, for example, were no longer needed to move armies and wartime supplies and went back into private hands.

Meanwhile, soldiers began returning home and looking for work. Men accustomed to receiving army pay suddenly found themselves without work or paychecks after discharge. Women, African Americans, and others who had filled their jobs on the home front while these men were absent at war suddenly were no longer needed. Making matters worse, a great epidemic of a deadly form of influenza, known as the "Spanish flu," struck the country in the winter of 1918–1919. This actually killed more Americans than the war itself. These factors combined to throw the country into an economic slowdown, known as the **Depression of 1920–1921**.

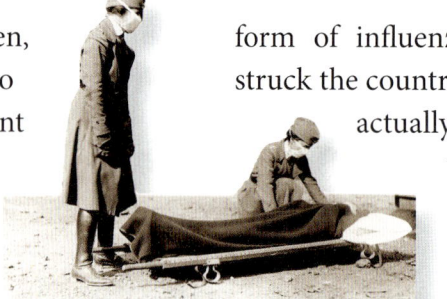
Nurses attend to an influenza victim

The "Red Scare"

A group of Russian Communists, at first known as the **Bolsheviks**, seized power in Russia in November 1917, while World War I was still raging. The Bolsheviks not only pulled Russia out of the war, they also opposed private property, religious beliefs, and free enterprise. They were therefore viewed as anti-American. President Wilson authorized troops in Russia to intervene on the side of the "Whites," the opponents of the Bolsheviks (or "Reds") in the Russian Civil War. American troops stayed in Siberia until 1920, but failed to prevent a Bolshevik victory. American leaders nevertheless refused to extend diplomatic recognition to the new Russian government. Meanwhile, Communists also threatened to seize power in both Germany and Hungary.

In the United States, many workers were concerned about their futures now that the war was over. In 1919, a wave of strikes took place across the United States. In Boston, police went on strike; in Seattle, workers staged a general strike. Ever since the collapse of the Homestead Strike, steel workers had lacked unions and were working 12–hour shifts, seven days a week.

Workers at U.S. Steel, many of whom were immigrants from Eastern Europe, now demanded the right to organize into unions and went on strike. So did coal workers in Indiana.

The success of the Bolsheviks in Russia, the Communist attempts in Central Europe, and the wave of strikes across the United States made many Americans fearful of a Communist revolution in their own country. Because Communists had adopted the color red as their symbol, this popular fear became known as the "**Red Scare**."

The "Palmer Raids" A. Mitchell Palmer, a Pennsylvania Quaker and a Progressive Democrat, was appointed as Attorney General by President Wilson in March 1919. Only a month after his appointment, several letter bombs, sent by Italian-born anarchists, were found in the mail. One of them was addressed to Palmer. In June, a bomb exploded on Palmer's porch while other bombs exploded in several cities.

Palmer created a new group inside the Justice Department, led by an energetic young lawyer, **J. Edgar Hoover**. In November, Hoover supervised the arrest of Russian workers suspected of radical activity in 12 cities: more than 200 of them were deported (*sent out of the country*). In January 1920, Hoover directed simultaneous raids in 30 cities, known as the "**Palmer Raids**." About 6,000 suspects were arrested. Most of them were foreign-born residents from Russia and Germany, who could be deported after only a short hearing and without a jury trial. Palmer would have deported most of them, but the Department of Labor believed that many of the arrests were illegal and

J. Edgar Hoover

194   Chapter 10 | The Roaring Twenties

refused to deport more than 556. Activist Emma Goldman was one of those deported. Palmer further predicted that there would be a Communist uprising in the United States, but this never occurred. Nevertheless the Palmer Raids weakened the labor unions and other worker organizations.

RADICALS DEPORTED TO RUSSIA IN DECEMBER 1919
From the reader's left to right—Emma Goldman, Ethel Berstein, Peter Bianki, Alexander Berkman

The Historian's Apprentice

"Like a prairie fire, the blaze of revolution was sweeping over every American institution of law and order a year ago. It was eating its way into the homes of the American workmen . . . burning up the foundations of society. Robbery, not war, is the ideal of communism. This has been demonstrated in Russia, Germany, and in America. . . . Obviously, it is the creed of any criminal mind . . . By stealing, murder and lies, Bolshevism has looted Russia, not only of its material strength but of its moral force . . . My information showed that communism in this country was an organization of thousands of aliens who were direct allies of Trotsky [a Russian Communist leader]. . . The Government is now sweeping the nation clean of such alien filth . . ."

—A. Mitchell Palmer, "The Case against the Reds" (1920)

"Every human being is entitled to hold any opinion that appeals to her or him without making herself or himself liable to persecution. . . . It requires no great prophetic gift to foresee that this new governmental policy of deportation is but the first step towards the introduction into this country of the old Russian system of exile for the high treason of entertaining new ideas of social life and industrial reconstruction. Today so-called aliens are deported, tomorrow native Americans will be banished."

—Emma Goldman, speaking at her deportation hearing (October 1919)

Imagine you are a newspaper editor in 1920. First read the excerpt from Palmer's pamphlet and from Goldman's speech above. Then write your own editorial on whether the Palmer Raids were justified.

Sacco and Vanzetti Two Italian immigrants, **Nicola Sacco** and **Bartolomeo Vanzetti** (a shoemaker and a fish seller) were arrested in 1920 for murders committed during a payroll truck robbery. Not only were they immigrants, Sacco and Vanzetti were also **anarchists** (*radicals who opposed organized government*). The trial judge showed extreme bias in his conduct of the trial, continually stressing the fact that Sacco and Vanzetti had shown disloyalty during the war by going to Mexico to escape the draft. Although the evidence was unclear, Sacco and Vanzetti were convicted and sentenced to death. Despite new evidence and multiple appeals, all requests for a retrial were denied. After a legal battle that lasted seven years, Sacco and Vanzetti were finally executed in

Nicola Sacco   Bartolomeo Vanzetti

Chapter 10 | The Roaring Twenties

1927. There were loud outcries of injustice both at home and abroad. Almost a century later, it remains a subject of controversy whether or not Sacco and Vanzetti were actually involved in the robbery, but there is general agreement that their trial was unfair.

"I would not wish to a dog or to a snake, to the most low and misfortunate creature of the earth—I would not wish to any of them what I have had to suffer for things that I am not guilty of. But my conviction is that I have suffered for things that I am guilty of. I am suffering because I am a radical and indeed I am a radical; I have suffered because I am an Italian and indeed I am an Italian."

—Bartolomeo Vanzetti, shortly before his execution

The Republican Presidents: Warren Harding

In March 1921, a Republican returned to the White House. Republicans remained in power for the next 12 years, overseeing the prosperity of the Twenties and its sudden demise. The three Republican Presidents who occupied the White House from 1921 to 1933—Harding, Coolidge, and Hoover—generally followed conservative policies favorable to American business.

Good looking and cheerful, Senator Warren Harding from Ohio had been selected as a compromise candidate by party bosses. A former newspaper publisher, Harding captured the national spirit when he called for a "**return to normalcy**"—with a greater emphasis on maintaining prosperity at home and a less ambitious foreign policy abroad.

Policies Favoring American Business

Harding introduced policies reminiscent of Republican governments before the Progressive Era. Businessmen figured prominently in his cabinet. His pro-business policies included higher tariffs, lower taxes, and minimal government interference in business activities. His government also enacted new immigration laws.

A Higher Tariff Wilson had dramatically lowered tariff rates in 1913 and had introduced income tax as an alternative source of revenue. Republicans were determined to reverse these policies. High tariff rates, they argued, would keep out foreign products and thus protect both American manufacturers and their workers. A high tariff could also benefit Midwestern farmers, who were concerned about growing competition from Canadian wheat. In 1922, Congress passed the **Fordney–McCumber Act**. Under the new tariff, those goods subject to customs duties (*taxes on imports*) paid an average duty of 38.5% of their value. Imported wheat, for example, had paid no duty at all between 1913 and 1921; under the new tariff, it now paid 30 cents a bushel. Other countries retaliated by raising their own tariffs on goods from the United States, with a detrimental impact on world trade.

Lower Taxes for the Wealthy Andrew Mellon, a wealthy banker and industrialist, served as Secretary of the Treasury under Harding and his Republican successors, Coolidge and Hoover. Mellon believed that wealthy Americans were more likely to invest in the economy than other social classes were. He therefore slashed taxes on the rich, reducing income and corporate taxes, abolishing the gift tax, and shifting more of the tax burden onto the shoulders of the average wage earner.

Lax Enforcement of Business Regulations Harding thought that government should interfere with business as little as possible, and Coolidge and Hoover later followed his example. They did not overturn existing laws regulating business; they simply failed to enforce them. Businessmen were appointed to regulatory commissions like the Interstate Commerce Commission and the Federal Trade Commission. The government also invited companies to share information and collaborate on prices. Business was given a free hand, and a large number of business mergers took place in the 1920s.

Restrictions on Immigration

During World War I, submarine warfare made it very dangerous to cross the Atlantic and the great flood of immigration was temporarily halted. In 1917, a literacy test was passed over President Wilson's veto. It required immigrants to read and write in their own language. This was intended to keep out poorer, uneducated, and unskilled immigrants from Southern and Eastern Europe. Even so, about 800,000 newcomers arrived between June 1920 and June 1921. Nativist sentiment, agitation by labor unions fearing competition from cheap labor, and popular prejudice against Southern and Eastern Europeans had all been growing in intensity for decades. These forces now led to the passage of a series of laws restricting immigration. Harding himself had called for limits on immigration in his election campaign, and soon after he took office Congress passed the **Emergency Quota Act of 1921**. A **quota** refers to any fixed number of people or things permitted to do something. The Emergency Quota Act of 1921 limited the total number of immigrants who could enter the United States in any one year to 350,000, fewer than half the number admitted in 1920. Each foreign country was assigned its own quota, or maximum number of immigrants, based on 3% of the number of immigrants from that country living in the United States in 1910. The new quota system was aimed at drastically reducing the number of immigrants from Southern and Eastern Europe. Immigration from Asia had already been banned in 1917, except for from the Philippines. Immigration from Latin America, however, remained unrestricted.

The Historian's Apprentice

Write a brief essay explaining how rejection of the League of Nations, higher tariffs, and the creation of new barriers to immigration were all signs of America's increasing isolationism.

Harding's Foreign Policy

Supporters of the League of Nations still hoped that the United States might someday join the League, even though the Versailles Treaty had been rejected. Shortly after becoming President, Harding dashed these hopes. Many historians nonetheless believe that Harding was not an isolationist but a moderate internationalist at heart. While rejecting League membership, Harding launched his own ambitious efforts to reduce the threat of war; he also worked hard to promote American business overseas.

The Washington Naval Conference

The dream of world peace was scarcely new. Many American groups favored such peace efforts. For example, the Woman's Peace Party was founded in 1915, before America entered World War I. In 1919, this organization renamed itself as the **Women's International League for Peace and Freedom**. The Women's International League for Peace condemned the Versailles Treaty as too vengeful, but moved its headquarters to Geneva to be close to the League of Nations, which it admired.

President Harding realized the Senate would never approve U.S. membership in the League of Nations. But in December 1920, a prominent Republican Senator proposed that America attempt a disarmament conference of its own with the other major naval powers: Britain and Japan. Petitions across the country flooded into Congress in support of his proposal. Harding agreed and invited Britain and Japan, as well as Italy, France, and several smaller countries, to a conference in Washington, D.C. in November 1921. In place of joining the League, Harding thus entered into a series of direct negotiations with the other major powers to promote world peace.

On the very first day of the **Washington Naval Conference**, Americans surprised the other delegates by proposing that the United States, Great Britain, and Japan each stop building new battleships and even scrap some of those they already had. It was the world's first proposal for partial **disarmament** (*reducing the number of weapons, or arms*). The United States and Britain eventually accepted parity (*equality*) in the number of battleships they possessed, while the Japanese accepted having slightly fewer. The ratio for the battleships of the three leading maritime powers was set at 5:5:3.

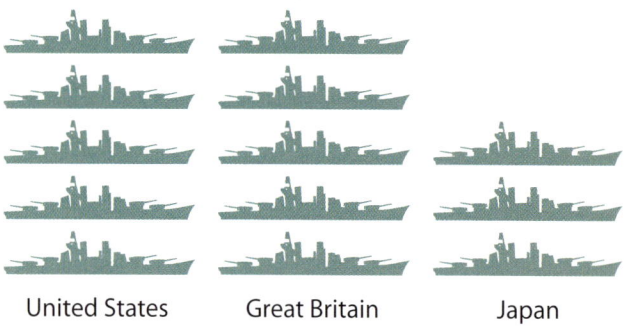

United States   Great Britain   Japan

The Japanese only accepted these terms when the Americans promised not to fortify Guam or the Philippines, giving the Japanese superiority in their home waters. The only other naval powers at this time, France and Italy, agreed to limit the number of their battleships to half the number of Japan's. The agreement only covered large battleships, not submarines and smaller warships, so these powers were still left with ample opportunities for competition.

The Four-Power Treaty

Fear of Russian expansion had led the British to sign an alliance with Japan in 1902. Americans feared that Japan and Britain might someday act together in the Pacific with a greater combined naval power than the United States. While representatives of these countries were at the Washington Naval Conference, the United States, Britain, and Japan therefore also worked out new arrangements for security in the Pacific. The Anglo-Japanese Alliance was dissolved and replaced by the **Four-Power Treaty**. The United States, Britain, Japan, and France agreed to respect each other's territories and rights in the Pacific region and to submit any disputes to a "joint conference" of all four powers. This agreement was reached on December 13, 1921. Only two days later, the Japanese agreed to possess fewer battleships at the Naval Conference.

Before leaving Washington, all the delegates to the Naval Conference also signed a **Nine-Power Treaty**, agreeing to respect the independence of China. American diplomats hoped by this means to receive international recognition for their earlier "Open Door" policy (see Chapter 8, page 151), but the new treaty proved impossible to enforce.

International Finance: Allied War Debts and German Reparations

One issue that greatly complicated U.S. foreign policy in these years was that of allied war debts. During World War I, the United States had lent $10 billion to Allied nations, mainly Britain, France, and Italy. These were loans, not grants or gifts, so the Allies were expected to repay the entire amount.

The Allies argued that in the early years of the war, they had sacrificed their soldiers' lives to the common cause at a time when Americans were only giving money. On these grounds, they urged that the war debts be cancelled. But Wilson and the Republican Presidents who followed him adamantly refused to do so. They were influenced by the fact that American taxpayers were still paying interest to the holders of the bonds that had raised the vast sums needed for these loans.

Under Harding, the United States did at least extend Britain's repayment period to 62 years and lowered the interest rate; similar arrangements were soon reached with the other debtor nations. The former Allies still did not have enough gold on hand to repay these debts. With higher American tariffs, they were also unable to sell enough goods in the United States to raise the cash or credit needed to make the loan payments. But Britain and France were entitled to reparations from Germany under the "War Guilt" Clause of the Treaty of Versailles. The amount that the Allies demanded from Germany was a staggering $32 billion (although they never recovered even a fraction of that sum). Britain and France used the money they received from Germany to pay their debts to the United States. The issue of repayment of war debts and of reparations thus became closely intertwined.

The Dawes Plan

In 1923, Germany was unable to pay its reparations, and France and Belgium occupied a part of western Germany. The German government then printed excessive amounts of paper money to make its reparations payments, leading to a wild **inflation** (*rise in prices*) inside Germany. Middle-class families lost their savings as money lost all value.

An American banker, Charles Dawes, came up with the **Dawes Plan** to fix the problem in 1924. Private American investors lent $200 million to Germany, while Germany's reparations payments were temporarily reduced to $250 million (with the plan of gradually increasing them over time). Germany used the American loan to make its reparations payments to Britain and France. Britain and France used this money, in turn, to make their loan payments to the United States. The same money thus circulated from private investors in the United States to Germany, then to Britain and France, and finally back to the United States Treasury. Germany also created a new currency to replace its old one, which had lost its value. The Dawes Plan gave Europe a sense of stability and a return to prosperity. In 1929, a new American plan reduced the German reparations down to $9 billion, to be paid over a period of 59 years.

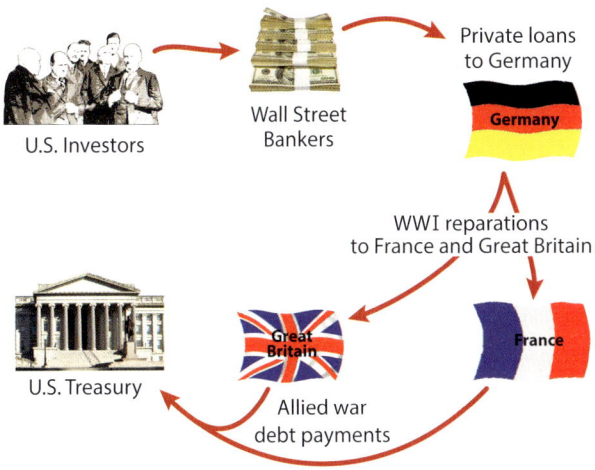

The question of the Allied war debts contributed to bad feelings between America and Europe. President Hoover announced a moratorium (*temporary postponement*) on the debt payments in 1931, after the Great Depression struck (see the next chapter). In 1933, all the European governments repudiated their war debts except Finland.

Promotion of American Investment Overseas

Although the United States was isolationist in many of its policies, Republican Presidents in the Twenties encouraged American investment abroad. Herbert Hoover, the energetic Secretary of Commerce under both Harding and Coolidge, actively promoted American economic expansion and investment in Europe, Latin America, and the Middle East. American businessmen not only made loans to Germany and other European countries, they also invested in Middle Eastern oil.

Relations with Latin America

During the Twenties, the Caribbean region continued to be treated like an "American lake." U.S. troops had been

Charles Dawes

occupying Nicaragua since 1912, Haiti since 1915, and the Dominican Republic since 1916. There was also friction between the United States and Mexico. Mexico's revolutionary government declared national ownership of all Mexican oil resources found below the ground. Some of these resources were claimed by American companies.

Scandal Rocks the Harding Administration

Harding appointed many of the "best minds" of his day to the cabinet, including Andrew Mellon, Herbert Hoover, and Charles Evans Hughes (a former Governor of New York and Supreme Court Justice). However, Harding also appointed his old friends, the "Ohio Gang," to important cabinet positions. They betrayed his trust by using their posts to make money for themselves. The head of the new Veterans' Bureau, for example, pocketed $200 million while building veterans' hospitals. The Secretary of the Interior arranged to have oil-rich lands at Teapot Dome, Wyoming, previously reserved for the Navy, transferred to his own department. He then secretly leased them to businessmen in exchange for personal bribes. Harding died of a heart attack in 1923, just before the "**Teapot Dome Scandal**" became widely reported in the press.

"Coolidge Prosperity"

Harding's Vice President, **Calvin Coolidge**, became the next President. Coolidge presented himself as a symbol of old-fashioned American values, like honesty and thrift. As Governor of Massachusetts, he had put down the Boston police strike in 1919. Continuing Harding's pro-business policies, his motto was: "**The business of America is business.**" Coolidge spoke so seldom in public that he became known as "Silent Cal." He was re-elected in 1924 on the slogan of "Coolidge Prosperity."

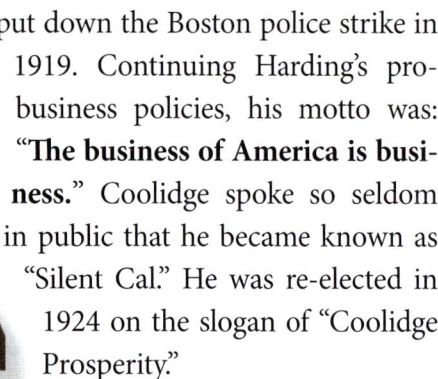

Coolidge reduced government expenditures and vetoed a bill to help farmers because he did not think the government should regulate farm prices. A veterans' bill, providing a life insurance policy to World War I veterans, was passed over his veto. Coolidge was given credit at the time for the business expansion of the 1920s, but he took no steps to curb the frenzy of stock market speculation and the continuation of high tariffs and regressive taxation that led to overproduction and under-consumption. Coolidge decided not to run for office again in 1928, without ever explaining why.

Further Restrictions on Immigration

Coolidge believed that "Nordics," or people from Northern and Western Europe, were superior to all other ethnic and racial groups. During his Presidency, restrictions on immigration were further tightened. Experts testified before Congress that people from Eastern and Southern Europe were genetically inferior. The **Immigration Act of 1924** lowered the total number of legal immigrants per year to 150,000 (2% the number of foreign-born residents living in the United States in 1890).

The quota for each country was also changed. The date on which it was based was pushed back from 1910 to 1890, a time before the large influx of "New Immigrants." The way in which the quota for each country was calculated was changed too. In 1921, this had been based on the percentage of *immigrants of that nationality* compared to *all immigrants* living in the United States. In 1924, it was based on the percentage of people of *that national origin* compared to *all Americans*. Thus, the 1924 law is sometimes known as the "**National Origins Act**."

The total effect of all these changes was to drastically reduce the number of immigrants to the

United States from Southern and Eastern Europe. For example, before World War I about 200,000 Italians migrated to the United States each year; the Emergency Quota Act of 1921 reduced this number to 40,000; under the 1924 Immigration Act, a mere 4,000 Italians could be legally admitted.

Coolidge's Foreign policy

The Geneva Disarmament Conference

The Washington Naval Conference had only been partially successful. The naval powers honored their pledges with respect to battleship construction but began an arms race in the building of cruisers and other smaller ships. Hoping to repeat Harding's success, Coolidge called for a new disarmament conference in Geneva, Switzerland—also the home of the League of Nations. The conference was held in 1927, but the participants refused to accept further limitations and nothing was achieved.

The Kellogg–Briand Pact

If no further progress could be made towards disarmament, what about the elimination of war itself? An American professor sent a letter to the French foreign minister, Aristide Briand, suggesting a treaty to outlaw war. In April 1927, Briand surprisingly responded by writing to the American Secretary of State, Frank

Frank Kellogg   Aristide Briand

Kellogg, with the news that France was ready to enter into a treaty with the United States to outlaw war. His suggestion was widely praised in the American press. A citizens' petition with two million signatures in favor of the proposal was submitted to Congress. Kellogg insisted that the number of nations signing the treaty be expanded beyond just France and the United States. In August 1928, 15 nations signed the Pact of Paris, more commonly known as the **Kellogg–Briand Pact**, promising not to use war as an instrument of policy. The Kellogg–Briand Pact was approved by Congress, and Kellogg won the **Nobel Peace Prize** (*a prize established in 1896 for promoting world peace*). The agreement, however, permitted nations to engage in defensive war and was therefore illusory. Only twelve years later, the most destructive war in human history would take place.

Herbert Hoover and "Rugged Individualism"

Herbert Hoover was a self-made millionaire and engineer. Before America entered World War I, Hoover had been in charge of distributing relief aid to Belgian children and others in Europe. During the war, he had ably headed the government's Food Administration, overseeing the production and distribution of food. Hoover then served as Secretary of Commerce under both Harding and Coolidge. He was therefore a logical successor to Coolidge. In his 1928 campaign, Hoover optimistically announced that America was on the verge of ending poverty. Like other Republican leaders, he was greatly impressed by the successes of American business in improving standards of living. He believed this was all the result of the "American system," which he defined as a society in which individuals are given an education and equal opportunities, benefitting those with a will to succeed.

Chapter 10 | The Roaring Twenties

This "**rugged individualism**," Hoover believed, spurred American progress. Hoover favored business cooperation to increase efficiency and avoid wasteful competition. He was more willing than Coolidge to use government to give some direction to the capitalist system—and supported promoting voluntary cooperation among farmers with government funds.

How the Boom of the Roaring Twenties Altered the American Economy

For many Americans, the 1920s were a prosperous period. Wages and employment opportunities increased. Profits and production soared. The economic boom of the Twenties changed consumers, businesses, manufacturing, and marketing practices.

Greater Efficiency in Manufacturing

One of the keys to success was the increasing efficiency of American industry. In 1914, **Henry Ford** introduced electric conveyor belts on his **assembly lines**. Each car moved along the belt to different groups of workers who completed one small portion of its assembly. Production time was astonishingly cut to one-sixth of what it had previously taken. In the 1920s, the conveyor belt and other new techniques were applied to a number of different industries, making American workers more productive than ever before.

The Rise of the Automobile

The product that most transformed American life during the Twenties was the automobile, which now came into widespread use. Henry Ford's vision of a complex machine, mass-produced on an assembly-line, brought the price of the automobile low enough to become affordable to middle-class purchasers. In 1920, there were 8 million cars on the road; by 1930, there were three times that number, or one car for every six Americans. The production of automobiles required vast amounts of steel, glass, and rubber, stimulating those industries. Motorists also required paved roads, bridges, garages, and gas stations. By 1929, one out of every nine workers was employed in an automobile-related industry.

The automobile had other effects as well. School buses allowed the creation of larger schools to serve wider areas. Tractors increased farm production. Cars gave people greater mobility, allowing farmers to drive into town for shopping or families to drive away on vacation.

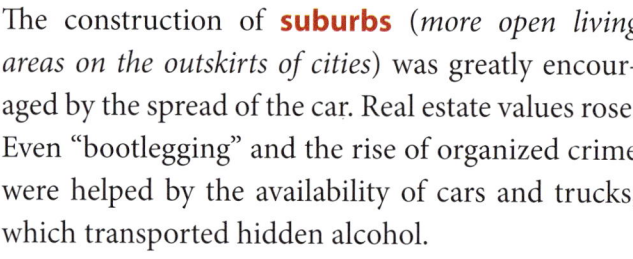

The construction of **suburbs** (*more open living areas on the outskirts of cities*) was greatly encouraged by the spread of the car. Real estate values rose. Even "bootlegging" and the rise of organized crime were helped by the availability of cars and trucks, which transported hidden alcohol.

The Expansion of Other New Industries

The use of electricity more than doubled in the 1920s. New electric household appliances, like the vacuum cleaner, refrigerator, and electric toaster, became available for the first time. The use of petroleum and natural gas increased. The American chemical industry greatly expanded. Commercial broadcasts on radio first began in 1920 and led to the manufacture and purchase of millions of radios. By the end of the decade the new motion picture business had also become one of the largest industries in the United States. The development of all these new industries created new jobs, produced immense profits, and changed the ways in which Americans lived, traveled, communicated, and enjoyed themselves.

New Marketing Practices in an Age of Consumerism

Mass production required mass consumption, which in turn required new ways to market goods. How would millions of consumers know what to buy? The growth of advertising informed potential consumers while stimulating their demand for products and services. New advertising agencies specialized in developing slogans and advertisements to attract customers. Advertisements were placed in newspapers and magazines, and on street signs and billboards. Businesses sponsored radio programs, so that they could read their advertisements to listeners. Homes also received mail-order catalogs, while shoppers in cities could visit giant department stores where clothing and household items from different manufacturers were displayed.

Retailers also developed new marketing practices. They had innovative plans to help consumers pay for products, such as **installment buying**. To pay in installments, the buyer had only to pay a small down payment to take home an item. The purchaser then paid the balance owed in small monthly payments (which included interest). People used installment purchasing to buy new products like cars, refrigerators, and household appliances. Customers also bought goods on credit.

American workers had higher average wages than before the war and could buy more products. Because the work week was shorter, people also had more leisure time. This led them to spend more money on entertainment. By 1930, more than half the population was going to the movies once a week. More than half of all American families also owned radios.

Speculation in the Stock Market and in Real Estate

Speculation is the buying of an item, not for personal use, but with the hope of reselling it later at a higher price. As you already know, **stocks** are shares in companies sold to the public. The owner of a stock has the right to sell it to someone else.

In the 1920s, speculation in stocks reached new heights. Corporate and personal profits were soaring and the federal government had reduced taxes on the rich. Many wealthy people invested part of their profits in the stock market. As the demand for stocks increased, their prices rose. Soon the price of a stock bore no relationship at all to its percentage of ownership in the company that issued it—it only represented what one buyer thought he or she could get from another buyer on the stock exchange.

As stocks went up in value, more and more people became tempted to buy them in the hope of getting rich quickly. This made stock prices climb higher still. By 1929, the prices of stocks were more than three times what they had been at the beginning of the Twenties. To make matters worse, people were buying on "**margin**." Instead of paying the full price of the stock, they paid only 10% and promised to pay the rest later. Before they paid the balance, they sold the stock to get the cash for the payment. If the stock went up in price, they made a handsome profit—far in excess of what their investment was worth. But if the stock went down in price, they risked losing all their investment and might not even be able to pay the 90% they still owed. With buying on margin, the stock market was quickly turning into a national casino.

People also invested in real estate—especially in Florida—with similar hopes and illusions. As long as stocks and real estate continued to climb in value, people felt rich and spent both cash and credit on other goods too. The frenzy of stock market speculation created an atmosphere of "easy money," which contributed to the prosperity of the 1920s. It made many individuals feel prosperous. However, as you will learn in the next chapter, such speculation eventually brought the entire economy down in collapse.

The Prosperity of the 1920s was Unevenly Distributed

Not all groups shared in the prosperity of the Roaring Twenties. The gap between the rich and poor remained wide. As many as half of all Americans lived at or below the poverty level. Some groups faced special difficulties.

Farmers

Farmers' problems were similar in some ways to those they faced in the Populist era. Advances in technology, especially the introduction of the tractor and the spread of electricity, led to overproduction and a catastrophic drop in farm prices. The revival of foreign competition, despite higher tariffs, also hurt farmers. Total farm income dropped from $22 billion in 1919 to only $8 billion in 1928. Many American farmers went bankrupt.

Workers in the Railroad, Coal, and Textile Industries

Railroads became increasingly unprofitable because of competition from cars and trucks. The coal industry faced new competition from oil and natural gas. The textile industry faced competition from foreign producers, especially as European manufacturers recovered from World War I.

Minority Groups

African Americans, Hispanic Americans, and American Indians shared the common experience of limited job opportunities, low pay, and high levels of unemployment. You will learn more about these groups later in this chapter.

Attempts to Preserve Traditional Values

The greater mobility and material comfort afforded by automobiles and electricity had an important impact on social patterns and contributed to the emergence of new values. Some groups felt a new sense of power and freedom. Others felt challenged by new currents of thought and strove to preserve traditional values.

At the start of the 1920s, it was the attempt to preserve traditional values that was most striking. Rural America continued to regard the rise of urban society with suspicion. The "Red Scare" and laws restricting immigration were expressions of this impulse. Two of the best examples of the effort to defend traditional values were Prohibition and the Scopes Trial.

Prohibition

The movement to ban alcoholic drinks, known as the **Temperance Movement**, began in the early 19th century. Temperance reformers saw alcoholic beverages as the root cause of poverty, crime, the breakdown of families, and sin. Protestant church groups and women reformers were especially active in this movement. Supported by Progressives, temperance especially appealed to small-town America. Several individual states had already banned alcohol in the late 19th century. The **18th Amendment** extended this "noble experiment"—a clear attempt to legislate public morality—to the national level. The amendment was ratified by the states at the beginning of 1919. It prohibited "the manufacture, sale, or transportation of intoxicating liquors," including their importation. The amendment granted both Congress and the state governments powers of enforcement. In October 1919, Congress passed the **Volstead Act**, which defined "intoxicating liquors" to include both wine and beer. The law provided penalties for the manufacture, sale, and transportation of alcoholic beverages (but not for their consumption). It also permitted limited production of alcohol for medical or religious purposes.

Authorities disposing of illegal alcohol

Prohibition proved difficult to enforce. There were very few enforcement agents. Most European immigrants and city-dwellers did not believe it was wrong to drink alcoholic beverages, and they refused to obey the law. "Bootleggers" brought beer and whiskey across from Canada. Others made their own brew in secret stills. Illegal nightclubs—known as "speakeasies"—served liquor in cities. Even President Harding secretly served alcohol to his guests in the White House.

As a result of Prohibition, people began to lose their respect for the law in general. The manufacture, transportation, and sale of alcohol was largely taken over by criminal gangs. Criminal bosses like Al Capone in Chicago made fortunes selling bootlegged liquor. Organized crime used its increased wealth and power to move into gambling, prostitution, and the collection of money from local businesses. Although Prohibition reduced social drinking, its side effects turned out to be far worse than its benefits. The "noble experiment" failed and Prohibition was finally repealed by the 21st Amendment in 1933.

Chicago Police Department mug shot of Al Capone

Fundamentalism and the Scopes Trial

In reaction to the rise of cities with new cultural values and greater freedom, there was an upsurge of traditional values in rural parts of the country. Some Protestant Christians declared their faith in the "Fundamentals," a term taken from a twelve-volume study, *The Fundamentals* (published between 1910 and 1915). These Christian **Fundamentalists** believed that the Bible—including its account of Creation—was to be taken literally. They thought that God had created the world in seven days, and that people and animals were created in their present form. They therefore opposed Darwin's theory of evolution—the view that organisms have existed on Earth for millions of years and that they have gradually evolved through a process of natural selection.

John Butler was a Tennessee farmer, a member of the state legislature, and a Christian Fundamentalist. In 1925, Butler was able to pass a bill in the state legislature that prohibited the teaching of evolution in state-funded public schools. Similar laws were passed in other Southern states. The **American Civil Liberties Union** (or ACLU) was formed in 1920 to protect freedom of speech and other civil liberties. It persuaded John Scopes, a high school teacher in Tennessee, to defy the **Butler Act**. Scopes was arrested for teaching evolution in violation of the law and put on trial. The ACLU brought in **Clarence Darrow**, a famous Chicago trial lawyer, to defend Scopes. **William Jennings Bryan**, the former Democratic candidate for President and President Wilson's Secretary of State, assisted the prosecution. Darrow cross-examined Bryan as an expert on the Bible, pointing to contradictions that seemed to arise when the Bible was interpreted literally. The confrontation between Darrow and Bryan received national attention in both the newspapers and radio. Scopes was convicted, but his fine of $100 was later set aside on a technicality. Tennessee never prosecuted any other teacher for giving lessons on evolution, even though the Butler Act was upheld by the Tennessee Supreme Court.

John Scopes

Clarence Darrow and William Jennings Bryan

Chapter 10 | The Roaring Twenties

New Values

Against these traditional rural values were newer urban ones. For the first time, half of all Americans were living in cities. Many sought greater openness and self-expression, and an abandonment of earlier restrictions. These new values were largely a product of the cosmopolitanism of city-life—higher levels of education, exposure to a greater number of ideas (especially from Europe), a greater mix of cultures due to the influx of immigrants, and freedom in general from the restraints of small town life. The sense of greater freedom had an especially strong impact on women, young adults, and African Americans.

Women

The decade opened with ratification of the **19th Amendment** in 1920, which guaranteed women the right to vote. Women's roles in the work force also began to change. Many women found increased employment opportunities as secretaries, sales clerks, telephone operators, nurses, and factory workers. A small number—graduates of women's colleges—became professional "career women," asserting their independence from men. New household appliances—such as the refrigerator, electric wash-ing machine, and vacuum cleaner—had only just appeared, giving women in the middle classes more leisure time.

Manners and morals were also changing. In the 1920s, women generally became more assertive. Many smoked and drank in public. They stopped wearing restrictive clothing like petticoats, corsets, broad hats, and long dresses. "**Flappers**" were fashionable young women who wore lipstick, short hair, and straight simple dresses or pleated skirts that just reached to their knees. The name "Flapper" referred to their greater freedom: they were birds "flapping" their wings. It was popularized by the 1920 film, *The Flapper*, about a teenage school girl in Florida.

Because of the greater number of women living in cities and the growing ownership of cars in the countryside, many young women now went out unchaperoned. Female movie stars began serving as popular role models. In general, women enjoyed far greater freedom of self-expression than before the war.

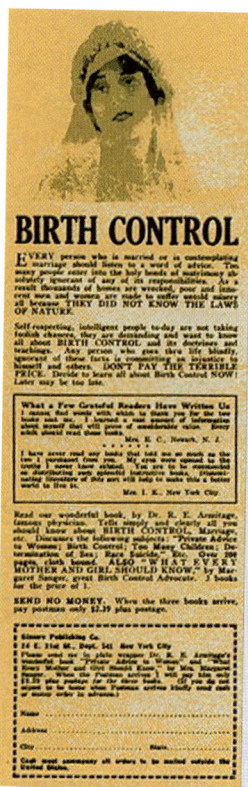

In the 1920s, greater awareness of birth control methods was also spreading. A woman reformer, **Margaret Sanger**, played a critical role in this development. In 1914, she wrote a series of articles about existing methods of birth control that shocked some readers. A federal law made it illegal to send information about birth control in the mail, and Sanger had to flee to England to avoid arrest. She returned to the United States and opened the first birth control clinic in America in 1916, staffed entirely by women doctors. In 1921, Sanger started the American Birth Control League, which later became Planned Parenthood.

The "Lost Generation"

Young adults in cities enjoyed greater freedom than ever before and gave the Twenties its reputation for craziness. They turned the materialism of their parents into a frenzied pursuit of pleasure. They were responsible for zany fads—such as goldfish swallowing, marathon dancing, and flagpole sitting. A group of young writers rejected the materialism of American life, which they viewed as superficial.

Young novelist Sinclair Lewis parodied the narrowness and hypocrisy of small-town middle-class American life in *Main Street* and *Babbitt*. F. Scott Fitzgerald revealed the confusions of his generation in *This Side of Paradise* and *The Great Gatsby*, showing how the search for purely material success could sometimes lead to tragedy. Some of these writers, including Fitzgerald, left the United States for Europe. Ernest Hemingway, a young American reporter in Paris, captured the feelings of these Americans living abroad in his novel *The Sun Also Rises*, published in 1926.

Hemingway

Hollywood and New Popular Heroes

Greater leisure time gave people more time for entertainment. People began attending organized sports in large numbers, where popular heroes like the baseball player Babe Ruth or the boxing champion Jack Dempsey appeared. People also began listening to radio and going to movies. Radio and motion pictures helped to forge a truly national popular culture as millions of Americans listened to the same voices on the radio or saw the same scenes in the movie theater.

Thomas Edison had developed the technology for moving pictures at the end of the nineteenth century. Most of the first film companies set up studios in New York, but several wanted to move away from Edison so that they did not get into disputes over patent rights. In 1910, the director D. W. Griffith took a group of famous actors to Los Angeles. They settled in **Hollywood**, which was then a small village. In 1915, Griffith filmed *Birth of a Nation*, a silent film epic about the Civil War and Reconstruction that was one of the most successful films of all time. Soon several other filmmakers, attracted by the warm and sunny weather, also moved to Hollywood.

In 1927, *The Jazz Singer*, the first "talkie" film with sound, was released. Movie studios like Paramount and Warner Brothers acquired their own movie theaters, where they showed their productions. Writers, directors, actors and actresses signed contracts with particular studios, received salaries, and only made films for that studio. Hollywood produced westerns, comedies, romances, and musicals. More and more Americans were attracted to the movies as a form of entertainment. Movie stars like Rudolph Valentino, Charlie Chaplin, Mary Pickford, and Greta Garbo became household names. Movie houses often showed newsreels before the main feature, and thus became places where Americans learned more about current affairs. They also saw how other people lived. Some people believed Hollywood was becoming a corrupt influence. A Republican leader, Will Hays, became a spokesperson for the motion picture industry and later wrote a moral code for movies to prevent states from introducing their own forms of censorship.

Mary Pickford with a movie camera

Movie stars and other popular heroes served as role models for many Americans. The rise of new popular heroes may have been influenced by the need to preserve a sense of personal identity in an increasingly impersonal age of machines. If people felt a loss of individuality on the assembly line or as part of a large corporate organization, they could at least vicariously enjoy the exploits of Charles Lindbergh, who made the first transatlantic flight in 1927, or of Gertrude Ederle, the first woman to swim the English Channel.

Chapter 10 | The Roaring Twenties

The Historian's Apprentice

Imagine you are a young person living in the Twenties. Write a letter to your cousin describing some aspect of popular culture: the Scopes trial, Prohibition, women's new roles, recent literature, or the movies.

The African-American Experience and the Harlem Renaissance

African Americans enjoyed new opportunities in the 1920s while continuing to face old prejudices.

Booker T. Washington vs. W.E.B. Du Bois

Two leaders who offered alternative responses to the challenges facing African Americans even before the Twenties began were Booker T. Washington and W.E.B. Du Bois.

Booker T. Washington (1856–1915), the elder of the two, had been born into slavery. After the Civil War, Washington and his mother moved to West Virginia. As a boy, he taught himself to read while working in a mine and then as a household servant. Because of his sharp intelligence, he was sent to the Hampton Agricultural Institute, a school for African Americans, but he had to make the 500-mile journey to the school alone on foot. Washington received vocational training, became a teacher, and later founded the Tuskegee Institute in Alabama, which taught agricultural and mechanical skills and teacher training. He also wrote about his own experiences in his popular autobiography, *Up from Slavery* (1901). Washington became the most famous African American of his generation, giving speeches, traveling with a large group of followers, and receiving support from wealthy white philanthropists, including Andrew Carnegie. Presidents like Theodore Roosevelt and William Howard Taft consulted him.

After witnessing the difficulties of Reconstruction and its aftermath, Booker T. Washington thought that African Americans should concentrate on achieving vocational skills rather than on demanding immediate social equality. He felt that racism could best be overcome by demonstrating that African Americans were honest, skilled and industrious. He therefore believed they should stay in the countryside and not attempt to compete with whites, advising them to "cast down your bucket where you are." In a famous speech given in Atlanta in 1895, he proposed the "Atlanta Compromise"—that African Americans would peacefully submit to segregation and white rule in the South, so long as they were given free vocational training in public schools and enjoyed their most basic legal rights.

W.E.B. Du Bois (1868–1963) was born in New England. Thirteen years younger than Booker T. Washington, he came to disagree strongly with the latter's approach. Du Bois believed that African Americans must agitate for full social equality and should not rest content, even temporarily, with an inferior social and economic status. He also believed that the most intelligent and capable blacks—whom he called the "Talented Tenth"—should receive a

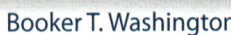
Booker T. Washington

W.E.B. Du Bois

liberal and professional education, both to demonstrate their ability and to lead the movement for full civil rights for all African Americans. Du Bois himself studied in the United States and Germany and received a Ph.D. at Harvard. He was Professor of History at the University of Atlanta from 1897 to 1919. He published *The Souls of Black Folk* in 1903, in which he opposed Booker T. Washington's views on education. After a meeting with Booker T. Washington in 1904, Du Bois launched the "Niagara Movement." The new movement condemned the "Atlanta Compromise." Its "Declaration of Principles" called for equal economic opportunities for African Americans and the right to vote. In 1909–1910, Du Bois joined with white Progressives in New York City to launch the **National Association for the Advancement of Colored People**, or "**NAACP**."

The Great Migration

When World War I broke out, nine out of ten African Americans were still living in the South, where most of them were sharecroppers or tenant farmers. A wartime shortage of workers led Northern manufacturers to send agents to the South to entice African Americans to move north. Others were encouraged to move by letters from relatives or by advertisements in African-American newspapers, or they just wanted to escape Southern segregation and racism. The spread of the boll weevil (*a beetle*) to cotton fields led to a loss of jobs in the South just when new restrictions on European immigration had created a growing demand for labor in the North. U.S. Steel used African-American workers as strike-breakers during the 1919 strike, while Henry Ford hired African Americans to work alongside white laborers in his auto plants in Detroit. Almost two million Southern blacks migrated to Northern cities—especially New York, Chicago, Detroit and Philadelphia—over the next two decades, in the "**Great Migration**."

Continuing Racism and Violence

African Americans felt a greater sense of freedom in the North, but they still faced considerable obstacles. They were forced to move to a limited number of neighborhoods because landlords and homeowners elsewhere refused to rent or sell to them. They continued to face racial hatred, discrimination, and even violence. As black veterans returned from World War I, there were increased tensions. In July 1919, an African-American teenager on a raft drifted towards a "white" beach on the shores of Lake Michigan in Chicago. A white bather threw rocks, hitting him on the head and causing him to drown. When police refused to arrest anyone, fighting broke out, which soon spread to rioting in black neighborhoods. White gangs invaded, destroying property and attacking residents. Over the next several days, 38 were killed and 500 were injured. Similar riots occurred in other cities, including Washington, D.C., Omaha, Nebraska, and Elaine, Arkansas, during "Red Summer."

Two years later, one of the worst race riots in the nation's history took place in Tulsa, Oklahoma. An African-American nineteen-year-old was arrested when he fell and grabbed the arm of a white female elevator operator. A white crowd showed up at the jail, ready to lynch the prisoner. But African-American veterans appeared with rifles, forcing the crowd to disperse. However, when news spread of the incident, angry whites attacked the black neighborhood of Greenwood, killing residents and

Greenwood burning, June 1921

Chapter 10 | The Roaring Twenties

burning the entire neighborhood to the ground. Estimates of the number who died vary from 39 to several hundred. More than 30 neighborhood blocks were destroyed, and 10,000 people were left homeless.

Meanwhile, lynchings continued across the South, averaging about thirty a year throughout the decade. Victims were often tortured before being murdered, and their dead bodies were frequently mutilated and burned. With the return of African-American veterans in 1919, many Southern whites became especially uneasy, and the number of lynchings briefly increased. Although many of these murders occurred in public, often in broad daylight, not a single person was ever charged under state law.

Will Brown was lynched by a mob in Omaha. This photo shows his body still burning.

The NAACP turned its efforts in support of the Dyer Bill, which would have made lynching a federal crime. The bill passed the House of Representatives but was held up in the Senate by filibustering (*giving long speeches so that a bill never comes before the Senate for a vote*). Opponents attacked the Dyer Bill as a violation of states' rights. Supporters pointed out that Congress had already passed laws making the sale of alcohol a federal crime, yet refused to pass a law against the far worse crime of lynching. In fact, the bill never passed.

The Harlem Renaissance

Despite these setbacks, African Americans developed a greater sense of pride in the 1920s. There were approximately 15 million African Americans living in the United States. More of them were being educated than ever before. The greatest concentration of African Americans was found in **Harlem**, a neighborhood in New York City. Because discrimination prevented them from residing in other parts of the city, African Americans of different occupations mixed together in Harlem where they lived side by side.

Roots

African-American communities in Northern cities started their own daily newspapers, such as *The Defender* in Chicago, which reached 300,000 subscribers by 1930, and the *Pittsburg Courier* with 100,000 readers. The NAACP published its own monthly magazine, *The Crisis*, edited by W.E.B. Du Bois, while a rival organization, the **National Urban League**, published the magazine *Opportunity*. These magazines not only reported news events and rallied supporters, they also published the work of African-American writers and poets, giving birth to a flourishing of black culture that has since become known as the "**Harlem Renaissance**."

Writers and Artists

Many of the writers and artists who made up the Harlem Renaissance were veterans of World War I. After fighting for democracy abroad, they resented second-class citizenship and white supremacy at home. The Harlem Renaissance began with the publication of the essay "Enter the New Negro," by **Alain Locke**, an African-American philosophy professor at Howard University. Locke's "New Negro" rejected the timidity and subservience of the "Old Negro"—African Americans who, like Booker T. Washington, attempted to reconcile themselves to white supremacy and were now seen as "Uncle Toms." Instead, the "New Negro" took great pride in being black and would rise above rac-

ism—"from some inner, desperate resourcefulness," wrote Locke, "has recently sprung up the simple expedient of fighting prejudice by mental passive resistance, in other words, by trying to ignore it." Harlem, according to Locke, had become the "Mecca of the New Negro."

One of the writers who participated in the movement was **Countee Cullen**, a poet who had studied English and French literature, and married Du Bois's daughter. Another, **Jean Toomer**, wrote *Cane* (1923)—a modern novel consisting of short stories, poems and a play, all of which described African-American experiences in both the South and the North. The most celebrated poet of the Harlem Renaissance was **Langston Hughes**. He aimed to capture "the spirit of the race" and inspire his people: "Most of my poems are racial in theme and treatment, derived from the life I know." Hughes was fluent in German, Spanish, and French. He had studied engineering at Columbia University and lived in Paris before returning to Harlem. His poems first appeared in the magazines *The Crisis* and *Opportunity*. In 1926, Hughes published his first complete volume of poetry.

Langston Hughes

Another writer, **Claude McKay**, came from Jamaica. He wrote *Home to Harlem* in 1928, a novel providing a realistic portrayal of African-American life in Harlem. Du Bois felt that McKay's description of the hardships of ghetto life actually set back the cause of civil rights since it depicted the conditions of the lowest, and not the most talented. Du Bois believed the aim of African-American literature should be to "uplift" the black community and to depict African Americans in a positive light. But Langston Hughes and other younger writers disagreed, arguing that the aim of the black artist should be to reveal the terrible consequences of racism and discrimination.

One of the underlying aims of the Harlem Renaissance was to disprove racial prejudice by demonstrating that African Americans were capable of creating great works of art and literature. Other important writers of the Harlem Renaissance included **Zora Neal Hurston**, who grew up in Florida, studied anthropology at Columbia University, and published short stories. Another writer, Wallace Thurman, believed that black writers should not have a specific agenda, other than to express themselves. He published a literary journal, *Fire!!!,* with Zora Neal Hurston and Langston Hughes.

Zora Neal Hurston

The painter Archibald Motley is often considered to belong to the Harlem Renaissance, although he lived in Chicago, where he painted African-American portraits and scenes of night life. Other notable painters were Palmer Hayden and Aaron Douglas.

The painting *Getting Religion* by Archibald Motley

Jazz

With its syncopated rhythms, use of notes from the blues scale, and emphasis on improvisation, jazz music also became popular. Jazz had its roots in old work songs, blues music from the South, and African-American spirituals. Langston Hughes tried to capture its pulse in his poems: "In many of them I try to grasp and hold some of the meanings and rhythms of jazz. Jazz to me is one of the inherent expressions of Negro life in America: the eternal

Billie Holiday

tom-tom of revolt against weariness in a white world." Musicians such as Louis Armstrong, Cab Calloway, and Duke Ellington played jazz music in Harlem night clubs. Ella Fitzgerald, Billie Holiday, and Bessie Smith became famous as jazz vocalists. Jazz became popular across the country. White New Yorkers flocked at night to the Cotton Club in Harlem, where black musicians played to a white audience. F. Scott Fitzgerald popularized jazz in his books.

Marcus Garvey

The most popular black leader of the early 1920s was another immigrant from Jamaica: **Marcus Garvey**. Born in Jamaica, Garvey traveled to both Latin America and England. Returning to Jamaica in 1914, he established the **Universal Negro Improvement Association**. In 1916, he moved to Harlem. Garvey believed that "black is beautiful," and that all people of African heritage should take pride in their race. He opposed cooperation with whites in organizations like the NAACP and encouraged blacks to form their own businesses and act independently. Garvey set up stores, restaurants, a hotel and his own newspaper, *The Negro World*. A frequent contributor was Carter G. Woodson, a graduate of Berea College and the second African American to earn a Ph.D. in history at Harvard. A noted scholar, Woodson became known as the "Father of Black History."

Garvey also established his own shipping line—the "Black Star Line," with routes to the Caribbean. Soon he had half a million followers. Garvey emphasized the achievements of African history: "Negroes, teach your children that they are the direct descendants of the greatest and proudest race that ever peopled the earth." He even started a "**Back to Africa**" movement. In 1920, he held the "International Convention of the Negro Peoples of the World" in Madison Square Garden, where he was proclaimed as the "Provisional President" of Africa. However, his shipping venture soon failed, and he made the mistake of meeting with Ku Klux Klan leaders in the South, enraging other African-American leaders. In 1923, Garvey was tried and convicted for mail fraud. He spent two years in prison and was deported to Jamaica in 1927. His movement never recovered, although some of his ideas would re-emerge 40 years later during the Civil Rights Movement.

The Historian's Apprentice

Booker T. Washington told African Americans to limit their ambitions for the moment to obtaining a vocational education and raising their standards of living. **W.E.B. Du Bois** urged African Americans to seek immediate equality with whites in all endeavors. Finally, **Marcus Garvey** told peoples of African heritage to separate from whites and to rely on themselves.

1. Make a chart or Venn diagram comparing the viewpoints of these three leaders on the African-American experience.
2. Select three members of your class to impersonate these three leaders. Then have all three hold a joint press conference in which they present their ideas. The rest of the class should act as reporters, asking them questions about their backgrounds, activities, and views. Each of the three main speakers should then provide a closing statement summarizing his own point of view.
3. Select one of these leaders and prepare a PowerPoint presentation or short biography based on your own research, using materials from the library or the Internet.
4. Select one of the writers from the Harlem Renaissance and read one of his or her works.

Other Minority Groups

African Americans were not the only minority group to experience discrimination and hardship in the 1920s. This was an era when most white Americans believed in the superiority of their own race.

Hispanic Americans

There were Hispanic Americans, especially in the Southwest, whose families had been living in these areas even before they were annexed by the United States. The number of Mexican workers crossing the border into the United States increased dramatically during World War I, when there was a shortage of labor on farms and in cities. There were no restrictions on immigration from Latin America (including Mexico). Landowners from Texas, Arizona, and California needed farm laborers and opposed all proposals to restrict immigration from the south. Their opponents argued that Mexicans were racially inferior and that their increasing numbers threatened American civilization. Although Congress refused to place limits on Latin American immigration, it created the U.S. Border Patrol in 1924, and required those entering America to pay $10 for a visa. Many Latin Americans could not afford this fee and began to cross the border illegally. Most of those who came worked as migrant farm laborers, picking sugar beets and cotton, or fruits and vegetables.

Some Hispanic immigrants found ways to fight discrimination and establish a place for themselves in American politics and culture. **Octaviano Larrazolo** was born in Mexico and migrated to the United States. He became a school teacher, a school principal, and a lawyer. He helped rewrite New Mexico's constitution to ban discrimination against Mexican Americans. In 1918, he became Governor of New Mexico. In 1928, he became the first Mexican American in the U.S. Senate. In the same year, Daniel Venegas, another Mexican immigrant, published *The Adventures of Don Chipote*, a novel describing the harsh conditions experienced by migrant laborers.

American Indians

During the 1920s, the goal of federal policy towards American Indian tribes remained the same as under the Dawes Act—to assimilate their members into "mainstream" society and turn them into small farmers. The government provided limited assistance, but only to those who held jobs, which were scarce on reservation land. Indians were only permitted to leave the reservation with the permission of the reservation agent. Because of the sale of reservation lands after passage of the Dawes Act, conditions on the remaining reservation lands were wretched, with high rates of alcoholism, crime and suicide. Ninety-six percent of Indian families had incomes of less than $200 a year (when an average family had twelve times as much). In 1928, a panel of sociologists reported that the Indians were "extremely poor," most of their homes were shacks without fresh water or toilets, their schools were inadequate, and diseases like tuberculosis and measles were killing thousands of them each year.

Some American Indian groups fought to preserve their traditions. The American Indian Defense Association was organized in 1921 to protect their rights. The new association successfully opposed a bill in Congress that would have taken away most of the land of the Pueblo Indians in New Mexico and Arizona. In 1924, the **Indian Citizenship Act** made all American Indians into United States citizens. In fact, many were already citizens after serving in World War I or for other reasons. The main effects of the Indian Citizenship Act were that Indians could vote in federal elections and became subject to federal income tax. Several states with reservation lands, including Arizona, New Mexico, and South Dakota, continued to bar American Indians from voting in state elections until the 1950s.

American Indians were excited in the 1920s by **Jim Thorpe** (1888–1953), a member of the Sac and Fox tribe. Thorpe attended an Indian agency school and the Carlisle Indian Industrial School, where he played football. Thorpe was so talented that his school team defeated both Harvard and the Army. In the 1912 Olympics, Thorpe won several events and was honored with a parade down Broadway. Later, he became a major league baseball player and then a football player in the new NFL. Because he had played a season in baseball, he was not considered an amateur and lost his Olympic medals, but Thorpe continued to play professional football until 1928. He is widely considered as one of the best athletes of the century. His Olympic medals were returned to his family in 1987.

Asian Americans

Just over 330,000 Asian Americans were living in the United States in 1920, making up less than one percent of the population. Most lived in the West—especially in California. The largest groups of Asian Americans were Japanese (220,596), Chinese (85,202), and Filipino (26,634). Asian immigrants could not become naturalized citizens, and further Asian immigration was barred by the Immigration Acts of 1921 and 1924. Those already living here continued to face discrimination. The Asiatic Exclusion League, formed in San Francisco in 1905, aimed to end Asian immigration and to segregate Asian children in public schools. California passed a law in 1913 that prohibited Asian residents from owning land because they could not become citizens. Other states quickly followed this example. In the 1920s, the U.S. Supreme Court upheld these laws as well as the general ban on naturalized citizenship for Asians. Asian Americans born in the United States, however, were citizens.

The Ku Klux Klan

The Ku Klux Klan, dead since the 1870s, was suddenly revived as an anti-immigrant, anti-Catholic, anti-Semitic, and anti-black movement. It especially represented the fears of the residents of the small towns of the Midwest and South, who saw themselves as the true "one hundred percent" Americans, but its membership also grew in some cities.

Rebirth of the Klan

William Simmons launched this resurgence of the Klan in 1915 when a Jewish convict in Georgia was lynched after his sentence to death for rape and murder was changed by the governor to life imprisonment. In the same year, the movie *The Birth of a Nation* glorified the Klan in its early history. The images of the film, which included the costumes and heroics of the Klan, became a popular propaganda tool for recruiting new Klan members.

The Klan in its Heyday

In the 1920s, the Klan organized on a national scale. It grew larger than it had been after the Civil War. Its structure stretched from coast to coast, with its strongest representation in the South and Midwest. In some areas, Klan membership constituted as much as 20% to 40% of the white male adult population. Klan members dressed in hooded robes, burned crosses, held parades and meetings, and spread their gospel of hatred.

In these years, the Klan's ideological stance also expanded. It not only included its traditional racism against African Americans but also embraced hatred of Jews, Catholics, unions, immigrants, and all

those advocating voting rights for women. The Klan's resurgence occurred in the aftermath of large-scale immigration to the United States in the late 19th and early 20th centuries, mostly from Eastern and Southern Europe. These immigrants were, for the most part, Jews and Catholics. They competed for jobs and housing during an uneasy time of rapid urbanization and industrialization. Women seeking equality ran counter to the traditional views of a male-dominated Anglo-Saxon society. Unions were progressive and were seen to be advancing the interests of immigrant laborers. Klan members championed white Anglo-Saxon Protestants as superior to everyone else. They claimed to represent "**one hundred percent Americanism**," which became their motto. African Americans, Catholics, Jews, and others who did not fit their ideal racial and cultural profile were considered outsiders and became the targets of the Klan's hatred.

With growing popular support, the Klan was able to play a greater role in politics nationwide. Klan members generally supported the Democratic Party. Klan members were elected to national, state and municipal offices. In Indiana, Klan member Edward Jackson was elected as Governor in 1924. In the same year, the Klan became a divisive element at the Democratic National Convention, forcing the supporters of William McAdoo, a Protestant, and Al Smith, a Catholic, to settle for a compromise candidate. Eventually, criminal activities, internal struggles, loss of public support, and new laws prohibiting some of the Klan's activities led to a collapse of its membership. By 1930, the number of its members had fallen back down to 30,000 (see chart).

The Ku Klux Klan
The Ku Klux Klan has actually occupied the national stage in three different periods: during and just after Reconstruction, from 1915 through the 1930s, and lastly, in the 1950s and 1960s, when it opposed the Civil Rights Movement.

Year	Membership
1868	550,000
1920	4,000,000
1924	6,000,000
1930	30,000
1965	35,000
2008	6,000
2012	5,000

Focus on Florida

By 1920, many Americans had come to think of Florida as a desirable place to visit or live. Advertisements, magazine articles, and the memories of those who had visited for business, pleasure, or military service had all done their part in promoting the state. Americans were aware of Florida's luxury hotels, parks, beaches, and other recreational opportunities. The state eliminated its inheritance and income taxes to provide additional appeal. Between 1923 and 1925, more than 300,000 Americans moved to Florida.

The increasing use of automobiles put pressure on the state to construct a roadway system. Florida's first highway department was established in 1915. The state's first concrete highway, between Jacksonville and Lake City, was completed in 1923. The Tamiami Trail, connecting Tampa and Miami, was completed in 1928. It was 273 miles long and took five years to build. In 1920 there had been fewer than 1,000 miles of paved roadways in Florida; by 1930, there were more than 3,800 miles.

Airplanes also arrived. The first airport was established at Miami Beach in 1912. By 1926, nine cities in Florida had their own airports, carrying both mail and passengers.

With trains, planes, and cars, "snowbirds" found they could escape the winter cold by coming south. Florida became a place where many people wanted to buy land. In the early Twenties, speculation in real estate led to a land boom in Miami Beach, which spread along the coasts and moved as far west as Tallahassee and Pensacola. Properties were bought and resold only a few days later at a profit. Land on Miami Beach, which the developer Carl Fisher had been willing to give away for free in 1915, was worth $26,000 an acre by 1925.

During these years, the land boom dominated Florida's economy. It affected transportation, construction, labor, and the allocation of resources. Architects designed luxurious mansions in the Mediterranean style for wealthy buyers, with tile roofs, wrought-iron balconies, fountains, and patios. Banks made speculative loans to developers and speculators without strict requirements. Inevitably, some loans went unpaid and a few banks began to fail. In 1925, a strike on the Atlantic Coast Line Railroad temporarily halted the movement of passengers and freight. A natural disaster struck a year later on September 18, 1926, when a deadly hurricane smashed Miami, Coral Gables, Fort Lauderdale, Dania, and Pompano. In Miami alone, as many as 2,000 buildings were destroyed, the city docks were demolished, and all the boats in the harbor were lost.

Real estate prices collapsed almost as rapidly as they had risen. Some people began to exit the state and more banks began to fail. The boom became a bust. There was a slight revival in 1927 and 1928, followed by another destructive hurricane in September 1928. The Mediterranean fruit fly arrived in 1929, destroying 80% of Florida's citrus crop. The stock market crash in October later the same year marked the beginning of the Great Depression, which would soon envelop the entire nation.

The Seminole Indians

The Seminole Indians are related to the Creek. Most once lived in Georgia and Alabama, but they were driven south into Florida by the Creek Wars. Several thousand Seminoles were living in Florida at the start of the Second Seminole War (1835–1842). Many were killed, but a few hundred survivors escaped into the Everglades. By the 1890s, the Seminoles were living peacefully in the Everglades and Big Cypress, surviving as hunters who traded their otter pelts, deerskins, egret plumes, and alligator hides with whites. The state and federal governments set aside reservation lands in Florida for the Seminoles, but few moved into them. As the scale of tourism and real estate development increased in the 1920s, the Seminole way of life became endangered. The Tamiami Trail, connecting Tampa and Miami, became the first road through the Everglades. Efforts to drain parts of the wetlands to create more farmland and build homes further threatened the Seminoles. The demand for their alligator hides and furs fell. The Seminoles began selling their patchwork art, baskets, and other crafts to tourists, who visited their roadside homes. The Seminoles themselves divided into two groups still existing today: the Miccosukee and the Seminoles.

Rosewood

In the early Twenties, Florida became the scene of some of the nation's worst racial violence. As much as 30% of the state's population was African American. Most lived inland in the "backcountry," where they were subjected to "Jim Crow" laws, economic exploitation, and terrible abuse. Florida historian Michael Gannon points out that Florida led the country in lynchings. The turpentine camps still relied on the practice of debt peonage, in which African-American workers could not leave because they owed the camp owners for their food and clothes.

Rosewood was a rural African-American community southwest of Gainesville. By 1923, it had about 350 residents, living in neat, wooden plank homes. Most worked in the timber industry: there were several turpentine mills, two pencil mills, and a sawmill nearby. Rosewood had two general stores, three churches, and its own turpentine mill. Early one January morning, a white woman in the nearby town of Sumner was attacked after her husband had gone to work. She claimed her attacker was an unknown African-American man; other witnesses said it was in fact a white train worker who often visited her and may have beaten her. The same day, a black prisoner had coincidentally escaped from a chain gang. The county sheriff organized white volunteers, who began searching for the escaped prisoner as the probable attacker. Trained dogs led a group of the search party to Rosewood. Under torture, one of the local residents told the men that he had helped to conceal the escaped convict. The unfortunate resident was lynched in the woods. The sheriff tried to disperse the growing mobs of angry white men, some of them drunk, who came pouring in from neighboring communities. They laid siege to one of the homes in Rosewood, which was defended by a resident who was a skilled hunter and marksman. Several were killed in the exchange of gunfire, including children. News of this local resistance spread, and crowds of white men descended on the town, where they burned its churches and houses. Men poured kerosene on the houses, ignited them, and shot those who came out. A few brave whites helped to smuggle some of Rosewood's surviving residents to safety. All of the survivors moved to other towns. On January 7, 1923, the mob returned to burn down all the remaining structures at Rosewood.

Despite coverage in several national newspapers at the time, the attack on Rosewood was quickly forgotten. Neither surviving victims nor neighboring whites spoke publicly of the incident for decades. In the 1980s, a survivor's child told the story to a reporter. At first, others tried to deny its truth. The Rosewood survivors filed for damages based on the state government's failure to protect them from the mob. The suit was dropped, but Florida's state legislature commissioned a special report. Afterwards, they voted to provide the survivors and their descendants with $1.5 million in compensation. It was the first time a state government had ever voted to compensate victims of racial violence.

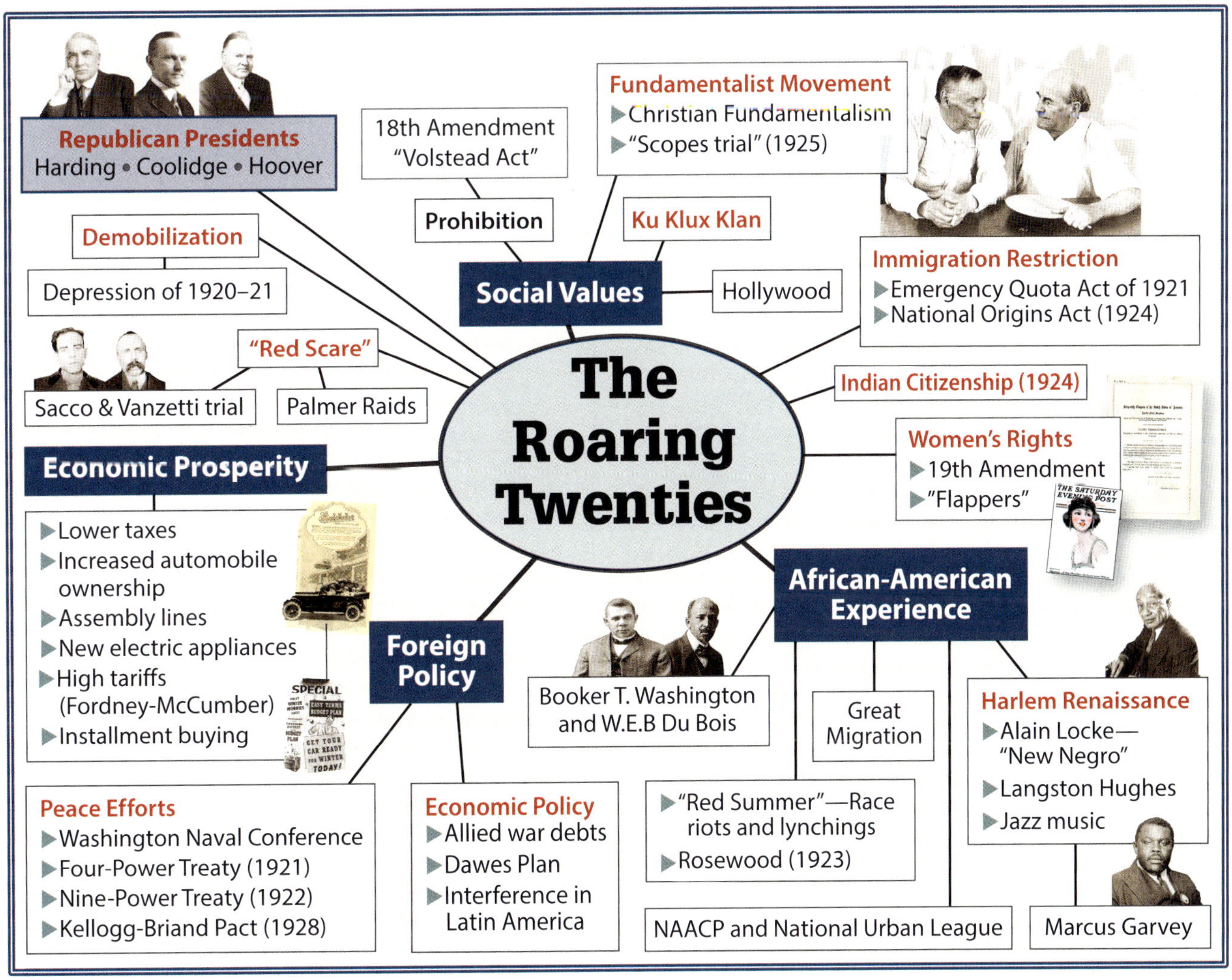

The Roaring Twenties

Republican Presidents: Harding • Coolidge • Hoover

Social Values
- 18th Amendment "Volstead Act"
- Prohibition
- Fundamentalist Movement
  - Christian Fundamentalism
  - "Scopes trial" (1925)
- Ku Klux Klan
- Hollywood
- Immigration Restriction
  - Emergency Quota Act of 1921
  - National Origins Act (1924)
- Indian Citizenship (1924)
- Women's Rights
  - 19th Amendment
  - "Flappers"

Demobilization
- Depression of 1920–21

"Red Scare"
- Sacco & Vanzetti trial
- Palmer Raids

Economic Prosperity
- Lower taxes
- Increased automobile ownership
- Assembly lines
- New electric appliances
- High tariffs (Fordney-McCumber)
- Installment buying

Foreign Policy

Peace Efforts
- Washington Naval Conference
- Four-Power Treaty (1921)
- Nine-Power Treaty (1922)
- Kellogg-Briand Pact (1928)

Economic Policy
- Allied war debts
- Dawes Plan
- Interference in Latin America

African-American Experience
- Booker T. Washington and W.E.B Du Bois
- Great Migration
- "Red Summer"—Race riots and lynchings
- Rosewood (1923)
- NAACP and National Urban League
- Harlem Renaissance
  - Alain Locke—"New Negro"
  - Langston Hughes
  - Jazz music
- Marcus Garvey

Review Cards

Economic Outcomes of Demobilization

- **Demobilization:** Soldiers retire from military service and economic production returns to civilian purposes.
- Returning soldiers looking for work, a series of strikes, and the end of wartime spending led to the **Depression of 1920–1921.**

Republican Presidents of the Twenties

Presidents **Warren Harding, Calvin Coolidge,** and **Herbert Hoover** each pursued policies favorable to business:
- Low taxation on companies and the rich
- High tariffs (**Ford–McCumber Act**)
- Lax enforcement of regulations

Harding called for a "return to normalcy," Coolidge said the "business of America is business," and Hoover favored "rugged individualism."

Harding died in office in 1923. Shortly after his death, the **Teapot Dome Scandal** exposed corruption in his administration.

How the Economic Boom Affected Manufacturing and Marketing

- The spread of automobiles and new electric appliances contributed to the general economic prosperity.
- **Assembly-line production** lowered prices.
- Advertising and **installment buying** encouraged greater consumption.
- **Speculation** on the stock market, including **buying on margin**, added to the feelings of prosperity.
- Florida experienced a boom from improvements in transportation, rising property values, and real estate speculation; but the state experienced an economic collapse in the late 1920s.

The "Red Scare"

The triumph of Bolshevism in Russia, a series of strikes, and random bombings by anarchists led many Americans to fear a Communist revolution at home during the **"Red Scare"** of 1919.

"Palmer Raids": Attorney General Palmer, assisted by J. Edgar Hoover, arrested and deported foreign-born radicals, including Emma Goldman.

Sacco and Vanzetti: Two Italian anarchists were arrested in 1920 for the murder of a guard during a robbery. After an unfair trial they were convicted on flimsy evidence and executed.

Immigration

- The Twenties saw the first restrictions on immigration from Europe. The **Emergency Quota Act of 1921** and the **National Origins Act of 1924** placed new restrictions on immigration to keep out Eastern and Southern Europeans and preserve America's existing ethnic composition. A quota was set for each country for the number of legal immigrants it could send. The 1921 Act limited total immigration to 350,000; the 1924 Act reduced this to 150,000. The quota system favored countries from Northern and Western Europe.
- No immigration at all was allowed from East Asia. On the other hand, no restrictions were placed on immigration from the Americas.

Minorities during the Twenties

Most minorities did not share in the prosperity of the 1920s.
- The number of Hispanic Americans increased since immigration from Mexico was still unrestricted. Many worked as migrant farm laborers.
- American Indians were made citizens in 1924 but continued to suffer from widespread poverty. The **Seminoles** of Florida increased their interaction with tourists to survive changes to the Everglades.
- Asian Americans were few in number and continued to face discrimination: for example, Asian immigrants could not own property.

U.S. Foreign Economic Policy in the Twenties

- While refusing to join the League of Nations, the Republican Presidents still attempted to promote world peace and U.S. business interests.
- **Washington Naval Conference (1921):** The world's leading naval powers agreed to limit the numbers of their battleships to fixed ratios proposed by the United States: United States $\times$ 5; Britain $\times$ 5; Japan $\times$ 3
- **Four-Power Treaty:** Guaranteed peace in the Pacific region.
- **Nine-Power Treaty:** Promised to respect China's sovereignty.
- **Kellogg–Briand Pact (1928):** Fifteen countries pledged to give up war except for self-defense.
- American Presidents also promoted U.S. business overseas and intervened in the Caribbean region.
- **Allied War Debts:** Americans had lent money to the Allies during the war and insisted on being repaid. France and Britain took the reparations money they received from Germany to pay their war debts to the United States. The Dawes Plan lent money to Germany while temporarily reducing German reparations payments.

Traditional Values vs. New Values

The inhabitants of small towns and even some cities supported the prohibition of alcoholic beverages and Fundamentalist Christianity:

- The **18th Amendment (1919)** and the **Volstead Act** introduced **Prohibition**, but many Americans failed to obey it.
- **Fundamentalists** took the Bible literally.
- **John Scopes** was put on trial and convicted for teaching the theory of evolution in Tennessee. Clarence Darrow and William Jennings Bryan participated in his trial.
- The **Ku Klux Klan** experienced a rebirth in 1915. Klan members opposed African Americans, immigrants, Catholics, Jews, unions, and women's suffrage.

Others, especially in the growing cities, supported greater freedom for women and young people:

- The **19th Amendment (1920)** gave women the right to vote, while **flappers** wore looser clothing and went out without chaperones. Women had increased opportunities in employment and education.
- The writers of the "**Lost Generation**"—such as Hemingway and Fitzgerald—expressed the feelings of many young Americans.
- **Hollywood**, center of the movie industry, helped circulate new values.

The African-American Experience

- African Americans continued to face "Jim Crow" laws, lynchings, racism, and economic inequality.
- **Booker T. Washington** urged African Americans to seek vocational training for the moment, but **W.E.B. Du Bois** favored an immediate struggle for full civil rights.
- Many African Americans moved to the North during the **Great Migration**.
- Even in Northern cities they faced racism, discrimination, and violence. Some of the worst race riots occurred in Chicago in 1919, Tulsa in 1921, and **Rosewood** in Florida in 1923.
- The **Harlem Renaissance**, based in New York City, saw a flourishing of African-American culture, with jazz music, the essays of **Alain Locke**, the novels of Jean Toomer, the poetry of **Langston Hughes** and Countee Cullen, and the stories of Zora Neal Hurston. African Americans demonstrated they could create great literary works. The "New Negro" took pride in being black and resisting racism. **Marcus Garvey** encouraged African Americans to rely more on themselves and to separate from whites.

What Do You Know?

SS.912.A.5.3

1. What did the rejection of the League of Nations, the higher tariffs imposed by the Fordney–McCumber Act, and the Emergency Quota Act all point to during the early 1920s?

   A. increasing militarism
   B. increasing isolationism
   C. increasing imperialism
   D. increasing internationalism

SS.912.A.5.1

The graph below provides information on the percentage of unemployed workers from 1914 to 1921.

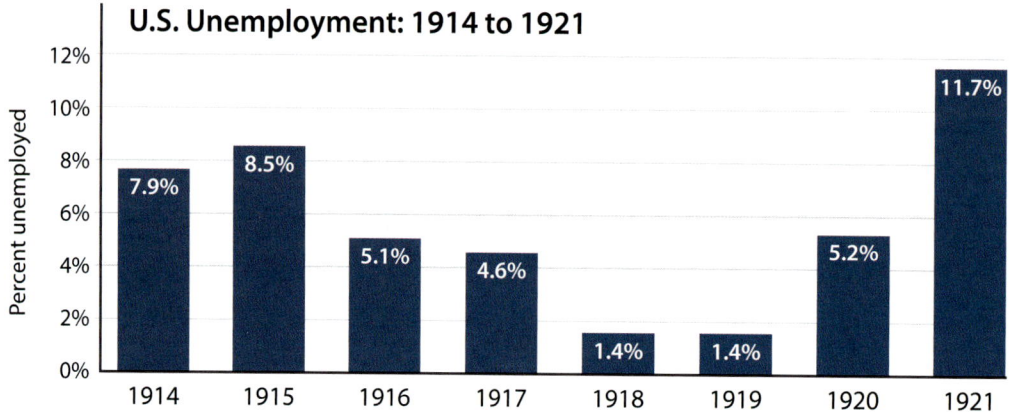

2. What was the primary cause of the changes to the unemployment rate in the United States in 1920 and 1921?

   A. the effects of demobilization
   B. the impact of the "Red Scare"
   C. the passage of the Emergency Quota Act
   D. the Bolshevik victory in the Russian Civil War

SS.912.A.5.2

3. Which event do these newspapers describe?

   A. Cold War
   B. Red Scare
   C. Prohibition
   D. Great Migration

Chapter 10 | The Roaring Twenties

SS.912.A.5.2

4. The political cartoon below depicts Uncle Sam in 1920.

What is the main idea of the cartoon?

A. The land of opportunity is not for Russian immigrants.

B. If an alien is from Latin America, he or she can be deported.

C. Packing vicious aliens like sardines is a serious violation of human rights.

D. Dangerous Communists and anarchists should be sent out of the country.

SS.912.A.5.10

5. Women had many new experiences as a result of World War I, including working at new jobs, wearing new fashions, and acting more independently. What other new change came to women just after World War I?

A. the right to vote

B. the right to drink alcoholic beverages

C. equal pay for equal work

D. the right to serve in military combat

SS.912.A.5.4

The graph below provides information about the value of U.S. agricultural goods sold overseas.

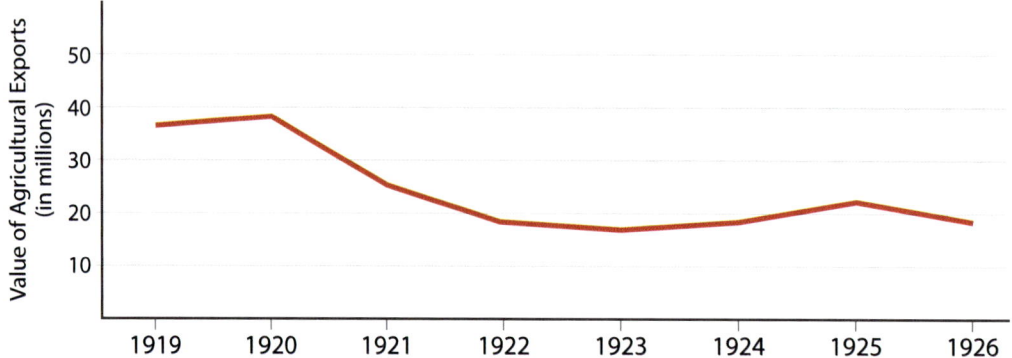

6. What was one impact of the changes shown in the graph?

   A. The U.S. government purchased the agricultural surplus from farmers.

   B. Farmers did not generally participate in the prosperity of the 1920s.

   C. Speculators bought up American farmland at inexpensive prices.

   D. Local food prices remained high because of domestic demand.

SS.912.A.5.4

7. Which groups did not generally participate in the prosperity of the 1920s?

   A. manufacturers and real estate developers

   B. stock brokers and automobile workers

   C. bankers and construction workers

   D. minorities and railroad workers

SS.912.A.5.10

8. Why was there racial unrest in Northern cities after World War I?

   A. African Americans had been given the right to vote for the first time.

   B. African-American baseball players were being allowed to play on previously all-white teams.

   C. The arrival of large numbers of immigrants from Eastern Europe caused tensions with African Americans.

   D. The migration of African Americans and returning African-American veterans had created greater competition for jobs and housing.

SS.912.A.5.4

9. The diagram below provides details about U.S. domestic policies in the 1920s.

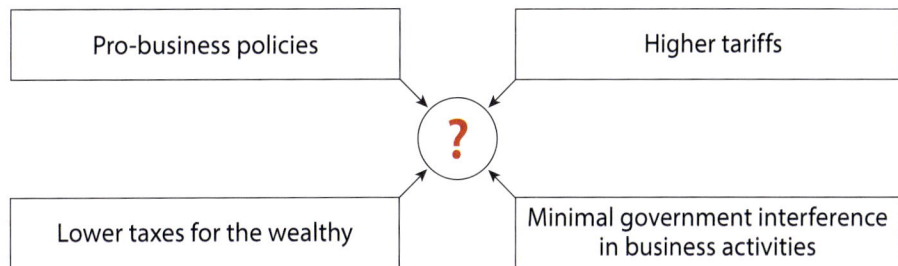

Which phrase best completes the diagram?

A. Led to a wave of strikes across the country

B. Stimulated a period of Progressive reforms

C. Spurred a period of economic growth and prosperity

D. Helped to bring about the Second Industrial Revolution

SS.912.A.5.9

10. Which best describes the activities of the Ku Klux Klan during the 1920s?

A. successfully achieved control of both the Congress and the Presidency

B. assisted Marcus Garvey in transporting African Americans "back to Africa"

C. were mainly directed at preventing African Americans from voting in the South

D. promoted anti-immigrant, anti-African-American, anti-Catholic, and anti-Jewish sentiments

SS.912.A.5.5

11. What did the Washington Naval Conference, the Nine-Power Treaty, and the Kellogg–Briand Pact have in common?

A. They were attempts at promoting world peace without the League of Nations.

B. They created secret alliances between the former Allied and Central Powers.

C. They were a series of naval disarmament treaties involving the Allied Powers of World War I.

D. They were disarmament treaties that limited the number of tanks, use of poison gas, and airplanes.

Chapter 10 | The Roaring Twenties   223

SS.912.A.5.8

Booker T. Washington	W.E.B. Du Bois	Marcus Garvey
• Founded the Tuskegee Institute • Wanted to achieve vocational skills rather than agitate for social equality • Submitted to segregation as long as given vocational training in public schools • Limited ambitions to obtaining a vocation and raising standards of living • Atlanta Compromise	• First African American to receive a Ph.D. from Harvard • Agitated for full social equality and refused to settle for an inferior social and economic status • African Americans should receive a liberal and professional education • Launched the Niagara Movement • Condemned the Atlanta Compromise • Launched the NAACP	• Established the Universal Negro Improvement Association • Believed "black is beautiful" • Opposed cooperation with whites in organizations like the NAACP • Founded African-American businesses such as the Black Star Line • Started a "Back to Africa" movement • Urged African Americans to separate from whites and rely upon themselves

12. What do the philosophies of these three African-American leaders suggest?

    A. African Americans believed that racial equality could not be achieved in the United States.

    B. Only Booker T. Washington felt that whites would accept African Americans as equals.

    C. Conditions were generally acceptable to the African-American community as they were.

    D. Frustrations with continuing inequality led African Americans to fight discrimination in different ways.

SS.912.A.5.6

13. What did African-American writers, artists, and musicians hope to achieve during the Harlem Renaissance?

    A. to display their ability as conscientious workers in the workplace

    B. to show that the pursuit of material success can often lead to tragedy

    C. to demonstrate that African Americans could produce great works of literature and art

    D. to reveal that conditions for African Americans in the South were almost as bad as in the North

SS.912.A.5.12

14. Which problem was demonstrated by events at Rosewood in 1923?

    A. the growing strength of the Ku Klux Klan in Southern states

    B. the continuing prevalence of racism in inland Southern towns

    C. racial tensions in Northern cities in the years after World War I

    D. the absence of agricultural employment in Southern communities

CHAPTER 11

The Great Depression and the New Deal

SS.912.A.5.11 Examine causes, course, and consequences of the Great Depression and the New Deal.

SS.912.H.1.1 Relate works in the arts (architecture, dance, music, theater, and visual arts) of varying styles and genre according to the periods in which they were created.

SS.912.H.1.3 Relate works in the arts to various cultures.

SS.912.H.1.5 Examine artistic response to social issues and new ideas in various cultures.

SS.912.A.5.12 Examine key events and people in Florida history as they relate to United States history.

Names and Terms You Should Know

- Economic boom
- Bull market
- Buying on margin
- Speculation boom
- Black Tuesday
- Smoot-Hawley Tariff
- Herbert Hoover
- "Hoovervilles"
- Great Depression and the New Deal
- Bonus Expeditionary Force
- Gross National Product (GNP)
- Dust Bowl
- Franklin D. Roosevelt
- Fireside chats
- New Deal
- Relief, Recovery, Reform
- Bank Holiday
- National Recovery Act (NRA)
- National Recovery Administration (NRA)
- Agricultural Adjustment Act (AAA)
- Civilian Conservation Corps (CCC)
- Works Progress Administration (WPA)
- Federal Deposit Insurance Corporation (FDIC)
- Social Security
- Tennessee Valley Authority (TVA)
- National Labor Relations Act (Wagner Act)
- Sit-down strike
- Court-packing plan

Florida "Keys" to Learning

1. The Great Depression was the greatest economic crisis in our nation's history. Production fell by half, and one quarter of the work force was unemployed.

2. Mass production created a surplus of goods. By the end of the Twenties, most people who could afford those goods had already bought them. Practices like buying stocks on margin had led to soaring speculation on the New York Stock Market. On "Black Tuesday" (October 29, 1929), the stock market crashed. People tried to sell their stocks but few were willing to buy them.

3. The stock market crash set off a "chain reaction." People who lost money on the stock market could no longer invest or buy as many goods. Businesses and consumers stopped making new purchases. Businesses fired workers, creating mass unemployment. Banks failed. Prices and the demand for goods fell. People lost their homes and many even had to beg for food.

4. On the Great Plains, a series of droughts combined with unsuitable plowing techniques to cause the disaster known as the "Dust Bowl."

5. President Hoover believed in *laissez-faire* economics and did not think the government should interfere too directly in the economy. He took some steps, such as establishing the Reconstruction Finance Corporation (RFC), but his actions were too little, too late. Hoover even used the army to break up a peaceful group of veterans and their families demanding a bonus from Congress.

6. Franklin D. Roosevelt won the Presidential election of 1932. His plan to end the Depression, called the "New Deal," had three goals: relief, recovery, and reform. Roosevelt declared a "Bank Holiday" to prevent bank runs and renew public confidence in banks. He created the Federal Deposit Insurance Corporation (FDIC) to insure bank deposits. The Securities and Exchange Commission was created to regulate the stock market. The National Recovery Administration (NRA) encouraged businesses to establish codes that set prices, wages, and working hours. The Agricultural Adjustment Act (AAA) limited production of crops and livestock to prevent surpluses and help farmers. The Civilian Conservation Corps (CCC) provided young men with work on public projects. The Tennessee Valley Authority (TVA) built dams to control floods and to provide electricity to one of the South's poorest areas. Many of his programs were aimed to "prime the pump"—to get the economy flowing again by placing money in consumers' hands.

7. The Supreme Court struck down several of Roosevelt's early New Deal programs. The "Second New Deal" aimed more at reform and security. The Social Security Act created a "safety net" for Americans by establishing unemployment insurance, retirement benefits, and aid to the disabled and orphaned. The Works Progress Administration (WPA) created new public works projects to increase employment and stimulate the arts. The National Labor Relations Act ("Wagner Act") gave workers the right to unionize. The Fair Labor Standards Act set maximum working hours, a minimum wage, and prohibited child labor.

8. Roosevelt attempted to save the New Deal from the Court with his "court-packing" scheme. His plan was widely condemned and rejected by Congress.

9. The Depression led to disillusionment with many traditional American values. John Steinbeck's novel *The Grapes of Wrath* depicted the plight of the "Okies." Langston Hughes was an African-American poet who wrote of the sufferings of African Americans. Dorothea Lange took photographs of poor migrants and sharecroppers. Their novels, poems and photos gave a human face to the Depression.

The Great Depression

The Great Depression was the worst depression in our nation's history. Production fell by half, one-quarter of the work force was unemployed, and prices plummeted. Behind these statistics was a great deal of suffering and misery. Only America's entry into World War II put a final end to the Great Depression.

The Causes of the Great Depression

What caused the economy to falter from the **economic boom** (*period of general prosperity*) of the 1920s and collapse into the Great Depression of the 1930s? Weaknesses in the economy in the 1920s actually set the process in motion for the breakdown. Historians still disagree on the main cause. When the New York Stock Market crashed in October 1929, it set off a chain reaction that first toppled the American economy and then spread to the rest of the world.

Overproduction/Underconsumption

The 1920s saw rapid economic expansion as manufacturers made and sold new products like cars, radios, and refrigerators. By the end of the 1920s, most of those who could afford these products or buy them on credit had already purchased them. Since such a large share of the national income went to a small, wealthy group at the top of society, not enough income went into the paychecks of average wage-earners to buy all that was being produced. Workers' wages had risen, but production had grown even faster. And many groups—such as farmers, African Americans, coal miners, and the elderly—were in economic difficulties even during the Roaring Twenties. Large numbers of American consumers lacked the "purchasing power" they needed to buy more goods and services. Inventories of unsold products began to pile up in stores and warehouses. Manufacturers were simply producing more goods than they could sell. With unsold inventory, manufacturers cut production and laid off workers, causing unemployment to rise.

High Tariffs Restricted International Trade

American producers might have sold their goods overseas, but they faced problems here as well. American tariffs protected American markets, but made it harder for producers to sell their goods abroad. Some countries retaliated against the United States by setting up high tariffs against American goods. Thus, the effect of high tariffs was to restrict international trade. The highest U.S. tariff of all, the **Smoot-Hawley Tariff**, went into effect in 1930 just after the stock market crash. It raised customs duties on thousands of goods and contributed to a reduction of U.S. trade by more than half.

Speculation, Shaky Banking and Inflated Stock Prices

Speculation refers to the practice of buying real estate (land or buildings), stocks, or anything else to sell later at a profit. During the 1920s, the government failed to regulate either banks or the stock market effectively, and speculation flourished. Bankers often placed their depositors' money in shaky, unsound investments. Private banks lent money to stock market speculators. Purchasers were able to "**buy stocks on margin**"—putting only 10% down and borrowing 90%. They sold the stocks after they went up in price to pay off the loan. This worked well in a "**bull market**"—a stock market in which stock prices were steadily increasing. In the bull market of the 1920s, stock prices became vastly inflated, reflecting the results of speculation rather than the true value of the stock based on company earnings. Others speculated by buying real estate and hoping to sell it after prices rose. Even ordinary consumers borrowed more than they could safely afford in order to buy consumer goods on credit, get mortgages from banks to buy homes, or buy stocks on margin. Widespread speculation and a vast over-extension of credit made the entire economy vulnerable. While speculation continued and credit kept expanding, people spent money and the economy prospered.

The "Crash of 1929" Triggers a Chain Reaction

By 1928 there were signs that the American economy was slowing down. Nevertheless, the election of Herbert Hoover in that year and the promise of four more years of Republican prosperity unleashed a frenzy of buying on the stock market. So long as people still wanted to buy stocks, their prices kept rising and the bull market continued. Stock prices continued to climb for almost another year. Then, in October 1929, the market turned sharply downward. On October 29, "**Black Tuesday**," the market crashed. Corporations and private shareholders all tried to sell their stocks at the same time. Prices kept going lower as people competed to sell and no one was willing to buy. In only three weeks, stocks lost half their value and $30 billion simply disappeared. This was as much as the United States had spent during all of World War I. And even then, the prices of stocks continued to fall.

Many historians believe that the stock market crash set off a chain reaction throughout the economy. Corporations could no longer raise funds. Business prospects became gloomy. As many as 26,000 businesses failed in 1930. Most important of all, people who lost money in the crash could no longer repay their loans. This led to a series of bank failures. Many people lost their entire life savings.

In this new economic climate, the demand for goods decreased. Prices fell. Manufacturers were forced to close their factories. More banks failed. Unemployment increased. The country became caught in the grip of a vicious downward spiral.

The Depression Becomes Worldwide

American banks and investors had invested overseas to help Europeans rebuild their economies after World War I. Now American banks and investors called in funds from Europe. New loans to Europe were canceled. At the same time, the Smoot-Hawley Tariff reduced international trade.

In 1929, monetary currencies around the world were still backed by gold. When American banks began calling in their debts, gold that was helping European economies was shipped off across the Atlantic. Germany therefore defaulted on its reparation payments to Britain and France, which meant that they weren't able to make payments on their debts to America. So the Depression quickly spread from America to Europe. It was a dramatic illustration of global financial interdependence.

The Human Experience of the Depression

The Depression was a national nightmare. Tens of thousands of businesses failed. Half a million farmers lost their farms. One quarter of American banks failed. More than ten million people were thrown out of work. What made matters worse was the fact that in those days there was no "safety net" as we have today—there was no federal system of unemployment relief, retirement benefits, or bank deposit insurance. People who had been working tirelessly

Men lined up for food in what was known as a "breadline."

Chapter 11 | The Great Depression and the New Deal

The Historian's Apprentice

Did the stock market crash cause the Great Depression? Historians have very different views on this question.

Opposing Viewpoints

"Much mythology surrounds these dramatic events in 1929. Perhaps the most [enduring] misconception portrays the Crash as the cause of the Great Depression. The disagreeable truth is that [historians] have been unable to demonstrate an appreciable cause-and-effect link between the Crash and the Great Depression. So, legend to the contrary, the average American—a description that in this case encompasses at least 97.5 percent of the population—owned no stock in 1929. Accordingly, the Crash had little direct economic effect on the typical American. The Depression, however, would be another story."

—David Kennedy, *Freedom from Fear* (1999)

"Most academic experts agree on one aspect of the crash: It wiped out billions of dollars of wealth in one day, and immediately depressed consumer buying. 'If you look at sales of consumer goods, particularly radios or automobiles, you will see they fell dramatically,' said Economics Professor John Galbraith. 'The crash had the impact of glass shattering, and while other more essential factors took over as the Depression wore on—universal fear, the slump in agricultural production because of drought, the decline in business investment—it is hard to argue that the collapse of the market did not start things in motion.'"

—Albert Scardino, *Did the '29 Crash Spark the Great Depression?* (1987)

▶ How do these views differ?

▶ With which historian would you most agree? Why?

---

for years might lose their jobs and savings, then lose their home, and finally find themselves on the street begging for food. Private charities and local relief agencies were simply overwhelmed by the scope of the disaster. Many Americans went hungry. Children suffered from malnutrition. Over a million men without work became "hoboes" riding railroad freight cars. Others sold apples on the street. Shantytowns of homeless people sprang up on the outskirts of cities. Millions of Americans depended on the soup kitchens and breadlines provided by local charities for their daily survival. Ironically, this widespread hunger occurred at a time when farmers were unable to sell their food crops and were going bankrupt in the thousands.

Minority groups were especially hard-hit because they typically suffered higher unemployment rates.

President Hoover Fails to Halt the Depression

Conservative economists, following *laissez-faire* principles, advised Hoover not to interfere directly in the economy. According to their theories, the market simply needed time to repair itself. When prices got low enough, people would start buying goods again. Once people resumed buying, manufacturers would start producing again. As production picked up, employment would increase. Unfortunately, these predictions turned out to be wrong. Instead, the Depression got worse month by month.

More people lost their jobs as production was cut back further and further.

Hoover's Response: Too Little, Too Late

Herbert Hoover

Hoover was a Republican who believed in *laissez-faire* economics. He did not think it was the federal government's job to interfere in the economy and he feared that federal aid would weaken individual character. Even so, he eventually took more active steps than any President before him to fight the economic downturn. The problem was that this was still not enough. The scope of the disaster was just too great.

Early Steps

Hoover held meetings with business leaders asking them not to lay off workers. He cut taxes and increased federal spending on public works projects (like Hoover Dam) by almost $1 billion. He called for a one-year international moratorium (*postponement*) on the payment of the war debts. He directed a federal agency to buy surplus farm crops.

Hoover Dam under construction

Hoover Rejects Direct Relief by the Federal Government

Hoover rejected, however, the demand that the federal government should provide direct payments to the unemployed and the needy. He feared this would create an unmanageable federal bureaucracy. He also believed this would reduce the incentive to work, undermining the "rugged individualism" that he saw as the key to American success. Instead, Hoover believed that emergency relief for the needy should come from local governments and private charities. But the public did not understand why the man who had once headed relief programs for Belgian children now refused to extend direct federal relief to his fellow Americans.

The Reconstruction Finance Corporation and the "Trickle-Down" Approach

By 1932, it was clear that Hoover's commitment to voluntary action rather than federal intervention was not working. Hoover now established the Reconstruction Finance Corporation ("RFC") to cope with the Depression. This agency gave emergency loans to banks and businesses. Hoover believed that cheap loans to businesses would save them from bankruptcy and help them to expand again. As they expanded, they would hire more workers. The benefits would then "trickle down" to the average American. However, the amount lent by the RFC under Hoover was only $2 billion. Losses on the stock market had reached $40 billion. The effect of these losses was greatly magnified because it led to a decline in spending. Hoover's efforts were therefore inadequate to cope with the magnitude of the problem.

Federal Reserve Policies Worsen the Depression

Matters were actually made worse by the Federal Reserve System. The Federal Reserve stood by as banks failed, without lending money to save them. In part this was because the currency was tied to the gold standard, so the Federal Reserve was limited in its options. In fact, the Federal Reserve mistakenly contracted the money supply, so that less money was available, making matters much worse.

Public Frustration Grows

Americans found Hoover's lack of leadership frustrating. The shantytowns that sprang up on the outskirts of cities were called "**Hoovervilles**." Some people demonstrated against the federal government's

relative inaction. About 40,000 unemployed veterans and their families—former members of the American Expeditionary Force during World War I—camped out in Washington, D.C. in the summer of 1932, hoping to persuade Congress to grant them a promised bonus. Fearing a possible riot, President Hoover used the army to disperse this "**Bonus Expeditionary Force**" (or "Bonus Army"). Many were shocked at this action.

Not surprisingly, just a few months later Democratic candidate Franklin D. Roosevelt defeated Hoover in a landslide election in November 1932. Roosevelt promised Americans a "**New Deal**."

Police attempt to evict former members of the American Expeditionary Force from their encampment in Washington, D.C. Later, Hoover sent the U. S. Army, including future World War II commanders MacArthur, Eisenhower, and Patton.

The New Deal

The "New Deal" was a major turning point in American history. It established the principle that the federal government bears ultimate responsibility for the smooth running of the American economy and for the protection of ordinary Americans against severe economic distress.

Franklin D. Roosevelt

Problems Facing the Nation in 1933

When Roosevelt took office in March 1933, the Depression was at its height. Americans were confronting a series of economic problems of catastrophic dimensions.

▶ **Widespread Unemployment** This was the most serious and immediate problem. Over one-quarter of the nation's workforce was unemployed. Local relief agencies were overwhelmed. Many feared that the frustrations of the unemployed might boil over into social revolution.

▶ **Collapse of the Banking System** Over ten thousand banks had failed since the Depression had started. Each bank failure meant hundreds or thousands lost their savings. Before Roosevelt took office, "runs" on banks began, in which many customers attempted to withdraw all their deposits. Since banks invest most of their depositors' money, these "runs" threatened to topple the entire banking system.

▶ **Decreased Production** Economists refer to the "**GNP**," or **Gross National Product**, which is the total value of all the goods and services produced by a nation in a single year (including income from U.S. investments abroad, but not income earned by foreigners in the United States). During the Great Depression, the GNP of the United States greatly decreased. Producers no longer made goods because there was no one who would buy them. Industrial production in 1932 was just half of what it had been in 1929. Many businesses went bankrupt.

▶ **Mortgage Foreclosures** Across America, people could no longer pay their mortgage payments on their homes or farms. Banks and lenders, also in grave financial difficulties, were forced to **foreclose** (*seize the property, throw people out of their homes and farms, and sell the property at an auction for whatever they could get*).

▶ **The** "**Dust Bowl**" Farmers on the Great Plains had to contend with an environmental disaster as well as the Depression. They had removed the tough

Chapter 11 | The Great Depression and the New Deal

grasses that once protected the soil. A series of droughts in the early 1930s dried up crops and topsoil, turning the soil into dust. The strong winds of the Great Plains then swept this dust eastwards. Blizzards of dust fell from the sky, choking farmers and livestock. Farmers had to abandon their farms. Many fled west to California, where they became known as "Okies" because so many of them came from Oklahoma. They hoped to find work on fruit farms or in cities, especially because government policies had cut off the influx of migrant workers from Mexico. Nevertheless the Okies were distrusted, and often had difficulty finding work.

Migrant workers

The President and His Advisers
The Character of the President

The new President was a fifth cousin to former President Theodore Roosevelt. His wife, Eleanor, was Theodore Roosevelt's niece. Roosevelt was born into a wealthy New York family. He had been a Progressive Democrat and had served as President Wilson's Assistant Secretary of the Navy. In 1920, Roosevelt was nominated as the Democratic candidate for Vice President, but the Democrats lost. In 1921, tragedy occurred when Roosevelt was struck with polio, a crippling disease. His legs were almost completely paralyzed. Slowly, with Eleanor's support, Roosevelt trained himself to stand with heavy metal braces. The experience gave Roosevelt an ability to empathize with suffering and the necessary patience and confidence to overcome the difficulties that confronted the nation during the Depression.

Roosevelt returned to politics and was elected as Governor of New York. When the Depression started, Eleanor Roosevelt served as her husband's eyes and ears by traveling around the state. As Governor, Roosevelt tried out many of the programs that he would later apply to the nation as President, including state spending on public works projects to create employment, and the use of radio talks to win public support.

A Team of Talented Advisers

Roosevelt realized the crucial importance of capable advisers, and he assembled a galaxy of talents to serve him in cabinet posts and as informal counselors. Much of the New Deal program was developed by a group of reform-minded professors. Roosevelt appointed Republicans to his cabinet as well as Democrats. He also appointed the first woman to a cabinet post: Frances Perkins, who became Secretary of Labor. The President's wife, Eleanor Roosevelt, also continued to play an important role, especially in advising him about the conditions of the poor and the problems of minority groups.

Roosevelt as Communicator

Roosevelt was an excellent speaker and communicator. Roosevelt's optimism and confidence were in striking contrast to the gloomy manner of Herbert Hoover. Roosevelt's 1932 campaign song was "Happy Days are Here Again." In his inaugural address, he told Americans that "the only thing we have to fear is fear itself." Part of Roosevelt's purpose was psychological—to restore the public confidence—so that people would return deposits to banks, begin buying and investing again, and resume all their normal economic activities, bringing the economy back to its feet.

Roosevelt came to the Presidency at a time when new means of communication—radio and motion pictures with

Eleanor Roosevelt

sound—made it possible for the President to reach out to more people than ever before. He gave informal radio addresses to millions of listeners, known as "**fireside chats**," in which he explained his policies in simple conversational terms. His chats were phrased to emphasize optimism, unity, and respect for his listeners. Roosevelt held frequent press conferences with newspaper reporters. Americans also learned about the New Deal from newsreels shown in cinemas.

New Deal Legislation: "Relief, Recovery, Reform"

The New Deal was pragmatic, making choices based on trial and error. Roosevelt was willing to try anything that worked. He created so many agencies so quickly during his first term in office that Americans referred to various New Deal programs (which used their initials for abbreviations) as "alphabet soup." The New Deal was novel, in both its size and its underlying assumption that the federal government had a major role in running the peacetime economy. Roosevelt explained New Deal measures in terms of three goals: "**Relief, Recovery, and Reform**."

The First New Deal

The "First New Deal" lasted from Roosevelt's inauguration in 1933 until 1935, and was mainly aimed at relief and recovery. As soon as Roosevelt took office, he assembled Congress for a special session to cope with the nation's economic problems. Democratic control of both Houses of Congress and the mood of the nation permitted Roosevelt to push through major legislation that would not have been possible in more normal times.

Resolving the Banking Crisis

▶ **The Bank Holiday** Roosevelt closed all the nation's banks just after his inauguration by declaring a "**Bank Holiday**." Each bank was permitted to reopen only after the government inspected its records and found it was financially sound. This gave banks an opportunity to avoid "runs" in which all their customers tried to withdraw their funds. In his fireside chats, Roosevelt encouraged the public to redeposit their savings in the reopened banks. The Emergency Banking Act authorized the federal government to assist threatened banks with emergency funds.

▶ **Federal Deposit Insurance Corporation (1933)** The **Federal Deposit Insurance Corporation (FDIC)** was created to insure deposits in banks so that people would no longer have to worry about losing their savings in the event of a bank failure. If a bank failed, the federal government would pay a depositor the value of the deposit up to a specified amount.

▶ **The Securities and Exchange Commission (1934)** The **Security and Exchange Commission (SEC)** was a new federal agency created to oversee the operations of the stock market, preventing fraud and guarding against the conditions that had led to the stock market crash. Companies selling securities were required to provide accurate information to potential investors.

Relief for the Unemployed

▶ **Work Relief: The CCC, PWA, and CWA** Roosevelt favored "**work-relief**"—government projects that gave people meaningful work. This preserved their sense of dignity and also improved the nation's economic foundations by providing needed roads and public buildings. The Federal Emergency Relief Act (1933) gave money to state and local governments to provide emergency relief, and provided for the hiring of millions on "make-work" projects. The **Civilian Conservation Corps** (1933) gave outdoor jobs to young men, such as planting trees and draining swamps. Members of the "**CCC**" lived in camps super-

A CCC crew at work in 1933

vised by army officers, and received free uniforms and food. They were required to send most of their pay home to their families. The **Public Works Administration** (1933) and the **Civil Works Administration** (1933) built highways, bridges, hospitals, airports, courthouses, and other public facilities.

▶ **Relief to Home and Farm Owners** The Homeowners Loan Corporation (1933) gave emergency loans at low interest rates to homeowners facing foreclosure. The **Agriculture Adjustment Act** (1933) provided loans to farm owners for the same purpose.

▶ **The Tennessee Valley Authority (1933)** The **Tennessee Valley Authority**, or **TVA**, was a major experiment in public ownership. The South was the region hardest hit by the Depression. Many areas still lacked electricity, running water or significant industry. The Tennessee Valley was an impoverished region covering parts of seven Southern states. The TVA built and maintained 21 large dams along the Tennessee River. These dams controlled floods, produced hydroelectricity, and manufactured fertilizers. Private electric companies complained about having to compete with the government in selling electricity. Meanwhile, the government used its own costs in generating hydroelectricity to judge whether the rates charged to consumers by private companies were fair. Construction of the dams and the introduction of conservation measures like the planting of trees brought greater prosperity to the region. Although the experiment was a success, Congress failed to extend this approach to other parts of the country.

Recovery Measures and "Priming the Pump"

All these relief measures were also meant to speed up recovery by rebuilding people's purchasing power. Roosevelt called this "pump priming": putting a little water into a dry pump to get it flowing again. Through its relief programs and public works projects, the government put money into the hands of consumers. It was hoped they would spend this money, increasing the demand for other products. Producers would start to produce again, and hire more workers. These workers would also spend money, increasing demand still further. Producers would step up production and hire more workers. Demand, production, and employment would then continue to increase until the Depression was over.

MORE PRIMING FOR THE PUMP

▶ **The National Recovery Administration (1933)** The **National Industrial Recovery Act** was designed to help industry recover from the Depression by increasing prices and reducing wasteful competition. The act created another new agency, the **National Recovery Administraton**. All businesses and companies in the same industry were asked to cooperate in drawing up a "code of fair practice." Each code set standard prices, limited production, reduced the work week to 40 hours, and established a minimum wage. President Roosevelt had the power to approve the code or suggest changes. Once the code was approved, businesses voluntarily following the code were allowed to display large posters with blue eagles, informing customers that they were NRA members. The NRA also guaranteed the rights of workers to organize into unions, established a National Labor Board to settle labor–management disputes, and abolished most forms of child labor.

The NRA approach differed from measures taken by the earlier Progressives, who had been suspicious of business combinations. In the atmosphere of economic crisis, the New Deal encouraged businesses to cooperate, and antitrust restrictions on price-fixing and collaboration were ignored. Some critics felt the NRA favored Big Business at the expense of smaller businesses, since Big Business was more influential in drawing up the "codes of fair practice." Although over 95% of all industries joined the NRA, in 1935 the Supreme Court declared the National Industrial Recovery Act unconstitutional on the grounds that the federal government had no power to interfere in businesses conducted within one state.

▶ **The Agricultural Adjustment Acts (1933 and 1938)** The purpose of the **Agricultural Adjustment Act** was to promote the recovery of farmers. Like the NRA, the AAA limited production. By creating artificial scarcity, it would encourage crop prices to rise. Under the first Agricultural Adjustment Act, the government simply paid farmers to plant fewer acres and kill extra livestock. Food prices did go up, but the Supreme Court declared the act unconstitutional in 1936 on the grounds that Congress could not control economic activities in a single state. Congress reacted by passing an act that paid farmers to grow crops like clover, which helped conserve the soil, instead of continuously growing the same food crops.

In 1938, Congress also passed a second Agricultural Adjustment Act. Under the second AAA, the government decided how much of a crop should be marketed each year. Each farmer was given a limited number of acres to plant. After the harvest, farmers' surpluses were stored by the government until prices rose to "parity" level (what farmers had received 1909–1914). Meanwhile, the government gave loans to farmers based on the value of their stored crops. Government experts also showed farmers new ways of soil conservation. This new act was successful both in raising prices and in increasing the fertility of the soil.

Other Recovery Measures

The New Deal included other recovery measures, such as creating a new agency to insure bank loans to homeowners for home improvements. Congress also authorized Roosevelt to negotiate with other countries to lower tariffs and stimulate international trade. Roosevelt continued to pour billions into the Reconstruction Finance Corporation, established by Hoover, which lent money to railroad companies, banks, industries, and insurance companies.

The Second New Deal

The Supreme Court struck down several of the First New Deal's programs, prompting Roosevelt to change his approach. The "Second New Deal" began in 1935. It was aimed more directly at reform and security. Reform measures were aimed at remedying defects in the structure of the American economy, to make sure that another Depression would never occur again. Roosevelt claimed he had to reform the capitalist system in order to save it. Security measures created a new system to protect ordinary citizens from economic disaster. Besides creating new employment opportunities for Americans, the Second New Deal made great strides in labor reform and in the creation of a system of social security.

▶ **The Works Progress Administration (1935)** The **Works Progress Administration**, or **WPA**, increased employment by creating new public works projects. It spent over $11 billion and gave nine million people jobs building public schools, courthouses, roads, and bridges. The WPA also hired unemployed artists, architects, writers, and musicians and paid them to paint murals, design buildings, write guidebooks, and produce plays and concerts. This policy greatly encouraged the creative arts during this difficult period.

The Social Security Act (1935)
The **Social Security Act** was the single most important law passed by the New Deal. Americans continue to be protected by Social Security today, which now makes up a large part of the federal budget.

One of the reasons the Depression had caused so much human suffering was that Americans had no "safety net" to fall back on when they were struck by unemployment, illness, or a death in the family. Social Security changed all this by adopting measures already in existence in several European countries:

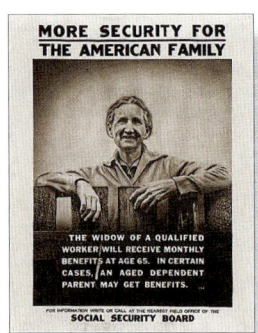

(a) *Unemployment insurance.* Workers received unemployment insurance, paid out of a tax on employer payrolls.

(b) *Retirement benefits.* Employees were to receive monthly payments after their retirement, paid for by a special tax on their own wages and contributions made by their employer. The same fund provided benefits to their spouses and children in the event of an untimely death. Because employees had paid in their own contributions to finance the program, it was not based on need and was not considered to be a relief program or charity.

(c) *The disabled and orphaned.* Disabled and orphaned Americans were eligible to receive special grants from Social Security.

The New Deal and Labor

National Labor Relations Act (1935)
This law, also known as the "**Wagner Act**," replaced several provisions of the National Industrial Recovery Act, which was declared unconstitutional in 1935. The NLRA gave workers the right to form unions, to bargain collectively, and to submit their grievances to the National Labor Relations Board. Employers could not engage in "unfair" anti-union practices. By allowing workers to organize, Roosevelt hoped to push up wages, increase workers' purchasing power, and create fair working conditions.

The "Sit-Down" Strike (1936)
In 1936, automobile workers held a "**sit-down**" **strike** at the General Motors plant in Flint, Michigan. In a sit-down strike, workers occupy the factory or plant and prevent the owners from using it. Roosevelt refused to use the federal government to intervene on behalf of General Motors. Eventually, as a result of the strike, General Motors agreed to recognize the automobile workers' union.

Fair Labor Standards Act (1938)
This act set maximum working hours and a minimum wage, while it prohibited child labor in factories.

Reactions to the New Deal

Roosevelt became very popular as President. Most people felt that, even if Roosevelt did not always succeed, at least he was taking an active approach to fight the Depression. The New Deal did not end the Depression, but things began to improve gradually. Roosevelt won a landslide victory in the 1936 Presidential election, with a majority in all but two states. He formed a new Democratic coalition composed of workers, the poor, African Americans and other minority groups, and the Democratic "Solid South."

Although the New Deal was generally popular, it did face criticism. Conservative critics charged Roosevelt with being a "traitor to his class." Radical critics, on the other hand, felt that Roosevelt did not go far enough in reforming American capitalism. One critic wanted to give all citizens over 65 years old a pension of $200 a month to be spent within the month. Senator **Huey Long** (former Governor of Louisiana), promised to give each American family an income of $5,000 a year, to be paid for by taxing the rich. Another popular critic gave radio addresses calling for the nationalization of banks and utility companies.

Roosevelt's "Court-Packing" Plan

The greatest threat to the New Deal came from the Supreme Court. The Court ruled that both the National Industrial Reconstruction Act and the Agricultural Adjustment Act were unconstitutional.

Roosevelt feared that the Supreme Court might overrule all of the New Deal legislation. By 1937, he was especially worried that it would overturn the Wagner Act and the Social Security Act. He therefore proposed to Congress that the President should be allowed to appoint a new Justice to the Court for each Justice who did not retire on reaching age 70. The proposal would have let Roosevelt appoint six new Justices. Roosevelt's "court-packing" plan was widely condemned by the public and rejected by Congress. The Senate refused to pass the provision for additional Justices.

Nonetheless, the legislation of the Second New Deal was subsequently upheld. Two Supreme Court Justices switched their votes in March 1937, while the court-packing plan was still being debated. This was a key turning point in Supreme Court history: ever since 1937, the Supreme Court has rarely declared economic laws unconstitutional.

The New Deal Comes to an End

Roosevelt's court-packing plan alienated Southern Democrats, who refused to back further New Deal measures. In 1936, when the economy seemed to be recovering, Roosevelt cut government spending. The result was an immediate worsening of the Depression. Roosevelt resumed federal spending and the Works Progress Administration began rehiring more of the unemployed. The New Deal itself never returned the country to full employment. This finally occurred only as America prepared to enter World War II.

Popular Culture of the Great Depression and the New Deal

The tremendous human suffering caused by the Great Depression was reflected in the popular culture of the time. It affected the way many Americans viewed the world. Instead of having confidence in the free market and a culture of consumerism, many became deeply disillusioned.

▶ **John Steinbeck** told the story of the "Okies," and their struggles in California in the most famous of all Depression novels, *The Grapes of Wrath* (1939). Steinbeck won the Pulitzer Prize and later won the Nobel Prize for literature. The book was also made into a popular movie. It tells the story of the Joads, a family who lose their farm and are driven from Oklahoma by the Dust Bowl. They move to California where they hope to find work, but they discover conditions are not as promised and become migrant laborers. Steinbeck's aim was to depict the suffering of the Depression and the greed and heartlessness that, in his eyes, had made it much worse.

▶ **Dorothea Lange** worked for the Farm Security Administration, a federal agency. She took remarkable photographs of people afflicted by poverty during the Depression, including sharecroppers and migrant workers. Her photograph, "Migrant Mother," is one of the most famous photographs in American history. Before the invention of television, these photographs gave a human face to the Great Depression and spurred calls for relief.

Dorothea Lange's portrait of a destitute migrant woman and her children

- **Langston Hughes** portrayed the hardships endured by African Americans in his poetry.
- **Walker Evans** photographed the plight of poor tenant farmers in Alabama.
- **Margaret Bourke White**'s photographs of the Depression were published in *Life* Magazine.

Other forms of popular culture provided a means of temporarily escaping the grim realities of the Depression:

- The "talkies" (*film with sound*) were first introduced in 1927 and quickly replaced silent movies. During the Depression, most Hollywood movies offered audiences "escapism." They often emphasized the enduring strength of the individual will and the American spirit, with common themes such as a poor man achieving economic success or a poor girl marrying a rich man. A few attacked serious social issues. Many American classic films were made in the 1930s, including "Gone with the Wind"—when Americans in another era overcame hardships—and "The Wizard of Oz"—a wonderful fantasy escape in which the child heroine ultimately prefers Dust Bowl Kansas to the magical land of Oz.

- Musical variety shows and popular dance halls also provided a means of escape. Popular crooners like Bing Crosby reached large audiences by performing upbeat, happy songs on the radio.

- Comic strips, offering light-hearted humor or adventure, also first appeared in the 1930s. So did the first Mickey Mouse cartoons.

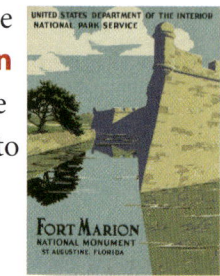

A WPA poster

- New Deal programs, especially the **Works Progress Administration** (or WPA), supported the arts. The Federal Arts Project hired artists to paint murals on public buildings; the Federal Writers' Project hired historians to write local histories and record the narratives of the shrinking ex-slave generation; the Federal Theater Project hired directors and actors to produce hundreds of plays; the Federal Music Project hired musicians and dancers for new orchestras and choruses; and the Federal Dance Project produced ballets and modern dance shows. In fact, more Americans went to the theater, the ballet or the movies than ever before, making the Great Depression a time of rich cultural activity despite economic troubles.

The Historian's Apprentice

In small groups, conduct research on one artist, writer, dramatist, dancer, film director, actor, singer, composer, or musician from the decade of the Great Depression (1930–1939).

- Each group should identify the genre, or type of works, their subject created.
- Members of each group should describe the style of one or more of these works.
- Each group should explain how these works related to the conditions of the Great Depression.
- Each group should analyze how these works represented an artistic response to the social issues of the Great Depression.

Present your group's findings in an illustrated oral presentation to the rest of class.

Consequences of the New Deal

Were the consequences of the New Deal generally positive or negative? Historians usually consider these major consequences:

Positive Effects:

 The New Deal reduced unemployment and gave immediate relief to those without food or shelter during the worst years of the Depression.

 The New Deal completed valuable public works like roads and the dams of the TVA.

 The New Deal established a "safety net" to protect ordinary Americans by establishing social security and insuring bank deposits.

 The New Deal introduced new regulatory agencies like the SEC (Securities and Exchange Commission).

 The New Deal increased the power of organized labor by giving workers the right to form unions, a minimum wage, and a maximum number of working hours per week.

 The New Deal established the principle that the federal government should oversee the smooth running of the economy and protect American citizens from economic disaster.

 The New Deal showed that increased government spending, lower taxes, and inflation could be used as tools to fight unemployment.

Negative Effects:

 The New Deal increased the national debt.

 The New Deal increased federal taxes.

 The New Deal increased the size of the federal bureaucracy.

The New Deal made citizens more dependent on government services, which some see as a negative and others as a positive effect. It also strengthened the federal government in its relationship with the states.

The Great Depression: Effects on Florida

In the last chapter, you learned how the Florida land boom had become a bust by 1926. In Florida, the Great Depression began even before the stock market crash. By the early 1930s, unemployment had risen and "Hoovervilles" had sprung up in Florida. In 1931, the Florida Legislature legalized gambling on horse and dog racing and Jai Alai games in hopes of improving the state economy. The measure raised additional revenues but failed to halt the Depression.

By 1932, 113 Florida banks had failed. The flow of out-of-state tourists into Florida dropped. In their place, desperate migrants without food or work began arriving. State police guarded roads and highways to prevent them from entering the state.

In the 1932 Presidential election, President Roosevelt won the State of Florida with three-quarters of the popular vote. Florida Governor David Scholtz declared a state bank holiday even before President Roosevelt announced a national one. On March 14, 1933, Florida's banks reopened their doors. New state banking regulations required greater solvency, higher reserve deposits, and more conservative lending practices. Alfred Du Pont, who inherited a fortune from his family's chemical business, helped to restore Florida's ailing banking system.

The Civilian Conservation Corps, or CCC, was especially active in Florida. Between 1930 and 1939, it employed 50,000 young men in Florida. They planted more than 13 million trees to develop the state's timber industry. The CCC also rebuilt the 100-mile long Overseas Railroad connecting Key West and Miami, which had been badly damaged by a hurricane in 1935. The CCC also left another important legacy. Public land used by the CCC formed the basis of the Florida state park system. In 1935, the Florida Legislature created the **Florida Park Service** and established its first four state parks: Myakka River State Park, Hillsborough River State Park, Torreya State Park and Gold Head Branch State Park.

Another New Deal agency, the Works Progress Administration, or WPA, employed 40,000 Floridians. It was responsible for the construction of hundreds of public buildings, bridges, roads, hospitals, and parks in Florida. The WPA built more than 500 schools and playgrounds in Florida and employed almost 16,000 teachers. It also built seawalls to protect beaches from erosion and encouraged the establishment of oyster beds and shrimp farms for commercial fishing. The WPA worked with the Federal Emergency Relief Administration, or FERA, to build dikes that reduced the threat of flooding in the Everglades. FERA also completed US Highway 1 in 1938.

The Florida Citrus Commission was established in 1935. It promoted the sale of the state's citrus products through extensive advertising. By 1940, proceeds from the sale of Florida's oranges, tangerines, and grapefruits totaled close to $35 million. FERA and the WPA also helped to start Florida's sugar industry and promoted the planting of corn, potatoes, peanuts, and cotton. Meanwhile, Alfred Du Pont bought forestland and launched the paper industry in Florida

By 1935, tourism in Florida showed some signs of recovery. In that year, more than two million tourists visited the state, spending more than $625 million. Airlines began to expand their operations in Florida. By 1939, several commercial airlines had regularly scheduled flights to Florida cities.

Florida also became an important cultural center in the 1930s. The famous writer **Ernest Hemingway** purchased a house in Key West in 1935. His novel *To Have and Have Not,* published in 1937, had a Florida setting. **Marjorie Kinnan Rawlings** was another notable writer who lived in Florida. She wrote about the local people in the interior of the state in her book *The Yearling* (1938), which won the Pulitzer Prize, as well as in her autobiographical *Cross Creek* (1942). The WPA supported writers such as **Zora Neale Hurston**, who moved back to Florida in the 1930s and wrote about her experiences growing up there.

The Historian's Apprentice

During the New Deal, the federal government learned that it can influence the nation's economy through its spending, taxing, and monetary policies. For example, if the federal government spends more money, the economy will generally speed up and increase production. This is because the government puts money into the hands of government employees and government contractors. They spend this money making their own purchases. The merchants who receive this money then make purchases of their own. All of this speeds up the economy. If the government lowers taxes, this has the same effect because taxpayers have more money to spend. When the Federal Reserve lowers interest rates, this makes it easier to borrow money and encourages people and businesses to spend. If prices start increasing too fast, the government can slow down the economy by increasing its taxes or by decreasing its spending. The Federal Reserve can also contract the money supply to slow the economy down.

Federal Tools for Managing The Economy

Goal	Tools	Effects
Speeding up the Economy	• Congress increases federal spending • Congress lowers taxes • Federal Reserve lowers interest rates	• Increases employment • Increases economic production • Increases inflation • Increases growth of national debt
Slowing Down the Economy	• Congress decreases federal spending • Congress raises taxes • Federal Reserve raises interest rates	• Lowers employment • Lowers economic production • Decreases inflation • Decreases growth of national debt

Look at any recent issue of a newspaper, news magazine, or Internet website and find one example of any of these policies. Describe your example, identify the policy, and determine if it was successful.

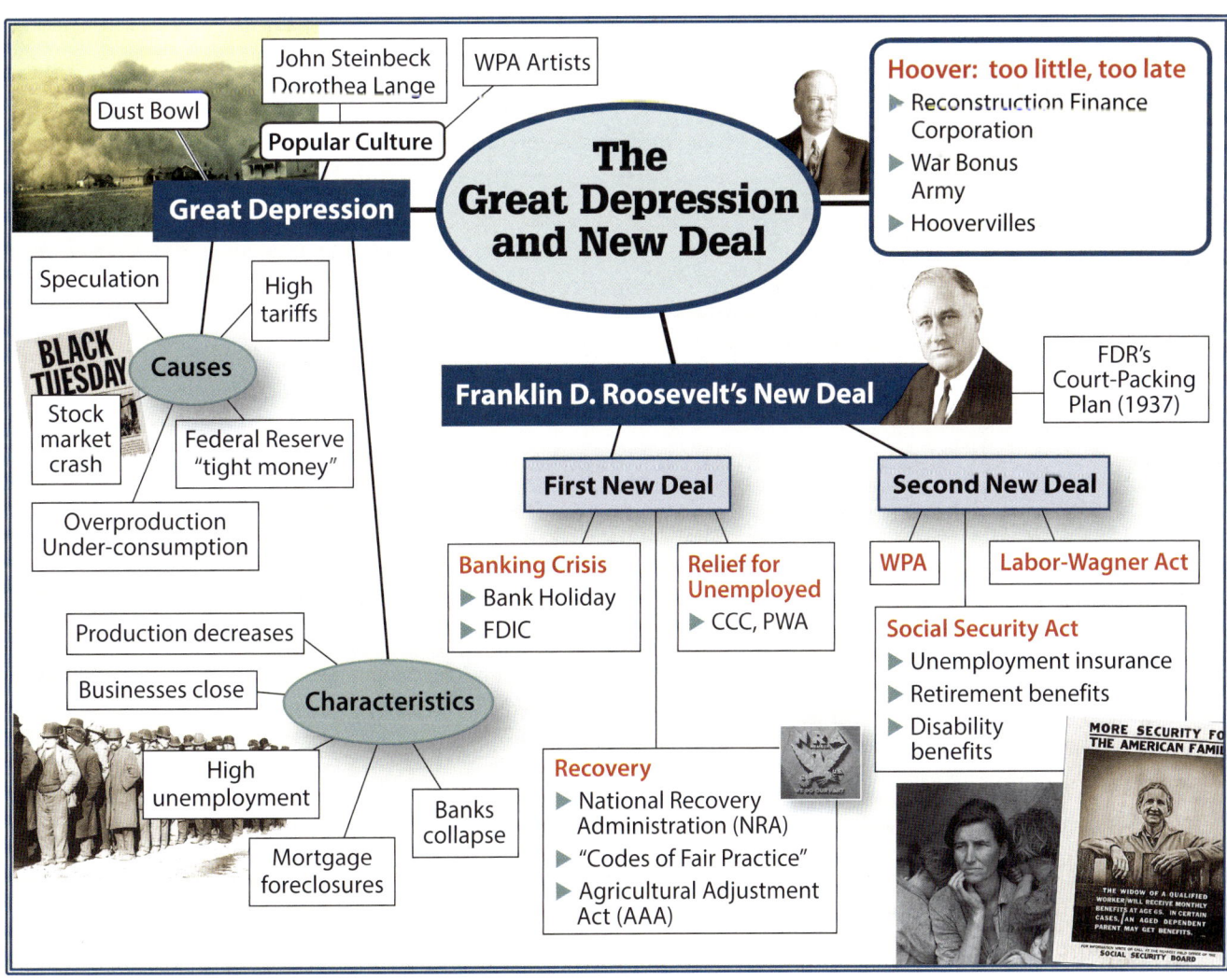

Chapter 11 | The Great Depression and the New Deal

Long-Term Causes of the Great Depression

▶ Economic weaknesses in the 1920s actually led to the Great Depression.
▶ Mass production created a surplus of goods. By the end of the 1920s, most people who could afford those goods had already bought them. Unsold goods piled up in warehouses and workers lost their jobs.
▶ High tariffs like the **Smoot-Hawley Tariff** (1930) protected American markets from foreign competition but also prevented surplus American goods from being sold abroad.
▶ An expansion of credit, practices like buying stocks on margin, and a lack of government regulation meant that speculation in the stock market soared.
▶ On October 29, 1929, known as **"Black Tuesday,"** the stock market crashed. Stock prices dropped suddenly. Everyone was trying to sell but no one wanted to buy.

Effects of the Stock Market Crash: From Wall Street to Main Street

▶ The stock market crash set off a "chain reaction" in the American economy. People who lost money on the market could no longer invest or buy as many goods. Businesses became nervous about the new economic environment.
▶ Businesses went bankrupt and laid off workers, creating mass unemployment. People lost their savings and could not pay off loans. Banks failed. Prices and demand for goods fell.
▶ American banks that had given loans to European countries to rebuild their war-torn economies now wanted their money back. The Depression spread to Europe when these loans were recalled.

The Human Impact of the Great Depression

▶ More than 10 million Americans became unemployed. There was no federal "safety net" of unemployment relief or insurance, and local or private charities were overwhelmed.
▶ Many people lost homes and some had to beg for food. Many jobless, homeless men became vagrant "hoboes." Others built shantytowns on the outskirts of cities. Minority groups particularly suffered, with the highest unemployment and the least savings.
▶ On the Great Plains, a series of droughts combined with the effects of unsuitable plowing techniques to cause the disaster known as the **"Dust Bowl."** Farmers could not grow their crops, livestock died, and farmers lost their fields and homes. Some fled west to California to find work. Known as "Okies," they were often mistreated and unemployed.

The First Presidential Response: Herbert Hoover

▶ **President Hoover** was a Republican who believed in *laissez-faire* economics. He did not think the federal government should interfere too directly in the free-market economy. Hoover believed the strong work ethic of independent Americans would end the crisis.
▶ Hoover still took early steps to help end the Depression, like cutting taxes, increasing federal spending, and meeting with business leaders. Later, he established the Reconstruction Finance Corporation (RFC) to give emergency loans to stop banks and businesses from going bankrupt. Hoover's steps were too few and too limited to stop the crisis.
▶ The Federal Reserve made the Depression worse by contracting (*shrinking*) the money supply.
▶ Hoover became so unpopular that Americans began calling the new shantytowns of homeless people **"Hoovervilles."** Hoover's defeat in the 1932 election was sealed when he used the army to break up a peaceful protest by the **"Bonus Expeditionary Force,"** a group of World War I veterans and their families.

The Second Presidential Response: Franklin Delano Roosevelt

- As Governor of New York, Franklin D. Roosevelt had introduced new programs to fight the Depression that he would later apply to the nation. His wife, Eleanor, was a close adviser who kept him informed about the problems of the poor and minority groups.
- Roosevelt possessed excellent communication skills. He came to office with a team of talented, reform-minded advisers. He used the radio to give reassuring **"fireside chats."**
- Roosevelt's **"New Deal"** was based on three goals: **relief, recovery,** and **reform.**

The First New Deal

- The "First New Deal," from 1933 to 1935, was focused on relief and recovery.
- So many new federal agencies were known by their abbreviations that they were called "alphabet soup."
- Many of these programs aimed to **"prime the pump"**—to get the economy flowing again by placing money into consumers' hands.
- Some "recovery" programs aimed to make banks and the stock market safer. Roosevelt declared a **"Bank Holiday"** to prevent bank runs, allow federal inspections, and renew public confidence in banks. The **Federal Deposit Insurance Corporation** (FDIC) insured bank deposits. The Securities and Exchange Commission was created to regulate the stock market.
- Other "recovery" programs aimed at assisting industry and agriculture. The **National Recovery Administration** (NRA) encouraged businesses to establish codes that set prices, wages, and work hours to promote cooperation and fairness. The **Agricultural Adjustment Act** (AAA) limited production of crops and livestock to prevent surpluses and protect farmers.
- Some "relief" programs aimed at helping the unemployed. The **Civilian Conservation Corps** (CCC), **Public Works Administration** (PWA), and **Civil Works Administration** (CWA) provided young men with work on public projects.
- Other "relief" programs sought to improve living conditions. The Home-owners Loan Corporation and Agricultural Adjustment Act gave emergency loans to homeowners and farmers facing foreclosure. The **Tennessee Valley Authority** (TVA) built dams to control floods and to provide electricity to one of the poorest areas in the South.

The Second New Deal

- The Supreme Court struck down many of Roosevelt's early New Deal programs. He began a "Second New Deal" in 1935, aiming more at reform and security.
- The **Works Progress Administration** (WPA) created new public works projects to increase employment and stimulate the arts. It hired construction workers, artists, writers and musicians.
- The **Social Security Act** was the most important and long-lasting achievement of the New Deal. It created a "safety net" for Americans in the event of another Depression. It established unemployment insurance, retirement benefits, and aid to the disabled and orphaned.
- The **National Labor Relations Act ("Wagner Act")** gave workers the right to unionize and to submit their grievances to the National Labor Relations Board. Other measures that benefitted labor were Roosevelt's refusal to use federal power to intervene in the successful "sit-down strike" at General Motors in 1936, and the passage of the Fair Labor Standards Act, which set maximum working hours, a minimum wage, and prohibited child labor.

Reactions to the New Deal

- The New Deal was supported by many Americans. Roosevelt created a new Democratic coalition: workers, the poor, minority groups such as African Americans, and the "Solid South."
- Some critics did not think the New Deal did enough. Senator Huey Long wanted to tax the rich and provide a guaranteed family income; another critic wanted to nationalize banks and utilities.
- The greatest threat to the New Deal was from the Supreme Court, which overturned some of the First New Deal. Roosevelt attempted to halt further attacks on the New Deal by the Court with his **"Court-packing" scheme.** He proposed that he should have the power to appoint new Justices. His plan was widely condemned and rejected by Congress. However, the Supreme Court stopped overturning New Deal programs.
- The New Deal did aid the economy, but only World War II ended the Depression.

The Cultural Impact of the Great Depression

- The Depression created disillusionment with traditional American beliefs in the free market and consumerism.
- **John Steinbeck**'s novel *The Grapes of Wrath* depicted the plight of the "Okies." Langston Hughes was an African-American poet who wrote of the sufferings of the African-American community.
- **Dorothea Lange** took photographs of poor migrants and sharecroppers, including the famous image "Migrant Mother." Walker Evans and Margaret Bourke also published famous photographs of suffering all around America.
- These photos, poems, and books gave a human face to the Depression and spurred calls for relief.
- Many people turned to popular culture for "escapism" during the Depression. Optimistic, fun movies, musical shows, radio singers, and comic strips were very popular.
- The WPA supported the arts by hiring artists, dancers, musicians, and actors. WPA historians traveled South to record narratives from a dying generation of former slaves.

What Do You Know?

SS.912.A.5.11

1. The diagram below provides details about the Great Depression.

Which phrase completes the diagram?

  A. War in Europe

  B. Agricultural Drought

  C. Overproduction of Goods

  D. Introduction of New Technologies

SS.912.A.5.11

2. Which statement best describes the American economy in the late 1920s?

   A. High tariffs stimulated international trade.

   B. Only the wealthiest Americans had access to credit.

   C. Mass production was not equally matched by consumption.

   D. Unemployment was higher than ever before in American history.

SS.912.A.5.11

3. On May 1, 1930, President Herbert Hoover addressed the annual dinner of the United States Chamber of Commerce.

   > While the crash only took place six months ago, I am convinced we have now passed the worst and with continued unity of effort we shall rapidly recover. There is one certainty in the future of a people of the resources, intelligence, and character of the people of the United States—that is prosperity.

   Based on these beliefs, what actions did President Hoover take in response to the Great Depression?

   A. He ordered emergency federal relief payments to the unemployed.

   B. He refused to take any measures at all as a violation of *laissez-faire* principles.

   C. He introduced a large number of public works projects to increase employment.

   D. He offered limited federal assistance directed primarily to businesses and banks.

SS.912.A.5.11

4. How did the plans of Presidents Herbert Hoover and Franklin D. Roosevelt compare for dealing with the Great Depression?

   A. Hoover gave emergency loans to banks and businesses while Roosevelt opposed such programs.

   B. Both Presidents believed the federal government should provide direct payments to the unemployed.

   C. Hoover increased federal spending on public works projects like Hoover Dam while Roosevelt opposed such projects.

   D. Roosevelt proposed that the federal government provide direct employment to the needy while Hoover relied more on local government and private charities.

Chapter 11 | The Great Depression and the New Deal

SS.912.A.5.11

5. The excerpt below is from President Franklin D. Roosevelt's First Inaugural Address in 1933.

> I shall ask the Congress for the one remaining instrument to meet the crisis—broad power to wage a war against the emergency as great as the power that would be given to me if we were in fact invaded by a foreign foe.

Based on this excerpt, what could be inferred about the direction that Roosevelt planned to take the executive branch of the federal government?

   A. He planned to increase its size and power to deal with the Depression.

   B. He planned to maintain its size in relationship to the other two branches.

   C. He planned to look to Congress for most of his ideas for ending the Depression.

   D. He planned to reduce its size to give greater power to state and local governments.

SS.912.A.5.12

6. The plaque on the left was displayed in 2010.

   It took the Great Depression and the New Deal to create the Florida State Park System. One of the New Deal's work programs was responsible for:
   - Constructing facilities in all eight original state parks
   - Constructing dams for flood control, reforestation and landscaping
   - Excavating sediment from caverns and establishing tourist routes for visitors
   - Fighting wildfires and creating wildfire breaks

   Which New Deal program was responsible for these accomplishments?

   A. The National Park Service

   B. The Civilian Conservation Corps

   C. The National Geographic Service

   D. The Florida Keys and Beach Preservation Act

SS.912.A.5.11

7. What was one effect of the dust storms across the Great Plains in the 1930s?

   A. growth of the banking industry from farm loans

   B. suspension of government assistance to farmers

   C. increase in farm production on the Great Plains

   D. migration of many to California and other states

SS.912.A.5.11

8. How did popular attitudes towards the federal government shift during the Great Depression?

   A. Public opinion turned against new federal programs because of increased taxes.

   B. People concluded that state governments were better at promoting economic growth.

   C. Voters grew distrustful of the federal government because they felt it favored the wealthy.

   D. Americans came to expect the federal government to help them solve their economic problems.

SS.912.A.5.11

9. The political cartoon on the left depicts President Franklin Roosevelt in 1937.

   Based on the cartoon, what was the reaction to President Roosevelt's "court-packing" plan?

   A. The public wanted President Roosevelt to act more quickly to save New Deal programs.

   B. Congress handed Roosevelt his first major defeat by upholding the separation of powers.

   C. A majority of Americans agreed that several of the Supreme Court Justices were too old.

   D. Most Americans agreed with the Supreme Court that the NRA and AAA were unconstitutional.

SS.912.A.5.11

10. Which New Deal agency constructed a series of dams that produced hydroelectricity?

    A. the Tennessee Valley Authority (TVA)

    B. the National Labor Relations Board (NLRB)

    C. the Securities and Exchange Commission (SEC)

    D. the Federal Deposit Insurance Corporation (FDIC)

SS.912.A.5.11

11. Which of these was NOT a long-term result of the New Deal?

    A. creation of a safety net to help American families in emergencies

    B. expanded political participation by farmers, workers and the poor

    C. a shift in national voting patterns in favor of the Democratic Party

    D. state ownership of basic industries such as steelworks and railroads

Chapter 11 | The Great Depression and the New Deal

SS.912.A.5.11

12. The graph below shows the unemployment rate in the United States between 1930 and 1945.

Based on the graph, what conclusion can be made about government policies in the 1930s?

   A. President Hoover's policies were more effective than the New Deal in dealing with the Depression.

   B. By 1938, the New Deal had successfully brought unemployment back down to pre-Depression levels.

   C. New Deal policies failed to improve the economy because of the interference of the Supreme Court.

   D. Despite Roosevelt's New Deal policies, the unemployment rate remained high throughout the 1930s.

SS.912.H.1.5

13. The book and movie below both first appeared in 1939.

How were these two works similar?

   A. Both were artistic responses to the hardships of the Depression.

   B. Both described the struggles of the "Okies" after moving to California.

   C. Both offered Americans a temporary comic escape from their problems.

   D. Both criticized the inability of traditional American values to end the Depression.

Unit IV: The Interwar Period (Chapters 10–11)

Identify or define each of the following terms.

"Palmer Raids" _____

Dawes Plan _____

National Origins Act (Immigration Act of 1924) _____

Kellogg–Briand Pact _____

Harlem Renaissance _____

Ku Klux Klan _____

Rosewood _____

"Black Tuesday" _____

Great Depression _____

Herbert Hoover _____

Dust Bowl _____

New Deal _____

Tennessee Valley Authority (TVA) _____

Social Security _____

Roosevelt's "Court-Packing" Plan _____

Crossword Puzzle

Across
1. Leader in car manufacturing in the 1920s and 1930s
6. Plan that gave Europe a sense of financial stability in 1924
8. A prize established in 1896 for promoting world peace
12. The early nineteenth-century movement to ban alcoholic beverages
14. This new industry helped producers sell their goods to a national market
15. W.E.B. DuBois helped launch this organization to help African Americans in 1909 (abbrev.)
17. _____ buying allowed consumers to pay small amounts monthly for goods
19. Fashionable women of the 1920s who were more assertive and less restricted than women of the past
21. Nickname for the shantytowns filled with poor people during the 1930s
24. The Four-Power Treaty consisted of America, France, Britain, and _____
25. An environmental disaster affecting farmers of the Great Plains during the 1930s
26. A stock market in which prices are steadily increasing
28. The Agricultural _____ Acts of 1933 and 1938 were set up to promote the recovery of farmers
29. The prosperous second decade of the 1900s was called the _____ Twenties
31. On October 29, 1929, the stock maket crashed on what became known as Black _____
32. The _____ trial prosecuted a teacher in Tennessee for giving his students a lesson about evolution

Down
2. Amendment that gave women the right to vote
3. National economic slowdown
4. Home of the League of Nations in Europe
5. Financial safety net set up to protect Americans in 1935
7. Public works projects were set up to create jobs by this agency (abbrev.)
9. The photographs of Dorothea _____ depicted people afflicted by poverty during the Great Depression
10. Buying something in the hope of reselling it later at a higher price
11. The _____ Valley Authority was a major experiment in public ownership of electricity
13. F. D. Roosevelt defeated Hoover in the November 1932 election promising a _____ _____ to the American people
16. The National Origins Act drastically cut the number of _____ arriving from Southern and Eastern Europe
18. Color associated with Communism
20. The Kellogg-Briand Pact promised not to use _____ as an instrument of policy
21. Named after the place where many African-American writers and poets lived, the _____ Renaissance saw a flourishing of African-American culture
22. The _____ Act defined intoxicating liquors to include wine and beer
23. Open living areas on the outskirts of cities
27. The 1920s period of economic boom collapsed in the 1930s during the _____ Depression
30. Total value of all goods and services produced by citizens of a nation in a single year, including income from investments abroad (abbrev.)

Unit IV | Activity 2

CHAPTER 12

World War II: America's Darkest and Brightest Hour

SS.912.A.6.1 Examine causes, course, and consequences of World War II on the United States and the world.

SS.912.A.6.2 Describe the United States' response in the early years of World War II (Neutrality Acts, Cash and Carry, Lend Lease Act).

SS.912.A.6.3 Analyze the impact of the Holocaust during World War II on Jews as well as other groups.

SS.912.A.6.4 Examine efforts to expand or contract rights for various populations during World War II.

SS.912.A.6.5 Explain the impact of World War II on domestic government policy.

SS.912.A.6.6 Analyze the use of atomic weapons during World War II and the aftermath of the bombings.

SS.912.A.6.7 Describe the attempts to promote international justice through the Nuremberg Trials.

SS.912.A.6.9 Describe the rationale for the formation of the United Nations, including the contribution of Mary McLeod Bethune.

SS.912.A.6.15 Examine key events and peoples in Florida history as they relate to United States history.

Names and Terms You Should Know

Fascism	"Four Freedoms"	Hiroshima	Ghetto
Nazism	Atlantic Charter	Nagasaki	Auschwitz
Benito Mussolini	Pearl Harbor	V-J Day	Nuremberg Trials
Adolf Hitler	Salerno	Home front	Tehran Conference
Spanish Civil War	Stalingrad	Japanese-American internment	United Nations
Appeasement	D-Day	*Korematsu v. U.S.*	Dumbarton Oaks Conference
Blitzkrieg	Normandy	"Double V" Campaign	San Francisco Conference
Neutrality Acts	Battle of the Bulge	A. Philip Randolph	Mary McLeod Bethune
Cash-and-carry	V-E Day	CORE	Security Council
Quarantine Speech	Coral Sea	Holocaust	General Assembly
Lend-Lease Act	Midway	Final Solution	

Florida "Keys" to Learning

1. Hitler and the Nazis came to power in Germany after the Great Depression had caused widespread unemployment. The League of Nations and the Western Allies failed to stop their aggressive acts.

2. Nazi Germany invaded Poland in September 1939. France and Britain declared war on Germany. Germany coordinated its airplanes, tanks, and motorized troop carriers in the new *Blitzkrieg* form of warfare. By June 1940, Germany had defeated France and occupied much of Europe.

3. The Neutrality Acts of 1935–1937 aimed at keeping the United States out of the war. The Neutrality Act of 1937 allowed Americans to sell non-military goods to countries at war on a "cash-and-carry" basis. The Neutrality Act of 1939 expanded "cash-and-carry" to include the sale of arms. In 1941, Roosevelt pushed "Lend-Lease" through Congress: the United States could supply the British with arms, to be paid for or returned after the war.

4. Japan launched a surprise attack on Pearl Harbor on December 7, 1941. Germany and Italy also declared war on the United States.

5. On the "home front," the United States created the Selective Service System to manage the draft. Women enlisted as WACS or WAVES. The War Production Board was placed in charge of production. Essential goods were reserved for the military. Even food was rationed. People grew their own in "Liberty Gardens."

6. When A. Philip Randolph planned a "March on Washington," President Roosevelt signed Executive Order 8802, throwing federal jobs and jobs with federal contractors open to African Americans. Through the "Double V" campaign, African Americans sought victory against Nazism abroad and racism at home. The *Braceros* program recruited Hispanic workers to work in the U.S.

7. Japanese Americans on the West Coast were sent by Executive Order 9066 to inland internment camps. The order was upheld by the Supreme Court in *Korematsu v. United States* (1944).

8. Nazi Germany murdered European Jews in the Holocaust. Jewish synagogues and businesses were closed in Germany after *Kristallnacht* in 1938. After Germany conquered Poland, Jews in Eastern Europe were crowded into ghettos. In 1942, Nazis adopted the "Final Solution": trains carried Jews and other victims to Auschwitz and other extermination camps where they were gassed and their bodies were burned.

9. In 1942, American forces landed in North Africa and helped defeat German and Italian troops. Afterwards, they advanced to Sicily and mainland Italy. Soviet forces defeated Germans at Stalingrad. American and British forces landed on the beaches of Normandy on "D-Day" (June 6, 1944). They advanced across France but faced a German counter-attack at the Battle of the Bulge. The counter-attack failed and the Western Allies advanced into Germany from the west as Soviet armies advanced from the east. Hitler committed suicide in April and Germany surrendered in May 1945.

10. In the Pacific, the Japanese advanced after their attack on Pearl Harbor. Captured U.S. forces in the Philippines were forced on the "Bataan Death March." Japanese and U.S. aircraft carriers fought at the Battle of the Coral Sea; a few months later, the U.S. sank four Japanese aircraft carriers at the Battle of Midway (1943), the turning point of the Pacific war.

11. The U.S. government secretly developed the atomic bomb in the "Manhattan Project." In August 1945, atomic bombs were dropped on the cities of Hiroshima and Nagasaki, and Japan surrendered.

12. Nazi leaders were put on trial at Nuremberg for "crimes against humanity." Germany was divided into four occupation zones while Japan was occupied by the United States.

13. The war led to the formation of the United Nations in 1945 and the signing of the Universal Declaration of Human Rights in 1948.

The Origins of World War II in Europe

The Rise of Dictatorships in Europe

The rapid changes caused by industrialization, the rise of nationalism, the harsh violence of World War I, the fragility of new democracies, and fear of Communism led to the rise of a new set of beliefs in Europe. This new way of thinking is generally known as "**fascism**," named after the Italian party that first introduced it. **Benito Mussolini** was the first of these fascist dictators, seizing power in Italy as early as 1922. Fascism combined feelings of intense nationalism, obedience to the party leader, racism, protection of the common people, and the worship of violent action. It often arose where people had been used to the strong leadership and the paternal protection of a monarchy, which had suddenly been replaced by democracy after World War I. The citizens of these weak new democracies feared for their future and were willing to surrender their newly won political power to forceful dictators who promised them prosperity and expansion.

Mussolini and Hitler

In Germany, the **Nazi** (National Socialist) Party was founded shortly after World War I. The Nazis and their leader, **Adolf Hitler**, believed that Germans were a superior race, destined to rule over Europe. The Nazis considered the peoples of Eastern Europe, such as the Poles and Russians, as ethnically inferior and fit to be enslaved. Hitler and the Nazis felt a special hatred for Jews, whom they blamed for Germany's defeat in World War I and other troubles. The Nazi Party also taught the doctrine of absolute personal obedience to the will of the party leader, or "*Führer*." They were Social Darwinists who despised weakness, and they were determined to use German technological superiority and military strength to achieve their own cold-blooded mastery of Europe. The Nazis also glorified violence. Their party included a paramilitary wing, first formed of unemployed veterans, known as the S.A. or "Storm Division" (*Stormabteilung*). They beat up opponents and boasted that they were not afraid to use force to obtain their ends.

The Historian's Apprentice

"Over against all this, the völkisch (Nazi 'folkish' or racist) concept of the world recognizes that the fundamental racial elements are of the greatest significance for mankind. In principle, the State is looked upon only as a means to an end and this end is the conservation of the racial characteristics of mankind. [W]e cannot admit that one race is equal to another. By recognizing that they are different, the völkisch concept separates mankind into races of superior and inferior quality. On the basis of this recognition it feels bound, in conformity with the eternal Will that dominates the universe, to postulate the victory of the better and stronger and the subordination of the inferior and weaker . . . On this planet of ours, human culture and civilization are indissolubly bound up with the presence of the Aryan [German and other Northern European peoples]. We all feel that in the distant future many may be faced with problems which can be solved only by a superior race of human beings, a race destined to become master of all the other peoples and which will have at its disposal the means and resources of the whole world."

—Adolf Hitler, *Mein Kampf* ("*My Struggle*"), 1925–1926

Mein Kampf outlines the Nazi philosophy. In the excerpt above, Hitler explains his views on racism.
- ▶ How did Hitler's views compare with American views in the same time period?
- ▶ How did Hitler's views make the outbreak of war more likely once he came to power?

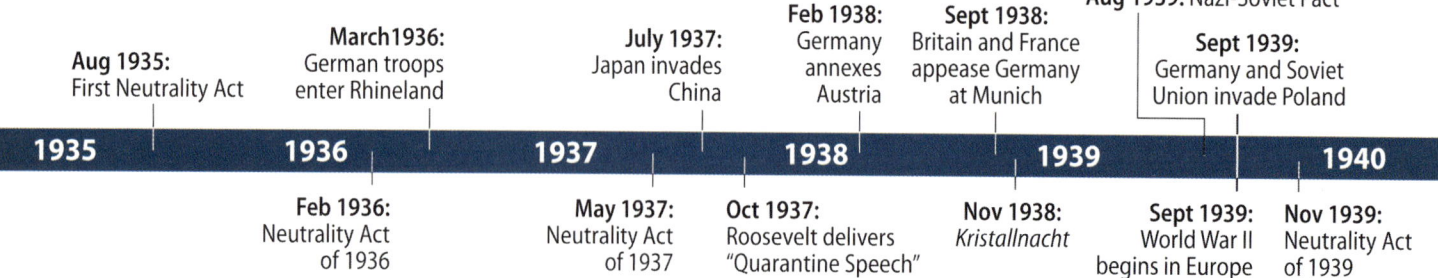

Although the Great Depression had begun in the United States, it quickly spread to Europe. Germany was especially shaken. German unemployment reached catastrophic proportions. Membership soared in both the German Communist and Nazi Parties—two parties with extreme views, but in opposite directions. People were looking for more radical solutions to their country's problems.

The Nazis were just one of several small political parties before the Great Depression. But in the 1933 elections, though still not a majority, the Nazis received more votes than any other party. Hitler was appointed as Chancellor (*head of the German government*) by conservative politicians who believed that they could control him. Only one month after his appointment, the building housing the German legislature, or *Reichstag*, was set on fire by an arsonist. Many historians believe the Nazis themselves were responsible for the *Reichstag* fire. The German legislature granted Hitler full dictatorial powers in the emergency—powers that he never surrendered. The Nazis began murdering opponents or imprisoning them in "concentration camps." They also began persecuting Jews, while all German institutions from unions to schools were either brought under Nazi control or closed. Opposition newspapers and political parties were banned. In a special ceremony, the German army took an oath of personal allegiance to Hitler.

Hitler addressing the German Legislature

The Failure of the League of Nations

The League of Nations, charged with responsibility for preventing another war, proved to be powerless before the aggressive acts of Hitler and other dictators. The League was based on the idea of **collective security**—that peaceful nations should band together against aggressors to prevent future wars. However, the League had no army of its own and depended on its members' actions. Several major countries, including the United States and the Soviet Union, failed to become members of the League. Germany and Japan were originally members but left the League in 1933. Hitler began to rebuild German military power in violation of the Treaty of Versailles, which he condemned. The Treaty prohibited German troops from entering the Rhineland, the area of Germany next to France. In 1936, Hitler sent German military forces into this region in open defiance of the Treaty. Britain, France, and the League of Nations failed to stop him. Indeed, only a few months later Britain, France and the United States even participated in the 1936 Olympics, which were held in Hitler's Berlin.

The League of Nations was similarly unable to stop the Japanese invasion of Manchuria (1931), the Italian invasion of Ethiopia (1935), or German, Italian, and Soviet intervention in the Spanish Civil War (1936–1939), where a right-wing general, Francisco Franco, was fighting to overturn his country's elected socialist government. In all of these instances, the League failed to halt aggression.

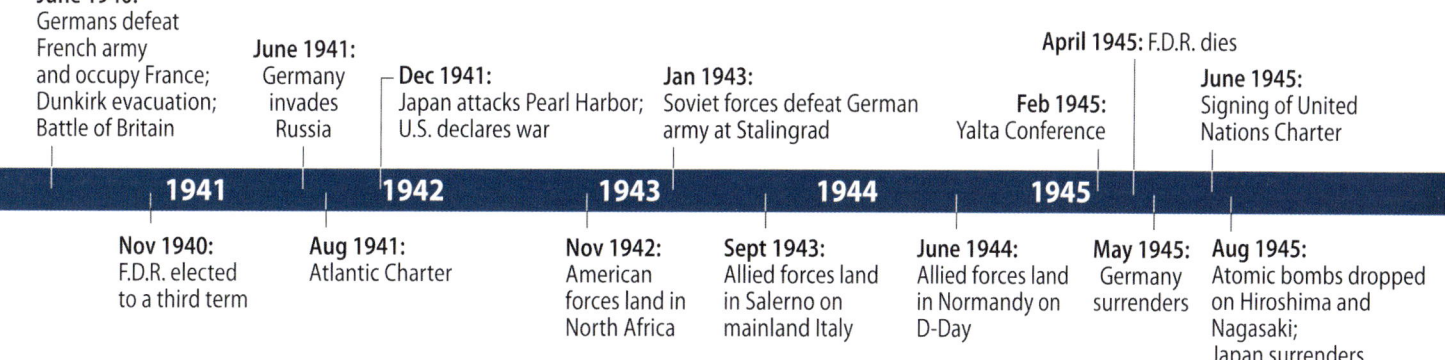

The Failure of Appeasement

In February 1938, Hitler annexed **Austria**, the small German-speaking republic that was left when the Austro-Hungarian Empire dissolved in 1919. Next, Hitler demanded the **Sudetenland**, a part of Czechoslovakia with a large number of German-speaking people. At first, France and Britain promised to protect Czechoslovakia, despite the fact that Hitler threatened war. Then Mussolini invited British and French leaders to meet with Hitler in the German town of Munich to work out a solution. At the **Munich Conference** in September 1938, British and French leaders, seeking to avoid war, agreed to hand over the western part of Czechoslovakia to Germany. This policy of giving in to the demands of a potential enemy has since become known as "**appeasement**." Neville Chamberlain, the British Prime Minister, returned to London promising his countrymen "peace in our time." However, his policy of appeasement only encouraged Hitler to make further demands. Hitler reached the conclusion that Britain and France were weak and would do almost anything to avoid war.

Kristallnacht

Surveying the damage

In November 1938, a German Jewish refugee assassinated a German diplomat in Paris. The German government used this event as an excuse to attack Jewish synagogues (*houses of worship*) and stores throughout Germany. Jews were attacked, Jewish businesses were closed, and Jewish communities were forced to pay a large fine for the assassination. Thousands of Jews were arrested and sent to concentration camps. So much broken glass fell into the streets that the event became known as *Kristallnacht* ("night of broken glass"). Historians often see this as the turning point when the Nazi government moved from propaganda and discrimination against Jews to more active measures of persecution. World opinion was shocked, and the United States withdrew its ambassador from Berlin in protest.

World War II Begins: The German Invasion of Poland

The annexation of the Sudetenland left the rest of Czechoslovakia weak and defenseless. In March 1939, Hitler persuaded the Slovaks in the east to declare their independence and sent a German army to occupy Prague and what was left of the country. Czech leaders surrendered without resistance. Hitler also began making new demands on Poland. He claimed the Free City of **Danzig** (present-day Gdańsk), which contained a large number of German-speaking residents.

By now, British and French leaders had reached the conclusion that Hitler's goal was the conquest of Europe. They therefore resisted his new demands and pledged to protect Poland. Hitler responded by negotiating a secret treaty with the Soviet dictator, **Joseph Stalin**. Under the terms of the **Nazi-Soviet Pact**, signed in August 1939, Hitler and Stalin agreed to divide Poland between themselves. In September 1939, Germany invaded Poland from the west, while the Soviet Union invaded from the east.

Chapter 12 | The United States in World War II

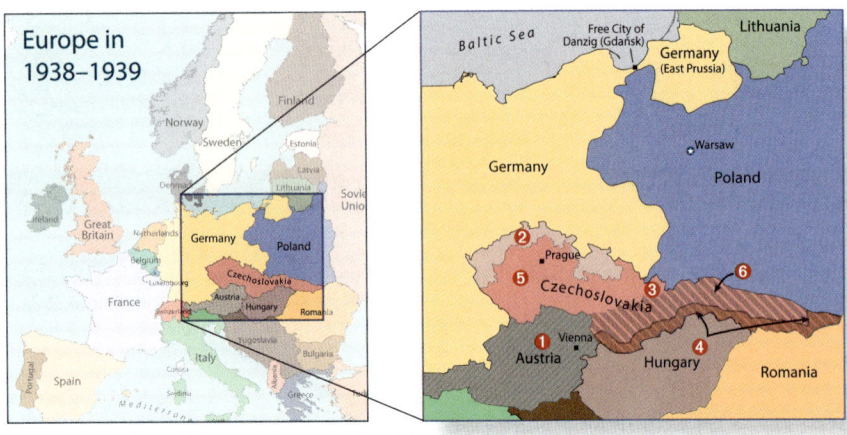

The expansion of Germany and the division of Czechoslovakia, 1938–1939

❶ Germany annexes Austria (March 1938).

❷ Germany annexes the Sudetenland after the Munich Conference (October 1938).

❸ Poland annexes Zaolzie (October 1938).

❹ Hungary annexes border areas (November 1938).

❺ The rest of western Czechoslovakia becomes a German protectorate.

❻ Eastern Czechoslovakia becomes Slovakia, a German satellite (March 1939).

Britain and France responded by declaring war on Germany, and **World War II** began in Europe.

Blitzkrieg The German army had developed new tactics for waging warfare based on the use of airplanes, tanks, motorized troop carriers, and communications by radio. German planes bombed Polish cities and troops from the air. German tanks and motorized artillery invaded Polish territory, followed by infantry forces. During World War I, troops had remained stationary in trenches, unable to advance without being mowed down by machine-gun fire. In this new type of warfare, planes, tanks, motorized artillery and motorized troop carriers—all applications of the internal combustion engine—were used to make rapid advances. The advantage in combat shifted back to the offense. Because of the speed of the German advance, this new form of warfare became known as *Blitzkrieg*, or "lightning warfare."

The Fall of France

France and Britain had declared war on Germany but did little to help Poland. During the first months of 1940, the French chose not to attack Germany and Germany's "Western Front" remained quiet. In April, Germany suddenly invaded Denmark and Norway; in May, the Germans attacked the Netherlands, Belgium, Luxembourg, and France. German troops avoided the strong defensive French barrier known as the **Maginot Line** by marching through the Ardennes Forest and across Belgium. French leaders had expected a German invasion through Belgium but farther north, and a large part of their army was trapped when the Germans surprisingly marched directly west to the coast. By June 1940, the French were forced to surrender. A British expeditionary force, cornered in the coastal town of Dunkirk, withdrew across the English Channel. The British sent

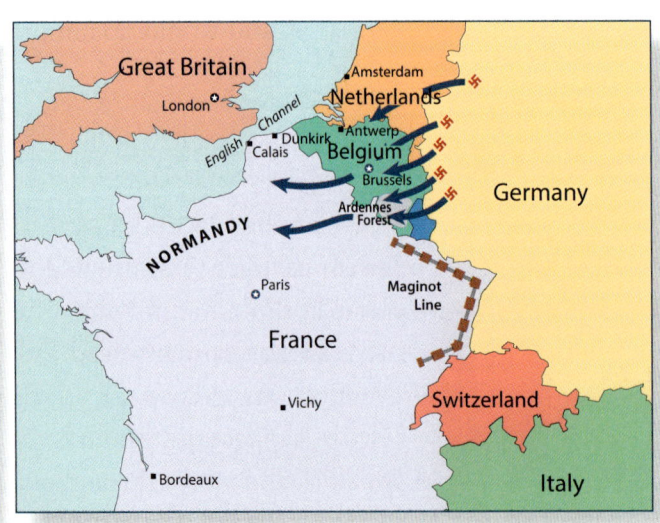

In 1939, Poland was invaded by Germany from the west and the Soviet Union from the east

The advance of the German Army and the defeat of France in June 1940

254 Chapter 12 | The United States in World War II

fishing boats, pleasure craft and everything else they could to ferry their soldiers back home.

The "Battle of Britain"

Having conquered most of Western Europe, Hitler now attempted to use his air force, the Luftwaffe, to bomb the British into submission. The Luftwaffe bombed London and other British cities to create a sense of terror. However, the fighter planes of the Royal Air Force were able to shoot down many of the attacking German planes, while the civilian population endured these attacks by crowding into bomb shelters or the deep shafts of the London Underground (*subway*). The British also used the new invention of **radar** to detect arriving planes and identify where attacks were likely to occur.

A rooftop observer in London

The Historian's Apprentice

1. Make your own illustrated chart or graphic organizer showing the causes of World War II in Europe. Classify each cause as social, political, or economic.
2. Hold a class debate on this topic: "Resolved: World War II could have been prevented." Evaluate the policies of appeasement, the weaknesses of the League of Nations, and U.S. isolationism. Would more active measures have prevented the expansion of Nazi Germany without war? If so, what might the world look like today?
3. How did innovations in technology affect warfare in World War II? Using the Internet, find pictures of warfare in both world wars. Then make observations about their similarities and differences. Share your findings with your class by giving a slide show, PowerPoint or oral presentation.

America Maintains a Partial Neutrality

In Chapters 9 and 10, you learned how Americans had become disillusioned by their involvement in World War I. They returned to their traditional policy of isolationism—refusing to join the League of Nations, insisting on the collection of war debts, passing high tariffs, and restricting immigration. Some Americans even became pacifists, renouncing all future wars. You also learned that there were some important exceptions to this general trend. For example, Americans hosted other powers at the Washington Naval Conference and promoted the Kellogg-Briand Peace Pact.

Continuing Isolationism

In the early 1930s, the United States was too absorbed in the problems of the Great Depression to become very active in world affairs. In 1936, the Nye Committee in the U.S. Senate issued a report revealing that many American munitions companies had profited greatly during the past war. Some of these companies had resorted to unfair practices, such as bribery. The report strengthened public feelings against involvement in Europe. The same year, Congress passed an act prohibiting new loans to Britain and France since they had stopped paying their debts to the United States from World War I.

The Neutrality Acts of 1935–1937

As the likelihood of war in Europe grew, Congress passed a series of acts designed to keep Americans out of the conflict. The United States had been drawn into World War I in part because Americans had been killed on Allied ships like the *Lusitania*. German submarines had attacked ships carrying supplies to Britain and France. The Neutrality Acts aimed at avoiding a repetition of this situation.

Neutrality Act of 1935 The first Neutrality Act was passed for a limited period of six months. It prohibited Americans from sending "arms, ammunition, and implements of war" to foreign nations that the President proclaimed were at war. In October 1935, this act was applied to both Italy and Ethiopia, even though Italy alone was the aggressor. The act also warned Americans traveling on the ships of nations at war that they did so at their own risk.

Neutrality Act of 1936 This act renewed the Neutrality Act of 1935 for another 14 months. Since it did not cover civil wars or prohibit the sale of non-military goods, it permitted American companies to sell trucks and oil to General Franco during the Spanish Civil War. However, it prohibited American loans to nations at war.

Neutrality Act of 1937 This act extended the prohibition on the sale of arms to parties engaged in civil wars, including the Spanish Civil War. It also prohibited Americans from traveling on the ships of nations at war. However, the new act permitted, at the discretion of the President, the sale of non-military goods to countries at war on a "**cash-and-carry**" basis—in other words, so long as the buyer paid in cash and arranged their transportation. When Japan invaded China in July 1937, Roosevelt refused to apply the terms of the Neutrality Act since war was not officially declared. This allowed Americans to continue sending supplies to China.

Roosevelt's Quarantine Speech

After the invasion of China, President Roosevelt thought it was time to test American opinion. In October 1937, he gave a speech announcing that peaceful nations must band together to **quarantine** (*isolate*) aggressive nations or their acts of aggression would increase. He seemed to suggest imposing economic sanctions. Public reaction was divided.

The Historian's Apprentice

The present reign of terror and international lawlessness began a few years ago. It began through unjustified interference in the internal affairs of other nations or the invasion of alien territory in violation of treaties; and has now reached a stage where the very foundations of civilization are seriously threatened. . . . Without a declaration of war and without warning or justification of any kind, civilians, including vast numbers of women and children, are being ruthlessly murdered with bombs from the air. In times of so-called peace, ships are being attacked and sunk by submarines without cause or notice. . . .

The peace-loving nations must make a concerted effort in opposition to those violations of treaties and those ignorings of humane instincts which today are creating a state of international anarchy and instability from which there is no escape through mere isolation or neutrality. It seems to be unfortunately true that the epidemic of world lawlessness is spreading. When an epidemic of physical disease starts to spread, the community approves and joins in a quarantine of the patients in order to protect the health of the community against the spread of the disease.

—Franklin D. Roosevelt, "Quarantine Speech," October 1937

▶ Many Americans rejected Roosevelt's message. They opposed any form of U.S. military action or involvement overseas. Yet others supported his view that the dictators posed an imminent threat. Imagine it is October 1937 and you have just heard Roosevelt's speech. Write a letter to a relative giving your own opinion.

The Neutrality Act of 1939

Even after the Nazi invasion of Poland two years later, most Americans still opposed involvement in any war. A majority in Congress, however, favored helping Britain and France with all measures short of war. Because the Neutrality Act of 1937 forbade all sales of arms to nations at war, Congress passed a new Neutrality Act in November 1939. The new act prohibited Americans from entering war zones. It also renewed the "cash-and-carry" provision of the 1937 act, extending it to the sale of arms as well as non-military goods. Roosevelt's goal was to help the Western Allies as much as possible, while keeping the United States out of war.

America Prepares for War

Americans began making preparations for war, just in case they were drawn into the conflict. Congress increased its spending on the army and navy. In 1940, after the German defeat of France, Congress even passed the first peacetime draft. All men between the ages of 21 and 35 had to register and became eligible for one year of military service.

A contest for the support of American public opinion was now waged. Isolationists and pro-German groups loudly challenged any efforts to assist the British. At the same time, the Committee to Defend America, the Century Group, and other groups lobbied for support for Britain. The British faced the threat of a German invasion across the English Channel, but they no longer had enough ships for their own defense. Acting as Commander-in-Chief, Roosevelt bypassed Congress and gave 50 destroyers (*mid-sized warships*) to the British in exchange for leases on British bases in Canada and the Caribbean.

The Lend-Lease Act of 1941

In the 1940 Presidential election, Roosevelt broke with tradition by running for a third term. Both Roosevelt and his Republican opponent advocated strong defense measures in their campaigns. By the time of Roosevelt's re-election, the British were desperate for food and arms. In December 1940, Roosevelt proposed in one of his fireside chats that America, as the "**arsenal of democracy**," should supply arms to the British. The British could pay for the arms later, he suggested, or simply return them after the war was over. "There is far less chance of the United States getting into war," the President explained to his listeners, "if we do all we can now to support the nations defending themselves against attack by the Axis . . ."

In March 1941, Roosevelt signed the **Lend-Lease Act**. This act repealed parts of the Neutrality Act of 1939 and authorized the United States to sell, lease, or lend war materials to "any country whose defense the President deems vital to the defense of the United States." Congress also voted new funds for the production of ships, tanks, planes, and other weapons. American battleships began protecting British merchant ships carrying American supplies across the Atlantic. Critics of the program feared that it might draw the United States into the war. Most Americans, however, supported Roosevelt's view that the United States must help beleaguered Britain. They hoped to keep the United States out of the war by strengthening British resistance to Nazi tyranny.

The Four Freedoms and the Atlantic Charter

In his State of the Union address in 1941, President Roosevelt told Americans that he hoped to establish a world based on **Four Freedoms**: (1) "freedom of speech and expression," (2) "freedom of every person to worship God in his own way," (3) "freedom from want," and (4) "freedom from fear," by which he meant freedom from the fear of war and the need to reduce armaments.

Several months later, Roosevelt met secretly with British Prime Minister **Winston Churchill** aboard a ship in the Atlantic off the coast of Canada. Roosevelt was now convinced that American entry into the war was inevitable. Roosevelt and Churchill discussed their objectives for a post-war world. They announced that they sought no territorial gains and wished to restore self-government to conquered peoples. They also favored free trade, freedom of the seas, economic development, social security, and a reduction of armaments. Finally, the **Atlantic Charter** laid the foundation for the future United Nations, a new international organization that would replace the League of Nations.

> ## The Historian's Apprentice
>
> ### The Atlantic Charter, August 14, 1941
>
> The President of the United States of America and the Prime Minister, Mr. Churchill . . . deem it right to make known certain common principles. . . .
>
> **First,** their countries seek no aggrandizement, territorial or other;
>
> **Second,** they desire to see no territorial changes that do not accord with the freely expressed wishes of the peoples concerned;
>
> **Third,** they respect the right of all peoples to choose the form of government under which they will live; . . .
>
> **Fifth,** they desire to bring about the fullest collaboration between all nations in the economic field with the object of securing, for all, improved labor standards, economic advancement, and social security;
>
> **Sixth,** after the final destruction of the Nazi tyranny, they hope to see established a peace which will afford to all nations the means of dwelling in safety within their own boundaries;
>
> **Seventh,** such a peace should enable all men to traverse the high seas and oceans without hindrance;
>
> **Eighth,** they believe that all of the nations of the world, for realistic as well as spiritual reasons must come to the abandonment of the use of force. . . . they believe, pending the establishment of a wider and permanent system of general security, that the disarmament of such nations is essential. They will likewise aid and encourage all other practicable measures which will lighten for peace-loving peoples the crushing burden of armaments.
>
> 1. How did the goals of the Atlantic Charter compare with those of President Wilson's Fourteen Points? How were they similar? How were they different?
> 2. How could Roosevelt agree to the Atlantic Charter before the United States was even at war? Was he acting within his constitutional powers as President?

Americans Move Closer to War

Roosevelt believed American entry into the war was necessary to defeat Hitler and save democracy. He also knew that he had to win wider public support before taking the country to war. So he proceeded in small steps. In 1941, armed American merchant ships began carrying supplies directly to Britain. U.S. troops also occupied Greenland and Iceland. It appeared as though American involvement in the war in Europe was just a matter of time.

The United States Enters the War

Surprisingly, it was events in Asia, not Europe, that finally brought the United States into the war.

Increasing U.S.-Japanese Tensions

Like the Nazis, Japan's military leaders believed they belonged to a superior race destined to rule over others. They had occupied Manchuria in 1931 and invaded the rest of China in 1937. Despite these aggressive acts, Roosevelt had not restricted American trade with Japan. In fact, Japan continued to import most of its oil from the United States.

Impressed by Hitler's stunning victories in Europe, the Japanese entered into a defensive alliance with Germany and Italy in September 1940. In June 1941, Hitler suddenly abandoned his pact with Stalin and invaded the Soviet Union. Japanese leaders debated whether to declare war on the Soviet Union or to advance southwards, seizing rice fields and rubber plantations, cutting supply routes to China, and extending their empire in the direction of the oil fields of the Dutch East Indies (present-day Indonesia).

Japanese leaders decided to send their forces into Southern Indochina. Roosevelt reacted by freezing Japanese assets in the United States and placing new restrictions on sales of oil, iron ore, steel, and rubber to Japan. This left Japan with a limited supply of oil. Roosevelt offered to restore normal trade relations, but only if the Japanese withdrew their forces from Indochina and China. As expected, Japan refused this demand.

Japan Plans a Surprise Attack

Japanese leaders decided instead to seize the Dutch East Indies so that they would have their own oil fields. They reasoned that such a daring act would first require their control of certain strategic locations—including Hong Kong, Singapore, and the Philippines. Realizing that these actions would bring the United States into the war, they decided to launch a surprise attack on America first. Prime Minister **Hideki Tojo** and other Japanese leaders believed that an attack on the naval base at Pearl Harbor would catch American forces unprepared and eliminate American naval power in the Pacific for a limited period of time. During this time, Japan could consolidate its conquests and strengthen its position. Japanese leaders believed they would then be able to negotiate a compromise peace with the United States, leaving Japan in control of East Asia.

The Attack at Pearl Harbor

In early December 1941, six aircraft carriers, a fleet of Japanese warships, and 360 airplanes secretly sailed north of the island of Oahu in Hawaii. The ships sailed without radio communication to avoid detection. The commander's ship proudly flew the same flag that had sailed with the fleet that defeated Russia in 1905. On the morning of December 7, 1941, two separate waves of Japanese airplanes attacked the U.S. Pacific fleet stationed in **Pearl Harbor**, Hawaii. The surprise attack destroyed six ships and 180 aircraft, took the lives of 2,403 Americans, and wounded 1,178 others. Almost half of those killed were on the *USS Arizona* when it was hit and sunk. The Japanese attackers rejoiced at their success, although they failed to destroy the repair yards or vast storage tanks used to refuel ships, and no aircraft carriers were at Pearl Harbor at the time. American opinion was enraged, making the negotiated peace that the Japanese sought very unlikely.

Japanese airplanes bomb the U.S. naval fleet at Pearl Harbor.

The next day, President Roosevelt asked Congress for a declaration of war on Japan.

The Historian's Apprentice

"Yesterday, December 7, 1941—a date which will live in infamy—the United States of America was suddenly and deliberately attacked by naval and air forces of the Empire of Japan.

The United States was at peace with that nation, and, at the solicitation of Japan, was still in conversation with its government and its Emperor looking toward the maintenance of peace in the Pacific. . . .

[T]he distance of Hawaii from Japan makes it obvious that the attack was deliberately planned many days or even weeks ago. During the intervening time the Japanese government has deliberately sought to deceive the United States by false statements and expressions of hope for continued peace.

The attack yesterday on the Hawaiian Islands has caused severe damage to American naval and military forces. I regret to tell you that very many American lives have been lost.

In addition, American ships have been reported torpedoed on the high seas between San Francisco and Honolulu. Yesterday the Japanese government also launched an attack against Malaya. Last night Japanese forces attacked Hong Kong, Guam, the Philippine Islands and Wake Island. And this morning the Japanese attacked Midway Island.

Japan has, therefore, undertaken a surprise offensive extending throughout the Pacific area. The facts of yesterday and today speak for themselves.

I ask that the Congress declare that since the unprovoked and dastardly attack by Japan on Sunday, December seventh, a state of war has existed between the United States and the Japanese Empire."

—Franklin D. Roosevelt before a Joint Session of Congress, December 8, 1941

1. Imagine you are a member of Congress who has just heard President Roosevelt's speech. Write a message to the voters in your district giving your views on the attack and how the country should respond.

2. In what ways was the attack on Pearl Harbor similar to the more recent attacks of Sepember 11, 2001? How were these attacks different? Prepare your answer in the form of a chart or Venn diagram.

Hitler now had a golden opportunity to let Americans become distracted by a war in the Pacific. Churchill feared such a war might draw American resources away from the Atlantic. However, four days later, Germany and Italy, acting as the allies of Japan, declared war on the United States. Hitler had greatly underestimated the capabilities, determination and endurance of the United States. Americans were now officially at war on two fronts—the Atlantic and Pacific.

The United States at War: The Home Front

In 1941, Americans faced enemies more ruthless and terrible than at any other time in history. With their doctrines of racial superiority and glorification of conquest, Nazi Germany, Imperial Japan, and Fascist Italy showed no mercy to the peoples they subdued. Their aim was world conquest and the extermination of many of their enemies through **genocide** (*murder of an entire people*). World War II became a contest to the death between the **Allied Powers** (Britain, the Soviet Union, and the United States) and the **Axis Powers** (Germany, Japan, and Italy).

Just as in World War I, the federal government now had to mobilize American manpower and production to meet enormous wartime needs.

The Draft

The first peacetime draft, as noted earlier, was introduced in 1940. After Pearl Harbor, the draft was extended to all able-bodied men between the ages of 18 and 45. The **Selective Service System**, with more than 6,000 local draft boards, was set up to oversee this system. One out of every ten Americans ended up in uniform during the war. By the time the war was over, more than 15 million men had voluntarily enlisted or been drafted. For the first time, women were also permitted to enlist. The **Women's Army Corps**, or "WACs," was established in 1942. WACs received uniforms and underwent basic training, although they did not serve in combat. WACS plotted aircraft paths, operated radios and telephone switchboards, organized supplies, drove army vehicles, and worked as stenographers, typists, and clerks. The Navy established their own Women Accepted for Volunteer Emergency Service, or "WAVES." Another 57,000 women served as nurses in the Army Nurse Corps.

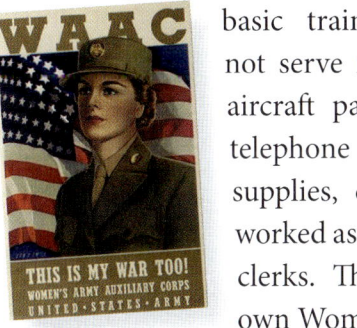

Minorities also played an important role in America's fighting forces. For example, about one million African Americans served, even though they suffered the indignity of being placed in segregated units and were not sent into combat until late in the war. The **Tuskegee Airmen**, a unit of African-American fighter pilots, flew more than 1,500 missions in Europe. One group of American Indians played a critical role because of their unique languages.

Najavo "**code talkers**" used the Navajo language to form secret codes in the Pacific campaign that Japanese code-breakers could not decipher.

Wartime Production

Many historians believe that America's greatest contribution to the Allied war effort was in its wartime production. Even before the war, American productive capacity had greatly exceeded that of the other great powers. U.S. coal production, for example, was double that of Germany. In 1937, Japan had manufactured 26,000 cars and Germany 330,000; in the same year, the United States had produced 4.8 million. During the war, American farms and factories were protected from bombing or invasion by the Axis Powers by distance and the oceans. America truly became, as Roosevelt had foreseen, the "arsenal of democracy."

The War Production Board

New federal agencies sprang up to manage the sprawling wartime economy, just as during World War I and the New Deal. The **War Production Board** was set up to ease the conversion from peacetime to wartime production. A hundred billion dollars in government contracts were awarded to private industry within the first six months of the war. An executive from General Motors was placed in charge of overall production. Henry Kaiser's shipyard in Richmond, California, built new "Liberty Ships" to carry men and supplies. Before long, a new ship was being rolled out every four and a half days. In Michigan, Henry Ford's plants began turning out thousands of bombers instead of cars.

Rationing

The War Production Board found it necessary to **ration** essential goods like gasoline, heating fuel, metals, and rubber. The Critical Materials Plan, adopted in 1942, allocated steel, copper, and aluminum. Later, canned, frozen, and processed foods were also rationed in order to ensure enough food for the soldiers. On the home front, people received ration booklets with coupons. Each rationed item was given a point value. Consumers paid money to the seller

Chapter 12 | World War II: America's Darkest and Brightest Hour

to cover the purchase of the product, but they also had to give the seller ration coupons to make the purchase. Consumers could buy no more of a good than the coupons in their ration books allowed.

Many Americans grew their own fruits and vegetables in "**Victory Gardens**," so that more food would be available for the troops.

The **Office of War Mobilization** was created in 1943 to oversee the allocation of both materials and manpower. Headed by former Supreme Court Justice James Byrnes, it supervised the War Production Board and other wartime agencies.

The Labor Force

The demands of war production brought a final end to the Great Depression. The draft, combined with the expansion of production, ended unemployment. Large numbers of workers entered the armed services and were sent overseas. Women, African Americans, and other minority workers stepped in to fill the gaps left by the men in uniform. For the first time, women took jobs in heavy industry. In the past, it had mainly been younger women who had worked outside the home, but now married, and older women also worked in factories. African Americans continued to migrate to Northern cities. The **National Labor War Board** oversaw the needs of workers.

Farm Production

Food was desperately needed by American troops, by the Allies in Europe, and by American consumers. Crop prices therefore rose, helping farmers. Farm production increased, based on improved techniques and the cultivation of new areas. Parts of the former Dust Bowl, for example, enjoyed a recovery from greater rainfall and better plowing techniques.

Paying for the War

The cost of the war to the United States was over $300 billion—more than eight times that of World War I. Almost half (45%) of this was paid for by revenues from tax receipts. In 1939, income taxes had raised about $1 billion and only 4 million Americans filed personal income tax returns. In 1942, changes in the tax laws added another 13 million taxpayers. By 1945, there were 43 million taxpayers filing income tax returns, and income taxes raised $40 billion. The practice of withholding taxes from workers' payrolls, a practice that still affects most Americans today, was also introduced during the war.

Whatever expenses could not be paid for out of tax revenues were financed by borrowing. As in World War I, patriotic Americans bought "**war bonds**," which were repaid with interest by the government after the war was over. In fact, only a quarter of the war bonds were sold to individuals. Most were bought by banks and other financial institutions.

Information and Propaganda

As in World War I, the government also made efforts to control the flow of information and to maintain popular support. The **Office of War Information** (OWI) created posters, controlled newsreels and even produced its own radio programs to promote patriotism and boost the war effort. The Office of War Information set up a "Motion Picture Bureau" in Hollywood to review movie scripts. Even children's comic books were recruited into the war effort, and Superman battled German and Japanese opponents.

The Forced Relocation of Japanese Americans

After the attack on Pearl Harbor, President Roosevelt ordered the internment of Japanese, German and Italian nationals either visiting or residing in the United States as "alien enemies." Many Americans on the West Coast further feared that the 120,000 Japanese Americans living there might commit acts of sabotage. These Japanese Americans included both residents born in Japan (*Issei*) and their American-born children (*Nisei*). Many *Nisei* had already been in the United States for several generations.

On February 19, 1942, President Roosevelt signed **Executive Order 9066**. This order permitted military commanders to designate "military areas" from which groups of people might be excluded. In May 1942, the Western Defense Commander ordered all persons of Japanese ancestry living in a 100-mile-wide zone along the West Coast to move to "relocation centers" farther

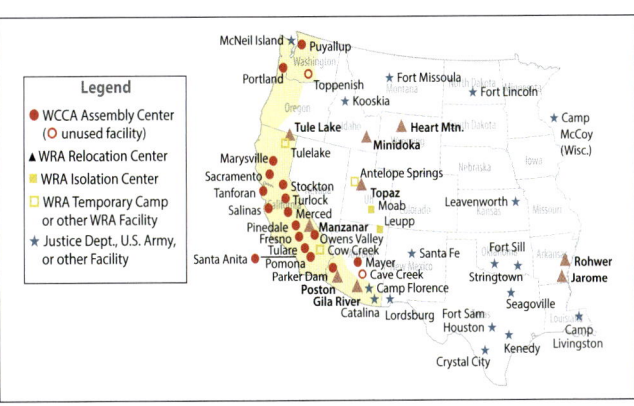

Locations of Japanese-American internment camps

Japanese-American family awaiting internment in a camp shown above.

inland, where they were required to remain until the end of the war. Most of these Japanese Americans were forced to sell their property and belongings on very short notice. Internment camps were established, in which the relocated families lived in wooden barracks, surrounded by barbed wire, in primitive and crowded conditions. Roosevelt justified this forced relocation as a military necessity. In reality, the widespread fear of Japanese Americans was largely racially motivated, since there was no actual evidence of acts of disloyalty. In contrast, only a few Italian Americans and German Americans were subject to internment during the war. Nor were any such steps taken against most of the many Japanese Americans living in Hawaii.

Although they were forced into internment camps, young Japanese-American men became eligible to enlist. Some refused to cooperate. Many more saw military service as an opportunity to distinguish themselves and their community, proving that their relocation had been unjust and that they were patriotic Americans. Japanese-American soldiers acted as interpreters, and the 442nd infantry regiment, a Japanese-American unit, fought with great distinction in Europe with one of the highest casualty rates.

Korematsu v. United States Fred Korematsu, a Japanese American, refused to relocate because he believed Executive Order 9066 was unconstitutional. He was arrested and convicted, but he challenged his conviction. The U.S. Supreme Court upheld his forcible relocation in *Korematsu v. United States* (1944). The Court viewed the government assessment of risk in wartime as reasonable and concluded that the suffering of the Japanese-American community was simply one of the burdens of the war. Almost 50 years later, Congress apologized and voted to pay compensation to the survivors of the relocated families.

The Historian's Apprentice

In *Korematsu v. United States*, Justice Hugo Black wrote the majority opinion:

"Korematsu was not excluded from the Military Area because of hostility to him or his race. He was excluded because we are at war with the Japanese Empire, because the properly constituted military authorities feared an invasion of our West Coast and felt constrained to take proper security measures, because they decided that the military urgency of the situation demanded that all citizens of Japanese ancestry be segregated from the West Coast temporarily . . . "

Justice Frank Murphy **dissented** (*disagreed*). Murphy argued that the forced relocations had unfortunately been based on nothing more than racial prejudice:

"I dissent . . . from this legalization of racism. Racial discrimination in any form and in any degree has no justifiable part whatever in our democratic way of life. It is unattractive in any setting, but it

Chapter 12 | World War II: America's Darkest and Brightest Hour

> *is utterly revolting among a free people who have embraced the principles set forth in the Constitution of the United States. All residents of this nation are kin in some way by blood or culture to a foreign land. Yet they are primarily and necessarily a part of the new and distinct civilization of the United States. They must, accordingly, be treated at all times as the heirs of the American experiment, and as entitled to all the rights and freedoms guaranteed by the Constitution."*

▶ Was the forced relocation of Japanese Americans justified? Have your class either hold a debate on this question or stage its own mock trial of Fred Korematsu.

▶ For evidence of racist attitudes, conduct your own research on the Internet by examining American propaganda posters from World War II. How do they depict the Japanese?

Other Minorities
African Americans

During the Great Depression, African Americans had suffered from even higher levels of unemployment than the rest of the country. As the nation prepared for war, there was fear that African Americans might remain excluded from new jobs.

A. Philip Randolph: A Famous Floridian

Randolph was born in Florida in 1889. He attended the Cookman Institute in East Jacksonville, then the only high school in Florida for African Americans. He moved to New York City in 1911, where he became interested in socialism and civil rights. He founded a magazine that campaigned against lynching. Afterwards, he became a union organizer.

The Pullman Company, which owned most of the country's overnight passenger cars, exclusively hired African-American men as porters. However porters were underpaid and relied on tips. In 1925, Randolph was elected as President of the Brotherhood of Sleeping Car Porters. Under his leadership, it became the first African-American union to sign a collective bargaining agreement with a major corporation in 1937. This success turned Randolph into a recognized leader in the struggle for African-American rights.

A. Philip Randolph came up with the idea of holding a "**March on Washington**" in favor of jobs for African Americans. The march was scheduled to be held on July 4, 1941, when more than 100,000 participants were expected to attend. President Roosevelt did not want the image of dissatisfied African Americans marching down Washington's streets just as he was preparing the nation for war. Instead, he negotiated an agreement with Randolph, NAACP leaders and Mary McLeod Bethune of the National Youth Administration. On June 25, Roosevelt issued **Executive Order 8802.** This order "reaffirmed" that no federal agency would discriminate in its hiring practices on the grounds of race, creed (religion), color or national origin. The order further stated that any company receiving a federal government contract could not discriminate on the same grounds. Finally, the order established the Committee on Fair Employment Practices, a new federal agency to oversee its enforcement. As a result, thousands of jobs were thrown open to African-American workers. Large numbers of African Americans continued to migrate north to fill them.

During the war, the *Pittsburgh Courier* (an African-American newspaper) called for the "**Double V campaign**" or "Democracy: Victory at Home, Victory Abroad." This meant fighting against Nazism overseas and against racism on the home front. Randolph kept his "March on Washington Movement" in operation until the end of the war, in order to support African-American rights.

Nevertheless, racism continued. The armed forces themselves remained segregated. In 1943, there were major race riots in Detroit, New York, and Los Angeles.

Hispanic Americans

Because of the increased demand for workers, Congress passed the "Mexican Labor Supply Program" in 1943, to import workers from Mexico and other Latin American countries. The workers under this program became known as the *braceros*. They not only worked on farms—planting and harvesting fruits and vegetables—they also worked in factories. Federal officials recruited them in Mexico but did not oversee their working conditions once they arrived here. The *braceros* were not protected by U.S. labor laws and were paid less than the minimum wage. The program finally ended in December 1947. By then, more than 200,000 workers had officially entered the United States as *braceros*.

An estimated 500,000 Hispanic Americans served in the armed forces during the war. Prejudice against Hispanic Americans nevertheless remained high in many communities. In June 1943, armed bands of sailors and soldiers roamed the Mexican-American **barrios** (*neighborhoods*) of Los Angeles and attacked fashionable Hispanic Americans wearing baggy zoot suits. The incident became known as the "**zoot suit** **riots**".

American Indians

More than 44,000 American Indians—or 10 percent of their population—served in the armed services during the war. Many of them volunteered, while others were drafted. Nazi racist ideology especially offended them, while military service appealed to their warrior traditions. Other American Indians left their reservations to take higher paying jobs on the home front. Increased contact with the outside world affected their outlook. The federal government also took mineral resources from Indian lands during the war. The National Congress of American Indians was formed to represent all tribes in November 1944, as the war was coming to a close. After the war, critics of federal policy felt that American Indians should be treated, not as tribal groups, but as individuals like everyone else. The Indian Claims Commission was established in August 1946 to evaluate all Indian claims in an attempt to reach a final settlement.

Jewish Americans

During World War II, more than half a million Jewish Americans entered the armed services. One of the great tragedies of the period was that the United States did not permit more Jewish refugees to enter its borders. Federal law severely restricted immigration, and there were no special exceptions for refugees at that time. A bill to admit 20,000 additional German Jewish children was defeated in Congress. In May 1939, a group of German Jews sailed on a German ocean liner, the *SS St. Louis,* to Cuba. The Cuban government refused to admit them even though they had purchased visas before leaving Germany. The boat next sailed to Florida, but both the United States and Canada refused to accept the Jewish passengers. Eventually the captain reluctantly sailed back to Europe, and half of the passengers later died in German concentration camps.

The War in Europe

Although it was Japan that had attacked the United States, Roosevelt still wanted to focus American energies on defeating Germany first. He saw Nazi Germany as the most dangerous of the Axis Powers and the only one that could threaten the survival of Britain or the Soviet Union. By the time that Americans entered the war, Hitler was already in control of most of Europe and North Africa.

Hitler's Plans and the Holocaust

As Hitler had revealed in his book *Mein Kampf*, he planned to reorganize Europe along racial lines. Germans would form the new ruling class. Other peoples would be turned into slaves. Jews, Gypsies, Poles, and several other groups were to be exterminated through mass murder.

These Nazi plans led to the **Holocaust**—the systematic slaughter of millions of Jews and other peoples. This policy of mass extermination evolved gradually. One of the first steps was to spread propaganda, whipping up **anti-Semitism** (prejudice against Jews). In 1935, Germany passed the Nuremberg Laws. These deprived German Jews of citizenship, prevented them from holding jobs in the professions, and prohibited marriages between Jews and non-Jews. After *Kristallnacht* in 1938, Jewish shops were closed, Jews were made to pay a large fine, and many Jews were arrested. With the conquest of Poland in 1939, millions of Polish Jews fell into Nazi hands. They were crowded into **ghettos**—restricted areas of Polish cities, sealed off from the outside, where many died from malnutrition, exposure, and disease. In 1941, all Jews were required to wear a yellow Star of David on their clothing. When German troops advanced into Russia in 1941, special firing squads were set up to kill Jewish residents through mass shootings. At the Wannsee Conference in Berlin at the beginning of 1942, Nazi leaders finally decided on the "**Final Solution**": the complete extermination of all the Jews in Europe. Special extermination camps were constructed, such as **Auschwitz** in southern Poland. Jews, gypsies and other victims across Nazi-occupied Europe were herded into tightly packed cattle cars and carried by train to these special camps. When they arrived, the tired and thirsty victims were shaved and stripped and led into what they were told were "showers," where they were gassed with Zyklon B, a form of cyanide. The victims included men, women, and children. Their bodies were then burned in large ovens. A few were spared to work themselves to death maintaining the camps or otherwise helping, as slave laborers, in the German war effort. Surrounded by electrified barbed wire and barking dogs, sleeping on crowded bunks in barely heated wooden barracks, and forced to stand for hours in meaningless roll calls in threadbare garments in sweltering heat or the freezing cold, these hapless camp inmates were beaten, starved, whipped, tortured, and hanged. Six million Jews and an equal number of others—Poles, Russians, Gypsies, political opponents, prisoners of war, homosexuals, Jehovah's Witnesses—perished under these cruel and barbaric conditions, which many consider to be the worst atrocity in human history.

U.S. Policy during the Holocaust

In 1942, Roosevelt summoned Jewish leaders to the White House when he received proof of Nazi measures to murder European Jews. However, few concrete steps were taken. The State Department turned down an offer to ransom 70,000 Romanian Jews. The Secretary of the Treasury, himself Jewish, was shocked. At his insistence, the government created the War Refugee Board, a new agency that saved the lives of several hundred thousand Jews in Hungary in 1944. Even so, some U.S. military officials rejected a proposal to bomb Auschwitz. Americans did not grasp the enormity of the crime until their troops began liberating the concentration camps.

The Historian's Apprentice

1. Use information from the websites of the U.S. Holocaust Memorial Museum, Yad Vashem, or other sources to research a topic about the Holocaust and present an oral report to your class. Possible topics include: the Warsaw Ghetto uprising, the Wannsee Conference, Auschwitz, daily life in a concentration camp, forced labor, children, Jewish resistance, medical experiments, non-Jewish heroes who helped Jews, and the trial of Adolf Eichmann.
2. Report on an example of genocide that has happened in the past ten years or that is happening today. What steps should nations take to ensure that acts of ethnic hatred and genocide do not ever occur again?
3. The number of Holocaust survivors is shrinking, but it still may be possible to interview a volunteer Holocaust survivor. The U.S. Holocaust Museum has a list of questions you might ask on their website. For example: please describe your life before the Holocaust; do you remember anti-Semitism when you were growing up; did you live in a ghetto or concentration camp; how did you cope with hunger; what happened to your family; were you liberated by Allied troops?

The Allied Campaign against Germany

President Roosevelt kept the American war effort focused on defeating Germany first.

Hitler Invades the Soviet Union

By late 1941, Hitler was the master of much of Europe with only Britain opposing him. He then committed his two greatest blunders: first, he invaded the Soviet Union in June 1941; second, he declared war on the United States in December 1941. Hitler had always planned to attack the Soviet Union, and he believed that the German army would quickly defeat the Soviets so that he could safely turn to an invasion of Britain without fear of attack from Germany's eastern side. At first the Nazi invasion of the Soviet Union made rapid progress, right according to plan. But by late 1941, the German advance halted just short of Moscow, stopped by the bitter cold of the Russian winter and insufficient supplies of gasoline.

The Battle for the Atlantic

While German tanks and troops were battling the Soviets, German **U-boats** (*submarines*) were causing havoc in the Atlantic Ocean and along the Eastern seaboard of the United States by sinking tankers and disrupting the American coastal trade. In April and May, German U-boats even surfaced off the beaches of Florida. Keeping the sea lanes across the Atlantic open was of vital concern to the Allies. They allowed Americans to send supplies to Britain. Stricter use of the **convoy system**, in which merchant ships sailed together, surrounded by an escort of better-designed warships and increased air support, as well as breaking the secret Nazi code for sending messages, finally reduced Allied shipping losses.

North Africa and Italy

Roosevelt and his military advisers were anxious to open up a "Second Front" in Western Europe to relieve German pressure on the Soviet army.

A Soviet soldier raising the Red Flag at Stalingrad

They began sending men and supplies to Britain to prepare for a grand assault. Churchill, however, remembered Britain's heavy losses on the battlefields of France during World War I. He preferred to wait for the Western Allies to build up more forces, for the Americans to have more combat experience, and for the Germans to exhaust themselves fighting the Soviets before he launched an invasion of France.

Churchill therefore proposed postponing the invasion. Instead, he wanted the Americans to help the British in North Africa, where the British were already fighting German and Italian troops. Roosevelt's leading military advisers were outraged by this proposal and recommended that the United States turn its focus on defeating Japan. But Roosevelt would not stray from his "Germany First" strategy. He agreed with Churchill that American forces were not yet ready for a landing in France. Because it was important for them to engage in combat to maintain public support for the war, Roosevelt accepted Churchill's alternative. Stalin was infuriated, even though Roosevelt promised to open a second front against Germany in France as soon as possible.

In November 1942, U.S. and British troops landed on the coasts of Morocco and Algeria. Much of the fighting in the North African campaign took place between tanks in the desert. Eventually, German and Italian forces were trapped in Tunisia, and 275,000 of them surrendered to the Allies in May 1943.

After defeating German forces in North Africa, American and British forces crossed the Mediterranean Sea to land in **Sicily** in July 1943. Allied success in Sicily led to the overthrow of Mussolini by his opponents. In September 1943, a new Italian anti-Fascist government surrendered to the Allies. By then, however, German troops had taken up most of the positions previously held by the Italian army. The Allies launched an amphibious attack on **Salerno**, on the mainland of Italy, on September 9, 1943. American generals expected the landing to be an easy one, but they met with fierce resistance from German troops and casualties were high.

The Allied Invasion of Italy, 1943

Stalingrad

Meanwhile, German and Soviet troops had been locked in deadly combat in the city of **Stalingrad** in the Soviet Union (August 1942–January 1943). This battle proved to be the turning point of the war in Europe. By now, the Soviet army had developed new tactics to counter German *Blitzkrieg* warfare. They fought close to Nazi lines, making German airpower ineffective, or fought from buildings, which could not be taken by tanks. They also had their own effective tanks and weaponry. In November 1942, a Soviet offensive encircled an entire German army. Hitler ordered his generals not to retreat from Stalingrad under any circumstances. After running out of food and ammunition, the last 100,000 men surrendered at the end of January 1943, in violation of Hitler's orders. Only 6,000 of them eventually survived Soviet imprisonment.

Tehran

Roosevelt crossed the Atlantic to meet with Churchill and Stalin at **Tehran** in November 1943. Against Churchill's advice, Roosevelt promised Stalin that the Western Allies would launch their long-awaited invasion of France by the spring of 1944.

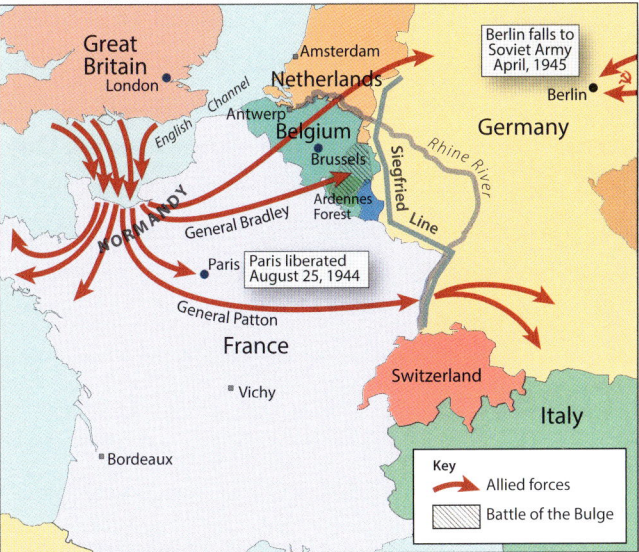

The Allied Advance, 1944–1945

Stalin in turn promised to declare war on Japan once Germany had surrendered.

D-Day

In early 1944, American and British troops began preparing for a massive amphibious invasion of France, known as "Operation Overlord." **General Dwight D. Eisenhower** was placed in supreme command of the Allied invasion. Large numbers of men, tanks, motorized troop carriers, and artillery gathered in Britain. Allied airplanes conducted bombing missions night and day to weaken German positions. The Western Allies even took steps to fool the German army into thinking their main assault would be farther north at Calais. Bad weather delayed the launching of the invasion. Finally, on "**D-Day**," June 6, 1944, more than 4,400 ships and other landing craft crossed the English Channel to bring Allied troops to the beaches of Normandy, France.

American troops landing in Normandy on D-Day

The Western Advance

Once they had established a foothold in France, the Allies moved quickly eastward. Paris was liberated just two months later with the help of the French resistance and the "Free French." Allied forces advanced even faster than they had expected. However, once some of their divisions reached the Ardennes Forest in northeastern France, the Germans launched a surprise counterattack. Hitler hoped he could divide and defeat the American and British armies, forcing each of them to sue for a separate peace. Then Germany would have a free hand to fight the Soviets. The "**Battle of the Bulge**" was fought with great ferocity for six weeks from December 16, 1944, until the end of January 1945. It saw the bloodiest action by U.S. forces in the war, with 19,000 killed, 62,000 wounded, and 26,000 missing. For the first time during World War II, African-American troops were sent into combat. In the end, vigorous American resistance, bitterly cold weather, Allied reinforcements, and unfavorable terrain caused the German offensive to collapse. Hitler's last attempt to bring the war to a successful conclusion failed. The Western Allies now advanced to the Siegfried Line, a series of defensive fortifications and bunkers along Germany's western frontier. In March 1945, they crossed the Rhine River.

New German Weapons

In June 1944, the Nazis began sending remote-controlled, unmanned jets to London and other Allied targets as bombs. In September, they also started firing V-2 rockets, the first liquid-propellant rockets. Hitler hoped these new weapons would save his empire. However, they were developed too late in the war to affect its final outcome.

The Collapse of Nazi Germany

While American, British and Free French forces were invading Nazi Germany from the west, Soviet forces continued their advance from the east. By the summer of 1944, the Soviet army had crossed into eastern Poland. Polish patriots rose up in resistance against their Nazi rulers during the Warsaw

Chapter 12 | World War II: America's Darkest and Brightest Hour

uprising of August 1944. Their rebellion was savagely repressed. Most of the city was destroyed by the retreating Nazis as Soviet troops, on Stalin's orders, watched passively from a distance. The Soviet army resumed its advance into Poland at the end of January, crossed the German border in February, and occupied Vienna in March. By April, the Soviet army reached Berlin, the capital of Germany. Hitler committed suicide at his underground bunker in Berlin on April 30, and Germany's military leaders surrendered to the Allies on May 7–8—known as **V-E Day**, or "Victory in Europe." President Roosevelt died of a heart attack on April 12, 1945—just two and a half weeks before Hitler committed suicide.

The Pacific Theater: The War against Japan

Back in December 1941 and early in 1942, the Japanese had made striking gains after their attack on Pearl Harbor. Japan had successfully conquered Hong Kong, Burma, Malaya, Borneo, the Solomon Islands, Java, and Singapore.

The Fall of the Philippines

Japanese forces also attacked the Philippines. General **Douglas MacArthur**, the U.S. Commander in the Far East, retreated to **Bataan** (a peninsula near the capital at Manila). MacArthur was personally ordered to leave for Australia. His troops remained in the Philippines, fighting bravely until they finally surrendered in April 1942. The Japanese forced their exhausted and half-starved American and Filipino prisoners-of-war to undertake the 80-mile "**Bataan Death March**" in the heat. Guards beat and bayoneted the prisoners, who were given no food and little water. Several thousand died along the way.

American war prisoners

Coral Sea and Midway

In April 1942, Americans cheered when they received the news that the famous aviator James Doolittle had led a daring daytime bombing mission over Tokyo, the capital of Japan. The following month, American and Japanese aircraft carriers fought one another in the **Battle of the Coral Sea**. It was the first time in history that aircraft carriers fought while separated by more than 100 miles of ocean. Planes from each side flew and attacked the other side's ships. Japanese bombers sank one American aircraft carrier and severely damaged a second.

In June 1942, the Japanese attempted to lure the U.S. Pacific fleet into a trap near the island of **Midway**. Their aim was to destroy all U.S. aircraft carriers operating in the Pacific and to capture the U.S. naval base on Midway. However, the Americans had deciphered part of the Japanese secret naval code and knew that they were planning a major attack on Midway. U.S. Admiral Chester Nimitz assembled several carriers and had rapid repairs made to the carrier that had been damaged at the Battle of the Coral Sea. The American carriers moved into position just northeast of Midway Island without detection. The Japanese began their attack on Midway not knowing that the U.S. Navy was nearby. Just when the Japanese carriers were least defensible, American dive-bombers suddenly appeared in the sky and bombed their decks. The Japanese lost four large aircraft carriers, while the Americans lost only one. The **Battle of Midway** was the turning point of the war in the Pacific.

In the distance below, a Japanese aircraft carrier burns following a U.S. airstrike at the Battle of Midway

World War II in the Pacific

Guadalcanal

The Japanese had occupied islands across the Pacific to create a defensive perimeter around their new conquests. In **Guadalcanal**, at the southwestern end of the Solomon Islands, they began building an airfield to protect their bases and enable their planes to threaten Australia. Two months after the Battle of Midway, American marines landed on the island, which they took by surprise. Despite a series of fierce land and naval attacks, the Japanese failed to retake Guadalcanal.

The Japanese Empire Crumbles

By 1943, the tide had turned in the Pacific. American forces began "island-hopping"—liberating some Pacific islands from Japanese control while bypassing others. In April 1944, they landed in Western New Guinea; early in 1945, they finally regained control of the Philippines. Once Germany was defeated, the United States was able to turn its full fury on Japan. Preparations began for a massive invasion of Japan's home islands. In April 1945, American forces landed in Okinawa, a large island only 340 miles from the Japanese home islands. After the German surrender in May 1945, the Soviet Union also declared war on Japan and invaded Manchuria.

Dawn of the Atomic Age

Just before the Nazi invasion of Poland, the famous scientist **Albert Einstein**—a German-Jewish refugee and a pacifist—wrote a personal letter to President Roosevelt recommending that the United States develop an atomic bomb. Einstein believed Nazi scientists were already working on one. "A single bomb of this type," wrote Einstein, "carried by boat and exploded in a port, might very well destroy the whole port together with some of the surrounding territory...." Einstein wrote to Roosevelt again in 1940 about signs of Nazi efforts to develop a weapon from uranium, based on a nuclear chain reaction.

Shortly after the attack on Pearl Harbor, the U.S. government launched its top-secret "**Manhattan Project**." Its goal was to develop an atomic bomb. Physicist Robert Oppenheimer was placed in charge of the secret weapons laboratory at Los Alamos, New Mexico, where the first atomic bomb was built. A team of scientists was assembled, which included refugee scientists who had fled Nazi Germany and Fascist Italy. By 1945, 6,000 people were working at the secret laboratories in Los Alamos. After the government invested $2 billion on the project, the first atomic bomb was successfully tested in the New Mexican desert in July 1945.

America Drops Two Atomic Bombs on Japan

The Manhattan Project was so secret that the new President, **Harry S. Truman**, only learned of it after Roosevelt's death. Fighting in the Pacific had been fierce and the Japanese were expected to fight even more tirelessly to defend their home islands. A planned Allied invasion of Japan was expected to cost close to a million American lives. To make such a costly invasion unnecessary, Truman turned to the new atomic bomb. He rejected the idea of exploding the bomb in the ocean, since it was unlikely to persuade the Japanese to surrender. Instead, Truman selected two cities that were centers of Japanese military production as targets. On August 6, the first atomic bomb was exploded over **Hiroshima.** Three days later, a second bomb was exploded over **Nagasaki**. As many as 100,000 people were killed in each explosion. Each city was totally destroyed. Japan surrendered on **V-J Day**, just after the second explosion, once the United States agreed to permit the Japanese Emperor to remain on his throne.

The Historian's Apprentice

In the book *Hiroshima*, reporter John Hersey tells the stories of six survivors from the blast. Here, a survivor runs through the city in search of his family immediately after the explosion:

"He was the only person making his way into the city; he met hundreds and hundreds who were fleeing, and every one of them seemed to be hurt in some way. The eyebrows of some were burned off and skin hung from their faces and hands. Others, because of pain, held their arms up as if carrying something in both hands. Some were vomiting as they walked. Many were naked or in shreds of clothing. On some undressed bodies, the burns had made patterns—of undershirt straps and suspenders and, on the skin of some women (since white repelled the heat from the bomb and dark clothes absorbed it and conducted it to the skin), the shapes of flowers they had had on their kimonos. Many, although injured themselves, supported relatives who were worse off. Almost all had their heads bowed, looked straight ahead, were silent, and showed no expression whatsoever."

—John Hersey, *Hiroshima* (1946)

1. Imagine you are a military adviser to President Truman at the beginning of August 1945. Write a short paper stating your recommendation on whether or not to use the atomic bomb on Japan.
2. Hersey wrote his account in 1946, less than one year after the war ended. Popular feelings against Japan were still high. What impact do you think his account had on American readers?
3. In your opinion, was the use of the atomic bomb justified?

The Consequences of World War II

World War II had many far-reaching effects. More than 50 million people lost their lives. Much of Europe, Asia and North Africa lay in ruins. The collapse of European and Japanese power left the United States and the Soviet Union as two superpowers in command of the world. The weakened condition of the older European powers, such as Britain and France, encouraged independence movements in their former colonies. Even the United States granted the Philippines its independence in 1946. Finally, the war led to the development of new weapons, such as jet aircraft, missiles, and the atomic bomb.

The Attempt to Promote International Justice at the Nuremberg Trials

The Allied leaders put surviving Nazi leaders on trial for "crimes against humanity"—making it clear that individuals are responsible for their crimes, even when committed with government authority in times of war. The liberation of the concentration camps by Allied forces at the end of the war added to the evidence of Nazi crimes and revealed the full extent of Nazi brutality.

Just over 20 of the leading Nazis were put on trial before a tribunal of Allied judges in **Nuremberg**, Germany, between 1945 and 1946. The accused included Herman Goering, former head of the Luftwaffe and one of the top Nazi leaders. They were charged with starting the war and committing such atrocities as the extermination of the Jews and the mistreatment of prisoners of war. Many of the accused Nazis tried to defend themselves by claiming that they had only been following orders. Most were convicted and sentenced to be hanged or imprisoned for life. Goering committed suicide in his cell just hours before his scheduled execution.

The Occupation of Germany and Japan

Germany was occupied by the United States, Britain, France, and the Soviet Union. Each Allied Power established its own occupation zone. The capital city of Berlin was similarly divided into separate sectors. The occupying powers introduced re-education programs, explaining the evils of Nazi beliefs to the German public to counter Nazi propaganda.

The United States also occupied Japan. General MacArthur was placed in charge of rebuilding that country. Important changes were imposed to make Japan less aggressive and imperialistic. Japan's overseas empire was taken away, and its military leaders were put on trial. Japan renounced the use of nuclear weapons and the waging of war. Japan was forbidden to have an army or navy, except for peacekeeping purposes. A new constitution went into effect in May 1947, turning Japan into a democracy.

Birth of the United Nations

One of the most important consequences of the war was the creation of the **United Nations**. Despite the failure of the League of Nations, the victorious Allies were committed to forming a new international peacekeeping organization. Roosevelt, who had served under President Wilson, was determined to ensure that the United States participated in this new body. He therefore strove to avoid all of Wilson's previous mistakes. For example, Roosevelt kept Republican Congressmen involved at every step. He continually negotiated with Soviet diplomats to make sure that the Soviet Union joined the United Nations, too.

Steps in the Formation of the U.N.

Early in the war, Roosevelt and Churchill agreed that the League of Nations needed to be replaced. In January 1942, 26 nations signed the United Nations Declaration, affirming their support for the ideals of the Atlantic Charter. A resolution was passed in the U.S. Senate in 1943, calling for the creation of a new peacekeeping organization. Roosevelt continued to discuss formation of the United Nations with Stalin at Tehran and Yalta. In the autumn of 1944, a conference was held in **Dumbarton Oaks** outside of Washington, D.C. There the leading Allied powers agreed on the general structure of the United Nations, including the formation of its "Security Council." The **United Nations Charter** was finally completed at the **San Francisco Conference** (April to June 1945), in which 50 nations participated. The United States became the first nation to sign the U.N. Charter.

> **Mary McLeod Bethune** was an African-American civil rights leader born in South Carolina in 1875. She moved to Daytona, Florida, where she opened a school for African-American girls in 1904. Later her school became a high school, then a junior college, and finally Bethune-Cookman College. Bethune became President of

the National Association of Colored Women (NACW), and helped found the National Council of Negro Women in 1935. She was appointed to national commissions by Presidents Coolidge and Hoover. As a friend of Eleanor and Franklin Roosevelt, Bethune later became a prominent member of—and the only woman on—the "Black Cabinet" of African-American community leaders that advised the Roosevelts on issues affecting African Americans. In 1945, McLeod was appointed by Truman as a delegate and adviser on interracial relations at the San Francisco Conference, which drafted the United Nations Charter. Bethune was the only black female delegate to attend; no other nation sent a woman of color to the conference.

Aims and Structure of the United Nations

According to its Charter, the major aims of the United Nations are the maintenance of peace and the encouragement of friendship and cooperation among nations. The United Nations also seeks to eliminate hunger, disease, and ignorance in the world. Like the earlier League of Nations, the United Nations relies on the concept of **collective security**. Unlike the League of Nations, the United Nations has its own peacekeeping forces, contributed by member nations.

All member nations belong to the **General Assembly**. Five nations serve as permanent members of the **Security Council.** These permanent members—the United States, Great Britain, Russia, China and France—enjoy special powers, including veto power over all U.N. peacekeeping operations. There are also ten nonpermanent members elected for two-year terms.

Other important bodies in the United Nations are the International Court of Justice and the Economic and Social Council. The U.N. Secretariat manages this complex organization. Its head, the **U.N. Secretary-General**, acts as spokesperson for the United Nations. Other institutions of the United Nations, such as UNESCO, support programs encouraging economic development and social reform.

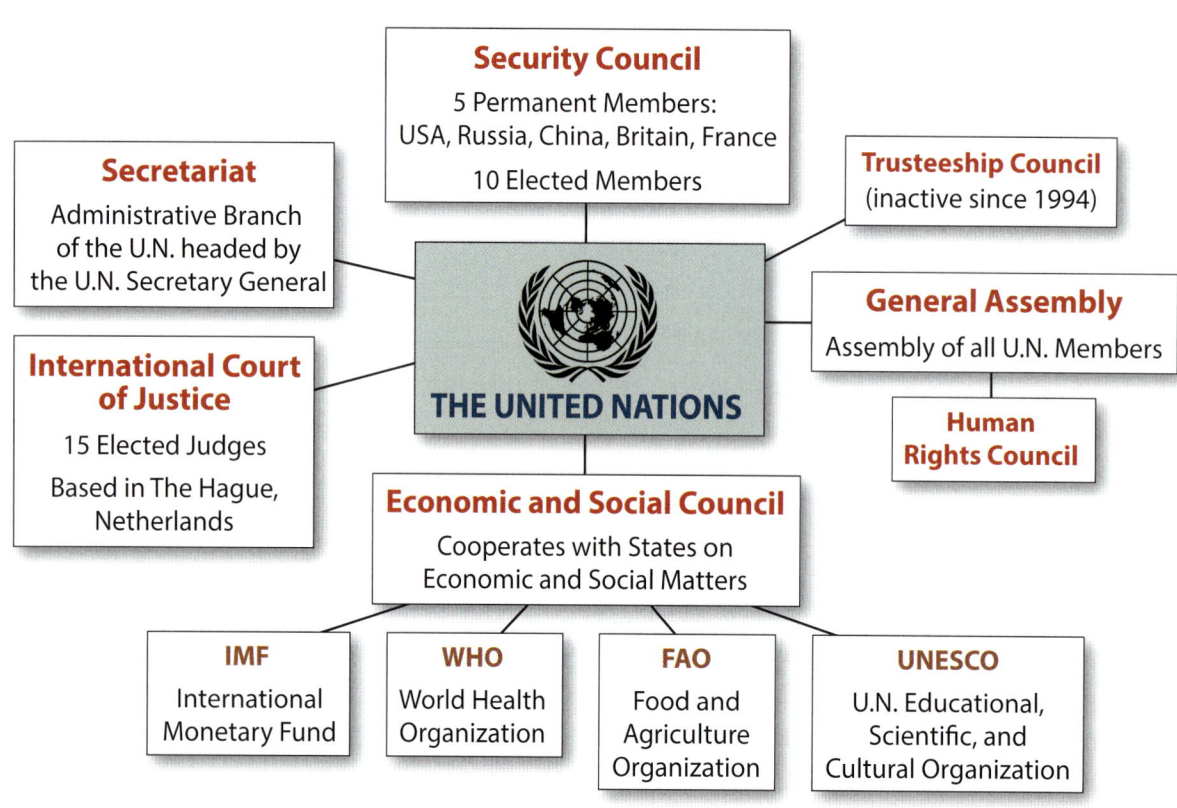

The Historian's Apprentice

Article 1
The Purposes of the United Nations are:

1. To maintain international peace and security, and to that end: to take effective collective measures for the prevention and removal of threats to the peace, and for the suppression of acts of aggression or other breaches of the peace, and to bring about by peaceful means, and in conformity with the principles of justice and international law, adjustment or settlement of international disputes or situations which might lead to a breach of the peace;
2. To develop friendly relations among nations based on respect for the principle of equal rights and self-determination of peoples, and to take other appropriate measures to strengthen universal peace;
3. To achieve international co-operation in solving international problems of an economic, social, cultural, or humanitarian character, and in promoting and encouraging respect for human rights and for fundamental freedoms for all without distinction as to race, sex, language, or religion; and
4. To be a center for harmonizing the actions of nations in the attainment of these common ends.

—Charter of the United Nations (1945)

▸ Which of these purposes do you think is most important? Why?
▸ How did the structure of the United Nations differ from the League of Nations?
▸ Do you think the organization of the United Nations is well adapted to its purposes?
▸ Why was Roosevelt more successful than Wilson in winning U.S. support for the U.N.?

Universal Declaration of Human Rights

After the barbarities of the Holocaust and World War II, one of the first acts of the new United Nations General Assembly was to draft the **Universal Declaration of Human Rights**. Eleanor Roosevelt was chairwoman of the committee that drafted the Declaration. Its 30 articles define those rights to which all human beings are entitled, including the right to life, the prohibition of slavery and torture, freedom of religion, freedom of movement, and freedom of association. It also establishes social, economic and cultural rights, such as the right to work, the right to an adequate standard of living, and the right to an education.

Focus on Florida

Almost as soon as war was declared, German U-boats began attacking ships in Florida's harbors and along its coasts. In 1942, 24 Allied oil tankers and merchant ships were sunk in Florida waters. Hundreds of sailors and large quantities of cargo, especially oil, were lost. A team of German saboteurs with explosives even landed on Florida's shores in that year. They were arrested by the FBI and later executed.

Florida played a vital role in the preparation and training of troops, sailors, and pilots. Florida had 172 military training centers, with air stations, naval piers and port facilities, bombing ranges, airfields, and army training grounds. More than 2 million Americans from all over the United States trained in Florida. When Lieutenant Colonel "Jimmy" Doolittle and his squadron bombed Tokyo in 1942, Floridians took great pride in the fact that Doolittle and his men had trained at Eglin Field near Valparaiso.

The economic impact of the war on Florida was immense. Between 1940 and 1945, the federal government spent more than $98 billion in the Florida economy to further the war effort. They bought hotels, such as the Breakers at Palm Beach and the Biltmore in Coral Gables, and rented tens of thousands of hotel rooms for troops. The Breakers became a military hospital. Camp Blanding became the fourth largest city in Florida. Shipyards began building "Liberty Ships." Nine million civilian workers flocked to Florida to work in construction and agriculture. Florida increased its agricultural production, especially of citrus fruits. Farmers began using a new pesticide—DDT.

Millions of Americans spent time in Florida during the war. This had a profound effect on the state by encouraging both tourism and population growth. In 1940, there were 1,897,414 people living in Florida. By 1950, this number had grown to 2,771,305—an increase of 46%, in a single decade.

276 Chapter 12 | World War II: America's Darkest and Brightest Hour

Review Cards

Rise of Nazism

- **Adolf Hitler,** the leader of the Nazi Party, believed that Germans were a superior race.
- After the Great Depression raised unemployment in Germany, the Nazis gained in popularity. In 1933, Hitler was appointed Chancellor. The German legislature gave Hitler emergency dictatorial powers after the *Reichstag* fire.
- All German institutions were brought under Nazi control or closed. The army took an oath of loyalty to Hitler. Opponents were sent to concentration camps or killed.

The Failure of the League of Nations and Appeasement

- The **League of Nations** failed to stop aggressors. It did nothing to stop Hitler from moving troops into the Rhineland, Japan from attacking Manchuria, Italy from attacking Ethiopia, or Germany, Italy, and the Soviet Union from acting in the Spanish Civil War.
- **Failure of Appeasement:** The Western powers also failed to stop the aggressive acts of the Fascist powers. At the **Munich Conference** in 1938, Britain and France attempted to appease Hitler by giving him part of Czechoslovakia. Hitler concluded that the Western powers were weak and would not stop him.

World War II Begins in Europe

- Nazi Invasion of Poland: After Hitler signed the Nazi-Soviet Pact with Stalin, he ordered the invasion of Poland in September 1939. France and Britain then declared war on Germany.
- *Blitzkrieg* Warfare: Germany had developed new tactics based on the coordinated use of airplanes, tanks, and motorized troop carriers. The rapid advance of German forces became known as *Blitzkrieg* (lightning warfare).
- Fall of France: In the spring of 1940, Germany attacked Denmark and Norway and marched through Holland and Belgium to defeat France. The British expeditionary force escaped at Dunkirk by sailing across the English Channel.
- "Battle of Britain": Hitler tried to use his air force to bomb the British into submission but failed. British fighter pilots attacked German planes. Radar helped the British defend themselves by pinpointing German attacks.

U.S. Neutrality

- The Neutrality Acts of 1935–1937 were aimed at keeping the United States out of war in Europe. The first Neutrality Acts prohibited Americans from sending arms to countries at war. The Neutrality Act of 1937 prohibited Americans from traveling on the ships of nations at war, but allowed Americans to sell non-military goods to countries at war on a **"cash-and-carry"** basis. The buyer had to pay cash and transport the goods.
- **Quarantine Speech:** When Japan invaded China in 1937, Roosevelt tested American public opinion with his "Quarantine Speech." He proposed isolating nations that violated treaties and attacked civilians.
- **The Neutrality Act of 1939** expanded "cash-and-carry" to include the sale of arms. Roosevelt was concerned to help the British, who faced Nazi Germany alone.
- In March 1941, Roosevelt pushed the **"Lend-Lease" Act** through Congress: the United States could supply arms to the British, who could pay for or return them after the war.
- **Four Freedoms:** Roosevelt promised Americans freedom of speech and expression, freedom of religion, freedom from want, and freedom from fear.
- **Atlantic Charter:** Roosevelt met Churchill in the Atlantic in August 1941 where they agreed to the Atlantic Charter, defining their post-war goals.

The Attack on Pearl Harbor

- In September 1940, Japan allied with Germany and Italy. Japan had only limited oil supplies after a U.S. embargo was imposed. They wanted to seize the oil fields of the Dutch East Indies, which would bring the United States into the war. They decided to attack the United States first and launched a surprise attack on the U.S. Pacific Fleet at **Pearl Harbor** on **December 7, 1941**—"a date that will live in infamy."
- Germany and Italy also declared war on the United States.

The War in Europe

- Roosevelt decided to defeat "Germany first" since he believed that Germany was the greater danger. Churchill persuaded Roosevelt to delay the invasion of France. Instead, British and American forces landed in **North Africa** in 1942, where they defeated German and Italian forces. Afterwards, the Allies conquered **Sicily** in Italy. When Mussolini's Fascist government collapsed, the Allies decided to invade mainland Italy. They landed at **Salerno,** where they met with fierce German resistance. Meanwhile, Soviet forces defeated a large German army at **Stalingrad,** often seen as the turning point of the war.
- American and British forces landed on the beaches of **Normandy** on June 6, 1944, known as **D-Day.** General **Dwight D. Eisenhower** acted as Supreme Commander.
- The Western Allies advanced rapidly and liberated Paris two months later. Allied forces faced a German counterattack at the **Battle of the Bulge.** The Nazi counterattack failed and American, British and French forces advanced into Germany from the west while Soviet armies advanced from the east. Soviet forces entered Berlin and Hitler committed suicide at the end of April 1945. Germany surrendered on May 7, 1945, known as **V-E Day.**

The War in the Pacific

- In the Pacific, the Japanese advanced into Southeast Asia and the Pacific after their attack on Pearl Harbor. In the Philippines, MacArthur retreated from Manila; surrendering U.S. forces went on the **"Bataan Death March."**
- Japanese and U.S. aircraft carriers fought at the **Battle of the Coral Sea** in May 1942; a few months later, the U.S. sank four Japanese aircraft carriers at the **Battle of Midway** (1943), the turning point of the war in the Pacific. American forces then began a process of island-hopping, pushing the Japanese back island by island.
- The U.S. government invested $2 billion in the **"Manhattan Project,"** a secret project to develop the **atomic bomb.** U.S. leaders feared Nazi Germany might develop such a bomb first. American scientists tested the bomb in New Mexico in 1945. Atomic bombs were dropped on the cities of **Hiroshima** and **Nagasaki** in August 1945. Japan surrendered on **V-J Day.**

Florida in World War II

- German U-boats sank ships near Florida's shoreline. German saboteurs were captured and executed.
- Florida became a training ground for the armed services. **Camp Blanding** became the fourth largest city in Florida. The U.S. government rented hotel rooms and other facilities to house troops, and spent $98 billion in Florida to further the war effort. Many of the people who trained or worked in Florida during the war came back later to visit or to live.
- Florida producers sold their orange juice, cattle, and other products to the armed forces. The use of the insecticide DDT to kill mosquitos was introduced during the war. Florida's shipyards helped build "Liberty Ships."

The Home Front

- The **Selective Service System** oversaw the draft. Eventually 15 million Americans served in the armed forces during the war. Women enlisted as **WACS** or **WAVES.**
- The **War Production Board** was placed in charge of wartime production. Factories began making tanks, "Liberty Ships," and other wartime goods. Essential goods like steel, copper, and aluminum were reserved for military purposes. Even food was **rationed.** People grew their own fruits and vegetables in makeshift **"Liberty Gardens."**
- Increased personal income taxes and the sale of **war bonds** helped pay for the war.
- The **Office of War Information** was in charge of maintaining popular support for the war.
- **A. Philip Randolph** planned a **"March on Washington"** to assure jobs for African Americans. To avoid the march, President Roosevelt signed **Executive Order 8802,** throwing all federal jobs and jobs with defense contractors open to African-American employees. More than a million African Americans served in the armed forces during the war, in segregated units. Through the **"Double V" campaign,** African Americans sought victory over Nazism abroad and over racism at home.
- Mexicans came to the United States to take wartime jobs. The *Braceros* program recruited Hispanic workers in Mexico and other Latin American countries to work as migrant field workers or in factories in the United States. In Los Angeles, fashionable Hispanic young men were attacked in the "zoot suit" riots.
- A large proportion of American Indians served during the war. **"Navajo code talkers"** communicated in a code based on the Navajo language, which was never broken by the Japanese.
- **Japanese Americans** on the West Coast were forcibly removed by **Executive Order 9066** and sent to internment camps further inland. President Roosevelt's order was upheld by the Supreme Court in *Korematsu v. United States* (1944). Most historians now agree that the relocation was motivated by racial prejudice rather than by any evidence of disloyalty.

The Holocaust

- Nazi **anti-Semitism** (*hatred of Jewish people*) led to the Holocaust. At first, German Jews were barred from many jobs and from intermarrying non-Jews. Jewish synagogues and businesses were closed and Jews had to pay a fine after *Kristallnacht* in 1938.
- After Germany conquered Poland, Jews from Germany and Eastern Europe were forced into **ghettos**—crowded, sealed-off sections of cities where people died of starvation and disease. After 1941, all Jews had to wear a yellow Jewish star on their clothing.
- Early in 1942, Nazis adopted the **"Final Solution"**: the murdering of all the Jews in Europe. Trains carried Jews to **Auschwitz** and other extermination camps where they were gassed and their bodies were burned. Those who were not immediately killed were starved, tortured, and worked to death. Six million Jews were killed, as well as an equal number of non-Jews (gypsies, Poles, Russians, political prisoners, homosexuals, individuals with disabilities, and others).

Consequences of World War II

- Nuremberg Trials: Nazi leaders were tried by an international tribunal of Allied judges for "Crimes against Humanity." Most of the accused were executed.
- Germany was divided into four occupation zones; Japan was occupied by the United States.
- The League of Nations was replaced by the **United Nations,** a new peacekeeping organization. The United Nations consists of the **Security Council, General Assembly, Secretariat,** and several other bodies. **Mary McLeod Bethune** assisted in its creation at the San Francisco Conference in 1945. The U.N. General Assembly drafted the **Universal Declaration of Human Rights.**

Chapter 12 | World War II: America's Darkest and Brightest Hour

What Do You Know?

SS.912.A.6.1

1. The political cartoon on the left appeared in England in December 1919. What was the main idea of this cartoon?

   A. The League of Nations should be replaced by the United Nations.

   B. The League of Nations should act more firmly in resisting acts of aggression.

   C. The League of Nations gives too much power to small countries like Belgium.

   D. The League of Nations is weak because the United States has failed to become a member.

THE GAP IN THE BRIDGE

SS.912.A.6.1

2. The diagram on the left provides details about Europe in the 1930s. Which phrase completes the diagram?

   A. French Responses to the Rise of Nazism

   B. Examples of German-Italian Cooperation

   C. Important Successes of the League of Nations

   D. Ways in Which Hitler Violated the Treaty of Versailles

[Diagram: Rearmed Germany, Sent troops into the Rhineland, Annexed Austria 1938, Took the Sudetenland — ?]

SS.912.A.6.2

3. The newspaper headlines below describe several laws passed by the U.S. Congress.

What common goal did the laws announced in these headlines share?

A. to maintain freedom of the open seas

B. to direct all sales of arms through the League of Nations

C. to keep America from being drawn into a war in Europe

D. to limit U.S. trade to countries in the Western Hemisphere

Chapter 12 | World War II: America's Darkest and Brightest Hour

SS.912.A.6.2

4. President Franklin Roosevevelt made the statement below in his annual message to Congress on January 6, 1941.

> I also ask this Congress for authority and for funds sufficient to manufacture additional munitions and war supplies of many kinds, to be turned over to those nations which are now in actual war with aggressor nations. Our most useful and immediate role is to act as an arsenal for them as well as for ourselves. They do not need man power, but they do need billions of dollars' worth of the weapons of defense. The time is near when they will not be able to pay for them all in ready cash. We cannot, and we will not, tell them that they must surrender, merely because of present inability to pay for the weapons which we know they must have.

What measure did President Roosevelt urge Congress to pass in this message?

   A. Neutrality Act
   B. Quarantine Act
   C. Lend-Lease Act
   D. Exchange of arms for leases to bases

SS.912.A.6.1

5. The statement below was made by Admiral Osami Nagano at the Imperial Conference of September 6, 1941 in Tokyo, Japan.

> From the standpoint of Imperial General Headquarters, based on the assumption that a peaceful solution has not been found and war is inevitable, the Empire's oil supply, as well as the stockpiles of many other important war materials, is decreasing day by day with the result that the national defense power is gradually diminishing. If this deplorable situation is left unchecked, I believe that, after a lapse of some time, the nation's vitality will deteriorate and ultimately fall into dire straits.

What event was planned to solve the problem identified by Admiral Nagano?

   A. attack on Pearl Harbor
   B. invasion of the Soviet Union
   C. dropping of the atomic bomb
   D. use of V-2 rockets against cities

SS.912.A.6.1

6. How did methods of warfare in World War II differ from those in World War I?

   A. Soldiers spent most of their time in trenches to avoid machine-gun fire.
   B. Because of a shortage of manpower, women fought overseas in combat roles.
   C. German submarines frequently attacked British and American shipping.
   D. Airplane, tank, and troop movements were coordinated for rapid advances.

SS.912.A.6.1

7. Which of the following shows the correct sequence of events in World War II?

   A. Pearl Harbor; Battle of Midway; D-Day; VE-Day; VJ-Day

   B. Pearl Harbor; Battle of Midway; VJ-Day; D-Day; VE-Day;

   C. Battle of Midway; D-Day; VE-Day; Pearl Harbor; VJ-Day

   D. D-Day; VE-Day; Pearl Harbor; Battle of Midway; VJ-Day

SS.912.A.6.1

8. The map below shows Western Europe from June 1944 to May 1945.

   Based on the map, what conclusion can be made about the Allied campaign in France in 1944–1945?

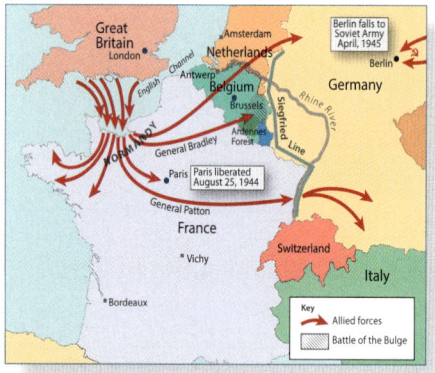

   A. Soviet air power over France contributed to the success of the Allies in the liberation of Paris.

   B. The D-Day landings prevented the "Free French" from ending the Nazi occupation in France.

   C. The Allies landed on D-Day at almost the same place where British forces had left France in 1940.

   D. The Allies faced the greatest resistance in the Ardennes Forest, where the Germans had also invaded in 1940.

SS.912.A.6.4

9. The diagram below provides details about events in the U.S. in June 1941.

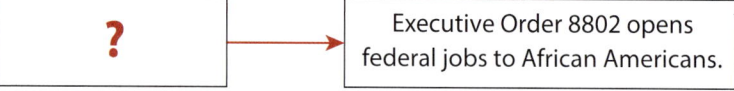

   Which sentence completes the diagram?

   A. Japanese Americans are relocated to internment camps.

   B. A. Philip Randolph proposes a "March on Washington."

   C. Three-quarters of the states ratify the 14th Amendment.

   D. The U.S. Supreme Court declares racial segregation unconstitutional.

SS.912.A.6.4

10. The posters below were created by the U.S. government during World War II.

    Which generalization do these posters support?

    A. Women refused to volunteer to assist in the war effort.

    B. The government urged women to fill jobs left vacant by men.

    C. The government tried to recruit women for combat in the war.

    D. Female military officers commanded both male and female troops.

SS.912.A.6.5

11. What was the purpose for rationing by the Office of Price Administration?

    A. to ensure that schools did not run out of supplies

    B. to ensure that children did not use too many products

    C. to ensure that enough products were available for military use

    D. to ensure that elderly citizens had an adequate supply of consumer goods

SS.912.A.6.4

12. The statement below by Justice Hugo Black is from the decision of the U.S. Supreme Court in *Korematsu v. United States* (1944).

    > Korematsu was not excluded from the military area because of hostility to him or his race. He was excluded because we are at war with the Japanese Empire, because the . . . authorities feared an invasion of our West Coast and felt constrained to take proper security measures.

    Based on this excerpt, with which statement would Justice Black have agreed?

    A. Individual rights can be restricted if a "clear and present danger" exists.

    B. Only the Supreme Court can legally deprive citizens of rights and liberties.

    C. Individual rights must be maintained at all costs, even in national emergencies.

    D. The Supreme Court lacks the power to block executive orders made during wartime.

SS.912.A.6.4

13. The statement below was made by Ms. Aiko Herzig-Yoshinaga in an interview in 1994. She recalls events from her childhood when her family was relocated during World War II.

    > [T]he army did not notify each family exactly where they would be going, what kind of weather they would be encountering, or exactly when they would be moving. Efforts within each family started to get rid of, sell, or store their household goods. And then trying to separate out what they thought they would need and what they thought they could either store or sell. It was a hectic, frantic time for all the Japanese families. In our family, my father, as a matter of fact, destroyed all of his Japanese language books because rumors spread that if the FBI came to your home and found Japanese language books, your father or uncle or mother would be taken away, and fear just gripped the community over things like that. My father destroyed almost all of his Japanese language books, including a book that he had written.

    Based on her statement, what conclusion can be drawn about the relocation of Japanese Americans?

    A. The U.S. Army had some limited evidence of sabotage by Japanese Americans.

    B. The removal of Japanese Americans from coastal areas was necessary for U.S. security.

    C. Japanese Americans were given very little time to take care of their personal possessions.

    D. The relocation of Japanese Americans was almost identical to the treatment of Jews under the Nazis.

SS.912.A.6.6

14. President Truman consulted four advisers about dropping an atomic bomb on Hiroshima. The excerpts below summarize the advice they gave.

Adviser A: "A planned Allied invasion of Japan is expected to cost close to a million American lives. These would be saved by dropping the bomb."	**Adviser B:** "There is little moral difference between dropping an atomic bomb on Hiroshima and our fire bombings of Dresden and Tokyo."
Adviser C: "We should demonstrate the bomb's effectiveness on a deserted island, but there is no guarantee that the Japanese will surrender even if the test is a success."	**Adviser D:** "Thousand of civilians will be instantly killed if we drop an atomic bomb on Hiroshima. Many of these are non-combatants, such as children, women and, elderly people."

Which advisers believed that dropping an atomic bomb on Hiroshima was an appropriate and justifiable military action?

A. Advisers A and B
B. Advisers A and C
C. Advisers B and D
D. Advisers C and D

SS.912.A.6.3

15. The chart below provides details on the Holocaust.

	Sequence of Leading Events in the Holocaust
▶	Jewish people cannot legally marry non-Jews or belong to most professions.
▶	**?**
▶	Jewish people are forced to move to restricted and crowded "ghetto" areas.
▶	Jewish people are forced to identify themselves by wearing yellow stars.
▶	Jewish people are sent by train to extermination camps in Eastern Europe.

Which sentence completes the chart?

A. Jewish people are permitted to emigrate with most of their belongings.
B. Jewish people are forced to act as personal slaves in non-Jewish homes.
C. Jewish people organize popular rebellions to overthrow the Nazi dictatorship.
D. Jewish synagogues and businesses are attacked in government-supported riots.

SS.912.A.6.9

16. Which civil rights leader helped to draft the United Nations Charter?

A. James Doolittle
B. Fred Korematsu
C. A. Philip Randolph
D. Mary McLeod Bethune

CHAPTER 13

The Cold War

SS.912.A.6.8 Analyze the effects of the Red Scare on domestic United States policy.

SS.912.A.6.10 Examine causes, course, and consequences of the early years of the Cold War (Truman Doctrine, Marshall Plan, NATO, Warsaw Pact).

SS.912.A.6.11 Examine the controversy surrounding the proliferation of nuclear technology in the United States and the world.

SS.912.A.6.12 Examine causes, course, and consequences of the Korean War.

SS.912.A.6.13 Analyze significant foreign policy events during the Truman, Eisenhower, [and] Kennedy . . . administrations.

SS.912.A.6.15 Examine key events and peoples in Florida history as they relate to United States history.

Names and Terms You Should Know

- Superpower
- Joseph Stalin
- Dumbarton Oaks Conference
- Yalta Conference
- Cold War
- Iron Curtain
- Harry S. Truman
- Potsdam Conference
- Containment
- Truman Doctrine
- Marshall Plan
- West Germany
- East Germany
- Berlin Blockade
- Berlin Airlift
- North Atlantic Treaty Organization (NATO)
- Warsaw Pact
- Nuclear Proliferation
- Korean War
- General Douglas MacArthur
- Panmunjom
- Loyalty Review Boards
- McCarthyism
- Dwight Eisenhower
- Eisenhower Doctrine
- Arms race
- Nikita Khrushchev
- John F. Kennedy
- Fidel Castro
- Bay of Pigs Invasion
- Alliance for Progress
- Cuban Missile Crisis
- Berlin Wall
- Peace Corps

Florida "Keys" to Learning

1. World War II left two superpowers: the United States and the Soviet Union. Their rivalry led to the Cold War as each promoted its own way of life.

2. The Cold War was rooted in political, economic, and social differences. The Soviet Union was a Communist dictatorship with a planned economy, collectivized farming, and state-owned factories. The United States was a capitalist democracy. People enjoyed individual rights and elected their own leaders.

3. Stalin mistrusted the West. He felt the Soviet Union had the right to control Eastern Europe for its own security. American leaders equally mistrusted Stalin. Stalin had promised free elections in Poland at Yalta but failed to honor his pledge.

4. An "Iron Curtain" fell on Eastern Europe. Trade, travel, and communications between Eastern and Western Europe were cut off. In 1947, Communists threatened the governments of Greece and Turkey. President Truman announced the Truman Doctrine: that the United States would provide assistance to free countries resisting Communism. Under the Marshall Plan, the United States gave economic aid to the countries of Western Europe.

5. Stalin cut off Western land routes to West Berlin in 1948. The United States responded with the "Berlin Airlift." After several months, Stalin reopened the roads to West Berlin.

6. The Western Allies formed NATO in 1949. The Soviet Union and its Eastern European satellites formed the Warsaw Pact in 1955.

7. China was taken over by Communist forces led by Mao Zedong in 1949. Chiang Kai-Shek and the Chinese Nationalists fled to the island of Taiwan.

8. Communist North Korea attacked South Korea in 1950. Truman decided to help South Korea resist the attack. General MacArthur chased the North Koreans to the borders of China, bringing China into the war. Truman dismissed MacArthur when he was openly critical of the President.

9. On the "home front," some began to fear Communist spies. Loyalty Review Boards and the House Committee on Un-American Activities interrogated citizens on their political activities. Alger Hiss, a prominent State Department official, was imprisoned. The Rosenbergs were executed for giving atomic secrets to the Soviet Union. Senator Joseph McCarthy claimed to have evidence of Communists in government, although he never produced it.

10. Nuclear proliferation—the spread of nuclear weapons—became a problem after the Soviet Union exploded its first atomic bomb. Both superpowers then developed hydrogen bombs.

11. President Eisenhower announced the Eisenhower Doctrine—that the United States would oppose the spread of Communism in the Middle East—and sent troops to Lebanon. The Soviet success in sending Sputnik into space in 1957 caused the United States to increase its spending on science education and to enter the space race.

12. In 1959, Fidel Castro successfully overthrew a dictator in Cuba and established a Communist state. When Castro seized some U.S. investments, Eisenhower began an economic boycott and the CIA trained Cuban exiles to overthrow Castro. Kennedy became President in 1961 and launched an invasion of Cuba by Cuban exiles at the Bay of Pigs. It failed.

13. In 1961, Soviet leader Nikita Khrushchev ordered the building of the Berlin Wall. When Kennedy later visited Berlin, he declared "I am a Berliner."

14. In October 1962, Americans discovered Cubans were about to install Soviet nuclear missiles. This led to the Cuban Missile Crisis—the closest the world has come to a nuclear war. America blockaded Cuba and Khrushchev removed the missiles when Kennedy pledged not to invade Cuba. They set up a "hot line" for emergency calls and agreed to a partial test ban treaty.

The end of World War II left two great "superpowers" in control of world affairs: the United States and the Soviet Union. The **Soviet Union** (or "U.S.S.R.") was formed after the Russian Revolution. It consisted of present-day Russia and neighboring countries that had once been part of the Russian empire. The United States and the Soviet Union were considered **superpowers** because they possessed far greater military strength, economic power, and political influence than other nations.

Although the United States and Soviet Union were allies during World War II, they quickly became rivals in a "**Cold War**" that would last for more than forty years. The war was "cold" only in the sense that, because of nuclear weapons, the two superpowers never confronted each other directly in open warfare. However, their global competition led to frequent world crises and regional confrontations on every continent.

The Social, Political, and Economic Causes of the Cold War

The roots of the Cold War lay in the competing ideological systems of the United States and the Soviet Union, and in their conflicting strategic needs. The United States wanted to spread its democratic, free-market system (also known as "capitalism"). The Soviet Union wanted to spread its system of Communism. It was inevitable that these two superpowers should clash in the pursuit of these objectives.

The Main Ideas of Communism

You may remember that the Soviet Union was the world's first Communist country. The Soviet system was based on the ideas of the 19th-century thinker Karl Marx, as interpreted by the Russian revolutionary Vladimir Lenin. Its main ideas are described below.

Class-Struggle and Revolution

Communists believe that in non-Communist societies, landowners and businessmen, known as "capitalists," use their wealth and power to exploit workers. They keep for themselves most of the wealth that workers create. The capitalists further use religious beliefs, which Communists see as mistaken or false, to fool workers into accepting their conditions. The conflict of interest between capitalists and workers leads to class struggle. The conditions of workers in capitalist societies grow increasingly worse until workers are finally driven to overthrow the ruling class of landowners and businessmen in a violent revolution. Soviet Communists claimed this was what happened in Russia in 1917.

From "Dictatorship of the Workers" to "Worker's Paradise"

After the revolution, Communist leaders are supposed to establish a dictatorship to educate the people in the ideas of Communism and to look after their true interests. Although this dictatorship is run for the benefit of the workers, the leaders of the Communist Party keep control in their own hands. Ownership of the means of production is taken over by the state. Unscientific religious beliefs are condemned. This "dictatorship of the workers" is meant to gradually create a new Communist society. In this ideal society, private property will be eliminated, government will wither away, and everyone will work happily for the good of society as a whole. In this "worker's paradise," each member of society will contribute according to his or her abilities and receive from society according to his or her needs.

Russian citizens march in 1917 ▶

Soviet Communism

In practice, the Soviet Union under Communism became a ruthless dictatorship. Lenin consolidated power after a brutal civil war but died shortly thereafter. His successor, **Joseph Stalin**, murdered political opponents or sent them to **gulags**—concentration-type camps located in the frozen wastelands of Siberia. Under Lenin, the Communists had confiscated major sources of wealth from Russian nobles, landowners and businessmen. All free organizations were suppressed, and only Communist views could be expressed. Stalin used force to confiscate peasant lands and to "collectivize" Soviet agriculture. He used a combination of propaganda and coercion to build up basic industries (like steel production) instead of providing for consumer needs. Stalin kept all power in his own hands and was responsible for the deaths of millions of Soviet citizens. Under Stalin, Communist ideology became a mere pretext for Stalin's own absolute power.

Joseph Stalin

A Clash of Systems

The United States had a far different social, political, and economic system. In the United States, people elected leaders democratically. People enjoyed free speech, freedom of the press, freedom of religious beliefs, and the right to a fair trial when accused of a crime. They were also free to own property and to make whatever they could afford to produce and sell. This system was the exact opposite of the Soviet system under Stalin. Americans hoped the war-torn countries of Europe would adopt their system. Stalin was determined to spread Soviet-style Communism.

The Historian's Apprentice

▶ Pretend you were a Soviet soldier during the war and became friends with an American soldier. Write a letter from Moscow in 1945 explaining how your social, political, and economic system works.

▶ Create a chart or table comparing the Soviet and American systems in 1945. Consider social, political, and economic differences.

The Cold War begins in Europe

The United States and the Soviet Union as Wartime Allies, 1941–1945

Both the United States and the Soviet Union had tried their best to keep out of World War II. Stalin had signed a "Non-Aggression Pact" with Hitler in August 1939, allowing the German army to march into Poland. However, Hitler had then ordered the invasion of the Soviet Union in June 1941. Six months later, after the Japanese attack on Pearl Harbor, Hitler had also declared war on the United States. The United States and the Soviet Union thus became allies in the struggle against Nazi Germany. The Soviets greatly resented the fact that the United States and Great Britain had waited until June 1944 to land their troops in France. All this time, the Soviet army had borne the main brunt of Nazi attacks. About 400,000 Americans were killed in the war; in sharp contrast, Soviet losses exceeded 23 million.

Stalingrad following the Soviet "victory"

Postwar Plans at the Yalta Conference (February 1945)

While American, British, and French troops marched through France into Germany from the west, the Soviet "Red Army" advanced from the east. The Red Army marched across Eastern Europe, liberating Poland, Romania, Czechoslovakia, Bulgaria, and Albania from Nazi rule. In February 1945, Roosevelt, Churchill, and Stalin met at Yalta in the Soviet Union. At the **Yalta Conference**, the "Big Three" laid plans for the postwar reconstruction of Europe. They agreed that Germany should be divided into four separate occupation zones. They confirmed the structure of the new United Nations organization, which had been negotiated at the **Dumbarton Oaks Conference** five months earlier. Finally, Stalin gave a pledge to his Western allies to allow free elections in Poland when the war ended.

Churchill, Roosevelt, and Stalin

The Potsdam Conference

President Roosevelt died in April 1945, just weeks before the surrender of Germany. The new President, **Harry S. Truman**, met with Stalin at Potsdam, Germany, in July and August 1945 in order to decide on the treatment of Germany, the final campaign against Japan, and the future of Europe. It was during this conference that Truman made the decision to drop the atomic bomb on Japan. Serious differences between the Soviet Union and the United States arose at Potsdam, mainly over the future of Eastern Europe.

The Soviet Point of View

Stalin believed the Soviet Union should have control over Eastern Europe to make sure that the Soviet Union was never invaded through Eastern Europe again. Just as the United States controlled Latin America with the "Monroe Doctrine," the Soviets claimed they had the right to a special "sphere of influence" in Eastern Europe. They felt the Western Powers had no direct interests in Eastern Europe and therefore should not interfere with Soviet activity there. Since the Soviet Red Army was already in occupation of Eastern Europe, Stalin saw this as a historic opportunity to achieve Communist control. Stalin also felt that he could not fully trust the United States and other Western countries, which had delayed their invasion of Europe, resulting in an unparalleled loss of Soviet lives.

American Points of View

President Truman felt that Stalin had promised free elections in Poland and should keep his word. He further believed that other European countries wanted to become democratic, free-market nations like the United States.

Most of Truman's advisers agreed that Communism was a dangerous system that should not be allowed to spread because it opposed American ideals. They saw Stalin as a brutal dictator, like Hitler, who could not be trusted. Truman's leading advisers therefore felt it would be a dangerous mistake for the United States to turn its back on European affairs as it had after World War I. They did not want to make the same error with Stalin that European leaders had made with Hitler. They felt it was important to resist Stalin's demands from the beginning, rather than to wait for the Soviet Union to grow even more powerful.

On the other hand, many Americans were frustrated by the loss of American lives in European armed conflicts. Some of them hoped the United States would once again retreat behind the oceans and return to its earlier policy of isolationism. Still others thought that the United States might try to win concessions from Stalin in Eastern Europe by offering economic assistance to the Soviet Union.

The Fate of Poland

Although the Soviet army had liberated Poland from Nazi rule, most Poles did not see the Soviet Union as their friend. Part of Poland had once been under the rule of the Russian Tsars. Stalin had cooperated with Hitler to divide Poland in half in 1939, and he had ordered the murder of more than 20,000 Polish military officers in the Katyn Forest in 1940.

In 1945, he had then let the German army destroy Warsaw, the Polish capital, before ordering Soviet troops to liberate what was left of it.

Despite his promise at Yalta, Stalin refused to hold free elections in Poland. Instead, the Red Army put local Polish Communists in charge.

The Historian's Apprentice

Imagine you are an American journalist at the end of World War II. Write an editorial on how American leaders should respond to Stalin's failure to allow free elections in Poland.

An "Iron Curtain" Falls on Eastern Europe

Meanwhile, the United States refused to share the secret of how to make an atomic bomb with the Soviet Union. With the failure of the Soviets to hold free elections in Poland and of the United States to share its atomic secrets, the "Cold War" began in earnest. Local Communists came to power throughout Eastern Europe. Trade and communications between Eastern and Western Europe were cut off. Winston Churchill told Americans in a speech in 1946 that an "**Iron Curtain**" had fallen, closing off Eastern Europe from the West. For the next forty years, travel and contact between the East and West was restricted, and Eastern European governments became "**satellites**" (*dependent states*) of the Soviet Union.

Truman Responds with Containment Policy

We have seen that there were differing views on how America should respond to the spread of Communism. A few Americans sympathized with Soviet sacrifices in World War II and believed that Soviet expansion into Eastern Europe was justified. Other Americans wanted to retreat into isolationism, as the United States had done after World War I. Truman and his closest advisers, however, feared that the Soviet seizure of power in Eastern Europe just might be the first step towards taking control of the world. They were determined to avoid the mistakes that Britain and France had committed in failing to stand up against Nazi Germany and Hitler. The American ambassador in Moscow warned Truman that the Soviet Union would attempt to expand and would only stop if it was threatened with force. Truman therefore resolved to react firmly against every Soviet effort to spread Communism to other countries. He did not attempt, however, to overturn Communism where it already existed. His goal was simply to "contain" it. This approach became known as "**containment**" policy.

The Truman Doctrine, 1947

In 1947, the Greek government was threatened by Communist rebels and the Soviet Union demanded that Turkey give it access to the Straits connecting the Black Sea and the Mediterranean. Britain, weakened by World War II, could no longer fulfill its traditional role of maintaining stability in this region. President Truman proposed to Congress that the United States give these countries financial assistance and military advice. In fact, Truman promised American support to any free people fighting Communism.

The Historian's Apprentice

Excerpts from President Truman's Address before Congress, March 12, 1947:

At the present moment in world history nearly every nation must choose between alternative ways of life. The choice is too often not a free one. One way of life is based upon the will of the majority, and is distinguished by free institutions, representative government, free elections, guarantees of individual liberty, freedom of speech and religion, and freedom from political oppression. The second way of life is based upon the will of a minority forcibly imposed upon the majority. It relies upon terror and oppression, a controlled press and radio; fixed elections, and the suppression of personal freedoms.

I believe that it must be the policy of the United States to support free peoples who are resisting attempted subjugation by armed minorities or by outside pressures.

I believe that we must assist free peoples to work out their own destinies in their own way.

I believe that our help should be primarily through economic and financial aid which is essential to economic stability and orderly political processes. . . .

It would be an unspeakable tragedy if these countries, which have struggled so long against overwhelming odds, should lose that victory for which they sacrificed so much. Collapse of free institutions and loss of independence would be disastrous not only for them but for the world. Discouragement and possibly failure would quickly be the lot of neighboring peoples striving to maintain their freedom and independence.

Should we fail to aid Greece and Turkey in this fateful hour, the effect will be far reaching to the West as well as to the East. We must take immediate and resolute action.

I therefore ask the Congress to provide authority for assistance to Greece and Turkey in the amount of $400,000,000 . . . In addition to funds, I ask the Congress to authorize the sending of American civilian and military personnel to Greece and Turkey, at the request of those countries, to assist in the tasks of reconstruction, and for the purpose of supervising the use of such financial and material assistance as may be furnished.

—Harry S. Truman

1. What differences does Truman see between the American and Soviet systems?
2. Why does Truman argue that aid is needed for Greece and Turkey?
3. What was the importance of sending civilian and military advisers as well as providing financial assistance?
4. Imagine you are a Congressman in 1947. Write a letter to your constituents explaining how you voted on President Truman's request for aid to Greece and Turkey.

To win support from the American public and avoid a return to isolationism, Truman thus promoted his program as a crusade on behalf of embattled democracies. His promise, known as the **Truman Doctrine**, marked the official beginning of "containment" policy.

The Marshall Plan, 1948

Europeans were still suffering from the enormous devastation of World War II. Truman feared that economic hardship might make Europeans more vulnerable to Communism. He wanted to help Europeans avoid the turmoil that had resulted from the economic dislocations following World War I. Truman's Secretary of State, **General George Marshall**, proposed that economic aid be given to the countries of war-torn Europe to help them rebuild their economies. In March 1948, Congress appropriated $12 billion for Marshall's proposal, which became known as the **Marshall Plan**. Supporters of the plan believed that economic aid would create strong European allies and trading partners for the United States. They also believed that by fighting poverty in Europe, they would make Europeans more resistant to the attractions of Communism.

The Marshall Plan was extremely successful. It speeded the economic recovery of Western Europe and built up good will towards the United States. Marshall Plan aid was also offered to the Soviet Union and Eastern Europe, but Soviet leaders refused to accept it and denounced the plan.

The Historian's Apprentice

Make a Venn diagram comparing the Truman Doctrine and the Marshall Plan. Consider both their goals and the means they used to carry out those goals. How were they similar? How did they differ?

The Division of Germany, the Berlin Blockade and the Berlin Airlift, 1948

In May 1948, the French, British, and Americans decided to merge their zones of occupation in Germany into a single state, the Federal Republic of Germany, also known as "**West Germany**."

Berlin, the old capital of Germany, was located deep in the Russian occupation zone. Because of its importance, the city had been divided into four sectors, each one occupied by one of the four allied powers—the Soviet Union, the United States, Great Britain, and France. The Soviets reacted to the merging of the western zones of Germany by announcing a **blockade of West Berlin** (the sectors of the city occupied by the three Western allies). They closed all highway and railroad links to the city from the West. The Western allies refused to abandon West Berlin. They began a massive airlift to feed and supply the city. The **Berlin Airlift** successfully defied Stalin. Within a year, the **Berlin blockade** was lifted. The Soviets then

Berliners watch as supplies are flown in by Western allies.

Cold War Alignments—1956
- NATO countries
- Warsaw Pact countries
- Other Communist countries

turned their occupation zone in Germany into an independent nation: the German Democratic Republic, also known as "**East Germany**."

The Formation of NATO and the Warsaw Pact

In response to the tensions of the Cold War, especially the Soviet testing of their first atomic bomb, the United States, Canada, and ten Western European countries formed the **North Atlantic Treaty Organization** (**NATO**) in 1949. Each member of NATO pledged to defend every other member if attacked. Through NATO, the United States extended its umbrella of nuclear deterrence to the countries of Western Europe.

When West Germany joined NATO in 1955, the Soviet Union responded by creating the **Warsaw Pact,** an alliance with its Eastern European "satellites." The Warsaw Pact was actually used by the Soviet Union to justify its interference in the affairs of Eastern Europe. The United States never directly interfered in this region where Soviet power was so firmly established. The United States admitted refugees from Eastern Europe as immigrants and loudly condemned Soviet acts of force, but it did not intervene when the Soviet Union sent troops to suppress an anti-Communist revolution in Hungary in 1956 or an independent government in Czechoslovakia in 1968.

Containment in Asia

Just when American statesmen believed they had succeeded in checking the spread of Communism in Europe, Communists took over China, the world's most populous nation. This raised new questions for American leaders. Could they check the spread of Communism, not only in Europe, but elsewhere around the globe? And would Communism hold a special appeal to the impoverished and struggling peoples of Asia, Africa, and Latin America? In many of these countries, leaders were angry at the West for the abuses they had experienced as colonies, while Communism seemed to offer a path towards rapid economic modernization and greater social equality.

The "Fall of China," 1949

Since 1927, Communist Chinese had been attempting to overthrow the Nationalist Chinese government. In 1937, when Japan invaded China, the Nationalists and Communists agreed to a temporary truce while they fought the Japanese. After the defeat of Japan, fighting immediately resumed between the Nationalists and Communists. The Communists, led by **Mao Zedong**, received supplies and support from the Soviet Union. The United States sent economic aid to the Nationalist government, led by General Chiang Kai-Shek, but the Chinese Nationalists were already greatly weakened by the war against Japan. Mao had adapted Communist ideas to appeal to China's peasants, who made up the vast majority of the population, and had generally won their support. In 1949, the Communists succeeded in defeating the Nationalists, and Chiang retreated to the island of Taiwan. He hoped one day to return to the mainland to defeat the Communists. Meanwhile, Mao turned mainland China into the world's most populous Communist state.

President Truman refused to extend diplomatic recognition to Mao's Communist government. The United States continued to treat Chiang's government on Taiwan as the official government of China. Because of its influence on the U.N. General Assembly, the United States was also able to keep Chiang's representatives in the United Nations and to keep out Mao's "Red China."

The Korean War (1950–1953)

Many Americans were shocked that the United States had not done more to prevent the fall of China into Communist hands. This affected the climate of opinion in the United States at the time of the outbreak of the Korean War.

Origins of the War

Korea is a mountainous peninsula jutting out from Manchuria and pointing towards Japan. Ruled by Japan from 1905 to 1945, it was divided at the **38th parallel** (of latitude) into two occupation zones at the end of World War II. Soviet forces occupied the North and American forces occupied the South. Like Germany, a Communist government was established in the Soviet zone. Elections in the South led to the creation of a non-Communist government there.

In June 1950, North Korea invaded South Korea in an attempt to unify the country under Communist rule. Communist leaders did not expect that the United States would help defend a country in Asia that seemed to have little to do with U.S. security. However, when Truman heard news of the invasion, it reminded him of Hitler's 1938 annexation of Czechoslovakia. Truman immediately decided to send U.S. troops to South Korea to resist the invasion.

The Soviet Union was then boycotting the United Nations Security Council in protest over its failure to seat Communist China. This coincidence permitted Truman to pass a resolution condemning the North Korean attack as an act of aggression. The Security Council invited member nations to assist South Korea. Truman was thus able to send troops to South Korea with United Nations authorization. Only five years after the end of World War II, Americans found themselves again in a major war.

The Course of the War and the Truman–MacArthur Controversy

By the end of June, North Korean forces had overrun most of South Korea. Truman sent **General Douglas MacArthur** to command American forces. MacArthur had commanded American forces in the Pacific against Japan during World War II, and had governed Japan during the occupation after the war.

General MacArthur landed his forces at Inchon Beach, north of the North Korean army. This took the North Koreans by surprise and forced them to retreat. Next, MacArthur counterattacked by marching into North Korea. He advanced almost up to the Yalu River, the border between North Korea and China. MacArthur's advance, however, brought China into the war. A large Chinese army forced MacArthur's smaller force to retreat southwards again, towards the 38th parallel.

General Douglas MacArthur (seated with binoculars) at Inchon Beach

General MacArthur wished to pursue the war vigorously. He planned to blockade mainland China and to assist Chiang Kai-Shek and the Chinese Nationalists on Taiwan in recapturing control of the mainland. MacArthur was even willing to use atomic bombs against the Communist Chinese to win these goals. Truman was also considering the possibility of using atomic weapons in extreme circumstances but was otherwise against taking such risks. When MacArthur criticized Truman publicly, Truman removed MacArthur from his command and ordered his return to the United States. Although MacArthur was a popular war hero, Truman successfully asserted civilian control over the military by dismissing him.

Consequences of the Korean War

Dwight D. Eisenhower, Allied Commander on D-Day, was elected as President of the United States the following year. In his campaign, Eisenhower promised voters he would find a way to end the Korean War. An **armistice** (or *cease-fire*) ending the war was finally signed in 1953 at **Panmunjom**, a village sitting on the **demilitarized zone** (**DMZ**) between North and South Korea. The armistice left Korea divided at the 38th parallel, exactly as it had been before the North Korean invasion three years earlier. American losses had not driven the Communists out of China or North Korea, but they had further shown American determination to resist the spread of Communism by force. Because neither side was able to defeat the other, Korea remains divided to this day. South Korea has a successful industrial economy, while North Korea is an isolated, Communist dictatorship, almost entirely cut off from international trade. Ironically, the "DMZ," 2½ miles wide and 160 miles long, now teems with rare wildlife.

Dwight D. Eisenhower

The Historian's Apprentice

▶ Write a short essay on whether or not American intervention in the Korean War was justified.
▶ Whose approach to fighting the Korean War was better—Truman's or MacArthur's? Imagine you are a journalist writing in 1951. Write an editorial on this question.

Nuclear Proliferation and the Nuclear Arms Race

To "**proliferate**" means to multiply rapidly. **Nuclear proliferation** refers to the spread of nuclear weapons and technology. Nuclear proliferation poses a danger because of the tremendous destructiveness of nuclear weapons. As more nations obtain these weapons, there is an increasing danger that one nation might someday use them. There is also a greater risk of an accidental explosion or of nuclear weapons falling into the hands of terrorists.

In 1945, the United States was the sole atomic power. Congress created the Atomic Energy Commission in 1946, giving the President control over atomic weapons. The United States refused to share the secret of the atomic bomb with the Soviet Union, but as early as August 1949, the Soviets exploded their first atomic bomb. American leaders anticipated that Soviet possession of the atomic bomb would result in more aggressive acts of Soviet behavior. This prediction further strengthened their resolve to resist all Soviet attempts to spread the Communist system.

- *The Hydrogen Bomb.* In 1952, the United States developed the hydrogen fusion bomb, which is much more destructive than the earlier atomic bomb. The Soviet Union exploded its first hydrogen bomb less than a year later, showing that the gap between American and Soviet nuclear technology was narrowing.
- *Deterrence and "Massive Retaliation."* Americans and Soviets also developed new missile technologies, making it possible to deliver atomic weapons by firing missiles at an enemy. American leaders in the 1950s decided to rely more on their nuclear weapons than on large numbers of troops. These nuclear weapons were supposed to act as a **deterrent**: the Soviet Union would be "deterred" from attacking the United States because Americans would retaliate by destroying the Soviet Union with nuclear weapons. American leaders believed this form of defense was cheaper than maintaining large numbers of conventional forces. However, it was also far less flexible. American leaders quickly realized that in almost all situations nuclear weapons could not be used because they were so very dangerous. Nuclear weapons were weapons of last resort, whose use could only be justified if the very survival of the nation were at stake. Even then, their use might not be justified because it could threaten the survival of humanity as a whole.
- Despite these drawbacks, the United States and the Soviet Union entered into a dangerous "**arms race**," in which each superpower began building and stockpiling as many nuclear weapons as possible to ensure its nuclear superiority.

The Historian's Apprentice

The controversy over nuclear proliferation remains with us today. Not only the United States and Russia, but also Britain, France, China, India, Pakistan, and several other nations now belong to the exclusive "nuclear club." Other countries, such as Iran, might also like to develop them. Should only powerful, developed countries be permitted to possess nuclear weapons? What gives them this right? Can the world afford to see every nation, no matter what its size, wealth or type of government, develop its own nuclear arsenal? Have your teacher divide your class into small groups. Each group should "brainstorm" to find an answer to this question: what steps should world leaders take to prevent nuclear proliferation? Then compare the solutions proposed by each group.

The Cold War on the "Home Front"

The Cold War affected everyday life in the United States just as earlier "hot wars" had done. As during World War I and the "Red Scare" of the 1920s, individual civil rights were often challenged in the name of national security.

A handful of Americans still believed that Communism or socialism offered a solution to the problems created by industrialization. The Soviet Union had been an ally during World War II and friendship with the Soviet Union had not been discouraged. Stalin's many atrocities were still unknown, and the American Communist Party numbered as many as 50,000 members during the war.

The Second "Red Scare"

As Communism spread in the postwar years, a majority of Americans became suspicious of those holding Communist beliefs at home. Fearing a possible Communist threat within the United States, President Truman created **Loyalty Review Boards** to conduct investigations of government employees suspected of "un-American" activities, such as membership in the American Communist Party. He also feared being called "soft on Communism" by his Republican opponents. Truman intended to fight Communism at home as well as abroad.

Congress also conducted its own investigations in the **House Committee on Un-American Activities**. This committee interrogated actors, directors, writers, government employees, union leaders, and other individuals about their political beliefs and activities. Leaders in the entertainment business were especially targeted because of their influence on American culture. Those questioned by the committee were often asked to report on the activities of others as well as themselves. Many were later blacklisted and unable to find work because they were suspected of being Communist sympathizers or refused to respond to the committee. The "**Hollywood Ten**" in 1947, for example, consisted of ten screenwriters and directors who refused to answer the committee's questions. These ten men were immediately fired by their employers; none found work in Hollywood for more than a decade afterwards.

The fall of China to Communism in 1949 and the development of nuclear weapons by the Soviet Union greatly increased American anti-Communist paranoia (*exaggerated fear and mistrust*). People wondered: Did Communist sympathizers in the U.S. State Department (*the department of the federal government that conducts foreign relations*) secretly ignore the Communist threat to China? Did Communist spies in the Department of Defense steal atomic secrets and give them to the Soviet Union?

In 1948, Whittaker Chambers, a former Communist, testified before the House Committee on Un-American Activities that **Alger Hiss**, an official in the State Department, had been a spy for the Soviet Union. F.B.I. Director Edgar Hoover began collecting information on suspected Communist sympathizers. In 1950, **Julius** and **Ethel Rosenberg** were formally charged with furnishing atomic secrets to the Soviets. The Rosenbergs were tried and executed, although some believe they may have been innocent.

McCarthyism

The anti-Communist hysteria continued throughout the early 1950s. In February 1950, **Joseph McCarthy**, the U.S. Senator from Wisconsin, shocked Americans by announcing in a speech that he had an actual list of Communist spies who had infiltrated the U.S.

Senator Joseph McCarthy

State Department. McCarthy used different forms of media to spread his message—including newspapers, pamphlets, radio, and television. A Senate Committee, led by Democrats, conducted an investigation of McCarthy's claims and called him a "fraud and a hoax." Republicans, however, backed McCarthy. They condemned the work of the Senate Committee as "the most brazen whitewash of treasonable conspiracy in our history." McCarthy later made similar accusations about other federal departments. He blamed former Secretary of State George Marshall for being weak on Communism and for losing China to the Communists. The public began to fear that Communists were everywhere in the government. People of liberal political views became afraid of being accused of being Communists. Those who came under suspicion could not work for the government and often could not find jobs in private industry. McCarthy became popular and helped other Republican candidates to Congress win their elections. Important families like the Kennedys gave him financial support. President Eisenhower disapproved of McCarthy but failed to criticize him openly.

McCarthy was put in charge of his own congressional subcommittee and continued to hold hearings. He bullied witnesses, disregarded their rights, exaggerated or falsified evidence, and destroyed people's careers. In 1953, he accused the U.S. Army of sheltering disloyal Communists. The army in turn accused McCarthy of using improper influence to have a friend promoted. Extensive hearings were held on the new medium of television. The American public saw McCarthy's bullying tactics first hand and he lost his popularity. McCarthy was challenged to produce evidence of his accusations and was condemned for his lack of "decency" in destroying other people's careers. People applauded when McCarthy was attacked. McCarthy's spell was broken. A famous journalist broadcast a special television program denouncing McCarthy's conduct for failing to distinguish between **dissent** (*disagreement*) and disloyalty. Finally, McCarthy was **censured** (*formally criticized*) by the Senate. Today, the term "**McCarthyism**" refers both to the height of anti-Communist hysteria in the 1950s and to the practice of making wild and unsound accusations against innocent people.

The Cold War Continues under Eisenhower and Kennedy

Containment under Eisenhower

President Eisenhower gave aid to France, then fighting Communist-leaning Vietnamese nationalists in Indochina. Eisenhower also authorized the **Central Intelligence Agency,** or **CIA**, to train exiles who overthrew the leftist government of Guatemala. The United States further gave a pledge to the Nationalist Chinese that it would protect the island of Taiwan from any attack by Communist China. On the other hand, Eisenhower and his Secretary of State, John Foster Dulles, felt unable to do anything but issue a harsh condemnation when Soviet troops invaded Hungary in Eastern Europe in 1956.

The Eisenhower Doctrine

In 1954, Eisenhower took a special interest in the Middle East. In 1956, he prevented Britain, Israel, and France from defeating Egypt and taking over the Suez Canal. The following year, Eisenhower announced that the United States would be "prepared to use armed force . . . [to counter] aggression from any country controlled by international communism." This extension of containment policy to the Middle East came to be known as the "**Eisenhower Doctrine**." Under this doctrine, 15,000 American troops were sent to Lebanon in 1958 to support its pro-Western President against the threat of revolution.

Sputnik

In 1957, the Soviets launched **Sputnik**, the first man-made satellite, into space. Americans were so shocked that the Soviets seemed to be ahead, that Congress passed an act providing funds for math and science education. Not only was this the beginning of the "space race," but it also had great military significance. With rockets that could travel into space, the Soviet Union had the ability to fire missiles that could carry nuclear weapons to the United States.

Nikita Khrushchev became the leader of the Soviet Union after Stalin's death in 1953. Although he seemed less extreme than Stalin, Khrushchev believed strongly in the superiority of the Communist system. He visited the United States in 1959. Plans for a Soviet-American summit conference in 1960 were abruptly called off when an American U2 spy plane flown by **Gary Powers** was shot down over the Soviet Union.

298   Chapter 13 | The Cold War

Cuba

In 1959, **Fidel Castro** and his guerilla fighters overthrew the Cuban dictator Batista. Castro had promised to establish a democracy in Cuba, but he set up a Communist dictatorship instead. Castro nationalized property in Cuba belonging to Americans. Eisenhower was infuriated and took counter-measures, eventually cutting off trade and diplomatic relations with Cuba. Eisenhower also gave his approval to a secret plot to train and support Cuban exiles, who hoped to topple Castro. The exiles were armed and given special training in Guatemala by the CIA. As Eisenhower's Presidency came to an end, the exiles were still being trained. Eisenhower's Vice President, Richard M. Nixon, lost the 1960 Presidential election to Democratic candidate John F. Kennedy.

Kennedy and Containment in Latin America

When Kennedy became President, one of the greatest problems he faced was the presence of Communism in Cuba, only 90 miles from the Florida shore. Kennedy feared that Communism might spread from Cuba to other Latin American countries.

The Bay of Pigs Invasion, 1961

In April 1961, about 1,400 CIA-trained Cuban exiles attempted their invasion of Cuba by landing at the Bay of Pigs. The night before the attack, CIA planes bombed Cuban airfields but failed to destroy all Cuban aircraft. American naval ships also staged decoy operations to confuse the Cuban government. The United States failed to give air support during the invasion, however, and the rebels were defeated. They were publicly interrogated in Cuba in order to lay blame on the United States for the invasion and to make Castro more popular. Although the operation had been planned while Eisenhower was President, Kennedy took the blame for its failure. Many thought the CIA was at fault.

The "Alliance for Progress," 1961

To meet the challenge posed by Communism, Kennedy created the **"Alliance for Progress,"** a program offering grants and loans to Latin American nations to promote economic progress, increased trade, and land reform. The program was generally unsuccessful, however, because local elites in Latin America were reluctant to make reforms.

The Cuban Missile Crisis

The Bay of Pigs invasion led Castro to strengthen his ties with the Soviet Union. In October 1962, the United States discovered from its spy planes that Cubans were secretly trying to build bases for Soviet nuclear missiles. This would have given the Soviet Union the ability to launch an immediate nuclear attack on the United States. Kennedy resolved to prevent the Soviets from setting up missiles with nuclear warheads on Cuba. But how could he do this without causing a nuclear war? After consulting with his advisers, Kennedy imposed a naval blockade around the island of Cuba and threatened to invade if the missiles were not withdrawn. Khrushchev agreed to withdraw the missiles for a pledge that the United States would not invade Cuba and that it would withdraw its own missiles from Turkey.

The **"Cuban Missile Crisis"** is often seen as Kennedy's greatest foreign policy success. Because of his cool handling of the crisis, Kennedy was able to persuade the Soviet Union and Cuba to back down. Critics, however, say he took the world too close to nuclear war. In the aftermath of the crisis, American and Soviet leaders set up a "hot line"—a special telephone connection so they could address one another in a crisis. They also began negotiations for a partial "test ban" treaty, which they signed the following year. It banned all testing of nuclear weapons except underground.

The Berlin Wall

The Cold War continued in other parts of the world as well as Latin America. In 1961, Khrushchev ordered the construction of the **Berlin Wall**—a wall of concrete and barbed wire, guarded by machine gun towers—that separated East and West Berlin. Its purpose was to prevent East Germans from escaping through Berlin to the West. Kennedy visited Berlin and told Berliners, "*Ich bin ein Berliner* [I am a Berliner]." He meant that the United States would not abandon West Berlin.

To better resist Communism, Kennedy created a new, special elite corps—the "Green Berets"—who would be able to combat Communism through guerilla warfare in the developing nations of Asia, Africa, and Latin America. Kennedy also started the **Peace Corps**, in which young Americans provided economic and social assistance to developing countries. In a later chapter, you will learn about Kennedy's policies in Vietnam.

One of the many guard towers along the Berlin Wall

Focus on Florida

Florida was greatly affected by the events of the Cold War. When a socialist government took over the country of Guatemala in 1954, the American Central Intelligence Agency, or "CIA," began secretly training exiles in Florida to overthrow it. The CIA operation in Guatemala was such a success that five years later, when Fidel Castro seized power in Cuba, the CIA began training teams of Cuban exiles in the Everglades, the Florida Keys, and Guatemala. This time, however, their effort led to disaster at the Bay of Pigs.

Because Cuba is less than 100 miles from Florida's shores, Florida became a focal point of the Cold War. During the Cuban Missile Crisis, U.S. troops flooded into South Florida. Afterwards, Florida's tropical forests continued to be used by the U.S. military to train soldiers preparing for Southeast Asia or Latin America. Radio stations in Florida were used to make broadcasts into Cuba.

Castro's Communist dictatorship in Cuba led to a stream of refugees to the United States. Between 1959 and 1962, more than 200,000 Cubans came to the United States—many of them professionals or business owners. Most of these immigrants settled in the Miami area. Immediately after the Cuban Missile Crisis, air travel between Cuba and the United States was cut off, but refugees continued to pour in from Cuba. In 1965, limited air travel was restored until 1973, and another 368,000 Cubans moved to the United States. In 1980, Castro announced that anyone who wished to leave Cuba could do so from the port of Mariel. Cuban Americans in Miami sent a fleet of small boats to pick up more than a hundred thousand "**Marielitos**." Most of these arrivals again settled in Dade County. Miami is now officially bilingual, and the area around Eighth and Flagler Streets has become known as "Little Havana."

Another impact of the Cold War on Florida was in the birth of the space industry. In 1949, the U.S. Air Force acquired **Cape Canaveral**, and in 1950, it began testing missiles there. In 1958, NASA was formed and America entered the "space race." Florida has played a key role because all of the American rockets launched into space took off from Cape Canaveral. In 1963, NASA acquired 90,000 acres on nearby Merritt Island, which became the **Kennedy Space Center**. The space program brought tens of thousands of scientists to Florida, turning Central Florida into the "Space Coast."

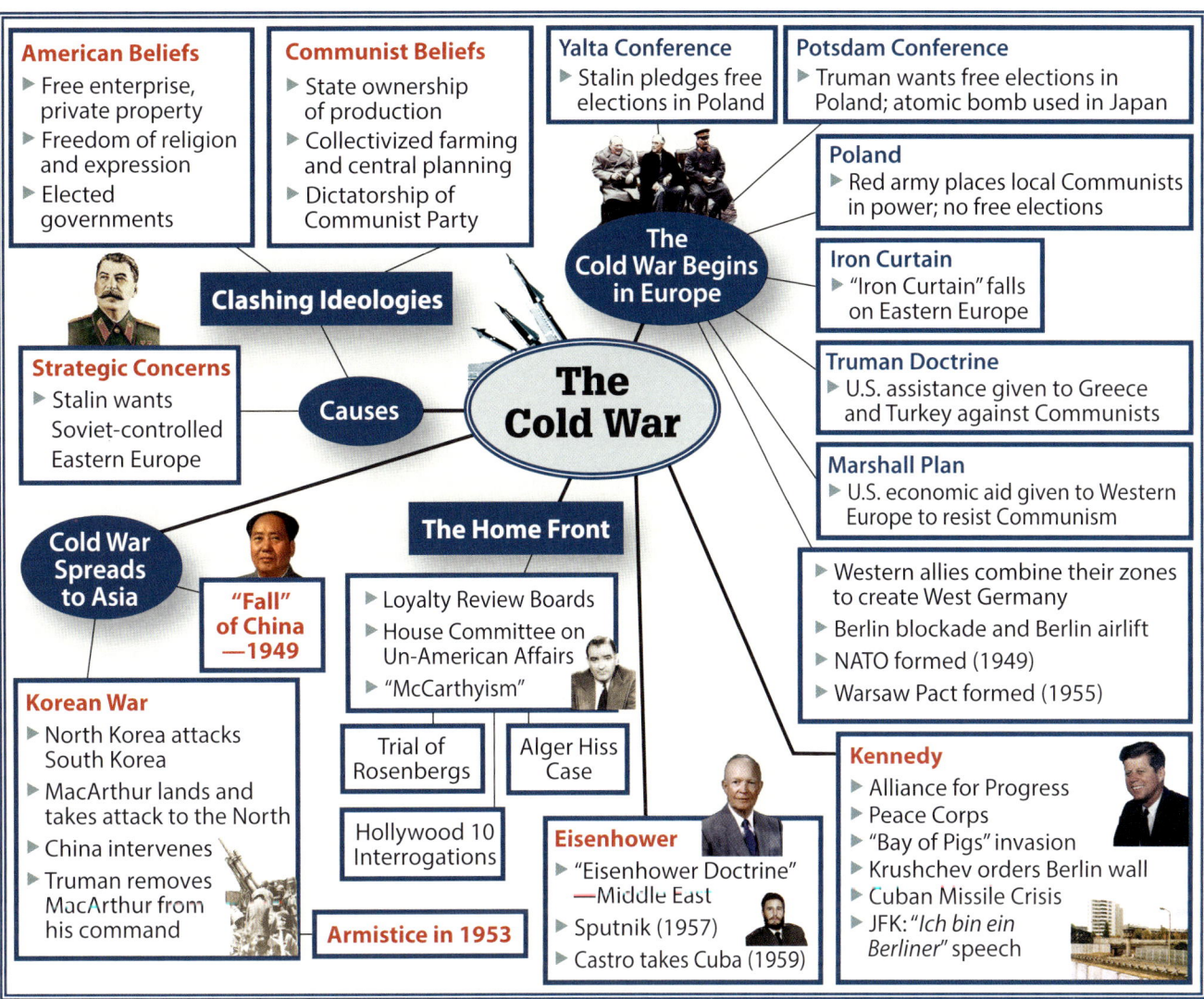

Review Cards

The Causes of the Cold War

The **Cold War** was rooted in the political, economic, and social differences between the two superpowers. Each superpower attempted to promote its way of life to other nations:

- The Soviet Union was a Communist country. Communists claimed that their society was run for the benefit of workers. In practice, the Soviet Union was a dictatorship run by Joseph Stalin. Citizens had limited rights and political opponents were imprisoned or killed. The country had a planned economy and collectivized agriculture. Factories were state-owned. Central planners told factory workers what and how much to produce.

- The United States was a capitalist democracy. People enjoyed individual rights, including free speech, freedom of press, and freedom of religion. They elected their own leaders. Americans could own property and run private businesses.

- Stalin mistrusted the West and resented the failure of Britain and the United States to open a second front before June 1944. He felt the Soviet Union had the right to control Eastern Europe to safeguard its own security.

- American leaders equally mistrusted Stalin. Stalin had promised free elections in Poland at Yalta but failed to honor his pledge. Americans refused to share the secret of the atomic bomb with the Soviets.

The Start of the Cold War in Europe

- Communists were placed in power in all those countries of Eastern Europe occupied by the Soviet ("Red") army after World War II.
- Trade, travel and communications between Eastern and Western Europe were cut. In 1946, Winston Churchill announced that an **"Iron Curtain"** had fallen on Eastern Europe.
- In 1947, Communists threatened the governments of Greece and Turkey.
- Truman announced the **Truman Doctrine** in March 1947: the United States would provide assistance to free peoples resisting Communism, including military and economic assistance to Turkey and Greece.
- In 1948, the United States announced the **Marshall Plan**: the United States would give economic aid to the countries of Western Europe to help them rebuild their economies, strengthen their resistance to Communism, and restore trade with the United States.
- **Containment Policy:** American leaders sought to "**contain**" Communism. They would not challenge Communism where it already existed, but they would prevent it from spreading further.

Events of the Early Cold War

The Division of Germany and the "Berlin Airlift":
- The Western Allies merged their occupation zones in Germany together to form **West Germany** (Federal Republic of Germany).
- Stalin reacted by cutting off all Western land routes to West Berlin in 1948.
- The United States and its allies responded with the "**Berlin Airlift**." Supplies were flown to West Berlin.
- After several months, Stalin reopened the roads to West Berlin.
- The Soviet occupation zone became **East Germany** (German Democratic Republic).

NATO vs. the Warsaw Pact:
- The Western Allies formed the North Atlantic Treaty Organization, or **NATO**, in 1949. NATO guaranteed the countries of Western Europe that they would be protected against Soviet attack by American nuclear weapons.
- The Soviet Union and its Eastern European **satellites** formed the **Warsaw Pact** in 1955.
- The Soviet Union sent its troops several times into Warsaw Pact countries to maintain Communism.

The Impact of the Cold War on Life in the United States

- In the United States, the Cold War led to a second "Red Scare." Many feared Communist spies.
- **Loyalty Review Boards** and the **House Committee on Un-American Activities** interrogated citizens on their political activities. After being investigated by the House Committee, the "**Hollywood 10**" lost their jobs.
- **Alger Hiss**, a prominent State Department official, was imprisoned for being a Communist.
- The **Rosenbergs** were tried and executed for giving atomic secrets to the Soviet Union.
- In the 1950s, **Senator Joseph McCarthy** claimed to have evidence of Communist spies in the State Department and other branches of government, but he never produced it. In 1953, McCarthy lost his influence when he challenged the army. The term "**McCarthyism**" now refers to anti-Communist hysteria.

The Cold War Spreads to Asia

The "Fall" of China:
- In 1949, China was taken over by Communist forces led by **Mao Zedong**. Mao declared the **People's Republic of China** in October 1949.
- Chiang Kai-Shek and the Chinese Nationalists fled to the island of Taiwan.
- The United States refused to recognize the Communist government of China.

The Korean War:
- Korea was divided in two after World War II along the 38th parallel. A Communist state was established in the North and a pro-Western government in the South.
- Communist North Korea attacked South Korea in June 1950.
- Truman decided to help the South Koreans resist the Communist attack. Truman acted with the approval of the U.N. Security Council.
- **General MacArthur** chased the North Koreans to the Yalu River on the border with China. His advance brought China into the war.
- MacArthur favored using nuclear weapons to defeat the Chinese. Truman dismissed MacArthur when he was openly critical of the President.
- A truce was signed at **Panmunjon** in 1953, leaving Korea divided along the 38th parallel just as before the war. The demilitarized zone, or **DMZ**, is the strip of land between the two countries.

Nuclear Proliferation and the Arms Race

- **Nuclear proliferation** refers to the spread of atomic weapons to other countries.
- This became a problem when the Soviet Union exploded its own atomic bomb in 1949. Within a few years, both superpowers developed much more destructive hydrogen bombs. Each power thought its nuclear arms served as a **deterrent** against attack.
- Nuclear weapons eventually spread to several other countries, including Britain, France, China, India, Pakistan, and Israel.
- The problem of nuclear proliferation remains today. How many more countries should have nuclear weapons? Should Iran have nuclear weapons? Does the spread of nuclear weapons increase the likelihood that these destructive weapons will be used, accidentally or deliberately, or fall into the hands of terrorists?

Foreign Policy Events under Eisenhower

- **Eisenhower Doctrine:** President Eisenhower announced the "**Eisenhower Doctrine**"—that the United States would oppose the spread of Communism in the Middle East—and sent troops to Lebanon.
- Sputnik: The Soviet success in sending *Sputnik* into space in 1957 caused the United States to increase its spending on science education.
- In Guatemala, CIA-trained exiles overturned a leftist government.
- **Castro and Cuba:** In 1959, **Fidel Castro** successfully overthrew **Batista**, a dictator in Cuba. Castro quickly imprisoned opponents and soon established a Communist state.
- When Castro seized some U.S. investments, Eisenhower began an economic boycott and let the CIA train Cuban exiles planning to overthrow Castro.

Foreign Policy Events under Kennedy	**The Cuban Missile Crisis**
▶ **Bay of Pigs Invasion:** In April 1961, a few months after John F. Kennedy became President, the Cuban exiles attempted to invade Cuba at the Bay of Pigs. However, Kennedy failed to give the exiles air cover and their invasion failed. ▶ **Berlin Wall:** In 1961, Soviet leader **Nikita Khrushchev** ordered the building of the **Berlin Wall** to prevent East Germans from escaping to West Berlin. ▶ **Kennedy's Berlin Speech:** When Kennedy later visited Berlin, he declared "I am a Berliner" to show his solidarity with the West Berliners. ▶ **Other Programs:** Kennedy started the Peace Corps, Alliance for Progress and "Green Berets" in his efforts to combat Communism.	▶ In October 1962, Americans discovered that Soviet nuclear missiles were about to be installed in Cuba. These missiles would have threatened Florida and other targets in the United States. This discovery led to the "**Cuban Missile Crisis**"—the closest the world has come to a nuclear war. ▶ America blockaded Cuba and threatened to invade the island. ▶ Khrushchev finally removed the missiles when Kennedy pledged not to invade Cuba and offered to remove U.S. missiles from Turkey. ▶ The United States and Soviet Union set up a "hot line" for emergency calls between their leaders; they also agreed to negotiate a partial test ban treaty.

What Do You Know?

SS.912.A.6.10

1. Which of these conditions was an economic cause of the Cold War in Europe?

    A. Stalin resented the fact that the Western Allies had delayed the invasion of France during the war.

    B. Truman failed to share the secrets of the atomic bomb at the Potsdam Conference.

    C. The United States had a capitalist system while the Soviet Union had a Communist system with central planning.

    D. Stalin felt the Soviet Union had the right to establish a "sphere of influence" in Eastern Europe.

SS.912.A.6.10

> At the present moment in history nearly every nation must choose between alternative ways of life. The choice is too often not a free one. . . .
>
> I believe it must be the policy of the United States to support free peoples who are resisting attempted subjugation [*overthrow*] by armed minorities or by outside pressures. . . . If we falter in our leadership, we may endanger the peace of the world—and we shall surely endanger the welfare of our own nation.
>
> —President Harry S. Truman, March 12, 1947

2. What threat was President Truman referring to in the speech above?

    A. a regional war between India and Pakistan

    B. the spread of Communism to Greece and Turkey

    C. Communist infiltration in the U. S. State Department

    D. Vietnamese resistance to the continuation of imperialism

SS.912.A.6.10

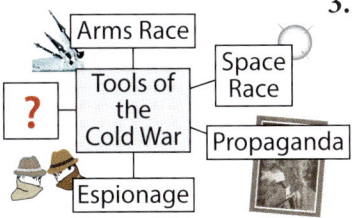

3. Which phrase best completes this graphic organizer?
   A. Military defeat of Nazi Germany
   B. Federal aid to American farmers
   C. Economic aid to other countries
   D. Free trade with Canada

SS.912.A.6.10

4. How was the Marshall Plan designed to discourage the spread of Communism in Europe?
   A. by joining European nations together into the European Union
   B. by restoring economic stability to the nations of Western Europe
   C. by providing military assistance to France, Great Britain, and Italy
   D. by establishing freely elected governments in Poland and Czechoslovakia

SS.912.A.6.13

The timeline below displays the sequence of several key events of the Cold War.

5. Which foreign policy did American leaders follow in response to these events?
   A. imperialism
   B. isolationism
   C. containment
   D. détente

SS.912.A.6.10

Article 5

The Parties agree that an armed attack against one or more of them in Europe or North America shall be considered an attack against them all and consequently they agree that, if such an armed attack occurs, each of them, in exercise of the right of individual or collective self-defense recognized by Article 51 of the Charter of the United Nations, will assist the Party or Parties so attacked by taking forthwith, individually and in concert with the other Parties, such action as it deems necessary, including the use of armed force, to restore and maintain the security of the North Atlantic area. —North Atlantic Treaty, April 4, 1949

6. Which action was a response to the organization created by this treaty?
   A. formation of the Warsaw Pact
   B. announcement of the Marshall Plan
   C. falling of the "Iron Curtain" over Eastern Europe
   D. application of the Eisenhower Doctrine to Lebanon

Chapter 13 | The Cold War

SS.912.A.6.13

? → Berlin Airlift, 1948

7. Which sentence best completes this diagram?

   A. Stalin cut off supply routes to democratic West Berlin.

   B. Stalin allowed free access to West Berlin by railroad and air.

   C. Stalin built a wall in Berlin to separate East and West Berliners.

   D. Stalin united all the Allied sectors of Berlin under one city government.

SS.912.A.6.13

This picture shows American soldiers placing milk on an airplane bound for Berlin in 1948.

8. What was the long-term significance of this airlift?

   A. It showed that the Western Allies had forgiven Germans for their actions in World War II.

   B. It demonstrated that the United States would resist any further attempts to spread Communism.

   C. It confirmed that Americans believed that Europe was more important than Asia.

   D. It indicated that air travel was becoming less expensive than travel by train or car.

SS.912.A.6.12

```
NR:   DA TT 3426                                          PAGE 2
      Detailed instructions reference Navy and Air Force follow
      All restrictions which have previously prevented the full utilization of the U.S.
Far East Air Forces to support and assist the defense of the South Korean territory
are lifted for operations below the 38th Parallel.  All North Korean tanks, guns,
military columns and other targets south of the 38th Parallel are cleared for attack
by U.S. Air Forces.  The purpose is to clear South Korea of North Korean military
forces.  Similarly U.S. Naval forces may be used without restriction in coastal waters
and sea approaches of Korea south of the 38th Parallel against forces engaged in
aggression against South Korea. (End DA-1)
Washington: DA-2
```

U.S. Army Teletype Conference, ca. June 1950, Library of Congress

9. Which foreign policy goal led to the instructions issued in the document above?

   A. American leaders wanted to prevent China from taking over North Korea.

   B. American leaders wanted to unite North and South into one democratic republic.

   C. American leaders wanted to maintain military bases in both North and South Korea.

   D. American leaders wanted to prevent Communist North Korea from taking over South Korea.

SS.912.A.6.12

10. Which statement best summarizes the outcome of the Korean War?

    A. North Korea made minor gains in the south but lost territory in the north to China.

    B. A majority of North Koreans fled southward causing a collapse of the North Korean government.

    C. North and South Korea remained divided at the 38th parallel, just as they had been before the war.

    D. Korea was reunited under a coalition government consisting of both Northerners and Southerners.

SS.912.A.6.13

The map below shows two alliances that existed in 1956.

11. Based on the information on the map, which action would have triggered American intervention in 1956?

    A. Soviet repression of an anti-Communist government in Hungary

    B. a declaration of independent statehood by the Belgian Congo

    C. Soviet intervention in support of a local Communist party in Turkey

    D. the outbreak of an armed conflict between China and Mongolia

SS.912.A.6.8

▶ The National Aeronautics and Space Administration (NASA) was created
▶ National Defense Education Act passed
▶ Increased federal money was provided to improve schools, especially in math and science
▶ More money was appropriated by Congress for research and development

12. Which event sparked these changes?

    A. The Soviet Union launched its satellite, *Sputnik*.

    B. Mao Zedong led a successful Communist revolution in China.

    C. North Korea crossed the 38th parallel to invade South Korea.

    D. Senator Joseph McCarthy announced the discovery of "Reds" in the State Department.

Chapter 13 | The Cold War

SS.912.A.6.13

> My fellow citizens of the world: ask not what America will do for you, but what together we can do for the freedom of man . . .
>
> —John F. Kennedy, Inaugural Address, 1961

13. Which program was started by President Kennedy to further the ideals expressed in this part of his Inaugural Address?

   A. Peace Corps
   B. the space program
   C. South East Asia Treaty Organization (SEATO)
   D. opening of relations with the People's Republic of China (PRC)

SS.912.A.6.13

14. What was an important consequence of the Cuban Missile Crisis?

   A. The Soviet Union secretly kept nuclear missiles in Cuba pointed at Florida.
   B. The United States kept missiles in Turkey and Greece pointed at the Soviet Union.
   C. Fidel Castro was removed from power in Cuba and all nuclear weapons were taken out of Cuba.
   D. Soviet and American leaders established an emergency "hot line" and negotiated a partial test ban treaty.

SS.912.A.6.11

15. This photograph shows missiles being displayed in a parade in East Berlin during the Cold War.

   Which problem of the Cold War is highlighted by this photograph?

   A. the dangers of nuclear proliferation
   B. the lack of free speech and freedom of religion under Communism
   C. the inability of Communist countries to supply enough consumer goods
   D. the failure of Eastern Europe to maintain trade and travel with the West

SS.912.A.6.15

16. How did the Cold War most affect Florida?

   A. Nuclear missiles installed in Cuba threatened the survival of Florida.
   B. People in Florida could no longer sell their products to Eastern Europe.
   C. Hundreds of thousands of refugees fled Castro's Communist dictatorship for Florida.
   D. Senator Joseph McCarthy accused a large number of people in Florida of being Communists.

Unit V: World War II and the Cold War (Chapters 12–13)

Identify or define each of the following terms.

Adolf Hitler _____

_____

Neutrality Acts _____

_____

Pearl Harbor _____

_____

D-Day _____

_____

Korematsu v. U.S. _____

_____

Holocaust _____

_____

Hiroshima _____

_____

United Nations _____

_____

Joseph Stalin _____

_____

Iron Curtain _____

_____

Truman Doctrine _____

_____

North Atlantic Treaty Organization _____

_____

Korean War _____

_____

McCarthyism_____

_____

Cuban Missile Crisis _____

_____

World War II Crossword Puzzle

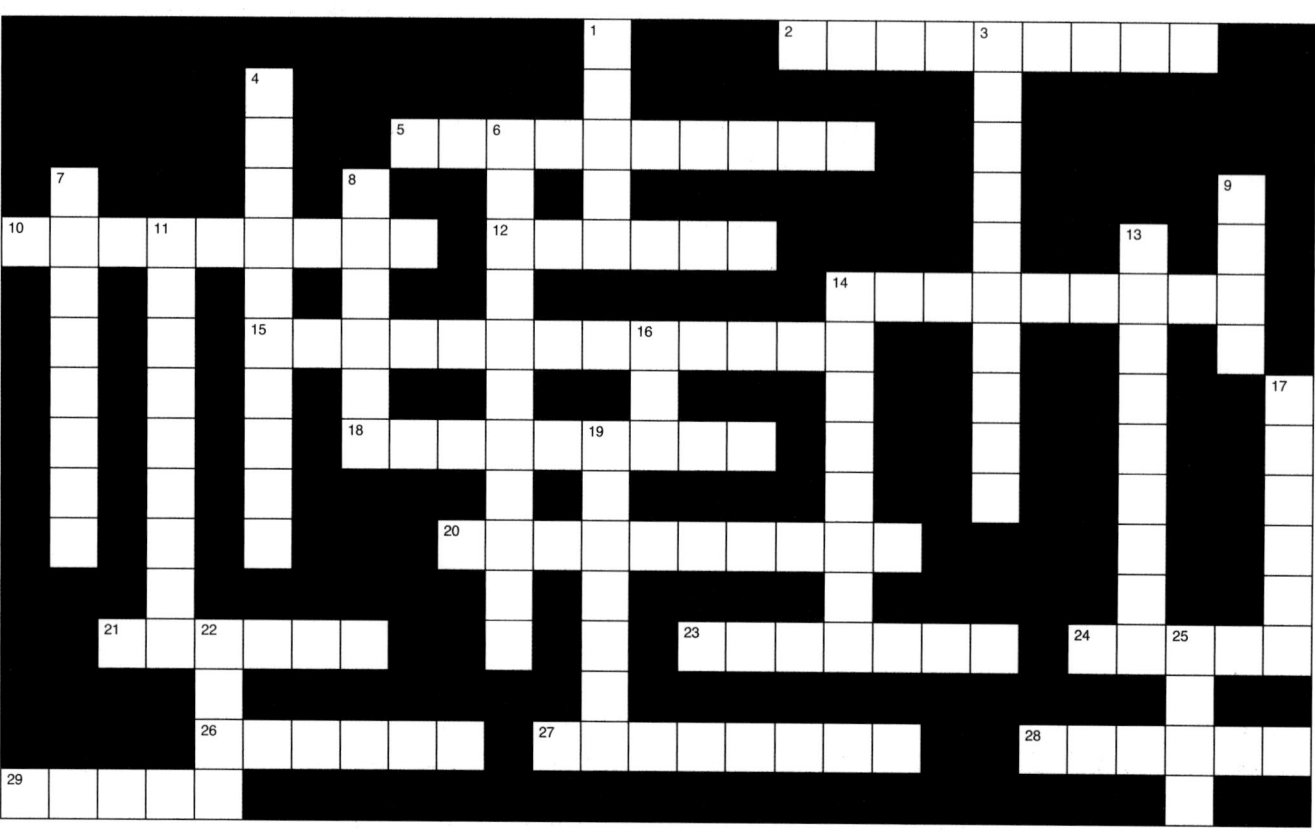

Across

2. British Prime Minister during World War II
5. Roosevelt's _____ Speech suggested that peaceful nations band together against aggressive nations to isolate them
10. The atomic bomb was developed in a top-secret operation called the _____ Project
12. World War II began when Germany and the Soviet Union attacked _____
14. Nazi extermination camp in southern Poland
15. Turning point when Nazi government began taking more active measures of persecution against Jews
18. Allies put surviving Nazi leaders on trial for crimes against humanity in the _____ Trials
20. A series of _____ Acts were passed from 1935–1937 to keep the United States out of World War II
21. Soviet dictator during World War II
23. Mussolini was a _____ dictator
24. Invention that helped detect flying aircraft
26. The Battle of _____ helped halt the Japanese advance in the Pacific
27. Murder of an entire race of people
28. In 1942, Japanese forced weak American and Filipino POWs to walk an 80-mile hike in the _____ Death March
29. Germany's military leaders surrendered to the Allies on May 7–8, 1944, known as _____

Down

1. On December 7, 1941, Japan attacked _____ Harbor, Hawaii
3. The United Nations relies partly on _____ security to keep peace in the world
4. "Lightning" warfare introduced by German forces in World War II
6. Giving in to the demands of a potential enemy
7. The second U.S. atomic bomb to explode in Japan was over _____
8. During World War II, _____ books were used to obtain essential goods such as canned foods, gasoline, and heating fuel
9. Political party that believed Germans were a superior race
11. Hitler's systematic slaughter of millions of Jews and other peoples
13. On August 6, 1945, a U.S. atomic bomb exploded over _____
14. The _____ Charter laid the foundation for the later formation of the United Nations
16. A Congressional Committee that in 1936 reported unfair practices by U.S. munitions companies in World War I
17. Author of *Mein Kampf*
19. The only black female delegate to attend the San Francisco Conference, which drafted the United Nations Charter
22. WAC: acronym for Women's _____ Corps
25. Massive amphibious invasion of France by American and British troops in 1944

CHAPTER 14

Postwar Prosperity and Civil Rights

SS.912.A.7.1 Identify causes for post-World War II prosperity and its effects on American society.

SS.912.A.7.2 Compare the relative prosperity between different ethnic groups and social classes in the post-World War II period.

SS.912.A.7.5 Compare nonviolent and violent approaches utilized by groups (African Americans . . .) to achieve civil rights.

SS.912.A.7.6 Assess key figures and organizations in shaping the Civil Rights Movement and Black Power Movement.

SS.912.A.7.7 Assess the building of coalitions between African Americans, whites, and other groups in achieving integration and equal rights.

SS.912.A.7.8 Analyze significant Supreme Court decisions relating to integration, busing [and] affirmative action . . .

SS.912.A.7.17 Examine key events and peoples in Florida history as they relate to United States history.

Names and Terms You Should Know

- Demobilization
- G.I. Bill of Rights
- Suburbs
- Birth rate
- Baby boomers
- Interstate Highway System
- NAACP
- National Urban League
- Congress of Racial Equality (CORE)
- *Brown v. Board of Education* (1954)
- Segregation
- Thurgood Marshall
- Integration
- Busing
- Rosa Parks
- Montgomery Bus Boycott
- Dr. Martin Luther King, Jr.
- Southern Christian Leadership Conference (SCLC)
- Social activism
- Sit-ins
- Student Nonviolent Coordinating Committee (SNCC)
- Freedom Riders
- March on Washington (1963)
- Civil Rights Act (1964)
- Voting Rights Act (1965)
- Affirmative action
- *Regents of the University of California v. Bakke* (1978)
- Black Power
- Nation of Islam
- Malcolm X
- Stokely Carmichael
- Black Panthers

Florida "Keys" to Learning

1. The end of the war led to demobilization and the "Baby Boom." The G.I. Bill of Rights gave returning veterans benefits such as low-interest loans to buy a home and money for education. With European economies devastated by the war, American manufacturers faced less competition. Government spending on defense remained high due to the Cold War. Americans experienced a long period of prosperity.

2. With greater purchasing power, Americans could afford refrigerators, cars, and televisions. Suburban housing developments like Levittown helped many Americans afford their own homes. The Federal Highway Act created highways that linked cities and suburbs. Prosperity, mass production, and mass consumption led to greater conformity. The media created a mass culture geared toward the middle class.

3. The Civil Rights Movement was launched in the postwar era and continued into the 1960s. African-American organizations, such as the NAACP, the National Urban League, and CORE (the Congress of Racial Equality) played an important role.

4. In 1948, President Truman desegregated the military. In 1954, the Supreme Court decision in *Brown v. Board of Education* held that segregation had no place in public education because it was inherently unequal. When the Governor of Arkansas tried to prevent nine black students from attending an all-white school in Little Rock in 1957, President Eisenhower sent in federal troops.

5. In 1955, Rosa Parks was arrested for refusing to move to the back of a city bus in Montgomery, Alabama. Dr. Martin Luther King, Jr., led a boycott of the city's buses. King believed in non-violent agitation to end oppression. The boycott ran for almost a year until a federal court ordered the public transit system to desegregate. King and others formed the Southern Christian Leadership Council (SCLC). A similar bus boycott occurred in Tallahassee, Florida, in 1956.

6. In 1960, black and white students staged a "sit-in" at a lunch counter in Greensboro, North Carolina, in which they sat together in a "white" section and refused to move. White and black students from 30 states formed the Student Nonviolent Coordinating Committee (SNCC). In 1961, CORE organized "Freedom Rides," in which interracial groups refused to sit in segregated sections of buses traveling across Southern states.

7. In 1963, Martin Luther King and other leaders led a march on Birmingham, Alabama. They were arrested, and King wrote his "Letter from Birmingham Jail." President Kennedy, alarmed by the police violence, proposed a civil rights bill. In 1963, civil rights leaders organized a "March on Washington" in support of Kennedy's bill. King delivered his "I Have a Dream" speech. After Kennedy's assassination, President Johnson pushed the Civil Rights Act of 1964 through Congress. It banned racial discrimination in hotels, restaurants, and unions. In 1965, President Johnson introduced "affirmative action" to increase opportunities for minorities and women.

8. The 24th Amendment (1964) prohibited poll taxes. "Freedom Summer" was a campaign to register black voters in Mississippi. Violence against marchers from Selma to Montgomery led President Johnson to introduce the Voting Rights Act of 1965.

9. In 1968, Dr. King was assassinated, causing riots across the nation. The "Black Power" Movement demanded that African Americans take control of their own communities, challenge racism more directly, and reduce contact with whites. Malcolm X urged African Americans to fight violence with violence and adopt "black nationalism." Stokely Carmichael introduced the term "Black Power." He favored black separatism and violence to combat racism. The Black Panther Party was formed to protect black neighborhoods in Oakland, California. The Panthers called for the arming of African Americans but also implemented social programs. The "Black Power" Movement called for greater pride in the African-American identity and led to the creation of new fashions, the "Afro" hairstyle, and black studies courses in universities.

The Postwar Prosperity

The late 1940s and early 1950s were a period of astonishing economic growth in the United States. One British Prime Minister called this period in America "the greatest prosperity the world has ever known." A combination of political, economic, and social factors contributed to this postwar prosperity.

Demobilization

At the height of World War II, there were eight million American men and women in uniform. American factories were producing enormous numbers of tanks, aircraft, battleships, guns, and ammunition in order to protect American lives. In August 1945, Japan surrendered and the war was over. Millions of American soldiers began returning home. Factories were converted to peacetime uses. **Demobilization** refers to the process of ending military operations, halting wartime production, and retiring troops from active service. By 1947, the armed forces had shrunk to 1.5 million; eventually, they wound down to 600,000. People whose lives had been disrupted by the war settled down to work and have families.

The "G.I. Bill of Rights"

In 1944, Congress passed the "Servicemen's Readjustment Act," better known as the "**G.I. Bill of Rights**." G.I. stood for "Government Issue"—the term applied to military equipment, like helmets and uniforms, furnished by the government. G.I. came to refer to the soldiers themselves during the war. The G.I. Bill gave special benefits to returning veterans, including unemployment payments while they were looking for work, mortgages at low rates so that they could buy their own homes, low interest loans to start businesses, and money to enable them to pursue further education ($500 a year for tuition and another $50 a month for living expenses while they attended school, at a time when prices were far less than today). Every veteran who served at least 90 days was qualified to receive these benefits. More than two million veterans eventually used G.I. benefits to go to college, while another five million used G.I. benefits to receive some other form of training.

The Baby Boom

Many war veterans quickly married and had children, leading to a surge in the **birth rate** (*the number of babies born per 1,000 people*) known as the "**baby boom**." Between 3.5 and 4.2 million babies were born each year for a period of more than a decade. Those born in these postwar years became known as the "baby boomers."

Postwar Economic Policies

In 1946, the nation was shaken by a series of strikes. In 1947, Congress passed the **Taft-Hartley Act**, which reversed some of the gains labor unions had made a decade earlier. The new law outlawed the "closed shop," in which businesses could hire only union members. It also prohibited secondary boycotts and other "unfair labor practices."

In these years, the Truman Administration laid the groundwork for the postwar economic order. The **Employment Act of 1946** announced that the goal of federal economic policy was to promote maximum production and full employment. The same law established the "Council of Economic Advisers," a group of experts that advises the President on economic matters.

America—the World's Leading Producer

With much of Europe and Asia in ruins, America became the world's largest producer. With less than 7% of the world's population, the United States became responsible for 50% of its manufacturing output. In these years, Americans produced 57% of the world's steel, 62% of its oil, 80% of its automobiles, and 43% of its electricity.

There was little foreign competition and American crops and manufactured goods were badly needed overseas. The Marshall Plan gave Europeans more purchasing power and expanded the demand for American goods. The demand for consumer goods within the United States was also at an all-time high. The use of assembly-line production methods had brought down the prices of many goods. With higher incomes and lower unemployment, American families bought vast quantities of mass-produced goods, from refrigerators and washing machines to cars and television sets. 50 million automobiles and 50 million television sets were sold in the decade after World War II.

Government spending also contributed to economic growth. Postwar spending by both federal and state governments was far above pre-war levels. When the Korean War began, government spending increased even further. The Federal Reserve increased the U.S. money supply, also encouraging economic growth.

New technologies and methods of production also contributed to American economic supremacy during these years. During the war, new drugs, new synthetic materials, and new inventions like the jet engine had been developed or improved. These innovations were now put to peacetime purposes. Many Americans found jobs in the aircraft, electrical, chemical, automobile, and food-processing industries. With restrictions on immigration, most of these new jobs went to workers already living in the United States. The **Gross National Product** (or GNP)—*the goods and services produced in one year by all Americans*—doubled in the fifteen years between 1945 and 1960. Real incomes rose by 59% between 1950 and 1962, while unemployment remained low (at about 4%).

Housing and the Growth of Suburbs

Home construction increased employment and also contributed to economic growth. The G.I. Bill and the Federal Housing Administration made it easier for Americans to secure loans for houses. Between 1945 and 1960, American home ownership increased by one-half.

In 1947, William Levitt built **Levittown**, New York—the first mass-produced housing development. Each house was built with an identical design and provided with a white fence, a green lawn, a refrigerator and washing machine, and other basic amenities. Levitt applied the techniques of assembly-line production to build these homes at low cost and at breakneck speed. With their housing benefits, veterans could often buy Levitt's houses for less than it cost to rent an apartment. Levitt built three other "Levittowns," and his ideas were quickly imitated by other developers.

Suburbs—residential communities with single-family houses, private lawns, and plenty of fresh air on the outskirts of cities—began to grow faster than the cities they surrounded. The movement of middle-income families from cities to suburbs contributed to a declining tax base in the nation's inner cities. Once vibrant downtown areas became increasingly poor as businesses and wealthy residents left these areas for the suburbs.

The Historian's Apprentice

▶ Which factors most contributed to the postwar prosperity?
▶ What lessons from the postwar period might be applied to encourage economic growth today?

The Eisenhower Years, 1953–1960

Dwight Eisenhower was elected President in November 1952. Despite being the first Republican President in 20 years, he preserved the programs of the New Deal. At the same time, he tried to reduce government spending and to promote American business interests.

One of Eisenhower's greatest achievements was a public project. During the war, Eisenhower had been impressed by the German highway system and its role in transporting troops. He believed that Americans needed a similar system, in part for the national defense, to be able to move troops or evacuate cities in case of war. In 1956, Congress passed the **Federal Highway Act**, which led to the construction of the **Interstate Highway System**—the network of highways that still unites our country today. The building of these highways contributed to prosperity and encouraged the migration of middle-class Americans to the suburbs. They could drive on the highway to get to work in the city each morning, and drive back along the same route to return to the suburbs each night.

The Age of Conformity

Prosperity led to a new emphasis on **conformity** in the postwar years. (To "conform" is to act like everyone else.) At work, many Americans were employees of large corporations with fixed expectations and little room for individuality. At home, a growing number of Americans lived in suburbs in houses that were similar or identical to those of their neighbors. Many suburban communities established their own rules, which residents were expected to obey. They also enforced racial, ethnic, and religious uniformity: white residents in suburbs signed agreements pledging not to sell their houses to people of color. Universities had quotas limiting the number of Jewish applicants they would admit. Americans purchased similar mass-produced cars, appliances, clothing, and food. The rise of the mass media—newspapers, magazines, movies, radio, and above all television—helped to create a new mass culture, which extolled the virtues of middle-class family life. Popular television programs, like "Father Knows Best" and "Leave it to Beaver," depicted what was supposed to be a typical American family—white, middle-class, living in the suburbs, with the father at work, the mother at home, and two or three children. Unusual ideas and independent thinking were frowned upon. Fear of Communism greatly strengthened the general dislike of non-conformist attitudes.

Limitations on the Postwar Prosperity

As in the 1920s, the postwar prosperity did not reach everyone. African Americans, Hispanic Americans, and American Indians were generally excluded from middle-class jobs or the opportunity to move to the suburbs. Minority veterans often found it more difficult to obtain the benefits to which they were entitled by the G.I. Bill. In the South, African Americans continued as tenant farmers; in the North, many were engaged in menial jobs. Many Hispanic Americans, especially in the West, worked as migrant farm workers. Members of minorities were rarely depicted in the movies, television, the radio or magazines except in subordinate or even demeaning roles.

The Civil Rights Movement

The **Civil Rights Movement** was a major turning point in American history, not only in achieving equal rights for African Americans but also in the transformation of the United States into a more pluralistic society. The struggle was long and hard because racism and prejudice were deeply ingrained in American life.

Chapter 14 | Postwar Prosperity and Civil Rights

Factors behind the Emergence of the Civil Rights Movement

Continuing Inequalities

A hundred years earlier, the Civil War and Reconstruction had held out the promise of equality for African Americans. But in the aftermath of Reconstruction, African Americans had been deprived of their political and civil rights. "**Jim Crow**" **laws** maintained racial segregation across the South, confining African Americans to the poorest neighborhoods and schools, and denying them higher education or better job opportunities. They were deprived of the right to vote, to hold office or to sit on juries. They were also subjected to a humiliating code of social conduct—Southern blacks were expected to take their hats off when addressing whites, while African-American men were addressed as "boy" even when they were adults. Poverty, inferior schools, and periodic acts of violence such as lynchings prevented Southern blacks from improving their conditions.

An African American drinking from a "colored" water fountain

In the early 20th century, many African Americans attempted to escape racism and poverty in the South by fleeing to cities in the North during the "Great Migration." But here, too, they faced racist attitudes and discrimination in employment and housing. They were often forced to take the worst jobs, to live in crowded urban ghettos, and to send their children to the worst schools. African Americans had twice the level of unemployment as whites, and many unions refused to accept them as members. Even the federal government discriminated against African Americans in its hiring policies and practiced segregation in the armed services.

American Egalitarian Ideals

Against these harsh realities stood the ideals expressed in the Declaration of Independence, the U.S. Constitution, and the Fourteenth and Fifteenth Amendments. These documents proclaimed that all people were "created equal" and that all citizens were entitled to the "equal protection of the laws." The full impact of these words, however, had yet to be realized.

The Role of African-American Organizations

Ever since emancipation, black leaders—with the help of sympathetic whites—had been fighting for their rights. The **NAACP** and **National Urban League** had both been founded in New York City in the first decade of the 20th century. The Urban League had originally aimed at increasing job opportunities for black Americans, while the NAACP had focused on advancing civil rights. African-American church organizations also played a major role in mobilizing the black community. They provided places where African Americans could interact as a community, freely discuss ideas, and develop leadership skills.

Howard University, founded in the 1870s, provided another training ground for African-American leaders. **Charles Hamilton Houston**, an African-American graduate of Harvard Law School and one of the first African-American officers in the U.S. Army, began training lawyers at Howard with the intention of overturning segregation in education. As early as the 1930s, Houston began taking photographs throughout the South to document the conditions of public schools for white and black children.

In the 1940s, **James Farmer** and other African Americans formed the **Congress of Racial Equality**, or "**CORE**." Influenced by Gandhi's campaign against the British in India, CORE members wished to use non-violent means of protest to fight segregation and racism.

The Impact of World War II

During World War II, the United States had struggled to defend democracy. More than one million

African Americans had joined the armed services during the war years. Half a million of them went overseas, where they experienced less racism than in many parts of the United States. Discriminatory hiring by defense contractors was prohibited, opening the door to jobs for African Americans on the Home Front. These developments encouraged African Americans to raise their voices in the fight for greater rights and equality at home. Meanwhile, the shocking atrocities committed by the Nazis during the war made many Americans more aware of the dangers of racism.

The Influence of Struggles in Asia and Africa

The Civil Rights Movement in the United States was closely tied to anti-colonial movements in Asia and Africa, where local peoples were struggling for independence from imperial rule. The use of non-violent methods of resistance to British rule in India by Mohandas ("Mahatma") Gandhi deeply influenced Civil Rights leaders like Dr. Martin Luther King. As African peoples fought for their independence from Europe, African Americans were fighting for their civil rights in the United States.

The Cold War

The Cold War made American leaders especially sensitive to the criticism that the United States was undemocratic, since they were claiming to be the champions of the "Free World." Acts of blatant racism and discrimination threatened to tarnish the American image overseas.

The Historian's Apprentice

▶ Make your own illustrated concept map or chart showing those factors that led to the birth of the Civil Rights Movement in the postwar years.

▶ Which of these factors do you think were the most important ones? Explain your answer in a brief essay.

The Struggle to End Racial Segregation

The modern Civil Rights Movement was launched in the postwar era and continued into the late 1960s, when it splintered into a variety of different and sometimes conflicting groups. Major gains were made, especially in the South. None of these were achieved without the intervention of the federal government and the participation of "grass-roots" movements of African Americans and sympathetic whites.

The Truman Years, 1945–1953

In 1947, **Jackie Robinson** became the first African-American Major League baseball player. In 1948, Truman ordered the desegregation of the armed forces and an end to discrimination in hiring by the federal government. Several Northern states, such as New York, passed their own laws outlawing discrimination in housing, employment, and the use of public services.

Brown v. Board of Education of Topeka, Kansas, 1954

Half a century earlier, Homer Plessy had challenged racial segregation in the South by sitting down in the white passenger car of a train. But in *Plessy v. Ferguson*, the U.S. Supreme Court had affirmed the constitutionality of segregation laws, so long as the facilities offered to each race were of "equal standards" (see Chapter 2, page 33). This became known as the "separate-but-equal" doctrine.

Chapter 14 | Postwar Prosperity and Civil Rights

Starting in the 1930s, black lawyers at the NAACP, led by Charles Hamilton Houston, began challenging the "separate-but-equal" doctrine in public education. They launched an ambitious strategy by filing a series of lawsuits challenging state laws. They began by questioning the exclusion of African Americans from law schools and graduate programs in state universities across the South. Since there were no state law schools for blacks, these states had failed to meet the "separate-but-equal" requirement. Last minute efforts by several states to set up separate programs for blacks failed to be "equal." The Supreme Court ruled in favor of the NAACP on the grounds that African Americans had not been offered "equal" alternatives by these states.

In the early 1950s, the NAACP moved to challenge the "separate but equal" policy itself. Linda Brown was a school girl in Topeka, Kansas. Her father sued the school board because she had been forced to attend an all-black school when an all-white school was closer to their home. In 1953, the NAACP appealed her case with a number of others to the U.S. Supreme Court. **Thurgood Marshall**, the NAACP lawyer handling the case, did not argue that the facilities given to African-American children were inferior (although this was generally the case). Instead, he argued that every system of segregated education by its very nature sent black children the psychological message that they were not "good enough" to be taught with whites.

Thurgood Marshall

Marshall supported his argument with the findings of a famous African-American psychologist, Kenneth Clark. Clark showed white and black dolls to African-American children and found that the children preferred the white dolls to black ones. Clark concluded that racial segregation had led to this painful sense of inferiority.

Earl Warren, former Governor of California, had only just been appointed as the Chief Justice of the Supreme Court. As Attorney General of California in the 1940s, Warren had assisted in the forced relocation of innocent Japanese Americans during the war. Regretting his earlier actions, he became a committed supporter of civil rights. As Chief Justice, Warren wanted to avoid a divided decision on the *Brown* case. With great effort, he obtained the support of all his fellow Justices. Warren wrote their unanimous decision, declaring that racial segregation in public schools was unconstitutional. "Separate but equal," he boldly announced, "has no place" in the field of public education:

Justice Earl Warren

> *"Does segregation of children in public schools solely on the basis of race, even though the physical facilities and other 'tangible' factors may be equal, deprive the children of the minority group of equal educational opportunities? We believe that it does. . . . Segregation of white and colored children in public schools has a detrimental effect upon the colored children. The impact is greater when it has the sanction of the law, for the policy of separating the races is usually interpreted as denoting the inferiority of the negro group. A sense of inferiority affects the motivation of a child to learn. . . . We conclude that, in the field of public education, the doctrine of 'separate but equal' has no place. Separate educational facilities are inherently unequal."*
>
> —U.S. Supreme Court, *Brown v. Board of Education of Topeka, Kansas* (1954)

▶ Why did Justice Warren conclude that segregated schools were "inherently" unequal?

▶ How was this conclusion important to the Court's judgment?

Southern Senators in Congress immediately signed a public protest against the *Brown* decision. Local officials across the South swore they would never enforce it. Violence in the South increased dramatically with a greater number of lynchings and an increase in

Emmet Till

membership in the Ku Klux Klan. Emmet Till, a 14-year old black boy from Chicago, visited his aunt in Mississippi in 1955: he was murdered after he whistled at a young white woman in a shop. Many were shocked, especially in the North, when the murderers were acquitted by an all-white Southern jury, despite the overwhelming evidence against them.

Southern resistance required the Supreme Court to make a separate ruling on how the *Brown* decision was to be implemented (*put into effect*) a year later. Enforcement of the *Brown* decision was handed over to the lower federal courts, which were to see that local school districts complied with the desegregation order "with all deliberate speed." Nonetheless, the *Brown* decision would take many years to carry out. Many Southern public schools closed rather than **integrate** (*bring people of different races together*). In some cases, courts later resorted to **busing**—requiring districts to send students in school buses to more distant schools in order to achieve a better racial mix.

The Montgomery Bus Boycott, 1955–56

In the 1950s, the system of segregation in the South extended far beyond education. African Americans were prevented from sharing restaurants, lunch counters, movie theaters, public restrooms, and even water fountains with whites. On public buses, African Americans were forced to sit in the back seats, while the front section of the bus was reserved for whites.

One evening in December 1955, **Rosa Parks** was riding home on a city bus in Montgomery, the state capital of Alabama. The bus became increasingly crowded. When a white passenger entered and there was no room left in the "white" section, the bus driver asked Parks to get up and move to the back of the bus. Parks,

Rosa Parks

an active member of the local branch of the NAACP, refused to do so and was arrested. Local NAACP leaders organized an immediate boycott of Montgomery's city buses to protest her arrest. They demanded courteous treatment, an end to segregation on the bus, and the hiring of African-American bus drivers.

Dr. Martin Luther King, Jr.

They formed the Montgomery Improvement Organization and elected as their leader an inspiring young Baptist minister, **Dr. Martin Luther King, Jr.** King had studied the writings of David Thoreau and Mahatma Gandhi on non-violence, as well as Christian teachings. He believed that passive resistance to unjust laws could change the attitudes of oppressors. The organizers arranged car pools and cabs to take boycotters to work; others walked. City buses sat idle. The boycott, which lasted just over a year, demonstrated that African Americans could act together in their determination to oppose segregation. At the same time, Parks and other bus riders sued in federal court, claiming that segregation on public buses was unconstitutional. In June 1956, the court ruled in their favor. Five months later, the U.S. Supreme Court refused to review the decision, in effect upholding it. The protestors had won the contest, and the city buses were integrated. After the boycott was over, Dr. King, Ralph Abernathy, and other African-American ministers formed the **Southern Christian Leadership Council**, or the "**SCLC**." The goal of this new organization was to fight for racial equality by using non-violent means.

Little Rock, Arkansas, 1957

Meanwhile, Southern state officials had deliberately delayed implementing the *Brown* decision. When the school board of Little Rock, Arkansas, admitted nine black children to its all-white high school, the Governor of Arkansas ordered the state's National Guard to prevent the children from entering

Chapter 14 | Postwar Prosperity and Civil Rights

Civil Rights Timeline

- **July 1948:** President Truman orders desegregation of U.S. armed forces
- **May 1954:** *Brown v. Board of Education of Topeka, Kansas*
- **May 1955:** US Supreme Court orders school desegregation "with all deliberate speed"
- **Dec 1955–Nov 1956:** Montgomery bus boycott
- **Jan 1957:** SCLC founded
- **Sept 1957:** Federal troops sent to Little Rock, Arkansas
- **Sept 1957:** Civil Rights Act of 1957
- **Feb 1960:** Greensboro, NC "Sit-in"
- **April 1960:** SNCC founded

the school. After pressure from President Eisenhower, the Governor removed the National Guard and allowed the children to attend the school, but he took inadequate steps to protect them. The "Little Rock Nine" (the nine students) were threatened by an angry white mob. This finally forced President Eisenhower to take decisive action: he sent 1,000 federal troops to Little Rock and ordered the Arkansas National Guard to defend the black students. Federal troops surrounded the high school, and for the rest of the year the students were given military escorts.

The Civil Rights Acts of 1957 and 1960

Southern resistance and continuing violence convinced Congress that new legislation was needed. The Civil Rights Act of 1957—the first federal civil rights act since Reconstruction—focused on voting issues. The law created the Civil Rights Commission, which led to formation of a new "Civil Rights" division in the Justice Department, and made it a federal crime to interfere with the rights of voters. The Civil Rights Act of 1960 strengthened the powers of the Commission and of the Justice Department to inspect voting records and to punish those who attempted to stop blacks from voting. Unfortunately, these acts proved ineffective.

"Sit-Ins" and SNCC

African-American organizations continued to push for racial equality through **social activism**—*efforts to promote political and social change through direct action*. In 1960, a group of African-American students sat at a "whites only" lunch counter in Greensboro, North Carolina. They refused to get up, even when they were surrounded and assaulted by an angry crowd. Their tactic, known as a "**sit-in**," was widely copied by other students throughout the South. They staged sit-ins at other lunch counters, libraries, parks, pools, and other public places, where they were often taunted, beaten, or arrested.

A group of students from 30 states, many active in the sit-ins, gathered in North Carolina in the spring of 1960. They formed another new civil rights organization: the **Student Nonviolent Coordinating Committee**, or "**SNCC**."

The Kennedy Years, 1961–1963

Senator John F. Kennedy actively campaigned for African-American support during the Presidential election of 1960. Once in office, he was reluctant to push for civil rights because he did not want to lose the support of Southern Democrats. But as the violence in the South escalated, Kennedy became more open in his support of civil rights. In 1962, he proposed a constitutional amendment to ban poll taxes in federal elections, since these had been used to keep African Americans from voting in the South.

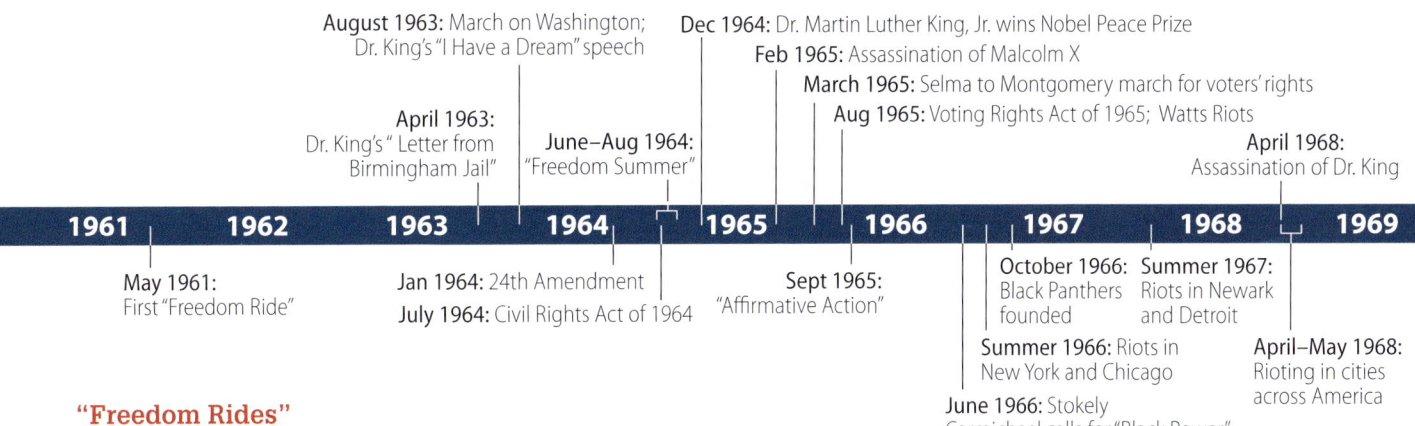

"Freedom Rides"

Since 1955, federal laws had prohibited segregated seating on buses traveling through more than one state, but these laws were difficult to enforce. CORE organized the first "**Freedom Ride**" in 1961. During a "Freedom Ride," a small interracial group rode a bus traveling through several Southern states. They sat together in interracial pairs or in sections often reserved for whites. The organizers of the "Freedom Rides" hoped to provoke a crisis so that the federal government would be forced to intervene. Freedom Riders often faced violence. They were attacked by angry mobs, arrested by hostile police, and even bombed. Young white students as well as blacks proved willing to risk injury and even death as Freedom Riders. Federal marshals eventually had to be sent in to protect them.

Letter from Birmingham Jail, 1963

In the spring of 1963, Dr. King and other Civil Rights leaders focused their efforts on Birmingham, the largest city in Alabama. King led a march into the city. He was arrested and put in solitary confinement. While a prisoner, he wrote his famous "Letter from Birmingham Jail," explaining why, after 340 years, African Americans could no longer delay their fight for equal rights.

As more demonstrators were arrested, they began to fill the jails of Birmingham. The new medium of television revealed to the rest of the nation the brutal

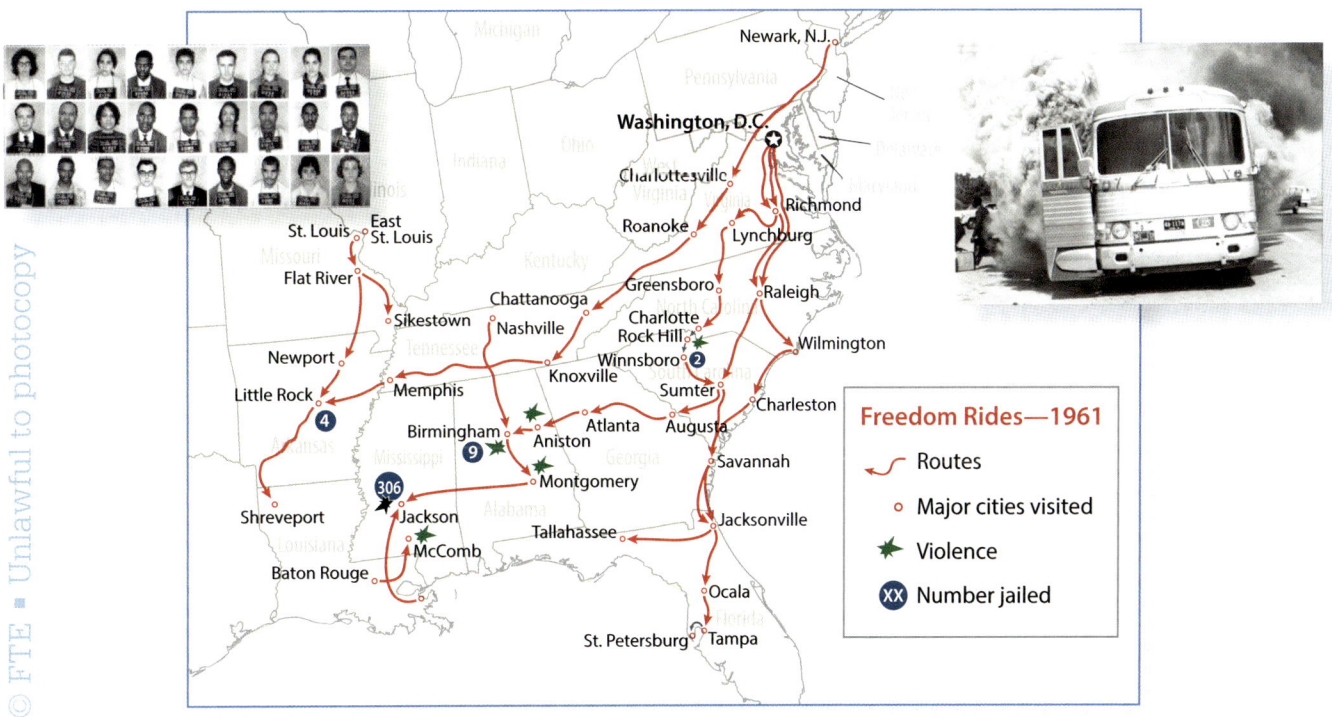

Chapter 14 | Postwar Prosperity and Civil Rights

The Historian's Apprentice

"For years now I have heard the word 'Wait!' It rings in the ear of every Negro with piercing familiarity. This 'Wait' has almost always meant 'Never.' We must come to see, with one of our distinguished jurists, that 'justice too long delayed is justice denied.'

We have waited for more than 340 years for our constitutional and God-given rights. . . . Perhaps it is easy for those who have never felt the stinging darts of segregation to say, 'Wait.' But when you have seen vicious mobs lynch your mothers and fathers at will and drown your sisters and brothers at whim; when you have seen hate-filled policemen curse, kick and even kill your black brothers and sisters; when you see the vast majority of your twenty million Negro brothers smothering in an airtight cage of poverty in the midst of an affluent society; when you suddenly find your tongue twisted and your speech stammering as you seek to explain to your six-year-old daughter why she can't go to the public amusement park that has just been advertised on television, and see tears welling up in her eyes when she is told that Funtown is closed to colored children, and see ominous clouds of inferiority beginning to form in her little mental sky . . . There comes a time when the cup of endurance runs over, and men are no longer willing to be plunged into the abyss of despair."

—Dr. Martin Luther King, Jr., "Letter from Birmingham Jail," 1963

▶ Why does Dr. King argue that African Americans can no longer wait to demand equal rights?

▶ Imagine you are the editor of a newspaper in 1963. Write an editorial supporting or criticizing King's letter.

---

tactics used by the Birmingham police to break up peaceful marches and protests, including the use of fire hoses and police dogs. To end the violence, the white owners of downtown stores in Birmingham agreed to desegregate their lunch counters and to hire African-American employees. Some residents objected to these concessions, and a large Ku Klux Klan rally was held in Birmingham. King's home was bombed, and riots broke out. President Kennedy again had to send in federal troops to restore order.

Kennedy's Civil Rights Bill, 1963

In the aftermath of these events, President Kennedy proposed a new civil rights bill to ban racial discrimination in public accommodations and to increase federal powers for enforcing school desegregation. Kennedy was unable, however, to get support for his bill from a majority in Congress.

The "March on Washington," August 1963

A. Philip Randolph, Dr. King, Bayard Rustin, and other Civil Rights leaders organized a "March on Washington" in support of Kennedy's civil rights bill. More than a quarter of a million people gathered along the Reflecting Pool in front of the Lincoln Memorial. King gave his most famous speech ("I have a dream"), in which he looked forward to the day when people of all races and backgrounds would live together peacefully as brothers and sisters.

The Historian's Apprentice

I have a dream that one day this nation will rise up and live out the true meaning of its creed: "We hold these truths to be self-evident, that all men are created equal."

I have a dream that one day on the Red Hills of Georgia, the sons of former slaves and the sons of former slave owners will be able to sit down together at the table of brotherhood.

I have a dream that one day even the State of Mississippi, a state sweltering with the heat of injustice, sweltering with the heat of oppression, will be transformed into an oasis of freedom and justice.

I have a dream that my four little children will one day live in a nation where they will not be judged by the color of their skin but by the content of their character.

I have a dream today! . . .

I have a dream that one day every valley shall be exalted, and every hill and mountain shall be made low, the rough places will be made plain, and the crooked places will be made straight; "and the glory of the Lord shall be revealed and all flesh shall see it together."

This is our hope, and this is the faith that I go back to the South with.

And this will be the day—this will be the day when all of God's children will be able to sing with new meaning . . .

Let freedom ring. And when this happens, and when we allow freedom to ring—when we let it ring from every village and every hamlet, from every state and every city, we will be able to speed up that day when all of God's children—black men and white men, Jews and Gentiles, Protestants and Catholics—will be able to join hands and sing in the words of the old Negro spiritual: 'Free at last! Free at last! Thank God Almighty, we are free at last!'

—Dr. Martin Luther King, Jr.

1. Based on this speech, how did Dr. King's religious beliefs give him courage?
2. How does this speech compare to his "Letter from a Birmingham Jail"?
3. To what extent has Dr. King's dream been realized?

Civil Rights Legislation under President Johnson

The Kennedy years came to a sudden and tragic end when President Kennedy was assassinated in November 1963. The new President—**Lyndon B. Johnson**—pushed Kennedy's stalled civil rights bill through Congress as a tribute to the former President. It was the most important civil rights legislation since Reconstruction. As a liberal Southern Democrat, Johnson took special pride in this accomplishment.

The Civil Rights Act of 1964

▶ Prohibited discrimination on the basis of race, color, religion, ethnic origin or sex (gender) in hotels, motels, restaurants, theaters, trade unions, and any places of employment doing business with the federal government or engaged in interstate commerce.

▶ Increased the power of the federal government to register voters.

▶ Cut off federal aid to all school districts with segregated schools.

▶ Established the Equal Employment Opportunity Commission to enforce its provisions on employment and trade unions.

The new act protected women and other minority groups as well as African Americans. Some people questioned whether the federal government had the power to outlaw discrimination in private businesses. In December 1964, the Supreme Court upheld the constitutionality of the act based on the power of the federal government to regulate interstate commerce.

The Struggle for Voting Rights

Despite the language of the Fifteenth Amendment, African Americans had been systematically stripped of the right to vote in the South ever since the end of Reconstruction. Southern states used poll taxes and literacy tests, as well as fear and ignorance, to withhold these rights. For years, the NAACP and other civil rights organizations had attempted to register greater numbers of African-American voters in the South, but with little success.

The **24th Amendment** was ratified in 1964. It prohibited states from denying citizens the right to vote in federal elections for failing to pay a poll tax or any other tax. That same year, SNCC joined with other leading Civil Rights organizations (NAACP, CORE, and SCLC) to plan a campaign for the registration of black voters. White and black college students from across the country traveled to Mississippi to register African Americans in what they called "Freedom Summer." The country was shaken when three of the volunteers—two white, Jewish students from New York, and an African-American student from Mississippi—were arrested, released in the middle of the night to a crowd of Ku Klux Klan members, and disappeared. Other civil rights workers were beaten or arrested, while many black homes and churches were bombed. Attorney General Robert Kennedy finally sent FBI agents to the area. After ten weeks, they found the missing bodies and those of several other victims of Klan violence.

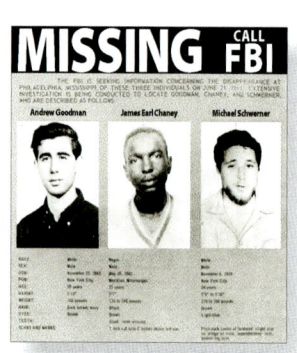

Murdered Civil Rights Volunteers

In December 1964, Dr. King won the Nobel Peace Prize. Four months later, he went to Alabama to lead a march from Selma to Montgomery, again demanding the right to vote for African Americans. The demonstrators were forced to start out several times because of police violence. They were only able to continue their march once they received the protection of federal troops. Americans were able to watch the marchers being clubbed and tear-gassed on national television. Outraged, President Johnson immediately summoned a joint session of Congress, where he proposed a new voting rights bill. Johnson dramatically ended his speech with a well-known slogan from the Civil Rights Movement: "We shall overcome."

The **Voting Rights Act of 1965** echoed the Fifteenth Amendment. States were prohibited from using any "test or device," such as a literacy test, to prevent their citizens from voting. The law prohibited all poll taxes used to deny African Americans the right to vote. The act further authorized the appointment of special "federal examiners" to register voters. The Voting Rights Act led to a large increase in the number of African-American voters. This eventually led to an increased number of African Americans in public office.

Affirmative Action, 1965

In 1965, President Johnson also issued an executive order requiring employers and institutions with federal contracts to raise the number of their minority and female employees. "**Affirmative action**" programs led to increased numbers of women and minorities in universities and the professions. Minority-owned businesses received a larger share of government contracts. Johnson also appointed Robert Weaver as the first African-American member of the Cabinet, and **Thurgood Marshall**, the NAACP attorney in the *Brown* case, as the first African-American Justice on the Supreme Court.

The *Bakke* Decision. Just over a decade later, some people felt that "affirmative action" programs had fulfilled their original purpose. They challenged the continuation of such programs as a form of "reverse discrimination" against whites. Allan Bakke was a white student from Florida who had served in Vietnam as an officer in the Marines and who had also worked for NASA. He applied to the medical school of the University of California at Davis but was twice rejected. Bakke sued the university on the grounds that his grades were better than those of minority students who had been admitted under a special race-based program. In *Regents of the University of California v. Bakke* (1978), the U.S. Supreme Court held that because of past racism, schools could take race into account in their admissions decisions to have greater diversity in their classrooms. However, a school could not set up a "quota" system setting aside a fixed number of places for candidates from any particular race or ethnic background. The Court therefore ordered the Davis medical school to admit Bakke.

The Historian's Apprentice

Should race still be taken into account in college admissions and hiring decisions, since it is more than fifty years since *Brown v. Board of Education*?

The Black Power Movement

Despite the successes of the Civil Rights Movement in fighting segregation in the South, little had been done to improve the economic conditions of African Americans, especially in Northern cities. Many younger African Americans believed that the goals of the Civil Rights Movement were too limited and that progress was too slow. They also disagreed with King's policy of non-violent protest in cooperation with sympathetic whites. In the late 1960s, the Civil Rights Movement splintered, and a more militant "Black Power" Movement identified new goals and took a new direction.

Northern Cities Erupt: Summers of Discontent

African Americans faced segregation in the North as well as the South, but in the North it was the result of residential living patterns rather than of state

Fires followed rioting in Watts and other American cities

laws. White Northerners had fled the inner cities for the suburbs; African Americans were left behind in decaying urban neighborhoods. Their frustrations finally boiled over in a series of riots that shook the country for four summers in a row. In the summer of 1965, rioting broke out in the Watts neighborhood of Los Angeles. The following summer, Harlem and Chicago became the scenes of rioting. In 1967, riots occurred in Newark and Detroit. The climax to these summer riots occurred in the spring of 1968, after Dr. Martin Luther King was assassinated by a white supremacist while he was standing on the balcony of his motel in Memphis, Tennessee. In cities across the nation, angry rioters smashed windows, overturned cars, and started fires. The worst riots took place in Washington, D.C., where the Capitol Building was lit up by the flames of nearby burning buildings. A special commission was appointed to investigate the causes of the unrest. It concluded that the lack of job opportunities for African Americans, urban poverty, and white racism were the chief factors behind the disturbances. The Civil Rights Act of 1968 (Fair Housing Act) prohibited racial discrimination in the sale or rental of housing. Its aim was to end the confinement of African Americans to particular neighborhoods or ghettos due to racial discrimination in housing.

"Black Power"

A new generation of African-American leaders believed in "Black Power." They wanted to use African-American votes to improve social and economic conditions. They also claimed to take greater pride in their own history and culture. Many of these leaders thought that African Americans should take control of their own communities, buy goods from their own businesses, and free themselves from the economic, cultural, and political control of whites. "Black Power" leaders were especially influenced by the progress of African nations, many of which had just won their independence. African-American intellectuals began searching for the roots of their own cultural identity. They did not want to simply imitate whites or be absorbed into mainstream American culture.

The Nation of Islam

The **Nation of Islam**, led by Elijah Muhammad, believed that Islam should be the religion of African Americans, and that they should form their own separate state, since they felt cooperation with whites was impossible.

Malcolm X

Malcolm Little was born in Omaha, Nebraska, where he had a troubled childhood: his father died when he was young; one of his uncles was lynched; and his mother was hospitalized. Although Malcolm excelled in school, he had limited opportunities. He led a reckless life as a youth, became involved with crime and drugs, and went to prison at the age of 20. In prison, he had a spiritual rebirth and converted to the Nation of Islam. He began using the name "**Malcolm X**," rejecting the name given to his family by their former slave owners. He also began to question Dr. Martin Luther King's ideas of non-violent resistance. Malcolm X thought that African Americans should respond to the violence of white racism with their own violence. He sought the separation of whites and blacks and advocated "black nationalism" (or black self-government). In 1964, he broke with the Nation of Islam, declared that he had been in error, and expressed his willingness to work again with more moderate Civil Rights leaders. Malcolm X visited Mecca, Europe, and Africa. On his return, he was assassinated in February 1965 by gunfire just before a speaking engagement. Three members of the Nation of Islam were convicted for the murder, although Elijah Muhammed denied any involvement.

Malcolm X

Stokely Carmichael

Stokely Carmichael attended Howard University and was one of the founders of the Student Non-Violent Coordinating Committee (SNCC), which had helped to organize the early "sit-ins," "Freedom Rides," and "Freedom Summer." Originally, Carmichael and other SNCC members had believed in non-violent methods and had recruited both white and black members. In 1966, Carmichael became chairman of SNCC. Under his leadership the organization became more militant. In 1967, Carmichael introduced the term "**Black Power**" at a rally. He later defined "Black Power" as "a call for black people in this country to unite, to recognize their heritage, to build a sense of community. It is a call for black people to define their own goals, to lead their own organizations." SNCC expelled its white members, and Carmichael broke with Dr. King and other Civil Rights leaders who wanted to integrate American society. Carmichael said that, after repeatedly watching non-violent protestors being beaten by police, he had come to the conclusion that African Americans should use violence when necessary. Looking back at both Marcus Garvey and Malcolm X, Carmichael also began to favor black separatism over the ideal of a multiracial society. Later, Carmichael joined the Black Panthers (see below); he finally left the Black Panthers to move to Africa.

The Black Panthers

In 1966, Bobby Seale and Huey Newton formed a new militant group, the **Black Panthers**, in Oakland, California. Their original purpose was to patrol black neighborhoods to protect residents from police violence. Eventually, the Black Panthers called for the arming of African Americans. They wore black pants, black leather jackets, and black berets. Some even carried guns. Yet the Black Panthers also initiated an ambitious social program to assist black youths. They published their own newspaper and started a free breakfast program to feed poor black children. The organization soon spread to other cities, and had 10,000 members by 1969. The Panthers created a ten-point program of demands, including the demand that the United States pay "reparations" to African Americans for centuries of unjust discrimination and exploitation. "Black Power" came to represent different things to different people. To some African Americans, it became a call for a violent revolution. To others, it was a call for "black capitalism," or for a greater appreciation of African-American culture. An important aspect of "Black Power" was sheer pride in being African American. There was a conscious effort to remove racist stereotypes and to eliminate racist language. The Black Power Movement led to the creation of a distinct hairstyle—the "Afro"—and new clothing fashions. Greater appreciation of African-American culture led to the introduction of black studies courses and departments at American universities, and to the appointment of more African-American professors.

By the late 1960s, the United States was a very different place than two decades earlier because of the Civil Rights and Black Power Movements. Their trail-blazing efforts inspired women, ethnic and religious minorities, American Indians, people with disabilities, and younger Americans, all of whom followed in their footsteps in transforming our country into a more open, heterogeneous society.

A Black Power convention on the steps of the Lincoln Memorial

The Ten-Point Program of the Black Panther Party, October 1966

1. We want freedom. We want the power to determine the destiny of our black community.
2. We want full employment for our people.
3. We want an end to the robbery by the white man of our black community.
4. We want decent housing, fit for shelter of human beings.
5. We want education for our people that exposes the true nature of this decadent American society. We want education that teaches us our true history and our role in the present-day society.
6. We want all black men to be exempt from military service.
7. We want an immediate end to police brutality and murder of black people.
8. We want freedom for all black men held in federal, state, county and city prisons and jails.
9. We want all black people when brought to trial to be tried in court by a jury of their peer group or people from their black communities, as defined by the Constitution of the United States.
10. We want land, bread, housing, education, clothing, justice and peace. And as our major political objective, a United Nations-supervised plebiscite to be held throughout the black colony in which only black colonial subjects will be allowed to participate for the purpose of determining the will of black people as to their national destiny.

The Historian's Apprentice

- How did these demands differ from those of Dr. Martin Luther King in his "I Have a Dream" speech only three years earlier?
- Make a chart comparing the Civil Rights Movement and the Black Power Movement. Be sure to include leaders, organizations, goals, beliefs, and accomplishments for each movement.
- Make a Venn diagram comparing the main beliefs of the Civil Rights Movement and the Black Power Movement. Were any of their beliefs the same? How did they differ?
- Imagine you are one of the leaders of the Black Power Movement. Write a short speech summarizing your views.
- Were "Black Power" leaders justified in declaring that violence might be necessary to end racism? Did they really use it?
- In his final essay, Dr. King wrote that the desegregation of the South was an easy task compared to the challenges posed by "inferior education, poor housing, unemployment, [and] inadequate health." Would you agree?

Chapter 14 | Postwar Prosperity and Civil Rights

Civil Rights Leader or Black Power Militant?

In the 1960s and 1970s, what made some individuals become Civil Rights leaders? What made others become Black Power militants? Examine the six leaders below and classify them.

Roy Wilkins (1901–1981) worked as a journalist and replaced W.E.B. Du Bois as the editor of *The Crisis* in 1934. He encouraged African Americans to deposit their money into a black-owned bank at a time when African Americans were having trouble getting bank loans. Wilkins later helped to organize the March on Washington in 1963, and became Executive Director of the NAACP in 1964. Although Wilkins was a tireless fighter for civil rights, he opposed the use of violence and was a strong anti-Communist. In the 1950s, Wilkins was a bitter opponent of the African-American Paul Robeson for his Communist views.

☐ Civil Rights leader, or
☐ Black Power militant?

Which facts helped you with your classification?

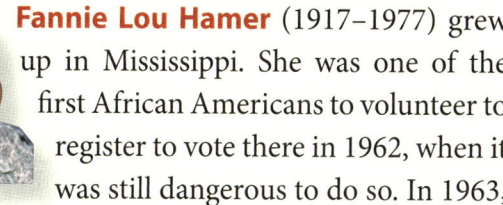

Fannie Lou Hamer (1917–1977) grew up in Mississippi. She was one of the first African Americans to volunteer to register to vote there in 1962, when it was still dangerous to do so. In 1963, she was sent to jail where she was beaten so badly by the police that she almost died and took months to recover. Nevertheless, in 1964 she helped to organize the Freedom Democratic Party, which sent delegates to the 1964 Democratic Convention to challenge the all-white Mississippi delegation. "All of this is because we want to register . . . if the Freedom Democratic Party is not seated now, I question America." The same year, Hamer was one of the principal organizers of "Freedom Summer"—the attempt to register African-American voters in Mississippi. "Nobody's free," she said, "until everybody's free."

☐ Civil Rights leader, or
☐ Black Power militant?

Which facts helped you with your classification?

Andrew Young was born in 1932 in New Orleans, attended Howard University, and became a pastor in Alabama. He encouraged African Americans to vote and became a friend of Dr. Martin Luther King. In 1961, he joined the SCLC (Southern Christian Leadership Conference). He participated in civil rights protests in Selma, Alabama, and St. Augustine, Florida. In 1964, he became the Executive Director of the SCLC, and he was with King when the latter was assassinated in 1968. Later, Young was elected to Congress from Georgia and was appointed as U.S. Ambassador to the United Nations by President Jimmy Carter in 1977. In 1981, Young was elected as the Mayor of Atlanta.

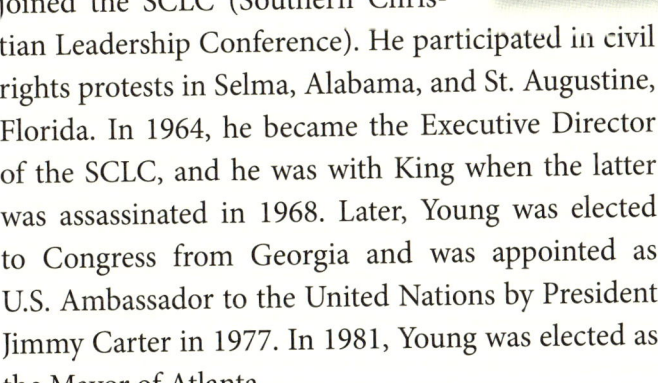

☐ Civil Rights leader, or
☐ Black Power militant?

Which facts helped you with your classification?

Constance Baker Motley (1921–2005) was an African-American female lawyer who wrote some of the original court documents in the case of *Brown v. Board of Education*. Hired by Thurgood Marshall, she was the first African-American woman to work in the legal department of the NAACP. Later, Motley argued several important Civil Rights cases before the U.S. Supreme Court. In 1966, she became the first African-American woman to be appointed as a federal judge.

☐ Civil Rights leader, or
☐ Black Power militant?

Which facts helped you with your classification?

Robert F. Williams (1932–1996) was the grandchild of a slave. He migrated to the North looking for work during World War II and became active in the Civil Rights Movement. Williams was shocked that local police did nothing when white racists fired gunshots at his home and those of other NAACP organizers. He organized a self-protection association, known as the "Black Armed Guard," since he felt that "citizens have to act in self-defense against lawless violence." In 1959, Williams held a debate with Dr. Martin Luther King in which he openly advocated armed resistance to racial oppression. When Williams was falsely accused of a kidnapping, he fled to Cuba. In 1962, he published a book, *Negroes with Guns*, which later influenced the founders of the Black Panther Party. During the Cuban Missile Crisis, Williams urged African-American soldiers to rebel. In 1964, he visited Hanoi, where he took the side of the North Vietnamese against the United States; the following year, Williams moved to China. In 1969, Williams finally returned to the United States. He was placed on trial for the earlier kidnapping, but the charges against him were quickly dropped. Later, he went to work at the University of Michigan.

☐ Civil Rights leader, or
☐ Black Power militant?

Which facts helped you with your classification?

H. "Rap" Brown was born in Louisiana in 1943. At the age of 24, he became chairman of SNCC in 1967; then he joined the Black Panthers. "I say violence is necessary," H. Rap Brown once proclaimed, "it is as American as cherry pie." Brown was charged with inciting a riot that same year and disappeared from public view after an attempt to blow up the courthouse where he was being tried. After a shootout with police in New York, he went to prison for five years. There, he converted to Islam and changed his name to Jamil Abdullah Al-Amin. He next moved to Atlanta, where he lived for several years. In March 2000, he fired a rifle at two African-American policemen who stopped his car. One of the police officers died. Brown was convicted and is currently serving a life sentence.

☐ Civil Rights leader, or
☐ Black Power militant?

Which facts helped you with your classification?

The Historian's Apprentice

▶ Write a short essay discussing why some of the individuals above became Civil Rights leaders and others became Black Power militants.

▶ Hold class discussions between Civil Rights and Black Power leaders. Have your teacher divide your class into small groups of six. Each member of the group should pretend to be one of the individuals above. Then imagine it is 1965 and have these six leaders present their views on where the Civil Rights Movement should go next. Or have six student volunteers pretend to be these leaders and hold a debate in front of the class on the same question.

Focus on Florida

Floridians played an important role in the struggle for civil rights even before the 1950s. **James Weldon Johnson** (1871–1938) was born in Jacksonville, Florida. He wrote the poem, "Lift Every Voice and Sing." It was set to music by his brother and became known as the "Negro National Anthem." Many African-

American schools across the South sang this anthem at the start of each day. Johnson became a field secretary of the NAACP in 1916 and led demonstrations and marches against lynching and racial injustice. In July 1917, he led a march of ten thousand African Americans down New York City's Fifth Avenue in protest. **Zora Neale Hurston** (1891–1960) was an African-American author who grew up in Eatonville, Florida, and became active in the Harlem Renaissance. Later, she returned to Florida. **A. Philip Randolph** (1889–1979) was born in Crescent City, Florida. At a time when many trade unions discriminated against African Americans, Randolph successfully led the Brotherhood of Sleeping Car Porters. In 1941, he challenged President Franklin D. Roosevelt to end racial discrimination in government employment and by government contractors. Randolph's efforts to end discrimination in the armed forces contributed to President Truman's decision to desegregate them in 1948. In 1963, Randolph was one of the organizers of the "March on Washington."

The strong desire for civil rights in Florida was partly in reaction to the harsh system of segregation that existed there. Like other Southern states, Florida denied African Americans their voting rights and limited their economic opportunities. Communities segregated their buses, schools, theaters, parks, and other public facilities. The Klu Klux Klan was powerful, and Florida led the South in lynchings in proportion to its population.

Harry T. Moore was an African-American teacher and school principal who was active in making African Americans in Florida more aware of their constitutional rights. He registered voters, founded the Brevard chapter of the NAACP, helped organize the Florida NAACP, and filed a series of lawsuits for civil rights. In 1937, he filed a lawsuit demanding equal pay for black and white school teachers. In 1941, Moore became the head of the Florida NAACP. Because of his efforts, a higher percentage of African Americans were registered to vote in Florida than in any other Southern state. Moore became involved in the case of four African-American males convicted of rape on flimsy evidence. Thurgood Marshal won an appeal in the U.S. Supreme Court overturning their convictions. But then two of the men were shot and killed by the sheriff, who claimed they were trying to escape. Moore called for the sheriff to be arrested. Shortly afterwards, on Christmas night in 1951, Moore and his wife were killed by a bomb planted under their house by Ku Klux Klan members. No one was ever charged with the murder.

School Desegregation In the 1940s, Florida's state legislature established the "Minimum Foundations Program" to improve its segregated schools. In part, this was to discredit the argument that Southern states were not providing equal resources to black schools. After the *Brown v. Board of Education* decision, Florida Governor LeRoy Collins managed to integrate the state's schools peacefully.

The Tallahassee Bus Boycott In May 1956—at the same time as the Montgomery bus boycott in Alabama—two African-American female students refused to give up their seats at the front of a bus in Tallahassee. Reverend C.K. Steele, a local NAACP leader, took charge of a boycott of the city's buses. Although a federal court struck down the segregated bus service in Montgomery, segregation continued on the buses in Tallahassee. Law enforcement officials attempted to arrest those running car pools for operating an illegal business. The actions of the U.S. Supreme Court resulted in their desegregation.

St. Augustine, 1964 In the early 1960s, race riots, sit-ins, wade-ins (to desegregate public beaches), and demonstrations took place in Jacksonville and Tallahassee. There was a sit-in in Miami as early as 1959. Rioting rocked **St. Augustine** in the summer of 1964 during the celebration of the city's 400th anniversary. Dr. King spent time in St. Augustine in 1964 to participate in demonstrations. Andrew Young said the treatment of African Americans in St. Augustine was worse than in Birmingham, Alabama. Segregationists shot into King's home and burned his beach cottage. King was arrested but under pressure from President Johnson, he was released. Only days later, President Johnson pushed the Civil Rights bill through Congress.

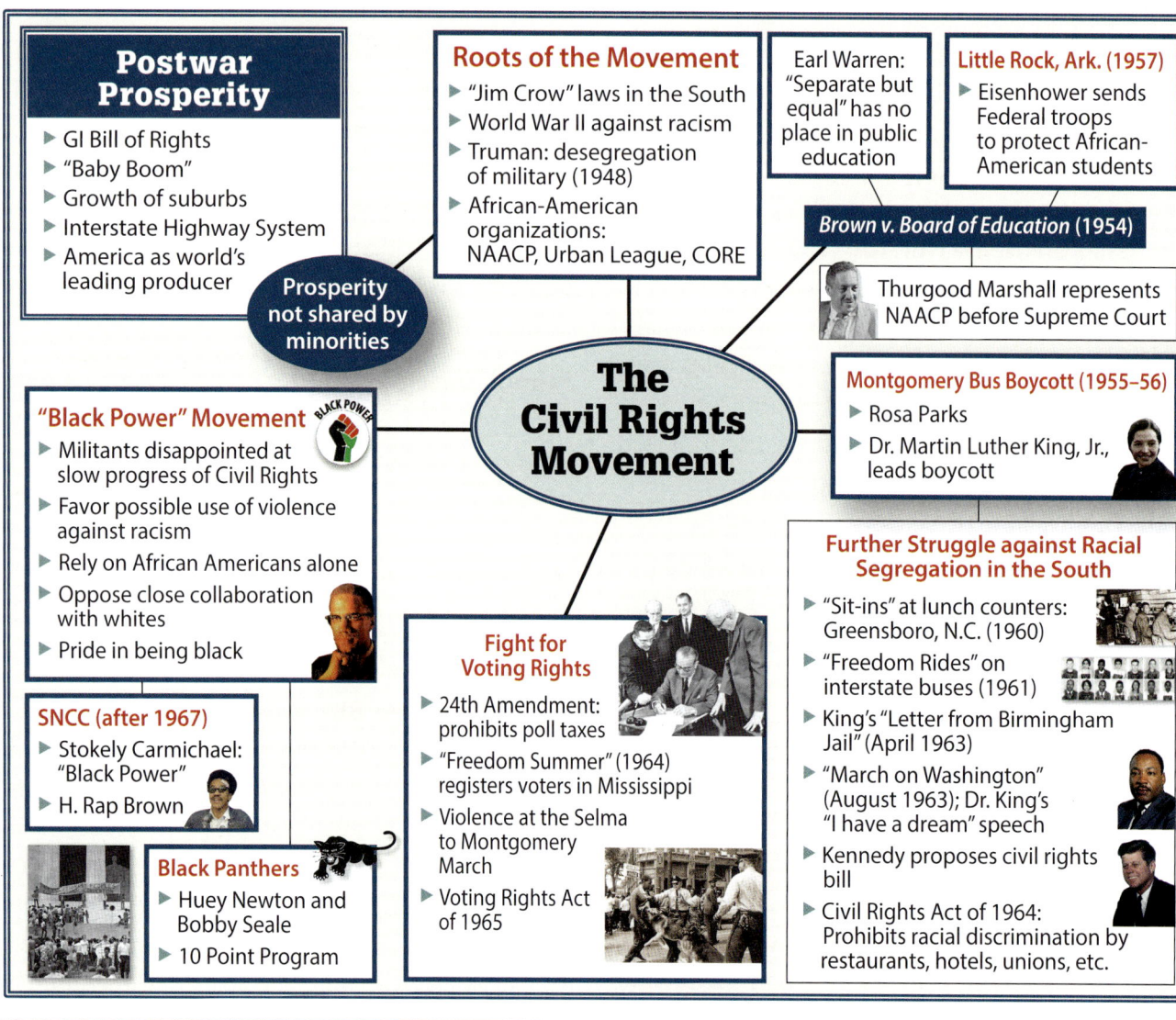

Reasons for Postwar Prosperity

- During the late 1940s and early 1950s, the U.S. **Gross National Product (GNP)** and average income grew while unemployment decreased. There were political, social, and economic reasons for this prosperity.
- **Political reason:** The **G.I. Bill of Rights** gave World War II veterans benefits like unemployment pay, loans to buy a home or start a business, and money for education.
- **Social reasons: Demobilization**—the return of soldiers to their civilian lives—and the **Baby Boom,** the huge surge in birth rates that resulted when returning veterans quickly married and had children. With the introduction of mass-produced housing developments like **Levittown,** many Americans were able to afford their own homes and moved to **suburbs.**
- **Economic reasons:** European economies had been devastated by the war. American manufacturers therefore faced less competition. The United States became the world's leading producer. New technologies developed during the war, such as plastics and drugs, continued to expand, and many Americans found jobs in the growing aircraft, electrical, and chemical industries. With their new purchasing power, Americans could afford more luxury items, including refrigerators, cars, and televisions, than ever before.
- **Political and economic reasons:** Government spending, which had increased during the Great Depression and World War II, continued to grow because of the Cold War and the Korean War. The **Employment Act of 1946** announced the goal of federal economic policy to be maximum production and full employment. The U.S. government also helped rebuild European economies by giving money through the **Marshall Plan.**

The Effects of Postwar Prosperity on American Society

- **Dwight D. Eisenhower,** the first Republican President in 20 years, preserved most New Deal programs but also promoted American business. He encouraged suburban growth and helped to unite the country by passing the **Federal Highway Act,** which created highways to link suburbs and cities.
- Prosperity, mass production, and mass consumption led to conformity. Many Americans worked at large corporations, lived in suburbs, and bought the same items. The mass media created a mass culture.
- Some new policies were harsh on labor: the **Taft-Hartley Act,** passed after a series of strikes in 1946, reversed many of the gains made by labor during the Great Depression.
- Prosperity was limited to some groups. Suburbs imposed restrictions on minorities. Mass media ignored them, and many jobs excluded them. Minority veterans often failed to obtain the benefits of the G.I. Bill.

Roots of the Civil Rights Movement

- **"Jim Crow" laws** had created a system of legally enforced racial segregation throughout the South. Some African Americans tried to escape by migrating to the North.
- African-American organizations, like the church, the **NAACP,** the **National Urban League,** and **CORE (the Congress of Racial Equality)** as well as African-American universities, such as **Howard,** worked to improve conditions and mobilize African Americans in the early 20th century.
- World War II contributed to the mobilization of African Americans. Black soldiers fought in the military, though in segregated units. On the home front, many worked in jobs previously barred to them. The horrors of Nazism revealed the dangers of racism to all.
- After the war, anti-colonial movements in Asia and Africa inspired African-American Civil Rights leaders.
- The Cold War made American leaders realize the need to curb racism to act as the champion of democracy.

The Struggle against Racial Segregation: 1945–1956

Beginnings
- The **Civil Rights Movement** began in the postwar era and continued into the 1960s. A combination of grass-roots activism and federal intervention produced great changes, especially in the South.
- President Truman desegregated the military in 1948 and prohibited job discrimination in the federal government. **Jackie Robinson** became the first African American to play Major League Baseball the year before.

Education and *Brown v. Board of Education of Topeka, Kansas*
- In 1954, the Supreme Court decision in *Brown v. Board of Education* overturned *Plessy v. Ferguson* (1896), which had permitted "separate but equal" facilities. In *Brown*, the NAACP lawyer **Thurgood Marshall** used evidence from a psychologist to show that segregation created feelings of inequality. Chief Justice **Earl Warren** wrote the unanimous opinion of the Court. The Court held that segregation had no place in public education because it led to facilities that were inherently unequal.
- The Court ordered states to desegregate their school systems with **"all deliberate speed."** In some cases, **busing** (taking students by bus to more distant schools) was used to desegregate schools.
- Southern reactions to *Brown* were violent. Senators swore not to enforce the decision. Murders, like that of young **Emmet Till,** increased. So did membership in the KKK. Some schools closed rather than **integrate**.
- In **Little Rock, Arkansas,** the state governor ordered the National Guard to prevent nine black students from attending an all-white school. President Eisenhower then sent federal troops to escort the **"Little Rock Nine"** and protect them throughout the year.

Chapter 14 | Postwar Prosperity and Civil Rights

The Montgomery Bus Boycott (1955-1956)

- The **Montgomery Bus Boycott** was a successful attempt to end segregation on public transit. **Rosa Parks**, an NAACP member, refused to sit in the "colored" part of the bus in Montgomery, Alabama, and was arrested. The NAACP organized a boycott of the bus system: African Americans refused to ride the buses until segregation was ended and African Americans were hired as drivers. The movement elected **Dr. Martin Luther King, Jr.** as its leader. King believed in non-violent agitation to end oppression. The boycott ran for almost a year until the local federal court ordered the public transit system to **desegregate** (*end racial segregation*).
- The success of the boycott caused several of its leaders, mostly ministers, to form the **Southern Christian Leadership Council (SCLC)** to fight for racial equality using non-violence.

The Struggle against Racial Segregation: From Sit-Ins to Affirmative Action, 1960–1965

- African-American students fought for equality through **social activism.** One famous tactic, begun at a lunch counter in Greensboro, N.C., was the **sit-in,** in which blacks and whites sat together in a "white" section and refused to move despite verbal and physical abuse.
- In 1960, white and black students from 30 states formed the **Student Nonviolent Coordinating Committee (SNCC)** to organize civil rights protests.
- In 1961, CORE organized **Freedom Rides,** in which interracial groups bravely refused to sit in segregated sections of buses traveling across Southern states. These riders were often attacked by mobs at stops and eventually had to be protected by federal marshals.
- In 1963, Martin Luther King and other leaders led a march on Birmingham, Alabama. They were arrested, and King wrote his famous **"Letter from Birmingham Jail"** demanding equality. Television showed the rest of the nation the horrible violence used by the Birmingham police against peaceful protesters.
- President Kennedy became alarmed by the violence and proposed a federal civil rights bill.
- A. Philip Randolph, Dr. Martin Luther King, and other leaders organized a **March on Washington** in support of Kennedy's civil rights bill. More than 250,000 people attended. King delivered his famous **"I Have a Dream"** speech.
- When Kennedy was assassinated in 1963, President **Lyndon B. Johnson** pushed the **Civil Rights Act of 1964** through Congress. It was the most important such measure since Reconstruction and banned racial discrimination in hotels, restaurants, unions, and federal contractors. It also protected other minority groups and women.
- In 1965, President Johnson implemented **"affirmative action,"** requiring employers with federal contracts to hire more women and minorities. President Johnson also appointed **Robert Weaver** as the first African-American Cabinet Member, and **Thurgood Marshall** as the first African-American Supreme Court Justice. Ten years later, the Supreme Court's *Bakke* decision declared racial quotas under "affirmative action" programs to be unconstitutional; however, universities could consider race in admissions decisions in order to overcome past discrimination and to provide student diversity.

The Struggle for Voting Rights

- African Americans in the South had been stripped of the vote by poll taxes, literacy tests, and violence.
- The **Civil Rights Acts of 1957 and 1960** tried to end voting discrimination, but proved ineffective.
- The **24th Amendment**, ratified in 1964, prohibited poll taxes.
- The same year, various civil rights organizations planned **"Freedom Summer,"** a campaign to register black voters in Mississippi. The volunteers were often attacked and three were killed by the KKK.
- Extreme violence against a peaceful march from **Selma to Montgomery** led President Johnson to introduce the **Voting Rights Act of 1965.** "Federal examiners" were sent to register black voters.

The Black Power Movement

- A series of events in the late 60s splintered the movement. Riots like the **Watts Riot** in L.A. broke out in the summers of 1965 and 1967. In 1968, Dr. King was assassinated, causing more riots.
- A commission appointed by President Johnson determined that the unrest had been caused by urban poverty and by job and housing discrimination. The **Civil Rights Act of 1968 (Fair Housing Act)** prohibited discrimination in housing.
- Many African Americans, especially youths in Northern cities, thought the Civil Rights Movement was too slow and limited despite its earlier successes. They disagreed with its program of non-violence and interracial cooperation. These activists began a more militant **Black Power Movement.**
- The Black Power Movement began with a group of leaders who wanted African Americans to take control of their own communities, fight racism directly, and avoid contact with whites. Many were inspired by the independence movements of African nations.
- **Malcolm X** joined the **Nation of Islam** while in jail, believing that African Americans should form a separate state because interracial cooperation was impossible. He wanted blacks to fight violence with violence, and advocated **"black nationalism,"** or black self-government. He was eventually assassinated by members of the Nation of Islam when he renounced their ideas.
- **Stokely Carmichael** was a Howard student who became the leader of SNCC. He made the organization more militant and introduced the term **"Black Power."** He was in favor of black separatism and the use of violence to fight racism.
- The **Black Panther Party** was formed by Bobby Seale and Huey Newton to protect black neighborhoods in Oakland, California. They called for the arming of African Americans but also implemented social programs. Their **10-Point Program** made radical demands on whites.
- Other African-American militants included **H. Rap Brown** and **Robert F. Williams.**
- **"Black Power"** meant more than violence. It called for greater pride in the African-American identity. It led to the creation of new fashions, the **"Afro"** hairstyle, and black studies courses in universities.

What Do You Know?

SS.912.A.7.1

1. The picture on the left shows President Franklin Roosevelt signing the Servicemen's Readjustment Act of 1944, better known as the "G.I. Bill."

What important benefits did this law provide to veterans returning from World War II?

   A. free medical care and a special retirement plan

   B. low-interest housing loans and a bonus payment after 5 years

   C. low-interest housing loans and payments towards high school, vocational school, or higher education

   D. the promise of a guaranteed job and payments towards high school, vocational school or higher education

SS.912.A.7.1

2. What was an important cause of American prosperity during the post-World War II period?

   A. Most American married couples postponed having children in order to work longer.

   B. American producers faced less competition because of destruction in Europe and Asia.

   C. Women remained in the workforce after the war in order to increase American production.

   D. The elimination of poverty through federal programs increased demand and stimulated production.

SS.912.A.7.1

3. The map on the left shows the transportation network initiated by the Federal Highway Act in 1956.

   What was an important impact of this network on the United States?

   A. State control of immigration routes has increased.

   B. Travel and trade between states became easier and faster than before.

   C. Towns bypassed by the interstate system generally grew just as fast as those on interstate highways.

   D. Increased traffic makes it more difficult for the armed forces to move troops around the country.

SS.912.A.7.6

4. This photo shows a segregated water fountain in Oklahoma in 1939.

   Which two organizations sought to overturn the conditions shown in this photograph by peaceful means?

   A. KKK and the Nation of Islam

   B. SNCC and the Black Panthers

   C. AFL-CIO and the Black Power Movement

   D. NAACP and the Congress of Racial Equality

SS.912.A.7.6

5. Executive Order 9981 (below) was issued by President Harry Truman in 1948.

> It is hereby declared to be the policy of the President that there shall be equality of treatment and opportunity for all persons in the armed services without regard to race, color, religion, or national origin.

   What was the immediate impact of Executive Order of 9981?

   A. The armed forces of the United States were desegregated.

   B. Free education was promised to veterans who had served in World War II.

   C. Southern members of the Democratic Party left and formed a new political party.

   D. Equal opportunity in education was established to promote advances in science and mathematics.

SS.912.A.7.5

6. Demonstrators attending the March on Washington, D.C. in 1963 are shown in this photograph.

   What was the main purpose of this event?

   A. to demand an end to racial discrimination by federal contractors

   B. to demand that Congress pass President Kennedy's Civil Rights Bill

   C. to demand enforcement of the Supreme Court's decision to desegregate schools

   D. to demand reparations for centuries of oppression experienced by African Americans

SS. 912.A.7.6

7. The timeline below shows several important events from the Civil Rights Era.

   Governor of Arkansas sends National Guard to prevent the "Little Rock Nine" from entering a white school — 1957

   CORE organizes "Freedom Rides" — 1961

   Dr. Martin Luther King, Jr. leads a march on Birmingham, Alabama, and writes "Letter from Birmingham Jail" — 1963

   Civil Rights groups organize "Freedom Summer" — 1964

   What was the reaction of federal officials to the events on the timeline?

   A. They sent emergency assistance in the form of troops and marshals to stop the violence.

   B. They immediately passed new laws ending discrimination in housing, employment, and voting.

   C. They failed to act because they needed the support of white Southerners to stay in office.

   D. They tended to side with white Southern segregationists against Civil Rights demonstrators.

SS. 912.A.7.6

8. The chart below summarizes important legislation in the 1960s.

Law or Amendment	Requirements
Civil Rights Act of 1964	Hotels and restaurants cannot discriminate on the basis of race
24th Amendment	States cannot impose poll taxes since these make it more difficult for African Americans to vote
Voting Rights Act of 1965	?

   Which phrase completes the chart?

   A. A state cannot deny citizens the right to vote on the basis of gender.

   B. A state cannot impose procedures that deny citizens the right to vote on account of age.

   C. A state cannot impose procedures that deny citizens the right to vote on account of race.

   D. A state cannot deny the right to vote to American Indians who choose to remain on federal reservations.

Chapter 14 | Postwar Prosperity and Civil Rights

SS.912.A.7.6

9. The bar graph below shows the number of registered African-American voters in several states.

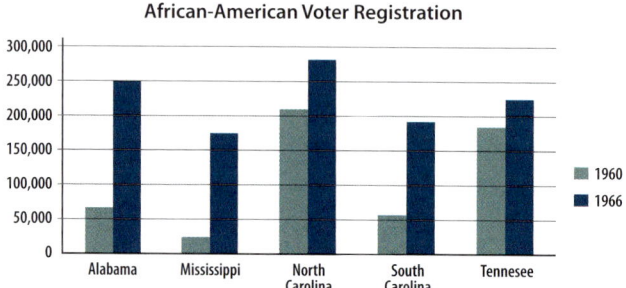

Which event caused the changes in African-American voter registration shown in the graph?

   A. Congress passed the Voting Rights Act of 1965.
   B. Southern states enacted their own new voting laws.
   C. Desegregated restaurants and hotels made voting easier.
   D. Newly integrated schools encouraged African Americans to vote.

SS.912.A.7.7

10. This photograph shows Dr. Martin Luther King, Jr., and other Civil Rights leaders at the "March on Washington" in 1963.

   What conclusion can be made from this photograph?

   A. A. Philip Randolph was unable to attend the March on Washington.
   B. Dr. King refused to work with whites in the struggle against segregation.
   C. Whites as well as blacks participated in the struggle against racial discrimination.
   D. The "March on Washington" successfully persuaded states to prohibit racial segregation.

SS.912.A.7.5

11. Which four organizations opposed the use of violence in the struggle for African-American civil rights?

   A. NAACP, Urban League, CORE, SCLC
   B. CORE, KKK, Black Panthers, Nation of Islam
   C. SNCC after 1967, SCLC, CORE, Black Panthers
   D. NAACP, Urban League, SNCC after 1967, Nation of Islam

SS.912.A.7.6

12. In the Civil Rights Act of 1964, Congress prohibited discrimination in restaurants and hotels on the basis of race, color, religion, or national origin. What else did Congress provide in the same act?

   A. an official definition for discrimination in housing
   B. accessibility rights for individuals with disabilities
   C. penalties for prohibited acts of racial discrimination
   D. penalties for those instituting "affirmative action" programs

336   Chapter 14 | Postwar Prosperity and Civil Rights

SS.912.A.7.8

13. The excerpt below comes from the opinion of the U.S. Supreme Court in *Brown v. Board of Education of Topeka, Kansas* (1954)

> We conclude that in the field of public education the doctrine of 'separate but equal' has no place. Separate educational facilities are inherently unequal.

What does this excerpt demonstrate about the power of the Supreme Court?

   A. It can limit the actions of Congress.
   B. It can rule state laws unconstitutional.
   C. It can dictate new laws to state legislatures.
   D. It can provide funding for public education.

SS.912.A.7.8

14. What did the Supreme Court decide in the case of *Regents of the University of California v. Bakke* (1978)?

   A. Schools can take race into account when making their admission decisions.
   B. A quota system should be set up to ensure a fixed number of places for candidates of each racial background.
   C. Schools should admit candidates solely on the basis of their academic qualifications and ability to pay.
   D. Any student whose parents or grandparents attended a state university should also be admitted.

SS.912.A.7.7

15. Which group of leaders discouraged cooperation with members of other racial groups in the struggle to improve conditions for African Americans?

   A. Malcolm X, Stokely Carmichael, and H. Rap Brown
   B. A. Philip Randolph, James Farmer and Fannie Lou Hamer
   C. Rosa Parks, Thurgood Marshall and Constance Baker Motley
   D. Roy Wilkins, Dr. Martin Luther King, Jr., and Dr. Ralph Abernathy

SS.912.A.7.6

16. The diagram below compares two groups.

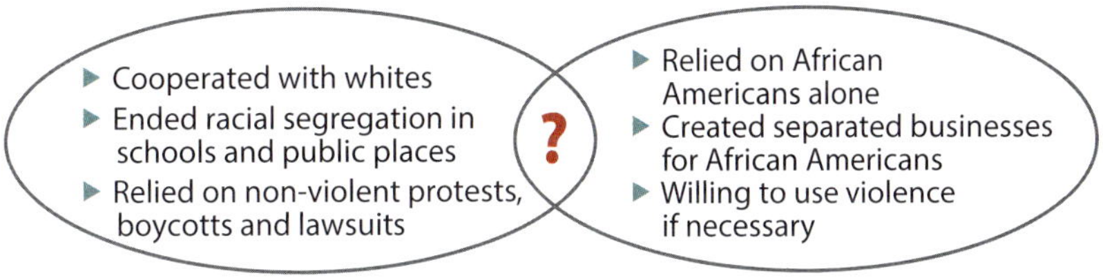

Civil Rights Groups: CORE, NAACP, Urban League, SCLC	Black Power Groups: Black Panthers, SNCC after 1967, Nation of Islam
▶ Cooperated with whites ▶ Ended racial segregation in schools and public places ▶ Relied on non-violent protests, boycotts and lawsuits	▶ Relied on African Americans alone ▶ Created separated businesses for African Americans ▶ Willing to use violence if necessary

Which phrase best completes the diagram?

   A. Opposed African-American participation in elections
   B. Expressed pride in being African-American
   C. Ignored racist attitudes in Northern cities
   D. Proposed emigration to Africa

Chapter 14 | Postwar Prosperity and Civil Rights

SS.912.A.7.6

17. The statement below was part of the "Ten-Point Program" of the Black Panther Party in 1966.

> We believe that this racist government has robbed us and now we are demanding the overdue debt of forty acres and two mules. Forty acres and two mules was promised 100 years ago as restitution for slave labor and mass murder of black people. We will accept the payment as currency which will be distributed to our many communities. The Germans are now aiding the Jews in Israel for the genocide of the Jewish people. The Germans murdered six million Jews. The American racist has taken part in the slaughter of over 50 million black people; therefore, we feel that this is a modest demand that we make.

Based on this statement, what is one way in which the Black Panthers differed from earlier Civil Rights groups like the NAACP?

A. The Black Panthers mainly pursued their goals by filing lawsuits in federal courts.

B. The Black Panthers demanded monetary reparations for past abuses of African Americans.

C. The Black Panthers opposed the practice of racial segregation by Southern state governments.

D. The Black Panthers demanded an end to discriminatory practices that made it difficult for African Americans to exercise their voting rights.

SS.912.A.7.1

18. The pictures below were in a magazine advertisement in 1957.

Which sentence describes neighborhoods like the one advertised above?

A. They welcomed Americans of all ethnic backgrounds.

B. Their construction was federally funded by the G.I. Bill.

C. Their spread was encouraged by the Federal Highway Act.

D. They were built for propaganda purposes during the Cold War.

CHAPTER 15

The Sixties: "The Times They are a-Changin'"

SS.912.A.6.13 Analyze significant foreign policy events during the . . . Kennedy, Johnson and Nixon administrations.

S.912.A.6.14 Analyze causes, course, and consequences of the Vietnam War.

SS.912.A.7.3 Examine the changing status of women in the United States from post-World War II to present.

SS.912.A.7.4 Evaluate the success of 1960s-era presidents' foreign and domestic policies

SS.912.A.7.10 Analyze the significance of the Vietnam War . . . on the government and people of the United States.

SS.912.A.7.13 Analyze the attempts to extend New Deal legislation through the Great Society and the successes and failures of these programs to promote social and economic stability.

SS.912.A.7.17 Examine key events and peoples in Florida history as they relate to United States history.

Names and Terms You Should Know

John F. Kennedy	Vietcong	Paris Peace Accords
Lyndon B. Johnson	Domino theory	Hawks vs. Doves
"War on Poverty"	SEATO (Southeast Asia Treaty Organization)	Media
"Great Society"		"Credibility Gap"
Project Head Start	Guerilla warfare	Anti-war protests
Medicare	Draft	War Powers Act
Medicaid	Conscientious objectors	Women's Liberation Movement
Warren Court	Gulf of Tonkin Resolution	Betty Friedan, *The Feminine Mystique*
Vietnam War	Tet Offensive	National Organization of Women (NOW)
Indochina	Richard M. Nixon	Women in the workforce
Ho Chi Minh	Vietnamization	Equal Rights Amendment (ERA)
Geneva Accords	Cambodia	*Roe v. Wade*
Demilitarized Zone (DMZ)	Dr. Henry Kissinger	

Florida "Keys" to Understanding

1. President John F. Kennedy wanted to use federal power to solve problems and defend freedom. He established a space program but other proposed reforms were stalled in Congress.

2. President Lyndon Johnson passed much of Kennedy's reform legislation. He also called for a "War on Poverty." After re-election in 1964, Johnson proposed his "Great Society" program. Medicare and Medicaid provided health insurance to seniors and others. Project Head Start helped low-income children. The Housing and Urban Development Act gave assistance to cities. The Appalachian Regional Development Act gave aid to one of America's most impoverished regions.

3. Under Chief Justice Earl Warren, the Supreme Court became an instrument of social change. The Court made important decisions on freedom of speech, freedom of religion, and rights for those accused of crimes.

4. In 1954, Vietnam was divided: North Vietnam became a Communist dictatorship under Ho Chi Minh and South Vietnam was placed under a pro-Western Emperor. Diem deposed the Emperor and refused to hold promised elections to reunite the country. The Vietcong (South Vietnamese Communists) began a campaign of guerrilla warfare against Diem.

5. American leaders believed in the "domino theory"—that if Vietnam fell to Communism, neighboring nations would also fall like a row of dominoes. Americans also had obligations under SEATO and wanted to reassure their allies. Kennedy sent military advisers. In August 1964, Congress passed the Gulf of Tonkin Resolution, which authorized Johnson to send in troops. Helicopters, napalm, Agent Orange, and bombing missions were used in support of U.S. troops. Nevertheless Americans were not used to the environment and often could not detect the enemy.

6. In 1968, the Vietcong launched the "Tet Offensive." The war dragged on because Americans refused to withdraw, while North Vietnam and the Vietcong were committed to their cause. American public opinion became increasingly divided. "Doves" thought the war was immoral; "Hawks" wanted to continue the war to contain Communism. The media covered the war closely, leading to a "credibility gap." In 1968, protests at the Democratic National Convention led to violence. In 1970, National Guardsmen killed four students at Kent State University.

7. Under President Nixon's policy of "Vietnamization," American troops were gradually replaced with South Vietnamese. In 1973, Dr. Henry Kissinger signed the Paris Peace Accords with North Vietnam. America withdrew its troops but continued to send aid. South Vietnam finally fell to Communist forces in 1975. Although Vietnam suffered the most from the war, 58,000 Americans were also killed. Congress passed the War Powers Act, limiting the President's power to intervene abroad.

8. The Women's Liberation Movement focused on achieving economic and social equality. In 1963, Betty Friedan published *The Feminine Mystique*, voicing the dislike of many middle-class women for their roles as housewives. In 1966, Friedan organized the National Organization for Women (NOW). Title IX (the Equal Opportunity in Education Act) pressured schools and universities to end discrimination against women. The Equal Pay Act required equal pay for men and women. Feminists fought sexual discrimination in language, pop culture, and private homes. Feminists also tried to pass the Equal Rights Amendment (ERA), but failed. Phyllis Schlafly led opponents who feared ERA would take away privileges like exemption from the draft. In *Roe v. Wade,* the Supreme Court established a woman's right to abortion in the early months of pregnancy.

In this chapter you will learn about the Sixties, a turbulent time for many Americans. The decade began full of hope. With startling improvements in science and technology and more than a decade of prosperity, many Americans believed they were living in a golden age. Social conflict and the Vietnam War soon shattered this illusion. At the same time, America continued to evolve into a more open and pluralistic society. The popular songwriter Bob Dylan captured the spirit of the times when he proclaimed: "The Times They are a-Changin'!"

John F. Kennedy and the "New Frontier"

The Presidential election of 1960 was contested by two younger politicians: Senator John F. Kennedy and Vice President Richard Nixon. Kennedy won a close election after a skillful performance in a series of television debates. Young, handsome, intelligent and rich, Kennedy set a new tone for the Presidency. In his Inaugural Address, he challenged Americans to "ask not what your country can do for you; ask what you can do for your country." Kennedy's speech was a bold attempt to ignite the spirit of American idealism.

Kennedy promised new solutions in the defense of freedom overseas and in grappling with problems at home. His slogan, the "New Frontier" was meant to symbolize the vigor of youth in contrast to what he considered the complacency of government during the Eisenhower years. Kennedy appointed a talented team of leading intellectuals and corporate managers to cabinet posts and as informal advisers. He immediately set to work harnessing the powers of the federal government to solve America's problems.

▶ **The Space Race:** Competing with the Russian space program, Kennedy announced that the United States would place a man on the moon by the end of the decade. During Kennedy's administration, Alan Shepard became the first American to travel into space and John Glenn became the first American to orbit the Earth.

▶ **Rights for the Disabled:** Kennedy brought new attention to the rights of disabled Americans with the President's Council on Mental Retardation and the beginning of the Special Olympics for athletes with disabilities.

▶ **Rights for Women:** Kennedy set up a federal commission to report on the status of women and signed the Equal Pay Act in 1963. You will learn more about these later in the chapter.

▶ **Stalled Domestic Programs:** Much of Kennedy's "New Frontier" legislation became tied up in Congress, where it was opposed by Republicans and Southern Democrats. Kennedy proposed a tax cut to stimulate the economy, a new Department of Urban Affairs, Medicare, a civil rights bill, housing subsidies, immigration reform, and increased federal aid to education. None of these measures passed (although several were later passed by Kennedy's successor, Lyndon Johnson).

The Kennedy Assassination

Americans were shocked when President Kennedy was assassinated in Dallas by Lee Harvey Oswald on November 22, 1963. Supreme Court Chief Justice Earl Warren later headed a Commission that investigated the murder. The **Warren Commission** concluded that Oswald had acted alone in murdering the President.

Lyndon B. Johnson and the "Great Society"

The new President, **Lyndon B. Johnson,** was a Texan with long experience in the U.S. Senate. Highly skilled at managing Congress, Johnson began his Presidency by calling on legislators to pass a civil rights bill and several other measures as a tribute to President Kennedy. Johnson also successfully pushed through the reduction in income taxes originally proposed by Kennedy. The purpose of this tax cut was to stimulate the economy by placing more money in the hands of consumers and investors.

The "War on Poverty"

As a young man, Johnson had taught impoverished students in Texas. One year he had taught the children of Mexican immigrants and concluded that the nation could not rest until it gave equal opportunity to all Americans, including the very poor. As President, Johnson now called for a **"War on Poverty**." The Economic Opportunity Act of 1964 created the Office of Economic Opportunity to administer the programs established by the act. These included:

- **Job Corps:** to train underprivileged youths
- **VISTA (Volunteers in Service to America):** a domestic "peace corps" of volunteers performing services in depressed areas
- Community action programs

The Presidential Election of 1964

In the election of 1964, Johnson faced a conservative politician, Senator Barry Goldwater of Arizona. Goldwater questioned the wisdom of the welfare state and criticized the growing influence of the federal government. At the same time, he wanted to strengthen American military power and even suggested that tactical nuclear weapons might be used by American commanders. Johnson won a landslide victory with 61% of the popular vote. His landslide victory also gave him control of both houses of Congress.

Johnson's "Great Society"

After the election, Johnson felt confident enough to propose even more comprehensive social legislation. In January 1965, Johnson introduced his **"Great Society"** programs. His aim was to turn the United States into a more egalitarian society by opening up opportunities for all Americans. His "Great Society" was the most ambitious program of social reform since the New Deal.

- **Medicare and Medicaid:** The most enduring part of Johnson's "Great Society" programs was the introduction of Medicare and Medicaid. **Medicare** provides hospital insurance and inexpensive health insurance to those over 65 years of age. **Medicaid** was a new partnership of states with the federal government. It provides health benefits to certain people with low incomes, including children, pregnant women, elderly people in nursing homes, and people with disabilities.

- **Federal Aid to Education:** The Elementary and Secondary Education Act gave over $1 billion to local school districts. The Higher Education Act provided funds for over 140,000 scholarships and created a National Teacher Corps. Johnson introduced **Project Head Start,** a project to help prepare underprivileged children between the ages of three and five for elementary school. All federal aid to education was made conditional on the desegregation of school districts.

- **Aid to Cities:** The Housing and Urban Development Act created a new cabinet post in charge of programs aimed at helping the nation's cities. Billions in aid were appropriated to urban planning, slum clearance, rental subsidies for the poor, and the reconstruction of dilapidated buildings.

- **Appalachian Regional Development Act:** This act provided federal funds to create new jobs and industries in **Appalachia,** one of the poorest regions of the United States at this time. The Appalachian Commission defined the region as stretching from Southern New York to Mississippi, with its center in West Virginia.
- **The Immigration Act of 1965:** One of the biggest changes Johnson introduced was in immigration policy. He ended the discriminatory "national origins" system, which had favored immigrants from Western Europe. In its place, the new act established a more equitable system by giving each country the same maximum number of immigrants it could send to the United States.
- **Other Programs:** Johnson created the National Foundation of the Arts and the Humanities. He raised the minimum wage and increased expenditures for both his "War on Poverty" and the space program. He signed the bill that created public television (PBS). Finally, his administration issued new regulations to reduce smog and water pollution.

The Great Society Falls Victim to the Vietnam War

Despite these federal programs, many Americans remained in poverty. Meanwhile, America's involvement in the Vietnam War (see below) forced President Johnson to withdraw funding from Great Society programs. Liberals who had supported Johnson's "Great Society" grew increasingly critical of his handling of the Vietnam War.

President Johnson signing the Immigration Bill of 1965

The Warren Court

In these same years, the U.S. Supreme Court under Chief Justice Earl Warren not only asserted the rights of African Americans but also expanded the rights of all Americans. The Court became a major instrument of social change, protecting individual rights that other institutions had failed to defend. Some critics opposed such "**judicial activism**," arguing that the Court should leave most of these questions to the elected branches of government (such as Congress).

- **Freedom of Speech:** In *Yates v. United States* (1957), the Court extended the right of free speech to members of the Communist Party.
- **Equal Representation:** In many states, new cities had arisen but they had proportionally fewer representatives in their state legislatures than older rural districts. Members of state legislatures often refused to redraw district lines to make districts more equal in the number of people they represented. In *Baker v. Carr* (1962), the Court ordered a reorganization of state legislatures on the principle of "one man, one vote." This ended general under-representation of urban voters and the over-representation of rural voters.
- **Freedom of Religion:** In *Engel v. Vitale* (1962), the Court outlawed the use of school prayers in public schools, which it saw as a violation of the First Amendment, which protected freedom of religious belief.

The Rights of Accused Persons:
- Clarence Gideon was arrested in Florida and accused of robbery. He faced a prison sentence but was too poor to afford a lawyer. He

requested a lawyer but was told that under the laws of Florida, the court would only pay for a lawyer if the accused faced the death penalty. Gideon defended himself and was sentenced to five years imprisonment. From prison, he appealed his case. In *Gideon v. Wainwright* (1963), the U.S. Supreme Court held that the government must provide a lawyer to anyone accused of a felony who cannot afford one. The Court held that the right to a lawyer was a fundamental right, essential to a fair trial. When he was tried again with the help of an attorney, Gideon was acquitted and released.

▶ In *Miranda v. Arizona* (1966), the Supreme Court announced that it would not permit the use of a confession obtained by the police as evidence in court, unless the suspect was first told of his constitutional rights to remain silent, to have an attorney present during questioning, and to have one provided if he could not afford his own attorney. These are now known as the "Miranda" rights.

The Historian's Apprentice

Inaugural Address of John F. Kennedy, January 20, 1961

"Let the word go forth from this time and place, to friend and foe alike, that the torch has been passed to a new generation of Americans—born in this century, tempered by war, disciplined by a hard and bitter peace, proud of our ancient heritage, and unwilling to witness or permit the slow undoing of those human rights to which this nation has always been committed, and to which we are committed today at home and around the world.

Let every nation know, whether it wishes us well or ill, that we shall pay any price, bear any burden, meet any hardship, support any friend, oppose any foe, to assure the survival and the success of liberty. . . .

In the long history of the world, only a few generations have been granted the role of defending freedom in its hour of maximum danger. I do not shrink from this responsibility—I welcome it. I do not believe that any of us would exchange places with any other people or any other generation. The energy, the faith, the devotion which we bring to this endeavor will light our country and all who serve it. And the glow from that fire can truly light the world.

And so, my fellow Americans, ask not what your country can do for you; ask what you can do for your country.

My fellow citizens of the world, ask not what America will do for you, but what together we can do for the freedom of man.

Finally, whether you are citizens of America or citizens of the world, ask of us here the same high standards of strength and sacrifice which we ask of you. With a good conscience our only sure reward, with history the final judge of our deeds, let us go forth to lead the land we love, asking His blessing and His help, but knowing that here on earth God's work must truly be our own."

▶ Discuss the following four questions in small groups. Then report your answers to the class as a whole. (1) Why was Kennedy's message so inspiring to listeners in 1961? (2) How do you think the same message would be perceived today? (3) How well were the goals stated in Kennedy's speech realized in his Presidency? (4) How would American history have been different if Kennedy had not been assassinated?

> **Inaugural Address of Lyndon B. Johnson, January 20, 1965:**
>
> *"In a land of great wealth, families must not live in hopeless poverty. In a land rich in harvest, children just must not go hungry. In a land of healing miracles, neighbors must not suffer and die untended. In a great land of learning and scholars, young people must be taught to read and write.*
>
> *For more than 30 years that I have served this Nation I have believed that this injustice to our people, this waste of our resources, was our real enemy. For 30 years or more, with the resources I have had, I have vigilantly fought against it. I have learned and I know that it will not surrender easily.*
>
> *But change has given us new weapons. Before this generation of Americans is finished, this enemy will not only retreat, it will be conquered.*
>
> *Justice requires us to remember: when any citizen denies his fellow, saying: "His color is not mine or his beliefs are strange and different," in that moment he betrays America, though his forebears created this Nation."*
>
> ▸ How does Johnson's Inaugural Address compare to Kennedy's, four years earlier? Which speech do you like better? Why?
>
> ▸ There are different types of leadership. Look again at the speeches of Kennedy and Johnson. Then think about the actions of each as leaders. How do these two speeches reflect their leadership styles?
>
> ▸ Make a Venn diagram or chart comparing the proposals and accomplishments of Kennedy and Johnson.
>
> ▸ From the Progressives to President Lyndon B. Johnson, the power and influence of the federal government over the American economy and society as a whole was increasing. Make your own timeline showing the major milestones in the growth of federal power from 1902 to 1968.
>
> ▸ Imagine it is 1965. Hold a class debate on whether or not Congress should pass President Johnson's "Great Society" programs.
>
> ▸ Select one of the decisions of the Warren Court described above. Using your school library or the Internet, find out more information about the case. Then write a summary. Be sure to include important background facts, the decision of the Supreme Court, and the reasoning behind the decision. You will learn more about the Supreme Court in Chapter 17.

The Vietnam War

Next to the Civil War, the Vietnam War was the most socially divisive war in American history. Why did Americans become involved in this distant Asian country, and why were they unable to achieve their goals there?

Background to the Conflict

Vietnam is located in the eastern part of **Indochina**, a large peninsula directly south of China. Vietnam consists of heavily forested mountains, highlands, and valleys. The Red River valley to the north and the Mekong Delta in the south provide fertile land for rice production. The country has warm, wet winters and hot, wet summers.

In the 19th century, the countries of **Indochina** (*Vietnam, Laos,* and *Cambodia*) came under French rule. The Vietnamese Emperor was permitted to remain on his throne, but the French governed the country for their own benefit. As early as 1900, a Vietnamese nationalist movement emerged. One leading Vietnamese nationalist was **Ho Chi Minh**, a dedicated revolutionary who left Vietnam in 1912, joined the French Communist Party in 1920, and served in the Communist Parties of Russia and China in the 1930s.

During World War II, Japan seized control of French Indochina. Ho Chi Minh led Vietnamese nationalists in an underground struggle against the Japanese. After the surrender of Japan, Vietnamese nationalist forces entered Hanoi. Ho Chi Minh declared the independence of Vietnam, and the Vietnamese Emperor abdicated in favor of the new republic.

France, however, refused to recognize the independence of Vietnam. Armed conflict between Vietnamese and French forces began in 1946 and lasted for nine years. Ho Chi Minh kept control of the North but was unable to establish control in the South, where the French had restored the Vietnamese Emperor. In 1950, the Soviet Union and Communist China recognized Ho Chi Minh's government. American leaders, viewing Ho Chi Minh as a Communist, gave assistance to the French. By 1954, the United States was paying for most of the French war effort, although President Eisenhower refused to commit U.S. troops. Vietnamese forces won a decisive victory in 1954, forcing France to withdraw from Indochina.

The Geneva Accords, 1954

In the spring of 1954, representatives from Indochina, France, China, the Soviet Union, Great Britain, and the United States assembled in Geneva, Switzerland, to negotiate a peace settlement. Laos and Cambodia were made into independent neutral states. The country of Vietnam was divided into two: Ho Chi Minh and the Vietnamese Communists were left in control of the North, while the Vietnamese Emperor was given control of the South. A special **Demilitarized Zone (DMZ)** separated the two. The division of Vietnam was meant to be temporary: free elections were supposed to be held and the country was to be re-united in 1956.

The Reasons for American Involvement

After the Geneva Conference, the United States replaced France as the chief supporter of South Vietnam. Why did American leaders assume this responsibility?

▶ **Fear of Communism—The "Domino Theory":** American leaders were afraid of the spread of Communism. They saw all the Communist nations of the world as part of the same monolithic bloc. Since the end of World War II, Communism had spread from the Soviet Union to Eastern Europe, China, North Korea and North Vietnam. American leaders were afraid that if they did not make a stand, it would spread further. They believed that if South Vietnam fell to Communism, other Southeast Asian countries—Laos, Cambodia, Thailand, Malaysia—would fall like a row of dominoes. Communism would continue to spread throughout the world until it posed a direct threat to the United States. These ideas became known as the "**domino theory**."

▶ **Belief in the Benefits of Democracy:** American leaders were also idealistic: they believed in the advantages of democracy. They hoped to introduce political, social and economic reforms that would benefit the Vietnamese people. They hoped this would provide an alternative to colonialism and Communism. American leaders thought they had an opportunity to build a successful democracy in Vietnam, which would provide an attractive model for other countries in Asia, Africa and Latin America.

▶ **An Example to Allies:** Once they had committed themselves to Vietnam, American leaders felt that their prestige as the leader of the "Free World" was at stake. If America deserted the government of South Vietnam, they argued, other nations would lose faith in America's ability to protect them. American leaders also felt obliged by their membership in **SEATO** (the Southeast

Asian Treaty Organization), an alliance of the United States and other countries similar to NATO, but with a focus on Southeast Asia.

▶ **Underestimation of the Enemy:** Another reason American leaders became involved was that they did not expect it to be difficult to win in Vietnam. They thought that the superiority of American democracy, combined with America's advanced technology and economic resources, would be sufficient to help South Vietnam resist Communism. They underestimated the strength of Vietnamese nationalism and the determination of Ho Chi Minh and the North Vietnamese to unify their country.

The Diem Government in South Vietnam, 1954–1963

After the Geneva Conference, Vietnam's Emperor remained in France and appointed a Catholic nationalist, **Ngo Dinh Diem,** as his prime minister. Diem deposed the Emperor the following year. Diem refused to hold elections in 1956, claiming that such elections would not be free in the North, where Ho Chi Minh had already established a Communist dictatorship. Thousands of North Vietnamese Catholics fled to South Vietnam with tales of Communist atrocities.

Diem established his own oppressive regime in the South, executing many political opponents. Diem's brother became the hated head of the secret police. Lands that had been distributed to the peasants were returned to the landlords. Diem, a Catholic, also began a policy of discrimination against Vietnamese Buddhists.

The Vietcong Revolt

When Diem refused to hold the elections required by the Geneva Accords, South Vietnamese Communists formed a revolutionary army, known as the **Vietcong**. They began a campaign of **guerilla warfare** (*a form of irregular fighting, in which smaller groups of forces suddenly strike and then disappear*) in the South, murdering officials and government sympathizers.

President Kennedy sent both military aid and several thousand military advisers to help Diem fight the Vietcong. Kennedy's aim was to show that the United States could prevent the expansion of Communism in the developing nations of Asia, Africa and Latin America through new "counter-insurgency" techniques. However, Diem's policies made him increasingly unpopular. He was overthrown and murdered by his own generals in 1963. Ironically, President Kennedy was assassinated in Dallas only a few weeks later.

President Johnson Escalates the War, 1964–1968

After the death of Diem, the United States became even more involved in the defense of South Vietnam. In August 1964, President Johnson announced that the North Vietnamese had attacked American ships in international waters in the Gulf of Tonkin. In the "**Gulf of Tonkin Resolution,**" Congress voted to give the President extraordinary powers to take all measures necessary to stop North Vietnamese aggression. Johnson saw this resolution as the legal basis for an escalation of the war. Years later it became clear that these American ships had been in North Vietnamese waters and that they were protecting South Vietnamese boats that had been bombing North Vietnamese targets.

In 1965, President Johnson sent the first American combat troops to Vietnam. By the end of the year 184,000 American soldiers were active in Vietnam. President Johnson also ordered bombing missions over North Vietnam to wear down North Vietnamese resistance and to destroy supply routes from North to South Vietnam. The missions failed to achieve either objective, even though Americans eventually dropped more bombs on Vietnam, Laos and Cambodia than they dropped on Europe in all of World War II. Bombing missions over Vietnam actually tended to strengthen rather than to weaken resistance. Resentment against the United States grew and the Vietnamese became more determined than ever to achieve their national independence.

The Nature of Combat

President Johnson hoped to use America's technological superiority and an overwhelming number of

U.S. Helicopter spraying **Agent Orange** over the jungle

troops to win the war. Jet planes bombed Vietcong supply routes and enemy forces. New destructive weapons like **napalm** (*gasoline mixed with a gel that sticks to skin as it burns*) and cluster bombs inflicted terrible damage on their victims. Herbicides, like **Agent Orange**, destroyed the jungle cover. Helicopters transported supplies, moved whole American units, and picked up wounded American soldiers.

Nevertheless, American soldiers faced immense obstacles in Vietnam. The climate was hot and uncomfortable. The jungles and forests of Vietnam provided cover for enemy movements and supply routes from North Vietnam and China. Booby traps set in rice paddies and jungles could go off at any time. The Vietcong, who were more familiar with the terrain, adopted the tactics of **guerilla warfare**. They seldom came out in the open. They persuaded or coerced other Vietnamese to cooperate with them. American soldiers were unable to distinguish the Vietcong from friendly Vietnamese. Any Vietnamese civilian, including women and children, might be a secret Vietcong. American units ocassionally destroyed whole villages in their search for the enemy. Some atrocities occurred, such as when American forces killed unarmed men, women and children in the village of **My Lai**.

American search-and-destroy missions and Vietcong terrorism drove many Vietnamese from the countryside to the cities. **Saigon** (the capital of South Vietnam) and other cities became clogged with refugees. A massive influx of supplies for American troops further subverted the South Vietnamese economy. These conditions encouraged the spread of bribery and corruption. Meanwhile, the South Vietnamese government never introduced effective land reform. None of the military governments that ruled South Vietnam after Diem's death ever commanded a strong base of popular support. This made it easier for the Vietcong to gain control over much of the countryside.

By the beginning of 1968, American military leaders thought they had finally broken the power of the Vietcong. However, during the "**Tet Offensive**"— launched on the Vietnamese New Year, January 30— the Vietcong seized control of many of South Vietnam's major cities. Although American forces were eventually able to drive the Vietcong out of these strongholds, the offensive showed that the Communists were far from beaten. When the American commander in Vietnam asked for another 200,000 troops, Johnson refused his request.

Paris Peace Talks Begin

North Vietnam agreed to begin peace talks in Paris when Johnson halted bombing missions in the spring of 1968. At the same time, Johnson decided not to run again for another term as President. By the end of 1968, over 500,000 American troops were in Vietnam, and the war was costing Americans $25 billion a year. Yet there were still no signs of future victory. Critics began calling Vietnam a "quagmire," or swamp.

Victims of My Lai massacre

President Nixon Continues the War

In the Presidential election of 1968, Democrats were deeply divided over the war. As a consequence, **Richard M. Nixon**, the same Republican who had lost the election to Kennedy in 1960, was elected President. Although Nixon promised Americans an early end to the war, accompanied by "peace with honor," the war in fact continued for another four years. Like Johnson, Nixon did not want to be the first American President to lose a war.

Under Nixon's policy of "**Vietnamization**," the South Vietnamese assumed the brunt of the fighting. Nixon gradually withdrew American combat troops from Vietnam and ended the "draft" (*military conscription*). At the same time, he increased American bombing missions over the North and the flow of military supplies and economic support to South Vietnam. Nixon believed the war could be shortened if supply routes from North to South Vietnam could be cut off. In 1970, American troops crossed over into neighboring Cambodia. Americans also began bombing Cambodia and Laos.

Nixon also tried to place new diplomatic pressure on the North Vietnamese by visiting Communist China and working out a policy of *détente* with Soviet leaders in 1972. You will learn more about these initiatives in the next chapter.

Cease-Fire and American Withdrawal

National Security Adviser **Dr. Henry Kissinger** continued secret negotiations with the North Vietnamese in Paris. In January 1973, he concluded the **Paris Peace Accords**, a cease-fire agreement with the North Vietnamese based on the withdrawal of all U.S. troops from Vietnam. Under the agreement, the United States was permitted to continue providing military and economic aid to South Vietnam.

Even after the American withdrawal, bitter fighting continued in Southeast Asia. In April 1975, both Cambodia and South Vietnam finally fell to Communist forces. Vietnam was united under Vietnamese Communist leadership, just as Ho Chi Minh had originally intended.

Why Were Americans Unable to Win the War?

Ho Chi Minh and other North Vietnamese leaders had been fighting to achieve control over a unified Vietnam since 1946. They were willing to sustain large losses to obtain their goal. Increasing casualties did not weaken their resolve. As the Americans sent in more troops, so did North Vietnam. The North Vietnamese were also able to obtain supplies from the Communist governments of China and the Soviet Union. Supply routes to the South like the Ho Chi Minh Trail were so primitive that they could be quickly rebuilt when they were bombed.

American leaders might have pulled out of a war they felt they could not win, but they were afraid of the effect this might have on their popularity inside the United States. Johnson did not want to be accused of giving in to Communists or of appearing to be weak, so he continued to escalate the war rather than abandon South Vietnam to Communism. Since American leaders would not pull out and North Vietnamese leaders would not give in, the war just dragged on and on.

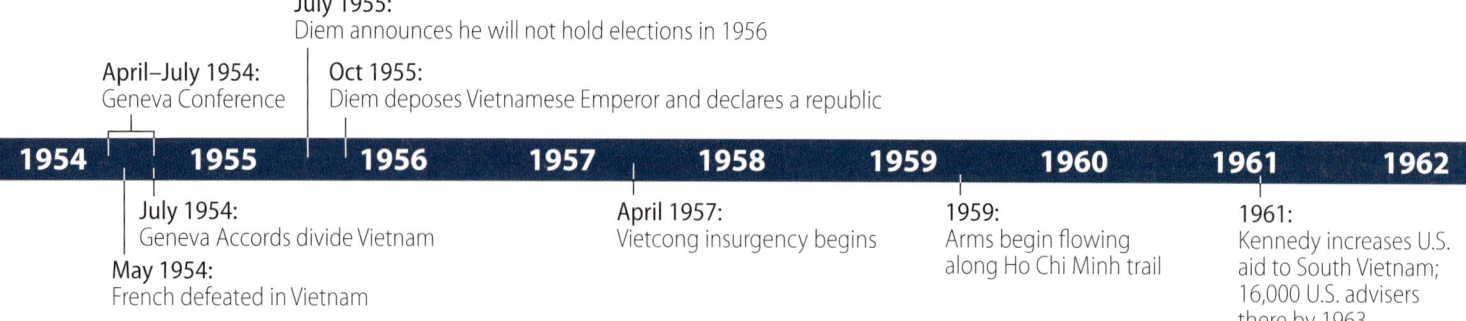

The Home Front: Discontent and Division During the Vietnam War

The Vietnam War became the most unpopular war in recent U.S. history. At first, most Americans supported the decision to help South Vietnam. But as the war dragged on and the troop commitment grew, many Americans grew disenchanted with the conduct of the war.

Doves and Hawks

"**Doves**" wanted the United States to withdraw from the war. They saw the contest as a civil war between Vietnamese in which the United States simply had no business. Many Doves, including Dr. Martin Luther King, Jr., thought the war was immoral. The United States was bombing so many civilians and burning down so many villages that it was destroying Vietnam in order to save it.

"**Hawks**" believed it was important to stop the spread of Communism. They saw the war as the defense of South Vietnam, a sovereign country, against an invasion from the North. Most Hawks thought that an all-out military effort in Vietnam could bring victory. They wanted to invade the North. A few favored the use of tactical nuclear weapons, which they thought would force the North Vietnamese to surrender.

The News Media and the "Credibility Gap"

Newspaper reporters and television journalists played an increasingly important role in presenting the Vietnam War to the American public. This was the first televised war. Modern television reporting brought the bloody horrors of war into the average American living room. Many Americans were influenced when CBS anchor Walter Cronkite turned against the war at the end of 1967.

American political leaders realized that they not only had to fight the war but also had to manage its public relations. Their concern to impress the public favorably often led to a twisting of the facts and to a growing "**credibility gap**." For example, President Johnson claimed that bombing had injured few North Vietnamese civilians, but a *New York Times* reporter in North Vietnam found just the opposite. Johnson told Americans that the United States was winning the war, but the public received a different impression from nightly broadcasts on television during the Tet Offensive. People began to lose faith in the trustworthiness of their own government. Nixon was even more secretive than Johnson, further widening the "credibility gap". Nixon attempted to prevent the *New York Times* from publishing the *Pentagon Papers*, a secret government study of American involvement in Vietnam. The Supreme Court ruled against him in *NY Times v. United States* (1971) on the basis of freedom of the press.

The "Baby Boomers" and the Anti-War Movement

Because of the postwar "baby boom," a large number of Americans reached their twenties in the late

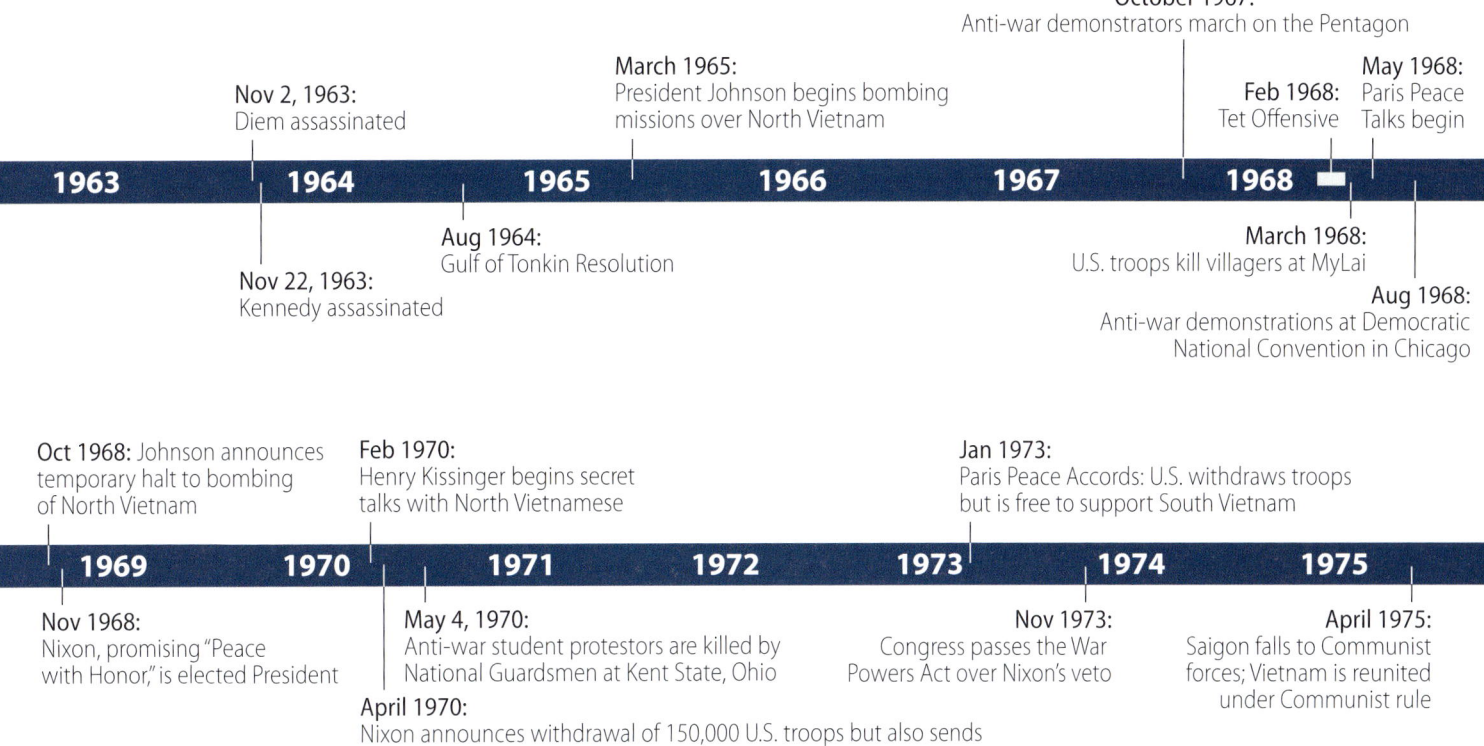

1960s and early 1970s. This new generation was influenced by the prosperity of the 1950s, the new permissive methods of childcare introduced by experts like Dr. Benjamin Spock, and the experience of watching television as they grew up. A larger number of Americans than ever before were going to college. Unlike the college students of the 1950s, the baby boomers had high expectations and an open, questioning attitude. They were not inclined to follow the social rules of their elders simply to conform. The baby boomers objected to the bureaucracy and impersonal, machine-like life-style of corporate America. They challenged the prevailing materialism of American society. The formation of student organizations, such as the Students for a Democratic Society (SDS) in 1960 and the "Free Speech" movement at the University of California at Berkeley in 1964 were symptoms of this new spirit. As the Sixties wore on, a new "Youth Culture" emerged. Young people were especially affected by rock music, greater sexual freedom, and the availability of recreational drugs like marijuana and LSD. Youths adopted new fashions, like long hair for men, bell-bottomed trousers, beads, and colorful clothing, to set themselves apart from traditional styles. Some dropped out of conventional society altogether to become "hippies."

An anti-war rally at the Pentagon in 1967

Many of these students became intensely political. In the late 1960s, their concerns focused on the escalating American involvement in Vietnam. Young men over the age of 18 were subject to compulsory military conscription, better known as the "**draft**." As in earlier conflicts, **conscientious objectors** who could prove they opposed all wars as a matter of religious belief were excused from service, but not those who were against the war on political grounds. Draft-aged men opposed to the war protested by burning their draft cards. Some draft resisters fled to Canada or Sweden. At the beginning of the war, college students were deferred from the draft until they completed their studies. A large number of draft resisters were middle-class college students, while many of those actually sent to Vietnam came from the working classes. This circumstance added tension to the debate over the war.

In the summer of 1968, anti-war protestors from around the country converged on Chicago to demonstrate at the Democratic National Convention. Police and demonstrators clashed violently outside the convention hall. Leading anti-war activists were put on trial for causing the disruption, although many witnesses believed that it was Chicago's mayor and the police who were at fault. One of the accused, a Black Panther, was bound and gagged in the courtroom to prevent his outbursts.

Anti-war protesters organized continual marches and demonstrations in the nation's capital, on college campuses, and in major cities.

In the spring of 1970, Nixon announced the invasion of Cambodia. At **Kent State University** in Ohio, local National Guardsmen were called in to control an anti-war demonstration. Several of the inexperienced Guards fired, killing four students and wounding nine others. American college students throughout the country shut down their campuses in protest. An estimated four million students went on strike.

Many younger Americans, especially on college campuses, became frustrated at their inability to stop the war. They began to ask what kind of society could wage such a war. This led them to question their fundamental values. A large number concluded that the war was caused by the American system of competitive capitalism. Some even decided to reject this society altogether, preferring to "drop out" and join in the new "counter-culture." The anti-war movement and the youth culture of the 1960s thus reinforced each other in encouraging the search for a better way of life.

The Consequences of the Vietnam War

The Vietnam War had profound consequences:

▶ The greatest effects of the war were felt in Vietnam itself. Estimates vary, but at least 1.3 million Vietnamese were killed during the war and a large proportion of the population of South Vietnam was left homeless. Herbicides destroyed rice paddies and forests. Cities were in ruins.

▶ 58,000 Americans were killed in the war. Their names are now inscribed on the Vietnam Veterans Memorial in Washington, D.C. Thousands more suffered physical and psychological injuries. A large number suffered from exposure to American herbicides used during the war, especially "Agent Orange." Many Vietnam veterans felt that their needs were subsequently ignored.

▶ Vietnamese Communists quickly introduced repressive policies in South Vietnam. Many people, fearful of persecution, fled on small boats to neighboring non-Communist countries. Some Vietnamese refugees immigrated to the United States.

▶ The extension of the Vietnam War into Cambodia led to the triumph of Cambodian Communists, known as the "Khmer Rouge." In 1975–1976, the Khmer Rouge murdered between two and four million Cambodians.

▶ Wartime expenses led to a reduction of the social welfare programs of Johnson's "Great Society." The war also caused rising inflation.

▶ Finally, the failure in Vietnam led to widespread American disillusionment in government. The war led to a crisis of confidence. American leaders realized that American power had its limits, but they were not sure where those limits were. The mood of the country became more isolationist. American leaders grew fearful of over-extending our commitments abroad. Young people were especially distrustful of their leaders.

▶ As a result of the failure in Vietnam and popular disillusionment, Congress attempted to claim a greater role in determining national policy. In 1973, Congress passed the **War Powers Act**, limiting the President's power to commit U.S. troops overseas. Within two days of committing troops to combat, the President must make a report to Congress. The troops must be withdrawn within 60 days, unless Congress authorizes a longer commitment.

The Historian's Apprentice

▶ Make your own illustrated map of Indochina in the 1960s. On your map, show countries, rivers, highlands, and rainforest areas. Then add the major cities and rivers of Vietnam. Finally, add important battles and other events with their dates. For example, mark where the Gulf of Tonkin incident occurred in August 1964, and the cities affected by the Tet Offensive in 1968.

▶ Watch one or more episodes of the PBS documentary, *Vietnam: A Television History*, or *The Vietnam War*, by Ken Burns and Lynn Novick. How does watching a documentary differ from reading a book? Is a television documentary more or less objective than a book? What do you think was the view of the producers of either of these documentaries? Explain your answers.

▶ Imagine it is 1969. Hold a class debate between "Hawks" and "Doves" on this topic—"Resolved: the United States should immediately withdraw from Vietnam."

▶ Using your school library or the Internet, find some newspapers from the 1960s. Look for opposing viewpoints on the war in Vietnam, expressed in editorials or articles. Then summarize the arguments you find in one of those editorials or articles.

▶ Using your school library or the Internet, find out more information about Daniel Ellsberg and *The Pentagon Papers*. What did they contain? Why was the federal government so concerned about their publication?

▶ Interview a parent, relative or neighbor who either fought in Vietnam or who participated in the anti-war movement. Be sure to formulate a series of good questions in advance. Then report the results of your interview to your class.

▶ Why do you think the Vietnam War remains a controversial topic today?

The Changing Status of Women

Another important development in the 1960s and 1970s was the **Women's Liberation Movement**. The earlier women's rights movement had aimed at achieving political and civil equality for women. The new women's movement focused on achieving economic and social equality between women and men.

Origins of the Women's Liberation Movement (or the Feminist Movement)

President Kennedy formed a commission on the status of women, chaired by Eleanor Roosevelt. Its report, issued in 1963, concluded that discrimination against women was widespread. It noted that

Chapter 15 | The Sixties: "The Times They are a-Changin'"

forty years after the passage of the 19th Amendment, women still did not receive equal pay for equal work and few held positions of high authority in business or the professions.

With the great postwar "baby boom," many women found fulfillment in traditional nurturing roles as wives and mothers. Movies, television, and popular magazines all reinforced the image of the woman as a middle-class housewife. Some educated, middle-class women, however, grew dissatisfied with their roles as housewives. They also felt that the division of labor between men and women within the home was unfair and stifling. These middle-class women wanted the freedom to express themselves in careers outside the home as men did. They wanted to "liberate" themselves from traditional roles. In 1963, their discontent came to the surface with the publication of **Betty Friedan**'s book, *The Feminine Mystique*. The "mystique" was the belief that women always found happiness as housewives and mothers rather than in careers—a belief that Friedan challenged. Meanwhile, social scientists, many of them women like Margaret Mead and Simone de Beauvoir, began to see women's status in Western society as the outcome of various social and cultural influences rather than as a biological necessity.

Betty Friedan

The success of the Civil Rights Movement inspired these women to strive for greater equality with men. Many of the leaders of the Women's Liberation Movement had been activists in the Civil Rights Movement or the anti-war movement. They read together, educated themselves, and formed women's groups to discuss issues and plan change. They adopted the same techniques as Civil Rights leaders to promote women's rights, such as forming organizations, lobbying, and engaging in demonstrations, boycotts, and strikes.

Highly educated, talented women like Betty Friedan, Gloria Steinem and Aileen Hernandez provided dynamic leadership. In 1966, Friedan and others formed the **National Organization for Women** (NOW), which became the chief voice of the modern women's movement. Gloria Steinem founded a monthly magazine, *Ms.,* devoted to women's issues.

The Women's Liberation Movement was also affected by the "**Sexual Revolution**" of the 1960s. Freudian psychology made people more open about their sexual feelings. "Sex education" began to be taught in the schools. The invention of the birth control pill gave women greater freedom to engage in sexual activity without fear of pregnancy. In this new atmosphere, women could more openly acknowledge their sexuality. This confirmed the new view that the differences between women and men were not as great as had once been supposed.

Goals and Accomplishments of the Women's Liberation Movement

The goals of the Women's Liberation Movement were far-reaching. Women demanded greater freedom and social and economic equality with men.

Education Feminists wanted to end discrimination in education. The **Equal Opportunity in Education Act** (1972), also known as **Title IX**, prohibited universities and schools receiving federal aid from discriminating in their educational programs, including athletics, on the basis of sex. In the 1970s, the U.S. military academies (such as West Point) and all but a small handful of colleges became co-educational. High school gym classes in public schools also became co-educational. "Affirmative action" programs further promoted the hiring of women professors. Finally a large number of women began being admitted to law schools, medical schools, and graduate business schools.

Women in the Workforce Feminists also wanted to end discrimination in hiring and establish equal opportunity in employment for women. They demanded laws requiring companies to grant maternity leave and federal aid for child day-care centers. They were successful in achieving many of these goals. In

1963, Congress passed the **Equal Pay Act,** requiring companies to pay women the same wages as men for the same work. The 1964 Civil Rights Act forbade discrimination in hiring on the basis of sex as well as race and nationality. Affirmative action further required companies with federal contracts to set goals for hiring more women. Today there are women police, television newscasters, business executives, and highway workers—in fact, women in almost every career. Athletes like tennis player Billie Jean King campaigned for equal prize money for women and men and showed that women's athletics were just as professional as men's were.

Popular Attitudes One of the main goals of the Women's Liberation Movement was to reshape popular attitudes. Feminists fought against sexual discrimination in social clubs, textbooks that ignored the contributions and experiences of women, and the use of women as "sex objects" in advertising. They even objected to female beauty contests. Feminists also introduced the title "Ms." to replace "Miss" and "Mrs." (which depended on marital status). They lobbied for funds for research on women's diseases, such as breast cancer, and for the study of women's special problems, such as rape and domestic violence. Finally, feminists urged that men and women should share equally in domestic duties like cooking and cleaning. Only by changing people's attitudes, these feminists argued, could women achieve true "liberation" from traditional roles and their historically inferior status. The changing position of women has had a dramatic impact on American life. Men today are more aware of their responsibilities at home, while women have assumed greater responsibilities in the workplace.

The Equal Rights Amendment (ERA)

One failure of the Women's Liberation Movement was its inability to secure the passage of the **Equal Rights Amendment (ERA)**. Feminists hoped to achieve many of their goals by passing a single constitutional amendment that guaranteed women equal rights with men. ("Equality of rights should not be denied . . . on account of sex.") The Equal Rights Amendment was first proposed by **Alice Paul** in 1923. It was submitted to Congress every year until it was approved by both houses of Congress in 1972. Congress gave the states seven years to ratify the amendment. Thirty-five states eventually ratified it, but three more were needed to satisfy the requirement of three-quarters of the states before the time period for ratification ran out. In November 1977, a National Conference of Women was held in Houston, Texas. Its 2,000 delegates were chosen by a series of state conventions. A burning torch was carried from Seneca Falls, New York—birthplace of the women's suffrage movement—to Houston. Three "First Ladies" (Mrs. Carter, Mrs. Ford, and Mrs. Johnson) were among the participants. The conference recommended approval of ERA and an extension of time for ratification. A rival conference was organized nearby by **Phyllis Schlafly** and other opponents of ERA, many of whom were women who favored traditional roles. Schlafly argued that the passage of ERA would subject women to the draft (*compulsory military service*) and take away other privileges, such as lower insurance rates and dependent social security benefits. Schlafly also feared that the language of ERA might be used to justify same-sex marriages. Other opponents of ERA insisted that women already had equal rights, and that enforcement of those rights was better left to the states. In the end, no additional states ratified ERA, and several states even attempted to rescind (*take back*) their ratifications. Florida was one of those states that never ratified ERA.

The Controversy over Abortion

Abortion is the early termination of an unwanted pregnancy. In 1970, abortions were illegal in most states. Feminists called for the repeal of state laws prohibiting abortion. Feminists argued that women should have control over their own bodies without the interference of the government.

***Roe v. Wade* (1973):** In *Roe v. Wade*, the U.S. Supreme Court ruled that a woman has a constitutional right to privacy under the Fourteenth Amendment. The Court held that this amendment guarantees "personal liberty and restrictions on state action." This right to privacy gives a woman an unrestricted right to have an abortion in the first three months of the pregnancy and restricted rights to have an abortion on health grounds in the second three months. The Court ruled that a woman had no rights to abort in the last three months of her pregnancy. The decision in *Roe v. Wade* overturned all state laws prohibiting abortion in the first three months.

The "Right-to-Life" versus "Pro-Choice" debate: "Right-to-Life" groups protested the *Roe v. Wade* decision. They argued that abortion was murder and that the state has the right to protect the unborn child. The Catholic Church and several Protestant and Jewish groups oppose abortion on the same grounds. Other religious and non-religious groups argue that abortion is a private matter, and that the religious beliefs of some should not be imposed on others. Most feminists continue to feel that women should be free to determine how their own bodies are used. Abortion continues to be one of the most divisive issues in the United States today.

Several later Supreme Court rulings have limited the reach of *Roe v. Wade*. For example, in *Webster v. Reproductive Health Services* (1989), the U.S. Supreme Court upheld a Missouri law prohibiting the use of state funds in clinics giving abortions. Other decisions have upheld laws banning some types of abortion procedures. You will review some of these more recent cases in Chapter 17.

A group of abortion-rights activists

The Historian's Apprentice

Have your class hold a debate on the Equal Rights Amendment. Do you think it should have been passed? Should it be passed today?

Section 1 Equality of rights shall not be denied or abridged by the United States or any state on account of sex.

Section 2 The Congress shall have the power to enforce, by appropriate legislation, the provisions of this amendment.

Section 3 This amendment shall take effect two years after ratification.

Focus on Florida

The launch of the Apollo 11 from Cape Canaveral on July 16, 1969, marked the end of a remarkable decade in Florida history. As Neil Armstrong stepped off the lunar module to become the first person to set foot on the moon, his famous words were: "That's one small step for [a] man, one great step for mankind." A similar description might have been applied to how Florida and perceptions of its future had changed in the Sixties. The Civil Rights Movement in Florida, highlighted by the Tallahassee bus boycott and the demonstrations in St. Augustine led by Dr. Martin Luther King, Jr., permanently altered race relations between the state's blacks and whites. The decade also saw the beginnings of a mass exodus of people from Cuba, which would change the politics and demographics of Florida for decades to come.

Finally, the 1960s saw an increase in the migration of retired people from other states to Florida. Today, people over 65 years of age make up one-fifth of Florida's population. They form a very active political group, often represented by the AARP (American Association of Retired Persons). A higher percentage of the elderly vote than members of other age groups. According to Florida's Department of Elder Affairs, more than 40% of those who vote are over 60 years of age. Seniors have exercised a tremendous influence on Florida from tourism to tax laws. They pay for half of all new home construction as well as $1 billion a year in local school taxes.

Review Cards

The Kennedy Years

- Young and idealistic, President **John F. Kennedy** was elected in 1960. He promised a **"New Frontier,"** using federal power to solve problems at home and defend freedom abroad.
- Kennedy's **Space Program** competed with the Soviets. The **President's Council on Mental Retardation** and the **Special Olympics** brought attention to disabled persons. Kennedy also set up a federal commission to report on the status of women and signed the **Equal Pay Act**.
- Other "New Frontier" reforms, involving taxes, housing, and civil rights, were halted in Congress.
- Kennedy was assassinated by **Lee Harvey Oswald** in November 1963.

The Johnson Years

- Lyndon B. Johnson became President in 1963. An experienced manager of the Senate, Johnson began his term by passing much of Kennedy's reform legislation as a tribute.
- Johnson called for a **War on Poverty**. The **Economic Opportunity Act** established programs like the **Job Corps,** to train youths, and **VISTA,** a domestic "peace corps."
- Johnson won a landslide victory against **Barry Goldwater** in 1964, giving him control of Congress. He proposed his **"Great Society"** reform program, the most ambitious since the New Deal.
- **Medicare** and **Medicaid** gave health insurance to seniors, the poor, children, pregnant women, and the disabled. These were the most enduring of all the "Great Society" programs.
- Federal money was given to education, like **Project Head Start** for low-income youths.
- The **Housing and Urban Development Act** gave federal aid to poor areas of cities. The **Appalachian Regional Development Act** gave aid to one of America's poorest regions.
- The **Immigration Act of 1965** replaced the previous system based on national origins by establishing the same immigration quota for all countries.
- Other achievements included the creation of the **National Foundation for the Arts and Humanities,** a higher minimum wage, environmental reform, and the creation of **PBS.**

The Warren Court

- The Supreme Court under **Earl Warren** became an instrument of social change, expanding the rights of all Americans. Some Americans opposed such **judicial activism.**
- The Court made important decisions on freedom of speech, freedom of religion, and rights for criminal suspects in cases like *Yates v. United States, Baker v. Carr, Engel v. Vitale, Gideon v. Wainwright,* and *Miranda v. Arizona.*

Background to the Vietnam War: the Struggle over Indochina

- **Indochina** was a French colony in the 19th century; it was then seized by Japan in 1940. Communist **Ho Chi Minh** led a nationalist resistance movement. After the war, he declared Vietnam to be independent. France refused to accept the new nation, leading to armed conflict for nine years.
- In 1954, France surrendered. In the **Geneva Accords,** Laos and Cambodia became independent. Vietnam was divided between Communist **North Vietnam** and **South Vietnam** under the Vietnamese Emperor. Elections and reunification were supposed to occur in 1956.

The Vietnam War: Early American Involvement

- In the South, Prime Minister **Ngo Dinh Diem** deposed the Emperor. Diem refused to hold elections in 1956, and established an oppressive, conservative regime in the South. South Vietnamese Communists formed a revolutionary army, the **Vietcong,** and began **guerrilla warfare.**
- The U.S. supported South Vietnam for a number of reasons. It feared the **"domino theory,"** had obligations under **SEATO,** believed that Vietnam would benefit from democracy, wanted to assure the "Free World" of its protection, and thought it could win the war easily.
- American involvement began when President Kennedy sent military advisers to Diem. When both leaders were assassinated in 1963, President Johnson escalated involvement. After a supposed attack on American ships, Congress passed the **Gulf of Tonkin Resolution.** This gave Johnson extraordinary powers of intervention. He sent the first troops to Vietnam in 1965.

The Vietnam War: Escalation

- Johnson hoped to win the war with American technological superiority. Bombs, skin-burning **napalm,** environmentally destructive **Agent Orange,** and helicopters were used.
- Americans still faced problems. They were not used to the environment. The Vietcong planned successful **guerilla attacks.** They often hid among civilians, so American **"search and destroy"** missions sometimes destroyed whole villages. Many civilians fled to cities like **Saigon,** which became overcrowded and corrupt. The U.S. became increasingly unpopular.
- In 1968, the Vietcong launched the **"Tet Offensive."** Although eventually driven out, the attack showed their strength. Johnson announced he would not run for another term as President.
- The war dragged on because America did not want to surrender and seem weak to the world, but the Communists were committed to their cause and were aided by China and Russia.
- Nixon was elected President in 1968. His policy of **"Vietnamization"** replaced American troops with South Vietnamese. Yet he also increased bombings in Vietnam, Cambodia, and Laos.
- In 1973, **Dr. Henry Kissinger** signed the **Paris Peace Accords** with North Vietnam. The U.S. withdrew all troops but continued to send aid. South Vietnam fell to the Communists in 1975.

A Divided Home Front

- As the war dragged on, the home front became divided. **"Doves"** thought the war was immoral and wanted the U.S to withdraw. **"Hawks"** wanted to continue the war to stop Communism.
- The Vietnam War was the first televised war. The media covered it closely, but the government sometimes twisted facts to impress the public. This led to a **"credibility gap."** Distrust in government grew, especially when Nixon tried to conceal the *Pentagon Papers,* a secret government war study.
- The "Baby Boom" generation created a new, anti-conformist **Youth Culture** in the 60s. Some created radical groups like **SDS**; others experimented with drugs like LSD, and still others became **"hippies."**
- Many students became political. They resented the **draft** and the war. In 1968, a protest at the **Democratic National Convention** turned violent. In 1970, National Guardsmen killed students at **Kent State University.** Government and police violence only increased resistance.

Consequences of the Vietnam War

- Vietnam suffered the most from the war. More than a million Vietnamese were killed, and villages, cities, and farmlands were destroyed.
- 58,000 Americans were killed. Others were badly injured and/or suffered psychological trauma.
- The Communist Vietnamese regime was repressive, and many fled. Some came to the United States.
- In Cambodia, the **"Khmer Rouge"** won power and committed acts of genocide.
- In America, war expenses ended many of the "Great Society" programs. Americans lost faith in their government and in the power of the military. American youth were especially disillusioned.
- Congress passed the **War Powers Act** in 1973, limiting the President's power to commit troops overseas without Congressional approval.

The Women's Liberation Movement: Formation

- The first phase of the women's movement in the early 20th century had aimed at political equality. The second phase in the '60s and '70s focused on economic and social equality.
- In 1963, President Kennedy's **Commission on the Status of Women** showed widespread gender discrimination. Women held lower-level jobs and did not receive equal pay.
- In 1963, Betty Friedan published *The Feminine Mystique.* She voiced the resentment of many educated, middle-class women's at their stifling roles as housewives and expressed their desire for careers.
- Many women, inspired by the Civil Rights Movement, formed women's groups and appointed leaders. In 1966, the **National Organization for Women (N.O.W.)** was organized.
- The movement was affected by the **Sexual Revolution.** People began to talk openly about sex, while the birth control pill allowed greater sexual freedom.

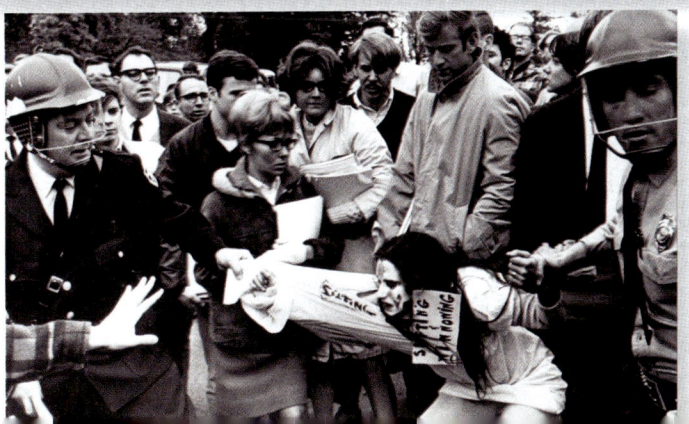

The Women's Liberation Movement: Goals and Accomplishments

- Feminists wanted to end discrimination in education. The **Equal Opportunity in Education Act,** or **Title IX,** required schools and universities to stop discrimination against women. Most schools became co-ed.
- Feminists also wanted to end employment discrimination. The **Equal Pay Act** required equal pay, the **Civil Rights Act** prohibited hiring discrimination, and "affirmative action" programs required hiring more women. Companies provided maternity leave and day-care to women workers.
- Feminists wanted to change social attitudes. They fought sexual discrimination in language, pop culture, and private homes. They called on men to respect women and share their duties.
- Feminists also tried but failed to pass the **Equal Rights Amendment (ERA),** a constitutional amendment. Many opposed it, fearing it would take away advantages like women's exemption from the draft. **Phyllis Schlafly** became a vocal supporter of women's traditional roles.
- In *Roe v. Wade,* the Supreme Court upheld the right to abortion in the first three months. **"Right to Life"** supporters argued that abortion was murder. **"Pro-Choice"** supporters argued that abortion was a private choice. Later rulings have limited *Roe v. Wade.* Abortion remains a very divisive issue.

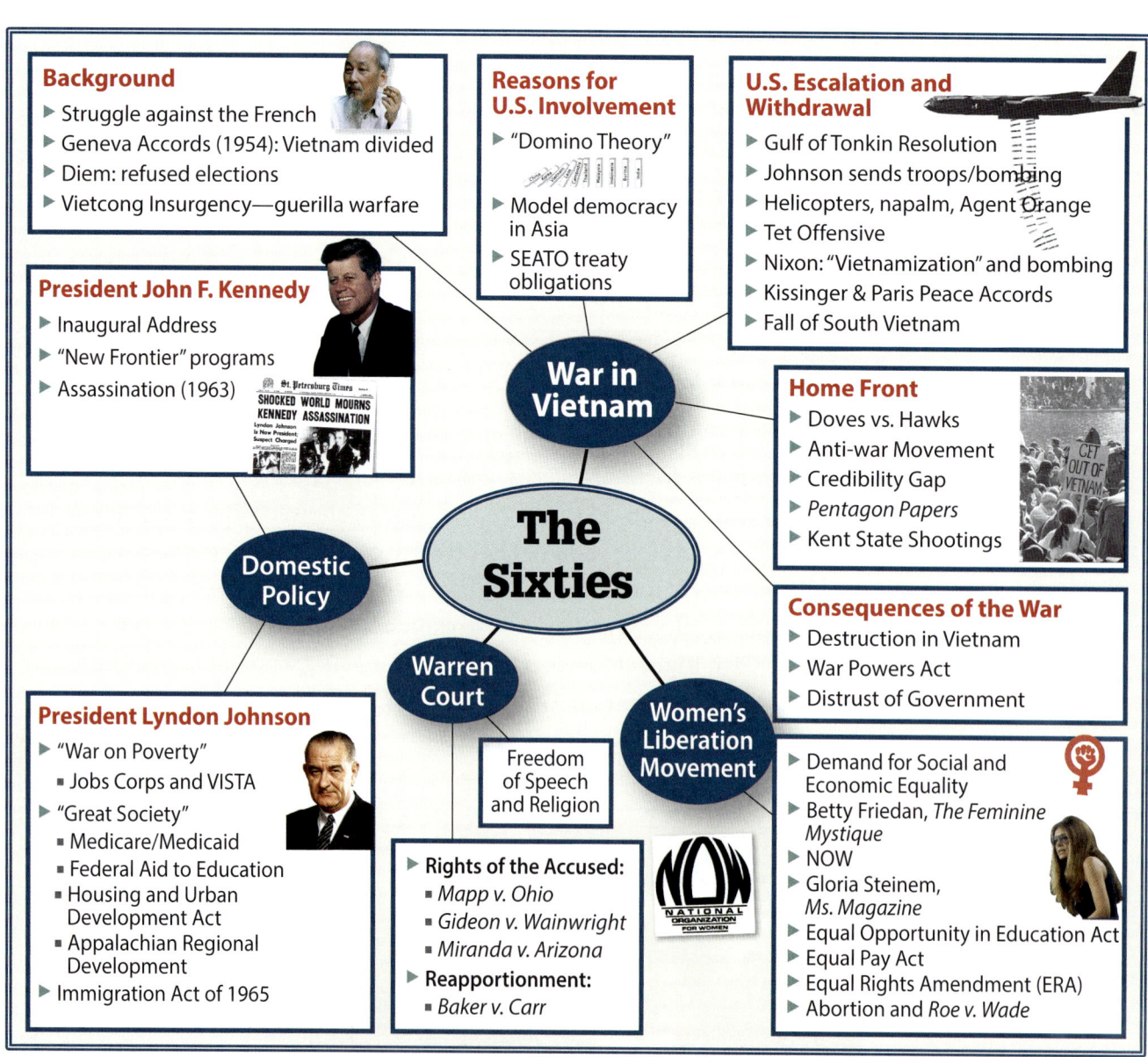

360   Chapter 15 | The Sixties: "The Times They are a-Changin'"

What Do You Know?

SS.912.A.7.13

1. The diagram below provides details about United States domestic policies.

   | ? | → | President Lyndon B. Johnson's "Great Society" |

   Which phrase completes the diagram?
   - A. Harry S. Truman's "Fair Deal"
   - B. Franklin Roosevelt's "New Deal"
   - C. Theodore Roosevelt's "Square Deal"
   - D. Warren Harding's "Return to Normalcy"

SS.912.A.7.13

2. What program did President Lyndon B. Johnson introduce to reduce economic inequalities among Americans?
   - A. New Deal
   - B. Great Society
   - C. Marshall Plan
   - D. Alliance for Progress

SS.912.A.6.14

3. The following statements were made by American leaders during the 1950s.

   > You have a row of dominoes set up, you knock over the first one, and what will happen to the last one is . . . that it will go over very quickly.
   > —President Dwight D. Eisenhower in a press conference on the strategic importance of Indochina, April 7, 1954
   >
   > [Vietnam is] the cornerstone of the free world in Southeast Asia, the keystone to the arch, the finger in the dike. Burma, Thailand, India, Japan, the Philippines, and obviously Laos and Cambodia are among those whose security would be threatened if the red tide of Communism overflowed into Vietnam.
   > —Senator John F. Kennedy in a speech, June 1956

   Which foreign policy do these two statements illustrate?
   - A. isolationism
   - B. containment
   - C. appeasement
   - D. Good Neighbor policy

SS.912.A.6.14

4. The excerpt below is from a resolution passed by both Houses of Congress on August 7, 1964.

> The Congress approves and supports the determination of the President, as Commander in Chief, to take all necessary measures to repel any armed attack against the forces of the United States and to prevent further aggression.
> —Tonkin Gulf Resolution

What was the significance of this resolution?

A. Congress showed its support for a policy of isolationism.

B. Congress authorized the President to take military action in Southeast Asia.

C. Congress provided the President with new constitutional powers to declare war.

D. Congress denied the President the revenues he needed to fight a war in Vietnam.

SS.912.A.6.14

5. What policy did President Richard Nixon introduce to remove American troops from South Vietnam without abandoning that country to Communist rule?

A. Vietnamization

B. "Arms for Bases"

C. Flexible Response

D. Operation Rolling Thunder

SS.912.A.6.14

6. The cartoon below illustrates a belief shared by many American leaders during the 1950s and 1960s.

Source: Public domain (found here: http://en.wikipedia.org/wiki/File:Domino_theory.svg)

Which action was taken as a result of this commonly held viewpoint?

A. The United States enacted the War Powers Act.

B. The United States sent troops to South Vietnam.

C. The United States attacked China during the Korean War.

D. The United States distributed economic aid under the Marshall Plan.

SS.912.A.6.14

7. The newspaper headline on the left describes a significant event in U.S. foreign affairs.

   What was the significance of this event to the Vietnam War?

   A. It demonstrated the superiority of United States forces over the Vietcong in South Vietnam.

   B. Its failure led to disagreements between the Vietcong and the government of North Vietnam.

   C. It showed that the Vietcong could mount a successful attack on South Vietnamese cities and were not close to defeat.

   D. United States and South Vietnamese troops were able to force the Vietcong to retreat to North Vietnam and Cambodia.

SS.912.A.6.14

8. Which of the following lists events from the Vietnam War in the correct chronological sequence?

   A. Paris Peace Accords—Gulf of Tonkin Resolution—Tet Offensive—Geneva Accords—Vietnamization

   B. Geneva Accords—Gulf of Tonkin Resolution—Tet Offensive—Vietnamization—Paris Peace Accords

   C. Vietnamization—Paris Peace Accords—Geneva Accords—Gulf of Tonkin Resolution—Tet Offensive

   D. Tet Offensive—Geneva Accords—Vietnamization—Paris Peace Accords—Gulf of Tonkin Resolution

SS.912.A.6.14

9. The photographs below were taken during the Vietnam War. What problem faced by American soldiers in Vietnam do these photographs illustrate?

   A. the popularity of Ho Chi Minh and Communist ideals

   B. the problem of obtaining medical supplies in a combat zone

   C. the difficulty of distinguishing Vietcong from ordinary villagers

   D. the widespread corruption of the South Vietnamese government

Chapter 15 | The Sixties: "The Times They are a-Changin'"

SS.912.A.7.10

10. What was the primary purpose of the War Powers Act of 1973?

   A. to use troops to defend against armed attacks on the United States

   B. to mobilize the National Guard to stop race riots in American cities

   C. to send troops to rescue American hostages held captive by foreign terrorists

   D. to limit the ability of the President to intervene militarily without the approval of Congress

SS.912.A.7.10

11. The diagram below provides details about United States foreign policy in the 1960s and 1970s.

58,000 American deaths	Americans distrust government leaders
Veterans face hostility and suffer stress disorders	Almost two million Southeast Asian immigrants pour into the United States

   Which phrase completes the diagram?

   A. The "Credibility Gap"

   B. The Domino Theory

   C. Causes of the Vietnam War

   D. Consequences of the Vietnam War

SS.912.A.7.4

President Lyndon B. Johnson watching Walter Cronkite on television

Walter Cronkite, News broadcast, February 27, 1968:

"For it seems now more certain than ever that the bloody experience of Vietnam is to end in a stalemate. "

President Johnson's response:

"If I've lost Cronkite, I've lost middle America."

12. Based on these statements, which conclusion can be made about the media during the Vietnam War?

   A. The mainstream media had little impact on the conduct of the war.

   B. President Johnson took secret steps to harass and silence the media.

   C. Criticism from the mainstream media contributed to the decision to withdraw from Vietnam.

   D. President Johnson was willing to violate freedom of the press to prevent criticism of the war.

SS.912.A.7.10

13. Which diagram best represents the "credibility gap" during the Vietnam War?

   A. Televised war images vs. Claims of government officials
   B. Baby Boom generation vs. Protests on college campuses
   C. Draft card burnings vs. Shootings at Kent State
   D. Doves vs. Hawks

SS.912.A.7.4

14. How successful were the domestic policies of Presidents Kennedy and Johnson?

   A. They failed to pass through Congress and left no lasting impact.
   B. They led to a credibility gap and growing distrust in government.
   C. They promoted greater social equality but failed to eliminate poverty.
   D. They prevented the United States from making overseas commitments.

SS.912.A.7.13

15. Which program was one of the most lasting impacts of President Lyndon Johnson's "Great Society"?

   A. Medicare
   B. Social Security
   C. Meat Inspection Act
   D. Federal Deposit Insurance

SS.912.A.7.3

16. This advertisement appeared in several magazines in the 1970s.

What does this advertisement illustrate?

   A. the triumph of the "Sexual Revolution"
   B. social attitudes against which feminists objected
   C. the influence of women advertisers in the media
   D. the success of employment laws against discrimination

SS.912.A.7.8

17. In which case did the Supreme Court rule that a person accused of a serious crime must be provided with an attorney if he or she was too poor to afford one?

   A. *Gideon v. Wainwright*
   B. *Yates v. United States*
   C. *Miranda v. Arizona*
   D. *Roe v. Wade*

Chapter 15 | The Sixties: "The Times They are a-Changin'"

SS.912.A.7.3

18. The table below shows the impact of Title IX on American society.

Impact of Title IX	
Before Title IX	After Title IX
1972: Women held 7% of all law degrees	2001: Women held 47% of all law degrees
1972: Women held 9% of all medical degrees	2001: Women held 43% of all medical degrees
1970: Women held 13.3% of all doctoral degrees	2000: Women held almost 50% of all doctoral degrees*
1970: One in 27 girls played varsity sports in high school	2012: One in 2.5 girls play varsity sports in high school
1970: 32,000 women athletes played on intercollegiate teams	2012: 150,000 women athletes play on intercollegiate teams
1972: College scholarships were virtually non-existent for women athletes	2012: More than $1 million in scholarships are awarded to women athletes

*Of these doctoral degrees held by women, most were in the education field. Only 17% of graduates with doctoral degrees in engineering and 18% with doctorates in computer science were women.

Based on the table, what was the impact of Title IX on American society?

A. While it led to greater gender equality, there is still work to be done.

B. It successfully increased gender equality in education but not in athletics.

C. It had little impact in improving gender equality in either education or athletics.

D. It successfully accomplished its goal of gender equality, both in education and athletics.

SS.912.A.7.3

19. Which statement correctly compares Betty Friedan and Phyllis Schlafly?

A. Friedan opposed the Supreme Court decision of *Roe v. Wade*, while Schlafly supported it.

B. Friedan was the author of *The Feminine Mystique*, while Schlafly was the lawyer who drafted the Equal Rights Amendment.

C. Friedan worked to end legal and political discrimination, while Schlafly focused on ending social and economic discrimination.

D. Friedan believed women should break out of their traditional roles as homemakers, while Schlafly argued that most women enjoyed them.

SS.912.A.7.3

20. Which demand was voiced by Betty Friedan, Gloria Steinem, and other members of the feminist movement in the 1960s and 1970s?

A. the demand for women's right to vote

B. the demand for social and economic equality

C. the demand to preserve women's traditional roles

D. the demand to defeat the Equal Rights Amendment

CHAPTER 16

American Foreign Policy Since 1972

SS.912.A.7.10 Analyze the significance of Vietnam and Watergate on the government and people of the United States.

SS.912.A.7.11 Analyze the foreign policy of the United States as it relates to Africa, Asia, the Caribbean, Latin America, and the Middle East.

SS.912.A.7.12 Analyze political, economic, and social concerns that emerged at the end of the 20th century and into the 21st century.

SS.912.A.7.14 Review the role of the United States as a participant in the global economy (trade agreements, international competition, impact on American labor, environmental concerns).

SS.912.A.7.15 Analyze the effects of foreign and domestic terrorism on the American people.

Names and Terms You Should Know

- *Détente*
- Watergate
- Apartheid
- OPEC
- PLO (Palestinian Liberation Organization)
- Jimmy Carter
- Panama Canal Treaty
- Camp David Accords
- Iranian Revolution
- Iran Hostage Crisis
- Ronald Reagan
- Reagan Doctrine
- Mikhail Gorbachev
- *Glasnost*
- *Perestroika*
- Iran-Contra Affair
- George H.W. Bush
- Persian Gulf War
- Saddam Hussein
- Bill Clinton
- Bosnia and Kosovo
- World Trade Organization
- NAFTA
- Election of 2000
- George W. Bush
- Terrorism
- September 11, 2001 ("9-11")
- Al-Qaeda
- Jihad
- Taliban
- Osama bin Laden
- Iraq War
- Barack Obama
- Migration
- Globalization

Florida "Keys" to Learning

1. President Nixon sought *détente*—an easing of tensions—with the Soviet Union. He visited Communist China to restore diplomatic relations. The Watergate Scandal ended Nixon's Presidency. Nixon was forced by the Supreme Court to hand over his tapes of White House conversations, which revealed that he had lied about the cover-up. Facing impeachment, Nixon resigned from office.

2. President Ford pardoned Nixon for his role in Watergate. Arab OPEC members boycotted the United States and oil prices soared. Ford's greatest foreign policy success was the signing of the Helsinki Accords.

3. President Carter attempted to bring a moral tone back to U.S. foreign policy. He signed a treaty agreeing to return the Panama Canal Zone to Panama by 2000. He negotiated the Camp David Accords between Egypt and Israel, which led to their later signing of a peace treaty. In 1979, the Shah of Iran was overthrown. Ayatollah Khomeini established an Islamic Republic and U.S. Embassy staff were held hostage for over a year.

4. President Reagan pledged to make America strong again. He withdrew troops from Beirut in response to suicide bombings. He launched an air strike on Libya for a terrorist act in Berlin. Reagan wanted to roll Communism back, not just contain it. Under the "Reagan Doctrine," he sent assistance to anti-Communist fighters in Grenada, Nicaragua, and Afghanistan. Some U.S. officials secretly sold arms to Iran for freeing American hostages in Lebanon; money received from Iran was secretly given to anti-Communist Contras in Nicaragua. The plan was discovered, leading to the Iran-Contra Affair. Reagan's announcement of the Strategic Defense Initiative led Soviet leader Mikhail Gorbachev to meet with Reagan in Iceland, where the two leaders agreed to reduce their nuclear arms.

5. During the Presidency of George H.W. Bush, the Cold War came to an end, Germany was reunited, the Soviet Union dissolved, and apartheid ended in South Africa. Bush sent U.S. troops to arrest Panamanian dictator Manuel Noriega, to chase Saddam Hussein's Iraqi forces out of Kuwait, and to bring food to millions of starving people in Somalia.

6. Under President Clinton, Americans enjoyed a "peace dividend." NAFTA and the World Trade Organization further promoted economic prosperity. When ethnic conflict arose in parts of the former Yugoslavia, the United States and its NATO allies intervened to prevent genocide. They were slower to react in preventing genocide in Rwanda. Clinton maintained friendly relations with China and intervened when democracy was threatened in Haiti.

7. George W. Bush came to power after a controversial election against Al Gore in 2000. A voting recount in Florida was halted by the U.S. Supreme Court. On September 11, 2001, al-Qaeda terrorists hijacked commercial planes and crashed them into the World Trade Center and Pentagon. President Bush declared a "War on Terror." American forces attacked Afghanistan and overthrew the Taliban. Fearing Saddam Hussein was hiding weapons of mass destruction, Bush ordered an invasion of Iraq.

8. President Obama tried to strengthen global ties. He withdrew the last U.S. troops from Iraq in 2011. His administration located and killed Osama bin Laden. During the "Arab Spring," Obama encouraged peaceful resolutions of revolts against dictatorships, leading to several democracies, but also to unrest.

9. America is no longer a superpower controlling the world, but it is still a global leader. Political, economic, and humanitarian factors shape its policies. Americans seek to prevent the spread of nuclear weapons, to defend democracy, to promote peace and stability, to foster world trade, and to fight pollution and global warming.

In this chapter, you will learn about American foreign policy from President Nixon to the present. You will also consider some of the global challenges facing Americans in the future.

In examining foreign policy, you should remember that American Presidents have to work with Congress and also have to win the support of the American people. To bring their message to the public, they often rely on the **media**, such as newspapers and television. The media influences public opinion through its reporting.

Our foreign-policy decision makers generally try to promote our national interests. This means, first and foremost, that they must protect our nation from invasion or attack. They also try to promote American economic interests—protecting American investments and encouraging American trade. Finally, they attempt to spread our cultural values—especially our system of individual freedom, democracy, and free enterprise.

How Presidents and Congress pursue these goals may differ. Some Presidents try to cooperate with other nations in the U.N. or by forming alliances to achieve these goals. Other Presidents have used military action to protect our interests and to ensure peace and stability in other parts of the world. American leaders have even tried to set up new democratic states in other parts of the world in order to serve as examples to neighboring countries. Still other Presidents have tried to limit American commitments abroad in order to marshal our resources at home.

Foreign Policy under President Nixon

You have already learned about the major foreign-policy problem that faced President Nixon in the last chapter: ending the Vietnam War.

Détente, China, and Chile

To place additional pressure on North Vietnam, Nixon took two steps that surprised many: Nixon sought *détente*, or an easing of tensions, with the Soviet Union. In 1972, Nixon became the first U.S. President to visit Moscow, and signed an agreement with Soviet leaders to limit the further development of nuclear arms, known as "SALT" (Strategic Arms Limitation Treaty).

In the same year, Nixon and Kissinger, now Secretary of State, also visited the Communist dictator **Mao Zedong** in "Red China" (mainland China) and began the process of normalizing diplomatic relations with that country. Nixon hoped that both Soviet and Chinese leaders would put pressure on North Vietnam to end the war. At the same time, his reopening of relations with China had tremendous effects. It opened the way for later U.S.-China trade, for the entry of Communist China into the United Nations, and for the normalization of relations between China and the rest of the world. Many historians believe this reopening of relations with China was Nixon's greatest accomplishment as President.

While making overtures to China, Nixon and Kissinger continued to act against those governments they saw as threatening American interests. They especially opposed the government of Salvador Allende, a socialist leader elected in Chile, who began nationalizing copper mines. Nixon and Kissinger instructed the CIA to cooperate with the Chilean military and other groups against Allende. General Pinochet seized power in a military coup and established a brutal dictatorship.

Chapter 16 | American Foreign Policy Since 1972

The Watergate Crisis

The foreign policy successes of Nixon and Kissinger were overshadowed by the **Watergate scandal** shortly after the beginning of Nixon's second term. During the Presidential election campaign of 1972, a group of ex-CIA agents broke into Democratic Party headquarters in the Watergate office complex in downtown Washington, D.C. Nixon tried to protect these agents from investigation by claiming that they were acting for national security. At Congressional hearings, it was revealed that Nixon had taped all his conversations in the White House. Nixon refused to hand over the tapes to investigators, claiming "Executive Privilege." His claim was overruled by the U.S. Supreme Court, which ordered him to hand over the tapes. These tapes revealed that Nixon was behind the "cover-up." Nixon resigned the Presidency rather than face impeachment.

The Historian's Apprentice

"A President and those who assist him must be free to explore alternatives in the process of shaping policies and making decisions, and to do so in a way many would be unwilling to express except privately. These are the considerations justifying a presumptive privilege for Presidential communications. . . . But this presumptive privilege must be considered in light of our historic commitment to the rule of law . . . To ensure that justice is done, it is imperative to the function of courts that compulsory process be available for the production of evidence needed either by the prosecution or by the defense."

—United States v. Nixon, 1974

▶ In *United States v. Nixon*, the Supreme Court weighed the President's need for confidentiality against the needs of the criminal justice system for evidence. Do you think they struck the right balance? Write a short essay giving your views on whether the Supreme Court was right in ordering Nixon to turn over the tapes.

▶ Nixon negotiated an end to the War in Vietnam, re-opened relations with China and worked for *détente* with the Soviet Union. He also bombed Laos and Cambodia, helped to topple the Allende government in Chile, and tried to cover up the Watergate burglars. What rating would you give Nixon as President?

The Ford and Carter Presidencies

Gerald Ford had been appointed as Vice President by Nixon and confirmed by Congress when Vice President **Spiro Agnew** had resigned. Although Ford had never been elected, after Nixon's resignation he suddenly became President. One step that Ford immediately took was to grant a Presidential pardon to Nixon. This action was unpopular with many Americans at the time.

In foreign policy, Ford kept Kissinger as his Secretary of State and continued Nixon's policy of *détente* with the Soviet Union. Ford faced problems, however, in the Middle East. **OPEC**, the Organization of Petroleum Exporting Countries, had been formed in 1960. During the Arab-Israeli War of 1973, the Arab members of OPEC boycotted the United States and other countries that traded with Israel. Even after the war ended, OPEC members continued to raise their oil prices, contributing to inflation in the United States at a time of high unemployment. Americans had to wait in long lines at gas stations because of fuel shortages, and many worried that the world's oil reserves might soon be exhausted. Smaller cars from Japanese and European manufacturers suddenly became more popular with Americans as gas prices soared.

President Ford was also forced to stand by passively when North Vietnamese Communist forces finally took over South Vietnam in April 1975. Movie cameras recorded the final American helicopters leaving the roof of the U.S. Embassy in Saigon. Vietnamese who had cooperated with the United States were left at the mercy of their sworn enemies, the Vietnamese Communists. In general, these were difficult times for the United States.

Ford had a major foreign policy success three months later in the **Helsinki Accords**. This agreement recognized the existing borders of Europe in an attempt to preserve peaceful relations between Western and Eastern Europe. The Helsinki Accords pledged "respect for human rights," providing a basis for later action by anti-Communist **dissidents** (*critics of the government*) in Eastern Europe.

The Panama Canal Treaty and the Camp David Accords

Democratic candidate **Jimmy Carter**, a former naval officer, farmer, and Governor of Georgia, was elected in 1976 as a Washington "outsider." At a time when Americans were distrustful of politicians, Carter's campaign slogan was, "I'll never lie to you." In foreign policy, Carter believed it was necessary for Americans to take a more moral tone. During the Cold War and even in Vietnam, past Presidents had been willing to back dictators to stop the spread of Communism. Carter thought that this was wrong. He tried to reassert American morality in foreign policy by signing a treaty with Panama in 1977. This agreement promised to hand over the Panama Canal to the government of Panama by 2000. Carter refused to help anti-Communist dictators like Somoza in Nicaragua, even when they had been friendly to the United States. In the Middle East, Carter tried to bring Israelis and Arabs together. In 1977, Carter invited **Menachem Begin** of Israel and **Anwar Sadat** of Egypt to Camp David in Maryland. With Carter's help, they were able to reach an agreement: under the **Camp David Accords**, Egypt recognized Israel. In exchange, Israel returned the Sinai Peninsula, which it had occupied since the 1967 War, to Egypt.

Despite these successes, relations with the Soviet Union deteriorated during the Carter Presidency. In 1979, Soviet leaders launched an invasion of Afghanistan, where Muslim rebels were attacking the pro-Soviet government. In retaliation, President Carter stopped U.S. grain sales to the Soviet Union and refused to let the United States participate in the Moscow Olympics.

The Iranian Revolution and the Hostage Crisis

In 1979, a popular revolution occurred in Iran. The pro-Western **Shah** faced mass demonstrations against his rule when people filled the streets in Tehran and other cities. The Shah fled the country. A religious leader, **Ayatollah Khomeini**, returned from exile and established an **Islamic Republic**. Iran became a theocracy governed by Islamic law. Khomeini blamed Americans and other Western powers for having supported the Shah. When the Shah sought medical treatment in the United States, Iranian students and other followers of Khomeini seized the staff at the U.S. Embassy in Tehran and held them as hostages. President Carter was unable to obtain their release, and the hostages were held captive for more than a year. Unknown to the American public, a secret attempt to free them in a daring helicopter mission failed. The hostage crisis and continuing problems with the economy at home led Carter to lose the Presidential election of 1980. The Watergate Crisis, the fall of Vietnam, and the **Iran Hostage Crisis** all seemed to confirm the collapse of American power and the weakness of American leaders.

The Historian's Apprentice

1. Using the Internet or your school library, research one of the foreign policy achievements or failures of Nixon, Ford or Carter. Then create a PowerPoint presentation for your class.

2. Your teacher should divide your class into groups. Each group should decide which President had the greatest successes in foreign policy—Nixon, Ford, or Carter. Each group should present its selection to the class and explain the reasons for its choice.

3. By the end of Jimmy Carter's Presidency, some experts believed the Presidency had become too difficult to handle. What is your opinion: why did American Presidents from Kennedy to Carter have so many foreign-policy difficulties?

Foreign Policy under Reagan and Bush

The new President, **Ronald Reagan**, was a former movie star and Governor of California. He pledged to take tough action to improve conditions for Americans both at home and abroad. Reagan was fortunate in that, on the day of his inauguration, Iran released its hostages from the U.S. Embassy.

Reagan and Terrorism

During Reagan's two terms in office, international terrorism became an increasing threat. **Terrorists** use acts of violence to attract media attention or coerce governments. When American and French troops went to Lebanon on a peace-keeping mission, opponents used terrorism to drive them out. In April 1983, a suicide bomber drove into the U.S. Embassy in Beirut, Lebanon, killing 63. A second bomber struck the U.S. Marine barracks in Beirut six months later, killing another 241 Americans. Four months later, Reagan withdrew the remaining U.S. troops from their peace-keeping mission. Reagan declared he would not negotiate with terrorists. When a bomb exploded in a West Berlin nightclub in 1986, Reagan launched punitive air strikes over Libya in retaliation.

The "Reagan Doctrine"

Reagan was a staunch anti-Communist and considered the Soviet Union to be an "evil empire." Rather than just contain Communism, he wanted to roll Communism back. He believed that other peoples around the world yearned to be free. This became known as the "**Reagan Doctrine**."

- **Afghanistan**. Reagan sent assistance to Muslim fighters opposing the Soviet army in Afghanistan.

- **Grenada**. When Communists took over the small island of Grenada in the Caribbean, Reagan sent in U.S. troops.

- **Nicaragua**. In Nicaragua, a country in Central America, a socialist government had seized power. Reagan gave support to anti-Communist rebels there known as "Contras." When Congress prohibited further aid to the Contras, some members of Reagan's administration violated the law by continuing to give secret aid to the Contras. This violation led to the Iran-Contra scandal that shook Reagan's second term.

The Iran-Contra Affair

Several Americans had been kidnapped by terrorist groups in Lebanon. These groups had connections with Iran. Iran was in a long war with Iraq, known as the **Iran-Iraq War**, and needed military supplies. In secret talks with Iran, some U.S. officials agreed to sell arms to Iran in return for release of the hostages in Lebanon. Money from the secret sales was then turned over to the Contras in Nicaragua. When news of this transaction leaked out, Congress and the American public were shocked. Not only had American officials negotiated with terrorists, they had also violated a Congressional ban on aiding the Contras. Several prominent officials resigned and faced criminal charges, but President Reagan claimed he had no knowledge of the bargain.

Changes in the Soviet Union

During Reagan's first term in office, there were several changes in leadership in the Soviet Union. In 1985, **Mikhail Gorbachev** assumed power as the new leader of the Soviet government. At that time, the Soviet Union was suffering from economic stagnation. It had not kept pace with the West. Central bureaucrats dictated what was to be produced, which often did not correspond with people's real needs. Workers had little incentive to work hard, and alcoholism and corruption had become chronic. Critics were afraid of being arrested and jailed. Meanwhile, Soviet resources were being drained in an unpopular war in Afghanistan. Gorbachev introduced two policies to deal with these problems:

- ▶ *Glasnost* ("openness"): Gorbachev introduced transparency, or openness, into the Soviet government. For the first time, people would be able to criticize the government and make suggestions without fear.

- ▶ *Perestroika* ("restructuring"): Gorbachev introduced limited free enterprise into the Soviet economy. For example, he allowed peasants to sell some of their crops in markets, allowed factory managers to set their own production levels, and permitted some private businesses.

Gorbachev also began withdrawing Soviet troops from Afghanistan. His policy of *glasnost* led to demands by some of the non-Russian peoples of the Soviet Union for independence. Rather than use force against the people of the Baltic States (Estonia, Latvia, and Lithuania), Gorbachev gave them their independence. The demand for greater freedom then spread to the countries of Eastern Europe and the other ethnic minorities in the Soviet Union.

Reagan-Gorbachev Summit Talks

Reagan proposed creating an expensive defensive system for the United States, perhaps using lasers, capable of withstanding a nuclear attack. This was at a time when the Soviets could not afford to take similar steps. Soviet leaders feared Americans intended to launch a "first strike" nuclear attack. Reagan's proposal for a *Strategic Defense Initiative* thus helped drive Gorbachev to seek discussions with the United States. Reagan and Gorbachev met for the first time in Reykjavik, Iceland, where both suddenly discussed dismantling their nuclear arsenals to make the world safer from the threat of nuclear destruction. They met several subsequent times and signed an agreement to reduce the number of nuclear missiles. It was the most successful arms reduction since the Cold War had begun.

The End of the Cold War

In 1987, speaking in Berlin and looking at the Berlin Wall, Reagan called on Gorbachev to "tear this wall down." One year later, Reagan's Vice President, **George H. W. Bush**, was elected President.

Over the next two years, the Cold War dramatically ended. Anti-government demonstrations spread through East Germany, Poland, and other Eastern European countries. Unlike earlier Soviet leaders, Gorbachev refused to use military power to prop up these unpopular regimes. The Berlin Wall was torn down in November 1989, allowing East and West Germans to pass back and forth freely. Poland became the first country behind the former Iron Curtain to elect a non-Communist government. Soon the other countries of Eastern Europe followed its lead. In October 1990, East and West Germany were reunited. Even in the Soviet Union, various ethnic groups demanded independence, including the Russians themselves. At the very end of 1991, the Soviet Union finally disintegrated. Russia, led by Boris Yeltsin, joined with several former Soviet republics to form a loose association known as the **Commonwealth of Independent States**.

Apartheid

In South Africa, laws strictly segregated white citizens from the vast majority of black South Africans. This system was known as **apartheid**. Opponents of apartheid in the United States and other foreign countries boycotted goods from South Africa and called for companies to withdraw their investments. As a result of these international protests, South Africa became increasingly isolated. President Reagan at first favored a policy of "**constructive engagement**": the United States would continue to negotiate and do business in South Africa, but it would pressure South Africans to make reforms. In 1986, Congress passed stiff sanctions over Reagan's veto. Almost at the same time that the Cold War ended in Europe, South Africa's new leader suddenly decided to end apartheid. Anti-apartheid leader **Nelson Mandela** was released from jail, and South Africa moved to majority rule.

Panama, Iraq and Kuwait, and Somalia

With the end of the Cold War and the collapse of the Soviet Union, the United States became the world's only remaining superpower. Many called for a "New World Order," based on democratic values. President Bush proved willing to use military power during these years to further American national interests. Shortly after becoming President, he sent U.S. forces into Panama to arrest Panamanian dictator **Manuel Noriega** to face drug charges in the United States.

In August 1990, Iraqi dictator **Saddam Hussein** invaded Kuwait, a small neighboring country with vast oil reserves. Bush organized an international coalition against the occupation and sent U.S. troops into Kuwait, where they defeated Iraqi forces in the **Persian Gulf War**. Once he had chased the Iraqis out of Kuwait, however, Bush refused to use U.S. military power to depose Hussein in Iraq. In the final months of his Presidency, Bush sent U.S. troops into Somalia (in East Africa), to help distribute food and save millions of people from starvation.

The Historian's Apprentice

Who should get credit for ending the Cold War? Hold a class debate on the following question: Did President Reagan's policies help to end the Cold War, or would Gorbachev have ended the Communist system anyway, since the Soviet Union was already falling behind the West?

Foreign Affairs under President Clinton

President Bill Clinton was elected in 1992, just after the Cold War had ended. Americans enjoyed a "peace dividend," as President Clinton closed military bases and reduced U.S. military expenditures. Nonetheless, the collapse of Communism led to rising unrest in many parts of the world. In Yugoslavia, warfare broke out between different ethnic groups. Christian Serbs attempted to kill Muslims in parts of **Bosnia** and **Kosovo** in a policy of genocide known as "**ethnic cleansing**." These conflicts brought bloodshed into the very heart of Europe. President Clinton stepped in to help negotiate a peace. He used American air power against Serbia when Serb leaders attacked Bosnia and caused ethnic Serbs to attack local Muslims in Kosovo. NATO intervention finally helped restore the peace.

Another case of near genocide occurred in **Rwanda**, a small country in Central Africa. In 1994 one of its ethnic groups, the Hutus, began slaughtering another group, the Tutsis. The United States and other Western Countries were slow to react, and as many as 850,000 people were killed.

During his two terms in office, Clinton's trade policies helped to foster economic prosperity. President Bush had previously negotiated an agreement with Canada and Mexico, known as the North American Free Trade Agreement, or **NAFTA**, to create a trade association that would rival the European "Common Market" (a free-trade area of European states). The United States, Canada, and Mexico agreed to gradually reduce their tariffs on one another's goods and to carry out other forms of cooperation. This agreement, however, had yet to be ratified. Clinton was able to persuade members of Congress to approve the NAFTA agreement. Meanwhile, in 1994, the **World Trade Organization** was created to help oversee international trade and settle trade disputes. During the early 1990s, U.S. trade with China increased. For the first time, China invited companies from the United States and other Western nations to invest in China. Over the next two decades, trade between the United States and China surged.

Like Reagan and Bush, President Clinton also supported democracy abroad. He maintained friendly relations with Russian leaders. When military leaders overthrew a democratically elected leader in **Haiti**, an island nation in the Caribbean, Clinton sent in American troops, who restored the elected leader to power. Like President Carter, Clinton also showed great concern for human rights. He attempted to pressure Chinese leaders to respect human rights in China. He encouraged other countries to show greater respect for women and civil rights and to provide more health care.

President George W. Bush and the "War on Terror"

The 2000 Election

In 2000, **George W. Bush**, the son of George H.W. Bush, was elected President after one of the closest contests in American history. Florida played a key role in the election results, since both Bush and his opponent, Democratic candidate **Al Gore**, had enough electoral votes to win the election if they could capture Florida. It was unclear who had won Florida's electoral votes because of inconsistencies in the voting in some districts. Gore demanded a recount, which was in progress until it was stopped by the U.S. Supreme Court in a close decision, in **Bush v. Gore** (2000).

Chapter 16 | American Foreign Policy Since 1972

The Attacks on September 11, 2001

The new President was in office only nine months when an event occurred that would shape the rest of his Presidency. **Al-Qaeda**, a terrorist organization founded by Islamic Fundamentalists in Saudi Arabia, opposed Western influence and especially resented the presence of U.S. troops in Saudi Arabia. They began what they considered to be a *jihad*, or "holy war," against the United States by committing terrorist acts. Al-Qaeda had secretly sent some of their members to the United States to attend flight-training school. On **September 11, 2001**, the terrorists boarded several commercial jets and used box cutters they had smuggled on board to threaten passengers and hijack the planes. Then they flew the planes themselves into the World Trade Center in New York City and the Pentagon Building in Washington, D.C. A fourth plane was meant to crash into the White House, but the passengers on board learned of the other crashes and fought the hijackers, causing the plane to crash in a wooded area in Pennsylvania. The two towers of the World Trade Center collapsed, leading to more than 3,000 deaths and closing down much of New York City.

The "War on Terror"

President Bush quickly responded by declaring a "**War on Terror**." He demanded that the **Taliban**—an Islamic Fundamentalist government ruling Afghanistan—turn over al-Qaeda leader **Osama bin Laden**, the mastermind behind the "**9-11**" attack. When the Taliban refused to surrender bin Laden, American forces attacked Afghanistan. They quickly overthrew the Taliban but failed to capture bin Laden. Meanwhile, Americans became so committed to maintaining peace and stability in Afghanistan that they found it difficult to leave.

The Historian's Apprentice

Imagine you are a newspaper reporter in September 2001. Write an article reporting on the events of September 11th. Use the Internet and your school library to gather more information as the basis for your report.

The Iraq War

President Bush was also concerned about the role of Iraqi dictator **Saddam Hussein**. Bush suspected that Hussein was concealing forbidden chemical and biological weapons of mass destruction from U.N. weapons inspectors, who had been making inspections since the previous Gulf War. American leaders feared that Hussein might make these weapons available to terrorists. After presenting the American position to the U.N. Security Council and issuing a final warning to Hussein, President Bush ordered U.S. forces to invade Iraq in March 2003. As in Afghanistan, they quickly overthrew the government but found themselves in a new situation that was difficult to leave.

Rival Iraqi groups competed for power, while former supporters of Hussein, radical Shiite Muslims, and other groups launched a resistance movement against the American occupation. No weapons of mass destruction were ever found, leading critics in the United States and abroad to claim that the whole invasion had been a mistake. Although Britain, Spain, Poland, and a few other countries had joined the United States in Iraq, Bush's intervention did not have the full support of the international community that his father had received when acting in Kuwait a decade earlier. As time went by, the occupation became increasingly unpopular among Americans, who were also shaken by a domestic financial crisis that began in 2007.

Foreign Policy under President Obama

In 2008, Senator **Barack Obama** was elected as President, becoming the first African-American President of the United States. It was just forty years after Dr. Martin Luther King, Jr.'s assassination. President Obama attempted to build stronger ties with other world leaders by taking a more collaborative approach. He had opposed Bush's intervention in Iraq and had campaigned on a promise to withdraw U.S. troops on a fixed timetable—a promise he largely kept. Obama's administration was also able to find and kill Osama bin Laden, the leader behind the September 11 attacks.

"The Arab Spring"

In the spring of 2011, demonstrations in favor of democracy began in Tunisia and spread to the rest of North Africa and other parts of the Arab world, including Egypt, Libya, Yemen, and Syria. President Obama encouraged existing governments not to use force and several dictators were overthrown. In Tunisia and Egypt, these changes were relatively peaceful; in Libya and Syria, they led to bloody conflicts. Violence later eruped in Egypt.

Iran, ISIS, Ukraine and Syria

In 2012, President Obama was elected to a second term. With other world leaders, he negotiated a treaty with Iran to halt its nuclear program for a lifting of sanctions. The rise of the violent Islamic State (ISIS) in Iraq and Syria, ISIS terrorist acts, Russian President Putin's seizure of Crimea, and the bloody civil war in Syria were all signs of increasing international instability. In the Presidential election of 2016, Democratic candidate Hillary Clinton lost a close race to **Donald Trump**, who was critical of Obama's policies.

Challenges Ahead

Americans face many challenges ahead in foreign affairs. In two World Wars, the United States had played a deciding role. During the Cold War, it was one of two superpowers and the acknowledged leader of the "Free World." In 1991, the United States emerged as the sole superpower. Gradually, however, other countries have been growing their economies, in some cases at faster rates than ours. Americans still play a dominant, if no longer a controlling, role in world events. The United States remains a **global leader**. Its policies affect events not only within its own borders but also around the world.

American policies towards other parts of the world are affected by a variety of factors. These include humanitarian concerns and both political and economic interests. Policies are often shaped by American public opinion, which in turn is influenced by reporting in the news media. Different ethnic groups sometimes have special interests in particular regions, such as African Americans in Africa, Hispanic Americans in Latin America, and Jewish and Arab Americans in the Middle East.

Africa

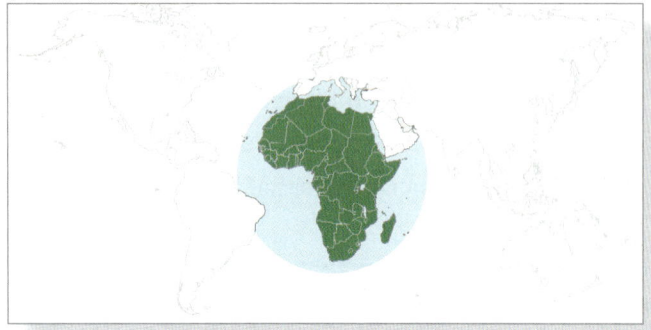

In Africa, democracy has been spreading. Many former military dictatorships in sub-Saharan Africa became democracies in the 1980s and 1990s. Several countries in North Africa became new democracies in 2011–2012. In Egypt, the most populous of these, the army reasserted control by toppling an elected Islamic Fundamentalist government.

In the decades ahead, Africans will need economic aid to improve their standards of living, health care, education, and transportation infrastructure. Humanitarian concerns such as the need to prevent starvation in Somalia or Darfur further shape American policy. The challenge for American leaders in Africa is how to best support local democracies, help eliminate poverty, and improve education and infrastructure.

The Middle East

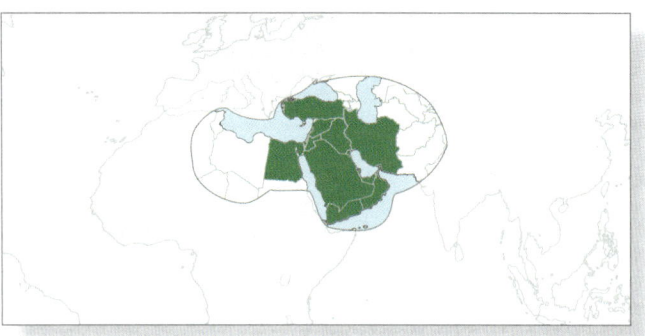

In the Middle East, American leaders remain concerned about the hostility felt by some groups toward the United States. U.S. leaders also hope to prevent Iran from acquiring nuclear weapons or promoting terrorism. The continuing civil war in Syria creates further uncertainty. Should the United States and its allies intervene to stop the bloodshed and remove Syrian dictator Bashar al-Assad? The conflict in Syria has led to the **migration** (*movement*) of millions of refugees seeking asylum in other countries. Should Americans accept more refugees from war-torn Syria, or does that expose them to terrorists? Increasing Russian influence poses further difficulties. In nearby Israel, Americans are encouraging Israelis and Palestinians to negotiate a lasting settlement that will give greater security to Israel and independent statehood to Palestine.

Economic factors (such as the need for oil from Saudi Arabia, Kuwait, and other Middle Eastern countries) as well as political and humanitarian concerns, especially the threat of war or acts of terrorism, continue to shape American policy in the Middle East.

Asia

Asia is the world's largest continent. China, with one fourth of the world's population, has one of the world's fastest growing economies. Both economic and political factors affect U.S. policy towards this giant. China is now our top trading partner after Canada. American leaders hope to maintain good relations with China while reducing the imbalance of trade between the two countries. They further seek to reduce the threat of Chinese militarism and preserve the independence of Taiwan. Humanitarian concerns also influence U.S. policy: Americans wish to help the people of Tibet and to encourage Chinese leaders to respect human rights. One of the greatest challenges is to cooperate with Chinese leaders to reduce pollution and slow down global climate change. Another challenge is to stop Chinese cyber-spying on American companies and individuals.

Elsewhere in Asia, American leaders strive to promote economic development. In the countries of Southeast Asia, for example, Americans provided important emergency assistance when parts of Thailand and Indonesia were affected by a **tsunami** (*tidal wave*).

North Korea poses a threat because of the dangers of nuclear proliferation. Although the country is poor, its unpredictable dictator has nuclear weapons and a large conventional army.

The Caribbean and Latin America

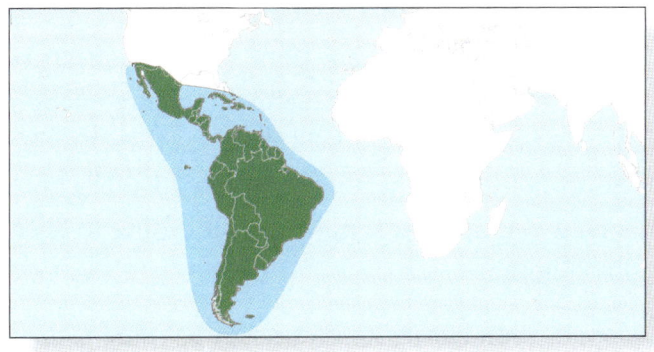

The United States is drawing increasingly closer to Latin America in its commercial relations. Mexico has become a close trading partner of the United States under NAFTA and is expected to continue this relationship under the USMCA trade agreement recently negotiated by the Trump Administration. Although President Trump plans to build a wall along the border with Mexico, he hopes to keep friendly relations.

The United States has especially strong interests in the Caribbean region. During the Cold War, American leaders feared the spread of Communism from Cuba and frequently intervened there. President Johnson sent troops to the Dominican Republic in 1964. President Reagan sent troops to Grenada in 1983. Even after the Cold War ended, President Bush sent troops into Panama and President Clinton sent troops to Haiti in 1994 to oust its military dictatorship.

More recently, Americans sent humanitarian aid to Haiti to help it recover from a catastrophic earthquake. As hurricanes increase in intensity, the islands of the Caribbean may be in more frequent need of international support. One of our greatest challenges remains our relations with Cuba, which is one of the world's last Communist strongholds, but which is now also showing signs of a transition to democracy and the process of normalization has slowed down under President Trump.

President Obama started normalizing U.S. relations with Cuba and reestablished diplomatic relations in July 2015. Nevertheless, an economic embargo remains in place and the process of normalization has slowed down under President Trump.

The Historian's Apprentice

▶ Choose one of these areas. Research the problems faced by the area and write a set of foreign policy recommendations for the President of the United States.

▶ Make a large chart with four columns and four rows. Label your chart: "Factors Affecting U.S. Foreign Policy." Across the top row write: Region, Political Factors, Economic Factors and Humanitarian Factors. Down the left column, write: Africa, Middle East, Asia, and Caribbean and Latin America. Then fill in the rest of your chart using information from this chapter, the Internet, and your school library. In each box explain how that factor influences American policy towards that region.

Globalization: America and the Global Economy

The world today is "shrinking," due to the processes of **globalization**. More countries are participating in global trade. Restrictions on trade have been lifted and tariffs have been reduced. The use of containerized cargo has made it easier and cheaper to ship goods across the oceans. Telephones, radio, and the Internet make it easier and faster to communicate.

In 1947, several leading nations signed GATT—an agreement to reduce tariffs and promote international

A busy port in Singapore

trade. The **World Trade Organization** (or **WTO**) replaced GATT at the beginning of 1995. China established normal trading relations with the United States in 2000. After agreeing to lower its own tariffs and to make other concessions, China was officially admitted to the WTO in 2001. WTO membership opened China to greater international trade and investment, while making it easier for China to export its own goods. A large number of goods sold in the United States, from clothes and furniture to Apple computers, are now made in China.

Today, large multinational companies manufacture goods wherever resources are available and production costs—including labor and taxes—are lowest. Often, different parts of a product will be manufactured in more than one country before they are assembled together. A computer, for example, might have a monitor that was manufactured in Japan, a hard drive from Taiwan, a keyboard from Mexico, and a microprocessor made in China. While globalization has lowered the prices of goods, it has also meant that American workers must now compete with laborers overseas. Either they compete with products from other countries or the work itself is shipped to a place where labor costs are cheaper. Even American manufacturers often produce parts or provide services overseas through "**outsourcing**" (*hiring other companies to do the work*), especially when those costs are significantly lower than making the same parts or providing the same services in the United States.

Globalization poses many problems. Will American companies be able to compete with producers in other countries, where labor costs are cheaper? Can American businesses maintain their reputation for superior products? Will American workers be able to hold onto their jobs? In the 2016 election, Donald Trump won support by promising to keep jobs at home.

Globalization has led to increases in world production and population which in turn have increased pollution, used up natural resources, and greatly affected the environment. You will learn more about the challenges posed by global climate change in the next chapter.

Globalization brings some important benefits that extend beyond economics. Economic interdependence and continuous contact between cultures often bring greater mutual understanding and make future armed conflict less likely.

Review Cards

The Cold War in the 70s

- Nixon made approaches to the Soviet Union and China to pressure North Vietnam.
- Nixon sought **"détente"**—an easing of tensions—with the Soviet Union and signed **SALT** to limit the arms race.
- Nixon visited the People's Republic of China to establish diplomatic relations. Many see Nixon's opening of relations with Communist China as his greatest accomplishment. This opened trade and eased China's entry to the U.N.
- The CIA helped **General Pinochet** overthrow socialist **Salvador Allende** in Chile. Pinochet then established a brutal dictatorship.
- **Watergate Scandal**: former CIA agents broke into Democratic headquarters. Nixon tried to cover up the burglary. He was forced by the Supreme Court to hand over his tapes of White House conversations. These showed that Nixon had lied about the cover-up. Nixon resigned from office rather than be impeached.

The Ford Presidency (1974–1977)

- **Gerald Ford** came to power when Vice President Spiro Agnew and then President Nixon resigned.
- Ford pardoned Nixon, kept **Dr. Henry Kissinger** as Secretary of State, and continued *détente*.
- Problems arose in the Middle East during the Arab-Israeli War. Arab **OPEC** members boycotted the United States and oil prices soared. Fuel shortages and gas lines worried Americans about the limits of world oil reserves. More Americans bought smaller Japanese and European cars.
- Inflation and unemployment were high.
- In 1975, South Vietnam fell to Communist North Vietnam.
- Ford's greatest success was with the **Helsinki Accords.** These recognized European boundaries and pledged respect for human rights.

The Carter Presidency (1977–1981)

- **Jimmy Carter** was elected as a Washington "outsider," who pledged honest and moral policies.
- Carter refused to back dictators just to stop Communism. He wanted to bring morality back into foreign affairs. Carter signed the **Panama Canal Treaty** promising to return the canal to Panama.
- Carter helped negotiate the **Camp David Accords** between Egypt and Israel. Egypt recognized Israel and Israel returned the Sinai Peninsula to Egypt.
- Relations with the Soviet Union deteriorated when it invaded Afghanistan. Carter stopped grain sales and refused U.S. participation in the Moscow Olympics.
- In 1979, **Ayatollah Khomeini** overthrew the Shah of Iran and established an **Islamic Republic.** When the Shah fled to the United States, Iranian rebels took U.S. Embassy workers hostage. The hostages were held for over a year. Carter was unable to free them.

The Reagan Presidency (1981–1989)

- Vietnam, Watergate, and the Iranian Hostage Crisis had made Americans feel weak. **Ronald Reagan,** a former movie star and Governor of California, pledged to make America strong again.
- International terrorism worsened in Lebanon, Beirut, and Libya. Reagan declared he would not negotiate with terrorists and organized punitive air strikes.
- Reagan called the Soviet Union an **"Evil Empire."** He wanted to roll Communism back and ensure a free world. He sent assistance to anti-Communist fighters in Afghanistan, Grenada, and Nicaragua. This became known as the "**Reagan Doctrine.**"
- The **Iran-Contra Affair**: American officials secretly sold arms to Iran, which was then engaged in the Iran-Iraq War, for help in freeing American hostages in Lebanon. Money secretly received from Iran for these arms was then handed over to the anti-Communist **Contras** in Nicaragua, despite a Congressional ban on U.S. aid to the Contras. When the plan was discovered, several high-ranking officials resigned, although Reagan himself claimed no knowledge of the deal.
- The Soviet Union was suffering from economic stagnation, corruption, expensive wars, and social problems like alcoholism. **Mikhail Gorbachev** assumed power in 1985 and attempted reforms. *Glasnost* ("openness") allowed people to openly criticize government and suggest change. *Perestroika* ("restructuring") allowed limited free enterprise to stimulate the economy.
- Gorbachev withdrew Soviet troops from Afghanistan.
- Reagan's plans for the **Strategic Defense Initiative,** to protect the United States against nuclear attack, would have been too expensive for the Soviet Union to match. Reagan and Gorbachev met in Iceland and agreed to reduce their nuclear arms.

The George H.W. Bush Presidency (1989–1993)

- **George H.W. Bush** was elected President in 1988. During his Presidency, independence movements spread across Eastern Europe. The Baltic states won their independence; Poland elected a non-Communist government; and the Berlin Wall came down in 1989. The Soviet Union dissolved in 1991 when Russia declared its independence and helped form the **Commonwealth of Independent States**. Meanwhile, Germany was reunited in 1990. The Cold War thus came to an end.
- South Africa ended **apartheid. Nelson Mandela** became its new leader based on majority rule.
- The United States became the sole superpower. Bush used military power to promote a **"New World Order."** He sent U.S. troops to arrest Panamanian dictator **Manuel Noriega,** and to chase **Saddam Hussein's** Iraqi forces out of oil-rich Kuwait in the **Persian Gulf War.** He also sent troops with food on a humanitarian mission to millions of starving people in Somalia.

The Clinton Presidency (1993–2001)

- The end of the Cold War brought a **"peace dividend"** with a reduction in military spending.
- In the former Yugoslavia, Christian Serbs attacked Muslims in **Bosnia** and **Kosovo** in a policy of **"ethnic cleansing."** The U.S. and NATO eventually intervened to prevent genocide and restore peace, but the death toll was still large. The United States and other countries were also slow to react in preventing genocide in **Rwanda** in Central Africa, where as many as 850,000 were killed.
- The creation of **NAFTA** and the **World Trade Organization** brought economic prosperity and increased trade with Canada, Mexico, and China.
- Clinton intervened when democracy was threatened in **Haiti.**

The George W. Bush Presidency (2001–2009)

- **2000 Presidential Election.** The closest Presidential election in history was settled by the U.S. Supreme Court's decision in *Bush v. Gore* (2000), which halted a recount of votes in Florida.
- **September 11, 2001.** Al-Qaeda terrorists hijacked commercial airplanes and crashed them into the World Trade Center and Pentagon. Osama bin Laden was the leader behind the attack.
- **Wars in Afghanistan and Iraq.** The U.S. attacked Afghanistan when Taliban leaders failed to hand over Osama bin Laden. The U.S. next invaded Iraq in 2003, suspecting dictator Saddam Hussein had "weapons of mass destruction" (WMDs). Hussein quickly fell, but Americans then faced an insurgency.

America and the World Today

- America is no longer a superpower controlling world events, though it is still a global leader.
- In 2008, **Barack Obama** was elected as the first African-American President. Obama tried to strengthen global ties. He withdrew U.S. troops from Iraq. His administration found and killed Osama bin Laden. During the **Arab Spring,** Obama encouraged peaceful resolutions of revolts against dictatorships. Nonetheless violence erupted in Libya, Syria, and Egypt.
- In Africa, democracy has been spreading, though the continent still needs greater stability and economic aid. The "Arab Spring" has brought both democracy and turmoil to North Africa.
- In the Middle East, America seeks to reduce hostility to the United States, prevent the spread of nuclear weapons to Iran, end the Syrian war, and establish peace between Israel and Palestine.
- In East Asia, American leaders hope to foster peaceful relations and trade with China while protecting other nations from Chinese militarism. They also hope to stop North Korea's nuclear program.
- Americans hope to maintain good trade relations with the nations of Latin America.

U.S. Foreign Policy Since 1972

Richard Nixon 
- *Détente* with Soviet Union
- Visit to Communist China
- Watergate Scandal

Gerald Ford 
- Pardoned Nixon
- Arab OPEC boycott of U.S.
- Helsinki Accords

Jimmy Carter 
- Panama Canal Treaty
- Camp David Accords
- Iranian Revolution—Ayatollah Khomeini
- Hostage Crisis

Challenges Ahead
- New Democracies
- Iran
- Israel/Palestine
- North Korea
- Globalization

Ronald Reagan
- Repeated terrorist attacks
- Air strike on Libya
- "Reagan Doctrine"—Grenada, Nicaragua, Afghanistan
- Iran-Contra Affair
- Strategic Defense Initiative
- Talks with Gorbachev

Barack Obama
- Withdrawal from Iraq
- Killing of Osama bin Laden
- "Arab Spring"

George W. Bush 
- 2000 Election; *Bush v. Gore*
- September 11, 2001: al-Qaeda attacks
- "War on Terror"
- Taliban overthrown in Afghanistan
- Iraq War

Bill Clinton
- NAFTA
- Bosnia & Kosovo: "ethnic cleansing"
- Rwanda: genocide
- Haiti: democratic government restored

George H.W. Bush
- End of Cold War
- U.S. interventions: Panama, Somalia
- First Gulf War: Kuwait

What Do You Know?

SS.912.A.6.13

1. What was the significance of President Nixon's visit to Communist China in 1972?

   A. It led to the reunification of Taiwan with Communist China.

   B. It persuaded Chinese leaders to introduce capitalism into the marketplace.

   C. It showed that the Cold War between the "Free World" and Communism was over.

   D. It opened the way for China's entry into the United Nations and trade with the United States.

SS.912.A.7.10

2. The cartoon on the right was published in May 1973.

   With which event was this cartoon associated?

   A. Teapot Dome Scandal

   B. Iran Hostage Crisis

   C. Watergate Scandal

   D. Iran-Contra Affair

Chapter 16 | American Foreign Policy Since 1972

SS.912.A.7.11

3. The photograph below shows foreign leaders meeting with President Carter at Camp David in 1978.

What was the outcome of this meeting?

A. The United States and its allies halted grain sales to the Soviet Union.

B. The United States persuaded Egypt and Israel to sign a future peace treaty.

C. The United States signed a treaty promising the return of the Panama Canal Zone.

D. The United States successfully rescued hostages held by Iranian students in Tehran.

SS.912.A.7.10

4. The diagram below gives details about the 1970s and 1980s.

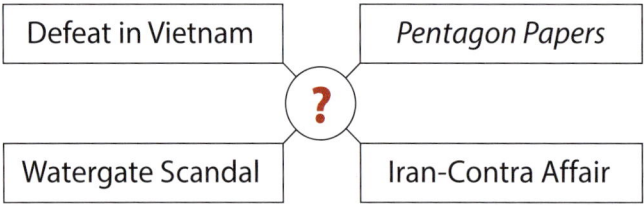

Which phrase completes the diagram?

A. Efforts to Reduce Presidential Power

B. Events that Weakened Public Trust in Government

C. Clashes between the Executive and Legislative Branches

D. Disagreements between the Supreme Court and the President

SS.912.A.7.12

5. The photograph on the left shows a newspaper being read at a gasoline service center in January 1974. Its headline states: "Gas Rationing Set Monday"

What was the primary cause of the shortages shown in the photograph?

A. A war in Afghanistan had cut oil supplies from Central Asia.

B. The Mexican government had nationalized its petroleum industry.

C. Arab members of OPEC had placed an oil embargo on the United States.

D. Iran had halted its oil exports after the former Shah was admitted into America.

Source: The National Archives.

SS.912.A.7.11

6. What was an important result of the Persian Gulf War of 1990?

    A. Kuwait was freed from occupation by Iraq.

    B. Relations between Israel and Iran improved.

    C. Kurdish rebels gained independence from Iraq.

    D. Saddam Hussein was removed from power in Iraq.

SS.912.A.7.12

7. Why did President Clinton propose cuts in defense spending in the 1990s?

    A. The SALT treaty had made it unnecessary to possess nuclear arms.

    B. The Communist government of the former Soviet Union had collapsed.

    C. The U.N. Security Council had taken over America's peacekeeping duties.

    D. Rising health care costs had taken funds normally used by the military.

SS.912.A.7.12

8. What step did Soviet leader Mikhail Gorbachev take in reaction to President Reagan's 1983 Strategic Defense Initiative?

    A. ending the system of apartheid in South Africa

    B. placing intermediate-range nuclear missiles in Cuba

    C. providing Soviet support to Communist China against Taiwan

    D. entering into talks with President Reagan to reduce armaments

SS.912.A.7.15

9. How were the attacks on Pearl Harbor in 1941 and on the World Trade Center in 2001 similar?

    A. Both resulted in global economic depressions.

    B. Both caused Americans to enter into armed conflicts.

    C. Both led to military conscription of adult American men.

    D. Both convinced American voters to retreat into isolationism.

SS.912.A.7.15

10. How were U.S. entry into World War I and the events of September 11, 2001 similar?

    A. They led to increased federal aid to private anti-terrorist groups.

    B. They limited Second Amendment rights in times of national crisis.

    C. They created special detention centers for holding aliens during wartime.

    D. They increased popular suspicions of some ethnic groups in the United States.

SS.912.A.7.15

11. How did President Bush respond to the acts of terrorism committed on September 11, 2001?

    A. He sent troops to Israel to protect it from terrorist attacks.

    B. He ordered a boycott of goods from Afghanistan and Iran.

    C. He invaded Iraq since he thought Saddam Hussein was behind the attacks.

    D. He sent troops to Afghanistan when it refused to surrender Osama bin Laden.

SS.912.A.7.14

12. The excerpt below is from Article 102 of the North American Free Trade Agreement (NAFTA):

> **Article 102: Objectives**
>
> 1. The objectives of this Agreement, as elaborated more specifically through its principles and rules, including national treatment, most-favored-nation treatment and transparency, are to:
>
>   a) eliminate barriers to trade in, and facilitate the cross-border movement of, goods and services between the territories of the Parties;
>
>   b) promote conditions of fair competition in the free trade area;
>
>   c) increase substantially investment opportunities in the territories of the Parties . . .

Why did Presidents Bush and Clinton support this agreement?

A. They believed that Japanese manufacturers intended to open factories in Mexico.

B. They thought it would stop the United States from joining the European Union (EU).

C. They believed it would help Canada and Mexico to resist the appeals of Communism.

D. They hoped more trade with Canada and Mexico would stimulate U.S. economic growth.

SS.912.A.7.14

13. This table provides information about U.S. trade with other nations in 2012.

Country	U.S. exports of goods in billions of dollars	U.S. imports of goods in billions of dollars	Percent of U.S. foreign trade in goods
Canada	292.4	324.2	16.1%
China	110.6	425.6	14.0%
Mexico	216.3	277.7	12.9%
Japan	70.0	146.4	5.7%
Germany	48.8	108.5	4.1%
United Kingdom	54.8	54.9	2.9%
South Korea	42.3	58.9	2.6%
Brazil	43.7	32.1	2.0%
Saudi Arabia	18.1	55.7	1.9%
France	30.8	41.6	1.9%

Source: U.S. Department of Commerce

Based on the table, which conclusion can be made about American trade today?

A. Americans export more goods to Germany than to Japan.

B. China imports more goods from the United States than it exports

C. Americans import more goods from Europe than from any other region.

D. Two of America's three strongest trading partners are members of NAFTA.

CHAPTER 17

American Social Issues

SS.912.A.7.5 Compare nonviolent and violent approaches utilized by groups (African Americans, women, Native Americans, Hispanics) to achieve civil rights.

SS.912.A.7.8 Analyze significant Supreme Court decisions relating to integration, busing, affirmative action, the rights of the accused, and reproductive rights.

SS.912.A.7.12 Analyze political, economic, and social concerns that emerged at the end of the 20th century and into the 21st century.

SS.912.A.7.9 Examine the similarities of social movements (Native Americans, Hispanics, women, antiwar protesters) of the 1960s and 1970s.

SS.912.A.7.15 Analyze the effects of foreign and domestic terrorism on the American people.

SS.912.A.7.16 Examine changes in immigration policy and attitudes toward immigration since 1950.

SS.912.A.7.17 Examine key events and key people in Florida.

Names and Terms You Should Know

Social movements	Gray Panthers	Terrorism
Cesar Chavez	Affirmative action	Oklahoma City bombing
United Farm Workers (UFW)	*Regents of the University of California v. Bakke* (1978)	September 11, 2001
American Indian Movement (AIM)	*Gideon v. Wainwright* (1963)	USA PATRIOT Act
Wounded Knee (1973)	*Roe v. Wade* (1973)	Climate change
Seminole Indians	Immigration and Naturalization Act of 1965	Gun control
26th Amendment	Illegal alien	
Americans with Disabilities Act	Refugee	

Florida "Keys" for Learning

1. In recent decades, other minorities have followed the example of African Americans in the Civil Rights Movement by demanding increased opportunities and equal rights.

2. American Indians have been greatly affected by changing federal policies. The American Indian Movement, or AIM, was founded in 1968. Other Indian activists occupied Alcatraz Island in 1969 and AIM occupied Wounded Knee in 1973. AIM demanded increased federal aid and improved treatment of American Indians in media and textbooks.

3. Cesar Chavez helped to organize Hispanic migrant farm workers. He started the United Farm Workers (UFW) and launched boycotts of grapes and lettuce to force growers to recognize the UFW and treat their migrant workers with greater dignity. Young Americans protesting the Vietnam War led to passage of the 26th Amendment, giving 18-year-olds the right to vote. Americans with disabilities formed DREDF, which sought greater accessibility. The Americans with Disabilities Act (1990) requires restaurants, hotels, theaters, and offices to make accommodations that make their facilities accessible to people with disabilities. The Gray Panthers was formed by Maggie Kuhn to fight against mandatory retirement laws and age discrimination (or "ageism"). The Age Discrimination in Employment Act of 1967 prohibits discrimination in the workplace on the basis of age.

4. The Supreme Court has played an important role in defending individual rights and the rights of minorities. It outlawed racial segregation in public schools and upheld busing as a way to integrate schools. It also upheld affirmative action admission programs, although it prohibited race-based quotas. The Court further upheld the rights of those accused of a crime, barring the police from using evidence in court that they had obtained illegally. The Supreme Court also established a woman's right to an abortion in the first trimester of her pregnancy.

5. The Immigration Act of 1965 abandoned the system based on national origins and permitted every country to have the same number of lawful immigrants. It also placed limits on immigration from Latin America for the first time. The Refugee Act of 1980 permitted refugees to immigrate to the United States, while the Immigration Reform and Control Act of 1986 gave amnesty to illegal immigrants already living in the United States. The Immigration Act of 1990 greatly expanded the number of legal immigrants admitted each year. Today, there are also millions of illegal aliens living in the United States. Americans struggle with how to deal with the large number of illegal immigrants and how to make our borders more secure.

6. Terrorism poses a special risk today. Domestic acts of terrorism include the bombing of the federal building in Oklahoma City in 1995. International acts of terrorism include the attack on the World Trade Center and Pentagon on September 11, 2001. The "Global War on Terror" led to changes at home as well as abroad. President Bush created a new cabinet-level department: the Department of Homeland Security. The Transportation Security Administration was established to screen passengers before boarding commercial airplanes. The USA PATRIOT Act gave federal officials new eavesdropping powers. The Bush administration used harsh interrogation techniques on detainees held outside the United States, some of which were later held to be unconstitutional by the Supreme Court.

7. Other important issues facing Americans today include: (1) how to reduce pollution and prevent climate change; (2) how to adjust taxation and spending to prevent further growth of the national debt; (3) what is the proper role of the federal government in American society; and (4) gun control.

American Social Issues

In this chapter, you will learn about recent social developments in the United States. Since the 1960s, various minority groups have struggled to achieve equal rights. The U.S. Supreme Court has often played an important role in these struggles. Meanwhile, our nation's immigration laws have signficantly evolved since 1950. Life in the United States has also been affected by threats of terrorism. Finally, Americans are being tested by the challenges of increasing global competition and climate change.

Social Activism by Minorities

Since the 1960s, American Indians, Hispanic Americans, younger and older Americans, and Americans with disabilities have all followed the example first set by African Americans by establishing **social movements** that demanded civil rights and the equal protection of the laws.

American Indians

The main challenge for American Indians continues to be whether to assimilate into mainstream society or to preserve traditional ways of life on reservations. Federal policies have vacillated between encouraging one or the other of these approaches.

The Indian Reorganization Act (Howard-Wheeler Act) of 1934

During the New Deal, the federal government tried to show greater respect for Indian traditions. **The Indian Reorganization Act** stopped the breaking up of reservations into individual plots of land under the Dawes Act. It restored elected tribal councils to govern the reservations. It also attempted to improve the quality of Indian education while encouraging traditional crafts, customs, and beliefs.

"Termination" Policy, 1953–1963

In Congressional hearings in the 1940s, critics complained that the Indian Reorganization Act had established American Indians as a separate entity within the nation. Instead, they argued, the government should just deal with them as individuals. In 1946, the Indian Claims Commission Act attempted to settle all remaining Indian claims against the federal government. Tribes were given a short time to gather records. Without these records as legal proof, all their tribal claims were dismissed.

In 1953, the federal government suddenly announced its intention of "**terminating**" (*ending*) its responsibilities to those Indians still living on reservations. These responsibilities were handed over to the states. The government also announced that it would provide job training and placement to help Indians assimilate into mainstream American life—a return to earlier efforts at "Americanization."

This new policy, however, was largely a failure. The government did not fulfill its promises. Indians attempting to enter mainstream society continued to face discrimination in employment and housing. On the reservations, state governments failed to supply many services once furnished by the federal government.

The American Indian Movement, 1960s and 1970s

In 1963, the federal government abandoned its "termination" policy. This time it swung back to encouraging tribal life on the reservations. In 1970, President Nixon announced that the federal government had solemn treaty obligations to the Indians which it had no right to "terminate." Indians were provided with federal funds for housing, medicine, education, and economic renewal. The Civil Rights Act (1964) and affirmative action programs reduced discrimination against American Indians in employment and education. Nevertheless, many Indians felt these programs were not enough.

Under the slogan of "**Red Power**," American Indians asserted greater pride and respect for their own heritage. They introduced the term "**Native American**," and objected to textbooks, television programs, and movies showing bias against them. They also sought more federal aid for Indian tribes on reservations. To dramatize their plight, Indian activists temporarily occupied **Alcatraz Island** in San Francisco Bay in 1969.

The **American Indian Movement**, or **AIM**, was founded in 1968 to mobilize public opinion behind tribal demands. In 1973, they took over **Wounded Knee**, **South Dakota**, to protest the failure of the federal government to fulfill its promises to the Indians. At Wounded Knee, there were even occasional exchanges of gunfire between the FBI and the protestors. Three people lost their lives during the occupation.

American Indian Tribes Today

In the 2000 Census, four million people identified themselves as American Indians or Alaskan Natives—more than in 1890. Of these, 2.5 million said they were full-blooded American Indians or Alaskan Natives. The two largest surviving tribes are the Navajo and Cherokee: each of these tribes has more than 280,000 full-blooded members.

Reservation and Indian-owned lands still constitute more than 50 million acres—about two percent of the land area of the United States. Much of this land, however, has poor soil and suffers from extremes of climate. The federal government continues to provide aid to Indians, including medical services, although many of these programs are underfunded. Many Indians living on reservations suffer from poverty, unemployment, and higher than average rates of diabetes and other illnesses.

Flag of the American Indian Movement

Seminole Indians The Seminole tribe of Florida continues to interact with tourists. Many Seminoles earn incomes by selling tax-free tobacco, growing citrus fruits, and running gaming enterprises. The Seminoles have several federal reservations in Florida with more than 90,000 acres. The Seminole tribe won a major settlement in 1992 based on land claims it had filed in 1947. The tribe operates the Ah-Tah-Thi-Ki Museum and the Ahfachkee Indian School and provides grants for tribal members attending college.

Hispanic Americans

In the 2000 Census, 35.3 million, or 12.5 percent of the U.S. population, considered themselves Hispanic. Spanish-speaking Americans come from many places—including Mexico, Puerto Rico, Cuba, the Dominican Republic, El Salvador, Chile, Argentina, and Peru. The three largest groups in 2000 were Mexican (about 7.3 percent of the U.S. population), Puerto Rican (1.2 percent), and Cuban (0.4 percent). The largest numbers of Hispanic Americans live in California, Texas, Florida, New Mexico, and Arizona, but Hispanic Americans are found in every state. They make up the fastest growing segment of the U.S. population today.

When Columbus arrived in the Americas, he thought he was in the East Indies and described the peoples he met as "Indians." In fact, the American Indians are not a single people but many different groups, or tribes. In the 1970s, Indian activists encouraged use of the name **"Native Americans"** instead of American Indians. This emphasized that the American Indian tribes were already living in the Americas when other groups, such as Europeans, began arriving in the 1490s. Today, **"Native Americans"** generally refers to American Indians, Alaskan Natives and Native Hawaiians as a single group. **"American Indians"** refers to those Native American tribes found in the continental United States.

 **Cesar Chavez** was born in Arizona in 1927. His grandfather migrated to the United States in the late 1880s. His family lost their store and ranch during the Great Depression and became migrant farm workers in California, where they picked peas, lettuce, cherries, beans, and grapes. They faced discrimination as well as poverty. In 1942, Cesar's father was killed in a car accident. Cesar later served in the navy for two years, but found that even there, Mexican Americans faced prejudice. Chavez became a community organizer and helped Mexican Americans register to vote. In 1962, he helped to start the **United Farm Workers Association**, or "**UFW**"—a union of migrant farm workers demanding better wages and living conditions. In 1965, Chavez organized a strike by grape pickers and a march to California's state capital in Sacramento. He also led a nationwide boycott of grapes. Similar unions of migrant farm workers were formed in Texas and the Midwest. In the 1970s, Chavez led the UFW in another strike for lettuce pickers. The UFW also demanded the use of less pesticide, which endangered the health of farm workers. Chavez conducted hunger strikes, once starving himself for 28 days in order to get better conditions. Eventually, Chavez was successful in gaining recognition for the United Farm Workers and the passage of laws protecting the rights of migrant farm workers.

Young Americans

During the Vietnam War, young American men were drafted at the age of 18 but did not enjoy the right to vote in some states until the age of 21. Many saw this as unjust. "Old enough to fight, old enough to vote," became a popular slogan. Congress passed a law lowering the voting age to 18, but the U.S. Supreme Court ruled that parts of the law violated the right of states to set their own election requirements. Congress responded by proposing the **Twenty-Sixth Amendment**, which was ratified by the states in July 1971—the shortest time ever required to ratify a constitutional amendment. It lowered the voting age to 18 in both federal and state elections.

Americans with Disabilities

Another group to demand equal rights were those with physical and mental disabilities. Some of them were unable to see, hear, or walk. They depended on a wheelchair or special training.

The American Federation for the Physically Handicapped, the first group to advocate rights for the disabled, was founded in 1940. In the 1960s, Ed Roberts, who had been severely paralyzed by polio, became the leader of the Berkeley Center for Independent Living, an advocacy group for people with severe disabilities.

The Rehabilitation Act of 1973 prohibited discrimination against people with disabilities by businesses and other organizations receiving federal funds. Disability activists staged a nationwide sit-in in 1977 to protest the fact that the federal government had delayed passing regulations to implement the act. The Disability Rights Education and Defense Fund, or DREDF, was a leading national civil rights group founded in 1979. It is led by individuals with disabilities and by the parents of children with disabilities. Like the NAACP, DREDF focused on legal actions to protect the civil rights of people with disabilities. DREDF points out that:

> "Americans with disabilities make up one of the United States' largest minorities. . . . Seventy-five percent are unemployed. Such economic and social disenfranchisement is not an inevitable consequence of the physical and mental limitations imposed by disability; it is the result of society's historic response to those limitations: lack of accessibility in the built environment and policies that encourage or even require exclusion, segregation, and institutionalization."

DREDF and its members demanded *accessibility*—the ability to *access*, or use, public and private facilities along with everyone else. In some cases, such accessibility required *reasonable accommodations*—adding special features, such as wider doors, lower counters, or ramps—in order to make facilities accessible to them.

Chapter 17 | American Social Issues

In 1990, Congress passed the **Americans with Disabilities Act**. This law prohibits discrimination against those with disabilities in employment and public accommodations. It requires restaurants, hotels, theaters, stadiums, and other public places to create paths of travel wide enough for wheelchairs, to have lower switches for light bulbs, to have some lower sinks in restrooms, and to make other "reasonable accommodations." Employers also have to make "reasonable accommodations" in order to employ people with disabilities. These accommodations must be paid for by the businesses themselves. If a business fails to make the required accommodations, it can be fined by the government. It can also be sued by individuals with disabilities who are unable to use that facility or work in that place of business.

Older Americans

Maggie Kuhn was forced, against her will, to retire at the age of 65. With five friends, she formed a group whose main goals were to raise the mandatory retirement age and to end the Vietnam War. In 1972, the organization officially adopted the name the "**Gray Panthers**." A talk show producer had once used this name, adapted from the "Black Panthers," to describe the group.

"Old age is not a disease. It is strength and survivorship, triumph over all kinds of vicissitudes and disappointments, trials and illnesses."
—Maggie Kuhn

The Gray Panthers fought against "ageism"—especially discrimination against older Americans. They established the National Media Watch Task Force to stop age stereotyping. The Gray Panthers also campaigned for affordable housing and a national health care system. They cooperated with well-known consumer advocate Ralph Nader to lower the prices of hearing aids. They also sued major drug manufacturers for blocking the production of generic drugs. More recently, the Gray Panthers have fought to protect the environment and to withdraw American forces from Iraq.

The American Association of Retired Persons, or **AARP**, is another organization that champions the interests of older Americans. Formed in 1958, it offers membership to Americans 50 years of age or older. AARP currently has more than 38 million members. It publishes a magazine and a bulletin, offers insurance and driver education programs, and lobbies in the interests of its members.

The Historian's Apprentice

▶ How have these social movements been influenced by the earlier Civil Rights Movement and the movement for women's rights? Write two or three paragraphs answering this question.

▶ Make a Venn diagram or chart showing how these various movements were similar and different.

▶ Draw a line and label the left side "non-violent" and the right side "violent." Then place each of the following groups in their proper location on your line: NAACP, SCLC, Black Panthers, NOW, anti-war movement, AIM, United Farm Workers, Gray Panthers, AARP, DREDF. Choose two of these organizations and write a paragraph for each justifying its placement on your line.

▶ Hold a class debate on this topic: "Resolved: Non-violence is more effective than violence in achieving social change." Use examples from this and earlier chapters as evidence to support your arguments.

A series of important federal laws now protects older Americans. The **Age Discrimination in Employment Act of 1967** prohibits discrimination on the basis of age in companies with 20 or more employees. It is similar in wording to the Civil Rights Act of 1964. Because of this act, companies cannot fire their employees on the basis of age. Whenever older workers are laid off, a company must prove that the layoff was based on reasonable factors. The Age Discrimination Act of 1975 extended these protections to students. Since 1986, age-based mandatory retirement has been prohibited in most occupations. The Fourteenth Amendment is now also seen as forbidding age discrimination.

The Role of the Supreme Court

While the actions of the President and Congress often grab the national headlines, the Supreme Court has also played a very important role in how we resolve modern social issues. This has been especially true since the landmark decision of *Brown v. Board of Education* (1954) ended the practice of legal racial segregation.

What does the Supreme Court Do?

First, it is important to understand just what the Supreme Court does. The role of any court is to determine if a specific law has been broken. Courts hold trials of people accused of crimes. Individuals and businesses can also sue one another in court if they believe a violation of law has taken place. If a person accused of a crime is convicted or a person or business loses a lawsuit, the losing party has the right to appeal the judgment of the trial court to a "court of appeal." The job of a court of appeal is to review the record of the trial and to ensure that everything was done properly. If the appellate court finds a serious error, it can send the case back to the lower court for a retrial. Usually, the appellate court is looking for errors in the interpretation or application of the law itself. Did the trial judge misinterpret the law? Did the trial judge give the wrong instructions to the jury? Did the judge admit evidence that should not have been presented?

The highest court of appeals in the land is the U.S. Supreme Court. In reaching its decisions, the Supreme Court interprets federal laws. In *Marbury v. Madison* (1803), the Supreme Court held that it

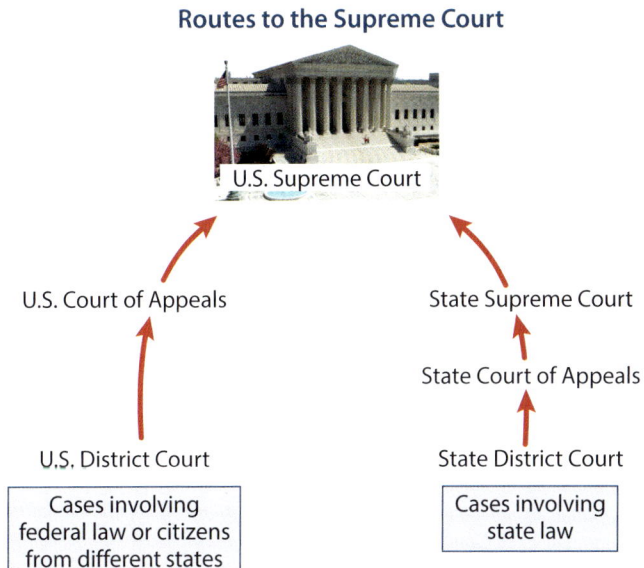

Routes to the Supreme Court

was "the province and duty" of the Court "to say what the law is. Those who apply the rule to particular cases must, of necessity, expound and interpret that rule." The most important federal law is the U.S. Constitution. It is the job of the U.S. Supreme Court to determine what the words of the Constitution mean. Look at the following examples:

▶ The 15th Amendment guarantees the right of "citizens" to vote. In this amendment, does the word "citizen" include women? In the 1870s, the Court thought that "citizens" with voting rights did *not* include women. Today, they clearly do.

▶ The First Amendment guarantees "free speech." Does this guarantee protect someone who shouts "fire!" in a crowded theater? Does "free speech" give someone the right to publish lies about a candidate to public office?

▶ The 14th Amendment guarantees "equal protection" of the laws by the states. Can state universities use different standards in admitting people of different races in order to make up for past discrimination? Does this violate "equal protection" even though it is trying to correct the results of past injustices?

The Court's views on what the Constitution means have changed over time. For a hundred years after Reconstruction, the Court failed to protect African Americans from state governments denying their right to vote and imposing racial segregation. The Supreme Court even upheld segregation in *Plessy v. Ferguson*. However, in 1954 the Court ruled against segregation in *Brown v. Board of Education*. This was the first in a series of landmark decisions protecting individual rights. The Court no longer waited for Congress or state legislatures to take action. The **Warren Court** (1953–1969) ended racial discrimination, ordered busing to equalize racial proportions in public schools, protected the rights of people accused of a crime, and even ordered the reapportionment of electoral districts to achieve greater equality. The **Burger Court** (1969–1986) upheld affirmative action programs and protected women's "reproductive rights" in the first months of pregnancy.

Some people refer to this practice, in which courts take a very active role in defending rights and promoting greater social equality, as **judicial activism**. Many believe such activism is needed because it protects individual rights. Critics argue that judicial activism can sometimes go too far: they believe many of these questions would be more appropriately resolved by Congress than by the courts.

Some Landmark Supreme Court Cases

Integration and Busing

Does the Constitution require children to be bused to distant schools in order to achieve racial balance?

Swann v. Charlotte-Mecklenburg Department of Education (1970)

Brown v. Board of Education outlawed state-ordered racial segregation in public schools. Many Southerners saw the *Brown* decision as an order not to segregate, but they did not see it as an order to integrate. They did not believe that a school district was required to take any positive steps towards mixing students of different races beyond prohibiting state-based racial discrimination.

The school district of Charlotte-Mecklenburg in North Carolina ended segregation and created a larger school district with more schools, but most African-American students still remained in racially segregated schools.

The NAACP filed a lawsuit in favor of James Swann, a 6-year-old African-American student. At first, the district court ruled in favor of the school district on the grounds that the district had no positive duty to increase racial mixing. On a second hearing, the court ordered busing: school districts were required to send their white and black students by bus to different schools until roughly the same proportion of races was found in all the schools in the district. This practice of "busing" students to more distant schools to achieve racial equality was upheld by the U.S. Supreme Court.

Affirmative Action

Is an "affirmative action" program an unlawful form of reverse racial discrimination?

Regents of the University of California v. Bakke (1978)

Earlier cases about racial discrimination had considered state actions that had harmed disadvantaged minorities, especially African Americans. The *Bakke* case judged the constitutionality of race-based government action intended to benefit groups that had suffered from past discrimination. The Supreme Court held that any race-based discrimination was questionable ("inherently suspect"). It could only be justified if: (1) it met a compelling interest; and (2) there was no other way to reach that goal. The Court ruled that the University of California could take race into consideration in its admissions policies, but it could not have a race-based quota.

You will probably only be required to know the Bakke decision above for Florida's EOC Assessment. However, the following cases show the further development of the law.

City of Richmond v. J. Croson (1989)

The city of Richmond, Virginia, has an African-American majority. The city established a special program that required 30% of all city construction contracts to go to companies owned by African Americans or other minorities. The Supreme Court held that Richmond's race-based program was not justified, despite its legacy of past discrimination. The city had not shown that its new race-based solution was "narrowly tailored" to remedy the effects of earlier discrimination. In other words, the city failed to show that (1) the law's goal was necessary; and (2) that race-based discrimination was the only way to achieve this goal. "We, therefore, hold that the city has failed to demonstrate a compelling interest in apportioning public contracting opportunities on the basis of race."

Adarand Constructors Inc. v. Pena (1995)

Richmond v. Croson dealt with race-based discrimination by a city. The *Adarand* case dealt with federal policies. The Supreme Court ruled that any race-based discrimination had to be subjected to "strict scrutiny." That is, it had to be judged carefully, based on very high standards. Even though the federal government's aim was to benefit minorities, the Court held it had no more right to discriminate than state governments did.

Grutter v. Bollinger and Gratz v. Bollinger (2003)

In *Grutter v. Bollinger*, the Supreme Court upheld the "affirmative action" policy of the University of Michigan Law School. Barbara Grutter was a white female resident of Michigan with high grades and a high score on the law school admissions test (LSAT). While she was denied admission to the law school, some applicants from minority groups with lower grades and test scores were admitted. She sued on the grounds that her rights under the Fourteenth Amendment had been violated. The Supreme Court held that the state had a compelling interest to have a "critical mass" of students from certain minority groups in its law school. Following *Bakke*, the Court held that quotas were unlawful but that a school could still take race into consideration in its admissions decisions. The state had "a compelling interest in obtaining the educational benefits that flow from a diverse student body." The Court warned that such race-based preferences, however, would probably become unnecessary within the next 25 years.

In a companion case, *Gratz v. Bollinger*, the Supreme Court struck down the undergraduate admissions policy of the University of Michigan, which awarded points to candidates on the basis of race. To be admitted generally, a student required 100 points. Each minority candidate automatically received 20 points. The Court held that this system violated the Fourteenth Amendment.

Rights of the Accused

Should evidence against criminals be permitted in a court trial when the police did not follow proper constitutional procedures to obtain it? Should a person have the right to remain silent or have an attorney present when interrogated?

Mapp v. Ohio (1961)

The Fourth Amendment protects us from police searches unless police have a search warrant, we consent to the search, or an established exception applies. Ohio police, looking for a bomb, searched Mapp's house. They did not have a search warrant or her permission. The search was also not based on any established exception. They did not find any bomb but they did find illegal child pornography.

The U.S. Supreme Court ruled that the police could not use this evidence in court since they had obtained it through an illegal search: "We hold that all evidence obtained by searches and seizures in violation of the Constitution [is] inadmissible in a state court." The purpose of this "**exclusionary rule**" is to take away all incentive for the police to conduct illegal searches.

Miranda v. Arizona (1966)

The Fifth Amendment protects us from **self-incrimination**, while the Sixth Amendment guarantees us the right to an attorney if we are accused of a crime. In 1963 Ernesto Miranda was arrested in Arizona for kidnapping and rape. After two hours of police questioning, Miranda signed a confession. However, he was never told that he had the right to remain silent or to have a lawyer present during the questioning. Miranda was convicted and sentenced to 20 to 30 years imprisonment. On appeal, his conviction was overturned because he had never been informed of his rights:

> "The person in custody must, prior to interrogation, be clearly informed that he has the right to remain silent, and that anything he says will be used against him in court; he must be clearly informed that he has the right to consult with a lawyer and to have the lawyer with him during interrogation, and that, if he is indigent [poor], a lawyer will be appointed to represent him. . . .
>
> If the individual indicates in any manner, at any time prior to or during questioning, that he wishes to remain silent, the interrogation must cease ... If the individual states that he wants an attorney, the interrogation must cease until an attorney is present. At that time, the individual must have an opportunity to confer with the attorney and to have him present during any subsequent questioning."

These rights are now known as the "Miranda" rights. Miranda himself was retried and convicted without the use of his confession. He was freed in 1972 but killed in a fight four years later.

Reapportionment

Does the Constitution require that each representative in a state legislature or Congress represent about the same number of voters?

Baker v. Carr (1962)

Over time, populations had grown more in urban than in rural districts. As a result, rural districts in most state legislatures were over-represented. Each representative from a rural district represented fewer voters than one from an urban district in the same state. Charles Baker lived in the city of Memphis, Tennessee. His urban district had ten times the number of voters than most districts in rural Tennessee—making his vote worth only one-tenth as much. For a long time, judges believed that the system of representation should be left to political processes rather than the courts. In *Baker v. Carr,* the U.S. Supreme Court announced that Tennessee should redesign its electoral districts so that each vote was approximately equal. The principle of "one person, one vote" was applied. As a result of this case, almost every state legislature had to reapportion its seats in the 1960s, and political power shifted from rural to urban areas. Florida was one of those states that had to reapportion its districts.

Wesberry v. Sanders (1964)

In this case, the U.S. Supreme Court applied the same principle of equality of representation to Congressional districts in the U. S. House of Representatives. The Court ruled that the Congressional districts of each state should be roughly equal in population.

Reproductive Rights

At what point in a pregnancy can a state prohibit abortion?

For Florida's EOC Assessment, you will probably only need to know the case of Roe v. Wade (1973). Nevertheless, you should be aware that the law continues to develop in this area.

Planned Parenthood v. Casey (1992)

In *Roe v. Wade,* the Supreme Court ruled that women have the right to an abortion in the first trimester on the basis of a consitutional right to privacy (see Chapter 15, pp. 355–356). Pennsylvania passed a law placing restrictions on this right. The woman seeking the abortion had to inform her husband or, if she were a minor, obtain the consent of her parents. Her doctor was also required to inform her about possible risks of an abortion to her health.

In this decision, the Supreme Court strongly upheld *Roe v. Wade*:

> "Liberty finds no refuge in a jurisprudence of doubt. Yet 19 years after our holding that the Constitution protects a woman's right to terminate her pregnancy in its early stages, [in] Roe v. Wade (1973), that definition of liberty is still questioned. . . . If the right of privacy means anything, it is the right of the individual, married or single, to be free from unwarranted governmental intrusion into matters so fundamentally affecting a person as the decision whether to bear or beget a child."

Nevertheless, the Court also upheld most of Pennsylvania's law, including its parental consent requirement and its 24-hour waiting period. The Court overturned the requirement that a wife must inform her husband to obtain an abortion.

Gonzalez v. Carhart (2007)

The Partial-Birth Abortion Ban Act was signed into federal law in 2003. This act prohibits doctors from performing a type of abortion sometimes used in the second trimester (*second three-month period*). Several federal courts held the act to be unconstitutional. The U.S. Supreme Court, however, upheld the ban. It ruled that "ethical and moral concerns," including the government's interest in the life of the unborn child, provided a reasonable basis for the prohibition.

The Historian's Apprentice

1. Select two of the Supreme Court decisions discussed in the last four pages. For each decision you select, research the facts of the case on the Internet. Then give your own opinion on whether the Supreme Court made the "right" judgment. For example, is the right to remain silent a fundamental right? Finally, identify one or more short-term and long-term effects of each decision.

2. Look at the cases in this section as a whole. Do you see the Supreme Court moving in any general direction? Is it moving towards more rights for the individual? Or towards more power for the federal government? Or in some other direction? Does it matter which Justices are on the Supreme Court? Now look at some of its more recent decisions on elections, health care, same-sex marriage, or any other current issue. Do the Court's most recent decisions confirm or refute your views?

3. How important has the Supreme Court become to our national life? Hold a class debate on the following topic: "Resolved: That the Supreme Court has become too involved in social issues." The affirmative side in this debate should argue that the Court has become too activist. The negative side should argue that the Court's involvement in social issues has had a positive impact.

Immigration

Our country is mainly made up of immigrants and their descendants. Less than two percent of the U.S. population today are American Indians. All others have either come from somewhere else or are descended from immigrants who did.

For most of its history, the United States had open borders and invited newcomers from all lands. There was plenty of open space for immigrants in the West, as well as available jobs in America's cities and factories. Prejudice against newcomers, however, was already present by the mid-nineteenth century. The Know-Nothing Party condemned Irish immigrants for being Catholic and poor. In 1882, the United States passed its first major law restricting immigration with the **Chinese Exclusion Act**. In the final decades of the nineteenth century and early twentieth century, lower steamship fares brought waves of immigrants from Southern and Eastern Europe. Many feared changes in the nation's general ethnic composition. As you know, Congress passed laws limiting immigration from Europe in 1921. The primary aim of these laws was to preserve the nation's existing ethnic make-up. Even after World War II, the McCarran-Walter Act had the same objective. However, the **Immigration and Nationality Act**

of 1965 marked a major turning point in American immigration policy. This act eliminated preferential quotas and entitled every country to the same number of immigrants. The law placed limits for the first time on the number of immigrants from the Western Hemisphere. It also placed a priority on family reunification. The goal of U.S. immigration policy shifted from the preservation of America's ethnic make-up to that of simply limiting the total number of immigrants.

The annual number of legal immigrants to the United States doubled between 1965 and 1970, and doubled again between 1970 and 1990. In 1986, President Ronald Reagan granted an **amnesty** to the three million illegal aliens then living in the United States. Since that time, there have been a number of additional amnesties. Meanwhile, the **Immigration Act of 1990** raised the number of legal immigrants permitted each year by another 40 percent. Between 1986 and 2008, about 400,000 legal immigrants were admitted to the United States annually. Since that time, more than one million people have become legal permanent residents each year.

Most of these immigrants are being reunited with their families. The average age of these newcomers is younger than the average age of the U.S. population. Most of the newcomers are also married. The largest group of recent immigrants comes from Mexico. They mainly come to the United States for economic reasons—to find better paying work.

Immigration to the United States Today

Attitudes towards immigration have changed in recent decades. The biggest concerns today are the presence of millions of illegal immigrants and the need to secure the nation's borders. About as many people enter the United States illegally each year as legally. Most illegal immigrants are hard-working members of the community. But because they live in fear of being deported, they cannot fully integrate into American society. Often they work at grueling, back-breaking jobs for low pay. Many pay taxes, but others work at "under the table" jobs in which their employers do not report their earnings. Their presence raises controversial issues. Should these illegal immigrants be able to obtain drivers' licenses and health insurance? Should the children of illegal immigrants be entitled to attend public schools? Are they receiving public services without paying taxes? After the attacks on September 11, 2001, does the presence of millions of undocumented, illegal immigrants pose any kind of threat to American security?

Most American leaders believe that something must be done to address these concerns. They generally agree on the need to secure the nation's borders and on the fact that the millions of illegal immigrants already living in the United States, often for many decades, cannot simply be sent back to their countries of origin. But how can they be turned into permanent residents without being unfair to those foreigners who have patiently waited to be admitted lawfully? This is the challenge facing Americans today.

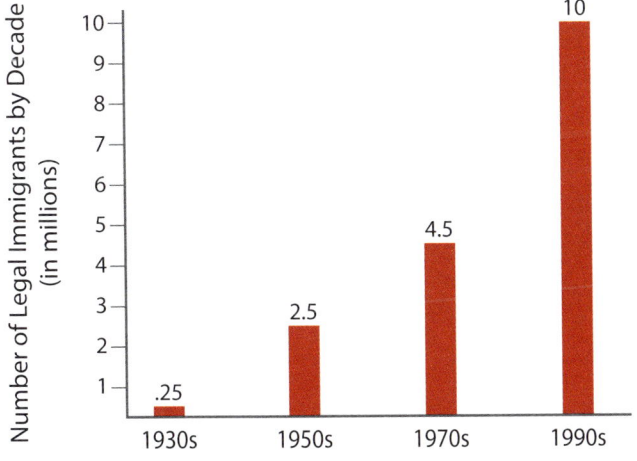

Source: U.S. Department of Homeland Security

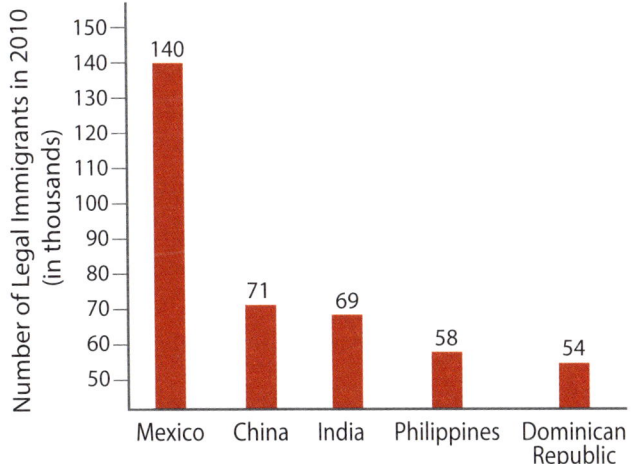

Source: U.S. Department of Homeland Security

Major Immigration Legislation Since World War II

McCarran–Walter Immigration and Nationality Act (1952)

This act kept quotas based on the 1920 census, thus allowing Britain, Germany, and Ireland to continue taking up two-thirds of all European immigration. Asian countries were allowed token immigration of 100 persons each. Special procedures were instituted to interview entering immigrants to keep out Communists. Total immigration from outside the Western Hemisphere was limited to 156,000. This act also created the U.S. Immigration and Naturalization Service.

Immigration and Nationality Act of 1965

This act was designed to be less biased than earlier immigration laws. Immigration from within the Western Hemisphere was limited to 120,000 per year, and from outside the Western Hemisphere was limited to 170,000. Each individual country was given an identical quota permitting a maximum of 20,000 immigrants. Preference was to be given to applicants with relatives in the United States or valuable occupational skills. The act allowed far greater immigration from Eastern and Southern Europe, Asia, and Africa than the McCarran-Walter Act. However, it became harder to immigrate from a large country than a small one. The act's new limits on immigration from Latin America led to a rise in illegal immigration from Mexico and Central America.

Refugee Act of 1980

This law gave special status to refugees—people fleeing persecution in their native countries. It allowed an additional 50,000 refugees to enter the country each year. The President could also admit an unlimited number of refugees in emergency situations.

Immigration Reform and Control Act of 1986

This act "legalized" all illegal aliens who had been in the United States continuously since 1981. Its purpose was to deal with the problems posed by massive illegal immigration. To discourage further illegal immigration, the law imposed penalties on employers who hired illegal aliens.

Immigration Act of 1990

This act limited total immigration to 700,000. It gave a priority to admitting those seeking family reunification. The act also created the "green card lottery" system, admitting approximately 50,000 immigrants per year from countries with traditonally low immigration rates.

Illegal Immigration Reform and Immigrant Responsibility Act of 1996

In 1994, California voters passed Proposition 187, which attempted to prevent illegal immigrants from attending public school or receiving other public benefits. Yet the U.S. Supreme Court had already overturned a similar Texas law barring undocumented children from attending public school in *Plyer v. Doe* (1982). The provisions of Proposition 187 were therefore overturned by a federal district court.

Based on the provisions of Proposition 187, Congress passed this new act. Aliens (*foreigners*) unlawfully present in the United States for 180 to 364 days had to remain outside the United States for three years before they could re-enter as legal immigrants. If they were unlawfully present for more than 364 days, they had to remain outside for ten years. The law also expanded the definition of terrorist activity as a basis for deportation. It further permitted "secret evidence" to be presented at deportation hearings.

In 2003, the Immigration and Naturalization Service was replaced by three agencies in the new Department of Homeland Security.

Challenges Ahead

Global and domestic events continue to shape U.S. political, economic, and social concerns. America's role as a global leader has often had important implications for Americans at home.

Terrorism

Terrorists use violence against innocent civilians to blackmail governments into making concessions, or to draw media attention to their grievances. They may set off car bombs, hijack airplanes, kidnap victims, or commit suicide bombings. Terrorism is not just a global phenomenon: there are also "domestic" terrorists. Often terrorists belong to groups based on ethnicity, religion, or political beliefs without the power to fight established governments more openly.

The Oklahoma City Bombing: One of the worst acts of terrorism in American history was in fact caused by domestic terrorists. In April 1995, **Timothy McVeigh** and Terry Nichols, assisted by two others, blew up the federal building in downtown Oklahoma City, killing 168 people (including 19 children), injuring another 680, and causing more than $600 million in property damage. McVeigh was a Gulf War veteran who resented the attack by federal agents two years earlier on a religious compound in Texas in a search for arms, which had resulted in a 51-day siege and 76 deaths. He and Nichols decided to bomb the federal building in revenge for the raid. They bought 40 bags of fertilizer, which they mixed with other chemicals to create an explosive mixture. McVeigh drove the 4,800 pounds of explosives in a rented truck to Oklahoma City, parked the truck in front of the federal building, and set the bomb off on April 19, 1995. In response to the bombing, Congress passed the Antiterrorism and Effective Death Penalty Act of 1996, which limited the power of federal judges to release prisoners accused of terrorism.

The "War on Terror": As you learned in the last chapter, an even greater tragedy was created by an international terrorist group, al-Qaeda, six years later. On September 11, 2001, al-Qaeda members hijacked four jet planes and flew two of them straight into the World Trade Center, leading both towers to collapse. A third team flew a jet into the Pentagon building in Washington, D.C. In response to these attacks, President George W. Bush declared a "**War on Terror**." Congress gave him the authority to use "all necessary and appropriate force against those nations, organizations or persons he determines planned, authorized, committed, or aided" the September 11th attacks. The war had effects on life within the United States as well as on U.S. foreign policy. President Bush created the **Department of Homeland Security** to better coordinate the work of several federal agencies. The head of this department became a member of cabinet. New procedures were instituted at airports to screen passengers and baggage before boarding aircraft. The **Transportation Security Administration** (or TSA) was created to conduct these screenings. Congress also passed the **USA PATRIOT Act** ("Uniting and Strengthening America by Providing Appropriate Tools Required to Intercept and Obstruct Terrorism Act of 2001"). This act gave the President special powers to combat terrorism. For example, the act made it easier for the government to set up wiretaps to eavesdrop on potential terrorists. The Bush administration also authorized the National Security Agency (NSA) to wiretap some callers without first obtaining a warrant. These warrantless wiretaps were later held to be unconstitutional.

Chapter 17 | American Social Issues

The Bush administration further adopted the use of harsh interrogation methods, such as "waterboarding" (pouring water into a cloth on the face of a prisoner to create the sensation of drowning) on high-level prisoners captured outside the United States. The same techniques were later used in Iraqi detention centers, such as the Abu Ghraib prison. The administration maintained that, while these methods were harsh, they were not torture. Some suspected terrorists, captured in Afghanistan or Iraq, were sent to the U.S. military base on Guantanamo Bay, Cuba, where similar practices were employed. Because Guantanamo Bay and the Iraqi detention centers were not on American soil, it was also argued that the detainees did not enjoy "due process" rights. Detainees were held for long periods without trial, or were convicted by military courts based on evidence not admissible in civilian courts. In 2006, the Supreme Court ruled in *Hamdan v. Rumsfield,* that the government did not have the authority to set up a military commission to try detainees at Guantanamo Bay. The Court also held that these prisoners were protected by the Geneva Convention and could not be subjected to "cruel treatment and torture" or to "outrages upon personal dignity, in particular, humiliating and degrading treatment." The practice of waterboarding was discontinued by Obama. He failed, however, to close the detention center at Guantanamo Bay because Congress would not permit the transfer of its prisoners.

The Historian's Apprentice

1. What factors make a person become a terrorist? Select an individual who became a terrorist and research his or her background, upbringing, involvement with terrorism, and terrorist acts. Write a research paper or give a PowerPoint presentation revealing your findings.
2. Hold a mock trial of Tim McVeigh or the terrorist leaders behind the September 11 attacks.
3. Do acts of terrorism justify the use of torture on suspected terrorist leaders? Can such techniques save lives or do they simply result in false confessions? Hold a class debate on this topic.

The Environment and Climate Change

Another major challenge facing Americans today is damage to the environment. For more than a million years, human beings have lived on Earth with minimal effect on its resources. However, in the past two hundred years, industrialization and population growth have suddenly escalated, severely straining our planet's air, water, and fragile ecosystems.

Water and Land Pollution

The rise of industry and accelerating population growth have led to the pollution of rivers, lakes, and oceans. Factories dump industrial wastes while cities send their sewage into lakes and rivers, which contaminate groundwater or drain into the ocean. As a result, many fresh water sources are no longer suitable for drinking, and large numbers of fish and shellfish have died.

Factories, farms, and cities also create immense amounts of solid waste. Some of this waste is placed in landfills or sent into the ocean. Waste in landfills is usually compacted and covered with soil, but can contaminate groundwater. Much of this waste, such as plastics, will not dissolve or disintegrate. The "Great Pacific Garbage Patch" is a vast area of plastics, chemicals, and sludge floating just below the surface in the middle of the Pacific Ocean. The plastic eventually breaks up into small particles, which are then eaten by birds, fish, jellyfish, and other marine life, causing illness and death.

Oil from tankers and drilling rigs poses another threat to seas and oceans. In 1989, the Exxon Valdez—a giant oil tanker—leaked as much as 30 million gallons of oil into the ocean bordering Alaska. In 2010, an explosion on an oil rig operated by BP in the Gulf of Mexico led to the worst oil spill in history—known as the "BP Oil Spill" or "Deepwater Horizon Spill." An oil well on the ocean floor continued to gush crude oil for 87 days, pouring about 200 million gallons of crude oil into the Gulf of Mexico. Fish, dolphins, turtles, and other wildlife were greatly affected. Even workers helping to clean up the spill suffered irritation, nausea, coughing, and other problems.

Blair Witherington of the Florida Fish and Wildlife Conservation Commission recovers an oiled, endangered Kemp's Ridley turtle within 20 miles of the Deepwater Horizon spill.
Photo: Carolyn Cole/LA Times

Air Pollution, Hydrocarbons, and Global Climate Change

Just as serious as water and land pollution is the problem of pollution of Earth's atmosphere. Homes, factories, offices, cars, trucks, and many power plants rely on burning hydrocarbon fuels—coal, oil, and natural gas—to provide energy and heat. Americans constitute a mere 5 percent of the world's population but cause as much as 25 percent of world pollution. As other countries, like China and Brazil, become more affluent, their levels of pollution also increase. When hydrocarbon fuels are burned, they release carbon dioxide and other pollutants into Earth's atmosphere. This carbon dioxide creates a blanket around Earth, preventing heat from escaping into space. Many scientists believe this is responsible for recent climate change—the heating of the Earth's surface, including ocean water. Warmer winters and hotter summers have led to the shrinkage of glaciers and of Earth's ice caps. Many scientists believe that the warming of the ocean's surface water has led to the increasing severity of hurricanes and other storms.

The use of chlorofluorocarbons (CFCs) in aerosol sprays has further led to a hole in the ozone layer surrounding the Earth. This layer protects human beings and other living things from harmful ultraviolent radiation. A series of international agreements has vastly reduced the production of CFCs.

To reduce pollution and damage to the environment, Congress passed the National Environmental Policy Act in 1969. President Nixon created the **Environmental Protection Agency**, or **EPA**, in 1970. The EPA enforces federal laws that protect the environment, such as the Clean Air and Clean Water Acts. Before government agencies can approve major construction or other changes that might affect the environment, they are required to complete an environmental impact statement—a report on how this change will affect the environment. The agency is also required to consider reasonable alternatives.

Americans are now searching for more sustainable forms of energy that produce less pollution than burning hydrocarbons. These include solar panels, wind mills that harness wind power, geothermal power, hydroelectric power, and even nuclear power. Meanwhile, devices using energy, such as cars, are becoming more efficient.

The Historian's Apprentice

1. What is causing climate change? Many scientists believe that pollution caused by human activities is one of the most important contributing factors. But scientists also recognize that some degree of climate change is normal, even without human activities. Research this question on the Internet and write a "White Paper" stating your own conclusions.
2. What steps is your community taking to conserve resources and to reduce pollution?

In 2015, representatives met in Paris to negotiate an international agreement on climate change. They agreed to set voluntary, national goals for reducing carbon emissions and to meet again every five years to evaluate progress. President Obama agreed to the accord but did not submit it to the Senate as a treaty. In 2017, President Trump announced he would withdraw from the accord.

Other Social Issues

A great variety of other issues both unite and divide different social, cultural, ethnic, religious, economic, and political groups in the United States.

Taxation, the National Debt and "Entitlements"

One of these issues has to do with how the government obtains and spends its money. Under President Clinton, there was a "peace dividend" from the end of the Cold War: military spending was reduced, and it seemed that the federal government might be able to stop its practice of **deficit spending** (*spending more each year than it receives in income*). However, after 9/11 the government spent massive amounts of money for military actions in Afghanistan and Iraq. When a financial crisis began in 2007, the government then spent large amounts of money to stimulate the economy.

In order to spend more money than it collects in taxes, the government issues interest-paying bonds. These are bought by investors. In the last few decades, many of these bonds have been bought by China. The amount owed by the federal government, based on these bonds, is known as the **national debt**. It is how much money is owed by the federal government.

As our national debt increases, more tax money goes towards paying interest to bondholders. Many critics fear that our national debt is already too high. They say the federal government must stop its practice of deficit spending. They also fear that a high national debt will lead to **inflation** (*rising prices*).

Almost everyone agrees that the President and Congress should try to reduce the national debt—but the question is how? One of the problems is that most of this money is now being spent on "entitlements"—Social Security payments to retirees and Medicare payments for health care. These payments are not supposed to be altered. Yet experts say there just isn't enough money saved in the Social Security system to pay everyone who will be entitled to collect Social Security in the future.

Some say that the federal government must simply cut the amounts it spends, even on entitlement programs or investments in the future like education and research. Others believe that the government should just raise taxes, especially on wealthy Americans. Government spending and taxation also affect job creation. The proper mix between taxation and government spending continues to be an important issue faced by all Americans.

The Role of the Federal Government

Some critics would like to see the role of the federal government reduced. They believe that many of its responsibilities should be handed back to state governments or to the private sector. Others believe that only the federal government can effectively deal with our largest problems, like unemployment.

Gun control

In recent years, a number of depressed or mentally-ill teenagers and adults have taken dangerous weapons into schools or to other public places and taken shots at students or other innocent bystanders. One of the worst tragedies occurred in December 2012, when a mentally-ill 20-year-old shot and killed 20 children and 6 adults at Sandy Hill Elementary School. Because of these incidents, Congress has frequently debated whether to pass laws restricting the ownership and use of firearms. For example, should individuals be able to purchase assault weapons? The National Rifle Association (NRA), a pro-gun group, argues that the right to own and use a gun is protected by the Second Amendment.

The Historian's Apprentice

1. Choose one of the social issues discussed in this chapter, or any other issue facing Americans today. Then prepare a written report or an oral presentation for your class. You might pretend to be a spokesperson for one side of the issue and deliver a speech to the class.

2. Select one of these topics or any other recent social issue and hold a class debate. For example, "Resolved: the United States should ban the sale of assault weapons."

3. Select one of these issues or any other and examine how that issue unites or divides various social, cultural, ethnic, religious, economic, or political groups in the United States. Then present your conclusions in the form of a letter to a penpal or friend who lives outside of the United States.

Focus on Florida

The issues described in this chapter all have their parallels in Florida. The Civil Rights Movement, culminating in demonstrations in St. Augustine led by Dr. Martin Luther King, Jr., permanently changed race relations across the state. Supreme Court decisions made Florida's state legislature more democratic by requiring a redrawing of election districts. Federal policies towards American Indians affected the Seminoles. The construction of highways, the invention of air conditioning and the arrival of jet travel increased the migration of retirees to Florida as well as the volume of out-of-state tourism. Events in Cuba during the Cold War led to a mass exodus that has greatly influenced Florida's demographics and politics.

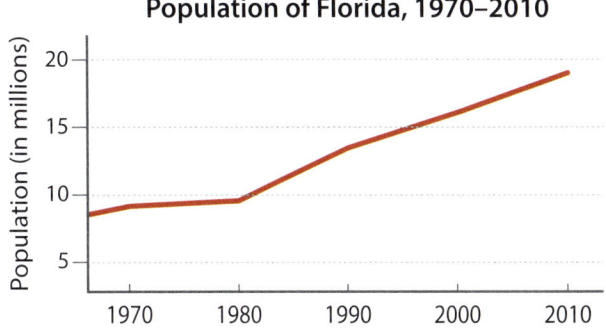

Tourism Today, Florida's largest industry is tourism. In addition to the state's mild winter climate, luxurious sand beaches, luxury hotels, Everglades National Park and Space Coast, the Walt Disney Company opened its Magic Kingdom theme park in Florida in 1971. Other entertainment complexes in the Orlando area soon followed. With close to 90 million visitors each year, Florida has become the number-one travel destination in the world. In 2011, tourism brought close to $67 billion to Florida's economy and accounted for one-quarter of the state's sales-tax revenues.

Immigration Much of Florida's recent increase in population has been due to immigration from Cuba and other Caribbean nations. Since Castro's takeover in 1959, more than 800,000 Cubans have fled to the United States. Most have settled in Florida. Today, two-thirds of the population of Florida's second largest city, Miami, is Hispanic.

Florida's Retirees With improvements in health care and life-style changes, the U.S. population is growing older. Many retirees from other states have moved to Florida. In 2010, residents over 65 years old were 17% of the state's total population; by 2030, they are expected to become a quarter of the state. Some of these retirees live in special retirement communities. A higher percentage of these citizens vote than in other age groups: in 2010, they constituted 31% of the statewide vote. Florida's growing number of retirees and immigrants may have important implications, and lead to future disagreements on priorities.

Terrorism The terrorists who piloted the planes that crashed into the World Trade Center in 2001 were flight-trained and lived for years in Florida. With its location on the southeastern border of the United States and its large immigrant and migrant populations, Florida poses special challenges to safeguard against terrorist acts.

The Historian's Apprentice

- What do you think will be the most important challenges for Florida in the future?
- What are your positions on these issues?
- Return to the paper you wrote at the beginning of the year (see the bottom of page xx) about what you wanted to learn about American history. Did you find out what you wanted to know?

Review Cards

The Impact of the Civil Rights Movement: Social Activism by Minorities

In recent decades, several minorities have followed the example of African Americans and women in fighting prejudice and demanding greater opportunities and equal rights. In general, these groups used non-violent means of protest.

American Indians and the American Indian Movement (AIM)

American Indians have been greatly affected by frequently changing federal policies:
- The Dawes Act (1887) allowed individual Indians to make claims on tribal lands.
- The Indian Reorganization Act of 1934 stopped the breaking up of tribal lands and encouraged Indians to preserve their traditional cultures.
- The Indian Claims Commission Act of 1946 attempted to settle all remaining Indian claims.
- In 1953, the federal government announced the termination of its obligations to the reservations.
- In 1963, the federal government reversed itself again. It ended the termination policy and attempted to encourage tribal life.
- In 1970, President Nixon recognized the obligations of the federal government towards the American Indians.
- The Seminoles have reservation lands in Florida, run a school and museum, and frequently interact with tourists.
- Indian activists introduced the term "Native Americans."

The American Indian Movement, or AIM, was founded in 1968 to mobilize public opinion on behalf of "Red Power."
- Indian activists occupied Alcatraz Island in 1969, and AIM members occupied **Wounded Knee** in 1973.
- AIM demanded increased federal aid and an improved treatment of American Indians in movies, television, and textbooks.

Hispanic Americans and the United Farm Workers Association (UFW)

- Migrant farm workers, many of whom were Hispanic Americans originally from Mexico, were badly paid and badly treated by growers. They performed back-breaking work like picking fruits and vegetables at harvest time.
- **Cesar Chavez** helped to organize the migrant farm workers. Chavez started the **United Farm Workers (UFW)** and launched national boycotts of grapes and lettuce to force growers to recognize the UFW and to treat their migrant workers with greater dignity. Chavez also went on personal hunger strikes.

Other Groups

- Young Americans protesting the Vietnam War led to passage of the **26th Amendment,** which gave eighteen-year-olds the right to vote.
- Americans with disabilities also demanded equal rights. They argued that society had created an artificial environment that had not taken into account their needs for **accessibility.** Individuals with disabilities and their relatives formed DREDF, which sought greater accessibility. The **Americans with Disabilities Act** (1990) requires restaurants, hotels, theaters, and offices to make their facilities **accessible** to people with disabilities. Employers also have to be willing to make **accommodations** to hire individuals with disabilities.
- The **Gray Panthers** were formed by **Maggie Kuhn** to fight against mandatory retirement laws and age discrimination (or "ageism"). The AARP also represents older Americans. The **Age Discrimination in Employment Act of 1967** prohibits discrimination in the workplace on the basis of age.

Immigration

- The **Immigration Act of 1965** was a major turning point in immigration law. It abandoned the system based on national origins introduced in the 1920s and permitted every country to have the same number of lawful immigrants. It also placed limits on immigration from Latin America for the first time.
- The **Refugee Act of 1980** permitted refugees to immigrate to the United States. The **Immigration Reform and Control Act of 1986** gave amnesty to illegal immigrants already living in the U.S.
- The **Immigration Act of 1990** expanded the number of legal immigrants admitted each year. People with close relatives already here or with special job skills are given a priority.
- Today, most immigrants come from Mexico, China, India, the Philippines and a few other countries. There are also a large number of illegal aliens—many from nearby Mexico and Central America. Americans struggle with how to deal with the large number of illegal immigrants now living in the United States, and how to keep our borders secure.

Other Issues

Other important domestic issues facing Americans today include:
- how to reduce pollution and prevent climate change
- the proper role of the federal government in American society
- how to adjust taxation and spending to prevent further growth of the national debt
- gun control: whether to ban assault weapons or place other limits on gun ownership

The Role of the Supreme Court

The Supreme Court rules on appeals of decisions from lower courts. The Supreme Court has played an important role in defending individual rights and the rights of minorities to the "equal protection of the laws."

- **Integration and Busing**
  - In *Brown v. Board of Education*, the Supreme Court outlawed racial segregation in public schools.
  - In *Swann v. Charlotte-Mecklenburg*, it upheld busing as a way to integrate schools.
- **Affirmative Action**
  - In *Regents of the University of California v. Bakke*, the Supreme Court upheld affirmative action admission programs but prohibited race-based quotas.

Other recent cases suggest affirmative action programs have to be narrowly focused on remedying past discrimination.

- **Rights of the Accused**
  - In *Mapp v. Ohio*, the Court held that police were barred from using any evidence in court that was unlawfully obtained.
  - *Miranda v. Arizona* held that the police must warn an accused person of his or her right to remain silent or to have a lawyer present during police questioning.
- **Legislative Reapportionment**
  - *Baker v. Carr* and *Wesberry v. Sanders* required reapportionment of legislative and Congressional districts.
- **Reproductive Rights**
  - *Roe v. Wade* established the right to an abortion in the first trimester of pregnancy. *Planned Parenthood v. Casey* upheld *Roe* but permitted states to add requirements like parental consent.

Terrorism

Terrorists use violence against innocent civilians to obtain concessions from governments or to gain the attention of the media. Terrorism now poses a special risk to all Americans.

- Domestic acts of terrorism include the bombing of the federal building in **Oklahoma City** by Timothy McVeigh and Terry Nichols in 1995.
- International acts of terrorism include the attack on the **World Trade Center** and **Pentagon** on September 11, 2001, by **al-Qaeda.**
- In addition to bringing the United States into war in Afghanistan and Iraq, the **"Global War on Terror"** led to changes at home.
- President Bush created a new cabinet-level department—the **Department of Homeland Security.**
- The **Transportation Security Administration** (TSA) was established to screen passengers before entering commercial airplanes.
- The **USA PATRIOT Act** (or **Patriot Act**) gave the federal government new eavesdropping powers to combat terrorism.
- The Bush administration also used harsh interrogation methods on detainees held outside the United States. Some of these methods were declared unconstitutional by the Supreme Court in *Hamdan v. Rumsfield* (2006).

American Social Issues

Minorities

American Indians

Changing Federal Policies
- Indian Claims Commission
- Termination Policy, 1953
- End of Termination Policy, 1963
- Recognition of Federal Obligations, 1970

American Indian Activists and AIM

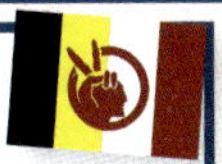

- Demand more aid & better treatment in movies, television, and textbooks
- Term "Native Americans"
- Occupations of Alcatraz (1969) and Wounded Knee (1973)

Hispanic Americans

- Cesar Chavez
- United Farm Workers (UFW)
- Boycotts of grapes and lettuce

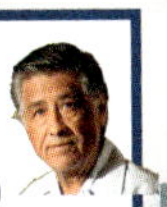

Other Groups

- 26th Amendment: Voting rights for 18-year-olds
- Americans with Disabilities Act (1990) requires accommodations/accessibility
- Gray Panthers—Maggie Kuhn: "fight ageism"
- Age Discrimination in Employment Act of 1967

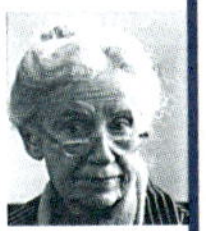

Supreme Court

- Integration/Busing: *Brown, Swann v. Charlotte-Mecklenburg*
- Affirmative Action: *Bakke*
- Rights of Accused: *Mapp, Gideon, Miranda*
- Legislative Reapportionment: *Baker v. Carr, Wesberry v. Sanders*
- Reproductive Rights: *Roe v. Wade*

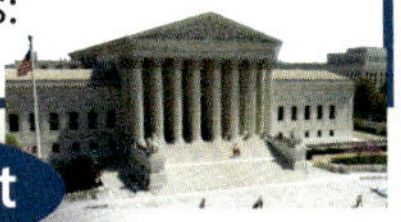

Other Issues

- Pollution/Climate change
- National debt
- Role of federal government
- Gun control

Immigration

- Immigration Act of 1965: Abandoned national origins system; every nation same quota
- Limits on immigration from Latin America
- Refugee Act of 1980
- Immigration Act of 1990 expanded the number of immigrants
- Most immigrants now from Mexico, China, India, and the Philippines
- Issues of borders/illegal aliens

Terrorism

Terrorism: Violence against civilians to win concessions from governments or to gain media attention
- Domestic terrorism: 1995 Bombing of federal building in Oklahoma City
- International terrorism: Attack on the World Trade Center and Pentagon on September 11, 2001, by al-Qaeda.

"Global War on Terror" led to changes at home and abroad
- Department of Homeland Security
- TSA: Screens all commercial air travelers
- USA PATRIOT Act

What Do You Know?

SS.912.A.7.9

1. Which was NOT one of the demands of AIM (American Indian Movement)?

A. more federal aid to American Indians living on reservations

B. revising school textbooks to include the American Indian perspective

C. division and distribution of remaining reservation lands to individuals

D. ending biased depictions of American Indians in movies and television

SS.912.A.7.9

2. The poster on the right was printed in 1978. Which social issue was addressed in this poster?

A. United States immigration policies

B. increasing health risks from pesticides

C. the conditions of migrant farm workers

D. the refusal of labor unions to admit minorities

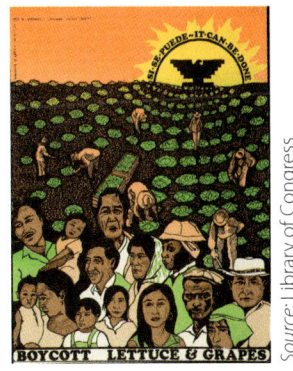

Source: Library of Congress

SS.912.A.7.12

3. The timeline below traces a century of federal policy towards American Indians.

- 1887: Dawes Act
- 1924: Indian Citizenship Act
- 1934: Indian Reorganization Act
- 1946: Indian Claims Commission
- 1953: Federal Government Adopts Termination Policy
- 1963: Federal Government Abandons Termination Policy
- 1970: Federal Government Recognizes Prior Treaty Obligations

Based on the timeline, what conclusion can be made about federal policy towards the American Indians?

A. Federal policy was mainly aimed at preserving American Indian traditions.

B. Federal policy consistently favored assimilation of American Indians into mainstream society.

C. Federal policy was based on the belief that American Indians were better off living on reservations.

D. Federal policy went back and forth between favoring American Indian independence or assimilation.

SS.912.A.7.5

4. What tactic was used by Cesar Chavez to further the goals of the United Farm Workers?

A. voting for new laws to protect workers

B. armed violence against rich farm owners

C. civil disobedience by lying down in fields

D. national boycotts of some types of produce

SS.912.A.7.9

5. How was the movement for rights for individuals with disabilities similar to the earlier Civil Rights Movement?

A. Both filed lawsuits based on the right to equal protection of the laws.

B. Both movements faced greater resistance in the South than the North.

C. Members of both movements faced physical violence from opponents.

D. Both movements required changes to make buildings more accessible.

SS.912.A.7.9

6. Which reform leader is correctly paired with his or her accomplishments?

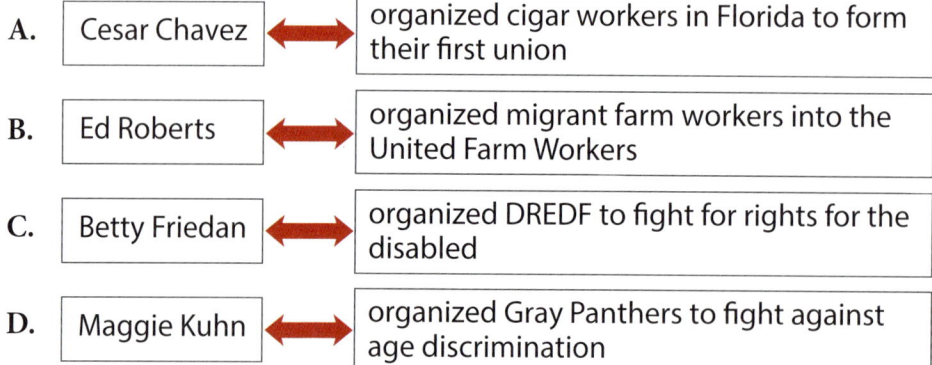

A. Cesar Chavez ↔ organized cigar workers in Florida to form their first union

B. Ed Roberts ↔ organized migrant farm workers into the United Farm Workers

C. Betty Friedan ↔ organized DREDF to fight for rights for the disabled

D. Maggie Kuhn ↔ organized Gray Panthers to fight against age discrimination

SS.912.A.7.8

> Jack Smith is arrested by the police. To obtain a confession, they interrogate Jack for several hours without telling him that has the right to remain silent or to have a lawyer present during the questioning.

7. Which Supreme Court decision did the actions of these police violate?

   A. *Bush v. Gore*

   B. *Mapp v. Ohio*

   C. *Miranda v. Arizona*

   D. *Gideon v. Wainwright*

SS.912.A.7.8

8. What was the reasoning of the U.S. Supreme Court in its opinion in *Roe v. Wade*?

   A. A balancing of the interests of the woman and the state give the woman the right to abort early in her pregnancy but not later.

   B. A woman's right to privacy prevents any outside interference with her right to abort her pregnancy.

   C. Because many religions teach that life begins with pregnancy, abortion cannot be permitted.

   D. The right to an abortion is a question that should be determined by state legislatures and not the courts.

SS.912.A.7.8

9. What did the Supreme Court decide in the case of *Mapp v. Ohio*?

   A. Police should inform suspects of their right to remain silent or have a lawyer present before taking their confession.

   B. If the police violate the law to obtain evidence, they cannot use that evidence against an accused person in court.

   C. The government cannot prevent a newspaper from printing a story without proving that this would be a clear threat to national security.

   D. State universities can consider race in their admissions policies, but they cannot establish a race-based quota system.

SS.912.A.7.8

10. Which Supreme Court decision is correctly paired with its subject?

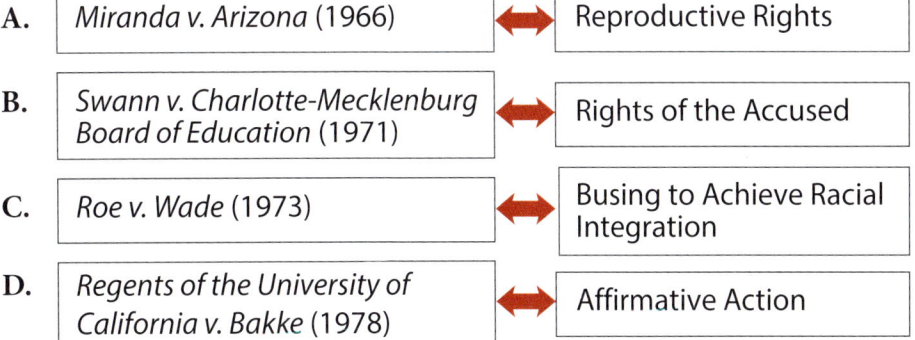

Chapter 17 | American Social Issues

SS.912.A.7.8

11. The excerpt below is from the Supreme Court decision of *Swann v. Charlotte-Mecklenburg Board of Education* (1971):

> All things being equal, with no history of discrimination, it might well be desirable to assign pupils to schools nearest their homes. But all things are not equal in a system that has been deliberately constructed and maintained to enforce racial segregation. The remedy for such segregation may be administratively awkward, inconvenient, and even bizarre in some situations and may impose burdens on some; but all awkwardness and inconvenience cannot be avoided in the interim period when remedial adjustments are being made to eliminate the dual [segregated] school systems.

According to this excerpt, which action was justified?

A. maintaining some racially segregated schools

B. sending students to the schools closest to their homes

C. substituting private and charter schools for public schools

D. busing students to more distant schools for racial integration

SS.912.A.7.8

| *Baker v. Carr* | *Wesberry v. Sanders* |

12. What has been the long-term effect of these decisions?

A. More women have been elected to public office.

B. Poll taxes and literacy tests have been prohibited.

C. Rural districts have generally gained in representation.

D. Representation in state legislatures and Congress has became more equal.

SS.912.A.7.16

13. Which law ended the system of quotas based on national origins and allowed every country an equal number of immigrants into the United States?

A. McCarran Walter Act

B. Immigration Act of 1965

C. Immigration Reform and Control Act of 1986

D. Illegal Immigration Reform and Immigrant Responsibility Act of 1996

SS.912.A.7.16

14. Which applicants were given priority for admission to the United States under the Refugee Act of 1980?

A. those with close relatives already living in the United States

B. those needing immediate medical treatment only offered in the United States

C. those looking for better economic opportunities than exist in their own country

D. those who fear political, social or religious persecution in their own country

SS.912.A.7.16

15. The graph below shows the number of legal immigrants admitted to the United States by decade.

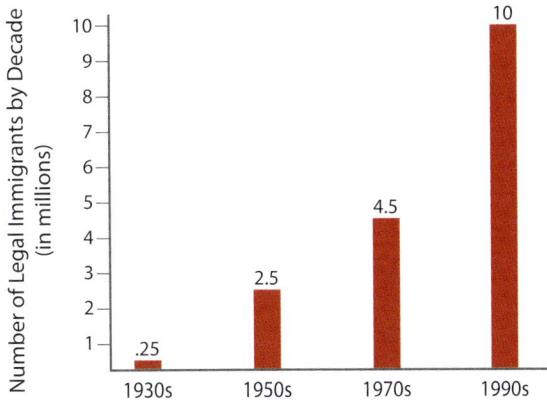

Source: U.S. Department of Homeland Security

Why has the number of legal immigrants to the United States increased since the 1980s?

A. Food shortages forced more people to migrate to the United States.

B. The United States has not secured its borders with Mexico and Canada.

C. More liberal immigration laws have allowed more legal immigrants to enter.

D. Television and the Internet have attracted more young people to the United States.

SS.912.A.7.16

16. What has been one of the effects of the Illegal Immigration Reform and Immigrant Responsibility Act of 1996?

A. Aliens suspected of terrorism can be deported based on secret evidence.

B. Illegal aliens in the United States can become legal immigrants more easily than those outside the United States.

C. The number of years a legal alien must wait before applying for United States citizenship has been reduced.

D. Applicants who pass an English language test are given priority over others for admission to the United States.

SS.912.A.7.15

17. How did the Bush administration justify the use of "waterboarding" and other harsh interrogation techniques on suspected terrorists?

A. Since terrorists had used torture on captured Americans, the United States was justified in using torture.

B. The torture of a few individuals can sometimes provide information that saves thousands of innocent lives.

C. Although these methods were harsh, they were not torture and they saved lives from possible terrorist attacks.

D. Harsh interrogation methods do not usually yield accurate information, but they deter other people from becoming terrorists.

Chapter 17 | American Social Issues

Unit VI: The Modern United States: Global Leadership and Domestic Issues (Chapters 14–17)

Identify or define each of the following terms.

Brown v. Board of Education (1954) _____

_____

Montgomery bus boycott _____

_____

Dr. Martin Luther King, Jr. _____

_____

Civil Rights Act of 1964 _____

_____

The "Great Society" _____

_____

Domino Theory _____

_____

Tet Offensive _____

_____

Vietnamization _____

_____

Richard M. Nixon _____

_____

Equal Rights Amendment _____

_____

Camp David Accords _____

_____

Election of 2000 _____

_____

September 11, 2001 ("9-11") _____

_____

Globalization _____

_____

United Farm Workers _____

_____

Unit VI | Activity 1

Crossword Puzzle

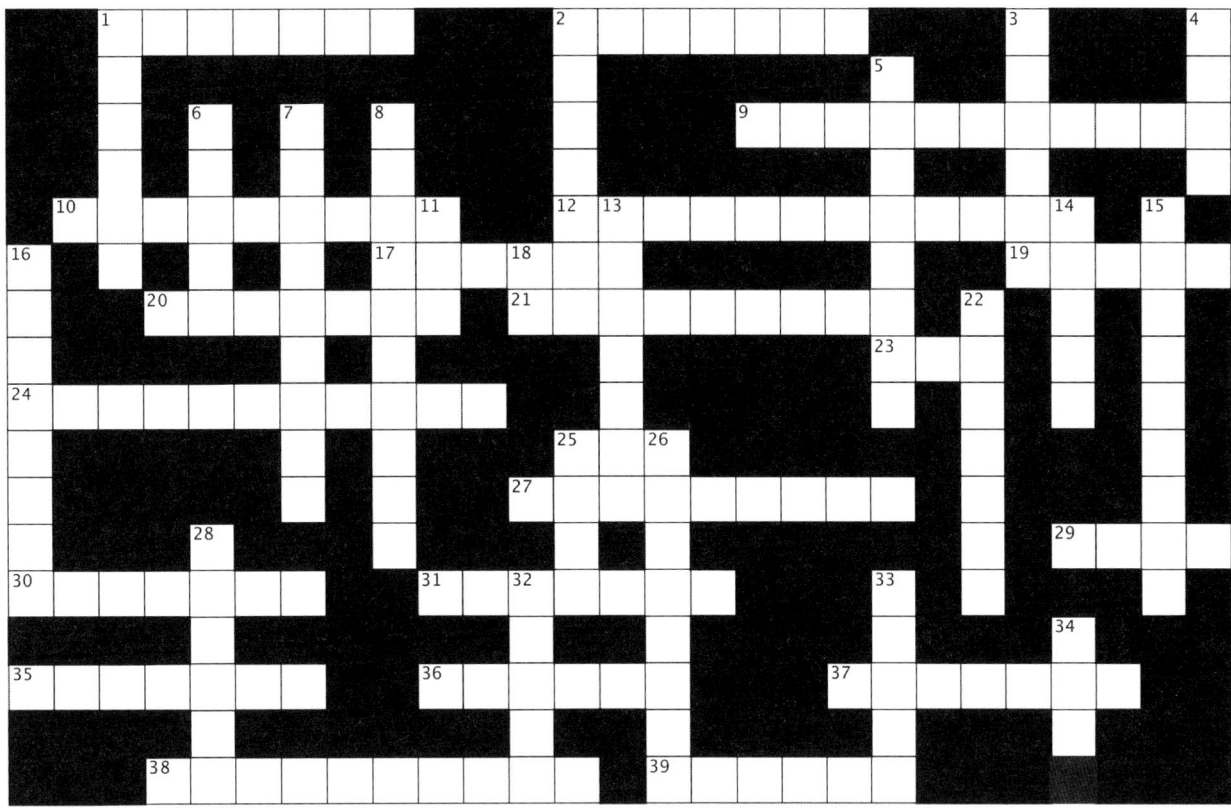

Across

1. To act like everyone else
2. Interracial groups whose members refused to sit in segregated sections of buses were called _____ Riders
9. Gorbachev's economic reform introduced in the Soviet Union
10. Project _____ _____ helped prepare underprivileged children for elementary school
12. The Americans with _____ Act requires that public spaces be physically accessible to all
17. Under the _____ Doctrine, aid was sent to anti-Communist fighters in Grenada, Afghanistan, and Nicaragua
19. President who withdrew America from the war in Vietnam
20. The _____ Act gave the federal government new powers to combat terrorism
21. French colony in the 19th century, later seized by Japan
23. _____ v. Wade guaranteed women the right to end a pregnancy in first trimester
24. _____ action programs led to more hiring of women and minorities
25. Goods and services produced annually by Americans (abbrev.)
27. Woman arrested for refusing to sit at back of segregated bus
29. Main speaker at the March on Washington (1963)
30. Group behind the 9-11 attacks
31. The easing of hostility or strained relations between countries
35. Iraqi dictator captured during the Iraq War
36. Herbicide used to kill jungle cover in Vietnam: Agent _____
37. President who called for a "War on Poverty"
38. A founder of the Student Non-Violent Coordinating Committee: Stokely _____
39. Capital of South Vietnam

Down

1. Cesar _____ organized Hispanic migrant farm workers
2. Author of *The Feminine Mystique*
3. Chief Justice Earl _____ expanded the rights of all Americans
4. The _____ Panthers formed to fight against age discrimination
5. Johnson's "Great Society" program enacted _____, health insurance for those over 65
6. Newspaper, television, and radio are forms of _____
7. Scandal that ended Nixon's Presidency
8. _____ use violence against innocent civilians to obtain concessions by governments or to gain media attention
11. The Vietcong seized control of many of South Vietnam's major cities in the _____ Offensive
13. AIM was founded to mobilize public opinion on behalf of _____
14. African-American students staged a __-__ at a Greensboro, North Carolina lunch counter
15. Vietnamese nationalist and revolutionary
16. McVeigh and Nichols were domestic terrorists responsible for the _____ City bombing
18. Servicemen's Readjustment Act, or _____ Bill of Rights
22. President John F. _____ proposed the Civil Rights Bill
25. George W. Bush came to the Presidency after a controversial election against Al _____
26. A militant group that patrolled black neighborhoods to protect residents from police violence: the Black _____
28. The division of Vietnam into North and South was enacted in the _____ Accords
32. WTO: World _____ Organization
33. _____ v. Board of Education (1954) case ended racial segregation in public schools
34. Association founded by Betty Friedan and others as the voice of the women's movement

Complete the chart below on some of the most important U.S. foreign policy events in the past 50 years.

Event	Description	Significance
Cuban Missile Crisis (1962)		
Nixon's Visit to China (1972)		
Camp David Accords (1977)		
Iran Hostage Crisis (1979–1980)		
Fall of Berlin Wall (1989)		
Persian Gulf War (1991)		
September 11, 2001 attacks		
Iraq War (2003–2010)		

Fill in the chart below on the struggles of various groups in American society to achieve equal rights.

Group	Demands	Strategies	Accomplishments
Civil Rights Movement (African Americans)			
Women			
American Indians			
Migrant Farm Workers			

Unit VI | Activity 3

A Practice End-of-Course Assessment in U.S. History, 1850–present

SS.912.A.2.1

1. What was the significance of the *Dred Scott* decision?

   A. The Supreme Court overruled attempts by Congress to limit the spread of slavery.

   B. The Supreme Court held that the practice of slavery was unconstitutional.

   C. While Lincoln objected to the decision, Stephen Douglas supported it.

   D. Dred Scott and his wife spent the rest of their lives in slavery.

SS.912.A.3.13

2. What was the main reason for fighting in Florida during the Civil War?

   A. The Union army wanted to prevent cattle and crops in Florida from reaching Confederate troops.

   B. Northern commanders planned to divide the South by marching through Florida.

   C. The main Southern fleet was stationed in ports along the Florida coast.

   D. Robert E. Lee, the Southern commander, owned land in Florida.

SS.912.A.2.3

3. How did President Andrew Johnson's views on Reconstruction differ from those of Congress?

   A. President Johnson refused to pardon former Confederate leaders, while Congress wanted to treat them leniently.

   B. President Johnson was shocked at the Southern "Black Codes," while Congressional leaders saw them as necessary to restore order.

   C. President Johnson accepted Southern "Black Codes," while Congress overturned them with a Civil Rights bill prohibiting racial discrimination.

   D. President Johnson thought the readmission of states into the Union should be decided by Congress, while Congressional leaders saw it as his responsibility.

SS.912.A.2.6

4. How did the "Black Codes" of 1865–1866 differ from the "Jim Crow" laws of the 1880s and 1890s?

   A. Black Codes created segregated public schools; Jim Crow laws prohibited African Americans from learning to read.

   B. Black Codes prohibited use of the same public facilities by different races; Jim Crow laws prohibited voting by African Americans.

   C. Black Codes prohibited freedmen from traveling freely, serving on juries or exercising civil rights; Jim Crow laws required racial segregation.

   D. Black Codes required "separate but equal" facilities for different races; Jim Crow laws stated some races were "not entitled to social and political equality."

SS.912.A.2.7

5. The painting on the left depicts the Battle of Little Bighorn in 1876.

   What was the primary objective of the U.S. policy that led to the conflict shown in the painting?

   A. to protect the safety of the transcontinental railroad from attack

   B. to force American Indian tribes on the Great Plains to live on reservations

   C. to remove remaining American Indian tribes from east of the Mississippi River

   D. to capture deserters from the Union and Confederate armies after the Civil War

SS.912.A.3.1

6. Which was NOT one of the ways in which 19th-century settlers dealt with the challenges of farming on the Great Plains?

   A. They used barbed wire for fencing.

   B. They burned cow and buffalo chips for fuel.

   C. They relied on irrigation from nearby lakes for water.

   D. They used steel plows to dig furrows into the tough soil.

SS.912.A.3.2

7. The patents below were filed by Alexander Graham Bell and Thomas Alva Edison.

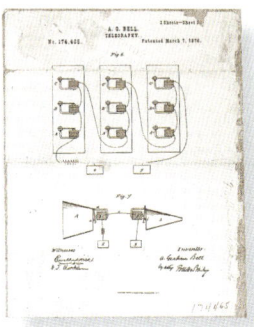 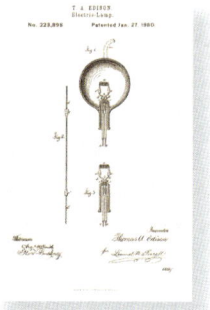

   How did these inventions affect the United States economy?

   A. They created a new demand for electricity.

   B. They prevented the growth of monopolies.

   C. They led to increased working hours in factories.

   D. They moved the center of American manufacturing to the South.

SS.912.A.3.5

8. Which American inventor became a millionaire by developing new hair-care and cosmetic products for African-American women?

   A. Sarah Goode   C. Garrett Morgan

   B. Madam C.J. Walker   D. Jan Ernst Matzeliger

SS.912.A.3.5

9. How did Andrew Carnegie, John D. Rockefeller, J. P. Morgan, and Henry Ford help to transform the American economy?

   A. They were the first to introduce interchangeable parts to manufacturing processes.

   B. They introduced the use of conveyor belts and assembly lines in their factories.

   C. Their willingness to engage in collective bargaining with unions improved conditions for workers.

   D. They created new industries requiring large investments, which resulted in cheaper products for consumers.

SS.912.A.3.9

10. Which statement best describes the American labor movement in the late 19th century?

    A. Workers organized their own labor unions against harsh conditions despite public hostility.

    B. Government officials encouraged workers to form labor unions because they distrusted business-owners.

    C. Union leaders were unable to recruit members because most workers were satisfied with their conditions.

    D. Disagreements between native-born and immigrant workers made the organization of labor unions almost impossible.

SS.912.A.3.10

11. Which ideology favored self-governing communities over organized government?

    A. Communism   C. Capitalism

    B. Anarchism   D. Socialism

SS.912.A.3.11

12. The cartoon on the left was published by Thomas Nast in the 1870s.

    What is the view of the cartoonist about the power of Tammany Hall in New York City?

    A. New York City government was unaffected by Tammany Hall.

    B. Tammany Hall maintained its power by falsifying vote counts in elections.

    C. Immigrants were happy to vote for Tammany Hall to repay it for its services.

    D. Many ordinary citizens felt powerful because Tammany Hall listened to them.

"THAT'S WHAT'S THE MATTER."
Boss Tweed: "As long as I count the votes, what are you going to do about it? Say?"

A Practice End-of-Course Assessment in U.S. History, 1850–present

SS.912.A.3.7

13. The graph below shows the population of Chinese immigrants and their descendants in the United States from 1860 to 1920.

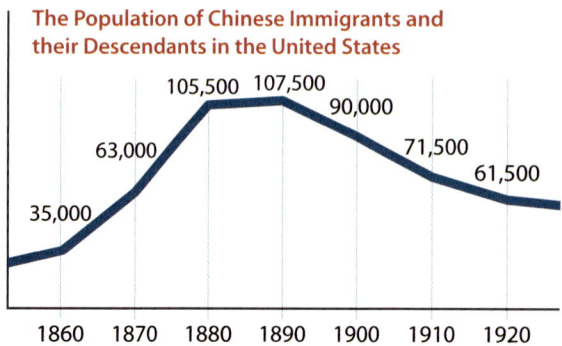

Why did the population of Chinese Americans decrease, as shown on the graph, when the populations of many other ethnic groups were increasing?

A. Improved economic conditions in China discouraged further emigration to the United States.

B. Congressional legislation in the 1880s banned any further immigration of workers from China.

C. After completion of the transcontinental railroad, there was a shortage of jobs in western states.

D. China entered into a "Gentlemen's Agreement" with the United States not to permit further emigration.

SS.912.A.3.1

14. The excerpt below is from William Jennings Bryan's speech at the Democratic National Convention in 1896.

> Having behind us the producing masses of this nation and the world, supported by the commercial interests, the laboring interests, and the toilers everywhere, we will answer their demand for a gold standard by saying to them: "You shall not press down upon the brow of labor this crown of thorns; you shall not crucify mankind upon a cross of gold."

Why did Bryan's rural supporters believe that the gold standard was oppressive?

A. They knew that railroad owners and grain elevator operators usually insisted on being paid with gold coin.

B. They believed that a policy of bimetallism would lead crop prices to rise, making farm debts less burdensome.

C. They feared that speculators like Jay Gould and James Fisk would manipulate prices by cornering the gold market.

D. They felt that reliance on the gold standard in international trade had made it difficult for farmers to export crops overseas.

SS.912.A.3.12

15. The excerpt below was written by Upton Sinclair in his novel *The Jungle* in 1905.

> There was never the least attention paid to what was cut up for sausage... There would be meat that had tumbled out on the floor, in the dirt and sawdust, where the workers had trampled and spit uncounted billions of consumption germs. There would be meat stored in great piles in rooms; and the water from leaky roofs would drip over it, and thousands of rats would race about on it. It was too dark in these storage places to see well, but a man could run his hand over these piles of meat and sweep off handfuls of the dried dung of rats. These rats were nuisances, and the packers would put poisoned bread out for them; they would die, and then rats, bread, and meat would go into the hoppers together.... and be sent out to the public's breakfast.

Which federal law was passed in reaction to this description?

- A. 17th Amendment
- B. Federal Reserve Act
- C. Meat Inspection Act
- D. Clayton Antitrust Act

SS.912.A.3.12

16. The excerpt below is from the Sherman Antitrust Act, enacted in 1890.

> Every contract, combination in the form of trust or otherwise, or conspiracy, in restraint of trade or commerce among the several States, or with foreign nations, is declared to be illegal.

What was the goal of this legislation?

- A. to prevent businesses from unfairly exploiting their laborers
- B. to use the power of government to promote economic growth and full employment
- C. to encourage companies to take advantage of their patent rights and natural monopolies
- D. to maintain fair competition and to halt unfair practices damaging to consumers and competitors

SS.912.A.3.12

17. The information on the left describes key events in the development of U.S. conservation policy.

- Withdrew 1.5 million acres of public lands from sale
- Designated the Devils Tower in Wyoming and the Petrified Forest and Grand Canyon in Arizona as National Monuments
- Created the National Conservation Commission

Which Progessive President was responsible for these achievements?

- A. Woodrow Wilson
- B. William McKinley
- C. Theodore Roosevelt
- D. William Howard Taft

SS.912.A.4.3

18. Which new technique for selling newspapers contributed to the outbreak of the Spanish-American War?

- A. muckraking
- B. yellow journalism
- C. jingoism
- D. Social Darwinism

SS.912.A.4.3

19. The newspaper headline on the left describes a significant event in U.S. foreign affairs.

How did this event contribute to the United States' entry into the Spanish-American War?

A. It led to anti-government demonstrations in the United States.

B. It enraged Cuban Americans in Florida who had lost their relatives.

C. It revealed that the United States needed to have colonies in the Caribbean.

D. It became difficult for President McKinley to resist demands to intervene in Cuba.

SS.912.A.4.2

20. The timeline below shows the dates of U.S. annexation of several territories.

Which argument did American imperialists make in favor of these annexations?

A. These territories were necessary for protection of the Panama Canal.

B. The local populations of these territories had asked to be annexed.

C. These territories would provide good coaling stations for trade with East Asia.

D. The United States should prepare them for self-government and independence.

SS.912.A.4.1

21. The excerpt below is from President Theodore Roosevelt's message to Congress in 1905.

> That our rights and interests are deeply concerned in the maintenance of the doctrine is so clear as hardly to need argument. This is especially true in view of the construction of the Panama Canal. . . . [I]t is very inadvisable to permit any foreign power to take possession, even temporarily, of the custom houses of an American republic in order to enforce the payment of its obligations; for such temporary occupation might turn into a permanent occupation. The only escape from these alternatives may at any time be that we must ourselves undertake to bring about some arrangement by which so much as possible of a just obligation can be paid.

Which policy is described in this message?

A. Roosevelt Corollary

B. "Open Door" Policy

C. Dollar Diplomacy

D. Watchful Waiting

SS.912.A.5

22. On January 31, 1917, the German Ambassador to the United States presented the following message to the United States.

> Since two years and a half England is using her naval power for a criminal attempt to force Germany into submission by starvation. . . . From February 1, 1917, sea traffic will be stopped with every available weapon and without further notice in the following blockade zones around Great Britain, France, Italy and in the Eastern Mediterranean.

Why did the use of unrestricted submarine warfare in the Atlantic by Germany, as announced in the note above, so enrage American public opinion?

   A. Submarine warfare was prohibited under international law.
   B. The United States did not have as large a submarine fleet as Germany.
   C. Submarines attacked without warning and did not have enough room to take on survivors.
   D. The use of submarines for a naval blockade was causing starvation in Great Britain and France.

SS.912.A.7

23. The photo on the left shows infantry soldiers in France during World War I.

   Which sentence best explains the conditions shown in the photograph?

   A. Shortages of fuel made it difficult for armies in France to use tanks or airplanes.
   B. The use of machine guns made it difficult for soldiers to advance across open fields.
   C. Lack of public support for the war made it safer for soldiers to remain isolated in trenches.
   D. Troops were kept separate from civilians as a safety precaution before the discovery of antibiotics.

SS.912.A.4.9

24. The excerpt below is from the Supreme Court in *Schenck v. United States* (1919).

> The most stringent protection of free speech would not protect a man in falsely shouting fire in a theatre and causing a panic. . . . The question in every case is whether the words used are used in such circumstances and are of such a nature as to create a clear and present danger that they will bring about the substantive evils that Congress has a right to prevent.

What action was taken in consequence of this decision?

   A. Conscientious objectors were forced to engage in combat because the United States was in danger.
   B. Charles Schenck was imprisoned for distributing thousands of leaflets urging young men to resist the draft.
   C. German Americans living on the East Coast were relocated to internment centers to avoid possible sabotage attempts.
   D. Charles Schenck was permitted to go free because the Court did not believe his actions created a "clear and present" danger.

SS.912.A.4.6

25. Which federal agency is correctly paired with its achievements during World War I (1917–1919)?

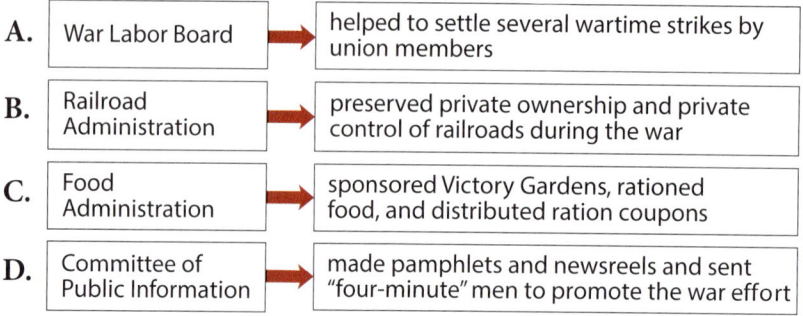

A. War Labor Board → helped to settle several wartime strikes by union members

B. Railroad Administration → preserved private ownership and private control of railroads during the war

C. Food Administration → sponsored Victory Gardens, rationed food, and distributed ration coupons

D. Committee of Public Information → made pamphlets and newsreels and sent "four-minute" men to promote the war effort

SS.912.A.4.10

26. The Treaty of Versailles, signed on June 28, 1919, included the article below.

> **Article 231** The Allied and Associated Governments affirm and Germany accepts the responsibility of Germany and her allies for causing all the loss and damage to which the Allied and Associated Governments and their nationals have been subjected as a consequence of the war imposed upon them by the aggression of Germany and her allies.

What was a consequence of this article?

A. German voters agreed to reduce the size of their armed forces.

B. Germany was required to pay reparations to the Allied Powers.

C. The League of Nations refused to admit Germany as a member.

D. The U.S. Senate failed to ratify the treaty in protest against this article.

SS.912.A.5.2

27. The diagram below provides details about United States history.

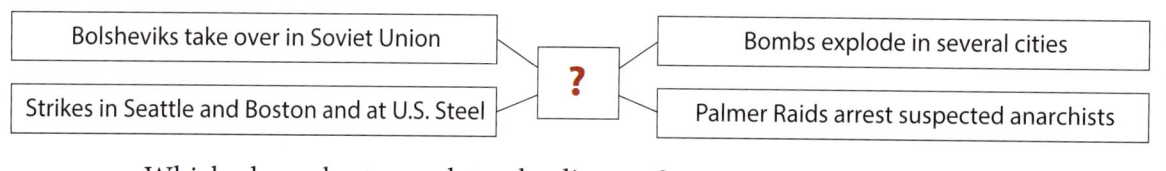

Which phrase best completes the diagram?

A. Red Scare
B. McCarthyism
C. Homestead Strike
D. Civil Rights Movement

SS.912.A.5.5

28. What was the goal of the Washington Naval Conference, the Geneva Disarmament Conference and the Kellogg-Briand Pact?

A. to promote American investment abroad

B. to achieve lasting peace without the League of Nations

C. to prepare the Western Allies against German rearmament

D. to strengthen U.S. naval power relative to the European powers and Japan

SS.912.A.5.4

29. Which phrase best completes the diagram?

   A. the construction of railroads
   B. the demobilization after World War I
   C. the spread of radio and automobiles
   D. the spread of televisions and jet travel

SS.912.A.5.10

30. Why are the Twenties often considered to have been a turning point for American women?

   A. Women were generally able to remain in the jobs they had filled while men were away during World War I.
   B. Women gained social and economic equality with men through new affirmative action programs and federal legislation.
   C. Women were guaranteed the right to vote, wore less restrictive clothing, and enjoyed increased employment opportunities.
   D. Women began taking more aggressive steps on behalf of women's suffrage, including marches and demonstrations in front of the White House.

SS.912.A.5.8

31. Based on these excerpts, in what way were the views of W.E.B. Du Bois and Alain Locke similar?

> The Negro race, like all races, is going to be saved by its exceptional men. The problem of education, then, among Negroes must first of all deal with the Talented Tenth; it is the problem of developing the best of this race . . .
>
> —W.E.B. Du Bois, *The Talented Tenth*, 1903
>
> Negro life is not only establishing new contacts and founding new centers, it is finding a new soul. There is a fresh spiritual and cultural focusing. We have, as the heralding sign, an unusual outburst of creative expression. There is a renewed race-spirit that consciously and proudly sets itself apart.
>
> —Alain Locke, *The New Negro*, 1925

   A. Both opposed sending African Americans for further vocational education.
   B. Both believed that the racist attitudes of the majority of Americans could not be changed.
   C. Both looked to the efforts of talented African Americans to overcome racial prejudice.
   D. Both believed that conditions for African Americans were just as bad in the North as in the South.

SS.912.A.5.11

32. The cartoon below, "Watch Your Step," appeared in November 1925.

The photograph below was taken in Chicago in February 1931.

Which event contributed to the changes from the time of the political cartoon to the conditions shown in the photograph?

A. demobilization after World War I
B. the rise of Nazism in Germany
C. "Black Tuesday"
D. the "Red Scare"

SS.912.A.5.11

33. The picture below shows a dust storm approaching Stratford, Texas, in 1933.

What was one effect of this and similar events across the Great Plains in the 1930s?

A. growth of the banking industry from farm loans
B. mass migration to California and other states
C. suspension of government assistance to farmers
D. increase in farm production on the Great Plains

SS.912.5.11

34. How did President Franklin D. Roosevelt's response to the Great Depression differ from Herbert Hoover's?

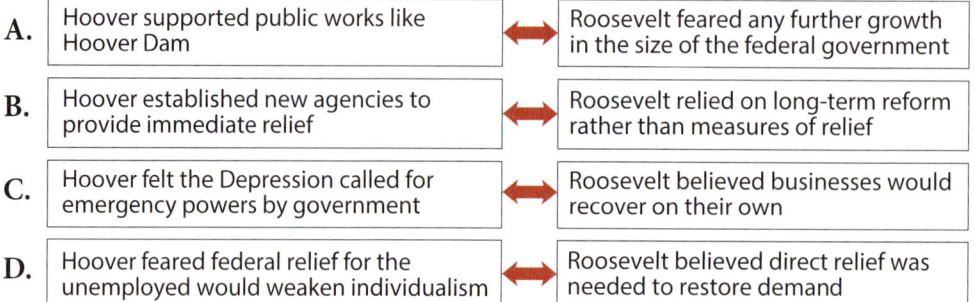

EOC-10   A Practice End-of-Course Assessment in U.S. History, 1850–present

SS.912.5.11

35. Which New Deal agency helped businesses draw up their own voluntary codes of fair practice, including standard prices and minimum wages, but was later held to be unconstitutional by the Supreme Court?

    A. Tennessee Valley Authority
    B. Civilian Conservation Corps
    C. Social Security Administration
    D. National Recovery Administration

SS.912.A.6.5

36. The list below provides information about conditions in the 1940s.

> - Migration to the West and the North
> - The selling of war bonds
> - Victory Gardens
> - Mandatory rationing
> - Increased employment
> - Enlistment of Women

Which conditions are identified in the list?

    A. causes of World War II

    B. effects of World War II on methods of warfare

    C. domestic effects of World War II

    D. social impact of the Progressive Era

SS.912.A.6.1

37. Which statement best explains the Allied victory over Germany in World War II?

    A. The massacre of European Jews and other groups made the war unpopular in Germany.

    B. The Soviets had a larger army, Americans manufactured more weapons, and Germany faced a war on several fronts.

    C. The Allies were able to use missiles, atomic weapons and other new weapons against Nazi Germany.

    D. The German army lacked experienced officers, training and supplies, and therefore quickly surrendered after the D-Day invasion.

SS.912.A.6.7

38. The excerpt below comes from an official indictment (*accusation*).

> All the defendants ... participated as leaders, organizers, instigators, or accomplices in the formulation or execution of a common plan or conspiracy to commit, or which involved the commission of, Crimes against Peace, War Crimes, and Crimes against Humanity.... [T]he defendants ... carried out ruthless wars against countries and populations ... including ... [the] murder, ill-treatment, [and] deportation for slave labor ... of civilian populations.

Based on the excerpt, where were these accusations made?

    A. trial of Sacco and Vanzetti
    B. Dumbarton Oaks Conference
    C. Nuremberg trials
    D. Munich Conference

SS.912.A.6.9

39. The diagram below provides information about an international organization.

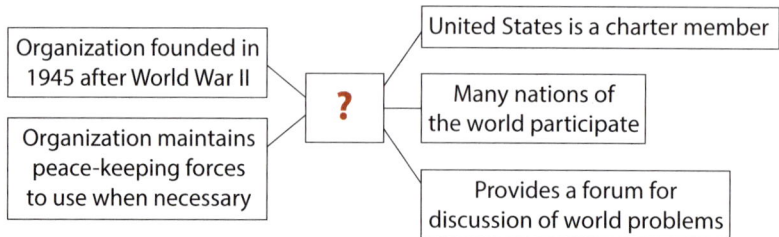

Which phrase best completes the diagram?

    A. United Nations   C. War Refugee Board

    B. League of Nations   D. Organization of American States

SS.912.A.6.10

40. The statement below was made by President Truman in an address to Congress in March 1947.

> I believe it must be the policy of the United States to support free peoples who are resisting attempted subjugation [overthrow] by armed minorities or by outside pressures. . . .

Which event was Truman referring to in this speech?

    A. Stalin's refusal to permit free elections in Poland

    B. the danger of a North Korean invasion of South Korea

    C. the threat of a Communist takeover in Greece or Turkey

    D. American participation in the trials of former Nazi leaders

SS.912.A.6.8

41. The timeline below displays a sequence of events in the late 1940s and early 1950s.

What would be the most appropriate title for this timeline?

    A. The Cold War Spreads to Asia and Latin America

    B. The Dangers of Nuclear Proliferation during the Cold War

    C. The Cold War Creates an Atmosphere of Suspicion at Home

    D. Soviet Spies Successfully Infiltrate the United States

SS.912.A.6.13

42. The memorandum on the left was written by President Kennedy in September 1961.

In the last paragraph, President Kennedy wrote:

"I am also interested in knowing when and under what circumstances we would expect to use West German forces if the East Germans confront us."

Which situation was President Kennedy addressing?

   A. The failure of the Soviet Union to permit elections in Poland.
   B. The Soviet blockade of all road and rail routes to West Berlin.
   C. The building of the Berlin Wall to separate East and West Berlin.
   D. The construction of silos for missiles with nuclear warheads in Cuba.

SS.912.A.6.13

43. What was the significance of the Cuban Missile Crisis?

   A. The world came close to a nuclear war.
   B. Khrushchev condemned the actions of Castro.
   C. The United States overthrew Communism in Cuba.
   D. The United States failed to give air cover to Cuban exiles.

SS.912.A.7.8

44. On what grounds did the Supreme Court rule that racial segregation in public schools was unconstitutional in *Brown v. Board of Education*?

   A. The practice of racial segregation is based on personal prejudices that Americans should strive to overcome.
   B. Southern states had not invested in African-American schools, which were not equal in quality to white schools.
   C. Segregated schools were by their nature unequal because they gave African-American children a sense of inferiority.
   D. The United States will not be able to compete internationally if it does not help all its citizens to reach their full potential.

SS.912.A.7.5

45. The excerpt below is from Dr. Martin Luther King, Jr.'s "Letter from Birmingham Jail" in 1963.

   > There comes a time when the cup of endurance runs over, and men are no longer willing to be plunged into the abyss of despair.

Which steps did Dr. King advocate African Americans should take to end those conditions they could no longer endure?

   A. taking hostages and launching terrorist attacks
   B. rioting in cities and forming armed bands for self-defense
   C. engaging in marches, boycotts, and non-violent civil disobedience
   D. adopting measures to separate from other groups in American society

SS.912.A.7.7

46. Which organizations favored independent actions by African Americans to improve their conditions without collaborating with sympathetic members of other races?

    A. Urban League and the NAACP
    B. Black Panthers and SNCC after 1967
    C. CORE and Mississippi Freedom Democratic Party
    D. Montgomery Improvement Association and SCLC

SS.912.A.7.3

47. Which of the following was an important gain for women in the 1970s?

    A. ratification of the Equal Rights Amendment
    B. equal representation of women and men in corporate management
    C. passage of the Equal Opportunity in Education Act, known as Title IX
    D. ratification of a constitutional amendment guaranteeing women's suffrage

SS.912.A.6.14

48. Which belief prompted American leaders to enter into the Vietnam War?

    A. They believed that Vietnamese Communists would be difficult to defeat.
    B. They felt that the United States had historic ties with the people of Vietnam.
    C. They saw the war as an opportunity to overturn the Communist government in nearby China.
    D. They feared if South Vietnam fell to Communists, other countries in Southeast Asia would also do so.

SS.912.A.7.10

49. Which argument was raised by domestic critics of the Vietnam War?

    A. Military service, even on behalf of a just cause, should never be compulsory.
    B. Most South Vietnamese welcomed establishment of a Communist government.
    C. An all-out military effort by the United States would quickly bring a military victory.
    D. The U.S. government had misrepresented facts about the war to the American public.

SS.912.A.6.13

50. What was the primary goal of President Nixon's policy of *détente*?

    A. to create stronger ties with Latin America
    B. to improve relations with Western Europe
    C. to decrease tensions with the Soviet Union
    D. to recognize the Communist government in China

SS.912.A.7.5

51. The excerpt below is from a speech on the problems of migrant farm workers.

> The road to social justice for the farm worker is the road of unionization. Our cause, our strike against table grapes and our international boycott are all founded upon our deep conviction that the form of collective self-help, which is unionization, holds far more hope for the farm worker than any other single approach, whether public or private.

Which leader proposed unionization as an answer for these workers?

- **A.** Cesar Chavez
- **B.** Malcolm X
- **C.** Martin Luther King, Jr.
- **D.** Rosa Parks

SS.912.A.7.16

52. The conversation below gives the views of two citizens on immigration policy.

Speaker 1: Immigrants are generally the hardest working people in their country. They want to improve conditions for themselves and their families. That is why they come to the United States. Even illegal aliens contribute to the American economy, often by taking the hardest jobs.

Speaker 2: It would be unfair to give an illegal alien priority in admission to the United States. These are people who broke our laws. If we reward them, then everyone will be tempted to come here illegally.

Which law would have been favored by Speaker 1 but opposed by Speaker 2?

- **A.** McCarran-Walter Act
- **B.** Immigration Act of 1965
- **C.** Immigration Reform and Control Act of 1986
- **D.** Illegal Immigration Reform and Immigrant Responsibility Act of 1996

SS.912.A.7.17

53. How was Florida affected by the invention of air conditioning, the construction of highways, and the expansion of jet travel?

- **A.** State officials refused to accept more exiles from Cuba to prevent overcrowding.
- **B.** Tourism and the migration of retirees from other states to Florida greatly increased.
- **C.** State officials were forced to raise state income taxes to pay for more social services.
- **D.** The average age of Florida residents became lower than the rest of the United States.

SS.912.A.7.15

54. Why was the Department of Homeland Security formed?

- **A.** to find and capture Osama bin Laden
- **B.** to conduct screenings of passengers at airports
- **C.** to capture those who caused the Oklahoma bombing
- **D.** to coordinate federal agencies in the fight against terrorism

A Practice End-of-Course Assessment in U.S. History, 1850–present

North America

The United States in 1877

The United States Today

The Constitution of the United States

We the People of the United States, in Order to form a more perfect Union, establish Justice, insure domestic Tranquility, provide for the common defence, promote the general Welfare, and secure the Blessings of Liberty to ourselves and our Posterity, do ordain and establish this Constitution for the United States of America.

Article I

Section. 1. All legislative Powers herein granted shall be vested in a Congress of the United States, which shall consist of a Senate and House of Representatives.

Section. 2. The House of Representatives shall be composed of Members chosen every second Year by the People of the several States, and the Electors in each State shall have the Qualifications requisite for Electors of the most numerous Branch of the State Legislature.

No Person shall be a Representative who shall not have attained to the Age of twenty five Years, and been seven Years a Citizen of the United States, and who shall not, when elected, be an Inhabitant of that State in which he shall be chosen.

Representatives and direct Taxes shall be apportioned among the several States which may be included within this Union, according to their respective Numbers, which shall be determined by adding to the whole Number of free Persons, including those bound to Service for a Term of Years, and excluding Indians not taxed, three fifths of all other Persons. The actual Enumeration shall be made within three Years after the first Meeting of the Congress of the United States, and within every subsequent Term of ten Years, in such Manner as they shall by Law direct. The Number of Representatives shall not exceed one for every thirty Thousand, but each State shall have at Least one Representative; and until such enumeration shall be made, the State of New Hampshire shall be entitled to chuse three, Massachusetts eight, Rhode-Island and Providence Plantations one, Connecticut five, New-York six, New Jersey four, Pennsylvania eight, Delaware one, Maryland six, Virginia ten, North Carolina five, South Carolina five, and Georgia three.

When vacancies happen in the Representation from any State, the Executive Authority thereof shall issue Writs of Election to fill such Vacancies.

The House of Representatives shall chuse their Speaker and other Officers; and shall have the sole Power of Impeachment.

Section. 3. The Senate of the United States shall be composed of two Senators from each State, chosen by the Legislature thereof, for six Years; and each Senator shall have one Vote.

Immediately after they shall be assembled in Consequence of the first Election, they shall be divided as equally as may be into three Classes. The Seats of the Senators of the first Class shall be vacated at the Expiration of the second Year, of the second Class at the Expiration of the fourth Year, and of the third Class at the Expiration of the sixth Year, so that one third may be chosen every second Year; and if Vacancies happen by Resignation, or otherwise, during the Recess of the Legislature of any State, the Executive thereof may make temporary Appointments until the next Meeting of the Legislature, which shall then fill such Vacancies.

No Person shall be a Senator who shall not have attained to the Age of thirty Years, and been nine Years a Citizen of the United States, and who shall not, when elected, be an Inhabitant of that State for which he shall be chosen.

The Vice President of the United States shall be President of the Senate, but shall have no Vote, unless they be equally divided.

The Senate shall chuse their other Officers, and also a President pro tempore, in the Absence of the Vice President, or when he shall exercise the Office of President of the United States.

The Senate shall have the sole Power to try all Impeachments. When sitting for that Purpose, they shall be on Oath or Affirmation. When the President of the United States is tried, the Chief Justice shall preside: And no Person shall be convicted without the Concurrence of two thirds of the Members present.

Judgment in Cases of Impeachment shall not extend further than to removal from Office, and disqualification to hold and enjoy any Office of honor, Trust or Profit under the United States: but the Party convicted shall nevertheless be liable and subject to Indictment, Trial, Judgment and Punishment, according to Law.

Section. 4. The Times, Places and Manner of holding Elections for Senators and Representatives, shall be prescribed in each State by the Legislature thereof; but the Congress may at any time by Law make or alter such Regulations, except as to the Places of chusing Senators.

The Congress shall assemble at least once in every Year, and such Meeting shall be on the first Monday in December, unless they shall by Law appoint a different Day.

Section. 5. Each House shall be the Judge of the Elections, Returns and Qualifications of its own Members, and a Majority of each shall constitute a Quorum to do Business; but a smaller Number may adjourn from day to day, and may be authorized to compel the Attendance of absent Members, in such Manner, and under such Penalties as each House may provide.

Each House may determine the Rules of its Proceedings, punish its Members for disorderly Behaviour, and, with the Concurrence of two thirds, expel a Member.

Each House shall keep a Journal of its Proceedings, and from time to time publish the same, excepting such Parts as may in their Judgment require Secrecy; and the Yeas and Nays of the Members of either House on any question shall, at the Desire of one fifth of those Present, be entered on the Journal.

Neither House, during the Session of Congress, shall, without the Consent of the other, adjourn for more than three days, nor to any other Place than that in which the two Houses shall be sitting.

Section. 6. The Senators and Representatives shall receive a Compensation for their Services, to be ascertained by Law, and paid out of the Treasury of the United States. They shall in all Cases, except Treason, Felony and Breach of the Peace, be privileged from Arrest during their Attendance at the Session of their respective Houses, and in going to and returning from the same; and for any Speech or Debate in either House, they shall not be questioned in any other Place.

No Senator or Representative shall, during the Time for which he was elected, be appointed to any civil Office under the Authority of the United States, which shall have been created, or the Emoluments whereof shall have been encreased during such time; and no Person holding any Office under the United States, shall be a Member of either House during his Continuance in Office.

Section. 7. All Bills for raising Revenue shall originate in the House of Representatives; but the Senate may propose or concur with Amendments as on other Bills.

Every Bill which shall have passed the House of Representatives and the Senate, shall, before it become a Law, be presented to the President of the United States; If he approve he shall sign it, but if not he shall return it, with his Objections to that House in which it shall have originated, who shall enter the Objections at large on their Journal, and proceed to reconsider it. If after such Reconsideration two thirds of that House shall agree to pass the Bill, it shall be sent, together with the Objections, to the other House, by which it shall likewise be reconsidered, and if approved by two thirds of that House, it shall become a Law. But in all such Cases the Votes of both Houses shall be determined by yeas and Nays, and the Names of the Persons voting for and against the Bill shall be entered on the Journal of each House respectively. If any Bill shall not be returned by the President within ten Days (Sundays excepted) after it shall have been presented to him, the Same shall be a Law, in like Manner as if he had signed it, unless the Congress by their Adjournment prevent its Return, in which Case it shall not be a Law.

Every Order, Resolution, or Vote to which the Concurrence of the Senate and House of Representatives may be necessary (except on a question of Adjournment) shall be presented to the President of the United States; and before the Same shall take Effect, shall be approved by him, or being disapproved by him, shall be repassed by two thirds of the Senate and House of Representatives, according to the Rules and Limitations prescribed in the Case of a Bill.

Section. 8. The Congress shall have Power To lay and collect Taxes, Duties, Imposts and Excises, to pay the Debts and provide for the common Defence and general Welfare of the United States; but all Duties, Imposts and Excises shall be uniform throughout the United States;

To borrow Money on the credit of the United States;

To regulate Commerce with foreign Nations, and among the several States, and with the Indian Tribes;

To establish an uniform Rule of Naturalization, and uniform Laws on the subject of Bankruptcies throughout the United States;

To coin Money, regulate the Value thereof, and of foreign Coin, and fix the Standard of Weights and Measures;

To provide for the Punishment of counterfeiting the Securities and current Coin of the United States;

To establish Post Offices and post Roads;

To promote the Progress of Science and useful Arts, by securing for limited Times to Authors and Inventors the exclusive Right to their respective Writings and Discoveries;

To constitute Tribunals inferior to the supreme Court;

To define and punish Piracies and Felonies committed on the high Seas, and Offences against the Law of Nations;

To declare War, grant Letters of Marque and Reprisal, and make Rules concerning Captures on Land and Water;

To raise and support Armies, but no Appropriation of Money to that Use shall be for a longer Term than two Years;

To provide and maintain a Navy;

To make Rules for the Government and Regulation of the land and naval Forces;

To provide for calling forth the Militia to execute the Laws of the Union, suppress Insurrections and repel Invasions;

To provide for organizing, arming, and disciplining, the Militia, and for governing such Part of them as may be employed in the Service of the United States, reserving to the States respectively, the Appointment of the Officers, and the Authority of training the Militia according to the discipline prescribed by Congress;

To exercise exclusive Legislation in all Cases whatsoever, over such District (not exceeding ten Miles square) as may, by Cession of particular States, and the Acceptance of Congress, become the Seat of the Government of the United States, and to exercise like Authority over all Places purchased by the Consent of the Legislature of the State in which the Same shall be, for the Erection of Forts, Magazines, Arsenals, dock-Yards, and other needful Buildings;—And

To make all Laws which shall be necessary and proper for carrying into Execution the foregoing Powers, and all other Powers vested by this Constitution in the Government of the United States, or in any Department or Officer thereof.

Section. 9. The Migration or Importation of such Persons as any of the States now existing shall think proper to admit, shall not be prohibited by the Congress prior to the Year one thousand eight hundred and eight, but a Tax or duty may be imposed on such Importation, not exceeding ten dollars for each Person.

The Privilege of the Writ of Habeas Corpus shall not be suspended, unless when in Cases of Rebellion or Invasion the public Safety may require it.

No Bill of Attainder or ex post facto Law shall be passed.

No Capitation, or other direct, Tax shall be laid, unless in Proportion to the Census or enumeration herein before directed to be taken.

No Tax or Duty shall be laid on Articles exported from any State.

No Preference shall be given by any Regulation of Commerce or Revenue to the Ports of one State over those of another: nor shall Vessels bound to, or from, one State, be obliged to enter, clear, or pay Duties in another.

No Money shall be drawn from the Treasury, but in Consequence of Appropriations made by Law; and a regular Statement and Account of the Receipts and Expenditures of all public Money shall be published from time to time.

No Title of Nobility shall be granted by the United States: And no Person holding any Office of Profit or Trust under them, shall, without the Consent of the Congress, accept of any present, Emolument, Office, or Title, of any kind whatever, from any King, Prince, or foreign State.

Section. 10.

No State shall enter into any Treaty, Alliance, or Confederation; grant Letters of Marque and Reprisal; coin Money; emit Bills of Credit; make any Thing but gold and silver Coin a Tender in Payment of Debts; pass any Bill of Attainder, ex post facto Law, or Law impairing the Obligation of Contracts, or grant any Title of Nobility.

No State shall, without the Consent of the Congress, lay any Imposts or Duties on Imports or Exports, except what may be absolutely necessary for executing it's inspection Laws: and the net Produce of all Duties and Imposts, laid by any State on Imports or Exports, shall be for the Use of the Treasury of the United States; and all such Laws shall be subject to the Revision and Controul of the Congress.

No State shall, without the Consent of Congress, lay any Duty of Tonnage, keep Troops, or Ships of War in time of Peace, enter into any Agreement or Compact with another State, or with a foreign Power, or engage in War, unless actually invaded, or in such imminent Danger as will not admit of delay.

Article II

Section. 1. The executive Power shall be vested in a President of the United States of America. He shall hold his Office during the Term of four Years, and, together with the Vice President, chosen for the same Term, be elected, as follows

Each State shall appoint, in such Manner as the Legislature thereof may direct, a Number of Electors, equal to the whole Number of Senators and Representatives to which the State may be entitled in the Congress: but no Senator or Representative, or Person holding an Office of Trust or Profit under the United States, shall be appointed an Elector.

The Electors shall meet in their respective States, and vote by Ballot for two Persons, of whom one at least shall not be an Inhabitant of the same State with themselves. And they shall make a List of all the Persons voted for, and of the Number of Votes for each; which List they shall sign and certify, and transmit sealed to the Seat of the Government of the United States, directed to the President of the Senate. The President of the Senate shall, in the Presence of the Senate and House of Representatives, open all the Certificates, and the Votes shall then be counted. The Person having the greatest Number of Votes shall be the President, if such Number be a Majority of the whole Number of Electors appointed; and if there be more than one who have such Majority, and have an equal Number of Votes, then the House of Representatives shall immediately chuse by Ballot one of them for President; and if no Person have a Majority, then from the five highest on the List the said House shall in like Manner chuse the President. But in chusing the President, the Votes shall be taken by States, the Representation from each State having one Vote; A quorum for this Purpose shall consist of a Member or Members from two thirds of the States, and a Majority of all the States shall be necessary to a Choice. In every Case, after the Choice of the President, the Person having the greatest Number of Votes of the Electors shall be the Vice President. But if there should remain two or more who have equal Votes, the Senate shall chuse from them by Ballot the Vice President.

The Congress may determine the Time of chusing the Electors, and the Day on which they shall give their Votes; which Day shall be the same throughout the United States.

No Person except a natural born Citizen, or a Citizen of the United States, at the time of the Adoption of this Constitution, shall be eligible to the Office of President; neither shall any Person be eligible to that Office who shall not have attained to the Age of thirty five Years, and been fourteen Years a Resident within the United States.

In Case of the Removal of the President from Office, or of his Death, Resignation, or Inability to discharge the Powers and Duties of the said Office, the Same shall devolve on the Vice President, and the Congress may by Law provide for the Case of Removal, Death, Resignation or Inability, both of the President and Vice President, declaring what Officer shall then act as President, and such Officer shall act accordingly, until the Disability be removed, or a President shall be elected.

The President shall, at stated Times, receive for his Services, a Compensation, which shall neither be encreased nor diminished during the Period for which he shall have been elected, and he shall not receive within that Period any other Emolument from the United States, or any of them.

Before he enter on the Execution of his Office, he shall take the following Oath or Affirmation:—"I do solemnly swear (or affirm) that I will faithfully execute the Office of President of the United States, and will to the best of my Ability, preserve, protect and defend the Constitution of the United States."

Section. 2. The President shall be Commander in Chief of the Army and Navy of the United States, and of the Militia of the several States, when called into the actual Service of the United States; he may require the Opinion, in writing, of the principal Officer in each of the executive Departments, upon any Subject relating to the Duties of their respective Offices, and he shall have Power to grant Reprieves and Pardons for Offences against the United States, except in Cases of Impeachment.

He shall have Power, by and with the Advice and Consent of the Senate, to make Treaties, provided two thirds of the Senators present concur; and he shall nominate, and by and with the Advice and Consent of the Senate, shall appoint Ambassadors, other public Ministers and Consuls, Judges of the supreme Court, and all other Officers of the United States, whose Appointments are not herein otherwise provided for, and which shall be established by Law: but the Congress may by Law vest the Appointment of such inferior Officers, as they think proper, in the President alone, in the Courts of Law, or in the Heads of Departments.

The President shall have Power to fill up all Vacancies that may happen during the Recess of the Senate, by granting Commissions which shall expire at the End of their next Session.

Section. 3. He shall from time to time give to the Congress Information of the State of the Union, and recommend to their Consideration such Measures as he shall judge necessary and expedient; he may, on extraordinary Occasions, convene both Houses, or either of them, and in Case of Disagreement between them, with Respect to the Time of Adjournment, he may adjourn them to such Time as he shall think proper; he shall receive Ambassadors and other public Ministers; he shall take Care that the Laws be faithfully executed, and shall Commission all the Officers of the United States.

Section. 4. The President, Vice President and all civil Officers of the United States, shall be removed from Office on Impeachment for, and Conviction of, Treason, Bribery, or other high Crimes and Misdemeanors.

Article III

Section. 1. The judicial Power of the United States, shall be vested in one supreme Court, and in such inferior Courts as the Congress may from time to time ordain and establish. The Judges, both of the supreme and inferior Courts, shall hold their Offices during good Behaviour, and shall, at stated Times, receive for their Services, a Compensation, which shall not be diminished during their Continuance in Office.

Section. 2. The judicial Power shall extend to all Cases, in Law and Equity, arising under this Constitution, the Laws of the United States, and Treaties made, or which shall be made, under their Authority;—to all Cases affecting Ambassadors, other public Ministers and Consuls;—to all Cases of admiralty and maritime Jurisdiction;—to Controversies to which the United States shall be a Party;—to Controversies between two or more States;— between a State and Citizens of another State,—between Citizens of different States,—between Citizens of the same State claiming Lands under Grants of different States, and between a State, or the Citizens thereof, and foreign States, Citizens or Subjects.

In all Cases affecting Ambassadors, other public Ministers and Consuls, and those in which a State shall be Party, the supreme Court shall have original Jurisdiction. In all the other Cases before mentioned, the supreme Court shall have appellate Jurisdiction, both as to Law and Fact, with such Exceptions, and under such Regulations as the Congress shall make.

The Trial of all Crimes, except in Cases of Impeachment, shall be by Jury; and such Trial shall be held in the State where the said Crimes shall have been committed; but when not committed within any State, the Trial shall be at such Place or Places as the Congress may by Law have directed.

Section. 3.

Treason against the United States, shall consist only in levying War against them, or in adhering to their Enemies, giving them Aid and Comfort. No Person shall be convicted of Treason unless on the Testimony of two Witnesses to the same overt Act, or on Confession in open Court.

The Congress shall have Power to declare the Punishment of Treason, but no Attainder of Treason shall work Corruption of Blood, or Forfeiture except during the Life of the Person attainted.

Article IV

Section. 1. Full Faith and Credit shall be given in each State to the public Acts, Records, and judicial Proceedings of every other State. And the Congress may by general Laws prescribe the Manner in which such Acts, Records and Proceedings shall be proved, and the Effect thereof.

Section. 2. The Citizens of each State shall be entitled to all Privileges and Immunities of Citizens in the several States.

A Person charged in any State with Treason, Felony, or other Crime, who shall flee from Justice, and be found in another State, shall on Demand of the executive Authority of the State from which he fled, be delivered up, to be removed to the State having Jurisdiction of the Crime.

No Person held to Service or Labour in one State, under the Laws thereof, escaping into another, shall, in Consequence of any Law or Regulation therein, be discharged from such Service or Labour, but shall be delivered up on Claim of the Party to whom such Service or Labour may be due.

Section. 3. New States may be admitted by the Congress into this Union; but no new State shall be formed or erected within the Jurisdiction of any other State; nor any State be formed by the Junction of two or more States, or Parts of States, without the Consent of the Legislatures of the States concerned as well as of the Congress.

The Congress shall have Power to dispose of and make all needful Rules and Regulations respecting the Territory or other Property belonging to the United States; and nothing in this Constitution shall be so construed as to Prejudice any Claims of the United States, or of any particular State.

Section. 4. The United States shall guarantee to every State in this Union a Republican Form of Government, and shall protect each of them against Invasion; and on Application of the Legislature, or of the Executive (when the Legislature cannot be convened), against domestic Violence.

Article V

The Congress, whenever two thirds of both Houses shall deem it necessary, shall propose Amendments to this Constitution, or, on the Application of the Legislatures of two thirds of the several States, shall call a Convention for proposing Amendments, which, in either Case, shall be valid to all Intents and Purposes, as Part of this Constitution, when ratified by the Legislatures of three fourths of the several States, or by Conventions in three fourths thereof, as the one or the other Mode of Ratification may be proposed by the Congress; Provided that no Amendment which may be made prior to the Year One thousand eight hundred and eight shall in any Manner affect the first and fourth Clauses in the Ninth Section of the first Article; and that no State, without its Consent, shall be deprived of its equal Suffrage in the Senate.

Article VI

All Debts contracted and Engagements entered into, before the Adoption of this Constitution, shall be as valid against the United States under this Constitution, as under the Confederation.

This Constitution, and the Laws of the United States which shall be made in Pursuance thereof; and all Treaties made, or which shall be made, under the Authority of the United States, shall be the supreme Law of the Land; and the Judges in every State shall be bound thereby, any Thing in the Constitution or Laws of any State to the Contrary notwithstanding.

The Senators and Representatives before mentioned, and the Members of the several State Legislatures, and all executive and judicial Officers, both of the United States and of the several States, shall be bound by Oath or Affirmation, to support this Constitution; but no religious Test shall ever be required as a Qualification to any Office or public Trust under the United States.

Article VII

The Ratification of the Conventions of nine States, shall be sufficient for the Establishment of this Constitution between the States so ratifying the Same.

The Word, "the," being interlined between the seventh and eighth Lines of the first Page, The Word "Thirty" being partly written on an Erazure in the fifteenth Line of the first Page, The Words "is tried" being interlined between the thirty second and thirty third Lines of the first Page and the Word "the" being interlined between the forty third and forty fourth Lines of the second Page.

Attest William Jackson Secretary

done in Convention by the Unanimous Consent of the States present the Seventeenth Day of September in the Year of our Lord one thousand seven hundred and Eighty seven and of the Independance of the United States of America the Twelfth In witness whereof We have hereunto subscribed our Names,

G°. Washington
Presidt and deputy from Virginia

Delaware
Geo: Read
Gunning Bedford jun
John Dickinson
Richard Bassett
Jaco: Broom

Maryland
James McHenry
Dan of St Thos. Jenifer
Danl. Carroll

Virginia
John Blair
James Madison Jr.

North Carolina
Wm. Blount
Richd. Dobbs Spaight
Hu Williamson

South Carolina
J. Rutledge
Charles Cotesworth Pinckney
Charles Pinckney
Pierce Butler

Georgia
William Few
Abr Baldwin

New Hampshire
John Langdon
Nicholas Gilman

Massachusetts
Nathaniel Gorham
Rufus King

Connecticut
Wm. Saml. Johnson
Roger Sherman

New York
Alexander Hamilton

New Jersey
Wil: Livingston
David Brearley
Wm. Paterson
Jona: Dayton

Pennsylvania
B Franklin
Thomas Mifflin
Robt. Morris
Geo. Clymer
Thos. FitzSimons
Jared Ingersoll
James Wilson
Gouv Morris

The 27 Amendments to the Constitution

I. Congress shall make no law respecting an establishment of religion, or prohibiting the free exercise thereof; or abridging the freedom of speech, or of the press; or the right of the people peaceably to assemble, and to petition the Government for a redress of grievances.

II. A well regulated Militia, being necessary to the security of a free State, the right of the people to keep and bear Arms, shall not be infringed.

III. No Soldier shall, in time of peace be quartered in any house, without the consent of the Owner, nor in time of war, but in a manner to be prescribed by law.

IV. The right of the people to be secure in their persons, houses, papers, and effects, against unreasonable searches and seizures, shall not be violated, and no Warrants shall issue, but upon probable cause, supported by Oath or affirmation, and particularly describing the place to be searched, and the persons or things to be seized.

V. No person shall be held to answer for a capital, or otherwise infamous crime, unless on a presentment or indictment of a Grand Jury, except in cases arising in the land or naval forces, or in the Militia, when in actual service in time of War or public danger; nor shall any person be subject for the same offence to be twice put in jeopardy of life or limb; nor shall be compelled in any criminal case to be a witness against himself, nor be deprived of life, liberty, or property, without due process of law; nor shall private property be taken for public use, without just compensation.

VI. In all criminal prosecutions, the accused shall enjoy the right to a speedy and public trial, by an impartial jury of the State and district wherein the crime shall have been committed, which district shall have been previously ascertained by law, and to be informed of the nature and cause of the accusation; to be confronted with the witnesses against him; to have compulsory process for obtaining witnesses in his favor, and to have the Assistance of Counsel for his defence.

VII. In Suits at common law, where the value in controversy shall exceed twenty dollars, the right of trial by jury shall be preserved, and no fact tried by a jury, shall be otherwise re-examined in any Court of the United States, than according to the rules of the common law.

VIII. Excessive bail shall not be required, nor excessive fines imposed, nor cruel and unusual punishments inflicted.

IX. The enumeration in the Constitution, of certain rights, shall not be construed to deny or disparage others retained by the people.

X. The powers not delegated to the United States by the Constitution, nor prohibited by it to the States, are reserved to the States respectively, or to the people.

XI. The Judicial power of the United States shall not be construed to extend to any suit in law or equity, commenced or prosecuted against one of the United States by Citizens of another State, or by Citizens or Subjects of any Foreign State.

XII. The Electors shall meet in their respective states and vote by ballot for President and Vice-President, one of whom, at least, shall not be an inhabitant of the same state with themselves; they shall name in their ballots the person voted for as President, and in distinct ballots the person voted for as Vice-President, and they shall make distinct lists of all persons voted for as President, and of all persons voted for as Vice-President, and of the number of votes for each, which lists they shall sign and certify, and transmit sealed to the seat of the government of the United States, directed to the President of the Senate;-The President of the Senate shall, in the presence of the Senate and House of

Representatives, open all the certificates and the votes shall then be counted;-The person having the greatest Number of votes for President, shall be the President, if such number be a majority of the whole number of Electors appointed; and if no person have such majority, then from the persons having the highest numbers not exceeding three on the list of those voted for as President, the House of Representatives shall choose immediately, by ballot, the President. But in choosing the President, the votes shall be taken by states, the representation from each state having one vote; a quorum for this purpose shall consist of a member or members from two-thirds of the states, and a majority of all the states shall be necessary to a choice. And if the House of Representatives shall not choose a President whenever the right of choice shall devolve upon them, before the fourth day of March next following, then the Vice-President shall act as President, as in the case of the death or other constitutional disability of the President-The person having the greatest number of votes as Vice-President, shall be the Vice-President, if such number be a majority of the whole number of Electors appointed, and if no person have a majority, then from the two highest numbers on the list, the Senate shall choose the Vice-President; a quorum for the purpose shall consist of two-thirds of the whole number of Senators, and a majority of the whole number shall be necessary to a choice. But no person constitutionally ineligible to the office of President shall be eligible to that of Vice-President of the United States.

XIII. Section 1: Neither slavery nor involuntary servitude, except as a punishment for crime whereof the party shall have been duly convicted, shall exist within the United States, or any place subject to their jurisdiction.

Section 2: Congress shall have power to enforce this article by appropriate legislation.

XIV. Section 1: All persons born or naturalized in the United States and subject to the jurisdiction thereof, are citizens of the United States and of the State wherein they reside. No State shall make or enforce any law which shall abridge the privileges or immunities of citizens of the United States; nor shall any State deprive any person of life, liberty, or property, without due process of law; nor deny to any person within its jurisdiction the equal protection of the laws.

Section 2: Representatives shall be apportioned among the several States according to their respective numbers, counting the whole number of persons in each State, excluding Indians not taxed. But when the right to vote at any election for the choice of electors for President and Vice President of the United States, Representatives in Congress, the Executive and Judicial officers of a State, or the members of the Legislature thereof, is denied to any of the male inhabitants of such State, being twenty-one years of age, and citizens of the United States, or in any way abridged, except for participation in rebellion, or other crime, the basis of representation therein shall be reduced in the proportion which the number of such male citizens shall bear to the whole number of male citizens twenty-one years of age in such State

Section 3: No person shall be a Senator or Representative in Congress, or elector of President and Vice President, or hold any office, civil or military, under the United States, or under any State, who, having previously taken an oath, as a member of Congress, or as an officer of the United States, or as a member of any State legislature, or as an executive or judicial officer of any State, to support the Constitution of the United States, shall have engaged in insurrection or rebellion against the same, or given aid or comfort to the enemies thereof. But Congress may by a vote of two-thirds of each House, remove such disability.

Section 4: The validity of the public debt of the United States, authorized by law, including debts incurred for payment of pensions and bounties for services in suppressing insurrection or rebellion, shall not be questioned. But neither the United States nor any State shall assume or pay any debt or obligation incurred in aid of insurrection or rebellion against the United States, or any claim for the loss or emancipation of any slave; but all such debts, obligations and claims shall be held illegal and void.

XV. Section 1: The right of citizens of the United States to vote shall not be denied or abridged by the United States or by any State on account of race, color, or previous condition of servitude.

Section 2: The Congress shall have power to enforce this article by appropriate legislation.

XVI. The Congress shall have power to lay and collect taxes on incomes, from whatever source derived, without apportionment among the several States, and without regard to any census or enumeration.

XVII. The Senate of the United States shall be composed of two Senators from each State, elected by the people thereof, for six years; and each Senator shall have one vote. The electors in each State shall have the qualifications requisite for electors of the most numerous branch of the State legislatures.

When vacancies happen in the representation of any State in the Senate, the executive authority of such State shall issue writs of election to fill such vacancies: Provided, That the legislature of any State may empower the executive thereof to make temporary appointments until the people fill the vacancies by election as the legislature may direct.

This amendment shall not be so construed as to affect the election or term of any Senator chosen before it becomes valid as part of the Constitution.

XVIII. Section 1: After one year from the ratification of this article the manufacture, sale, or transportation of intoxicating liquors within, the importation thereof into, or the exportation thereof from the United States and all territory subject to the jurisdiction thereof for beverage purposes is hereby prohibited.

Section 2: The Congress and the several States shall have concurrent power to enforce this article by appropriate legislation.

Section 3: This article shall be inoperative unless it shall have been ratified as an amendment to the Constitution by the legislatures of the several States, as provided in the Constitution, within seven years from the date of the submission hereof to the States by the Congress.

XIX. The right of citizens of the United States to vote shall not be denied or abridged by the United States or by any State on account of sex.

Congress shall have power to enforce this article by appropriate legislation.

XX. Section 1: The terms of the President and Vice President shall end at noon on the 20th day of January, and the terms of Senators and Representatives at noon on the 3d day of January, of the years in which such terms would have ended if this article had not been ratified; and the terms of their successors shall then begin.

Section 2: The Congress shall assemble at least once in every year, and such meeting shall begin at noon on the 3d day of January, unless they shall by law appoint a different day.

Section 3: If, at the time fixed for the beginning of the term of the President, the President elect shall have died, the Vice President elect shall become President. If a President shall not have been chosen before the time fixed for the beginning of his term, or if the President elect shall have failed to qualify, then the Vice President elect shall act as President until a President shall have qualified; and the Congress may by law provide for the case wherein neither a President elect nor a Vice President elect shall have qualified, declaring who shall then act as President, or the manner in which one who is to act shall be selected, and such person shall act accordingly until a President or Vice President shall have qualified.

Section 4: The Congress may by law provide for the case of the death of any of the persons from whom the House of Representatives may choose a President whenever the right of choice shall have devolved upon them, and for the case of the death of any of the persons from whom the Senate may choose a Vice President whenever the right of choice shall have devolved upon them.

XXI. Section 1: The eighteenth article of amendment to the Constitution of the United States is hereby repealed.

Section 2: The transportation or importation into any State, Territory, or possession of the United States for delivery or use therein of intoxicating liquors, in violation of the laws thereof, is hereby prohibited . . .

XXII. Section 1: No person shall be elected to the office of the President more than twice, and no person who has held the office of President, or acted as President, for more than two years of a term to which some other person was elected President shall be elected to the office of the President more than once. But this Article shall not apply to any person holding the office of President, when this Article was proposed by the Congress, and shall not prevent any person who may be holding the office of President, or acting as President, during the term within which this Article becomes operative from holding the office of President or acting as President during the remainder of such term . . .

XXIII. **Section 1:** The District constituting the seat of Government of the United States shall appoint in such manner as the Congress may direct:

A number of electors of President and Vice President equal to the whole number of Senators and Representatives in Congress to which the District would be entitled if it were a State, but in no event more than the least populous State; they shall be in addition to those appointed by the States, but they shall be considered, for the purposes of the election of President and Vice President, to be electors appointed by a State; and they shall meet in the District and perform such duties as provided by the twelfth article of amendment . . .

XXIV. **Section 1:** The right of citizens of the United States to vote in any primary or other election for President or Vice President for electors for President or Vice President, or for Senator or Representative in Congress, shall not be denied or abridged by the United States or any State by reason of failure to pay any poll tax or other tax.

Section 2: The Congress shall have power to enforce this article by appropriate legislation.

XXV. **Section 1:** In case of the removal of the President from office or of his death or resignation, the Vice President shall become President.

Section 2: Whenever there is a vacancy in the office of the Vice President, the President shall nominate a Vice President who shall take office upon confirmation by a majority vote of both Houses of Congress.

Section 3: Whenever the President transmits to the President pro tempore of the Senate and the Speaker of the House of Representatives his written declaration that he is unable to discharge the powers and duties of his office, and until he transmits to them a written declaration to the contrary, such powers and duties shall be discharged by the Vice President as Acting President.

Section 4: Whenever the Vice President and a majority of either the principal officers of the executive departments or of such other body as Congress may by law provide, transmit to the President pro tempore of the Senate and the Speaker of the House of Representatives their written declaration that the President is unable to discharge the powers and duties of his office, the Vice President shall immediately assume the powers and duties of the office as Acting President.

Thereafter, when the President transmits to the President pro tempore of the Senate and the Speaker of the House of Representatives his written declaration that no inability exists, he shall resume the powers and duties of his office unless the Vice President and a majority of either the principal officers of the executive department or of such other body as Congress may by law provide, transmit within four days to the President pro tempore of the Senate and the Speaker of the House of Representatives their written declaration that the President is unable to discharge the powers and duties of his office. Thereupon Congress shall decide the issue, assembling within forty-eight hours for that purpose if not in session. If the Congress, within twenty-one days after receipt of the latter written declaration, or, if Congress is not in session, within twenty-one days after Congress is required to assemble, determines by two-thirds vote of both Houses that the President is unable to discharge the powers and duties of his office, the Vice President shall continue to discharge the same as Acting President; otherwise, the President shall resume the powers and duties of his office

XXVI. **Section 1:** The right of citizens of the United States, who are eighteen years of age or older, to vote shall not be denied or abridged by the United States or by any State on account of age . . .

XXVII. No law varying the compensation for the services of the Senators and Representatives shall take effect, until an election of Representatives shall have intervened.

Index

A

Abolitionists, 5, 13, 16
Addams, Jane, 120, 125, 134–135, 147
Affirmative Action, 319, 323, 355, 394–395
African-American Migration, see Great Migration
Agricultural Adjustment Act (AAA), 235, 237
Airplanes, 168, 181, 215, 259, 269, 401
Al-Qaeda, 376, 401
Alliance for Progress, 299, 304
Alliance system, 169
Allied Powers, 168–169, 292
American Expeditionary Force (AEF), 171, 177, 181, 231
American Federation of Labor, 85, 90, 173
American Indian Movement (AIM), 405
Americanization, 53, 101, 113
Americans with Disabilities Act, 392
Anarchism, 87–88, 122, 133
Angel Island, 103
Anti-Imperialist League, 147
Anti-war protests, during World War I, 174, during Vietnam War, 350–352
Apartheid, 374
Appeasement, 253, 255, 276, 361
Appomattox, 15
Arms race, 201, 295–296, 380
Assembly line, 69, 202, 207, 217, 312
Atlantic Charter, 253, 257–258, 273, 276
Auschwitz, 266–267
Austria-Hungary, 100, 168, 178–179

B

Baby boomers, 350–351
Bank Holiday, 233, 240
Barbed wire, 50–51, 106, 168, 263, 266, 300
Battle of the Bulge, 269, 276
Bay of Pigs invasion, 299
Bell, Alexander Graham, 65, 67
Berlin Airlift, 292
Berlin Blockade, 292
Berlin Wall, 300, 374
Bessemer process, 64–65, 70, 75
Bethune, Mary McLeod, 264, 273
Betty Friedan: *The Feminine Mystique,* 354
"Big Stick" policy, 154–155
Bin Laden, Osama, 376–377
Black Codes, 26–27, 34, 85
Black Panthers, 319, 325, 328, 392
Black Power, 319, 323–328
Black Tuesday, 228
Blitzkrieg, 254, 268, 276
Bonus Expeditionary Force, 321
Booker T. Washington, 130, 208–210, 212, 217
Boom town, 49
Bosnia and Kosovo, 375
Boss Tweed, 98–99
Boxer Rebellion, 151, 156
Broward, Napoleon Bonaparte 134
Brown v. Board of Education (1954), 315–316, 318, 323, 327, 329, 393–394
Bryan, William Jennings, 110, 147, 205
Buffalo Soldiers, 45–46
Bull Market, 227–228
Bush, George W., 375, 401
Bush, George H.W., 375
Busing, 317, 394
Buying on margin, 193, 203

C

Cambodia, 345–346, 349, 351–352, 370
Camp David Accords, 371
Capitalism, 62, 75, 83, 85, 89, 122, 236, 287, 325, 352
Carnegie, Andrew, 70, 74, 88, 146–147, 156, 208
Carpetbagger, 29–30
Carter, Jimmy, 327, 371–372
Castro, Fidel, 299–300
Central Powers, 168–169, 179
Chavez, Cesar, 391
Chemical warfare, 168
Child labor, 83, 85, 90, 127, 133, 235–236
Chinese Exclusion Act, 103–104, 398
City manager, 125
Civil Rights Act
    of 1866, 27, 34
    of 1957 and 1960, 318
    of 1964, 320–322, 354–355
    of 1968, 324
Civilian Conservation Corps (CCC), 233, 240
Clayton Antitrust Act, 133–134
Climate change, 378, 380, 402–403
Clinton, Bill, 375
Coal Strike of 1902, 129
Cold War, 291, 293–300, 315, 371, 373–375, 377, 379–380, 404
Committee of Public Information, 172, 175, 181
Communism, 122, 133, 195, 251, 293, 295–300, 313, 346–347, 349–350, 371–372, 375, 379
Compromise of 1850, 7
Congress of Racial Equality (CORE), 314, 319, 322
Congressional Reconstruction, 27, 34
Conscientious objectors, 172, 181, 351
Conscription, 12, 171, 349
Consumerism, 203, 237
Consumers, 64, 68, 73–74, 105, 122–123, 129–131, 202–203, 227, 234, 261–262, 342
Containment, 290, 292–293, 298–299, 302
Convoys, 169–170
Coral Sea, 270–271, 276
Corporation, 68–70, 74–75, 84, 129, 133, 173, 228, 230, 233–235, 243, 264, 313
Court-packing plan, 237
Cowboy, 49–50
"Credibility Gap," 350
"Cross of Gold" Speech, 110
Cuba, 128, 148–150, 154, 265, 299–300, 328, 357, 379, 390, 402
Cuban Missile Crisis, 299–300, 328

D

D-Day, 253, 269, 276
Davis, Jefferson, 10
Dawes Act, 53, 213, 289, 405
Dawes Plan, 199, 217
De Lôme letter, 144, 156
Debs, Eugene, 89–90, 122, 131, 174
Debt peonage, 30, 34, 216
Demobilization, 193, 217
Dewey, Commodore George, 144
Direct primary, 126, 134
Disarmament, 198, 201, 258
"Dollar Diplomacy," 154–156
"Domino theory," 346
"Double V" campaign, 264
Douglass, Frederick, 5, 13, 16
Drake, Edwin, 66
Dred Scott decision, 8, 27
Du Bois, W.E.B., 208–210, 212, 327
Due process, 27, 34, 107, 402
Dumbarton Oaks Conference, 289
Dust Bowl, 231, 237, 262

E

East Germany, 290, 292–293, 374
Economic boom, 202, 227
Edison, Thomas, 66–67, 76, 181, 207
Eighteenth Amendment, 204
Eisenhower Doctrine, 298
Eisenhower, Dwight, 313
Election of 2000, 375
Ellis Island, 100–101, 103
Emancipation Proclamation, 13, 29
Entrepreneur, 70, 72, 75, 89
Equal protection, 27, 34, 314, 389, 394
Equal Rights Amendment (ERA), 128, 355–356
Espionage Act, 174, 181
Everglades, 134, 215–216, 240

F

Fascism, 276
Federal Deposit Insurance Corporation (FDIC), 233
Federal Reserve Act, 132, 134
Federal Trade Commission, 133, 197
Ferdinand, Archduke Francis, 168
Fifteenth Amendment, 28, 32, 314, 322–323
Final Solution, 266
Fireside chat, 233, 257
Flagler, Henry, 72, 75, 155
Flappers, 206, 217
Fordney–McCumber Act, 196
Fort Sumter, 11–12
Four Freedoms, 257, 276–277
Four-Power Treaty, 198, 217
Fourteen Points, 178–179, 181, 258
Fourteenth Amendment, 24, 27, 38–39, 355, 393, 395
Freedman, 30
Freedmen's Bureau, 27, 34
Freedom Riders, 319, 322
Frontier, 48–50, 178, 269, 357
Fugitive Slave Act, 7
Fundamentalist Movement, 217

G

Garvey, Marcus, 212, 217, 25
General Assembly, 274–276, 279
Geneva Accords, 346–347
Gentlemen's Agreement, 103, 134, 152

German Americans, 169, 173, 175, 181, 263
Gettysburg, 14
Ghetto, 101, 211, 266–267, 314, 324
G.I. Bill of Rights, 311–312
Glasnost, 373
Globalization, 379–380
Gompers, Samuel, 85, 90, 146–147, 173
Gorbachev, Mikhail, 368, 373, 381, 385
Government regulation, 73, 130–131
Graduated income tax, 132, 134, 173
"Grandfather clauses," 32
Grange Movement, 107
Granger laws, 107–108
Gray Panthers, 392
Great Depression, 199, 216, 229, 231–240, 252, 255, 262, 264, 300, 391
Great Migration, 166, 177, 181, 184, 192–193, 209, 217, 219, 221, 314
Great Plains, 43–45, 47, 49–52, 64, 101, 105, 107, 110, 231–232
"Great Society," 342–343, 345, 352, 357
Gross national product (GNP), 231, 312, 330
Guerilla warfare, 148, 300, 347–348
Gulf of Tonkin Resolution, 347, 351
Gun control, 404

H

Harding, Warren, 196
Harlem Renaissance, 208, 210–212, 217, 329
Hawaii, 145–146, 148–149, 151, 156, 159–161, 177, 259–260, 263, 271, 390
Hawks vs. Doves, 350
Haymarket Riot, 88, 90
Hearst, William Randolph, 143
Hiram Rhodes Revels, 29
Hiroshima, 253, 271–272, 276
Hitler, Adolf, 251–253, 255, 258–260, 265, 267–270, 276, 288–290, 294
Ho Chi Minh, 346–347, 349–350
Holmes, Oliver Wendell, 174
Holocaust, 265–267, 275–276
Home front, 174–176, 181, 194, 260–261, 264–265, 276, 296, 315, 350
Homestead Act, 48, 50, 62, 75
Homestead Strike, 71, 88, 194
Hoover, Herbert, 172, 199–201, 228, 230, 232
Hoover, J. Edgar, 194, 297
Hoovervilles, 230, 239
Horizontal integration, 71
Hussein, Saddam, 374, 376

I

Ida Tarbell, 124, 134, 175
Ideology, 74, 89–90, 265, 288
Illegal alien, 399–400
Immigration and Naturalization Act of 1965, 343, 398–400
Impeachment, 27–29, 370
Imperialism,
Indian Wars, 45, 47
Indochina, 259, 271, 298, 345–346, 349, 353
Initiative, 75, 109, 126, 131, 134, 349, 368, 373
Innovation, 62, 64, 66, 68, 75, 255, 312
Installment buying, 203, 217
Integration, 70–71, 394
Interstate Commerce Act, 73, 108, 130

Interstate highway system, 313
Iran Hostage Crisis, 372
Iran-Contra Affair, 373
Iranian Revolution, 371
Iraq War, 373, 376
Iron Curtain, 290, 374

J

Japanese-American internment, 263
Jazz, 211–212
Jihad, 376
"Jim Crow" laws, 32–33, 176–177, 216, 314
John Brown's raid, 7, 9
Johnson, Andrew, 26–29, 131
Johnson, Lyndon B., 321, 342, 345, 357

K

Kansas–Nebraska Act, 7–8
Kellogg-Briand Pact, 201, 217
Kennedy, John F., 299, 318, 344, 357
Khrushchev, Nikita, 298
King, Dr. Martin Luther, Jr., 315, 317, 319–321, 324, 326–328, 350, 377
Kissinger, Dr. Henry, 349, 370
Knights of Labor, 84–85, 88–90
Korean War, 294–295, 312
Korematsu v. U.S., 276
Ku Klux Klan, 31–32, 104, 212, 214–215, 217, 320, 322, 329

L

La Follette, Robert, 125, 173
Labor union: see union
League of Nations, 178–181, 197–198, 201, 252, 255, 258, 273–276, 279–280
Lend-Lease Act, 257, 276
Lincoln, Abraham, 10, 14
Literacy tests, 32, 34, 322
Little Big Horn, 47
Lockout, 86
Lusitania, 170, 181, 255

M

MacArthur, General Douglas, 270, 294
Mahan, Alfred Thayer, 145, 156
Mail-order house, 68
Maine (U.S.S.), 144, 156
Malcolm X, 319, 324–325
Manila Bay, 144
Mapp v. Ohio (1961), 396
March on Washington (1963), 320–321
Market economy, 62, 75
Marshall Plan, 292, 311, 330
Marshall, Thurgood, 316, 323, 327
Marti, José, 155
McCarthyism, 297–298
McCoy, Elijah, 66
Meat Inspection Act, 130
Media, 297, 313, 350, 372, 377, 392, 401
Medicaid, 342, 357
Medicare, 342, 357, 404
Midway, 149, 151, 156, 260, 270–271, 276
Militarism, 169, 178, 181, 378
Miranda v. Arizona (1966), 344, 396
Missouri Compromise, 6, 8
Mobilization, 171, 217, 262, 276

Monopoly, 70, 73–74, 106
Monroe Doctrine, 153–155, 158, 289
Montgomery bus boycott, 317–318, 32
Morgan, J. P., 71–72, 110, 129
Morse, Samuel, 65
Muckrakers, 123–125, 134
Municipal reform, 125
Munn v. Illinois, 73, 107
Mussolini, Benito, 251

N

NAACP (National Association for the Advancement of Colored People), 125, 128, 209–210, 212, 217, 264, 314, 316–317, 322–323, 327–329, 391–392, 394
NAFTA, 375, 379
Nagasaki, 253, 271–272, 276
Nation of Islam, 324
National Industrial Recovery Act, 234–235, 237
National Labor Relations Act (Wagner Act), 236–237
National Organization of Women (NOW), 354
National Origins Act (Immigration Act of 1924), 200–201
National Recovery Administration (NRA), 234–235, 237
National Urban League, 210, 217, 314
National Woman Suffrage Association, 125–127
Nationalism, 181, 324, 347
Nativism, 104
Naval blockade, 12, 168–170, 299
Nazism, 264, 276
Neutrality Acts, 255–256, 276
"New Deal," 231–233, 235 240, 261, 313, 342, 357
"New Immigrants," 100–102, 104
"New South," 30
Nineteenth Amendment, 193
Nixon, Richard M., 299, 349
"Normalcy," return to, 196
Normandy, invasion of, 269
North Atlantic Treaty Organization (NATO), 293
Nuclear proliferation, 295–296, 378
Nuremberg trials, 273, 276

O

Obama, Barack, 377
Oklahoma City bombing, 401
"Old Immigrants," 100
Omaha Platform, 109
OPEC, 370–371
"Open Door" policy, 151, 156, 198
Open range, 49–50
Ostend Manifesto, 144

P

Palmer raids, 194–195, 217
Panama Canal Treaty, 371
Panama Canal, 75, 152–153, 155–156, 371
Panmunjom, 295
Paris Peace Accords, 349, 351
Parks, Rosa, 317
Peace Corps, 342, 357
Pearl Harbor, 253, 259–262, 270–271, 276, 288
Perestroika, 373
Persian Gulf War, 374
Philippines, 144, 146–149, 151–152, 177, 197, 259

Platt Amendment, 150
Plessy v. Ferguson (1896), 33, 315
Palestinians, 378
Political machine, 98–99, 122, 125
Poll taxes, 32, 318, 322–323
Populist Party, 108
Potsdam Conference, 289
Presidential Reconstruction, 26, 34
Progressives, 123, 125–127, 132–134, 173, 176, 204, 209, 235
Prohibition, 139, 180, 193, 204–205, 208, 217, 256
Project Head Start, 342, 357
Puerto Rico, 144, 149, 156
Pullman Strike, 89, 110
Pure Food and Drug Act, 130
Push-and-pull factors, 52

Q

Quarantine Speech, 252, 256, 276
Queen Liliuokalani, 148
Quota system, 197, 323

R

Radical Republicans, 27–28
Randolph, A. Philip, 264, 282, 329
Reagan Doctrine, 372
Reagan, Ronald, 372, 399
Recall, 1206–127, 131, 134
Reconstruction, 15, 25–34, 195, 207–208, 215, 230, 235, 237, 289, 291, 314, 321–322, 342, 394
"Red Scare," 194, 204, 217, 296
Referendum, 109, 126–127, 131, 134
Refugee, 253, 265–266, 271, 293, 300, 348, 352, 387–388, 400
Regents of the University of California v. Bakke (1978), 323, 395
Relief, recovery, reform, 233
Republican Party, 6, 8, 10, 129, 131
Reservations, 46–47, 50, 53–54, 175–176, 213, 216, 389–390
Riis, Jacob, 124, 134
Roaring Twenties, 204, 217
Rockefeller, John D., 71, 74, 124
Roe v. Wade (1973), 355–356, 397
Roosevelt Corollary, 153–156
Roosevelt, Franklin D., 231, 241, 256, 260, 329
Roosevelt, Theodore, 126, 128, 133–134, 144, 146, 152, 155, 208, 232
Rosewood, 215–217
Rough Riders, 128, 144, 156

S

Sacco and Vanzetti, 195–196
Salerno, 268, 276
Salvation Army, 122
San Francisco Conference, 273–274
San Juan Hill, 128, 144
Sand Creek Massacre, 46
Scalawag, 29–30
Schenck v. United States, 189
Scopes trial, 205
SEATO (Southeast Asia Treaty Organization), 346, 360
Secession, 10, 12, 16, 62
Second Industrial Revolution, 63–64, 67, 70, 74–75, 105, 223
Secret ballot, 109, 126, 134

Sectionalism, 16
Security Council, 273–274, 276, 294, 376
Sedition Act, 174, 181
Segregation, 31–34, 131, 134, 176, 181, 208–209, 314–323, 329, 394–395
Selective Service Act, 171, 181
Seminole Indians, 16, 134, 216, 390
September 11, 2001, ("9-11"), 376, 383, 385, 387–388, 399, 401
Serbia, 168, 178–179, 375
Settlement house, 122–123, 125, 134
Seventeenth Amendment, 126
Sharecropping, 30
Sherman Antitrust Act, 73–74, 87, 129, 133
Sherman Silver Purchase Act, 107
Sioux Indians, 47
Sit-down strike, 236
Sit-in, 318, 325, 329
Sixteenth Amendment, 131
Smoot-Hawley Tariff, 227–228
Social activism, 318, 389
Social Darwinism, 61–75
Social Gospel Movement, 122–123, 134
Social Security, 90, 235–237, 239, 258, 355, 404
Socialism, 87, 122, 133, 264, 296
Sod house, 51
Solid South, 32
Southern Christian Leadership Conference (SCLC), 317, 322, 327
Spanish Civil War, 252, 256
Spanish-American War, 128, 143–146, 148–152, 155–156
Speculation, 72, 200, 203, 215, 227–228
Spheres of influence, 146, 151
"Square Deal," 128–130, 134
Stalin, Joseph, 253, 285, 288
Stalingrad, 253, 267–268, 276
Stock, 69, 73, 203, 227–229
Stokely Carmichael, 319, 325
Strike, 83–89, 129, 194, 209, 236, 311, 391
Student Nonviolent Coordinating Committee (SNCC), 318
Suburbs, 202, 312–313, 324
Superpower, 272, 296, 377
Swann v. Charlotte-Mecklenburg Board of Education (1971), 394

T

Taft, William Howard, 128, 130, 134, 208
Taliban, 376
Tammany Hall, 98–99, 125
Tehran Conference, 268–269, 273
Telegraph, 44, 65, 68–70, 75, 108–109, 130, 145
Teller Amendment, 145, 149–150, 156, 159
Temperance Movement, 126–127, 204
Tenement, 98
Tennessee Valley Authority (TVA), 234
Terrorism, 31, 348, 372, 378, 401–402
Tet Offensive, 340, 348, 350–351, 353, 358, 360, 363
Thirteenth Amendment, 25, 29
Transatlantic cable, 65, 75
Transcontinental railroad, 44–46, 62–63
Treaty of Portsmouth, 152, 156
Treaty of Versailles, 179–181, 199, 252
Trench warfare, 168, 181

Truman Doctrine, 290, 292
Truman, Harry S., 271, 289, 291
Trusts, 73–74, 106, 129, 131
Twain, Mark, 70, 147, 156
Tweed, William Marcy, 98–99
Twenty-sixth Amendment, 391

U

Union, 73, 84, 89–90, 133, 195, 197
United Farm Workers (UFW), 391–392
United Nations, 253, 258, 273–276, 289, 294, 326–327, 369
Universal Negro Improvement Association, 212
Unrestricted Submarine Warfare, 170–171, 181
Upton Sinclair, 124, 130, 134
Urbanization, 97, 215
USA PATRIOT Act, 401
U.S. Constitution, C-1

V

V-E Day, 270, 276
V-J Day, 272, 276,
Vertical Integration, 70–71
Vicksburg, 14
Vietcong, 347–348, 350
Vietnam War, 343, 345, 350, 352–353, 391–392
    anti-war protests, 350–352
"Vietnamization," 349
Volstead Act, 204, 217
Voting Rights Act (1965), 323

W

Wabash v. Illinois, 108
Walker, Madam C. J., 67
War bonds, 173, 175–176, 181, 262, 276
War Guilt Clause, 179, 199
War Industries Board, 172, 181
"War on Poverty," 342–343, 357
War Powers Act, 351, 353
Warren Court, 343, 345, 394
Warsaw Pact, 293
Washington Naval Conference, 197, 201, 217, 255
"Watchful Waiting," 154–156
Watergate, 370, 372, 380
West Germany, 290, 292–293, 374
"White Man's Burden," 146–147, 156
Wilson, Woodrow, 126, 128, 131, 133–134, 154, 178, 180
Women's International League for Peace and Freedom, 197
Women's Liberation Movement, 353–355
Women's suffrage, 123, 126–128, 131, 133, 175, 355
Works Progress Administration (WPA), 235, 237–238, 240
World Trade Organization, 375, 379
Wounded Knee, 47, 390, 405

Y

Yalta Conference, 253, 289
Yellow fever, 150, 152
Yellow journalism, 143, 156

Z

Zimmerman telegram, 52–53